Fundamental
MANAGERIAL ACCOUNTING
Concepts

First Canadian Edition

Thomas P. Edmonds
University of Alabama – Birmingham

Cindy D. Edmonds
University of Alabama – Birmingham

Bor-Yi Tsay
University of Alabama – Birmingham

David E. Eliason
Southern Alberta Institute of Technology

McGraw-Hill Ryerson

Toronto Montréal Boston Burr Ridge, IL Dubuque, IA Madison, WI New York San Francisco St. Louis
Bangkok Bogotá Caracas Kuala Lumpur Lisbon London Madrid Mexico City Milan New Delhi
Santiago Seoul Singapore Sydney Taipei

McGraw-Hill
Ryerson Limited
A Subsidiary of The **McGraw·Hill** *Companies*

Fundamental Financial Accounting Concepts
First Canadian Edition

ISBN: 0-07-090049-3

1 2 3 4 5 6 7 8 9 10 TCP 0 9 8 7 6 5 4 3

Printed and bound in Canada

Care has been taken to trace ownership of copyright material contained in this text; however, the publisher will welcome any information that enables them to rectify any reference or credit for subsequent editions.

Vice President and Editorial Director: Pat Ferrier
Executive Editor: Nicole Lukach
Sponsoring Editor: Lenore Gray Spence
Developmental Editor: Brook Nymark
Director of Marketing: Jeff MacLean
Senior Supervising Editor: Margaret Henderson
Copy Editor: Rohini Herbert
Production Coordinator: Madeleine Harrington
Composition: VISU*TronX* Services
Cover Design: Greg Devitt
Cover Image: Chris McElcheran/Masterfile
Printer: Transcontinental Printing Group

National Library of Canada Cataloguing in Publication

Main entry under title:

    Fundamental managerial accounting concepts / Thomas P. Edmonds ... [et al.]. – 1st Canadian ed.

Includes index.
ISBN 0-07-090049-3

    1. Managerial accounting. I. Edmonds, Thomas P.

HF5657.4.F85 2002   658.15'11   C2002-902205-3

Thomas P. Edmonds

Thomas P. Edmonds, Ph.D. holds the Friends and Alumni Professorship in the Department of Accounting at the University of Alabama at Birmingham (UAB). He has been actively involved in teaching accounting principles throughout his academic career. Dr. Edmonds has coordinated the accounting principles courses at the University of Houston and UAB. He currently teaches introductory accounting in mass sections that frequently contain more than 180 students. Dr. Edmonds has received five prestigious teaching awards including the UAB President's Excellence in Teaching Award and the distinguished Ellen Gregg Ingalls Award for excellence in classroom teaching. He has written numerous articles that have appeared in many publications including *Issues in Accounting*, the *Journal of Accounting Education*, *Advances in Accounting Education*, *Accounting Education: A Journal of Theory, Practice and Research*, the *Accounting Review*, *Advances in Accounting*, the *Journal of Accountancy*, *Management Accounting*, the *Journal of Commercial Bank Lending*, the *Banker's Magazine*, and the *Journal of Accounting, Auditing, and Finance*. He has published four textbooks, five practice problems (including two computerized problems), and a variety of supplemental materials including study guides, work papers, and solutions manuals. Dr. Edmonds' writing is influenced by a wide range of business experience. He has been a successful entrepreneur. He has worked as a management accountant for Refrigerated Transport, a trucking company. Dr. Edmonds also worked in the not-for-profit sector as a commercial lending officer for the Federal Home Loan Bank. In addition, he has acted as a consultant to major corporations including, First City Bank of Houston, AmSouth Bank in Birmingham, Texaco, and Cortland Chemicals. Dr. Edmonds began his academic training at Young Harris Community College in Young Harris, Georgia. He received a B.B.A. degree with a major in finance from Georgia State University in Atlanta, Georgia. He obtained a M.B.A. degree with a concentration in finance from St. Mary's University in San Antonio, Texas. His Ph.D. degree with a major in accounting was awarded by Georgia State University. Dr. Edmonds' work experience and academic training has enabled him to bring a unique user perspective to this textbook.

Cindy D. Edmonds

Cindy D. Edmonds, Ph.D., is an Associate Professor of Accounting at the University of Alabama at Birmingham. She serves as the coordinator of the introductory accounting courses at UAB. She has written a variety of supplemental text materials including practice problems, a study guide, work papers, and test banks. Dr. Edmonds' articles appear in numerous publications including: *Advances in Accounting Education*, *Journal of Education for Business*, *Journal of Accounting Regulation*, *Advances in Accounting*, *Management Accounting*, *CMA Journal*, *Disclosures*, and *Business & Professional Ethics Journal*. Her manuscript "Running a City on a Shoe String" received a certificate of merit award from the Institute of Management Accountants. The manuscript was used by the City of Vestavia in its application for Moody's Municipal Bond Rating. Dr. Edmonds has worked in the insurance industry, in a manufacturing company, and a governmental agency. This work experience has enabled her to bring a real-world flavor to her writing. Dr. Edmonds holds a B.S. degree from Auburn University, a M.B.A degree from the University of Houston and a Ph.D. degree from the University of Alabama.

Bor-Yi Tsay

Bor-Yi Tsay, Ph.D., CPA, CMA is a Professor of Accounting at The University of Alabama at Birmingham (UAB) where he has taught since 1986. He has taught principles of accounting courses at the University of Houston and UAB. Currently, he is teaching a cost and control course at UAB's Master of Business Administration (MBA) program. Dr. Tsay received the 1996 Loudell Ellis Robinson Excellence in Teaching Award. He has also received numerous awards for his writing and publications including John L. Rhoads Manuscripts Award, John Pugsley Manuscripts Award, Van Pelt Manuscripts Award, and three certificates of merits from Institute of Management Accountants. His articles appeared in *Journal of Accounting Education, Management Accounting, Journal Managerial Issues, CPA Journal, CMA Magazine, Journal of Systems Management,* and *Journal of Medical Systems.* He currently serves as a member on the board of the Birmingham Chapter, Institute of Management Accountants. He is also a member of American Institute of Certified Public Accountants and Alabama Society of Certified Public Accountants. Dr. Tsay received a B.S. in agricultural economics from National Taiwan University, an M.B.A. with a concentration in Accounting from Eastern Washington University, and a Ph.D. in Accounting from the University of Houston.

David E. Eliason

David E. Eliason, CMA, is an Instructor and Academic Program Coordinator–Accounting, in the Business and Tourism Department at the Southern Alberta Institute of Technology, Calgary, Alberta. He has been in the Department since 1976. He has taught introductory financial accounting courses, managerial, and cost accounting courses, as well as advanced level courses in both the CMA and CGA course of study. He is also one of the first in the department to teach business courses using technology-enhanced delivery methods to classes where each student has their own laptop computer. Mr. Eliason has represented SAIT and the technology and resources of the institute in Russia, delivering information seminars in Moscow and St. Petersburg. Mr. Eliason has also worked with an international oil company in Kazakstan, developing and delivering training programs in accounting and business. He has consulted with Kyzylorda State University in Kazakstan on curriculum design, pedagogy, and delivery techniques. He has been a faculty representative on the Southern Alberta Institute of Technology Board of Governors, and President of the Faculty Association. Besides his long teaching career, Mr. Eliason has also worked in the oil industry, heavy-duty equipment industry, and was in private practice offering accounting, consulting, and tax advice.

Contents in Brief

Contents

CHAPTER 5

Cost Accumulation, Tracing, and Allocation 162

CHAPTER 6

Cost Management in an Automated Business Environment: ABC and TQM 200

During the past decade, the effects of technology, globalization, and the concentration of power have acted to create a new business environment. This environment is characterized by rapid change and fierce competition. Managers are under extreme pressure to produce consistent earnings growth and employees are expected to make meaningful contributions to profitability early in their careers. To be able to succeed in this environment, students must develop critical thinking, communication, and computer skills as well as an understanding of accounting procedures and practices. The goal of *Fundamental Managerial Accounting Concepts* is to better prepare students for entry into the new business environment by providing an appropriate balance between skill development and technical competence.

Traditionally, accounting education has emphasized a content-based approach. Specifically, skill development has been held at a relatively low level (focused primarily on comprehension and recall skills) and rigour has been measured by the quantity of content covered. More and more topics have been added to the curricula and textbooks grow ever larger. Unfortunately, this model provides little opportunity for professors to help students develop the skills that the new business environment demands. The number of classroom hours available is limited—students can feel lost in a crowd of processes and content, with no overarching tools to guide the way. With so much material to cover, there just is not time available to work on skill development. By contrast, the brief table of contents below is designed to facilitate a better understanding of critical core concepts. This enables students to rise above the crowd and step into the light of understanding.

Chapter 1 Management Accounting: A Value-Added Discipline

Chapter 2 Cost Behaviour, Operating Leverage, and Profitability Analysis

Chapter 3 Analysis of Cost, Volume, and Pricing to Increase Profitability

Chapter 4 Relevant Information for Special Decisions

Chapter 5 Cost Accumulation, Tracing, and Allocation

Chapter 6 Cost Management in an Automated Environment: AB and TQM

Chapter 7 Planning for Profit and Cost Control

Chapter 8 Performance Evaluation

Chapter 9 Responsibility Accounting

Chapter 10 Planning for Capital Investments

Chapter 11 Product Costing in Service and Manufacturing Entities

Chapter 12 Job-Order, Process, and Hybrid Cost Systems

Chapter 13 Financial Statement Analysis

Chapter 14 Cash Flow Statement

This text offers you an opportunity to shift the traditional educational paradigm. Content is focused on essential concepts, thereby reducing the quantity of material that must be covered. As a result, you have more time to work on skill development. Indeed, the Instructors' Resource Manual provides step-by-step instructions for the implementation of innovative teaching methodologies such as active learning and group dynamics. It offers a rich set of short discovery learning cases, which provide a forum for illuminating class-opening experiences that are highly effective in stimulating interest and developing critical thinking skills. In addition, the text itself contains many innovative features to better prepare students to face the challenges of a new business environment.

▌ Innovative Features

A Separate Section of Innovative End-of-Chapter Materials Encourages Students to Analyze, Communicate, and Think (ACT)

An innovative *act*ivities section entitled Analyze, Communicate, Think (ACT) is included in the end of chapter materials. The ACT section is composed of business application cases, group exercises, writing assignments, ethics cases, and Excel spreadsheet applications. This section lets you decide the appropriate level of emphasis for innovative approaches to accounting education. Further, the material in this section permits you to stress computer applications to the extent you deem appropriate. While the text is not designed to teach spreadsheet technicalities, Excel problems and exercises do include teaching tips that facilitate the student's ability to use spreadsheets. Excel templates (SPATS) are available on the OLC for the Spreadsheet Assignments, as indicated by the Technology icon.

By focusing on the materials in the ACT section, you can place heavy emphasis on analytical skills and/or computer technology. However, there is also a healthy supply of traditional exercises and problems included in the end-of-chapter materials. Accordingly, you can emphasize the traditional approach by selectively choosing the end-of-chapter materials that contain conventional requirements. The ACT section of end-of-chapter materials permits you to emphasize those areas that you consider to be most important for your particular academic environment. Examples of the ACT materials are provide below for your review!

WRITING ASSIGNMENT *Operating Leverage, Margin of Safety, and Cost Behaviour*   **ACT 3-3**

The article "Up Front: More Condensing at the Digest?" in the October 19, 1998, issue of *Business Week* reported that Thomas Ryder, CEO of Reader's Digest Association, was considering a spinoff of Reader's Digest's direct-marketing operations into a joint venture with Time Warner. The article's author, Robert McNatt, noted that the direct marketing of books, music, and videos is a far larger part of the Reader's Digest business than is its namesake magazine. Further, the article stated that 1998 direct-marketing sales of $1.6 billion were down 11 percent from 1997. The decline in revenue caused the division's operating profits to decline by 58 percent. The article stated that the contemplated alliance with Time Warner could provide some fast help. Gerald Levin, Time Warner chairman, has said that his company's operations provide customer service and product fulfillment far better than other Web sellers do because of Time Warner's established 250 Web sites.

Required

a. Write a memo explaining how an 11 percent decrease in sales could result in a 58 percent decline in operating profits.

b. Provide a brief explanation as to how the decline in revenue will affect the company's margin of safety.

c. Provide a logical explanation as to why a joint venture between Reader's Digest's direct-marketing division and Time Warner could work to the advantage of both companies. (*Hint:* Consider the effects of fixed-cost behaviour in formulating your response).

SPREADSHEET ASSIGNMENT   *Using Excel*

Dorina Company makes cases of canned dog food in batches of 1,000 cases and sells each case for $15. The plant capacity is 50,000 cases; the company currently makes 40,000 cases. DoggieMart has offered to buy 1,500 cases for $12 per case. Because product-level and facility-level costs are unaffected by a special order, they are omitted.

Required
a. Prepare a spreadsheet like the following one to calculate the contribution to income if the special order is accepted. Construct formulas so that the number of cases or the price could be changed and the new contribution would be automatically calculated.
b. Try different order sizes (such as 2,000) or different prices to see the effect on contribution to profit.

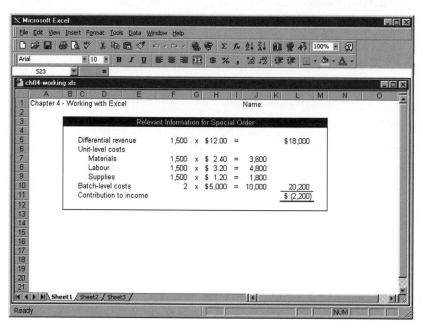

Spreadsheet Tips
1. The numbers in Cells F7 to F9 should be formulas that refer to F5. This allows the number of cases to be changed in Cell F5 with the other cells changing automatically.
2. The formula in Cell F10 uses a function named ROUNDUP to calculate the even number of batches. The formula should be =ROUNDUP(F5/1000,0), where the zero refers to rounding up to the nearest whole number.

ACT 6-2   GROUP ASSIGNMENT   *Use of ABC in a Service Business*

A dialysis clinic provides two types of treatment for its patients. Hemodialysis (HD) is an in-house treatment that requires patients to visit the clinic three times each week for dialysis treatments. Peritoneal dialysis (PD) permits patients to self-administer their treatments at home on a daily basis. On average, the clinic serves 102 HD patients and 62 PD patients. A recent development caused clinic administrators to develop a keen interest in cost measurement for the two separate services. Provincial Insurance plans began to pay treatment providers a fixed payment per insured participant, regardless of the level of services provided by the clinic. With fixed fee revenues, the clinic was forced to control costs to ensure profitability. As a result, knowing the cost to provide HD versus PD services was critically important for the clinic. It needed accurate cost measurements to answer the following questions: Were both services profitable, or was one service carrying the burden of the other service? Should advertising be directed toward the acquisition of HD or PD patients?

Unfortunately, the existing cost allocation system was believed to be inaccurate in the measurement of the true cost to provide the respective services; it had been developed in response to provincial insurance reporting requirements. It allocated costs between HD and PD on the basis of the ratio of cost to charges (RCC). In other words, RRC allocates indirect costs in proportion to revenues. To illustrate, consider the allocation of $1,766,560 of indirect nursing service costs, which are allocated to the two treatment groups in relation to the revenue generated by each group. Given that the clinic generated total revenue of $6,013,550, an allocation rate of $0.2937633 per revenue dollar was established ($1,766,560 ÷ $6,013,550). This rate was multiplied by the proportionate share of the revenue generated by each service category to produce the following allocation:

Type of Service	Service Revenue	×	Allocation Rate	=	Allocated Cost
HD	$3,720,574	×	0.2937633	=	$1,092,968
PD	2,292,976	×	0.2937633	=	673,592
Total	6,013,550	×	0.2937633	=	$1,766,560

To better assess the cost to provide each type of service, the clinic initiated an activity-based costing (ABC) system. The ABC approach divided the nursing service cost into four separate cost pools. A separate cost driver (allocation base) was identified for each cost pool. The cost pools and their respective cost drivers follow:

	Total	HD	PD
Nursing services cost pool categories		?	?
RNs (Registered Nurses)	$ 478,240	?	?
LPNs (Licensed Practical Nurses)	808,128	?	?
Nursing administration and support staff	230,336	?	?
Dialysis machine operations (tech. salaries)	249,856	?	?
Total	$1,766,560	?	?

	Total	HD	PD
Activity cost drivers (corresponding to cost pools)			
Number of RNs (Registered Nurses)	14	10	4
Number of LPNs (Licensed Practical Nurses)	38	30	8
Number of treatments (nursing administration)	69,934	28,686	41,248
Number of dialyzer treatments (machine operations)	28,686	28,686	
Total	$1,766,560	?	?

Required

a. Organize the class into four sections and divide the sections into groups of four or five students each. Assign Task 1 to the first section of groups, Task 2 to the second section, Task 3 to the third section, and Task 4 to the fourth section.

Group Tasks

1. Allocate the RN cost pool between the HD and PD service centres.
2. Allocate the LPN cost pool between the HD and PD service centres.
3. Allocate the nursing administration and support staff cost pool between the HD and PD service centres.
4. Allocate the dialysis machine operations cost pool between the HD and PD service centres.

b. Have the class determine the total cost to allocate to the two service centres in the following manner. Select a spokesperson from each section and have the selected representatives go to the board. Each spokesperson should supply the allocated cost for the cost pool assigned by her respective section. The instructor should total the amounts and compare the ABC cost allocations with those developed through the traditional RCC system.

c. The instructor should lead the class in a discussion that addresses the following questions:

(1) Assuming that the ABC system provides a more accurate measure of cost, which service centre (HD or PD) is overcosted by the traditional allocation system and which is undercosted?

(2) What is the potential impact on pricing and profitability for both service centres?

(3) How could management respond to the conditions described in the problem?

A variety of writing, group, technology, and ethics assignments are included. These problems are marked appropriately for easy identification.

Isolating Concepts

How do you promote the understanding of concepts? We believe that concepts should be isolated and discussed within a decision-making context. The implementation of this strategy has caused us to deviate from the traditional approach in many respects. For example, notice that the traditional chapter covering cost terminology (i.e., usually Chapter 2) has been eliminated from this textbook. We believe that introducing a plethora of detached cost terms in a single chapter is an ineffective teaching strategy. At best, students tend to memorize a few definitions. Indeed, the primary theme of a *terms chapter* seems to be: "Here are some definitions. Memorize them now and you will use them later." This sets a bad precedent. The appropriate educational expectation is comprehension, not memorization.

In contrast, we isolate concepts and introduce them singly. For example, we separate the concept of *product costing* from the related issues of manufacturing cost flow and the corresponding recording procedures. We assume that all materials purchased are used during the accounting period and that all products started are completed during the accounting period. Accordingly, the only inventory account used is a finished goods account. Within this context, students can clearly see how amortization on manufacturing equipment is accumulated in an inventory account while amortization on administrative equipment is expensed. Similarly, differences between administrative salaries and production wages are readily apparent. We use a financial statements model to highlight these critical comparisons (see Exhibit 5 in Chapter 1 as an example). Manufacturing cost flow is discussed in a separate chapter after students have had time to digest the distinction between a product cost versus a general, selling, administrative expense.

Interrelationships between Concepts

While isolating concepts facilitates the learning process, students must ultimately understand how the concepts are interrelated in business practice. The text has been written so that knowledge builds in a stepwise fashion to the point of full integration. For example, notice how the definitions of relevant costs are compared to those of cost behaviour on page 125 of Chapter 4 and how the definitions of direct costs are contrasted to those of cost behaviour and cost relevance on pages 166–167 of Chapter 5. The commitment to integrated learning is evident not only in the text material but also in exercises and problems. The aim of this text is to develop a pedagogical format that facilitates the students' ability to apply accounting concepts to increasingly complex organizational environments.

Avoid Logical Inconsistencies

What is a period cost and how does it differ from a product cost? Traditionally a period cost is defined as a cost that is expensed in the period in which it is incurred. This definition fails to distinguish period costs from product costs because product costs are also expensed in the period in which they are incurred (i.e., sold). Indeed, both period and product costs are accumulated in asset accounts until such time that the assets are used. More specifically, there is no conceptual difference in the way prepaids, supplies, depreciable assets, and inventory are treated in the financial statements. The fact is, the term "period" cost is a false identifier. We avoid this inconsistency by focusing on the true distinction, which is between product costs versus general, selling, and administrative costs. This is not an isolated incident but an example of a consistent commitment to avoid logical inconsistencies that thwart the comprehension of concepts.

Avoid Inconsistent Terminology

It is highly confusing when the same term is used to identify different concepts. Even so, many textbook authors have been careless in the use of terminology. For example, the term *fixed cost* is generally used to mean that a cost stays the same regardless of the volume of activity. However, within the context of a special order decision the term *fixed* is used to imply that the cost stays the same regardless of whether the special order is accepted or rejected. Similarly, the term *direct cost* is frequently used interchangeably with the term *variable cost*. For example, books frequently compare "direct or variable" costing with full absorption costing. This terminology implies that direct and variable costing are the same thing. We have made every effort to avoid the use of conflicting terminology in this text.

Context Sensitive Nature of Terminology

Students are frequently confused by the fact that same exact cost can be classified as fixed, variable, direct, indirect, relevant, or not relevant. For example, the salary of a store manager is fixed regardless of the number of customers that enter the store. However, the same salary is variable relative to the number of stores operated by a company. The salary is directly traceable to a particular store but not traceable to particular sales made in the store. The salary is relevant to a decision regarding whether to eliminate the store, but not relevant to a decision as to whether a department within the store should be eliminated. Students must learn to identify the circumstances that determine the classification of costs. The chapter material, exercises, and problems in this text are designed to encourage students to analyze the decision-making context rather than to memorize definitions. Problem 4-A in Chapter 2 provides an example of how the text teaches students to make appropriate interpretations of differential decision making environments.

L.O. 1   **PROBLEM 2-4A**   *Context-Sensitive Nature of Cost Behaviour Classifications*

Patty Stark operates a sales booth in computer software trade shows, selling an accounting software package, *EZRecords*. She purchases the package from a software manufacturer for $50 each. Booth space at the convention hall costs $4,000 per show.

Required

a. Sales at trade shows in the past have ranged between 50 and 250 units per show. Determine the average cost of sales per unit if Ms. Stark sells 50, 100, 150, 200, or 250 units of *EZRecords* at a trade show. Use the following chart to organize your answer:

a	Sales Volume in Units (a)				
	50	100	150	200	250
Total cost of software (a × $50)	$2,500				
Total cost of booth rental	4,000				
Total cost of sales (b)	$6,500				
Average cost per unit (b ÷ a)	$130.00				

b. If Ms. Stark wants to earn $20 for each package of software sold at a trade show, what price would she be required to charge at sales volumes of 50, 100, 150, 200, and 250 units?

c. Record the total cost of booth space if Ms. Stark attends one, two, three, four, or five trade shows. Record your answers in the following chart:

	Number of Trade Shows Attended				
	1	2	3	4	5
Total cost of booth rental	4,000				

d. Ms. Stark provides decorative shopping bags to customers who purchase merchandise. Some customers take the bags; others do not. Some customers stuff more than one software package into a single bag. The number of bags varies in relation to the number of units sold, but the relationship is not proportional. Assume that she uses $20 of bags per 50 units sold. What is the additional cost per unit sold? Is the cost fixed or variable?

Excel Applications

Spreadsheet applications are an essential component of contemporary accounting practice. Students must be aware of the power of spreadsheet software and know how accounting data is presented in spreadsheet format. Toward this end, we have included a discussion of Microsoft® Excel® spreadsheet applications wherever appropriate in the text. In most instances, actual spreadsheets are shown in the text. Refer to Exhibit 1 in Chapter 8 and Exhibit 6 in Chapter 10 for examples. These exhibits are shown on the following pages for your review. Also, end-of-chapter materials include problems and exercises that can be completed with spreadsheet software.

Exhibit 8-1 *Static and Flexible Budgets in Excel Spreadsheet*

	Static Budget		Flexible Budgets				
			16,000	17,000	18,000	19,000	20,000
Number of Units	18,000		16,000	17,000	18,000	19,000	20,000
	Per-Unit Standards						
Sales Revenue	$80.00	$1,440,000	$1,280,000	$1,360,000	$1,440,000	$1,520,000	$1,600,000
Variable Manuf. Costs							
Materials	$12.00	216000	192000	204000	216000	228000	240000
Labour	$16.80	302400	268800	285600	302400	319200	336000
Overhead	$5.60	100800	89600	95200	100800	106400	112000
Variable G,S,&A	$15.00	270000	240000	255000	270000	285000	300000
Contribution Margin		550,800	489,600	520,200	550,800	581,400	612,000
Fixed Costs							
Manufacturing		201,600	201,600	201,600	201,600	201,600	201,600
G,S,&A		90,000	90,000	90,000	90,000	90,000	90,000
Net Income		$259,200	$198,000	$228,600	$259,200	$289,800	$320,400

Interesting and Lively Writing Style

The text frequently conveys information through scenarios that permit students to view managers in action. In Chapter 3, a management team uses cost, volume, profit (CVP) analysis to evaluate the potential profitability of a new product. Along the way, the team confronts an ethical dilemma. Should substandard materials be used to accomplish a target-costing objective? In Chapter 5, a group of department heads advocates the use of allocation bases that serve their self-interest. Tempers fly and anger prevents one participant from reaching a compromise that would benefit his unit. The importance of the human side of the decision process becomes readily apparent. Interesting vignettes such as these are interspersed throughout the text. While this is not a novel, neither is it your typical dull textbook. Managerial accounting tools are introduced in a fashion that arouses and maintains student interest.

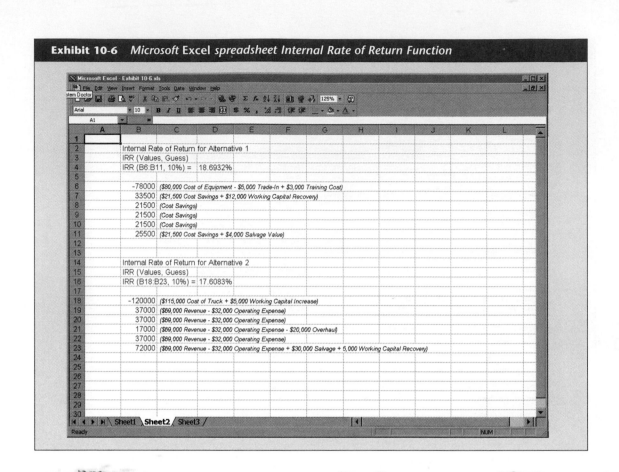

Exhibit 10-6 *Microsoft Excel spreadsheet Internal Rate of Return Function*

Real World Applications

Student interest is further piqued through the use of real-world illustrations. Each chapter opens with a feature titled *The Curious Manager*. This feature poses an interesting question that relates to the general content of the chapter. The questions involve real-world companies and include pictures that stimulate student interest. The question is answered in a text box located a few pages after the page containing the question. Real-world applications that relate to specific topics covered within each chapter are introduced through a feature titled *Reality Bytes*. This feature may contain survey results, graphics, quotes from business leaders, and other information that relates the text material to accounting practice. The objective here is to stimulate student interest by demonstrating the usefulness of managerial accounting tools in the management of real-world organizations. Examples of **The Curious Manager** and **Reality Bytes** are shown on the following page for your review.

the *curious* manager

© Photodisc/Phillip Spears

An ABC pilot project was undertaken in the die-cast engine parts area of the Volkswagen Canada Inc. plant in Barrie, Ontario, Volkswagen was ripe for ABC: it made about 25 engine parts, ranging from mass-produced gear housings to highly specialized camshaft-bearing caps. The cost analysis turned up numerous profit laggards. "A lot of them came out negative," says George Waddell, a cost accountant who led the project team. "The whole die-cast operation was profitable then, but that was because maybe only five or six of those parts were making a lot of money and covering for the ones that were losing money."

How can this happen?

reality bytes

Lisa de Wilde does not look like a mafiosa. And you would never mistake the president and CEO of Astral Media's pay-TV channels for a modern mob-moll character in *The Sopranos*, which airs on Astral's The Movie Network (TMN) from Ontario to Newfoundland. (Western viewers are out of luck, since Superchannel, the region's pay-TV station, does not air the crime drama.) However, if de Wilde has her way, every time Canadians think of the mobster melodrama, they will think of the pay-TV network. Astral is hoping the opportunity to watch new episodes of the award-winning television series, and its Hollywood movies, will be an offer TV junkies cannot refuse, convincing them to fork over the extra $12.95 a month subscription fee.

Source: John Gray, "Mob Makeover," *Canadian Business*: Feb. 19, 2001.

Managerial Orientation

This is not your typical cost accounting textbook approach. Service, financial, and not-for-profit entities are placed on equal footing with manufacturing companies. For example, a retail sales company is used as the background for the introduction of the budgeting chapter. A quick view of the table of contents reveals an early emphasis on decision making. In the first chapter, product costing is related to financing opportunities, managerial incentives, and income tax considerations. More traditional topics such as manufacturing cost flow and recording procedures are presented at the end of the text rather than at the beginning. Technical terminology is introduced within a decision-making context. For instance in Chapter 2, cost behaviour is related to operating leverage through an example where fixed cost structure is used to provide a competitive operating advantage. The interpretation rather than the computation of variances is emphasized in Chapter 8. The overall theme of the text is to introduce concepts in the context of decision making.

Information Overload

The proposed table of contents reflects our efforts to address the information overload problem. We believe that existing managerial textbooks contain significantly more material than can be digested by the typical student. Education research suggests that information overload leads to memorization. Very little is accomplished when students are exposed to such a volume of material that they are unable to comprehend the basic concepts. This text seeks to emphasize the comprehension of concepts by reducing the volume of content. You will notice that we have limited the number of chapters to fourteen. This contrasts with traditional texts that normally contain between 18 and 20 chapters.

Flexibility in Sequencing of Material

The arrangement of material in the table of contents represents only one of many alternatives for the sequence in which material can be covered. For example, after establishing a conceptual foundation by covering Chapters 1, 2, 4, and 5, you could proceed with coverage of Chapter 11 (i.e., product cost flow) followed by Chapter 12 (i.e., job order and process costing). With the exception of the foundation chapters (i.e., 1, 2, 4, and 5) all chapters stand alone. More specifically, you can skip around or omit Chapters 3, and 6 through 14 as you deem appropriate. Indeed, Chapters 7, 13, and 14 can be covered prior to Chapter 1. If your students do not cover cash flow concepts in their financial accounting course, we recommend that you begin your course by covering Chapter 14, Cash Flow Statement. Several of the chapters in this text assume that students have had an exposure to cash flow concepts. Accordingly, it will be necessary to skip cash flow topics in certain chapters or to establish a foundation that will enable your students to identify cash flow concepts. Incidentally, we emphasize the direct method with the primary objective of having students identify events as financing, investing, or operating. Accordingly, gaining the exposure needed to cover the cash flow applications presented in the text is not a difficult task. Even so, if you choose to skip cash flow coverage, rest assured that you can do so without negative consequences. The text is designed to permit the maximum level of instructor flexibility.

Some instructors believe that management accounting begins with the budgeting process. Further, they recognized the logical link between the coverage of financial statements in the financial accounting course and the coverage of pro forma statements in the budgeting chapter. Since our budgeting chapter is explained within the context of a retail establishment, you can start your managerial accounting course with Chapter 7 (i.e., planning for profit and cost control) if you are inclined to do so.

▌ Supplemental Materials

The text is supported by a complete package of supplements. The package includes the following items:

For Instructors

Solutions Manual: Prepared by David E. Eliason, Southern Alberta Institute of Technology
The Solutions Manual has been prepared and Canadianized by the author and contains the complete answers to all questions, exercises, problems and cases. The Manual has been tested using a variety of quality-control procedures to ensure accuracy. It was proofed and checked for accuracy.

Instructor's CD-ROM This integrated CD allows instructors to customize their own classroom presentations. It contains key supplements such as:

- **Instructor's Manual.** The text is suitable to teaching approaches such as group dynamics and active pedagogy. The Instructor's Manual, prepared by Doug Ringrose, Grant MacEwan College, provides step-by-step, explicit instructions as to how the text can be used to implement these alternative teaching methodologies. Guidance is also provided for those instructors who choose to use the traditional lecture method. The Manual includes lesson plans and demonstration problems with student work papers, as well as solutions for them.
- **Computerized Test Bank**. A computerized version of the Test Bank, this supplement is a valuable resource for instructors who prepare their own quizzes and examinations.
- **Solutions Manual.** Prepared in MSWord, these files are downloadable.
- **PowerPoint® Slides.** These slides may be used in class as presentation material and to review chapter concepts.
- **SPATS.** Available in Instructor version and Student version, Spreadsheet Application Templates make it easier for students to solve the technology-identified problems using Excel®.

Combining these resources, this Instructor's CD makes it easy for instructors to create multi-media presentations.

Test Bank: Prepared by Brian Winter, Southern Alberta Institute of Technology The Test Bank includes an expansive array of true/false, multiple choice, short discussion questions, and open-ended problems. The material is coded by learning objective and level of difficulty.

Online Learning Centre (www.mcgrawhill.ca/college/edmonds) The textbook's Online Learning Centre includes valuable downloadable instructor supplements, including:

- Instructor's Manual
- Solutions Manual
- PowerPoint® Slides
- SPATS

Primis Online McGraw-Hill's Primis Online, the world's largest and best resource, is available at your fingertips, literally! Select from our online database of over 350,000 pages of content, including the First Canadian Edition of Edmonds, *Fundamental Managerial Accounting Concepts*. With a few mouse clicks, create customized learning tools simply and affordably. When you adopt a Primis Online text, you decide the best medium for your students: printed textbooks or electronic e-books.

WebCT/Blackboard For faculty requiring online content, *Fundamental Managerial Accounting Concepts* is available in two of the most popular delivery platforms: WebCT and Blackboard. These platforms are designed for instructors who want complete control over course content and how it is presented to students. They provide instructors with more user-friendly and highly flexible teaching tools that enhance interaction between students and faculty.

PageOut PageOut is a McGraw-Hill online tool that enables instructors to create and post class-specific Web pages simply and easily. No knowledge of HTML is required.

The supplements listed here may accompany *Fundamental Managerial Accounting Concepts*, First Canadian Edition. Please contact your local McGraw-Hill Ryerson representative for details concerning policies, prices, and availability as some restrictions may apply.

For Students

Study Guide. Prepared by Michael Hockenstein, Vanier College (ISBN 0-07-091492-3) Each chapter of the Study Guide includes a review and an explanation of the chapter's learning objectives, as well as multiple-choice problems and short exercises. Also included is a series of articulation problems that require students to indicate how accounting events affect (i.e., increase, decrease, no effect) the elements of financial statements. They not only reinforce the student's understanding of how events affect statements but also help them to understand how the income statement, balance sheet, and cash flow statement interrelate.

Student Solutions Manual (ISBN 0-07-0905021-5) Extracted from the Instructor's Solutions Manual, the Student Solutions Manual contains solutions to odd-numbered exercises and problems in the text. The large type makes these solutions easy to read.

Online Learning Centre (www.mcgrawhill.ca/college/edmonds).
The Student Online Learning Centre follows the text chapter by chapter. Students will find:

- Additional self-assessment quizzes
- Learning objectives and their explanations
- Key terms
- Spreadsheet Application Template Software (SPATS) or Excel templates
- Check figures
- Internet application questions
- PowerPoint slides

Acknowledgements

Why do geese fly in a V-shape? Because the effort of the lead goose provides an uplifting draft that eases the burden of flight for the birds that follow. We are deeply indebted to the reviewers and class testers who have selflessly contributed their time and effort to the development of this book. Like the lead goose, their work has made the road of progress easier to travel for all who follow. We extend our deepest gratitude to those who have shared with us the frustrations and excitement associated with the development of innovative teaching materials. Our class testers included, Tim Nygaard of Madisonville Community College, Bob Smith of Florida State University, Phil Olds of Virginia Commonwealth University, Mark Lawrence of the University of Alabama at Birmingham, Nancy Schneider of Lynchburg College, Walt Doehring and Bruce Lindsey of Genesee Community College, Jeffrey Galbreath of Greenfield Community College, Leonard Stokes of Siena College, Dorcas Berg of Wingate College, Pat McMahon of Palm Beach Community College, and Jad Ashley of Grossmont College.

The text underwent an extensive review process that included a diverse group of instructors located at schools across Canada and the U.S.A. The comments and suggestions of the reviewers have significantly influenced the writing of the text. Our efforts to establish a meaningful but manageable level of content was greatly influenced not only by their suggestions regarding what to include, but also by their opinions regarding what to leave out. This edition underwent an intense review process from a number of Canadian instructors. Without their input, we would not have the text that we have today. They include:

Gerry Dupont	*Carleton University*
Fathi Elloumi	*Athabasca University*
Doug Ringrose	*Grant MacEwan College*
Peter Lubka	*University of Waterloo*
David E. Allwright	*Mount Royal College*
Judith K. Harris	*St. Clair College*
Ted Carney	*Humber College of Applied Arts & Technology*
Terry Fegarty	*Seneca College of Applied Arts & Technology*
Rob Harvey	*Algonquin College of Applied Arts & Technology*
Jerry Aubin	*Algonquin College of Applied Arts & Technology*

Many others have contributed directly or indirectly to the development of the text. Participants in workshops and focus groups have provided useful feedback. Colleagues and friends have extended encouragement and support. Among these individuals our sincere appreciation is extended to: Lowell Broom, University of Alabama at Birmingham; Bill Schwartz and Ed Spede of Virginia Commonwealth University; Doug Cloud, Pepperdine University—Malibu; Charles Bailey, University of Central Florida; Bob Holtfreter, Central Washington University; Kimberly Temme, Maryville University; Beth Vogel, Mount Mary College; Celia Renner, The University of Northern Iowa; Robert Minnear, Emory; Larry Hegstad, Pacific Lutheran University; Shirish Seth, California State University at Fullerton; Richard Emery, Linfield College; Gail Hoover, Rockhurst; Bruce Robertson, Lock Haven University; Jeannie Folk, College of Dupage; Marvelyn Burnette, Wichita State University; Ron Mannino, University of Massachusetts; John Reisch, Florida Atlantic University; Rosalie Hallbaurer, Florida International University; Lynne H. Shoaf, Belmont Abbey College; Jayne Maas, Towson University; Ahmed Goma, Manhattan College; John Rude, Bloomsburg University; Jack Paul, Lehigh University; Terri Gutierrez, University of Northern Colorado; Khondkar Karim, Monmouth University; Carol Lawrence, University of Richmond; Jeffrey Power, Saint Mary's University; Joanne Sheridan, Montana State University; and George Dow, Valencia Community College.

For the Canadian Edition, I would like to thank Professor Thomas P. Edmonds for introducing me to this wonderful text. Although he doesn't know me, and doesn't realize he met me at a workshop, he showed me the way. I would also like to acknowledge my office mate, Brian Winter, fellow Academic Coordinator Tony Mallette, and instructors Jan Nyholt, Ron Hill, Susan Baxter, and Connie Hahn at the Southern Alberta Institute of Technology. They had a significant effect on the focus and direction as the revision was taking place. This all could not have taken place without Nicole Lukach, Katherine Goodes, Brook Nymark, and Margaret Henderson, all of McGraw-Hill Ryerson Limited. Rohini Herbert, my copy editor, deserves huge thanks. She was patient, helpful, and led me by the hand. The technical checker, Ted Carney deserves my thanks as well. No matter how careful you are, someone else can always find something that has been overlooked. Last, but certainly not least, my wife and best friend, Hazel. When I want to hit the computer, and throw something, she quietly shows me the error of my ways, and gently sets me back on the road to completing this journey. To all of you, thank you.

Thomas P. Edmonds
Cindy D. Edmonds
Bor-Yi Tsay
David E. Eliason

McGraw-Hill Ryerson
Online Learning Centre

McGraw-Hill Ryerson offers you an online resource that combines the best content with the flexibility and power of the Internet. Organized by chapter, the EDMONDS Online Learning Centre (OLC) offers the following features to enhance your learning and understanding of Accounting:

- Self-Assessment Quizzes
- Microsoft® Excel® Templates
- SPATS and Microsoft® PowerPoint® Presentations
- Internet Application Questions

By connecting to the "real world" through the OLC, you will enjoy a dynamic and rich source of current information that will help you get more from your course and improve your chances for success, both in the course and in the future.

For the Instructor

Downloadable Supplements

All key supplements are available, password-protected for instant access!

PageOut **PageOut**

Create your own course Web page for free, quickly and easily. Your professionally designed Web site links directly to OLC material, allows you to post a class syllabus, offers an online gradebook, and much more! Visit www.pageout.net

Primis Online **Primis Online**

Primis Online gives you access to our resources in the best medium for your students: printed textbooks or electronic ebooks. There are over 350,000 pages of content available from which you can create customized learning tools from our online database at www.mhhe.com/primis

WebCT/Blackboard *WebCT* **Bb**

If you require online content, *Fundamental Managerial Accounting Concepts* is available in two of the most popular delivery platforms: WebCT and Blackboard. These platforms are designed to give you complete control over course content and how you present it to your students. These user-friendly and highly flexible teaching tools enhance interaction between you and your students.

For the Student

Online Quizzes

Do you know the material? You can consult the Key terms for each chapter as well as having handy access to the Learning Objectives. Need some practice? Work through the eLearning Sessions contained in every chapter. If that isn't enough for you, test your knowledge with the Multiple Choice quizzes to maximize the effect of the time spent reviewing text concepts.

SPATS and Microsoft® PowerPoint® Presentations

View and download presentations created for each chapter, then work through selected Technology problems from the text with the Spreadsheet Application Template Software (SPATS). A great way to improve your skills while preparing for class or for post-class review.

Internet Application Questions

Go online to learn how companies use the Internet in their day-to-day activities. Answer questions based on current organization Web sites and strategies.

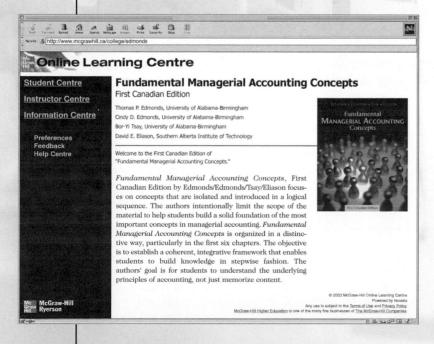

Your Internet companion to the most exciting educational tools on the Web!

The Online Learning Centre can be found at:

www.mcgrawhill.ca/college/edmonds

Management Accounting
A Value-Added Discipline

Learning Objectives

After completing this chapter, you should be able to:

1 Distinguish between managerial and financial accounting.

2 Identify the components of the cost of a product made by a manufacturing company, including the cost of materials, labour, and overhead.

3 Understand the need to determine the average cost per unit of a product.

4 Understand the difference between a cost and an expense.

5 Explain how product versus general, selling and administrative costs affect financial statements.

6 Understand how cost classification affects financial statements and managerial decisions.

7 Appreciate the need for a code of ethical conduct.

8 Distinguish product costs from upstream and downstream costs.

9 Understand how products provided by service companies differ from products made by manufacturing companies.

10 Explain how emerging trends, including activity-based management, value-added assessment, and just-in-time inventory, are affecting the managerial accounting discipline.

the *curious* manager

Courtesy Mercedes Benz

Mercedes-Benz spent millions of dollars to promote its new 4x4 M-Class sports utility vehicle. Suppose the president of the company has asked you to determine the unit cost of making an M-Class vehicle. Would you consider the promotional costs to be part of the cost of the vehicle? Assume that Mercedes prices its products at cost plus a designated markup above cost. Would you consider the promotional costs in determining the appropriate sales price?

Andy Grove, president and CEO of Intel Corporation, is credited with the motto "Only the paranoid survive." Mr. Grove describes a wide variety of concerns that make him paranoid. Specifically, he states the following:

> *I worry about products getting screwed up, and I worry about products getting introduced prematurely. I worry about factories not performing well, and I worry about having too many factories. I worry about hiring the right people, and I worry about morale slacking off. And, of course, I worry about competitors. I worry about other people figuring out how to do what we do better or cheaper, and displacing us with our customers. But these worries pale in comparison to how I feel about what I call strategic inflection points.[1]*

Mr. Grove describes strategic inflection points as "a time in the life of a business when its fundamentals are about to change."[2] The forces of change can be so powerful that they transform the very essence of conducting business. Consider the ways the airplane changed the transportation industry, television affected radio, satellites altered television programming, fast-food restaurants altered the

[1] Andrew S. Grove, *Only the Paranoid Survive* (New York: Bantam Doubleday Dell, 1996), p. 3.
[2] Ibid, p. 3.

food-processing industry, automated tellers changed the banking industry, plastic debit cards affected cheque printers, superstores affected the small retail industry, and the Internet is changing the communications industry.

*Most students have completed an introductory financial accounting course prior to reading this text. Considering what you have learned about financial accounting, do Intel's financial statements contain the information Mr. Grove needs to address his worries? Clearly, the historical-based financial information contained in the income statement, balance sheet, statement of shareholders' equity, and cash flow statement is insufficient to effectively manage a business. **Financial accounting** is not designed to satisfy the full range of needs of business managers. Its scope is limited to the needs of external users, including creditors, investors, government agencies, financial analysts, news reporters, and so on. The field of accounting that is designed to satisfy the information needs of managers and other individuals working inside the business is called **managerial accounting**. This text is designed to introduce you to the fundamental concepts associated with accounting information that is useful in managing the operations of a business.*

▍ Differences between Managerial and Financial Accounting

LO1
Distinguish between managerial and financial accounting.

Clearly, the information needs of internal and external users overlap. For example, both investors and managers are affected by strategic inflection points. Even so, the information needed to operate a business can be quite different from the information necessary to evaluate its investment potential. Some of the distinguishing characteristics of management accounting are discussed in the following section.

Users

As indicated, financial accounting provides information that is primarily used by investors, creditors, and others who work *outside* the business. In contrast, managerial accounting focuses on information that is used by executives, managers, and operators who work *inside* the business. The two user groups need different types of information.

Level of Aggregation

Investors and creditors frequently use general economic indicators as well as company-specific financial information when making their investment and credit decisions. For example, an investor considering the purchase of stock versus bond securities may be interested in the government's monetary policy, the growth rate of the gross domestic product, changes in the level of disposable income, tax policy, and the trend of corporate profits. In addition to general economic data, investors also use company-specific financial statement information. With respect to company-specific financial data, investors generally desire *global information* that reflects the performance of the company as a whole. They are much less interested in data regarding the performance of specific subunits, such as particular divisions, stores, or departments. For example, an investor is not so much interested in the performance of a particular Sears store as she is in the performance of Sears Canada versus the performance of The Bay.

　Internal users need information that facilitates the decision making necessary to *plan*, *direct*, and *control* the operations of a particular enterprise. The type of information needed by internal personnel is related to their job level in the organizational hierarchy. At the base level of a business organization, workers need information that is useful in making products or delivering services to customers. For example, the manager of the children's department of a particular Bay store needs to know how many pairs of blue jeans to have available for a back-to-school sale. When preparing the work schedule, the departmental manager may need information regarding the availability of staff and the company policy regarding overtime pay. Other considerations include the availability of supplies, such as shopping bags, cash register tapes, sales tags, and so forth. Indeed, the vast majority of information used at the operating level is nonfinancial.

As you move up the organizational ladder, financial information becomes increasingly important. Middle managers need information regarding the financial as well as the operating performance of their responsibility centres. For example, the manager of a Bay store is likely to be held responsible for achieving growth in the store's revenue and for controlling its expenses. The store manager is also interested in nonfinancial data, such as operating hours, the types of merchandise sold, the store layout, the image created by advertising campaigns, customer return policies, and employee training.

Senior executives make extensive use of the company's financial statements. Top executives use financial data when comparing the performance of their companies against that of their competitors. Financial information is also important in communicating companywide goals, objectives, and accomplishments to shareholders and in providing information necessary to obtain financing from creditors. Executives also use financial information in making strategic decisions regarding mergers and acquisitions as well as for decisions regarding the sale of subsidiaries, divisions, or product lines. To a lesser degree, executives may also use economic indicators and operating information. However, even these data are normally presented in summary form, which enables executive-level managers to assess the condition of the overall organization. Exhibit 1–1 summarizes the information needs of different user groups.

In summary, the financial accounting system is a component of the managerial accounting system. The managerial accounting system provides a much richer data set that includes economic and nonfinancial data as well as financial statement data. Information provided to insiders becomes increasingly disaggregated and nonfinancial as you move down the organizational hierarchy.

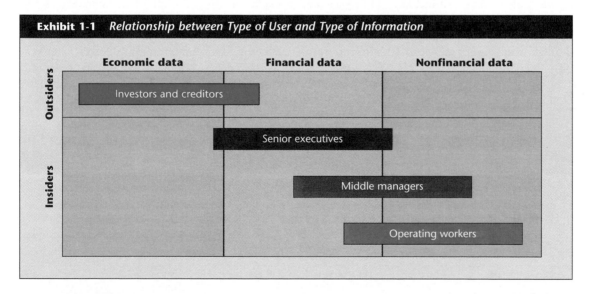

Exhibit 1-1 *Relationship between Type of User and Type of Information*

Regulation

Financial accounting is designed to generate information for the general public. Publicly traded companies in Canada must conform to the rules of disclosure as defined by the various provincial securities commissions, stock exchanges (e.g., TSE, CDNX) as well as GAAP. Canadian **GAAP (generally acepted accounting principles)** is defined by the **Canadian Institute of Chartered Accountants (CICA)**. GAAP severely restricts the accounting procedures and practices that can be applied to the preparation of published financial statements. Beyond financial statement data, much of the information generated in management accounting systems is proprietary information that is not made available to the public. Since this information is not distributed to the public, regulation designed to protect the public interest is not needed. Indeed, management accounting is restricted only by the **value-added principle**. Management accountants are free to engage in any information-gathering and reporting activity so long as the activity adds value in excess of its cost. For example, management accountants are free to make forecasts that enable managers to set production schedules to be able to satisfy customer demand. In contrast, financial accounting as prescribed by GAAP does not permit forecasting.

Characteristics of Information

Management's responsibilities include planning, directing, and controlling the operations of the business. Meeting these responsibilities requires future as well as historical information. Predicting the future frequently requires subjective judgment. While financial accounting is characterized by its objectivity, reliability, consistency, and historical nature, managerial accounting is more concerned with relevance and timeliness. Managerial accounting includes more estimates and fewer facts than does financial accounting. Financial accounting reports what happened yesterday; managerial accounting reports what is expected to happen tomorrow.

Time Horizon

Financial information is reported on a delayed basis for a specified time period. The normal accounting period is one year. This reporting time frame is acceptable for historical reports, but it is inadequate for operating purposes. Management cannot wait until the end of the year to discover problems. Planning, controlling, and directing must be continual. Therefore, to promote effective operations, many companies have implemented **total quality management (TQM)** programs. TQM is a two-dimensional management philosophy that includes (1) a systematic problem-solving philosophy that encourages front-line workers to achieve *zero defects*, and (2) an organizational commitment to achieving *customer satisfaction*. A key component of TQM is **continuous improvement**, which refers to an ongoing process through which employees learn to eliminate waste, reduce response time, minimize defects, and simplify the design and delivery of products and services to customers. Continuous improvement requires continuous feedback. Accordingly, managerial accounting information is necessarily captured and delivered in a more timely fashion than financial accounting information. Exhibit 1–2 summarizes the critical differences between financial and managerial accounting.

Exhibit 1-2 *Comparative Features of Managerial versus Financial Accounting Information*		
Features	**Managerial Accounting**	**Financial Accounting**
Users	Insiders, including executives, managers, and operators	Outsiders, including investors, creditors, government agencies, analysts, and reporters
Level of aggregation	Local information on subunits of the organization	Global information on the company as a whole
Information type	Economic and physical data as well as financial data	Financial data
Regulation	Unregulated, limited only by the value-added principle	Regulated by provinces, exchanges, CICA
Information characteristics	Estimates that promote relevance and enable timeliness	Factual information that is characterized by objectivity, reliability, consistency, and accuracy
Time horizon	Past, present, and future	Past only, historically based
Reporting frequency	Continuous reporting	Delayed, with emphasis on annual reports

▮ Product Costing

While there are significant differences between managerial and financial accounting, the two disciplines also overlap in many areas. One such area is that of estimating **product cost**.[3] Managers need to know the cost of their products for a variety of reasons. Cost information is often useful in pricing decisions; knowing what you paid for a product certainly influences your decision regarding the price at which you are willing to sell that product. Indeed, **cost-plus pricing** is a common business practice.[4] **Product costing** is also an essential part of the control process. To effectively manage the business, executives must know how actual costs compare with budgeted costs. Are costs higher or lower than expected? Who is responsible for the variances between expected and actual costs? What action can be taken to control the variances? These questions cannot be answered unless executives understand product costing practices and procedures.

Product costing also affects financial reporting. For example, the cost of merchandise is accumulated in an inventory account before it is expensed as cost of goods sold. Accordingly, expense recognition is delayed until the point of sale. As a result, the classification of costs as inventory or expense can affect the amount of assets shown on the balance sheet and the amount of net income shown on the income statement. Since product costing affects financial reporting, it can influence investors, creditors, and taxing authorities as well as managers.

▮ Product Costs in Manufacturing Companies

LO2

Identify the components of product cost for a manufacturing entity.

To this point, your experience with product costing is likely limited to merchandising businesses. Determining the amount of product cost for these businesses is a relatively simple matter. The cost of the product is usually the price paid plus some adjustment for transportation costs incurred to acquire the goods. Manufacturing companies are more complex; instead of buying their products, they make them. The cost of making products includes the cost of materials, labour, and other resources (i.e., overhead) that are used in the production process. This means that some of the costs you are accustomed to treating as expenses will now be treated as assets. To understand the accountant's distinctions between a cost and an expense, consider the case of Tabor Manufacturing Company.

Tabor Manufacturing Company

Tabor Manufacturing Company was started when it acquired $1,200 cash from its owners. Tabor was organized for the purpose of manufacturing wooden tables. The company spent $1,000 to build four tables, the cost included $390 for materials, $470 for work performed by a carpenter, and $140 for tools used in making the tables. What is the amount of expense incurred by Tabor? The answer is, zero. The costs of materials, labour, and overhead (i.e., tools) are *product costs*. The $1,000 cash has been transformed into products (i.e., four tables). Accordingly, the payments of cash for materials, labour, and tools were *asset exchange* transactions. One asset (cash) decreased, while another asset (tables) increased. An expense will not be recognized until the tables are used (sold); in the meantime, the cost of the tables will be shown in an inventory (asset) account known as **Finished Goods**. Exhibit 1–3 provides a graphical image of the way cash is transformed into inventory.

---

[3] This text uses the term *product* in a generic sense to mean both goods and services.
[4] Other pricing strategies will be introduced in subsequent chapters.

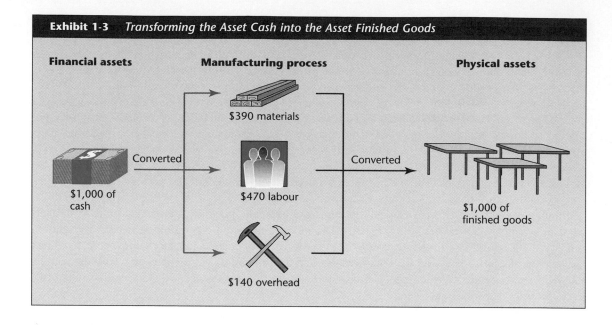

Exhibit 1-3 *Transforming the Asset Cash into the Asset Finished Goods*

Financial assets

Manufacturing process

Physical assets

$1,000 of cash

Converted

$390 materials

$470 labour

$140 overhead

Converted

$1,000 of finished goods

Cost per Unit

How much did each table made by Tabor Manufacturing cost? The actual cost for each of the four tables is different. The carpenter probably spent a little more time on some of the tables than others. Likewise, the tools were used in different proportions on each table. Finally, it is likely that mistakes were made on some of the tables that were not made on others. Accordingly, more materials were probably used to make some of the tables. Determining the exact cost of each table requires an unreasonable amount of record keeping, indeed, it is virtually impossible. Minute details, such as a millisecond of labour, cannot be effectively measured. Even if we could determine the exact cost of each table, the information would be of little use. Minor differences in the cost per unit would make no difference in terms of pricing or other decisions that management needs to make. For these reasons, accountants normally calculate cost per unit as an average. In the case of Tabor Manufacturing, the cost per table is $250 (i.e., $1,000 ÷ 4 units). Unless stated otherwise, you should assume that the term *cost per unit* means *average cost per unit*.

Costs Can Be Assets or Expenses

It may seem odd that wages paid to production workers are included in an inventory account instead of being expensed on the income statement. Remember, however, that an expense is incurred when an asset *is used* in the process of earning revenue. Note that the cash paid to production workers was not used to produce revenue. Instead, the cash was used to produce inventory. The revenue will be earned when the inventory is used (sold). So long as the inventory remains on hand, the amount of production wages and other product costs (i.e., materials and overhead) should remain in an inventory account. This means that at the end of an accounting period, some portion of the *product cost* may be on the balance sheet in an asset account (i.e., inventory), while the other portion will be shown as an expense (i.e., cost of goods sold) on the income statement. Costs that are not classified as product costs are normally expensed in the period in which the economic sacrifice is incurred. These costs include *general operating costs, selling and administrative costs, interest costs,* and *the cost of taxes.* To illustrate, return to the example of Tabor Manufacturing. Recall that Tabor made four tables at an average cost per unit of $250. Assume that Tabor pays an employee a $200 sales commission to sell three of the tables. The sales commission is expensed immediately. The total product cost for the three tables sold is $750 (i.e., 3 tables × $250 each). This cost (i.e., $750) is expensed on the income statement as cost of goods sold. The portion of the total product cost remaining in inventory is $250 (1 table × $250). Exhibit 1–4 shows the relationship between the costs incurred and the expenses recognized for Tabor Manufacturing Company.

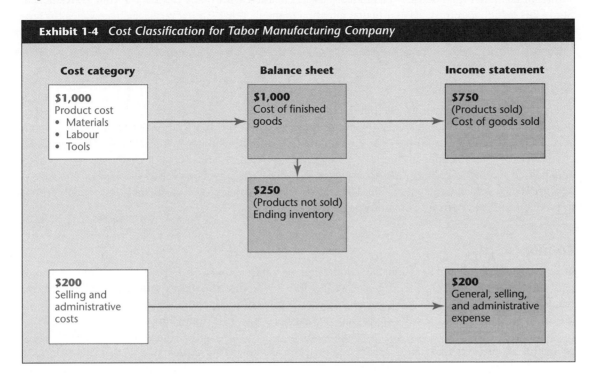

Exhibit 1-4 *Cost Classification for Tabor Manufacturing Company*

The Effect of Product Costs on Financial Statements

To illustrate the unique features of accounting for product costs in manufacturing companies, assume that Patillo Manufacturing Company was started on January 1, 2001. Patillo experienced the following accounting events during its first year of operations. *Assume that all transactions are cash transactions.*[5]

1. Acquired $15,000 of capital from the owners.
2. Paid $2,000 for the materials that were used to make its products. All products started were completed during the period.
3. Paid $1,200 for salaries of selling and administrative employees.
4. Paid $3,000 for wages of production workers.
5. Paid $2,800 for furniture used in selling and administrative offices.
6. Recognized amortization expense on office furniture purchased in Event 5. The furniture acquired on January 1 had a $400 estimated salvage value and a four-year useful life. The annual amortization charge is $600 (i.e. [$2,800 − $400] ÷ 4).
7. Paid $4,500 for manufacturing equipment.
8. Recognized amortization expense on equipment purchased in Event 7. The equipment was acquired on January 1. It had a $1,500 estimated salvage value and a three-year useful life. The annual amortization charge is $1,000 (i.e. [$4,500 − $1,500) ÷ 3).

LO5
Explain how product versus G, S, & A costs affect financial statements.

[5] The illustration assumes that all inventory started during the period was completed during the period. Accordingly, Patillo has only one inventory account entitled Finished Goods Inventory. Many manufacturing companies normally have three levels of inventory at the end of an accounting period, including raw materials inventory, work-in-process inventory (i.e., inventory of partially completed units), and finished goods inventory. A detailed discussion of these inventory items is included in Chapter 11.

9. Sold inventory to customers for $7,500.
10. The inventory sold in Event 9 cost $4,000 to make.

The effects of these transactions on the balance sheet, income statement, and cash flow statement are shown in Exhibit 1–5. The flow of product costs is marked with black arrows for your convenience. Study this exhibit carefully. Pay particular attention to the fact that similar costs, such as wages for production workers and salaries for administrative personnel, can have radically different effects on the financial statements.

Material Costs

The purchase price of materials used in the manufacturing process is a *product cost*. Materials used to make products are normally called **raw materials**. The cost of raw materials is accumulated in an asset account (i.e., inventory) until the time the products are sold. Remember that materials cost is only one component of total manufacturing costs. When goods are sold, the total cost of producing those goods is expensed as *cost of goods sold*. Accordingly, raw materials cost is a part of the *cost of goods sold* expense recognized at the point of sale. The costs of materials that can be easily and conveniently traced to products are called **direct raw materials** costs.

Labour Costs

Note that the salaries paid to selling and administrative employees are treated differently from the wages paid to production workers (i.e., Event 3 versus Event 4). Salaries paid to selling and administrative employees are expensed immediately, but the cost of wages of production workers is added to an inventory account. These wages are expensed as part of cost of goods sold at the time the goods are sold. Prior to the point of sale, labour costs of production employees remain on the balance sheet in an inventory account. Labour costs that can be easily and conveniently traced to products are called **direct labour**

Exhibit 1-5 *Effect of Product versus Selling and Administrative Costs on Financial Statements*

Event No.	Cash	+ Manuf. Equip.*	+ Office Furn.	+ Inventory	= Cont. Cap.	+ Ret. Ear.	Rev.	− Exp.	= Net Inc.	Cash flow
1	15,000				15,000					15,000 FA
2	(2,000)			2,000						(2,000) OA
3	(1,200)					(1,200)		− 1,200	(1,200)	(1,200) OA
4	3,000			3,000						(3,000) OA
5	(2,800)		2,800							(2,800) IA
6			(600)			(600)		− 600	(600)	
7	(4,500)	4,500								(4,500) IA
8		(1,000)		1,000						
9	7,500					7,500	7,500		7,500	7,500 OA
10				(4,000)		(4,000)		− 4,000	(4,000)	
Totals	9,000	+ 3,500	+ 2,200	+ 2,000	= 15,000	+ 1,700	7,500 −	5,800 =	1,700	9,000 NC

*Negative amounts in these columns represent accumulated amortization.
†The letters in the far right-hand column of Exhibit 1–5 designate different types of cash flow activities. The letters FA represent financing activities, IA represents investing activities, and OA represents operating activities. The letters NC on the bottom row represent the net change in cash. If you have not studied the cash flow statement, we recommend that you study Chapter 14 prior to continuing your study of the material in this chapter.

costs. The cost flow of wages for production employees versus salaries for selling and administrative personnel is shown in Exhibit 1–6.

Overhead Costs

Although the cost of amortization totalled $1,600 ($600 on office furniture and $1,000 on manufacturing equipment), only the $600 of amortization on office furniture appears directly on the income statement. The amortization on manufacturing equipment is split between the income statement (i.e., cost of goods sold) and the balance sheet (i.e, inventory). The cost flow associated with the amortization of the manufacturing equipment versus office furniture is shown in Exhibit 1–7.

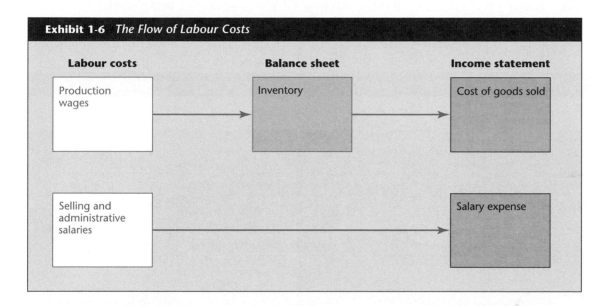

Exhibit 1-6 *The Flow of Labour Costs*

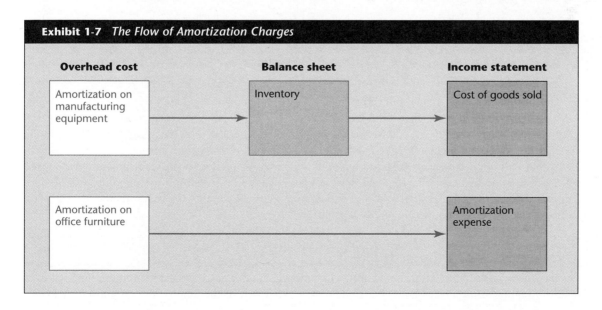

Exhibit 1-7 *The Flow of Amortization Charges*

Exhibit 1-8 *Schedule of Inventory Costs*

Materials	$2,000
Labour	3,000
Manufacturing overhead*	1,000
Total product costs	6,000
Less: Cost of goods sold	(4,000)
Ending inventory balance	$2,000

* Depreciation ([$4,500 − $1,500] ÷ 3)

Total Product Cost A summary of the total product cost incurred by Patillo Manufacturing is shown in Exhibit 1–8.

General, Selling, and Administrative Costs

The **general**, **selling**, **and administrative costs** (G, S, & A) are normally expensed *in the period* in which the associated economic sacrifice is made. Accordingly, the salary expense for selling and administrative employees and the amortization on office furniture are shown on the income statement. Because of this recognition pattern, non-product expenses are sometimes called **period costs**. The income statement, balance sheet, and cash flow statement for Patillo Manufacturing are shown below in Exhibit 1–9:

Exhibit 1-9

PATILLO MANUFACTURING COMPANY
Financial Statements
December 31, 2001

Income Statement		Balance Sheet		Cash Flow Statement	
Revenue	$7,500	Cash	$ 9,000	Operating Activities	
Cost of Goods Sold	4,000	Finished Goods Inv.	2,000	Inflow from Revenue	$ 7,500
Gross Margin	3,500	Office Furniture	2,800	Outflow for Inventory	(5,000)
G, S, & A Expenses		Accumulated Amort.	(600)	Outflow for S&A Salaries	(1,200)
Salaries Expense	(1,200)	Manuf. Equipment	4,500	Net Inflow from Operating Acts.	1,300
Dep. Exp. 2 O. Furn.	(600)	Accumulated Amort.	(1,000)	Investing Activities	
Net Income	$1,700	Total Assets	$16,700	Outflow for Equip. and Furn.	(7,300)
		Equity		Financing Activities	
		Contributed Capital	$15,000	Inflow from Capital Acquisitions	15,000
		Retained Earnings	1,700	Net Change in Cash	9,000
		Total Equity	$16,700	Beginning Cash Balance	-0-
				Ending Cash Balance	$ 9,000

The $4,000 of cost of goods sold shown on the income statement includes a portion of the materials, labour, and **overhead** costs. Similarly, the $2,000 of finished goods inventory on the balance sheet is composed of materials, labour, and overhead. These product costs will be recognized as expense in the next accounting period when the goods are sold. Accordingly, classifying a cost as a product cost may delay, but will not eliminate, its recognition as an expense. All product costs are ultimately recognized as expense. Note that cost classification does not affect cash flow. Cash inflows and outflows are recognized in the period that cash is collected or paid, regardless of whether the cost is recorded in an asset account or is expensed on the income statement.

Overhead Costs: A Closer Look

Such costs as depreciation on manufacturing equipment cannot be easily traced to products. Suppose that Patillo Manufacturing makes both chairs and tables. What part of the amortization is caused by manufacturing tables versus manufacturing chairs? Similarly, suppose that a production supervisor oversees the labour of employees who work on both tables and chairs. How much of the supervisor's salary should be assigned to tables and how much to chairs? Remember that the supervisor did not work directly on either product line. Likewise, the cost of a tub of glue used in the production department would be difficult to trace to tables versus chairs. You could count the drops of glue used on each product, but the information would not be useful enough to merit the time and money spent collecting the data. Costs that cannot be traced to products and services in a *cost-effective* manner are called **indirect costs**. The indirect costs required to make products are called **manufacturing overhead**. Some of the items commonly included in manufacturing overhead are indirect materials, indirect labour, factory utilities, rent of manufacturing facilities, amortization on manufacturing assets, and production planning and setup costs.

Since indirect costs cannot be effectively traced to products, they are normally distributed to products through a process known as **cost allocation**, which is the process of dividing a total cost into parts and assigning the parts to relevant objects. To illustrate, suppose that production workers spend an eight-hour day making a chair and a table. The chair requires two hours to complete and the table requires six hours. Now, suppose that $120 of utilities is consumed during the day. How much of the $120 should be assigned to each piece of furniture? The utility cost cannot be directly traced to each specific piece of furniture, but the piece of furniture that required more labour also likely consumed a larger part of the utility cost. Using this line of reasoning, it is rational to distribute the utility cost to the two pieces of furniture on the basis of *direct labour hours*. Specifically, the utility cost could be allocated at a rate of $15 per hour ($120 ÷ 8 hours). The chair would be assigned $30 of the total cost ($15 per hour × 2 hours). The remaining $90 of cost ($15 × 6 hours) would be assigned to the table. The allocation of the utility cost is shown visually in Exhibit 1–10.

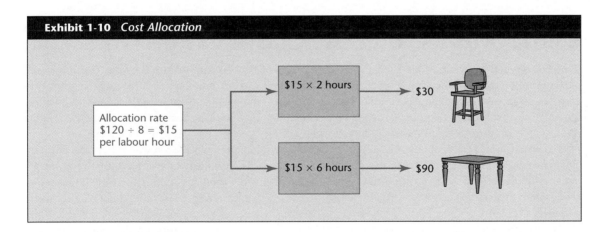

Exhibit 1-10 *Cost Allocation*

We will discuss the details of cost allocation in Chapter 5, but at this stage, you should understand that overhead costs are normally allocated to products, rather than being traced directly to them.

Manufacturing Product Cost Summary

As indicated, the cost of a product made by a manufacturing company is normally composed of three categories: direct materials, direct labour, and manufacturing overhead. The relevant information regarding these three cost components is summarized in Exhibit 1–11.

Exhibit 1-11 *Components of Manufacturing Product Cost*

Component 1—Direct Materials
Sometimes called *raw materials*. In addition to basic resources, such as wood or metals, it may include manufactured parts. For example, engines, glass, and car tires may be considered raw materials for an automotive manufacturer. If the amount of a material in a product is known, it can usually be classified as a direct material. The cost of direct materials can be easily traced to specific products.

Component 2—Direct Labour
The cost of wages paid to factory workers involved in "hands-on" contact with the products being manufactured. If the amount of time employees worked on a product can be determined, this cost can usually be classified as direct labour. Like direct materials, direct labour costs must be easily traced to a specific product.

Component 3—Manufacturing Overhead
Costs that cannot be easily traced to specific products. Accordingly, these costs are called *indirect costs*. They may include, but are not limited to, the following:
1. **Indirect materials**, such as glue, nails, paper, and oil. Indeed, note that indirect materials used in the production process may not appear in the finished product. An example is a chemical solvent used to clean products during the production process but is not a component material found in the final product.
2. **Indirect Labour**, such as the cost of salaries paid to production supervisors, inspectors, and maintenance personnel.
3. Rental cost for manufacturing facilities and equipment.
4. Utility costs.
5. Amortization.
6. Security.
7. The cost of preparing equipment for the manufacturing process (i.e., setup costs).
8. Maintenance cost for the manufacturing facility and equipment.

▌Importance of Cost Classification

LO6

Understand how cost classification affects financial statements and managerial decisions.

Who cares whether a cost is classified as an asset or an expense? To answer this question, begin by considering how cost classification affects financial statements. Accumulating costs in asset accounts as opposed to recognizing them as expenses produces, at least in the short term, more favourable financial statements. Specifically, *the amount of total assets and net income is higher if a cost is classified as an asset than if it is expensed.* As a result, anyone who has an interest in a company's financial statements is concerned with how costs are classified. For example, managers who are rewarded on the basis of financial performance are motivated to classify costs as assets. Similarly, a company that is trying to show a favourable financial position to acquire capital or borrow money is motivated to delay expense recognition. In contrast, a company trying to avoid taxes tries to expense costs, rather than classify them as assets.

Marion Manufacturing Company

To illustrate some of the practical implications of cost classification, assume that Marion Manufacturing Company (MMC) was started when it acquired $12,000 from its owners. During its first year of operation, the company incurred specifically identifiable product costs (i.e., materials, labour and overhead) amounting to $8,000. MMC also incurred $4,000 of costs to design the product and plan the manufacturing process. During the accounting period, MMC made 1,000 units of product and sold 700 units at a price of $18 each. All transactions were cash transactions.

Exhibit 1–12 shows financial statements for MMC under two alternative scenarios. The first scenario treats the $4,000 of design and planning costs as selling and administrative expenses. In contrast, the second scenario treats the $4,000 of design and planning costs as product costs; accordingly, these costs are accumulated in the Inventory account and expensed when the goods are sold.

Statement Differences

The first difference between the income statements is the amount of cost of goods sold. Under Scenario 1, the total product cost is $8,000, which results in a cost per unit of $8 each (i.e., $8,000 ÷ 1,000 units). Since 700 units were sold, the cost of goods sold amounts to $5,600 ($8 × 700). In contrast, total product cost under Scenario 2 is $12,000 ($8,000 specifically identifiable product costs + $4,000 of design and planning costs classified as product cost). Accordingly, the cost per unit becomes $12 ($12,000 ÷ 1,000 units), and the cost of goods sold becomes $8,400 ($12 × 700 units).

The second difference between the income statements is the amount of selling and administrative expense. Under Scenario 1, the $4,000 of design and planning costs is classified as selling and administrative expense. In contrast, there is no selling and administrative expense under Scenario 2 because the $4,000 of design and planning costs is classified as a product cost. Under Scenario 2, the design and planning costs constitute $4 per unit ($4,000 ÷ 1,000 units) of the total product cost. As a result, only $2,800 ($4 × 700) of the total design and planning costs are expensed because they are included in cost of goods sold. Therefore, a $2,800 difference exists between the

Exhibit 1-12 *Financial Statements under Alternative Cost Classification Scenarios*		
Income Statements	**Scenario 1**	**Scenario 2**
Revenue (700 × $18)	$12,600	$12,600
Cost of Goods Sold	(5,600)	(8,400)
Gross Margin	7,000	4,200
Selling and Administrative Expense	(4,000)	0
Net Income	$ 3,000	$ 4,200
Balance Sheets		
Assets		
Cash	$12,600	$12,600
Inventory	2,400	3,600
Total Assets	$15,000	$16,200
Equity		
Contributed Capital	$12,000	$12,000
Retained Earnings	3,000	4,200
Total Equity	$15,000	$16,200
Cash Flow Statements		
Operating Activities		
Inflow from Customers	$12,600	$12,600
Outflow for Inventory	(8,000)	(12,000)
Outflow for S&A	(4,000)	0
Net Inflow from Operating Activities	600	600
Investing Activities	0	0
Financing Activities		
Acquisition of Capital	12,000	12,000
Net Change in Cash	12,600	12,600
Beginning Cash Balance	0	0
Ending Cash Balance	$12,600	$12,600

amounts of cost of goods sold under the two scenarios (i.e., $8,400 − $5,600). The remaining $1,200 (i.e., $4 × 300) of the design and planning costs is contained in an Inventory account under Scenario 2. This explains the $1,200 difference in the amounts of inventory reported under the two scenarios ($3,600 − $2,400). Since net income is larger under Scenario 2, retained earnings is also higher under that scenario.

Clearly, the Scenario 2 income statement and balance sheet provide a more favourable portrayal of business operations. Note, however, that cash flow is not affected by the classification of cost. The same amount of cash was collected and paid under both scenarios. Since cost of goods sold and selling and administrative expense are both considered to be operating items, no difference exists in the amount of cash flow from operating activities, regardless of whether the $4,000 of design and planning costs is classified as a product cost or a selling and administrative expense.

Practical Implications

The financial statement differences shown in Exhibit 1–12 are merely *timing differences*. Indeed, when the remaining inventory is sold, the $1,200 portion of the design and planning costs included in inventory under Scenario 2 will be expensed through cost of goods sold. In other words, once all of the inventory is sold, total expenses and retained earnings will be the same under both scenarios. The accumulation of cost in an Inventory account acts only to delay the ultimate expense recognition. Even so, the temporary effects on the financial statements can have important implications with respect to the (1) availability of financing, (2) motivations of management, and (3) payment of income taxes.

Availability of Financing

The willingness of creditors and investors to provide capital to a business is influenced by their expectations of the business's future financial performance. If a business is able to generate sufficient cash flows, it will be able to make interest payments and to repay the principal balance of its liabilities. Investors are interested in future earnings because they will share in the wealth. Because creditors and investors use financial statement data to predict future performance, their credit and investment decisions may be influenced by the way costs are classified (i.e., asset versus expense). In general, more favourable financial statements enhance a company's ability to obtain financing from creditors or investors.

The **efficient markets hypothesis** supports the argument that creditors and investors look to the substance of business events, regardless of the way the transactions are reported in financial statements; therefore, the credit and investment markets are efficient. Whether creditors and investors are deceived by spurious reporting practices is a matter of unresolved debate.[6] Even if we assume that markets are efficient, we must acknowledge the fact that many restrictive covenants[7] in credit agreements use financial statement data. Executive compensation can also be influenced by financial statement data. Accordingly, financial statement data may affect the type of executive talent that a company is able to attract. As a result, financial reporting practices can have real economic consequences that impact investment and credit decisions, regardless of whether the market is efficient. In other words, classifying costs as assets, rather than expensing them, may affect the willingness of creditors and investors to provide capital to a business.

Management Motivation

As suggested, financial statement data may affect executive compensation. For example, assume that Marion Manufacturing has a management incentive plan that provides a bonus pool equal to 10 percent of net income. Under Scenario 1, managers would receive $300 ($3,000 × 0.10). In contrast, managers would receive $420 ($4,200 × 0.10) under Scenario 2. Do not be deceived by the relatively small numbers. We could illustrate with hundreds of thousands of dollars just as well as hundreds of dollars; the amounts in the illustrations are small to facilitate communication. Under these circumstances, managers would clearly favour Scenario 2. Indeed, managers may be tempted to misclassify costs to manipulate the content of financial statements.

Since accumulating costs in asset accounts merely delays expense recognition, why would a manager be tempted to misclassify costs? After all, isn't the benefit only temporary? Not necessarily. A manager who repeats the practice year after year can maintain a continual delay. In other words, even as the old costs reach the point of expense recognition, new costs are being added to asset accounts. Accordingly, the old delay is replaced with a new delay. The delay can be maintained so long as the practice continues. It is also important to recognize that even temporary delays can make a difference. Suppose that the manager classifies costs in a manner that provides him a compensation bonus in 2001 and then changes jobs in 2002. Under these circumstances, the manager receives a bonus that he other-

---

[6] There is widespread acceptance of the weak and semistrong forms of the efficient markets hypothesis. These forms relate to efficient assimilation of public information. There is considerable controversy regarding the strong form, which suggests efficiency with respect to insider information.

[7] A restrictive covenant is an agreement or clause in a debt contract that provides assurance to creditors regarding the payment of principal and interest. Such agreements frequently involve restrictions that are measured by financial ratios. These ratios are based on financial statement data.

wise would not have obtained. Even if the delay of expense recognition serves only to benefit the manager by allowing him to receive a bonus in 2001 that he will otherwise obtain in 2002, the manager will gain a *time value of money* benefit. In other words, receiving the bonus early has a value. At a minimum, the manager could invest the bonus money and earn interest during the time of the delay.

To reduce the temptations of statement manipulation, many companies tie bonus plans to the company's stock price, rather than to its financial statements. To the extent that the market is efficient, it rewards performance that adds true value to the company by bidding up the company's stock price. An efficient market is not deceived by accounting practices that are designed solely to manipulate financial statements. The growing number of companies using stock options in their incentive programs may suggest that today's business organizations believe that stock prices are better indicators of performance than are financial statements.

Income Tax Considerations

Since income taxes are determined by taking a designated percentage of taxable income, managers seek to minimize taxes by reporting the minimum amount of taxable income. Accordingly, Scenario 1 in Exhibit 1–12 depicts the most favourable tax condition. In other words, with respect to taxes, managers prefer to classify costs as expenses, rather than assets. Obviously, the Canadian Customs and Revenue Agency (CCRA) prefers the opposite treatment. Disagreements between the CCRA and taxpayers are ultimately settled in the courts.

❚ Ethical Considerations

The preceding discussion provides a glimmer of insight into the conflicts of interest that management accountants face in the course of performing their duties. Accountants hold positions of trust within their organizations and the business community. The information they generate is used to make decisions that can have a significant financial impact on many individuals. Accordingly, management accountants must be prepared not only to make hard choices between legitimate alternatives but also to face conflicts of a more sinister nature. Some of the more common conflicts that accountants may encounter include requests or pressure to

LO7
Appreciate the need for a code of ethical conduct.

1. Perform duties for which they have not been trained to perform competently.
2. Disclose confidential information.
3. Compromise their integrity through falsification, embezzlement, bribery, and so on.
4. Distort objectivity by issuing misleading or incomplete reports.

Yielding to such temptations can have disastrous consequences. The primary job of a management accountant is to provide information that is useful in making decisions. Information is worthless if its provider cannot be trusted. Accordingly, accountants have an obligation to themselves, their organizations, and the public to maintain high standards of ethical conduct.

❚ Common Features of Criminal and Ethical Misconduct

People who become involved in unethical or criminal behaviour usually do so unexpectedly. They start with small indiscretions that evolve gradually into more serious violations of trust. Accordingly, *awareness* constitutes a key ingredient for the avoidance of unethical or illegal conduct. In a effort to increase awareness, Donald Cressey studied hundreds of criminal cases to identify the primary factors that lead to trust violations.[8] He found these three factors were common to all cases:

- The existence of a secret problem
- The presence of an opportunity
- The capacity for rationalization

It is important to note that individuals have different ideas about what they think must be kept secret. Consider two responses to the problem of an imminent business failure. One person may feel so ashamed that she cannot discuss the problem with anyone. Another person in the same situation may want to talk to anyone, even a stranger, in the hope of getting help. Cressey's findings suggest that the person who is inclined toward secrecy is more likely to accept an unethical or illegal solution. In other words, secrecy increases vulnerability.

Few individuals like to think of themselves as evil. Accordingly, they develop rationalizations to justify their misconduct. Cressey found a significant number of embezzlers who contended that they were only "borrowing the money" even after being convicted and sentenced to jail. Some of the more common rationalizations include peer pressure, loyalty to unscrupulous superiors, family needs, revenge, and personal vices, such as drug addiction, gambling, and promiscuity. To avoid involvement in ethical misconduct, accountants must develop a strong sense of personal responsibility. They cannot allow themselves to blame other people or unfair circumstances for their problems. They must learn to hold themselves personally accountable for their actions.

Ethical misconduct is a serious offence in the accounting profession. Accountants must realize that in this arena, their careers are vulnerable to a single mistake. A person caught in white-collar crime loses the opportunity to hold a white-collar job. Second chances are rarely granted to them. Given this condition, it is extremely important that you learn how to recognize and avoid the common features of ethical misconduct. To help you prepare for the real-world ethical dilemmas that you are likely to encounter, we have included an ethics case at the end of each chapter. When working on these cases, you should attempt to identify the effects of (1) secrecy, (2) opportunity, and (3) rationalization.

▌ Upstream and Downstream Costs

LO8

Distinguish product costs from upstream and downstream costs.

Product costing as described thus far pertains to the measurement of cost for financial reporting purposes. In other words, we have been interested in deciding which costs go on the balance sheet versus the income statement. Product costing for financial reporting focuses on the measurement of costs incurred during the manufacturing process. Most companies incur product-related costs before and after, as well as during, the manufacturing process. For example, Ford Motor Company incurs significant research and development costs prior to starting to mass produce a new model car. These **upstream costs** occur before the manufacturing process begins. Similarly, companies normally incur significant costs after the manufacturing process is complete. Examples of **downstream costs** include the costs of transportation, advertising, sales commissions, and bad debts.

Profitability analysis requires attention to upstream and downstream costs as well as manufacturing product costs. To be profitable, a company must recover the total cost of developing, producing, and delivering its products to its customers. To illustrate, assume that Pearson Electronics incurs $30,000,000 in research and development costs leading to the production of a new computer-processing chip. Manufacturing costs, including materials, labour, and overhead costs, are expected to be approximately $150 per chip. Furthermore, the company expects to pay a sales commission of $25 per chip to its sales staff. The company expects to produce and sell 1,500,000 chips before the processor becomes technologically obsolete. Assuming the company desires to earn a profit margin equal to *20 percent of cost*, what price should it charge per processor? To answer this question, we must first determine what

---

[8] D. R. Cressey, *Other People's Money* (Montclair, NJ: Patterson Smith, 1973).

is meant by 20 percent of cost. More specifically, what is cost? Do we mean manufacturing product cost (i.e., $150), or do we mean the total of all costs associated with the product, which amounts to $195 ($150 manufacturing cost + upstream research and development of $20 [$30,000,000 ÷ 1,500,000 units] + downstream sales commissions of $25)?

If the sales price is based solely on manufacturing product cost, the sales price is $180 ($150 + [150 × 20%]). A $180 sales price is insufficient to cover the $195 total cost per unit of developing, manufacturing, and selling the product. Clearly, the pricing decision must include *all* costs associated with the product. The manufacturing product cost is only a subset of the total cost that must be considered in the pricing decision. Indeed, the effective management of a business organization requires careful analysis of the costs of all activities performed by the business entity.

▌ Product Costs in Service Companies

Service companies differ from manufacturing companies in that they provide assistance, rather than goods, to their customers. For example, a doctor prescribes a treatment to help the patient to get well. Similarly, Bell Canada provides a communication system that permits conversations between individuals who are separated by a distance that would otherwise prohibit interaction. Likewise, an airline provides transportation service, and a bank aids customers with financial transactions. Service businesses differ from manufacturing entities in that they have no inventory. How does product costing relate to a service company that has no tangible output? In other words, how can a company have product costs when it has no inventory?

First, cost accumulation is not restricted to tangible output. For example, providing a movie for customers to view costs money as does providing customers shirts to buy. Likewise, making a movie costs the production company money just the same as making a shirt costs a manufacturing company money. Indeed, *service companies, like manufacturing companies, incur materials, labour, and overhead costs* in the process of providing services to their customers. For example, in the process of making a film, Disney Studios incurs the cost of materials (film, costumes, and props), the cost of labour (salaries paid to actors, directors, and technicians) and overhead (amortization, utilities, and insurance). Similarly, a hospital providing medical service to a patient incurs costs for medical supplies (materials), salaries of doctors and nurses (labour), and amortization, utilities, insurance, and so on (overhead).

The *primary difference between manufacturing entities and service companies is that the products provided by service companies are consumed immediately*. In contrast, products made by manufacturing companies can be retained in the form of inventory prior to being purchased by customers. Like their counterparts in manufacturing, managers of service companies are under increasing pressure to lower costs, improve quality, and increase productivity. Information regarding product costing is useful in the accomplishment of these goals, regardless of whether the consumption of the product is immediate or delayed. Although service companies may not report product costs in the form of inventory on their financial statements, they certainly segregate and analyze product costs for internal decision-making purposes.

LO9

Understand how products provided by service companies differ from products made by manufacturing companies.

▌ Cost Measurement in Managerial Reports

Your background in financial accounting may mislead you with respect to the way that cost data are likely to appear in managerial reports. Financial accounting suggests that costs are used solely for the development of a single set of financial statements. This is not true with respect to managerial reporting. Managers are interested not only in the profitability of the business as a whole but also in the profitability of its various subcomponents. For example, managers may be interested in the profitability of particular products, customers, departments, equipment purchases, and business strategies. Because managers analyze different subcomponents of a business, the same cost may be viewed from different perspectives. For instance, although research and development costs are usually included in general, selling, and administrative expenses for the purpose of financial reports, these costs may be considered a component of product cost for the purpose of making a pricing decision. In addition, research and development could be considered a departmental cost if management were trying to assess the effectiveness of the research department. Likewise, the same research and development costs may be included in a social responsibility report when the president of the company is trying to convince consumers that the company is concerned with the development of environmentally safe products. Be prepared to broaden your perspective regarding the measurement and use of cost data. You must *interpret* cost data in a variety of different contexts. Accordingly, *thinking* will serve you more effectively than *memorizing*.

▌ Trends in Managerial Accounting

LO10

Explain how emerging trends are affecting the managerial accounting discipline.

Many factors are contributing to the development of a *global economy*. Satellites enable worldwide communication; superships move vast supplies of merchandise swiftly and efficiently across oceans. Delivery companies, such as Federal Express and United Parcel Service, guarantee overnight delivery to virtually every corner of the world. Executives move across international boundaries in supersonic aircraft. Trade agreements reduce or eliminate tariffs, quotas, and other barriers to free trade. As a result, many companies face worldwide competition. The new competitive environment has forced these companies to reengineer their production and delivery systems to eliminate waste, reduce errors, and minimize costs.

One of the key ingredients to successful **reengineering** is a practice known as *benchmarking*. **Benchmarking** involves the identification of the **best practices** used by world-class competitors. By studying and mimicking these practices, a company uses benchmarking to implement the most effective methods of accomplishing various tasks. Three widely recognized *best practices* identified by world-class companies include activity-based management (ABM), value-added assessment, and just-in-time inventory (JIT). These best practices are discussed in a later chapter (Chapter 6).

focus on International Issues

Where in the World Do New Managerial Accounting Practices Come from?

Many of the emerging practices in managerial accounting have their foundations in Asian companies. These companies established employee relationships that achieve continuous improvement by encouraging employees to participate in the design as well as the execution of their work. Employee empowerment through the practice known as *kaizen management* recognizes gradual, continuous improvement as the ultimate key to cost reduction and quality control. Employees are encouraged to identify and eliminate nonvalue-added activities, idle time, and waste. The response is overwhelming when employee suggestions are taken seriously. For example, the Toyota Motor Corporation reported the receipt of approximately two million employee suggestions in one single year alone.

Source: Takao Tanaka, "Kaizen Budgeting: Toyota's Cost Control System Under TQC," *Journal of Cost Management*, Winter 1996, p. 62.

Activity-Based Management

Andy Grove's strategic inflection points discussed at the beginning of this chapter are frequently based on simple changes in perspective. For example, imagine how the realization that the world is round, instead of flat, changed people's approach to travel. A developing strategic inflection point for management accounting stems from realizing that an organization cannot manage *costs*. Instead, it manages the *activities* that cause costs to be incurred. **Activities** are the actions taken by an organization to accomplish its mission. The primary mission of all organizations is to provide products (i.e., goods and services) that their customers *value*. Accordingly, the sequence of activities through which an organization provides products to its customers is called a **value chain**. **Activity-based management** seeks to manage the value chain to create new or to refine existing **value-added activities** and to eliminate or reduce *nonvalue-added activities*. As its name implies, a value-added activity is any unit of work that contributes to a product's ability to satisfy customer needs. Cooking adds value to food served to a hungry customer. **Nonvalue-added activities** are tasks undertaken that do not contribute to a product's ability to satisfy customer needs. Waiting for the oven to preheat so that food can be cooked does not add value. Most customers value cooked food, but they do not value waiting for it.

Value-Added Assessment

Activity-based management requires a critical assessment of the full range of activities that cause the customers of a business to *value* its products. To illustrate, consider the value-added activities associated with a pizza restaurant. Begin with its products. To illustrate, consider the value-added activities associated with a pizza restaurant. Begin with a customer who is hungry for pizza; certain activities must be performed to satisfy that hunger. These activities are outlined in Exhibit 1–13. At a minimum, the restaurant must conduct some type of research and development (obtain a recipe), obtain the raw materials (gather the ingredients), manufacture the product (mix and cook the ingredients), market the product (i.e., advise the consumer of its availability), and deliver the product (transfer the pizza to the customer).

Businesses are able to gain competitive advantages by adding activities that effectively satisfy customer needs. For example, Domino's Pizza grew rapidly as a result of its recognition of the value customers placed on the convenience of having a pizza delivered to their homes. Alternatively, Little Caesar's has been highly successful at satisfying the value customers place on low prices. Other restaurateurs may seek to satisfy customer values pertaining to taste, ambiance, or location. Businesses can also gain competitive advantages by identifying and eliminating nonvalue-added activities. By eliminating nonvalue-added activities, a business can provide products of equal quality at a lower cost than its competitors. Some of the more common nonvalue-added activities and approaches taken to eliminate them are discussed in the next section of this text.

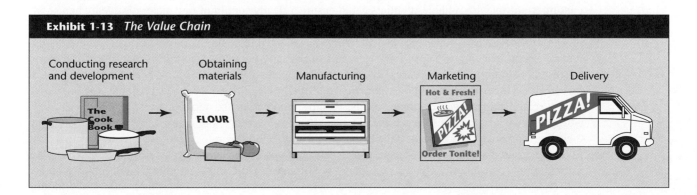

Exhibit 1-13 *The Value Chain*

| Conducting research and development | Obtaining materials | Manufacturing | Marketing | Delivery |

Just-in-Time Inventory

A common nonvalue-added activity found in many types of business organizations is maintaining excess amounts of inventory. Consumers want inventory to be available when they need it, but they do not benefit when more inventory is stored than is necessary to meet their demands. Indeed, the customer may suffer from excessive inventory holdings because some of the cost of inventory maintenance is passed on in the form of higher prices. Many businesses have been able to simultaneously reduce their **inventory holding costs** and increase customer satisfaction by making inventory available **just in time (JIT)** for customer consumption. For example, hamburgers that are made to order are fresher and more individualized than those that are made in advance and stored until a customer places an order. Many fast-food restaurants have discovered that JIT systems lead not only to greater customer satisfaction but also to reduced costs through the elimination of waste.

Traditionally, manufacturing companies have maintained large amounts of inventory to avoid production disruptions. Large supplies of raw materials are maintained to ensure their availability in case suppliers are unable to provide the materials when they are needed. Large numbers of finished goods are also maintained to ensure the ability to meet unexpected customer demands. Some companies even maintain inventories of partially completed goods as a buffer against the possibility of internal disruptions, such as strikes or mechanical failures. For example, the entire production process of Ford Motor Company could be halted if employees working in the brake factory went out on strike. This potential disaster can be avoided if Ford maintains a large enough supply of brakes to provide a cushion of time before a strike can be settled.

Unfortunately, maintaining large amounts of inventory is expensive. Many costs are obvious: financing, warehouse space, supervision, theft, damage, and obsolescence. Other costs are hidden: diminished motivation, sloppy work, inattentive attitudes, and increased production time. Employees are less concerned with avoiding problems that create shortages if they feel there is an ample supply of inventory available to cover unanticipated shortfalls. For example, a purchasing agent was overheard making the comment, "I'm not sure if the clerk got that order right. Anyway, it doesn't really matter. If they send us the wrong stuff, we have a large enough supply of parts on hand that we have time to send back the wrong parts and reorder the right ones." The agent failed to consider the cost of processing a new order. Someone must be paid to inspect the goods when they arrive. If the order is wrong, someone must repackage the merchandise and return it to the supplier. Someone must spend time reordering the right parts. These costs could be avoided if the supply of inventory were low enough to motivate the purchasing agent to get the order right in the first place.

To increase efficiency and profitability, many managers are asking whether the value added by inventory buffers is sufficient to justify the costs incurred. It may cost less to solve the problems that create the need for inventory than it costs to maintain the inventory. For example, avoiding a strike may cost less than maintaining enough inventory to wait out its settlement. Similarly, establishing **most-favoured customer status** with reliable suppliers could ensure a steady supply of raw materials even when shortages exist for other customers. Such assurances can eliminate the need for maintaining raw materials inventories. Likewise, proper mechanical maintenance can reduce the likelihood of mechanical disruptions, thereby reducing the need for inventories of partially completed goods. Furthermore, communication and commitments from customers can stabilize demand and minimize the need for finished goods inventories. Under ideal conditions, materials and finished products are made available *just in time* to satisfy manufacturing and customer needs, thereby eliminating the requirement for inventories. Few companies have been able to reach the JIT ideal of zero inventory, but many have reduced the size of their inventories and the holding costs associated with them.

The increased security measures implemented in the wake of September 11, 2001, tragedy in New York City and Washington created problems for auto makers in Canada and the United States who use JIT. Automobile parts manufacturers located in the Windsor area of Canada that supply automobile assembly plants in the Detroit area of the United States experienced slowdowns in the delivery system. The terrorism threat caused increased cross-border slowdowns due to increased security measures.

Trucks that normally travelled between plants hourly were being held up for several hours each way. This caused slowdowns in production and assembly because the parts being produced could not be delivered on time, and because deliveries were delayed, assembly was also slowed down. The normal cross-border trade in the Windsor–Detroit corridor is estimated to be $1 billion per day.

Just-in-Time Illustration

To illustrate the benefits of a JIT system, consider the case of Paula Elliot, a student at a large urban university. She helps support herself by selling flowers on a street corner. In the late afternoon, she purchases flowers from a florist, drives them to a downtown location, and sells them to people who are on their way home from work. She pays $2 for a single stem rose and sells each rose for $3. She purchases 25 roses per day and works three days per week. Some days she does not have enough flowers to meet customer demand. On other days, she must throw away one or two flowers. She believes that quality is important and refuses to sell flowers that are not fresh. During the month of May, she purchased 300 roses and sold 280. She calculated her driving cost to be $45. Her income statement for the month is shown in Exhibit 1–14.

After studying just-in-time inventory systems in her managerial accounting class, Paula was convinced that she could apply the concepts to increase the profitability of her own small business. She began by *reengineering* her distribution system. Specifically, she began purchasing her flowers from a florist located within walking distance of her sales location. She had considered purchasing from this florist earlier but had rejected the idea because the florist's normal selling price was $2.25 per rose. That price was too high considering her current cost of $2 per rose. After learning about *most-favoured customer status*,

Exhibit 1-14 *Income Statement*	
Sales Revenue (280 units × $3 per unit)	$840
Cost of Goods Sold (300 units × $2 per unit)	(600)
Gross Margin	240
Driving Expense	(45)
Net Income	$195

however, she decided to discuss the matter with the prospective florist. By guaranteeing the new florist that she would buy at least 30 roses per week, she was able to convince him to match her current cost of $2 per rose. The florist agreed that she could make purchases in batches of any size so long as the total amounted to at least 30 per week. Under this arrangement, Paula was able to buy roses *just in time* to meet customer demand. Each day, she purchased a small number of flowers. When she ran out of flowers, she simply returned to the florist for additional ones. The JIT system also enabled her to eliminate the *nonvalue-added activities* associated with driving to the old florist, thereby eliminating the driving expense. Customer satisfaction actually improved because no one was ever turned away for lack of inventory. In June, Paula was able to buy and sell 310 roses with no waste and no driving expense. The June income statement is shown in Exhibit 1–15.

Paula was ecstatic about the $115 increase in profit (i.e., $310 in June − $195 May = $115 increase), but she was puzzled as to exactly what had caused the change. Clearly, she had saved $40 by avoiding waste (20 flowers × $2 each). She had also eliminated $45 of driving expenses. However, these two factors explained only $85 ($40 waste + $45 driving expense) of the $115 total. What had caused the remaining $30 ($115 − $85) increase in profit? Paula decided to ask her accounting professor to help her understand the remaining $30 difference.

Exhibit 1-15 *Income Statement*	
Sales Revenue (310 units × $3 per unit)	$930
Cost of Goods Sold (310 units × $2 per unit)	(620)
Gross Margin	310
Driving Expense	0
Net Income	$310

The professor explained that the May sales suffered from *lost opportunities*. Recall that under the old inventory system, Paula had to turn away some prospective customers because she ran out of flowers before all customers were served. Note that sales increased from 280 roses in May to 310 roses in June. The most logical explanation for the 30 unit difference (310 − 280) is that customers who would have purchased flowers in May were unable to do so because of a lack of availability. Accordingly, May's sales suffered from a lost opportunity to earn a gross margin of $1 per flower on 30 roses. In accounting terms, May's profit suffered from a $30 **opportunity cost**. This cost provides the missing link in explaining the difference in the profitability between May and June. The total $115 difference is composed of (1) savings of $40 from the elimination of waste, (2) driving expense of $45, and (3) opportunity cost of $30.

In summary, companies that carry inventory incur two types of cost. The first category is explicit holding cost that includes financing charges, warehouse space, personnel, and lost, damaged, stolen, or otherwise wasted inventory. The second is the hidden cost of lost opportunities, such as lost sales or employee inefficiency. Just-in-time inventory systems eliminate or diminish these costs by managing resources so that they are consumed immediately, thereby eliminating the need for inventories.

Value Chain Analysis across Companies

Comprehensive value chain analysis extends from obtaining raw materials to the ultimate disposal of finished products. It encompasses the activities performed not only by a particular organization but also by that organization's suppliers and those who service its finished products. For example, PepsiCo. must be concerned with the activities of the company that supplies the containers that hold its soda as well as the retail companies that sell its products. If cans of Pepsi fail to open properly, the customer is likely to blame PepsiCo., rather than the supplier of the cans. Likewise, a customer who receives a bad glass of Pepsi in a restaurant may conclude that the soda brand is distasteful, rather than blaming the restaurateur for failing to properly mix carbonated water with the soft drink syrup. Comprehensive value chain analysis can lead to the identification and elimination of nonvalue-added activities that occur between companies. For example, container companies could be encouraged to build manufacturing facilities near Pepsi's bottling factories, thereby eliminating nonvalue-added activities associated with transporting empty containers from the manufacturer to the bottling facility. The result is a cost saving that benefits the customer by lowering costs without affecting quality.

---

a look
back

Managerial accounting primarily concerns the information needs of *internal* users, and *financial accounting* primarily concerns the information needs of *external* users. Managerial accounting uses a wider range of information, such as economic, operating, nonfinancial, and financial data. Managerial accounting information is local (i.e., pertains to the company's subunits), is limited by cost/benefit considerations, is more concerned with relevance and timeliness and is future oriented. Financial accounting information, on the other hand, is more global than managerial accounting information. In other words, it supplies information that applies to the whole company. Financial accounting is regulated by numerous authorities, is characterized by objectivity, is focused on reliability and accuracy, and is historical in nature.

Both managerial and financial accounting are concerned with product costing. Financial accountants need product cost information to determine the amount of inventory shown on the balance sheet and the amount of cost of goods sold shown on the income statement. Managerial accountants need to know the cost of products for pricing decisions and for control and evaluation purposes. When determining the unit cost of products, managers use the average cost per unit. The actual cost of each product requires an unreasonable amount of time and record keeping and makes no difference in product pricing and product costs control decisions.

Product costs are the costs incurred in the process of making products. They include the costs of direct labour, direct materials, and overhead. *Overhead costs* are product costs that cannot be cost effectively traced to the product; therefore, they are assigned to products through a process known as *cost allocation*. Examples of overhead include indirect materials, indirect labour, amortization, rent, and utilities on manufacturing facilities. Product costs are first accumulated in an asset account (inventory). They are expensed as cost of goods sold in the period the inventory is sold. The difference between the sales revenue and cost of goods sold is called *gross margin*.

General, *selling*, *and administrative costs* are classified separately from product costs. They are subtracted from the gross margin to determine net income. General, selling and administrative costs can be divided into two categories. The costs that occur before the manufacturing process begins (e.g., research and development costs) are called *upstream costs*. The costs that occur after manufacturing is complete (e.g., transportation) are called *downstream costs*.

Service companies, like manufacturing companies, incur materials, labour, and overhead costs, but the products provided by service companies are consumed immediately. Therefore, service company product costs are not accumulated in an inventory account.

A *code of ethical conduct* is needed in the accounting profession because accountants hold positions of trust and face conflicts of interest. In recognition of the temptations that accountants face, the IMA has issued the statement *Standard of Ethical Conduct for Management Accountants*, which provides accountants guidance in resisting temptations and in making difficult decisions.

Such trends as *just-in-time inventory* and *activity-based management* are methods that many companies have used to reengineer their production and delivery systems to eliminate waste, reduce errors, and minimize costs. Activity-based management seeks to eliminate or reduce *nonvalue-added activities* and to create new *value-added activities*. Just-in-time inventory seeks to reduce inventory holding costs and to lower prices for customers by making inventory available just in time for customer consumption.

a look
forward

Now that you have gained an appreciation for one type of cost classification (i.e., product versus G, S, & A), you are ready to see how other classifications can be used to facilitate managerial decision making. In the next chapter, you will learn how to classify costs according to the *behaviour* costs exhibited when the number of units of product increases or decreases (i.e., volume of activity changes). More specifically, you will learn to distinguish between costs that vary with activity volume changes versus costs that remain fixed with activity volume changes. You will learn not only to recognize *cost behaviour* but also how such recognition can facilitate the evaluation of business risk and opportunity.

KEY TERMS

Activities The actions taken by an organization to accomplish its mission. *(p. 21)*

Activity-based management (ABM) The management of the activities of an organization so as to add the greatest value by developing products that satisfy the needs of that organization's customers. *(p. 21)*

Benchmarking The identification of the best practices used by world-class competitors. *(p. 20)*

Best practices Practices used by world-class companies. *(p. 20)*

CICA Canadian Institute of Chartered Accountants. *(p. 5)*

Continuous improvement A total quality management (TQM) feature that refers to an ongoing process through which employees learn to eliminate waste, reduce response time, minimize defects, and simplify the design and delivery of products and services to customers. *(p. 6)*

Cost allocation The process of dividing a total cost into parts and assigning the parts to relevant objects. *(p. 13)*

Cost-plus pricing A strategy that establishes the price by referring to the cost of the product. Normally, the price is set at cost plus a designated percentage of cost. *(p. 7)*

Direct labour Wages paid to production workers whose efforts can be easily and conveniently traced to products. *(p. 10)*

Direct raw materials The costs of raw materials used to make products that can be easily and conveniently traced to those products. *(p. 10)*

Downstream costs Costs incurred after the manufacturing process is complete. Examples include delivery costs and sales commissions. *(p. 18)*

Efficient markets hypothesis The line of reasoning that holds that (1) creditors and investors look to the substance (economic consequences) of business events, regardless of how the transactions are reported in financial statements, and (2) all publicly available information is immediately incorporated into the price of stock. Acceptance of the strong form of this hypothesis suggests that creditors and investors are not deceived by spurious reporting practices and that stock prices reflect the true value of the company's stock (stock prices are not over- or undervalued). *(p. 16)*

Financial accounting The field of accounting designed to meet the information needs of external users of business information (creditors, investors, governmental agencies, financial analysts, etc.). Its objective is to classify and record business events and transactions to facilitate the production of external financial reports (income statement, balance sheet, cash flow statement, and statement of changes in equity). *(p. 4)*

Finished goods The end result of the manufacturing process. Measured by the accumulated cost of raw materials, labour, and overhead. *(p. 7)*

General, selling, and administrative costs All costs that are not associated with obtaining or manufacturing a product. In practice, these costs are sometimes referred to as *period costs* because they are normally expensed in the period in which the economic sacrifice is incurred. *(p. 12)*

Generally accepted accounting principles (GAAP) The rules and regulations that accountants agree to follow when preparing financial reports for public distribution. *(p. 5)*

Indirect cost A cost that cannot be easily traced to a specific product. *(p. 13)*

Inventory holding costs The costs associated with acquiring and retaining inventory including the costs of storage space; lost, stolen, or damaged merchandise; insurance; personnel and management; and interest. *(p. 22)*

Just in time (JIT) An inventory flow system that minimizes the amount of inventory on hand by making inventory available for customer consumption on demand, therefore eliminating the need to store inventory. The system reduces explicit holding costs, including financing, warehouse storage, supervision, theft, damage, and obsolescence. It also eliminates hidden opportunity costs, such as lost revenue due to the lack of availability of inventory. *(p. 22)*

Managerial accounting The field of accounting designed to meet the information needs of managers and other individuals working inside the business. It is concerned with information gathering and reporting that adds value to the business. Managerial accounting information is not regulated or made available to the public. *(p. 4)*

Manufacturing overhead Production costs that cannot be traced directly to products. *(p. 13)*

Most-favoured customer status An arrangement wherein a supplier and customer achieve mutual benefit by providing each other with favourable treatment that is not extended to other associates. *(p. 22)*

Nonvalue-added activities Tasks undertaken that do not contribute to a product's ability to satisfy customer needs. *(p. 21)*

Opportunity cost The cost of lost opportunities, such as the failure to make sales due to an insufficient supply of inventory. *(p. 24)*

Overhead Costs associated with producing products that cannot be cost effectively traced to products; includes indirect costs, such as indirect materials, indirect labour, utilities, rent, depreciation on manufacturing facilities and equipment, and planning, design, and setup costs related to the manufacture of products. *(p. 12)*

Period costs General, selling, and administrative costs that are expensed in the period in which the economic sacrifice is made. *(p. 12)*

Product costs All costs related to obtaining or manufacturing a product intended for sale to customers. These costs are accumulated in inventory accounts and expensed as costs of goods sold at the point of sale. For a manufacturing company, product costs include direct materials, direct labour, and manufacturing overhead. *(p. 7)*

Product costing The classification and accumulation of individual inputs (i.e., materials, labour, and overhead) for the purpose of determining the cost of making a good or providing a service. *(p. 7)*

Raw materials The physical commodities (e.g., wood, metal, paint, and so on.) used in the manufacturing process. See also *direct raw materials*. *(p. 10)*

Reengineering Business practices designed by companies to make production and delivery systems more competitive in world markets by eliminating or minimizing waste, errors, and costs. *(p. 20)*

Total Quality Management (TQM) A management philosophy that includes (1) a continuous systematic problem-solving philosophy that engages personnel at all levels of the organization in eliminating waste, defects, and nonvalue-added activities, and (2) a continuous organizational commitment to the accomplishment of customer satisfaction. *(p. 6)*

Upstream costs Costs incurred before the manufacturing process begins, for example, research and development costs. *(p. 18)*

Value-added activity Any unit of work that contributes to a product's ability to satisfy customer needs. *(p. 21)*

Value chain The linked sequence of activities that create value for the customer. *(p. 21)*

Value-added principle The benefits attained (i.e., value added) by the accounting process should exceed the cost of the process. *(p. 6)*

1. What is the difference between financial and managerial accounting?
2. What does the value-added principle mean as it applies to managerial accounting information? Give an example of value-added information that may be included in managerial accounting reports but is not shown in publicly reported financial statements.
3. What are the two dimensions of a total quality management program? Why is it being used in business practice?
4. How does product costing used in financial accounting differ from product costing used in managerial accounting?
5. What does the statement "costs can be assets or expenses" mean?
6. Why are the salaries of production workers accumulated in an inventory account instead of being expensed on the income statement?
7. How do product costs affect the financial statements?
8. What is an indirect cost? What are examples of product costs that would be classified as indirect?

9. How does a product cost differ from a general, selling, and administrative cost? Give examples of each.
10. Why is cost classification important to managers?
11. What does the term *reengineering* mean? Name some reengineering practices.
12. What is cost allocation? Give an example of a cost that needs to be allocated.
13. What are some of the common ethical conflicts that accountants encounter?
14. What costs should be considered in determining the sales price of a product?
15. What does the term *activity-based costing* mean?
16. What is a value chain?
17. What do the terms *value-added activity* and *nonvalue-added activity* mean? Provide an example of each type of activity.
18. What is a just-in-time (JIT) inventory system? Name some inventory costs that can be eliminated or reduced by its use.

EXERCISE 1-1   *Features of Financial versus Managerial Accounting*   **L.O. 1**

Required

Indicate whether each of the following items is a feature of managerial or of financial accounting:

a. Information is global and pertains to the company as a whole.
b. Information is provided to insiders, including executives, managers, and operators.
c. Information is factual and is characterized by objectivity, reliability, consistency, and accuracy.
d. Information is reported continuously with a current or future orientation.
e. Information is provided to outsiders, including investors, creditors, government agencies, analysts, and reporters.
f. Information is regulated by the provinces, exchanges, and CICA.
g. Information is based on estimates that are bounded by relevance and timeliness.
h. Information is historically based and usually reported annually.
i. Information that pertains to subunits of the organization is local.
j. Information includes economic and nonfinancial data as well as financial data.

EXERCISE 1-2   *Identification of Product versus General, Selling, and Administrative Costs*   **L.O. 5**

Required

Indicate whether each of the following costs should be classified as a product cost or as a general, selling, and administrative cost:

a. The cost of supplies used in a doctor's office.
b. Amortization on the office furniture of the president of a company.
c. Direct material used in a manufacturing company.
d. Indirect materials used in a manufacturing company.
e. Salaries of employees working in the accounting department.
f. Commissions paid to sales staff.
g. Interest on the mortgage for the company's corporate headquarters.
h. Indirect labour used to manufacture inventory.
i. Attorney's fees charged to a client.
j. Research and development costs incurred to create new drugs for a pharmaceutical company.

L.O. 5 EXERCISE 1-3 *Classification and Treatment of Costs: Product or GS&A/Asset or Expense*

Required

Use the following table to indicate whether each event results in the incurrence of a product cost or a general, selling, and administrative (G, S, & A) cost. Also indicate whether the cost would be placed in an asset or expense account. Assume that all transactions are cash transactions. The first cost has been recorded as an example.

Cost Category	Product/ G, S, & A	Asset/ Expense
Paid wages to production workers	Product	Asset
Paid for advertising		
Paid for the promotion of customer relations		
Purchased production supplies		
Recognized amortization on administration building		
Recognized amortization on manufacturing equipment		
Paid for research and development		
Paid for setup of manufacturing equipment		
Paid for utilities used in factory		
Purchased cars for sales staff		
Paid distributions to stockholders		
Used general office supplies		
Used raw materials in the manufacturing process		
Recognized use of prepaid rent on office equipment		

L.O. 5 EXERCISE 1-4 *The Effect of Product versus General, Selling, and Administrative Costs on Financial Statements*

Required

Bledsoe Industries recognized $4,000 of accrued compensation cost. Using the following horizontal financial statement model, record this event under the following two assumptions: (1) the compensation is for office personnel, and (2) the compensation is for production workers.

	Assets	=	Liab.	+	Equity	Rev	+	Exp	+	Net Inc.	Cash Flow
1.											
2.											

L.O. 5 EXERCISE 1-5 *The Effect of Product versus General, Selling, and Administrative Costs on Financial Statements*

Required

Aaron Industries recognized the annual cost of depreciation on December 31, 2008. Using the following horizontal financial statement model, indicate how this event affected the company's financial statements under the following two assumptions: (1) the amortization was on office furniture, and (2) the amortization was on manufacturing equipment. Indicate whether the event acts to increase (I), decrease (D), or not affect (NA) each element of the financial statements. Also, in the Cash column, indicate whether the cash flow is associated with operating activities (OA), investing activities (IA), or financing activities (FA). (*Note:* Accumulated amortization is shown as a decrease in the book value of the appropriate asset account.)

Event No.	Assets					Equity						
	Cash	+ Manuf. Equip.*	+ Office Furn.	+ Inventory	=	Cont. Cap.	+ Ret. Ear.	Rev	− Exp	= Net Inc.	Cash flow
1											
2											

EXERCISE 1-6   Components of Product Cost in a Manufacturing Company   L.O. 2

Kay Simmons was talking to another accounting student, Dean Dillard. Upon discovering that the accounting department offered an upper-level course in cost measurement, Kay remarked to Dean, "How difficult can it be? My parents own a toy store. All you have to do to figure out how much something costs is to look at the invoice. Surely you don't need an entire course to teach you how to read an invoice."

Required
a. Identify the three main components of product cost for a manufacturing entity.
b. Explain why measuring product cost for a manufacturing entity is more complicated than measuring product cost for a retail toy store.
c. Assume that Kay's parents rent a store for $4,000 per month. Note that different types of toys use different amounts of store space. For example, displaying a bicycle requires more store space than displaying a deck of cards. Also, some toys remain on the shelf for longer periods of time. Fad toys sell out rapidly, but traditional toys require a longer time period to sell. Under these circumstances, how would you determine the amount of rental cost required to display each type of toy? Identify two other costs incurred by a toy store that may be difficult to allocate to individual toys.

EXERCISE 1-7   Product versus General, Selling, and Administrative Costs   L.O. 5

A review of the accounting records of Kelly Manufacturing indicated that the company incurred the following payroll costs during the month of February:
1. Salary of the company president—$16,000.
2. Salary of the vice-president of manufacturing—$8,000.
3. Salary of the chief financial officer—$9,400.
4. Salary of the vice-president of marketing—$7,800.
5. Salaries of middle managers in manufacturing plant (i.e., department heads, production supervisors)—$98,000.
6. Wages of production workers—$469,000.
7. Salaries of administrative secretaries—$56,000.
8. Salaries of engineers and other personnel responsible for the maintenance of production equipment—$89,000.
9. Commissions paid to sales staff—$126,000.

Required
a. Determine the amount of the payroll that would be classified as general, selling, and administrative expense.
b. Assuming that Kelly made 2,000 units of product and sold 1,800 of them during the month of February, determine the amount of the payroll that would be included in cost of goods sold.

EXERCISE 1-8   Process of Recording Product versus General, Selling, and Administrative Costs in a   L.O. 2, 4, 5
Financial Statements Model

Brady Manufacturing experienced the following events during its first accounting period:
1. Acquired cash from its owners.
2. Paid cash to purchase raw materials that were used to make products.
3. Paid wages to production workers.
4. Paid salaries to administrative staff.
5. Recognized amortization on manufacturing equipment.
6. Recognized amortization on office furniture.

7. Recognized revenue from cash sale of products.
8. Recognized cost of goods sold from sale referenced in Event 7.

Required

Use a horizontal statement model to show how each event affects the balance sheet, income statement, and cash flow statement. Indicate whether the event acts to increase (I), decrease (D), or not affect (NA) each element of the financial statements. Also, in the Cash column, indicate whether the cash flow is associated with operating activities (OA), investing activities (IA), or financing activities (FA). The first transaction has been recorded as an example. (*Note:* Accumulated amortization is shown as a decrease in the book value of the appropriate asset account.)

Event No.		Assets				Equity						
	Cash	+ Manuf. Equip.*	+ Office Furn.	+ Inventory =	Cont. Cap.	+ Ret. Ear.	Rev	− Exp	= Net Inc.		Cash flow	
1	I	n/a	n/a	n/a	I	n/a	n/a	n/a	n/a		I	FA

L.O. 2, 3, 4 EXERCISE 1-9   *Allocation of Product Costs between Ending Inventory and Cost of Goods Sold*

Clevland Manufacturing Company began operations on January 1. During the accounting period, Clevland started and completed 4,000 units of product. The company incurred the following costs:
1. Raw materials purchased and used—$2,000.
2. Wages of production workers—$3,000.
3. Salaries of administrative and sales personnel—$1,200.
4. Amortization on manufacturing equipment—$3,600.
5. Amortization on administrative equipment—$1,400.

Clevland sold 3,000 units of product.

Required

a. Determine the total product cost for the period.
b. Determine the amount of ending inventory.
c. Determine the amount of cost of goods sold.

L.O. 4, 5 EXERCISE 1-10   *Financial Statement Effects for Manufacturing versus Service Organizations*

The following financial statements model shows the effects of recognizing amortization under two different circumstances. One of the events represents the recognition of amortization for a machine used in a manufacturing company. The other event represents the recognition of amortization for X-ray equipment used in a doctor's office. The effects of each event have been recorded using the letter (I) to represent increase, (D) for decrease, and (n/a) for not affected.

Event No.		Assets		Equity						
	Cash	+ Equip.	+ Inventory =	Cont. Cap.	+ Ret. Ear.	Rev	− Exp	= Net Inc.	Cash flow	
1	n/a	D	n/a	n/a	D	n/a	I	D	n/a	
2	n/a	D	I	n/a	n/a	n/a	n/a	n/a		

Required

a. Identify the event that represents amortization of the X-ray equipment.

b. Explain why the recognition of amortization for equipment used in a manufacturing company affects financial statements differently from the recognition of depreciation for equipment used in a service organization.

EXERCISE 1-11   *Effect of Product versus General, Selling, and Administrative Cost on the Income*   **L.O. 5**
                     Statement and Cash Flow Statement

Required

Each of the following events describes the acquisition of an asset that requires a year-end adjusting entry. Explain how the acquisition of the asset and the adjusting entry affect the amount of net income and the cash flow shown on the year-end financial statements. Also, in the Cash column, indicate whether the cash flow is associated with operating activities (OA), investing activities (IA), or financing activities (FA). Assume a December 31 annual closing date. The first event has been recorded as an example.

	Net Income	Cash Flow
Event No.	**Amount of Change**	**Amount of Change**
1. Acquisition of computer equipment	N/A	($14,000) IA
1. Adjusting Entry	($3,000)	N/A

1. Paid $14,000 cash on January 1 to purchase computer equipment that was used for administrative purposes. The equipment had an estimated expected useful life of four years and a $2,000 salvage value.
2. Paid $14,000 cash on January 1 to purchase manufacturing equipment. The equipment had an estimated expected useful life of four years and a $2,000 salvage value.
3. Paid $4,500 cash in advance on May 1 for a one-year rental contract on administrative offices.
4. Paid $4,500 cash in advance on May 1 for a one-year rental contract on manufacturing facilities.
5. Paid $600 cash to purchase supplies to be used by the marketing department. At the end of the accounting period, $150 of supplies was still on hand.
6. Paid $600 cash to purchase supplies to be used in the manufacturing process. At the end of the accounting period, $150 of supplies was still on hand.

EXERCISE 1-12   *Upstream and Downstream Costs*   **L.O. 8**

During 2002, Mendez Manufacturing Company incurred $45,000,000 of research and development (R&D) costs to create a long-life battery to use in computers. In accordance with CICA standards, the entire R&D cost was recognized as an expense in 2002. Manufacturing costs including direct materials, direct labour, and overhead are expected to be $130 per unit. Packaging, shipping, and sales commissions are expected to cost $25 per unit. Mendez expects to sell 1,000,000 batteries before new research is expected to render the battery design technologically obsolete. During 2002, Mendez made 220,000 batteries and sold 200,000.

Required

a. Identify the upstream and downstream costs.

b. Determine the amount of cost of goods sold and the ending inventory balance.

c. Determine the sales price assuming that Mendez desires to earn a profit margin that is equal to 25 percent of the *total cost* of developing, making, and distributing the batteries.

d. Prepare an income statement for 2002. Use the sales price developed in Part *c*.

e. Provide a logical explanation as to why Mendez would price the batteries at a level that would generate a loss for the 2002 accounting period.

L.O. 10 EXERCISE 1-13   *Value Chain Analysis*

Sonic Speaker Company (SSC) manufactures and sells high-quality audio speakers. The speakers are encased in solid walnut cabinets supplied by Cranston Cabinet, Inc. Cranston packages the speakers in durable moisture-proof boxes and ships them by truck to SSC's manufacturing facility, which is located 50 miles from the cabinet factory.

Required

Identify the nonvalue-added activities that occur between the companies described in the preceding scenario. Provide a logical explanation as to how these nonvalue-added activities could be eliminated.

L.O. 10 EXERCISE 1-14   *The Effect of a Just-in-Time Inventory System on Financial Statements*

After reviewing the financial statements of GRAYCO, Paul Nelson concluded that the company was a service company. Mr. Nelson based his conclusion on the fact that GRAYCO's financial statements contained no inventory accounts.

Required

Explain how GRAYCO's implementation of a 100 percent effective just-in-time inventory system could have led Mr. Nelson to a false conclusion regarding the nature of GRAYCO's business.

L.O. 10 EXERCISE 1-15   *Use of JIT to Minimize Waste and Lost Opportunity*

Yen Wong, a teacher at Billington Middle School, is in charge of ordering the T-shirts to be sold for the school's annual fund-raising project. The T-shirts are printed with a special Billington School logo. In some years, the supply of T-shirts was insufficient to satisfy the number of sales orders. In other years, T-shirts were left over. Excess T-shirts are normally donated to some charitable organization. T-shirts cost the school $8 each and are normally sold for $12 each. Mr. Wong has decided to order 1,000 shirts.

Required

a. If the school receives actual sales orders for 900 shirts, what is the amount of profit that the school will earn? What is the cost of waste due to excess inventory?

b. If the school receives actual sales orders for 1,100 shirts, what is the amount of profit that the school will earn? What is the amount of opportunity cost that will be incurred?

c. Explain how a JIT inventory system could be used to maximize profitability by eliminating waste and opportunity cost.

L.O. 10 EXERCISE 1-16   *Use of JIT to Minimize Holding Costs*

Alice's Pet Supplies purchases its inventory from a variety of suppliers, some of which require a six-week lead time before delivering the goods. To ensure that she has a sufficient supply of goods on hand, Ms. Exter, the owner, is required to maintain a large supply of inventory. The cost of this inventory averages $12,000. She usually finances the purchase of inventory and pays a 9 percent annual finance charge. Ms. Exter's accountant has suggested that she establish a relationship with a single large distributor who can satisfy all of her orders within a two-week time period. Given this quick turnaround time, she will be able to reduce her average inventory balance to $4,000. Ms. Exter also believes that she could save $2,000 per year by reducing phone bills, insurance, and warehouse rental space costs associated with ordering and maintaining the larger level of inventory.

Required

a. Is the new inventory system available to Ms. Exter a pure or approximate just-in-time system?

b. On the basis of the information provided, how much of Ms. Exter's inventory holding cost could be eliminated by taking the accountant's advice?

PROBLEMS—SERIES A

PROBLEM 1-1A   *Product versus General, Selling, and Administrative Costs*   **L.O. 2, 3, 4, 5, 6**

Schneider Manufacturing Company was started on January 1, 2001, when it acquired $45,000 cash from its owners. Schneider immediately purchased office furniture and manufacturing equipment costing $5,000 and $14,000, respectively. The office furniture had a five-year useful life and a zero salvage value. The manufacturing equipment had a $2,000 salvage value and an expected useful life of three years. The company paid $6,000 for salaries of administrative personnel and $8,000 for wages to production personnel. Finally, the company paid $9,000 for raw materials that were used to make inventory. All inventory was started and completed during the year. Schneider completed production on 5,000 units of product and sold 4,000 units at a price of $6 each in 2001. (Assume that all transactions are cash transactions.)

Required
a. Determine the total product cost and the average cost per unit of the inventory produced in 2001.
b. Determine the amount of cost of goods sold that would appear on the 2001 income statement.
c. Determine the amount of the ending inventory balance that would appear on the December 31, 2001, balance sheet.
d. Determine the amount of net income that would appear on the 2001 income statement.
e. Determine the amount of retained earnings that would appear on the December 31, 2001, balance sheet.
f. Determine the amount of total assets that would appear on the December 31, 2001, balance sheet.
g. Determine the amount of net cash flow from operating activities that would appear on the 2001 cash flow statement.
h. Determine the amount of net cash flow from investing activities that would appear on the 2001 cash flow statement.

PROBLEM 1-2A   *The Effect of Product versus Period Costs on Financial Statements*   **L.O. 2, 4, 5**

Harrison Manufacturing Company experienced the following accounting events during its first year of operation. With the exception of the adjusting entries for depreciation, assume that all transactions are cash transactions.
1. Acquired $25,000 of capital from the owners.
2. Paid $4,000 for the materials used to make its products, all of which were started and completed during the period.
3. Paid salaries of $2,200 to selling and administrative employees.
4. Paid wages of $3,500 to production workers.
5. Paid $4,800 for furniture used in selling and administrative offices. The furniture was acquired on January 1. It had an $800 estimated salvage value and a four-year useful life.
6. Paid $6,500 for manufacturing equipment. The equipment was acquired on January 1. It had a $500 estimated salvage value and a three-year useful life.
7. Sold inventory to customers for $12,500 that had cost $7,000 to make.

Required
Explain how these events would affect the balance sheet, income statement, and cash flow statement by recording them in a horizontal financial statements model as indicated here. The first event is recorded as an example.

Financial Statements Model												
			Assets				Equity					
Event No.	Cash	+ Manuf. Equip.*	+ Office Furn.	+ Inventory =	Cont. Cap.	+ Ret. Ear.	Rev	− Exp	= Net Inc.		Cash Flow	
1	25,000				25,000						25,000	FA

* Record accumulated amortization as negative amounts under these columns.

L.O. 2, 3, 4, 5   **PROBLEM 1-3A**   *Product versus General, Selling, and Administrative Costs*

The following transactions pertain to 2003, the first year operations of Gould Company. All inventory was started and completed during the accounting period. Assume that all transactions are cash transactions.

1. Acquired $1,000 of contributed capital from its owners.
2. Paid $200 for materials used to produce inventory.
3. Paid $300 to production workers.
4. Paid $100 rental fee for production equipment.
5. Paid $80 to administrative employees.
6. Paid $40 rental fee for administrative office equipment.
7. Produced 300 units of inventory of which 200 units were sold at a price of $3.50 each.

Required

Prepare an income statement, a balance sheet, and a cash flow statement.

L.O. 2, 3, 4, 5   **PROBLEM 1-4A**   *Service versus Manufacturing Companies*

Robertson Company began operations on January 1, 2002, by issuing common stock for $15,000 cash. During 2002, Robertson received $20,000 cash from revenue and incurred costs that required $30,000 of cash payments.

Required

Prepare an income statement, a balance sheet, and a cash flow statement for Robertson Company for 2002, under each of the following scenarios:

a. Robertson is a promoter of rock concerts. The $30,000 was paid to provide a rock concert that produced the revenue.

b. Robertson is in the car rental business. The $30,000 was paid to purchase an automobile. The automobile was purchased on January 1, 2002, has a four-year useful life, with no expected salvage value. Robertson uses straight-line amortization. The revenue was generated by leasing the automobile.

c. Robertson is a manufacturing company. The $30,000 was paid to purchase the following items:
   (1) Paid $4,000 cash to purchase materials that were used to make products during the year.
   (2) Paid $10,000 cash to workers who laboured to make products during the period.
   (3) Paid $1,000 cash for salaries of sales and administrative employees.
   (4) Paid $15,000 cash to purchase manufacturing equipment. The equipment was used solely for the purpose of making products. It had a three-year life and a $3,000 salvage value. The company uses straight-line amortization.
   (5) During 2002, Robertson started and completed 2,000 units of product. The revenue was earned when Robertson sold 1,500 units of product to its customers.

d. Refer to Part *c* above. Could Robertson determine the actual cost of making the 907th product? How likely is it that the actual cost of the 907th product was exactly the same as the cost of producing the 908th product? Explain why management may be more interested in average cost than in actual cost.

L.O. 2, 3, 4, 5, 6   **PROBLEM 1-5A**   *Importance of Cost Classification*

Kidd Manufacturing Company (KMC) was started when it acquired $20,000 from its owners. During the first year of operations, the company incurred specifically identifiable product costs (i.e., materials, labour, and overhead) amounting to $12,000. KMC also incurred $8,000 of engineering design and planning costs. There was a debate regarding how the design and planning costs should be classified. Advocates of Option 1 believe that the costs should be included in the general, selling, and administrative cost category. Advocates of Option 2 believe it would be more appropriate to classify the design and planning costs as product costs. During the accounting period, KMC made 4,000 units of product and sold 3,000 units at a price of $7 each. All transactions were cash transactions.

Required

a. Prepare an income statement, a balance sheet, and a cash flow statement under each of the two options.

b. Identify the option that results in financial statements that are more likely to leave a favourable impression on investors and creditors.

c. Assume that KMC provides an incentive bonus to the company president equal to 10 percent of net income. Compute the amount of the bonus under each of the two options. Identify the option that provides the president with the higher bonus.

d. Assume a 35 percent income tax rate. Determine the amount of income tax expense under each of the two options. Identify the option that minimizes the amount of the company's income tax expense.

e. Comment on the conflict between the interest of the company president as determined in Part *c* and the interest of the owners of the company as indicated in Part *d*. Describe an incentive compensation plan that would avoid conflicts between the interests of the president and the owners.

PROBLEM 1-6A   *Value Chain Analysis*   L.O. 10

Kerr Company invented a new process for manufacturing ice cream. Basically, the ingredients are mixed in high-tech machinery that forms the product into small round beads. Like a bag of balls, the ice cream beads are surrounded by air pockets when placed into packages. This design has numerous advantages. First, each bite of ice cream melts rapidly when placed into a person's mouth, creating a more flavourful sensation when compared with ordinary ice cream. Also, the air pockets mean that a smaller amount of ice cream is included in a typical serving. This not only lowers materials cost but also provides the consumer with a low-calorie snack. A cup looks as if it is full of ice cream, but it is really half full of air. The consumer eats only half the ingredients that are contained in a typical cup of blended ice cream. Finally, the texture of the ice cream makes scooping it out of a large container a very easy task. The frustration of trying to get a spoon into a rock-solid package of blended ice cream has been eliminated. Kerr Company named the new product Sonic Cream.

Like many other ice cream producers, Kerr Company purchases its raw materials from a food wholesaler. The ingredients are mixed in Kerr's manufacturing plant. The packages of finished product are distributed to privately owned franchise ice cream shops that sell Sonic Cream directly to the public. Kerr provides national advertising and is responsible for all research and development costs associated with making new flavours of Sonic Cream.

Required

a. On the basis of the information provided, draw a comprehensive value chain for Kerr Company that includes its suppliers and customers.

b. Identify the place in the chain where Kerr Company is exercising its opportunity to create added value beyond that currently being provided by its competitors.

PROBLEM 1-7A   *Use of JIT to Reduce Inventory Holding Costs*   L.O. 10

Reliable Manufacturing Company obtains its raw materials from a variety of suppliers. Reliable's strategy is to obtain the best price by letting the suppliers know that it does comparative shopping and buys from the lowest bidder. Approximately four years ago, unexpected increased demand resulted in materials shortages. Reliable was unable to find the materials it needed, even though it was willing to pay premium prices. Because of the lack of raw materials, Reliable was forced to close its manufacturing facility for two weeks. Reliable's president made a vow that her company would never again be at the mercy of its suppliers. She immediately ordered her purchasing agent to perpetually maintain a one-month supply of raw materials. Compliance with the president's orders resulted in a raw materials inventory amounting to approximately $1,000,000. Warehouse rental and personnel costs to maintain the inventory amounted to $5,000 per month. Reliable has a line of credit with a local bank that calls for a 12 percent annual rate of interest. Assume that the line of credit was used to finance the increased raw materials inventory.

Required

a. On the basis of the information provided, determine the annual holding cost of the raw materials inventory.

b. Explain how a JIT system could reduce Reliable's inventory holding cost.

c. Explain how most-favoured customer status could enable the establishment of a JIT inventory system without risking the raw materials shortages experienced in the past.

PROBLEM 1-8A   *Use of JIT to Minimize Waste and Lost Opportunity*   L.O. 10

Course Technologies, Inc. (CTI), provides review courses twice each year for students who desire to take national exams in financial planning. The price of textbooks is included in the registration fee. Text material requires constant updating and is useful for only one course. To minimize printing costs and ensure availability of books on the first day of class, CTI has books printed and delivered to its offices two weeks in advance of the first class. To ensure that an adequate supply of books is available, CTI normally orders enough books to cover a 10 percent increase over expected enrollment. Usually, there is an oversupply of books that is thrown away. However, demand occasionally exceeds expectations by more than 10 percent and there is an insufficient supply of books available for student use. Indeed, CTI has been forced to turn away students simply because of a lack of textbooks. CTI expects to enroll approximately 100 students per course. The tuition fee is $800 per student. The cost of teachers is $25,000 per course, textbooks cost $60 each, and other operating expenses are estimated to be $35,000 per course.

Required

a. Prepare an income statement, assuming that 95 students enroll in the course. Determine the amount of waste associated with unused books.

b. Prepare an income statement, assuming that 115 students attempt to enroll in the course. Note that five students are denied entry into the course because of an insufficient supply of textbooks. Determine the amount of lost profit resulting from the inability to serve the five additional students.

c. Suppose that textbooks can be produced through a high-speed copying process that permits delivery *just-in-time* for class to start. The cost of books made using this process, however, is $65 each. Assume that all books must be made under the same production process. In other words, CTI cannot order some of the books under the regular copy process and the rest under the high-speed process. Prepare an income statement under the JIT system assuming that 95 students enroll in a course. Compare the income statement under JIT with the income statement prepared in Requirement *a*. Comment on how the JIT system would affect profitability.

d. Assume the same facts as in Requirement *c* with respect to a JIT system that enables immediate delivery of books at a cost of $65 each. Prepare an income statement under the JIT system, assuming that 115 students enroll in a course. Compare the income statement under JIT with the income statement prepared in Requirement *b*. Comment on how the JIT system would affect profitability.

e. Discuss the possible effect of the JIT system on the level of customer satisfaction.

PROBLEMS—SERIES B

L.O. 2, 3, 4, 5, 6

PROBLEM 1-1B   *Product versus General, Selling, and Administrative Costs*

Quill Manufacturing Company was started on January 1, 2005, when it acquired $67,000 cash from its owners. Quill immediately purchased office furniture and manufacturing equipment costing $10,000 and $19,000, respectively. The office furniture had a four-year useful life and a zero salvage value. The manufacturing equipment had a $1,000 salvage value and an expected useful life of six years. The company paid $7,000 for salaries of administrative personnel and $9,000 for wages of production personnel. Finally, the company paid $12,000 for raw materials that were used to make inventory. All inventory was started and completed during the accounting period. Quill completed production on 8,000 units of product and sold 6,000 units at a price of $7 each in 2005. (Assume that all transactions are cash transactions.)

Required

a. Determine the total product cost and the average cost per unit of the inventory produced in 2005.

b. Determine the amount of cost of goods sold that would appear on the 2005 income statement.

c. Determine the amount of the ending inventory balance that would appear on the December 31, 2005, balance sheet.

d. Determine the amount of net income that would appear on the 2005 income statement.

e. Determine the amount of retained earnings that would appear on the December 31, 2005, balance sheet.

f. Determine the amount of total assets that would appear on the December 31, 2005, balance sheet.

g. Determine the amount of net cash flow from operating activities that would appear on the 2005 cash flow statement.

h. Determine the amount of net cash flow from investing activities that would appear on the 2005 cash flow statement.

PROBLEM 1-2B   *The Effect of Product versus General, Selling, and Administrative Costs on*   **L.O. 2, 4, 5**
Financial Statements

Powell Company experienced the following accounting events during its first year of operation. With the exception of the adjusting entries for amortization, all transactions were cash transactions.
1. Acquired $58,000 of capital from the owners.
2. Paid $13,000 for the materials that were used to make its products. All products started were completed during the period.
3. Paid salaries of $5,400 to selling and administrative employees.
4. Paid wages of $8,600 to production workers.
5. Paid $8,000 for furniture used in selling and administrative offices. The furniture was acquired on January 1. It had a $1,000 estimated salvage value and a seven-year useful life.
6. Paid $17,000 for manufacturing equipment. The equipment was acquired on January 1. It had a $2,000 estimated salvage value and a five-year useful life.
7. Sold inventory to customers for $39,000 that had cost $23,500 to make.

Required
Explain how these events would affect the balance sheet, income statement, and cash flow statement by recording them in a horizontal financial statements model as indicated here. The first event is recorded as an example.

Financial Statements Model											
	Assets				Equity						
Event No.	Cash	+ Inventory +	Manuf. Equip.* +	Office Furn.	=	Cont. Cap. +	Ret. Ear.	Rev	– Exp	= Net Inc.	Cash Flow
1	58,000					58,000					58,000 FA

* Record accumulated amortization as negative amounts under these columns.

PROBLEM 1-3B   *Product versus General, Selling, and Administrative Costs*   **L.O. 2, 3, 4, 5**

The following transactions pertain to 2004, the first year of operations of Compton Company. All inventory was started and completed during the accounting period. All transactions were cash transactions.
1. Acquired $28,000 of contributed capital from its owners.
2. Paid $4,800 for materials used to produce inventory.
3. Paid $2,200 to production workers.
4. Paid $2,500 rental fee for production equipment.
5. Paid $750 to administrative employees.
6. Paid $1,600 rental fee for administrative office equipment.
7. Produced 1,900 units of inventory of which 1,500 units were sold at a price of $8.70 each.

Required
Prepare an income statement, a balance sheet, and a cash flow statement.

PROBLEM 1-4B   *Service versus Manufacturing Companies*   **L.O. 2, 3, 4, 5**

Mayflower Company began operations on January 1, 2007, by issuing common stock for $47,000 cash. During 2007, Mayflower received $38,500 cash from revenue and incurred costs that required $45,000 of cash payments.

Required
Prepare an income statement, a balance sheet, and a cash flow statement for Mayflower Company for 2007, under each of the following scenarios.
a. Mayflower is an employment agency. The $45,000 was paid for employee salaries and advertising.
b. Mayflower is a trucking company. The $45,000 was paid to purchase two trucks. The trucks were purchased on January 1, 2007, had five-year useful lives and no expected salvage value. Mayflower uses straight-line amortization.

c. Mayflower is a manufacturing company. The $45,000 was paid to purchase the following items:
   (1) Paid $9,000 cash to purchase materials that were used to make products during the year.
   (2) Paid $14,000 cash to workers who laboured to make products during the period.
   (3) Paid $2,000 cash for salaries of sales and administrative employees.
   (4) Paid $20,000 cash to purchase manufacturing equipment. The equipment was used solely for the purpose of making products. It had a six-year life and a $2,000 salvage value. The company uses straight-line amortization.
   (5) During 2007, Mayflower started and completed 2,600 units of product. The revenue was earned when Mayflower sold 2,200 units of product to its customers.
d. Refer to Part c. Could Mayflower determine the actual cost of making the 500th product? How likely is it that the actual cost of the 500th product was exactly the same as the cost of producing the 501st product? Explain why management may be more interested in average cost than in actual cost.

L.O. 2, 3, 4, 5, 6   **PROBLEM 1-5B**   *Importance of Cost Classification*

Jones Company was started when it acquired $35,000 from its owners. During the first year of operations, the company incurred specifically identifiable product costs (i.e., materials, labour, and overhead) amounting to $20,000. Jones also incurred $10,000 of product development costs. There was a debate regarding how the product development costs should be classified. Advocates of Option 1 believed that the costs should be included in the general, selling, and administrative cost category. Advocates of Option 2 believed it would be more appropriate to classify the product development costs as product costs. During the first year, Jones made 10,000 units of product and sold 8,000 units at a price of $7 each. All transactions were cash transactions.

Required
a. Prepare an income statement, a balance sheet, and a cash flow statement under each of the two options.
b. Identify the option that results in financial statements that are more likely to leave a favourable impression on investors and creditors.
c. Assume that Jones provides an incentive bonus to the company president that is equal to 8 percent of net income. Compute the amount of the bonus under each of the two options. Identify the option that provides the president with the higher bonus.
d. Assume a 35 percent income tax rate. Determine the amount of income tax expense under each of the two options. Identify the option that minimizes the amount of the company's income tax expense.
e. Comment on the conflict between the interest of the company president as determined in Part c and the interest of the owners of the company as indicated in Part d. Describe an incentive compensation plan that would avoid conflicts between the interests of the president and the owners.

L.O. 10   **PROBLEM 1-6B**   *Value Chain Analysis*

Karan Cross visited her personal physician for treatment of flu symptoms. She was met by the receptionist, who gave her personal history and insurance forms to complete. She needed no instructions; she completed these same forms every time she visited the doctor. After completing the forms, Ms. Cross waited for 30 minutes before being ushered into the patient room. After she had been waiting there for an additional 15 minutes, Dr. Smith entered the room. The doctor ushered Ms. Cross into the hallway where he weighed her and called her weight out to the nurse for recording. Ms. Cross had gained 10 pounds since her last visit, and the doctor suggested that she consider going on a diet. Dr. Smith then took her temperature and asked her to return to the patient room. Ten minutes later, he returned to take a throat culture and a blood test. She waited another 15 minutes for the test results. Finally, the doctor returned and told Ms. Cross that she had strep throat and bronchitis. Dr. Smith prescribed an antibiotic and told her to get at least two days of bed rest. Ms. Cross was then ushered to the accounting department for settlement of her bill. The accounting clerk asked her several questions; the answers to most of them were on the forms that she had completed when she first arrived at the office. Finally, Ms. Cross paid her required co-payment and left the office. Three weeks later, she received a bill indicating that she had not paid the co-payment. She called the accounting department, and, after a search of the records, the clerk verified that the bill had, in fact, been paid. The clerk apologized for the inconvenience and inquired as to whether Ms. Cross's health had improved.

Required
a. Identify at least three value-added and three nonvalue-added activities suggested in this scenario.
b. Provide a logical explanation as to how the nonvalue-added activities could be eliminated.

PROBLEM 1-7B *Use of JIT to Reduce Inventory Holding Costs*

Honest Automobile Dealership, Inc. (HAD) buys and sells a variety of cars made by Famous Motor Corporation. HAD maintains about 30 new cars in its parking lot for customers' selection; the cost of this inventory is approximately $480,000. Additionally, HAD hires security guards to protect the inventory from theft and a maintenance crew to keep the facilities attractive. The total payroll cost for the guards and maintenance crew amounts to $120,000 per year. HAD has a line of credit with a local bank that calls for a 15 percent annual rate of interest. Recently, Joe Johnson, the president of HAD, learned that a competitor in town, Emerson Dealership, has been attracting some of HAD's usual customers because Emerson could offer them lower prices. Mr. Johnson also discovered that Emerson carries no inventory at all but shows customers a catalogue of cars as well as pertinent information from online computer databases. Emerson promises to deliver any car that a customer identifies within three working days.

Required
a. On the basis of the information provided, determine HAD's annual inventory holding cost.
b. Name the inventory system that Emerson uses and explain how the system enables Emerson to sell at reduced prices.

PROBLEM 1-8B *Use of JIT to Minimize Waste and Lost Opportunity*

Judy's Hamburger is a small fast-food shop in a busy shopping centre that operates only during lunch hours. Judy Wonders, the owner and manager of the shop, is very confused. On some days, she does not have enough hamburgers to satisfy customer demand. On other days, she has more hamburgers than she can sell. When she has an excess of hamburgers, she has no choice but to dump them. Usually, Ms. Wonders prepares about 160 hamburgers before the busy lunch hour. The product cost per hamburger is approximately $0.75; the sales price is $2.50 each. Ms. Wonders pays general, selling, and administrative expenses that include daily rent of $50 and $40 in wages per day.

Required
a. Prepare an income statement based on sales of 100 hamburgers per day. Determine the cost of wasted hamburgers if 160 hamburgers were prepared in advance.
b. Prepare an income statement assuming that 200 customers attempt to buy a hamburger. Since Ms. Wonders has prepared only 160 hamburgers, she must reject 40 customer orders because of the insufficient supply. Determine the amount of lost profit.
c. Suppose that hamburgers can be prepared quickly after each customer order. However, Ms. Wonders must hire an additional part-time employee at a cost of approximately $20 per day. The per unit cost of each hamburger remains at $0.75. Prepare an income statement under the JIT system assuming that 100 hamburgers are sold. Compare the income statement under JIT with the income statement prepared in Requirement *a*. Comment on how the JIT system would affect profitability.
d. Assume the same facts as in Requirement *c* with respect to a JIT system that requires additional labour costing $20 per day. Prepare an income statement under the JIT system, assuming that 200 hamburgers are sold. Compare the income statement under JIT with the income statement prepared in Requirement *b*. Comment on how the JIT system would affect profitability.
e. Explain how the JIT system might be able to improve customer satisfaction as well as profitability.

ANALYZE, THINK, COMMUNICATE

BUSINESS APPLICATIONS CASE *Financial versus Managerial Accounting*

ACT 1-1

In the July 20, 1998, edition of *Business Week* magazine, Harold Ruttenberg, founder and CEO of Just For Feet, Inc., referred to some information that highlighted his company's success. When comparing his "big box stores" with his mall-based rivals, he noted that the size of a typical Just For Feet store is between 15,000 and 25,000 square feet, while rival stores such as Foot Locker and Footaction USA, Inc. average between 4,000 and 6,000. Ruttenberg noted that the larger size lets Just For Feet buy in bulk and negotiate discounts of between 15 percent and 20 percent. These discounts are passed on to customers in each store's Combat Zone, where discounts can reach 70 percent. Such discounting has enabled Just For Feet to retain a highly competitive pricing advantage. Ruttenberg also highlighted the company's selection and training programs that have produced employees whose performance far outpaces the competition. The average Just For Feet store produces sales of $650 per square foot; the typical mall store produces only $250 per square foot. On the down side, Ruttenberg noted that Just For Feet experienced a sharp increase in inventory holding costs until an information system was installed to help bring the inventory stock level down. It fell 22 percent, from $152 of inventory per square foot in 1996 to $119 of inventory per square foot in 1997.

Required

a. Indicate whether the information described in this narrative would be best described as financial or managerial accounting information. Support your answer with appropriate commentary.

b. Provide some additional examples of managerial and financial accounting information that could apply to Just For Feet, Inc.

c. Explain why the manager of a Just For Feet store needs different kinds of information than investors or creditors need. Give an example of information that would be useful to a store manager but irrelevant to an investor or creditor.

ACT 1-2

GROUP ASSIGNMENT *Product versus Upstream and Downstream Costs*

Bob Beeland, the accounting manager of Wexler Inc., gathered the following information for 2003. Some of it can be used to construct an income statement for 2003. Ignore items that do not appear on an income statement. Some computation may be required. For example, the total cost of manufacturing equipment would not appear on the income statement. However, the cost of manufacturing equipment is needed to compute the amount of depreciation. All units of product were started and completed in 2003.

1. Issued $432,000 of common stock.
2. Paid engineers in the product design department $5,000 for salaries that were accrued during the previous accounting period.
3. Incurred advertising expenses of $35,000.
4. Paid $360,000 for materials used to manufacture the company's product.
5. Incurred utility costs of $80,000. These costs were allocated to different departments on the basis of square footage of floor space. Mr. Beeland identified three departments and determined the square footage of floor space for each department to be as the right table.

Department	Square Footage
Research and Development	10,000
Manufacturing	60,000
Selling and Administrative	30,000
Total	100,000

6. Paid $440,000 for wages of production workers.
7. Paid cash of $329,000 for salaries of administrative personnel. There was $8,000 of accrued salaries owed to the administrative personnel at the end of 2003. There was no beginning balance in the Salaries Payable account for administrative personnel.
8. Purchased manufacturing equipment two years ago at a cost of $5,000,000. The equipment had an eight-year useful life and a $1,000,000 salvage value.
9. Paid $195,000 cash to engineers in the product design department.
10. Paid a $129,000 cash dividend to owners.
11. Paid $40,000 to set up manufacturing equipment for production.
12. Paid a one-time $93,000 restructuring cost to redesign the production process to enable the company to implement a just-in-time inventory system.
13. Prepaid the premium on a new insurance policy covering nonmanufacturing employees. The policy cost $36,000 and had a one-year term with an effective starting date of May 1. Four employees work in the research and development department and eight employees in the selling and administrative department. Assume a December 31 closing date.
14. Made 69,400 units of product and sold 60,000 units at a price of $35 each.

Required

a. Divide the class into groups of four or five students per group, and then organize the groups into three sections. Assign Task 1 to the first section of groups, Task 2 to the second section of groups, and Task 3 to the third section of groups.

Group tasks

1. Identify the items that are classified as product costs and determine the amount of cost of goods sold shown on the 2003 income statement.
2. Identify the items that are classified as upstream costs and determine the amount of upstream cost expensed on the 2003 income statement.
3. Identify the items that are classified as downstream costs and determine the amount of downstream cost expensed on the 2003 income statement.

b. Have the class construct an income statement in the following manner: Select a member of one of the groups assigned the first group task identifying the product costs. Have that person go to the board and list the costs included in the determination of cost of goods sold. Anyone in the other groups who disagrees with one of the classifications provided by the person at the board should voice an objection and explain why the item should be classified differently. The instructor should lead the class to a consensus on the disputed items. After the amount of cost of goods sold is determined, the student at the board constructs the part of the income statement showing the determination of gross margin. The exercise continues in a similar fashion with representatives from the other sections explaining the composition of the upstream and downstream costs. These items are added to the income statement started by the first group representative. The final result is a completed income statement.

WRITING ASSIGNMENT *Emerging Practices in Managerial Accounting*

ACT 1-3

The 1998 annual report of the Maytag Corporation contained the following excerpt:

> *During the first quarter of 1996, the Company announced the restructuring of its major appliance operations in an effort to strengthen its position in the industry and to deliver improved performance to both customers and shareowners. This included the consolidation of two separate organizational units into a single operation responsible for all activities associated with the manufacture and distribution of the Company's brands of major appliances and the closing of a cooking products plant in Indianapolis, Indiana, with transfer of that production to an existing plant in Cleveland, Tennessee.*

The restructuring cost Maytag $40 million and disrupted the lives of many of the company's employees.

Required

Assume that you are Maytag's vice-president of human relations. Write a letter to the employees who are affected by the restructuring. The letter should explain why it was necessary for the company to undertake the restructuring. Your explanation should refer to the ideas discussed in the section "Trends in Managerial Accounting" of this chapter.

ETHICAL DILEMMA *Product Cost versus Selling and Administrative Expense*

ACT 1-4

Eddie Emerson is a proud woman with a problem. Her daughter has been accepted into a prestigious law school. While Ms. Emerson beams with pride, she is worried sick about how to pay for the school; she is a single parent who has worked hard to support herself and her three children. She had to go heavily into debt to finance her own education. Even though she now has a good job, family needs have continued to outpace her income and her debt burden is staggering. She knows she will be unable to borrow the money needed for her daughter's law school.

Ms. Emerson is the controller of a small manufacturing company. She has just accepted a new job offer. Indeed, she has not yet told her employer that she will be leaving in a month. She is concerned that her year-end incentive bonus may be affected if her boss learns of her plans to leave. She plans to inform the company immediately after receiving the bonus. She knows her behaviour is less than honourable, but she believes that she has been underpaid for a long time. Her boss, a relative of the company's owner, makes twice what she makes and does half the work. Why should she care about leaving with a little extra cash? Indeed, she is considering an opportunity to boost the bonus.

Ms. Emerson's bonus is based on a percentage of net income. Her company recently introduced a new product line that required substantial production startup costs. Ms. Emerson is fully aware that GAAP requires these costs to be expensed in the current accounting period, but no one else in the company has the technical expertise to know exactly how the costs should be treated. She is considering misclassifying the startup costs as product costs. If the costs are misclassified, net income will be significantly higher, resulting in a nice boost in her incentive bonus. By the time the auditors discover the misclassification, Ms. Emerson will have moved on to her new job. If the matter is brought to the attention of her new employer, she will simply plead ignorance. Considering her daughter's needs, Ms. Emerson decides to classify the startup costs as product costs.

Required

a. On the basis of this information, indicate whether Ms. Emerson believes the number of units of product sold will be equal to, less than or greater than the number of units made. Write a brief paragraph explaining the logic that supports your answer.

b. Explain how the misclassification could mislead an investor or creditor regarding the company's financial condition.

c. Explain how the misclassification could affect income taxes.

d. Identify the factors that contributed to the breach of ethical conduct. When constructing your answer, you may want to refer to the section "Common Features of Criminal and Ethical Misconduct" of this chapter.

ACT 1-5 SPREADSHEET ASSIGNMENT *Using Excel*

Refer to the data in Problem 1–3A.

Required

Construct a spreadsheet that includes the income statement, balance sheet, and cash flow statement.

ACT 1-6 SPREADSHEET ASSIGNMENT *Mastering Excel*

Refer to the data in Problem 1–2A.

Required

Construct a spreadsheet of the financial statements model as shown here:

Place formulas in Row 16 to automatically add the columns. Also add formulas in Column S to calculate net income after each event, and add formulas in Row 18 to compute total assets and equity. Note that you must enter the events since only the first is shown as an example.

Spreadsheet Tips

1. The column widths are set by choosing Format, then Column, and then Width.
2. The shading in columns B, N, and T is added by highlighting a column and choosing Format, then Cells, and then clicking on the tab titled Patterns and choosing a colour.
3. The sum function is an easy way to add a column or row. For example, the formula in Cell C16 is = SUM(C6:C15).
4. As an example of the formulas in Column S (net income), the formula in Cell S7 is = S6 + O7 − Q7.
5. If you find that some of the columns are too far to the right to appear on your screen, you can set the zoom level to show the entire spreadsheet. The zoom is set by choosing View, then Zoom, and then clicking on Custom and typing 100 percent in the box. The shortcut method to set the zoom is to click in the box on the right side of the top tool bar that appears immediately below the menu.

Cost Behaviour, Operating Leverage, and Profitability Analysis

Learning Objectives

After completing this chapter, you should be able to:

1 Distinguish between fixed and variable cost behaviour.

2 Understand how operating leverage affects profitability.

3 Understand how cost behaviour affects profitability.

4 Prepare an income statement under a contribution margin approach.

5 Calculate the magnitude of operating leverage.

6 Use cost behaviour to create a competitive operating advantage.

7 Understand how cost behaviour is affected by the relevant range and the decision-making context.

8 Select an appropriate time period for the calculation of the average cost per unit.

9 Define the term *mixed costs*.

10 Use the high-low method, scattergraphs, and regression to estimate fixed and variable costs.

the *curious* manager

Most people would expect an increase in a company's revenues to cause an increase in its profits, but they may be surprised that a small percentage of change in revenue can generate a dramatic difference in profits. Consider the following data for Westjet Airlines, an airline that operates primarily in Western Canada.

Year	Revenues (Millions)	Percentage increase from previous year	Net Earnings (Millions)	Percentage increase from previous year
1998	$125.4	N/A	$6.5	N/A
1999	$203.6	62.4%	$15.8	143%
2000	$332.5	63.3%	$15.8	91.8%

Note that profitability numbers shown are for net earnings. Considering this, what could possibly explain how a 63.8% increase in revenues could result in a 91.8% increase in net earnings?

*Three college students have decided to take a short vacation. They are considering inviting a fourth person to join them. One student remarks that they will all save money if the fourth person goes along because many of the costs necessary to make the trip will be the same, regardless of whether three or four people go. For example, the cost of the hotel room is $90 per night. If three people stay in the room, the cost per person is $30 ($90 ÷ 3 = $30). If four people stay in the room, the cost is only $22.50 per person ($90 ÷ 4 = $22.50). In accounting terms, the cost of the hotel room is a **fixed cost**. In other words, the total cost is fixed at $90 even if the number of people staying in the room changes. Other costs* vary, *depending on how many people participate. Food costs will likely be more* *for four people than for three. The food cost is an example of **variable cost**. If the fixed costs are high in relation to the variable costs, adding additional participants will significantly reduce the cost per person. Indeed, the differential could be so significant that it would influence a person's decision as to whether to make the trip. Accordingly, the way a cost behaves (i.e., is fixed or variable) can have a significant impact on decision making.*

▌ Fixed Cost Behaviour

LO1

Distinguish between fixed and variable cost behaviour.

This chapter examines the effect of cost behaviour on the risks and rewards of operating a business. Just as fixed and variable cost behaviour can impact personal choices, it can also affect business decisions, such as these. How much more will it cost to send one more employee to a sales meeting? If more people buy our products, can we charge less? If sales increase by 10 percent, how will profits be affected? Managers seeking answers to such questions must consider the relationships between costs and activities. Examples of activity measures include the number of people attending a training program, the amount of goods sold, the number of clients served, the number of orders processed, the number of sales calls made, the number of products made, and the number of patients treated. Knowing how costs behave in relation to a given level of business activity enables management to maximize profitability through more effective planning and control. To illustrate, consider the case of Star Productions, Inc. (SPI).

SPI is an entertainment company that specializes in promoting rock concerts. The company is considering paying a band $48,000 to play a concert. Obviously, SPI must sell enough tickets to cover this cost. In this case, the relevant activity base is the number of tickets sold. The cost of the band is a *fixed cost* because it does not change with the number of tickets sold. Exhibit 2–1 demonstrates fixed cost behaviour patterns by showing the *total cost* and the *cost per unit* at three different levels of activity.

Exhibit 2–1	*Fixed Cost Behaviour*		
Number of tickets sold (a)	2,700	3,000	3,300
Total cost of band (b)	$48,000	$48,000	$48,000
Cost per ticket sold (b ÷ a)	$17.78	$16.00	$14.55

Note that fixed cost in *total* and fixed cost *per unit* exhibit distinctly different behaviour patterns. The total cost of the band remains constant (i.e., fixed) at $48,000 regardless of the number of tickets sold. Accordingly, there is logical consistency between the term *fixed cost* and the cost behaviour pattern with respect to *total cost*. In other words, *total fixed cost remains constant (i.e., fixed) when activity changes*. In contrast, *fixed cost per unit* changes inversely each time the number of tickets sold changes. As the number of tickets sold increases, the fixed cost per ticket decreases. As ticket sales decrease, fixed cost per ticket increases. This means that there is a contradiction between the term *fixed cost per unit* and the behaviour pattern that is implied in the terminology. Specifically, *fixed cost per unit* is *not fixed*. Instead, it changes each time the number of tickets changes. This contradiction in terminology can cause untold confusion. We strongly recommend that you carefully study the behaviour patterns shown in Exhibit 2–2 before proceeding with your reading assignment.

Exhibit 2–2	*Fixed Cost Behaviour*	
When Activity	**Increases**	**Decreases**
Total fixed cost	Remains constant	Remains constant
Fixed cost **per unit**	Decreases	Increases

Clearly, the fixed cost data shown in Exhibit 2–1 are useful in helping management decide whether to sponsor the concert. For example, the information could be used to examine potential pricing scenarios. The per-unit cost data represent the mini-

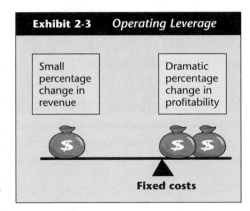

Who cares if costs exhibit fixed or variable behaviour? Andrew Farkas cares. Mr. Farkas has used the concept of fixed cost to establish a successful real estate property management company, Insignia Financial Group. Mr. Farkas's stake in Insignia is reported to be worth approximately $160 million. Property management companies existed before Mr. Farkas started Insignia, but the property management business was considered to have a relatively low profit potential because the costs of operating such companies were high relative to the level of revenue they were able to generate. Mr. Farkas spent millions of dollars to develop a standardized computer management process. The investment was substantial, and the cost was basically fixed. When Mr. Farkas implemented an aggressive plan to expand Insignia's client base, revenues soared but costs remained relatively stable. The result was a highly profitable business that earned Mr. Farkas recognition as the "first new real-estate mogul in a decade."

Source: Fred Vogelstein, "A Real-Estate Tycoon for the '90s," *U.S. News & World Report*, May 19, 1997, p. 52.

mum ticket prices required to cover the fixed cost at various levels of activity. These data could be compared with the prices of other events that would compete for the customer's business (movie prices, prices of sporting events, prices of theatre tickets, etc.). If the concert prices are not competitive, sales will not materialize and the business venture will lose money. Similarly, management must assess the likelihood of being able to sell the various numbers of tickets. How do these data compare with the band's track record for ticket sales at other concerts? Although decision making always involves uncertainty, applying appropriate analytical techniques, such as those discussed in this chapter, can reduce risk.

■ Operating Leverage

You probably know that large objects can be moved with little effort when *physical leverage* is properly applied. In business, managers apply **operating leverage** to convert small changes in revenue into dramatic changes in profitability. Fixed costs constitute the *lever* that managers use to accomplish the disproportionate changes between revenue and profitability. The leverage relationships between revenue, fixed costs, and profitability are depicted in Exhibit 2–3.

LO2
Understand how operating leverage affects profitability.

When *all costs are fixed*, every additional sales dollar contributes one dollar toward the potential profitability of a project. In other words, once fixed costs have been covered, each sales dollar represents pure profit. As a result, a small change in the volume of sales can have a significant effect on profitability. To illustrate, assume that SPI estimates that it will sell 3,000 tickets for $18 each. Given this starting point, a 10 percent difference in actual versus estimated sales volume will produce a 90 percent difference in profitability. This fact can be verified by examining the data shown in Exhibit 2–4.

Exhibit 2–4 *Effect of Operating Leverage on Profitability*					
Number of tickets sold	2,700	⇐−10%⇐	3,000	⇒+10%⇒	3,300
Sales revenue ($18 per ticket)	$48,600		$54,000		$59,400
Cost of band (fixed cost)	(48,000)		(48,000)		(48,000)
Gross profit	$ 600	⇐−90%⇐	$ 6,000	⇒+90%⇒	$11,400

The percentages shown in Exhibit 2–4 are computed by comparing a base measure with one of the alternative measures. To illustrate, we compute the percentage change in the gross profit at 3,000 units (i.e., base measure) with the gross profit at 3,300 units (i.e., the alternative measure). The percentage change is computed in two steps. First, subtract the gross profit at the base measure ($6,000) from the gross profit at the alternative ($11,400). The difference is $5,400 ($11,400 − $6,000). Next, divide the difference by the base measure of gross profit. The result is a 90 percent increase in profitability ($5,400 ÷ $6,000 = 0.90). The percentage decline in profitability is computed in a similar manner. First, determine the difference in the base measure of gross profit and the alternative measure of gross profit ($600 − $6,000 = $5,400). Divide the difference by the base ($5,400 ÷ $6,000 = 0.90). The minus sign indicates that profitability *declined* by 90 percent. The general formula for the computation of the percentage change is as follows:

$$[(\text{Alternative measure} - \text{Base measure}) \div \text{Base measure}] \times 100 = \% \text{ change}$$

Students frequently miscalculate percentages because they do not carefully consider the identification of the base measure versus the alternative measures. It may help to think of the base measure as the starting point and the alternative measure as the final destination. In the preceding example, the starting point (base measure) was the data set at estimated sales of 3,000 units. The alternative measures were the data sets if actual sales ended up being either 2,700 units or 3,300 units. You should force yourself to distinguish between the *base measure* and the *alternative measures* before you make any computations. Rushing into the calculations can lead to errors. Your motto should always be *think before you calculate.*

The concept of operating leverage is consistent with what economists call the **economies of scale**. This concept recognizes that *the cost per unit can be reduced by taking advantage of opportunities that become available when the size of an operation increases*. In SPI's case, the cost per ticket decreases as the number of tickets sold increases. Since the level of sales affects the cost per ticket, it affects pricing and profitability as well. Clearly, SPI can charge less if 3,000 people buy tickets than if only 2,700 do so. Lower prices may, in turn, spark higher levels of customer demand, which then lowers unit cost even further. Accordingly, managers must pay careful attention to the expected behaviour patterns as well as the amounts of the cost components of a particular business venture. The relationship between fixed cost and the level of expected activity is a significant factor in many managerial decisions.

Risk and Reward Assessment

LO2

Understand how operating leverage affects profitability.

Risk refers to the possibility that sacrifices may exceed benefits. Once incurred, a fixed cost is an unalterable economic sacrifice. As such, it represents the ultimate risk associated with a particular business project. If SPI pays the band but nobody buys a ticket, the company will lose $48,000. It can avoid this risk by converting the *fixed cost* into a *variable cost*.

To illustrate variable cost behaviour, assume that SPI is able to convince the band to play for compensation equal to $16 per ticket sold. Exhibit 2–5 shows the total cost of hiring the band and the cost per ticket sold at three different levels of activity.

Since the band is paid $16 for each ticket sold, the *total variable cost* increases in direct proportion to the number of tickets sold. A total cost of $16 will be incurred if

Exhibit 2–5	Variable Cost Behaviour		
Number of tickets sold (a)	2,700	3,000	3,300
Total cost of band (b)	$43,200	$48,000	$52,800
Cost per ticket sold (b ÷ a)	$16	$16	$16

SPI sells one ticket (1 × $16); the total cost if two tickets are sold is $32 (2 × $16); ticket sales of three results in total cost of $48 (3 × $16), and so on. This explains why the total cost of the band increases proportionally as ticket sales move from 2,700 to 3,000 to 3,300. The *variable cost per ticket* remains at $16, however, regardless of whether the number of tickets sold is 1, 2, 3, or 3,000. Note that variable cost per unit behaves in a manner that is contradictory to the behaviour implied in the terminology. Specifically, *variable cost* per unit *remains constant,* regardless of how many tickets are sold. Here also, you should carefully study the behaviour patterns of a variable cost that are shown in Exhibit 2–6 before proceeding with your reading assignment.

Exhibit 2–6	*Variable Cost Behaviour*	
When Activity	**Increases**	**Decreases**
Total variable cost	Increases proportionately	Decreases proportionately
Variable cost **per unit**	Remains constant	Remains constant

Note that shifting the cost structure from fixed to variable has enabled SPI to avoid the fixed cost risk. If no one buys a ticket, SPI loses nothing because the company incurs no cost. If only one person buys a ticket at the $18 ticket price, SPI earns a $2 profit ($18 sales revenue − $16 cost of band). Does this mean that managers should avoid fixed costs whenever possible? Not necessarily. Shifting the cost structure from fixed to variable reduces not only the level of risk but also the potential for profits. In other words, managers cannot avoid the downside risk of a fixed cost operating structure without also losing the upside benefit. Exhibit 2–7 shows that when the cost structure is variable, the relationship between sales and profitability is proportional. A 10 percent increase in sales results in a 10 percent increase in profitability. Likewise, a 10 percent decline in sales produces a corresponding 10 percent decline in profitability. Variable costs do not provide opportunities for operating leverage.

Exhibit 2–7	*Variable Cost Eliminates Operating Leverage*					
Number of tickets sold	2,700	⇐−10%⇐	3,000	⇒+10%⇒	3,300
Sales revenue ($18 per ticket)	$48,600		$54,000		$59,400
Cost of band (16 per ticket)	(43,200)		(48,000)		(52,800)
Gross profit	$ 5,400	⇐−10%⇐	$ 6,000	⇒+10%⇒	$ 6,600

Relationship between Cost Behaviour and Revenue

Exhibit 2–8 compares the relationship between revenue and total fixed cost with the relationship between revenue and total variable cost. Clearly, a pure fixed cost structure offers greater risk and higher potential rewards. A company will incur a loss until it has generated enough revenue to cover its fixed cost. Thereafter, every dollar of revenue represents pure profit. As volume increases, income becomes disproportionately larger than total costs. In contrast, a pure variable cost structure offers security (a profit is earned at any level of sales). Unfortunately, costs increase proportionately with increases in revenue, thereby eliminating disproportionate growth in profitability.

LO1
Distinguish between fixed and variable cost behaviour.

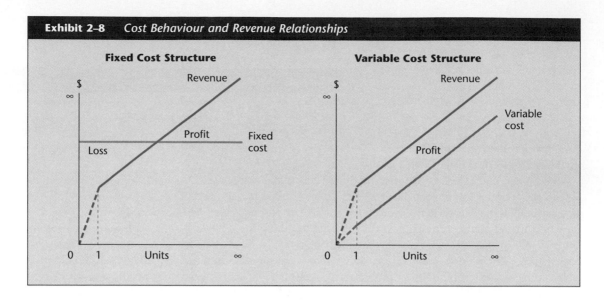

Exhibit 2-8   *Cost Behaviour and Revenue Relationships*

▌ Effect of Cost Structure on Profit Stability

LO3

Understand how cost behaviour affects profitability.

The preceding discussion suggests that companies with higher levels of fixed costs are more likely to experience earnings volatility. To further illustrate this point, consider the following scenario. Suppose that three companies produce and sell the same product. Each company sells 10 products for $10 each. Further, each company incurs $60 of cost in the process of making and selling its products. Despite these similarities, the companies operate under radically different **cost structures**. The entire $60 of cost incurred by Company A is fixed. Company B incurs $30 of fixed cost and $30 of variable cost ($3 per unit). All $60 of cost incurred by Company C is variable ($6 per unit). The income statements of the three companies are shown in Exhibit 2–9.

When sales change, the size of the corresponding change in net income is directly related to the company's cost structure. The more the fixed cost, the higher is the fluctuation in net income. To illustrate, assume that sales increase by one unit; the resulting income statements are shown in Exhibit 2–10.

Company A, which had the highest level of fixed costs, experienced a $10 ($50 − $40) increase in profitability; Company C, which had the lowest level of fixed cost (zero), had only a $4 ($44 − $40) increase in profitability. Company B, which had a 50/50 mixture of fixed and variable cost, had a mid-range $7 ($47 − $40) increase in net income. The effect of fixed cost on volatility holds for decreases as well as increases in sales volume. To illustrate, assume that sales decrease by one unit (from 10 to 9 units). The resulting income statements are shown in Exhibit 2–11.

Exhibit 2-9   Income Statements

	Company Name		
	A	B	C
Variable Cost per Unit (a)	$0	$3	$6
Sales Revenue (10 units × $10)	$100	$100	$100
Variable Cost (10 units × a)	0	(30)	(60)
Fixed Cost	(60)	(30)	0
Net Income	$ 40	$ 40	$ 40

Exhibit 2-10   Income Statements

	Company Name		
	A	B	C
Variable Cost per Unit (a)	$0	$3	$6
Sales Revenue (11 units × $10)	$110	$110	$110
Variable Cost (11 units × a)	0	(33)	(66)
Fixed Cost	(60)	(30)	0
Net Income	$ 50	$ 47	$ 44

After reading the previous material, you should understand that Westjet Airlines, dramatic growth in net earnings was due to operating leverage. You now know that a company's cost structure affects the relationships between changes in its revenues and changes in its net earnings. Companies with relatively high fixed costs have relatively high operating leverage. More specifically, a given percentage change in revenues can cause a much larger change in its net earnings. Airlines have many fixed costs. For example, the costs of the planes (amortization) stays constant, regardless of the number of passengers on a given flight. Other assets that are likely to result in fixed amortization charges include the cost of computer systems, office furniture, fuel trucks, and other equipment. Indeed,

although the increase in numbers of passengers caused revenue to soar, fixed assets, though they grew significantly in the same period, grew at a pace that was less than the increase in net earnings. The following data is from the annual report of Westjet Airlines:

Year	Total Assets	Percentage Change from the Previous Year
1998	$108,242,000	N/A
1999	$186.598,000	72.4%
2000	$337,172,000	80.7%

Here, also, Company A experienced the largest variance in earnings ($10 decrease). Company B had a moderate decline of $7, and Company C had the least volatility with only a $4 decline. Clearly, the stability of earnings is directly related to a company's cost structure. So, what is the best structure? If given a choice, should a manager select fixed or variable costs? There is no definitive answer to this question. However, rational responses can be given for specific sets of circumstances. Highly leveraged companies (those with high levels of fixed cost) experience higher profits when sales increase and higher losses when sales decline. Companies with low leverage have more stable earnings. Revenue changes trigger corresponding increases and decreases in net income, but the magnitude of those swings is lower if the degree of operating leverage is low. A manager who believes that revenues are likely to increase should create a highly leveraged cost structure. If the manager locks costs in, when sales grow, she will reap significant rewards. On the other hand, if there is a great deal of uncertainty about earnings growth or if the manager believes that revenue is likely to decline, it would be wise to develop a low leverage cost structure.

Exhibit 2–11   Income Statements

	Company Name		
	A	B	C
Variable Cost per Unit (a)	0	$3	$6
Sales Revenue (9 units × $10)	$90	$90	$90
Variable Cost (9 units × a)	0	(27)	(54)
Fixed Cost	(60)	(30)	0
Net Income	$30	$33	$36

▌Determination of the Contribution Margin

The relationships between cost structure and profitability are so important that managerial accountants frequently construct income statements in which costs are categorized according to their behaviour patterns. The first step under this approach is to subtract variable costs from revenue; the result is called the **contribution margin**. This margin represents the amount that is available to pay fixed expenses and thereafter to provide profits to the enterprise. The amount of net income is computed by subtracting the fixed costs from the contribution margin. The contribution margin approach is not acceptable for public reporting (i.e., GAAP prohibits its use in external financial reports), but it is widely used for internal reporting purposes.

LO 4

Prepare an income statement under the contribution margin approach.

▌Measurement of Operating Leverage Using the Contribution Margin

LO5

Calculate the magnitude of operating leverage.

The contribution margin approach has many applications that will be discussed in later chapters of this text. One application that is pertinent to the material in this chapter is the measurement of operating leverage. To illustrate, assume that the comparative income statements shown in Exhibit 2–12 are available for Bragg Company and Biltmore Company. The formula for determining the magnitude of the operating leverage is as follows:

Exhibit 2–12   Income Statements

	Company Name	
	Bragg	**Biltmore**
Variable Cost per Unit (a)	$6	$12
Sales Revenue (10 units × $20)	$200	$200
Variable Cost (10 units × a)	(60)	(120)
Contribution Margin	140	80
Fixed Cost	(120)	(60)
Net Income	$ 20	$ 20

$$\text{Operating leverage} = \frac{\text{Contribution margin}}{\text{Net income}}$$

Applying this formula to the income statement data reported for Bragg and Biltmore produces the following measures:

Bragg Company	Biltmore Company
$\text{Operating leverage} = \dfrac{\$140}{\$20} = \mathbf{7}$	$\text{Operating leverage} = \dfrac{\$80}{\$20} = 4$

The computations indicate that Bragg is more highly leveraged than Biltmore. Given a percentage change in revenue, Bragg's corresponding change in profitability is seven times greater than the change in revenue. In contrast, Biltmore's profits change only at the rate of four times the percentage change in revenue. More specifically, a 10 percent increase in revenue produces a 70 percent increase (10 percent × 7) in profitability for Bragg Company and 40 percent increase (10 percent × 4) in profitability for Biltmore Company. This condition is verified by the income statements shown in Exhibits 2–13 and 2–14.

Exhibit 2–13   Comparative Income Statements for Bragg Company

Units (a)	10	11
Sales Revenue ($20 × a)	$200⇒+10%⇒	$220
Variable Cost ($6 × a)	(60)	(66)
Contribution Margin	140	154
Fixed Cost	(120)	(120)
Net Income	$ 20⇒+70%⇒	$ 34

Exhibit 2–14   Comparative Income Statements for Biltmore Company

Units (a)	10	11
Sales Revenue ($20 × a)	$200⇒+10%⇒	$220
Variable Cost ($12 × a)	(120)	(132)
Contribution Margin	80	88
Fixed Cost	(60)	(60)
Net Income	$ 20⇒+40%⇒	$ 28

As previously indicated, operating leverage is neither good nor bad; it is a condition that can work to a company's advantage or disadvantage, depending on how it is used. The following section explains how operating leverage can be used to create a competitive advantage in business practice.

■ Use of Fixed Cost to Provide a Competitive Operating Advantage

Mary MaHall and John Strike have established tutoring services companies to support themselves while they are attending university. Both Ms. MaHall and Mr. Strike act as business managers and hire other students to provide the tutoring services provided by their companies. Ms. MaHall pays her tutors salaries; her labour costs are fixed at $16,000 per year, regardless of the number of hours of tutoring performed. Mr. Strike pays his employees $8 per hour; accordingly, his labour is a variable cost. Both currently provide 2,000 hours of tutoring services at the price of $11 per hour. As indicated in Exhibit 2–15 both companies currently produce the same profit.

LO6
Use cost behaviour to create a competitive operating advantage.

Suppose that each company embarks on a strategy to take over the other company's students by reducing the price of tutoring servic-

Exhibit 2–15 *Comparative Profitability at 2,000 Hours of Tutoring*			
	MaHall		**Strike**
Number of hours of tutoring provided	2,000		2,000
Service revenue ($11 per hour)	$22,000		$22,000
Cost of tutors	Fixed (16,000)	Variable ($8 × 2,000)	(16,000)
Net income	$ 6,000		$ 6,000

es to $7 per hour. First, consider what happens to Ms. MaHall if she successfully implements this strategy. Then consider what happens to Mr. Strike if he successfully implements this strategy. Look at each case independently. In other words, what happens if MaHall's company takes over Mr. Strike's customers, thereby raising its services to 4,000 hours? Next, what happens to Mr. Strike if he takes over MaHall's customers (i.e., he provides 4,000 hours of tutoring)? The profitability for each scenario is shown in Exhibit 2–16.

Exhibit 2–16 *Comparative Profitability at 4,000 Hours of Tutoring*			
	MaHall		**Strike**
Number of hours of tutoring provided	4,000		4,000
Service revenue ($7 per hour)	$28,000		$28,000
Cost of tutors	Fixed (16,000)	Variable ($8 × 4,000)	(32,000)
Net income (loss)	$12,000		$ (4,000)

Ms. MaHall's fixed cost structure enables her company to operate at significantly higher levels of activity without increasing the cost of providing services. Unfortunately for him, Mr. Strike's costs increase proportionally with increases in sales volume. This situation places Ms. MaHall at a competitive advantage when activity increases. However, do not forget that operating leverage works both ways. Suppose that a new computer-assisted tutoring services company enters the market. The new service is more expensive, but it is technologically superior to the services that Ms. MaHall and Mr. Strike provide. Accordingly, some of their customers choose to spend the extra money necessary to obtain the computer-assisted instruction. Ms. MaHall and Mr. Strike can continue to provide services at the original price of $11 per hour. However, total demand falls to 1,000 hours. Even if Ms. MaHall could capture the entire market, her operations would produce a loss as indicated in Exhibit 2–17. On the other hand, Mr. Strike can produce a profit at any number of hours from one to infinity. This fact is demonstrated by showing his profit picture at 1,000 hours in Exhibit 2–17.

Exhibit 2–17	*Comparative Profitability at 1,000 Hours of Tutoring*			
		MaHall		**Strike**
Number of hours of tutoring provided		1,000		1,000
Service revenue ($11 per hour)		$11,000		$11,000
Cost of tutors	Fixed	(16,000)	Variable ($8 3 1,000)	(8,000)
Net income (loss)		$ (5,000)		$ 3,000

No absolute rules exist as to whether a company should operate with fixed versus variable costs. Management accountants are required to exercise judgment in performing their duties; they must understand how **cost behaviour** can affect profitability under different operating scenarios. They must also make predictions as to the business conditions that are likely to prevail once their operating strategy is implemented.

▌ Cost Behaviour Summarized

The previous illustrations introduced the terms *fixed* and *variable costs*. These terms will be used repeatedly throughout this textbook. It is critically important that you gain a thorough understanding of the behaviour patterns of these two cost categories. The following section provides a graphical presentation and a summary chart that highlight the differences between fixed and variable costs. You should study these graphs and the summary chart carefully before proceeding with your course of study.

With respect to fixed costs, the term *fixed* refers to the behaviour of *total cost*. The *cost per unit* of a fixed cost *varies inversely* with changes in the level of activity. As activity increases, fixed cost per unit decreases. As activity decreases, fixed cost per unit increases. These relationships are shown graphically in Exhibit 2–18.

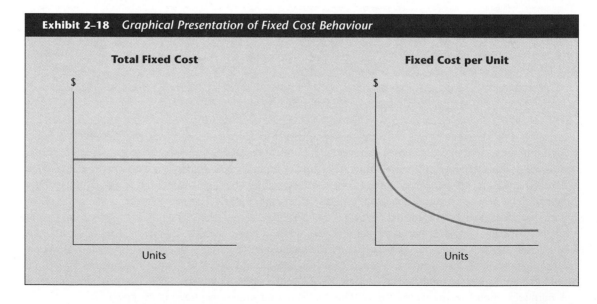

Exhibit 2–18   *Graphical Presentation of Fixed Cost Behaviour*

With respect to variable cost, the term *variable* refers to the behaviour of *total cost*. Total variable cost increases or decreases proportionally with changes in the volume of activity. In contrast, *variable cost per unit remains fixed* at all levels of activity. These relationships are shown graphically in Exhibit 2–19.

The relationships between fixed and variable costs are summarized in the chart in Exhibit 2–20. Again, we urge you to study these relationships carefully.

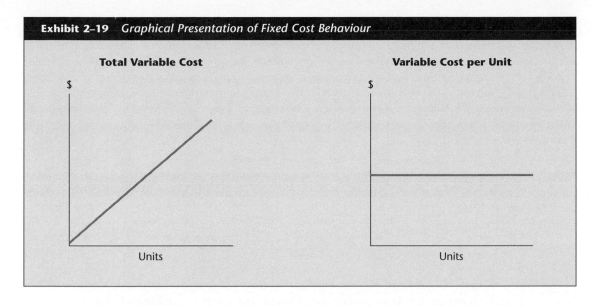

Exhibit 2–19   *Graphical Presentation of Fixed Cost Behaviour*

Total Variable Cost

Variable Cost per Unit

Exhibit 2–20   *Fixed and Variable Cost Behaviour*

When Activity Level Changes	Total Cost	Cost per Unit
Fixed costs	Remains constant	Changes *inversely*
Variable costs	Changes in *direct* proportion	Remains constant

The Relevant Range

Suppose that SPI is required to rent a concert hall at a cost of $5,000. The facility has a capacity to seat 4,000 people. Is the cost of the concert hall a fixed or variable cost? Since total cost remains the same, regardless of whether one ticket, 4,000 tickets, or any number in between are sold, the cost is a fixed cost relative to ticket sales. However, what happens if significantly more than 4,000 people desire to attend the concert? Under these circumstances, SPI may choose to rent a larger facility at a higher cost. In other words, *the cost is fixed only for a designated range of activity.*

A similar condition exists for many variable costs. Suppose that SPI is purchasing 1,800 T-shirts at a cost of $12 each. The supplier may offer a discount to buyers who purchase more than 2,000 units. In this case, the company's variable cost per unit would decrease if it increased its order size to exceed 2,000 units. The point to remember is that cost behaviour applies to a specified range of activity. The range of activity over which the definitions of fixed and variable costs apply is commonly called the **relevant range**. Also note that the definitions of fixed and variable are bound by a specified period of time. With respect to the concert hall, the time period is one day. If the time period is changed from one to two days, the total cost of rental is no longer fixed. Instead, it moves from $5,000 to $10,000. It is fixed at $5,000 for one day only. As this discussion implies, *the classification of fixed versus variable can have meaning only within the context of a specified relevant range of activity for a defined period of time.*

LO7

Understand how cost behaviour is affected by the relevant range and the decision-making context.

Context-Sensitive Definitions of Fixed and Variable

LO7

Understand how cost behaviour is affected by the relevant range and the decision-making context.

The behaviour pattern of a particular cost may change from fixed to variable or vice versa, depending on the context in which the cost is considered. For example, the cost of the band was considered to be fixed at $48,000 when SPI was considering hiring it to play at a single concert. Regardless of how many tickets it sells, the total cost remains fixed at $48,000. However, a variable behaviour pattern occurs if SPI decides to use the band to perform at a series of concerts. The total cost and the cost per concert if the band plays one, two, three, four, or five concerts at a cost of $48,000 per concert are shown in Exhibit 2–21.

Exhibit 2–21 *Cost Behaviour Relative to Number of Concerts*					
Number of concerts (a)	1	2	3	4	5
Cost per concert (b)	$48,000	$48,000	$ 48,000	$ 48,000	$ 48,000
Total cost (a × b)	$48,000	$96,000	$144,000	$192,000	$240,000

Within this context, the total cost of hiring the band increases proportionally with the number of concerts, while cost per concert remains constant. Accordingly, the cost is a variable cost. Clearly, the same cost can behave as a fixed cost or as a variable cost, depending on the **activity base** used to define the cost. When trying to identify a cost as fixed or variable, you must first ask yourself, *"fixed or variable" relative to what activity base?* The cost of the band is fixed *relative* to the number of tickets sold for a specific concert; it is variable *relative* to the number of concerts produced.

▌ Cost Averaging

LO8

Select an appropriate time period for the calculation of the average cost per unit.

Lake Resorts, Inc. (LRI) provides water skiing lessons for its guests. Since the demand for lessons is seasonal (there is more demand in July than in December), LRI has decided to rent equipment (boat, skis, ropes, life jackets, etc.) on an as-needed basis. LRI's accountant has collected the following data regarding the expected cost of providing ski lessons:

1. The daily rental fee for equipment is $80.
2. Instructors are paid $15 per hour.
3. Fuel costs amount to $2 per hour of operation.
4. Each lesson requires one hour of time. Ten hours of effective ski time are available each day.

Suppose management wants to know the cost per lesson if 2, 5, or 10 lessons are provided per day. The appropriate computations are shown in Exhibit 2–22.

It is important to recognize that the cost per lesson shown in Exhibit 2–22 is an *average cost.* Accountants focus on average costs because they are relatively easy to compute and are frequently more relevant to decision making than are actual costs. Consider some of the difficulties that would be encountered in trying to determine the actual cost of each individual lesson. Because the cost of equipment rental covers any number of lessons within the relevant range, it cannot be identified as an actual cost of any particular lesson. Because some skiers weigh more than others, pulling them behind the boat requires the use of more gas. Likewise, wind con-

Exhibit 2–22 *Analysis of Total and Unit Costs*			
Number of Lessons (a)	2	5	10
Cost of equipment rental	$ 80	$ 80	$ 80
Cost of instruction (no. hrs. × $15)	30	75	150
Cost of fuel (no. hrs. × $2)	4	10	20
Total cost (b)	$114	$165	$250
Cost per lesson (b ÷ a)	$ 57	$ 33	$ 25

Natasha Bell is a business student who works part time to help pay for her university expenses. She is currently taking her first accounting course. Natasha often hears managers at her employer's company refer to amortization as a *fixed cost*. The instructor in her accounting course requires students to study the financial statements of several real-world companies, including those of America Online (AOL). While reviewing AOL's income statement, Natasha noticed that the company's amortization did not appear to be fixed. In fact, it went from $2.8 million in 1994 to $12.3 million in 1995 to $33.4 million in 1996. What could possibly explain why this *fixed cost changed* so radically over a three-year period?

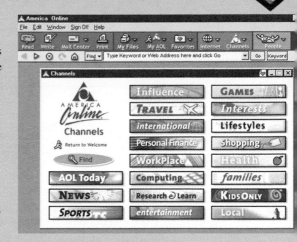

When an accountant says a cost is fixed, remember that it can stay the same (i.e, be fixed) in relation to one factor but change (i.e., be variable) in relation to other factors. Also, fixed costs are fixed only within a relevant range. The amortization cost for a single network server is fixed for a certain range of activity, but the capacity of each server is limited. AOL's client base has been growing so rapidly that the top end of server capacity (i.e., the upper end of the relevant range) is exceeded regularly. To provide service to a rapidly expanding customer base, AOL purchased many new servers and other amortizable assets from 1994 to 1996. The balance of Capital Assets at AOL for these three years follows:

Year	Capital Assets
1994	$ 20,306,000
1995	70,919,000
1996	101,277,000

Clearly, amortization charges can be expected to increase as the investment in amortizable assets increases. In this case, *fixed* means "stays the same" relative to a certain number of customers. When the number of customers exceeds the relevant range, additional investments and corresponding amortization charges increase.

ditions, water currents, the number of times a skier falls, and the presence of other boats affect cost factors, such as the actual time required to administer a lesson, the use of equipment, and the consumption of fuel. Determining the exact amount of each resource used for each lesson is an impossible task.

Average cost data are also useful for performance evaluation and for control. Knowing whether an instructor spent a few minutes more or less on a particular lesson is of little use. Knowing, however, that an instructor averages 10 extra minutes on virtually every lesson taught signals the need for corrective action. Knowing what happens *on average* is more useful than knowing what happened in one particular instance.

Computing the average cost per unit requires considering the span of time from which data are drawn. Suppose that during one day in the 2007 season, an instructor administered 10 lessons for a total cost of $250. During the 2006 season, LRI administered a total of 589 lessons at a cost of $19,437. Furthermore, assume that the records indicate that during the last five seasons, LRI administered 2,500 lessons at a total cost of $55,000. What is the average cost per lesson for the day, the year, and the five-year period? The answers are provided in Exhibit 2–23.

Exhibit 2–23 *Cost per Lesson*			
	Span of Time		
	One Day	**One Year**	**Five Years**
Total cost of lessons (a)	$250	$19,437	$55,000
Number of lessons (b)	10	589	2,500
Cost per lesson (a ÷ b)	$ 25	$ 33	$ 22

Assuming that management has decided to price ski lessons at $5 above the average cost per lesson, which of the cost per lesson figures should be used to establish the price? Should the price be $30 ($25 + $5), $38 ($33 + $5) or $27 ($22 + $5)?[1] The shorter interval (i.e., one day) represents the most current information, but it may also be the least relevant. Suppose that the one-day average cost was computed on a Sunday when the demand for ski lessons was extremely high. This would explain why the daily cost per lesson figure is lower than the yearly amount. The fixed cost of equipment rental is spread over a large number of lessons, making the cost per lesson small. Unfortunately, the Sunday average has little relevance for setting Monday's prices. This is true because customer demand drops sharply on Monday when many weekend vacationers return to work.

An average based on yearly data is probably more appropriate. If last year's season is a good predictor of this year's demand, pricing lessons at $38 provides a return that approximates the $5 average that management desires to earn. On days when demand is high, cost per unit will be low, and the resort will earn more than $5 per lesson. On days when demand is low, it will earn less than $5. However, on average, it will earn the desired return. Distortions can also result from the use of long as well as short time spans. For example, data drawn from the five seasons may not reflect current costs or recent changes in customer demand. For example, equipment rental cost was probably less five years ago than it is today. As this discussion implies, the selection of the most appropriate time span requires considerable judgment. A *good management accountant provides much more than number crunching.*

▌ Use of Estimates in Real-World Problems

LO9

Define the term *mixed costs.*

Identifying fixed and variable costs in real-world contexts normally requires the use of estimated, rather than actual, costs. Imagine the difficulty of trying to classify all the different costs incurred by a large company, such as Delta Airlines, as fixed or variable. Record keeping would be horrendous. The volume of the work required would be complicated by the fact that some costs are neither purely fixed nor variable. Instead, they contain a mixture of fixed and variable components. These costs are called **mixed costs** or **semivariable costs**. Consider, for example, the charges for cellular phone service. Customers are typically charged a flat rate plus an amount for each minute that they use the phone. The flat rate stays the same, no matter how long the phone is used. Even if no calls are made, the customer must pay the flat rate fee. This portion of the phone cost behaves as a fixed cost. However, the total bill increases for each minute that the phone is in use. The more the phone is used, the higher is the bill. With respect to this portion of the bill, the cost behaviour is variable.

Dividing a mixed cost into its respective fixed and variable components may be difficult if many phones are in use simultaneously. For example, suppose that the annual phone expense for a multinational sales company is $1,280,000. The company uses thousands of phones that are serviced by a variety of cellular companies that charge different rates for phone usage. Dividing the total expense into

[1]The cost plus method is only one of several possible pricing strategies. Other pricing practices will be discussed in subsequent chapters.

fixed and variable components would require the analysis of thousands of separate phone bills. Fortunately, this tedious task usually is unnecessary because a company may find estimated, rather than actual, costs to be adequate for decision making. The next section describes a method of dividing total cost into estimated fixed and variable components.

▌High-Low Method of Estimating Fixed and Variable Costs

Suppose that Rainy Day Books is interested in expanding its operations by opening a new store. The company president, who is attempting to evaluate the risk of opening it, wants to know the level of fixed cost likely to be incurred. To satisfy the president's request, the accountant gathered the data shown in Exhibit 2–24 regarding the sales volume and cost history of an existing store. Assuming that the new store can operate with approximately the same cost structure, the data can be used to estimate the amount of fixed cost likely to be incurred by the new store. The procedures used to make the estimate will be discussed in the following paragraphs.

LO10

Use the high-low method, scattergraphs, and regression to estimate fixed and variable costs.

Exhibit 2–24 *Cost Data*		
Month	**Units Sold**	**Total Cost**
January	30,000	$450,000
February	14,000	300,000
March	12,000	150,000
April	25,000	440,000
May	10,000	180,000
June	11,000	240,000
July	20,000	350,000
August	18,000	400,000
September	17,000	360,000
October	16,000	320,000
November	27,000	490,000
December	34,000	540,000

The first step is to identify the high and low activity points in the data set. Indeed, the procedure used is called the **high-low method**. The total cost of operating the store *depends* on the number of books sold (i.e., the more books sold, the higher the total cost). Accordingly, the number of books sold is called the *independent variable*, and the total cost is called the *dependent variable*.

Applying the high-low method begins with identifying the highest and lowest *activity* points in the data set. The lowest point in units sold occurred in May. The determining factor is the independent variable. Since cost depends on sales volume, we must focus our attention on the number of units sold. The high point in sales volume occurred in December. The relevant number and cost data for the December and May high and low points follow:

The variable cost per unit is determined by dividing the difference in the total cost by the difference in the number of units sold, as follows:

	Units Sold	**Total Cost**
High	34,000	$540,000
Low	10,000	$180,000

$$\text{Variable cost per unit} = \frac{\text{Change in total cost}}{\text{Change in volume}} = \frac{(\$540,000 - \$180,000)}{(34,000 - 10,000)} = \frac{\$360,000}{24,000} = \$15$$

The fixed cost component can now be determined by subtracting the variable cost from the total cost. The computation can use the high point or the low point. Either reference point yields the same result. Computations using the high point are as follows:

Fixed Cost + Variable Cost = Total Cost
Fixed Cost = Total Cost − Variable Cost
Fixed Cost = $540,000 − ($15.00 × 34,000 units)
Fixed Cost = $30,000

The high-low method is easy to use, but it is vulnerable to inaccuracies. Note that although the data set has 12 data points, only two of them are used to develop the fixed and variable cost estimates. If either or both of these points are not representative of the true relationship between fixed and variable costs, the estimates produced by the high-low method will be inaccurate. Accordingly, *the chief advantage of the high-low method is simplicity of use; its chief disadvantage is vulnerability to inaccuracy.* Rainy Day's accountant decides to use a scattergraph to test the accuracy of the high-low method.

▌Scattergraph Method of Estimating Fixed and Variable Costs

LO10

Use the high-low method, scattergraphs, and regression to estimate fixed and variable costs.

Scattergraphs are sometimes used as an estimation technique for dividing total cost into fixed and variable cost components. In this case, Rainy Day's accountant constructs a scattergraph by recording the number of books sold along the horizontal axis. Cost data are recorded along the vertical axis. The 12 data points are then plotted on the graph, and a line is drawn through the high and low points in the data set. The result is shown in Exhibit 2–25.

After viewing the scattergraph in Exhibit 2–25, the accountant is certain that the high and low points are not representative of the data set. Note that most of the data points are above the high-low line. The line should be shifted upward to reflect the influence of the other data points. The accountant constructs a second scattergraph to accomplish this objective. This graph is shown in Exhibit 2–26. It is identical to the graph in Exhibit 2–25, except that the straight line is plotted through the centre of the entire data

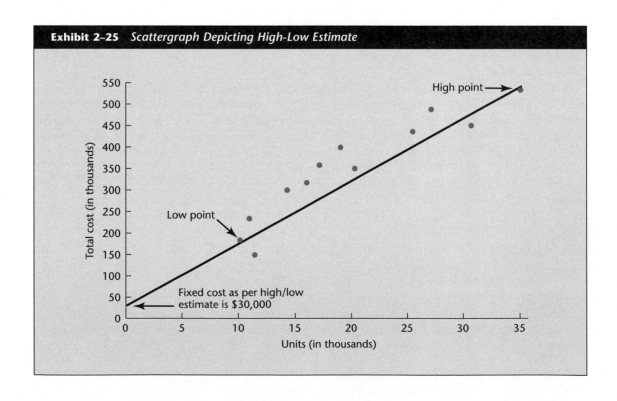

Exhibit 2–25 *Scattergraph Depicting High-Low Estimate*

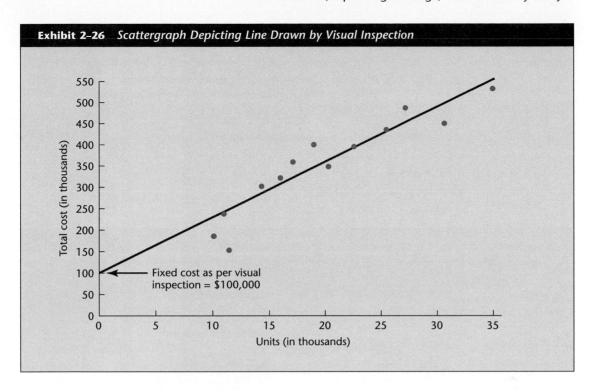

Exhibit 2–26   *Scattergraph Depicting Line Drawn by Visual Inspection*

set, rather than just the high and low points in the data set. The new line is called a **regression line.** Although the line is drawn by visual inspection, it should be placed to minimize the total distance between the data points and the line. This usually means that approximately half of the data points appear above and half below the regression line. The estimated variable cost per unit is represented by the slope (i.e., steepness) of the regression line. The fixed cost is determined by the point (the *intercept*) where the regression line crosses the vertical axis (i.e., the total cost line). Therefore, the variable and fixed cost components are determined by the slope and the intercept of the regression line.

The intercept shown in Exhibit 2–26 provides an estimate of fixed cost amounting to $100,000. Although the amount of fixed cost is the only item that the company president had asked to see, the variable cost can be easily determined by subtracting the fixed cost from the total cost at any point along the regression line. For example, at 15,000 units, total cost amounts to $300,000. Variable cost is determined as follows:

Fixed Cost + Variable Cost = Total Cost
Variable Cost = Total Cost − Fixed Cost
Variable Cost = $300,000 − $100,000
Variable Cost = $200,000

Variable cost per unit is $13.33, calculated by dividing the total variable cost by the number of units ($200,000 ÷ 15,000 units = $13.33 per unit).

■ Regression Method of Cost Estimation

LO10

Use the high-low method, scattergraphs, and regression to estimate fixed and variable costs.

Since the regression line is drawn by simple visual inspection, it is subject to human error. A better fit can be obtained using a statistical procedure known as **least-squares regression**.[2] Many of today's spreadsheet programs include a regression procedure. For example, the regression estimates shown in Exhibit 2–27 were generated in an *Excel* spreadsheet by performing the following functions:

1. Enter the data in spreadsheet columns[3] (see Columns B and C, Rows 3 through 14 in Exhibit 2–27).
2. Click *Tools*.
3. Click *Data Analysis*.[4]
4. Click *Regression* and then *OK*.
5. Define data ranges and click *Line Fit Plot*.
6. Click *OK*.

Exhibit 2–27 *Excel Spreadsheet Showing the Results of Least-Squares Regression*

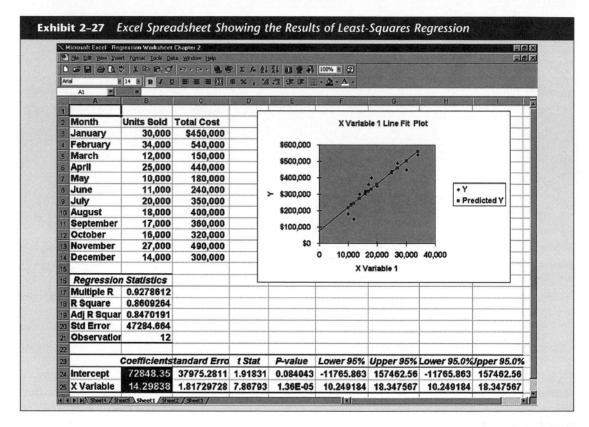

[2]Although the least-squares regression is a more accurate method than the high-low method and the visual scattergraph method, the three methods follow the same logical reasoning. Basically, the procedure locates a straight line on a coordinate with the *Y* axis representing the cost in dollars and the *X* axis representing the cost driver. In the examples shown in this chapter, the measurement of production in units is used as the cost driver and appears on the *X* axis. The basic regression model can be explained in the following equation:

$Y = a + bX$

where

$a =$ total fixed cost, or the *Y* intercept of the regression line
$b =$ variable cost per unit of *X*, or the slope of the regression line
$X =$ independent variable
$Y =$ dependent variable

[3]Statistical reliability requires an information set that includes more than 30 data points. The illustration shown here has been limited in size to simplify the demonstration.

[4]If the pull-down menu does not contain a data analysis option, it is likely that the statistical functions have not been activated in your program. You will need to consult the *Excel* user manual or help routine for instructions to activate the statistical functions.

The regression function returns an estimate of $72,848 for fixed cost and $14.30 per unit for variable costs. These estimates are highlighted in blue in the spreadsheet shown in Exhibit 2–27. The regression statistics and other information shown in the worksheet output are provided to enable the assessment of the quality of the estimates. A detailed discussion of this topic is beyond the scope of this text. For more in-depth discussion of the reliability issue, please refer to a statistics textbook.

a look back

Cost behaviour patterns can play a critically important role in a company's profitability. It is important to understand how different costs behave in relation to changes in the volume of activity. Total *fixed cost* remains constant when activity changes. Fixed cost per unit decreases with increases in activity and increases with decreases in activity. In contrast, total *variable cost* increases proportionately with increases in activity and decreases proportionately with decreases in activity. Variable cost per unit remains constant, regardless of how activity changes. The definitions of fixed and variable costs have meaning only within the context of a specified range of activity (i.e., the relevant range) for a defined period of time. In addition, cost behaviour depends on the measure of volume being considered (e.g., a store manager's salary is fixed relative to the number of customers visiting a particular store but is variable relative to the number of stores operated). A mixed cost contains a mixture of fixed and variable cost components.

Fixed costs allow companies to take advantage of *operating leverage*. With operating leverage, each additional sale decreases the cost per unit. This principle allows a small percentage change in volume of revenue to have a significantly larger percentage change on profits. The *magnitude of operating lever-*

age can be determined by dividing the contribution margin by net income. When revenues have covered fixed costs and all costs are fixed, each dollar of revenue represents pure profit. Having a fixed cost structure (i.e., operating leverage) has risks and rewards for a company. If the volume of sales is increasing, costs do not increase, allowing profits to soar. Alternatively, if the volume of sales is decreasing, costs do not decrease and profits decline significantly more than revenues. Companies with high variable costs in relation to fixed costs do not experience as great a level of operating leverage. Their costs increase or decrease in proportion to increases in revenue. These companies experience less risk but fail to reap disproportionately higher profits when volume soars.

Under the contribution margin approach, variable costs are subtracted from revenue to determine the amount of *contribution margin*. Fixed costs are then subtracted from the contribution margin to determine the amount of net income. Accordingly, the contribution margin represents the amount available to pay fixed costs and provide a profit. This format is used for internal reporting purposes.

Cost per unit is an average cost that is easier to compute than the actual cost of each unit and is more relevant to decision making than the actual cost. Computation of the average cost per unit must consider the span of time from which data are drawn. Distortions can result from the use of long as well as short time spans.

Fixed and variable costs can be estimated by using such methods as the *high-low method*, *scattergraphs*, and *regression*. The high-low method, and scattergraphs are easier to use but do not provide the accuracy of regression methods of costs estimation.

a look forward

The next chapter will show you how changes in cost, volume, and pricing affect profitability. You will learn to determine the number of units of product that must be produced and sold in order to break even (i.e., the number of units that will produce an amount of revenue that is exactly equal to total cost). You will learn to establish the price of a product using a cost-plus-pricing approach and to establish the cost of a product using a target-pricing approach. Finally, the chapter will show you how to use a break-even chart to examine potential profitability over a range of operating activity and how to use a technique known as *sensitivity analysis* to examine how simultaneous changes in sales price, volume, fixed costs, and variable costs affect profitability.

KEY TERMS

Activity base The factor that causes changes in variable cost; is usually some measure of volume when used to define cost behaviour. *(p. 56)*

Contribution margin The difference between a company's sales revenue and total variable cost; represents the amount available to cover fixed costs and thereafter to provide a profit. *(p. 51)*

Cost averaging A method to determine the average cost per unit of a product or service by dividing the total cost by the activity base used in defining the cost. Using the average cost per unit is often more relevant to decision making than using actual costs. Pricing, performance evaluation, and control are most often based on average costs. *(p. 56)*

Cost behaviour The way a cost reacts (i.e., goes up, goes down, or remains the same) relative to changes in some measure of activity. For example, the behaviour pattern of the cost of raw materials is to increase as the number of units of product made increases. *(p. 54)*

Cost structure A company's cost mix (the relative proportion of variable and fixed costs to total cost). When sales change, the size of the corresponding change in net income is directly related to the company's cost structure. Companies with a large percentage of fixed cost to variable costs have more fluctuation in net income with changes in sales revenue. *(p. 50)*

Economies of scale The concept by which the unit cost of production can be reduced by taking advantage of opportunities that become available when an operation's size is increased. Increased size usually results in an increased volume of activity that drives the per-unit fixed cost down, resulting in a lower total cost of production. *(p. 48)*

Fixed cost A cost that in total remains constant when volume of activity changes. Fixed cost per unit varies inversely with changes in the volume of activity. *(p. 45)*

High-low method A method of estimating the fixed and variable components of a mixed cost;

determines the variable cost per unit by dividing the difference between the total cost of the high and low points by the difference in the corresponding high and low volumes. The fixed cost component is determined by subtracting the variable cost from the total cost at either the high or low volume. *(p. 59)*

Least-squares regression A statistical procedure used to determine the regression line to achieve a better fit through the data points. Because of the mathematical computations required in least-squares regression, computers are usually used to calculate the line. *(p. 62)*

Mixed costs (semivariable costs) Costs composed of a mixture of fixed and variable components. *(p. 58)*

Operating leverage An operating condition in which a percentage change in revenue produces a proportionately larger percentage change in net income; measured by dividing the contribution margin by net income. The higher the proportion of fixed cost to total costs, the greater is the operating leverage. *(p. 47)*

Regression line A line, represented by the equation $Y = a + bX$, drawn through observed points (Y, total cost, and X, volume of activity) plotted on a graph with the horizontal axis representing volume of activity and the vertical axis representing total costs. The line is drawn so that the total distance between the data points and the line is minimized. A fixed cost estimate (a) is represented by the point where the regression line crosses the vertical axis (intercept). The slope (b) of the line represents an estimate of the average variable cost per unit of activity. *(p. 61)*

Relevant range The range of activity over which the definitions of fixed and variable costs apply. *(p. 55)*

Scattergraph method A method of estimating the variable and fixed components by which cost data are plotted on a graph and a regression line is visually drawn through the points so that the total distance between the data points and the line is minimized. *(p. 60)*

Variable cost A cost that in total changes in direct proportion to changes in volume of activity; remains constant per unit when volume of activity changes. *(p. 46)*

QUESTIONS

1. Define *fixed cost* and *variable cost* and give an example of each.
2. How can knowing cost behaviour relative to volume fluctuations affect decision making?
3. Define the term *operating leverage* and explain how it affects profits.
4. How is operating leverage calculated?
5. Explain the limitations of operating leverage in predicting profitability.
6. If volume is increasing, would a company benefit more from a pure variable or a pure fixed cost structure? Which cost structure would be advantageous if volume is decreasing?
7. When are economies of scale possible? In what types of businesses would you most likely find economies of scale?
8. Explain the risk and rewards to a company that result from having fixed costs.
9. Are companies with predominately fixed cost structures likely to be most profitable?
10. How is the relevant range of activity important to fixed and variable cost? Give an example of how the definitions of these costs become invalid when volume goes outside the relevant range.
11. Sam's Garage is trying to determine the cost of providing an oil change. Why would the average cost of this service be more relevant information than the actual cost for each customer?
12. When would the high-low method be the appropriate method for estimating variable and fixed costs? When would least-squares regression be the most desirable?
13. The president of Bright Corporation tells you that he sees a dim future for his company. He feels that his hands are tied because fixed costs are too high. He says that fixed costs do not change and therefore the situation is hopeless. Do you agree? Explain.
14. All costs are variable because if a business ceases operations, its costs fall to zero. Do you agree with the statement? Explain.
15. Because of seasonal fluctuations, Norel Corporation has a problem determining the unit cost of the products it produces. For example, high heating cost during the winter months causes the cost per unit to be higher than per-unit cost in the summer months even when the same number of units of product is produced. Suggest several ways that Norel can improve the computation of per-unit costs.
16. Vern Salsbury tells you that he thinks the terminology for fixed cost and variable cost is confusing. He notes that fixed cost per unit changes when the number of units changes. Further, variable cost per unit remains fixed, regardless of how many units are produced. He concludes that the terminology seems to be backward. Is Mr. Salsbury correct in his description of the behaviour of the per-unit fixed and variable costs? If not, what is the correct description for the behaviour of fixed and variable costs? If he is correct, explain why the terminology appears to be contradictory.

EXERCISES

L.O. 1 EXERCISE 2-1   *Identification of Cost Behaviour*

Pasta Palace is a fast-food restaurant company that operates a chain of restaurants across the nation. Each restaurant employs eight people; one is a manager paid a salary plus a bonus equal to 2 percent of sales. Other employees, including two cooks, one dishwasher, and four waitresses, are paid salaries. Each manager is budgeted $1,000 per month for advertising cost.

Required

Classify each of the following costs incurred by Pasta Palace as being fixed, variable, or mixed:

a. The cooks' salaries at a particular location relative to the number of customers.

b. The cost of supplies (cups, plates, spoons, etc.) relative to the number of customers.

c. The manager's compensation relative to the number of customers.

d. Waitresses' salaries relative to the number of restaurants.

e. Advertising costs relative to the number of customers for a particular restaurant.

f. Advertising costs relative to the number of restaurants.

L.O. 1 EXERCISE 2-2   *Identification of Cost Behaviour*

Kalite Company incurred the following costs:

		100	200	300	400	500
				Units Sold		
a.	Total salary cost	$2,200.00	$ 3,400.00	$ 4,600.00	$ 5,800.00	$ 7,000.00
b.	Total cost of goods sold	5,000.00	10,000.00	15,000.00	20,000.00	25,000.00
c.	Cost per unit for amortization	180.00	90.00	60.00	45.00	36.00
d.	Total rent cost	4,500.00	4,500.00	4,500.00	4,500.00	4,500.00
e.	Total cost of shopping bags	5.00	10.00	15.00	20.00	25.00
f.	Cost per unit of merchandise	50.00	50.00	50.00	50.00	50.00
g.	Rental cost per unit of merchandise sold	45.00	22.50	15.00	11.25	9.00
h.	Total phone expense	125.00	225.00	325.00	425.00	525.00
i.	Cost per unit of supplies	1.00	1.00	1.00	1.00	1.00
j.	Total insurance	1,000.00	1,000.00	1,000.00	1,000.00	1,000.00

Required

Identify each of these costs as being fixed, variable, or mixed.

L.O. 1 EXERCISE 2-3   *Determination of Fixed Cost per Unit*

Allen Thomas Corporation has the following annual fixed costs:

Item	Cost
Amortization expense	$220,000
Officers' salaries	480,000
Long-term lease expenses	120,000
Property taxes	40,000

Required

Determine the fixed cost per unit of production, assuming that Allen Thomas produces 50,000; 60,000; and 70,000 units. (Round your answer to the nearest cent.)

EXERCISE 2-4   *Determination of Total Variable Cost*   **L.O. 1**

The following variable costs apply to the production of goods made by Scott Manufacturing Corporation:

Item	Cost per Unit
Materials	$2.00
Labour	1.80
Variable overhead	.40
Total	$4.20

Required

Determine the amount of total variable cost, assuming levels of production at 20,000; 24,000; and 28,000 units.

EXERCISE 2-5   *Fixed versus Variable Cost Behaviour*   **L.O. 1**

A company had the following costs for two items of overhead in two recent months:

	May	June
Production (units)	100	200
Rent	$1,000	$1,000
Utilities	$1,000	$2,000

Required

a. For each of the two items of cost, calculate the cost per unit for both May and June.
b. On the basis of both total cost and cost-per-unit, identify which cost is variable and which is fixed. Explain your answer.

EXERCISE 2-6   *Fixed versus Variable Cost Behaviour*   **L.O. 1**

Taylor Trophies makes and sells trophies distributed to little league ballplayers. The company normally produces and sells between 20,000 and 23,000 trophies per year. The following cost data were drawn from the company's accounting records:

	Number of Units			
	20,000	21,000	22,000	23,000
Total costs incurred				
Fixed	$ 45,000			
Variable	100,000			
Total costs	$145,000			
Cost per unit				
Fixed	$2.25			
Variable	5.00			
Total cost per unit	$7.25			

Required

a. Complete the preceding table by filling in the missing amounts for the levels of activity shown in the first row of the table. Round all cost-per-unit figures to the nearest whole penny.
b. Explain why the total cost per unit decreases as the number of units increases.

L.O. 1 EXERCISE 2-7   *Fixed versus Variable Cost Behaviour*

Pistol Productions sponsors rock concerts. The company is considering a contract to hire a band at a cost of $20,000 per concert.

Required
a. What are the total band cost and the cost per person if attendance is 500, 1,000, 1,500, 2,000, and 2,500?
b. Is the cost of hiring the band a fixed or a variable cost?
c. Draw a graph and plot total cost and cost per unit if attendance is 500, 1,000, 1,500, 2,000, and 2,500.
d. Identify Pistol's major business risks and explain how they can be minimized.

L.O. 1 EXERCISE 2-8   *Fixed versus Variable Cost Behaviour*

Pistol Productions sells souvenir T-shirts at each rock concert that it sponsors. The shirts cost $5 each.

Required
a. What are the total cost of shirts and cost per shirt if sales amount to 500, 1,000, 1,500, 2,000, and 2,500?
b. Is the cost of T-shirts a fixed or a variable cost?
c. Draw a graph and plot total cost and cost per shirt if sales amount to 500, 1,000, 1,500, 2,000, and 2,500.
d. Identify Pistol's major business risks and explain how they can be minimized.

L.O. 1 EXERCISE 2-9   *Creation of Graphs of Fixed Cost Behaviour*

The following graphs depict the dollar amount of fixed cost on the vertical axes and the level of activity on the horizontal axes:

Total fixed cost   **Fixed cost per unit**

$ $

Units   Units

Required
a. Draw a line that depicts the relationship between total fixed cost and the level of activity.
b. Draw a line that depicts the relationship between fixed cost per unit and the level of activity.

L.O. 1 EXERCISE 2-10   *Creation of Graphs of Variable Cost Behaviour*

The following graphs depict the dollar amount of variable cost on the vertical axes and the level of activity on the horizontal axes:

Total variable cost

Variable cost per unit

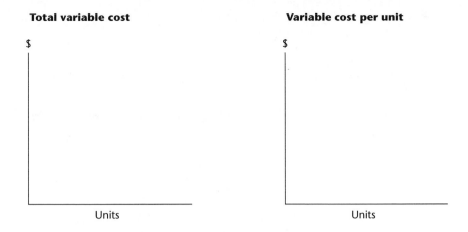

Units

Units

Required

a. Draw a line that depicts the relationship between total variable cost and the level of activity.

b. Draw a line that depicts the relationship between variable cost per unit and the level of activity.

EXERCISE 2-11   *Mixed Cost at Different Levels of Activity*

L.O. 1

Telemarketers, Inc. paid one of its sales representatives $3,600 during the month of June. The rep is paid a set salary plus $20 per unit of product sold. During June, 100 units were sold.

Required

Calculate the total monthly cost of the sales representative's salary for each of the following months:

	Month			
	July	Aug.	Sept.	Oct.
Number of units sold	120	80	140	90
Total variable cost				
Total fixed cost				
Total salary cost				

EXERCISE 2-12   *Use of Fixed Cost as a Competitive Business Strategy*

L.O. 1, 2, 3, 6

The following income statements reveal different cost structures for two competing companies:

Income Statements		
	Company Name	
	Blue	Green
Number of Customers (a)	50	50
Sales Revenue (a × $800)	$40,000	$40,000
Variable Cost (a × $600)		(30,000)
Variable Cost (a × $0)	0	
Contribution Margin	40,000	10,000
Fixed Costs	(30,000)	0
Net Income	$10,000	$10,000

Required

a. Recalculate Blue's income statement, assuming that it serves 100 customers when it lures 50 customers away from Green by lowering the sales price to $500 per unit.

b. Recalculate Green's income statement, assuming that it serves 100 customers when it lures 50 customers away from Blue by lowering the sales price to $500 per unit.

c. Explain why the price-cutting strategy increased Blue Company's profits but caused a net loss for Green Company.

L.O. 4, 5 EXERCISE 2-13   *Use of a Contribution Margin Format for an Income Statement to Measure the Magnitude of Operating Leverage*

The following income statement was drawn from the records of Margan Company, a merchandising firm:

MARGAN COMPANY Income Statement for the Year Ended December 31, 2001	
Sales Revenue (5,200 units × $180)	$936,000
Cost of Goods Sold (5,200 units × $100)	(520,000)
Gross Margin	416,000
Sales Commissions (20% of sales)	(187,200)
Administrative Salaries	(104,400)
Advertising Expense	(34,400)
Amortization Expense	(25,000)
Shipping and Handling Expenses (5,200 units × $2)	(10,400)
Net Income	$ 54,600

Required

a. Reconstruct the statement using the contribution margin format.

b. Calculate the level of operating leverage.

c. Use the measure of operating leverage to determine the amount of net income that Margan will earn if sales increase by 20 percent.

L.O. 5 EXERCISE 2-14   *Assessment of the Magnitude of Operating Leverage*

The following income statement applies to Drake Company for the current year:

Income Statement	
Sales Revenue (480 units × $60)	$28,800
Variable Cost (480 units × $35)	(16,800)
Contribution Margin	12,000
Fixed Costs	(8,000)
Net Income	$ 4,000

Required

a. Calculate the magnitude of operating leverage.

b. Use the operating leverage measure computed in Requirement *a* to determine the amount of net income that Drake Company will earn if it experiences a 25 percent increase in revenue. The sales price per unit was not affected.

c. Verify your answer to Requirement *b* by constructing an income statement based on a 25 percent increase in sales revenue. The sales price was not affected. Calculate the percentage change in net income between the two income statements.

EXERCISE 2-15   *Cost Averaging*   L.O. 8

Carington Camps, Inc. leases the land on which it builds camp sites. Carington is considering opening a new site on land that rents for $2,000 per month. The variable cost of providing service is expected to be $4 per camper. The following chart shows the number of expected campers for the first year of operation of the new site.

Jan.	Feb.	Mar.	Apr.	May	June	July	Aug.	Sept	Oct.	Nov.	Dec.	Total
200	100	300	300	400	600	800	800	500	300	200	300	4,800

Required

Assuming that Carington wants to earn $10 per camper, determine the price it should charge for a camp site in February and August. Assume that Carington does not employ a seasonal pricing strategy.

EXERCISE 2-16   *Estimation of Fixed and Variable Cost Using the High-Low Method*   L.O. 10

Biltmore Boat Company makes inexpensive aluminum fishing boats. Production is seasonal, with considerable activity occurring in the spring and summer. Sales and production tend to decline in the fall and winter months. During 2001, the high point in activity occurred in April when it produced 200 boats at a total cost of $140,000. The low point in production occurred in December when it produced 40 boats at a total cost of $44,000.

Required

Use the high-low method to estimate the amount of fixed cost per month incurred by Biltmore Boat Company.

PROBLEMS—SERIES A

PROBLEM 2-1A   *Identification of Cost Behaviour*   L.O. 1

Required

Identify the following costs as fixed or variable:

Costs related to plane trips between Toronto, Ontario, and Vancouver, British Columbia. Pilots are paid on a per-trip basis.
a. Cost of a maintenance check relative to the number of passengers on a particular trip.
b. Fuel costs relative to the number of trips.
c. Pilots' salaries relative to the number of trips flown.
d. Amortization relative to the number of planes in service.
e. Cost of refreshments relative to the number of passengers.
f. Pilots' salaries relative to the number of passengers on a particular trip.

National Bank operates several branch offices in grocery stores. Each branch employs a supervisor and two tellers.
g. Supervisors' salaries relative to the number of branches operated.
h. Supervisors' salaries relative to the number of customers served in a particular branch.
i. Facility rental costs relative to the size of customer deposits.
j. Tellers' salaries relative to the number of tellers in a particular district.
k. Supplies cost relative to the number of transactions processed in a particular branch.
l. Tellers' salaries relative to the number of customers served at a particular branch.

Costs related to the operation of a fast-food restaurant.
m. Amortization of equipment relative to the number of customers served at a particular restaurant.
n. Amortization of equipment relative to the number of restaurants.
o. Building rental cost relative to the number of customers served in a particular restaurant.
p. Manager's salary of a particular store relative to the number of employees.

q. Food cost relative to the number of customers.
r. Utility cost relative to the number of restaurants in operation.
s. Company president's salary relative to the number of restaurants in operation.
t. Land costs relative to the number of hamburgers sold at a particular restaurant.

L.O. 1   **PROBLEM 2-2A**   *Cost Behaviour and Averaging*

Billy Preston has decided to start Preston Cleaning, a residential housecleaning service company. He is able to rent cleaning equipment at a cost of $500 per month. Labour costs are expected to be $50 per house cleaned and supplies are expected to cost $4 per house.

Required
a. Determine the total expected cost of equipment rental and the average expected cost of equipment rental per house cleaned, assuming that Preston Cleaning cleans 15, 20, or 25 houses during one month. Is the cost of equipment a fixed or a variable cost?
b. Determine the total expected cost of labour and the average expected cost of labour per house cleaned, assuming that Preston Cleaning cleans 15, 20, or 25 houses during one month. Is the cost of labour a fixed or a variable cost?
c. Determine the total expected cost of supplies and the average expected cost of supplies per house cleaned, assuming that Preston Cleaning cleans 15, 20, or 25 houses during one month. Is the cost of supplies a fixed or a variable cost?
d. Determine the total expected cost of cleaning houses, assuming that Preston Cleaning cleans 15, 20, or 25 houses during one month.
e. Determine the average expected cost per house, assuming that Preston Cleaning cleans 15, 20, or 25 houses during one month. Why does the cost per unit decrease as the number of houses increases?
f. If Mr. Preston tells you that he prices his services at 30 percent above cost, would you assume that he means average or actual cost? What factors lead you to this conclusion?

L.O. 1   **PROBLEM 2-3A**   *Context-Sensitive Nature of Cost Behaviour Classifications*

Western Bank has a startup division responsible for establishing new branch banks. Each branch opens with three tellers. Total teller cost per branch is $45,000 per year. The three tellers combined can process up to 90,000 customer transactions per year. If a branch does not attain a volume of at least 60,000 transactions during its first year of operations, it is closed. If the demand for services exceeds 90,000 transactions, a new teller is hired, and the branch is transferred from the startup division to the regular operations division.

Required
a. What is the relevant range of activity for the startup division?
b. Determine the amount of teller cost in total and the average teller cost per transaction for a branch that processes 60,000, 70,000, 80,000, or 90,000 transactions. In this case (i.e., the activity base is the number of transactions for a specific branch), is the teller cost a fixed or a variable cost?
c. Determine the amount of teller cost in total and the average teller cost per branch for Western Bank, assuming that the startup division operates 10, 15, 20, or 25 branches. In this case (i.e., the activity base is the number of branches), is the teller cost a fixed or a variable cost?

L.O. 1   **PROBLEM 2-4A**   *Context-Sensitive Nature of Cost Behaviour Classifications*

Patty Stark operates a sales booth in computer software trade shows, selling an accounting software package, *EZRecords*. She purchases the package from a software manufacturer for $50 each. Booth space at the convention hall costs $4,000 per show.

Required
a. Sales at trade shows in the past have ranged between 50 and 250 units per show. Determine the average cost of sales per unit if Ms. Stark sells 50, 100, 150, 200, or 250 units of *EZRecords* at a trade show. Use the following chart to organize your answer:

a	Sales Volume in Units (a)				
	50	100	150	200	250
Total cost of software (a × $50)	$2,500				
Total cost of booth rental	4,000				
Total cost of sales (b)	$6,500				
Average cost per unit (b ÷ a)	$130.00				

b. If Ms. Stark wants to earn $20 for each package of software sold at a trade show, what price would she be required to charge at sales volumes of 50, 100, 150, 200, and 250 units?

c. Record the total cost of booth space if Ms. Stark attends one, two, three, four, or five trade shows. Record your answers in the following chart:

	Number of Trade Shows Attended				
	1	2	3	4	5
Total cost of booth rental	4,000				

d. Ms. Stark provides decorative shopping bags to customers who purchase merchandise. Some customers take the bags; others do not. Some customers stuff more than one software package into a single bag. The number of bags varies in relation to the number of units sold, but the relationship is not proportional. Assume that she uses $20 of bags per 50 units sold. What is the additional cost per unit sold? Is the cost fixed or variable?

PROBLEM 2-5A *Effects of Operating Leverage on Profitability*   L.O. 2

Technical Training Services (TTS) provides instruction on the use of computer software for the employees of its corporate clients. It offers courses in the clients' offices on the clients' equipment. The only major expense TTS incurs is instructor salaries; it pays instructors $4,000 per course taught. TTS recently agreed to offer a course of instruction to the employees of Bullington Incorporated at a price of $250 per student. Bullington estimated that 20 students would attend the course.

Part 1: On the basis of the preceding information.

Required
a. Relative to the number of students in a single course, is the cost of instruction a fixed or a variable cost?
b. Determine the profit, assuming that 20 students attend the course.
c. Determine the profit, assuming a 10 percent increase in enrollment. What is the percentage change in profitability?
d. Determine the profit, assuming a 10 percent decrease in enrollment. What is the percentage change in profitability?
e. Explain why a 10 percent shift in enrollment produces more than a 10 percent shift in profitability. Use the term that identifies this phenomenon.

Part 2: The instructor has offered to teach the course for a percentage of tuition fees. Specifically, she wants $200 per person attending the class. Assume that the tuition fee remains at $250 per student.

Required
a. Is the cost of instruction a fixed or a variable cost?
b. Determine the profit, assuming that 20 students take the course.
c. Determine the profit, assuming a 10 percent increase in enrollment. What is the percentage change in profitability?

d. Determine the profit, assuming a 10 percent decrease in enrollment. What is the percentage change in profitability?

e. Explain why a 10 percent shift in enrollment produces a proportional 10 percent shift in profitability.

Part 3: TTS sells a workbook with printed material unique to each course to each student who attends the course. Those that are not sold must be destroyed. Because the workbooks had to be completed prior to the start of class, TTS printed 20 copies of the books on the basis of the client's estimate of the number of people who would attend the course. Each workbook costs $20 and is sold to workshop participants for $30. This cost includes a royalty fee paid to the author and the cost of duplication.

Required

a. Calculate the workbook's total cost and the cost per student, assuming that 18, 20, or 22 students attend the class.

b. Classify the cost of workbooks as fixed or variable relative to the number of students attending the workshop.

c. Discuss the risk of holding inventory as it applies to the workbooks.

d. Explain how a just-in-time inventory system can reduce the cost and risk of holding inventory.

L.O. 2, 3, 6 PROBLEM 2-6A   *Effects of Fixed and Variable Cost Behaviour on the Risk and Rewards of Business Opportunities*

Western and Eastern Universities offer executive training courses to corporate clients. Western pays its instructors $10,000 per course taught. Eastern pays its instructors $400 per student enrolled in the class. Both universities charge executives a $600 tuition fee per course attended.

Required

a. Prepare an income statement for Western and Eastern, assuming that 25 students attend a course.

b. Western University embarks on a strategy to entice students from Eastern University by lowering its tuition to $300 per course. Prepare an income statement for Western, assuming that the university is successful and therefore is able to enroll 50 students in its course.

c. Eastern University embarks on a strategy to entice students from Western University by lowering its tuition to $300 per course. Prepare an income statement for Eastern, assuming that the university is successful and therefore is able to enroll 50 students in its course.

d. Explain why the strategy described in Part *b* produced a profit but the same strategy described in Part *c* produced a loss.

e. Prepare an income statement for Western and Eastern Universities, assuming that 15 students attend a course.

f. It is always better to have fixed than variable cost. Explain why this statement is false.

g. It is always better to have variable than fixed cost. Explain why this statement is false.

L.O. 5 PROBLEM 2-7A   *Analysis of Operating Leverage*

Albert Brett is a venture capitalist facing two investment opportunities. He intends to invest $2 million in a new startup firm. He is nervous, however, about future economic volatility. Albert asks you to analyze the following financial data for the past year's operations of the two firms he is considering and give him some business advice:

	Company Name	
	Morgan	**Sanders**
Variable cost per unit (a)	$18	$9
Sales revenue (10,000 units × $24)	$240,000	$240,000
Variable cost (10,000 units × a)	(180,000)	(90,000)
Contribution margin	$ 60,000	$150,000
Fixed cost	(30,000)	(120,000)
Net income	$ 30,000	$ 30,000

Required

a. Compute the operating leverage for the two firms.

b. If the economy expands in the following years, Morgan and Sanders will both enjoy a 10 percent per year increase in sales, assuming that the selling price remains unchanged. Compute the change in net income for each firm in dollar amount and in percentage.

c. If the economy contracts in the following years, Morgan and Sanders will both suffer a 10 percent decrease in sales volume, assuming that the selling price remains unchanged. Compute the change in net income for each firm in dollar amount and in percentage.

d. Write a memo to Albert Brett with your advice and analyses.

PROBLEM 2-8A   *Selection of the Appropriate Time Period for Cost Averaging*   **L.O. 8**

Atlantic Movies is considering signing a contract to rent a movie for $1,500 per day. The contract requires a minimum one-week rental period. Estimated attendance is as follows:

Monday	Tuesday	Wednesday	Thursday	Friday	Saturday	Sunday
300	300	100	400	800	1,000	600

Required

a. Determine the daily average cost per person of the movie rental contract.

b. Suppose that Atlantic chooses to price movies at cost as computed in Part *a* plus $2. What price would it charge per ticket on each day of the week?

c. Use weekly averaging to determine a reasonable price to charge for movie tickets.

d. Comment on why weekly averaging may be more useful to business managers than daily averaging.

PROBLEM 2-9A   *Identification of Relevant Issues for Cost Averaging*   **L.O. 8**

Expeditions, Inc. offers mountain-climbing expeditions for its customers, providing food, equipment, and guides. Climbs normally require one week to complete. The company's accountant is reviewing historical cost data to establish a pricing strategy for the coming year. The accountant has prepared the following table regarding the cost data for the most recent climb, the company's average cost per year, and the five-year average cost:

	Span of Time		
	Recent Climb	**One Year**	**Five Years**
Total cost of climbs (a)	$7,500	$502,427	$1,555,000
Number of climbers (b)	10	569	2,500
Cost per climber (a ÷ b)	$ 750	$ 883	$ 622

Required

Write a memo that explains the potential advantages and disadvantages of using each of the per-unit cost figures as a basis for establishing a price to charge climbers during the coming year. What other factors must be considered in developing a pricing strategy?

PROBLEM 2-10A   *Estimation of Fixed and Variable Costs*   **L.O. 8**

Green Valley Computer Services, Inc. has been in business for six months. The following are basic operating data of the period:

	Month					
	Jan.	**Feb.**	**Mar.**	**Apr.**	**May**	**June**
Service hours	120	136	260	420	320	330
Revenue	$6,000	$6,800	$13,000	$21,000	$16,000	$16,500
Operating costs	4,200	5,200	7,000	11,100	9,000	10,500

Required

a. What is the average service revenue per hour for the six-month time period?
b. Use the high-low method to estimate the total monthly fixed cost and the variable cost per hour.
c. Determine the average contribution margin per hour.
d. Use the scattergraph method to estimate the total monthly fixed cost and the variable cost per hour.
e. Compare the results of the two methods and comment on the difference.

PROBLEMS—SERIES B

L.O. 5 PROBLEM 2-1B   *Identification of Cost Behaviour*

Required

Identify the following costs as fixed or variable:

Costs related to the operation of a retail gasoline company.
a. Property and real estate taxes relative to the amount of gasoline sold at a particular station.
b. Amortization of equipment relative to the number of stations.
c. Cashiers' wages relative to the number of customers served in a station.
d. Manager's salary of a particular station relative to the number of employees.
e. Gasoline cost relative to the number of customers.
f. Utility cost relative to the number of stations in operation.
g. The company's cost of national TV commercials relative to the number of stations in operation.
h. Amortization of equipment relative to the number of customers served at a station.

Costs related to shuttle bus trips between Calgary International Airport and downtown Calgary. Each bus driver receives a specific salary per month. A manager schedules bus trips and supervises drivers, and a secretary receives phone calls.
i. Fuel costs relative to the number of passengers.
j. Drivers' salaries relative to the number of trips driven.
k. Office staff salaries relative to the number of passengers on a particular trip.
l. Amortization relative to the number of buses in service.
m. A driver's salary relative to the number of passengers on a particular trip.
n. Fuel costs relative to the number of trips.

Jody's Barbershop operates several stores in shopping centres. Each store employs a supervisor and three barbers. Each barber receives a specific salary per month plus a 10 percent commission based on the service revenues each barber has earned.
o. Store rental costs relative to the number of customers.
p. Barbers' commissions relative to the number of customers.
q. Supervisory salaries relative to the number of customers served in a particular store.
r. Barbers' salaries relative to number of barbers in a particular district.
s. Supplies cost relative to the number of hair services provided in a particular store.
t. Barbers' salaries relative to the number of customers served at a particular store.

L.O. 1 PROBLEM 2-2B   *Cost Behaviour and Averaging*

Tammy Edwards asks you to analyze the operating cost of her lawn services business. She has bought the needed equipment with a cash payment of $10,080. Upon your recommendation, she agrees to adopt straight-line amortization. The equipment has an expected life of two years and no salvage value. Ms. Edwards pays her workers $15 per lawn service. Material costs, including fertilizer, pesticide, and supplies, are expected to be $6 per lawn service.

Required

a. Determine the total cost of equipment amortization and the average cost of equipment amortization per lawn service, assuming that Ms. Edwards provides 25, 30, or 35 lawn services during one month. Is the cost of equipment a fixed or a variable cost?

b. Determine the total expected cost of labour and the average expected cost of labour per lawn service, assuming that Ms. Edwards provides 25, 30, or 35 lawn services during one month. Is the cost of labour a fixed or a variable cost?

c. Determine the total expected cost of materials and the average expected cost of materials per lawn service, assuming that Ms. Edwards provides 25, 30, or 35 lawn services during one month. Is the cost of fertilizer, pesticide, and supplies a fixed or a variable cost?

d. Determine the total expected cost per lawn service, assuming that Ms. Edwards provides 25, 30, or 35 lawn services during one month.

e. Determine the average expected cost per lawn service, assuming that Ms. Edwards provides 25, 30, or 35 lawn services during one month. Why does the cost per unit decrease as the number of lawn services increases?

f. If Ms. Edwards tells you that she prices her services at 40 percent above cost, would you assume that she means **L.O. 1** average or actual cost? What factors lead you to this conclusion?

PROBLEM 2-3B   *Context-Sensitive Nature of Cost Behaviour Classifications*

John Crane sells a newly developed camera, Super Image. He purchases the cameras from the manufacturer for $150 each and rents a store in a shopping mall for $3,000 per month.

	Sales Volume in Units (a)				
	1100	200	300	400	500
Total cost of cameras (a × $150)	$15,000				
Total cost of store rental	3,000	_____	_____	_____	_____
Total cost of sales (b)	$18,000	_____	_____	_____	_____
Average cost per unit (b ÷ a)	$180.00				

Required

a. Determine the average cost of sales per unit if Mr. Crane sells 100, 200, 300, 400, or 500 units of Super Image per month. Use the following chart to organize your answer:

b. If Mr. Crane wants to make a gross profit of $50 for each camera, what price should he charge at sales volumes of 100, 200, 300, 400, or 500 units?

c. Record the total cost of store rental if Mr. Crane opens a camera store at one, two, three, four, or five shopping malls. Record your answers in the following chart:

	Shopping Malls				
	1	2	3	4	5
Total cost of store rental	$3,000				

d. Mr. Crane provides decorative ornaments to customers who purchase cameras. Some customers take the ornaments; others do not, and some take more than one. The number of ornaments varies in relation to the number of cameras sold, but the relationship is not proportional. Assume that he gives $50 of ornaments per 100 cameras sold as an average. What is the additional cost per camera sold? Is the cost fixed or variable?

PROBLEM 2-4B   *Effects of Fixed and Variable Cost Behaviour on the Risk and Rewards of Business*   **L.O. 2, 3, 6** *Opportunities*

River Club and Hill Club are competing health and recreation clubs in Brampton. They both offer tennis training clinics to adults. River pays its coaches $6,000 per season. Hill pays its coaches $200 per student enrolled in the clinic per season. Both clubs charge a tuition fee of $300 per season.

Required

a. Prepare income statements for River and Hill, assuming that 30 students per season attend each clinic.

b. The ambitious new director of River Club tries to expand his market share by lowering the club's tuition per student to $180 per course. Prepare an income statement for River, assuming that the club has attracted all of Hill's customers and therefore is able to enroll 60 students in its clinics.

c. Independent of Part *b*, Hill Club tries to lure River's students by lowering its price to $180 per student. Prepare an income statement for Hill, assuming that the club is successful and therefore is able to enroll 60 students in its clinics.

d. Explain why the strategy described in Part *b* produced a profit while the same strategy described in Part *c* produced a loss.

e. Prepare an income statement for River Club and Hill Club, assuming that 18 students attend a clinic at the original $300 tuition price.

f. It is always better to have fixed than variable cost. Explain why this statement is false.

g. It is always better to have variable than fixed cost. Explain why this statement is false.

L.O. 7, 8 PROBLEM 2-5B   *Analysis of Operating Leverage*

Martha Thompson has invested in two startup companies. At the end of the first year, she asks you to evaluate the operating performance of the two companies. The following are some operating data for the first year:

	Company Name	
	Julio	Leeds
Variable cost per unit (a)	$22	$13
Sales revenue (25,000 units × $30)	$750,000	$750,000
Variable cost (25,000 units × a)	(550,000)	(325,000)
Contribution margin	$200,000	$425,000
Fixed cost	(100,000)	(325,000)
Net income	$100,000	$100,000

Required

a. Compute the operating leverage for the two firms.

b. If the economy expands in the following year, Julio and Leeds will both enjoy a 10 percent per year increase in sales volume, assuming that the selling price remains unchanged. Compute the change in net income for each firm in dollar amount and in percentage.

c. If the economy contracts in the following year, Julio and Leeds will both suffer a 10 percent decrease in sales volume, assuming that the selling price remains unchanged. Compute the change in net income for each firm in both dollar amount and percentage.

d. Write a memo to Martha Thompson with your advice and analyses.

L.O. 8 PROBLEM 2-6B   *Selection of the Appropriate Time Period for Cost Averaging*

The City Fairground Parks and Recreation Department is considering the possibility of signing a contract to hire a circus at a cost of $2,500 per day. The contract requires a minimum performance period of one week. Estimated attendance is as follows:

Monday	Tuesday	Wednesday	Thursday	Friday	Saturday	Sunday
500	400	260	640	910	1,290	1,000

Required

a. Determine the daily average cost of the circus contract per person attending.
b. Suppose that the commission prices tickets at cost as computed in Part *a* plus $1.50. What would be the price per ticket charged on each day of the week?
c. Use weekly averaging to determine a reasonable price to charge for the circus tickets.
d. Comment on why weekly averaging may be more useful to business managers than daily averaging.

PROBLEM 2-7B   *Identification of Relevant Issues for Cost Averaging*   **L.O. 7**

Mojave Tours, Inc. organizes adventure tours for people interested in trips to a desert environment. A tour program generally lasts three days. Mojave provides food, equipment, and guides. For the purpose of setting prices for the next year, Susan Jennings, the president of Mojave Tours, has received from her accountant the company's past cost data in the following table:

	Span of Time		
	Recent Tour	**One Year**	**Ten Years**
Total cost of tours (a)	$6,600	$333,200	$2,179,125
Number of tourists (b)	30	1,360	11,175
Cost per tourist (a ÷ b)	$ 220	$ 245	$ 195

Required

Write a memo to Ms. Jennings that explains the potential advantages and disadvantages of using each of the different per-tourist cost figures as a basis for establishing a price to charge tourists during the coming year. What other factors must be considered in developing a pricing strategy?

PROBLEM 2-8B   *Estimation of Fixed and Variable Costs*   **L.O. 10**

Dixon Legal Services provides legal advice to clients. The following are basic operating data of the first six months of operation:

	Month					
	Jan.	**Feb.**	**Mar.**	**Apr.**	**May**	**June**
Service hours	80	102	135	156	186	170
Revenue	$4,800	$6,120	$8,100	$9,360	$11,160	$10,200
Operating costs	6,800	7,520	8,000	8,050	8,814	8,800

Required

a. What is the average service revenue per hour for the six-month time period?
b. Use the high-low method to estimate the total monthly fixed cost and the variable cost per hour.
c. Determine the average contribution margin per hour.
d. Use the scattergraph method to estimate the total monthly fixed cost and the variable cost per hour.
e. Compare the results of the two methods and comment on any differences.

ANALYZE, THINK, COMMUNICATE

BUSINESS APPLICATIONS CASE   *Operating Leverage*   **ACT 2-1**

The following information was drawn from the recent annual reports of Air Canada and Marks Work Wearhouse Ltd:

Description of Business for Air Canada

Air Canada is Canada's largest domestic and international full-service airline, providing scheduled and char-ter air transportation for passengers and cargo. Air Canada acquired Canadian Airlines International in 2000 becoming the seventh largest North American airline and 12th largest airline in the world. With the acquisi-tion of Canadian, Air Canada is carrying 30 million passengers annually and at year-end (Dec. 2000), employed approximately 45,000 employees.

Operating revenues and income for two recent accounting periods are as follows (in millions):

	2000	1999
Operating revenues	$9,283	$6,443
Operating income	86	377

Description of Business for Marks Work Wearhouse Ltd.

Mission Statement

Being the most customer-sensitive and responsive specialty retail organization in the markets within which we operate; Having a people-oriented work environment where our people are allowed the greatest possible free-dom to carry out their responsibilities, take ownership of what they do, have fun, learn and earn fair financial rewards; and Providing a superior financial return to investors as a result of being customer-driven and peo-ple-oriented.

Core Values

The company's divisions are committed to building their respective customer bases and creating shareholder value over time through increasing revenues and earnings, while honouring the Company's three Core Values:
- *Product integrity,*
- *Respect for people, and*
- *Continuous improvement.*

Operating revenues and income for two recent accounting periods are as follows (for retail sales business in millions):

	2001	2000
Operating revenues	$487	$437
Operating income	8	6

Required

a. Identify the company with the higher operating leverage.
b. Write a brief paragraph providing a logical explanation as to why one of the companies would have a higher level of operating leverage than the other company.
c. If revenues for both companies were declining, which company would most likely experience the greatest decline in operating income? Explain your answer.

ACT 2-2 GROUP ASSIGNMENT *Operating Leverage*

The Student Government Association (SGA) of Lawton University is planning a fund-raising campaign. SGA is considering the possibility of hiring Andrew Antonucci, a world-renowned investment counsellor, to address the public. It would sell tickets for $20 each. The university has agreed to let the SGA use Diltmore Auditorium at no cost. Mr. Antonucci is willing to accept one of two compensation arrangements. He will sign an agreement to receive a fixed fee of $12,000, regardless of the number of tickets sold. Alternatively, he will accept a payment of $15 per ticket sold. In communities similar to that in which Lawton is located, Mr. Antonucci has drawn an audi-ence of approximately 800 people.

Required

a. In front of the class, prepare a statement showing the expected net income, assuming 800 people buy tickets.

b. The instructor will divide the class into groups and then organize the groups into four sections. The instructor will assign one of the following tasks to each section of groups:

Group Tasks

1. Assuming that SGA pays Mr. Antonucci a fixed fee of $12,000, determine the amount of net income that SGA will earn if ticket sales are 10 percent higher than expected. Calculate the percentage change in net income.

2. Assuming that SGA pays Mr. Antonucci a fixed fee of $12,000, determine the amount of net income that SGA will earn if ticket sales are 10 percent lower than expected. Calculate the percentage change in net income.

3. Assuming that SGA pays Mr. Antonucci $15 per ticket sold, determine the amount of net income that SGA will earn if ticket sales are 10 percent higher than expected. Calculate the percentage change in net income.

4. Assuming that SGA pays Mr. Antonucci $15 per ticket sold, determine the amount of net income that SGA will earn if ticket sales are 10 percent lower than expected. Calculate the percentage change in net income.

c. Have each group select a spokesperson. Have one of the spokespersons in each section of groups go to the board and present the results of the analysis conducted in Part *b*. Resolve any discrepancies between the computations presented at the board and those developed by the other groups.

d. Draw conclusions regarding the risks and rewards associated with operating leverage. At a minimum, answer the following questions:

(1) Which type of cost structure (fixed or variable) produces the higher growth potential in profitability for a company?

(2) Which type of cost structure (fixed or variable) faces the higher risk of declining profitability for a company?

(3) Under what circumstances should a company seek to establish a fixed cost structure?

(4) Under what circumstances should a company seek to establish a variable cost structure?

WRITING ASSIGNMENT   *Cost Averaging*

ACT 2-3

Susan McGillis is a veterinarian. She has always felt sorry for the pets of low-income families. These families love their pets, but frequently they do not have enough money to properly provide for pet care. She decides to do something about the problem by opening a part-time veterinary practice in a low-income neighbourhood. She plans to volunteer her services free of charge two days per week. Clients will be charged only for the actual costs of materials and overhead. She leases a small space for $200 per month. Utilities and other miscellaneous costs are expected to be approximately $160 per month. She estimates the variable cost of materials to be approximately $10 per pet served. A friend of Dr. McGillis who runs a similar type of clinic in another area of town indicates that she should expect to treat the following number of pets during her first year of operation:

Jan.	Feb.	Mar.	Apr.	May	June	July	Aug.	Sept	Oct.	Nov.	Dec.
15	30	30	40	50	65	70	90	50	30	20	10

Dr. McGillis's friend explains that visits increase significantly in the summer because children who are out of school tend to bring their pets to the vet more often. Furthermore, the friend explains that business tapers off during the winter and reaches a low point in December when people spend what little money they have on Christmas presents for their children. After looking at the data, Dr. McGillis becomes concerned that the people in the neighbourhood will not be able to afford pet care during some months of operation even if it is offered at cost. For example, the cost of providing services in December would be approximately $46 per pet treated (i.e., $360 overhead ÷ 10 pets = $36 per pet + $10 materials cost). She is willing to provide her services free of charge, but she realizes that she cannot afford to subsidize the practice further by personally paying for the costs of materials and overhead in the months of low activity. She decides to discuss the matter with her accountant to find a way to cut costs even more. Her accountant tells her that her problem is cost *measurement,* rather than cost *cutting*.

Required

Assume that you are Dr. McGillis's accountant. Write a memo that describes a cost-plus-pricing strategy that will resolve the problem of high costs during months of low volume. Recommend in your memo the price to charge per pet treated during the month of December.

ACT 2-4

ETHICAL DILEMMA   *Profitability versus Social Conscience (Effects of Cost Behaviour)*

Advances in biological technology have enabled two research companies, Bio Labs, Inc. and Scientific Associates, to develop an insect-resistant corn seed. Neither of the companies is financially strong enough to develop the distribution channels necessary to bring the product to world markets. World Agra Distributors, Inc. has negotiated a contract with both companies for the exclusive right to market their seed. Bio Labs signed an agreement to receive an annual royalty of $1,000,000. In contrast, Scientific Associates chose an agreement that provided for a royalty amounting to $0.50 per kilogram of seed sold. Both agreements carried a 10-year term. During 2002, World Agra sold approximately 1,600,000 kilograms of the Bio Labs Inc. seed and 2,400,000 kilograms of the Scientific Associates seed. Both types of seed were sold for $1.25 per kilogram. At this point, it was becoming increasingly apparent that the seed developed by Scientific Associates was superior. Although the insect infestation was virtually nonexistent for both types of seed, the seed developed by Scientific Associates produced corn that was sweeter and resulted in consistently higher yields.

World Agra Distributors' chief financial officer, Roger Weatherstone, recently retired. To the astonishment of the annual planning committee, Mr. Weatherstone's replacement, Ray Borrough, adamantly recommended that the marketing department develop a major advertising campaign to promote the seed developed by Bio Labs Inc. The planning committee reluctantly approved the recommendation. A $100,000 ad campaign was launched; its ads emphasized the ability of the Bio Labs' seed to avoid insect infestation. The campaign was silent with respect to the taste or crop yield. Indeed, no mention of any kind was made regarding the seed developed by Scientific Associates. World Agra's sales staff was instructed to push the Bio Labs' seed and to sell the Scientific Associates seed only on customer demand. Although total sales remained relatively constant during 2003, sales of the Scientific Associates seed fell to approximately 1,300,000 kilograms while sales of the Bio Labs, Inc. seed rose to 2,700,000 kilograms.

Required

a. Determine the amount of increase or decrease in profitability experienced by World Agra as a result of the promotion of the Bio Labs seed. Support your answer with appropriate commentary.

b. Did World Agra's customers in particular and society in general benefit or suffer from the decision to promote the Bio Labs seed?

ACT 2-5

SPREADSHEET ASSIGNMENT   *Using Excel*

Brandon Walker rented a truck for his business on two different occasions. Since he will soon be renting a truck again, he would like to analyze his bills and determine how the rental fee is calculated. His two bills for truck rental show that on September 1, he drove 1,000 kilometres and the bill was $1,500, and on December 5, he drove 600 kilometres and the bill was $1,380.

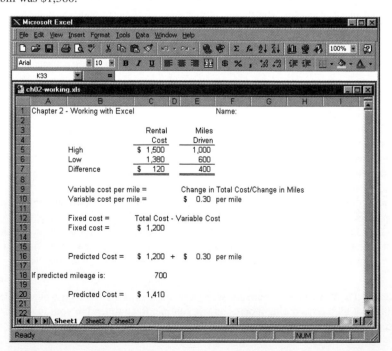

Required

Construct a spreadsheet to calculate the variable and fixed costs of this mixed cost that will allow Mr. Walker to predict his cost if he is to drive the truck 700 kilometres. The cells that show as numbers should all be formulas, except C5, C6, E5, E6, and C18. Constructing the spreadsheet in this manner will allow you to change numbers in these five cells to recalculate variable cost, fixed cost, or predicted total cost.

> **Spreadsheet Tip**
>
> To format cells to show dollar signs, commas, or both, choose Format, then Cells, then click on the tab titled Numbers, and choose Currency or Accounting.

SPREADSHEET ASSIGNMENT   *Mastering Excel*

ACT 2-6

Ferraro Company makes and sells decorative ceramic statues. Each statue costs $50 to manufacture and sells for $75. Ferraro spends $3 to ship the statue to customers and pays the salesperson a $2 commission for each statue sold. The remaining yearly expenses of operation are administrative salaries, $70,000; advertising, $20,000; and rent, $30,000. Ferraro plans to sell 9,000 statues in the coming year.

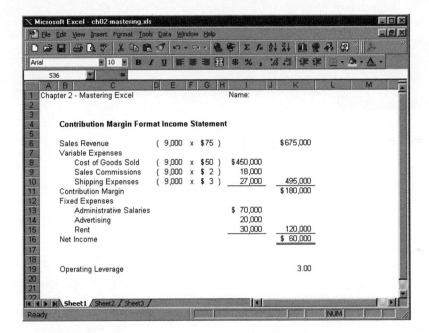

Required

Construct a spreadsheet that shows a contribution margin format income statement and that calculates operating leverage. Place formulas in the spreadsheet to allow changes to any of the preceding information to be automatically reflected in the income statement and operating leverage.

Analysis of Cost, Volume, and Pricing to Increase Profitability

Learning Objectives

After completing this chapter, you should be able to:

1 Determine the sales price of a product using a cost-plus-pricing approach.

2 Use the contribution-per-unit approach to calculate the break-even point.

3 Use the contribution-per-unit approach to calculate the sales volume required to attain a target profit.

4 Use the contribution-per-unit approach to assess the effects of changes in sales price, variable costs, and fixed costs.

5 Understand the concept of target pricing.

6 Consider the ethical considerations associated with misleading advertising.

7 Draw and interpret a cost-volume-profit graph.

8 Calculate the margin of safety in units, dollars, and percentages.

9 Understand how spreadsheet software can be used to conduct sensitivity analysis for cost-volume-profit relationships.

10 Conduct cost-volume-profit analysis using the contribution margin ratio and the equation method.

11 Identify the limitations associated with cost-volume-profit analysis.

12 Perform multiple-product break-even analysis.

the *curious* manager

© SuperStock

Barbara Malki, owner of Cahaba Cycles, is considering the possibility of establishing a racing team to promote her stores. She plans to sponsor two riders, each of whom will be given a $1,200 bicycle, $200 of decorative clothing, and a $100 racing helmet. In addition, Ms. Malki plans to pay each rider $2,000 to cover the costs of travel and race entry fees. Finally, she plans to spend $5,000 for banners, water bottles, and other promotional items that will be displayed and distributed at races. The average price and costs of bicycles sold at Cahaba Cycles are $900 and $600, respectively. In trying to decide whether she should establish the team, Ms. Malki needs to know how many bicycles her company must sell to cover the costs of the promotional program. Can you provide the information she needs?

Suppose that Ms. Malki finds a bike manufacturer who agrees to co-sponsor the bike team by providing free bicycles to the team members. The manufacturer's advertising decals will be displayed on the bikes, and Cahaba's decals will be displayed on the clothing. All other costs remain constant. Under these circumstances, how many bicycles must Cahaba sell to recover the cost of co-sponsoring the team?

The president of Bright Day Distributors recently took a managerial accounting course. He was fascinated by the operating leverage concept. *His instructor had demonstrated how a small percentage increase in sales volume could produce a significantly higher percentage increase in profitability. Unfortunately, the discussion had been limited to the effects of changes in sales volume. In practice, changes in sales volume are often related to changes in sales price. For example, cutting prices often causes increases in sales volume. Costs as well as sales frequently change. For example, increases in the advertising budget often result in increases in sales volume. Further, higher levels of sales can exceed the relevant range, thereby leading to increases in the fixed costs, such as the inventory holding costs incurred for warehouse space, personnel, and interest. Indeed, Bright Day's president discovered that increases in sales volume may even affect the company's variable costs. By increasing the size of its inventory purchases, the company could attain volume discounts that would lower its variable cost per unit. Bright Day's president quickly realized that operating leverage represented only one aspect of the business environment. He needed to know more. He needed to understand how changes in prices and costs as well as volume affects profitability. In accounting terms, Bright Day's president is interested in what is commonly called cost-volume-profit (CVP) analysis.*

▎Determining the Contribution Margin per Unit

LO1

Determine the sales price of a product using a cost-plus-pricing approach.

The contribution margin approach for constructing an income statement introduced in the previous chapter is an extremely useful mechanism for analyzing the relationships between the CVP (cost-volumne-profit) variables. Recall from Chapter 2 that the *contribution margin* is the difference between sales revenue and variable costs. It is a measure of the amount available to cover fixed costs and thereafter to provide profits for the enterprise. To illustrate, consider the following scenario.

Bright Day Distributors is a medium-sized health food sales company. The company distributes non-prescription health food supplements, including vitamins, herbs, and natural hormones, through a tele-marketing program in Central Canada. Bright Day recently obtained the rights to distribute the new herb mixture Delatine. A recent research report found that Delatine slowed the aging process in laboratory animals. The research scientists speculated that the substance would have a similar effect on human subjects. Their hypothesis could not be confirmed because of the relatively long span of the human life cycle. The news media picked up the findings of the research report; as stories appeared on network news, on talk shows, and in magazines, the demand for Delatine increased.

Delatine costs $24 per bottle. Bright Day uses a **cost-plus-pricing strategy**; it sets prices at cost plus a markup equal to 50 percent of cost. Accordingly, a bottle of Delatine is priced at $36 per bottle ($24 + [.50 × $24]). The **contribution margin per unit** can be computed as follows:

Sales revenue per unit	$36
Variable cost per unit	24
Contribution margin per unit	$12

For every bottle of Delatine it sells, Bright Day earns a $12 contribution margin. Bright Day's first concern is whether it can sell enough units to produce a total contribution margin sufficient to cover fixed costs. If fixed costs were $120, it would have to sell 10 bottles (10 bottles × $12 per bottle = $120). The president made the point clear when he said, "We don't want to lose money on this product. We have to sell enough units to pay for our fixed costs." After the fixed costs have been covered, the $12 contribution margin represents the amount of dollars added to profits each time a bottle of Delatine is sold. The per unit contribution margin can be used to analyze a variety of cost-volume-profit relationships.

▮ Determining the Break-Even Point

Bright Day's management team believes that enthusiasm for the product will diminish rapidly as the attention of the news media shifts to other subjects. The team is concerned about the capacity of the company's telemarketing department to reach large segments of the population rapidly. The company simply has too few sales operators to enable rapid market penetration. Furthermore, time constraints will not permit the company to employ and train additional sales staff. Bright Day needs to reach customers immediately. Accordingly, the managers decided to investigate an immediate television advertising campaign. The company's marketing manager believes that several hundred ads running on various local cable channels would be required to inform customers that they could purchase Delatine through Bright Day. The chief accountant estimates the cost of the proposed campaign to be $60,000. The company president immediately asks, "How many bottles of Delatine would have to be sold to *break even?*"

LO2

Use the contribution-per-unit approach to calculate the break-even point.

The **break-even point** is the point where *total revenue equals total costs*. A company neither earns a profit nor incurs a loss at the break-even point. Net income at breakeven is zero. Bright Day's president wants to know what sales volume (i.e., number of bottles of Delatine sold) would be required to *equate sales revenue with total cost*. The cost of the advertising campaign is fixed relative to the level of sales. The cost remains at $60,000, regardless of the number of bottles of Delatine that Bright Day sells. Since Bright Day expects to earn a $12 contribution margin for each bottle it sells, the sales volume required to break even can be calculated by dividing the fixed costs by the contribution margin per unit. The appropriate computations follow:

$$\text{Break-even volume in units} = \frac{\text{Fixed costs}}{\text{Contribution margin per unit}}$$

$$= \frac{\$60,000}{\$12} = 5,000 \text{ Units}$$

The break-even point expressed in *sales dollars* can be determined by multiplying the number of units that must be sold to break even by the sales price per unit. Accordingly, the break-even point expressed in dollars is $180,000 (5,000 units × $36). The following income statement confirms these results:

Sales Revenue (5,000 units × $36)	$ 180,000
Total Variable Expenses (5,000 units × $24)	(120,000)
Total Contribution Margin (5,000 units × $12)	60,000
Fixed Expenses	(60,000)
Net Income	$ 0

Once fixed costs have been covered (i.e., 5,000 units have been sold), net income will increase by the amount of the *per-unit contribution margin* for each additional unit sold. In other words, every bottle of Delatine sold in excess of the break-even point will add $12 to net income. Similarly, each lost sale below the break-even point will reduce the company's net income by $12. Test your comprehension of the effect of the per-unit contribution margin on profitability by studying the following income statements:

	Number of Units Sold (a)				
	4,998	**4,999**	**5,000**	**5,001**	**5,002**
Sales Revenue ($36 per unit × a)	$ 179,928	$ 179,964	$ 180,000	$ 180,036	$ 180,072
Total Variable Expenses ($24 per unit × a)	(119,952)	(119,976)	(120,000)	(120,024)	(120,048)
Total Contribution Margin ($12 per unit × a)	$ 59,976	$ 59,988	$ 60,000	$ 60,012	$ 60,024
Fixed Expenses	(60,000)	(60,000)	(60,000)	(60,000)	(60,000)
Net Income	$ (24)	$ (12)	$ 0	$ 12	$ 24

As sales increase from 5,000 to 5,001, net income increases from zero to $12. When sales increase by one additional unit, net income again rises by $12 (i.e., moves from $12 to $24). Income continues to increase by the $12 per-unit contribution margin each time an additional unit is sold. This pattern suggests that beyond the break-even point, the effect of an increase in sales on net income can be computed quickly by multiplying the amount of the change times the contribution margin per unit. Suppose sales increase from 5,400 units to 5,600 units. How will this change affect profitability? Profits will increase by $2,400 ([5,600 − 5,400] × $12). The following comparative income statements illustrate this result:

| | Number of Units Sold (b) | | |
	5,400	5,600	200 Unit Difference
Sales Revenue ($36 per unit)	$ 194,400	$ 201,600	$ 7,200
Total Variable Expenses ($24 per unit)	(129,600)	(134,400)	(4,800)
Total Contribution Margin ($12 per unit)	64,800	67,200	2,400
Fixed Expenses	(60,000)	(60,000)	0
Net Income	$ 4,800	$ 7,200	$ 2,400

■ Using the Contribution Approach to Estimate the Sales Volume Necessary to Attain a Target Profit

LO3

Use the contribution-per-unit approach to calculate the sales volume required to attain a target profit.

After considering Bright Day's usual return on investment target, its president decides that the campaign should produce a $40,000 profit. He asks the accountant to determine the sales volume that would be required to achieve this level of profitability. In this case, the contribution margin must be sufficient to cover the fixed cost and to provide the desired profit. The required sales volume expressed in units can be computed by dividing the amount of the fixed costs plus the desired profit by the contribution margin per unit. The appropriate computations are shown here:

$$\text{Sales volume in units} = \frac{\text{Fixed costs} + \text{desired profit}}{\text{Contribution margin per unit}}$$

$$= \frac{\$60,000 + \$40,000}{\$12} = 8,333.33 \text{ units}$$

The required sales volume expressed in sales dollars can be determined by multiplying this number of units by the sales price per unit. Accordingly, the level of required sales expressed in dollars is $300,000 (8,333.33 units × $36). The following income statement confirms these results; all amounts are rounded to the nearest whole dollar:

Sales Revenue (8,333.33 units × $36)	$ 300,000
Total Variable Expenses (8,333.33 units × $24)	(200,000)
Total Contribution Margin (8,333.33 units × $12)	100,000
Fixed Expenses	(60,000)
Net Income	$ 40,000

In practice, the company does not sell a partial bottle of Delatine. Accordingly, the accountant rounds the 8,333.33 bottles to the nearest whole unit. Recall that we are working with estimated data used for planning and decision making. Accuracy is desirable, but it is not as important as relevance. Accordingly, you should not be concerned when computations do not produce whole numbers. Rounding and approximation are common characteristics of managerial accounting data.

After reviewing the accountant's computations, the president turns to the marketing manager and asks, "What are our chances of reaching a sales volume of 8,333 units?" The manager replies, "Slim to none." Indeed, the marketing manager is concerned about the possibility of reaching the 5,000 unit break-even point. She notes that Bright Day has never had a product that sold more than 4,000 bottles during its initial offering. Also, tests conducted by the telemarketing staff indicated that customers are resistant to a $36 per bottle price. The test group included many customers who had heard about the product and expressed an interest in buying it, but when they were told the price, they consistently rejected the offer. On the basis of experience with similar products, the marketing manager believes that customers would be willing to pay $28 per bottle for Delatine. The company president immediately asks how the change in sales price will affect the sales volume required to produce the $40,000 target profit.

▮ Using the Contribution Approach to Estimate the Effects of Changes in Sales Price

Changing the sales price from $36 to $28 will have a significant effect on the contribution margin. Recall that the original contribution margin was $12 per unit ($36 − $24). The contribution margin will drop to a mere $4 per unit if the sales price is reduced to $28 per bottle ($28 sales price − $24 cost per bottle = $4 contribution margin per bottle). The significant drop in contribution margin per unit will cause a dramatic increase in the sales volume necessary to attain the target profit. The appropriate computations are shown here:

LO4
Use the contribution-per-unit approach to assess the effects of changes in sales price, variable costs, and fixed costs.

$$\text{Sales volume in units} = \frac{\text{Fixed costs} + \text{Desired profit}}{\text{Contribution margin per unit}}$$

$$= \frac{\$60,000 + \$40,000}{\$4} = 25,000 \text{ units}$$

The required sales volume expressed in sales dollars can be determined by multiplying the above number of units by the sales price per unit. Accordingly, the required sales volume *expressed in dollars* is $700,000 (25,000 units × $28). The following income statement confirms these results:

Sales Revenue (25,000 units × $28)	$ 700,000
Total Variable Expenses (25,000 units × $24)	(600,000)
Total Contribution Margin (25,000 units × $4)	100,000
Fixed Expenses	(60,000)
Net Income	$ 40,000

The marketing manager concludes that it would be impossible to sell 25,000 bottles of Delatine at any price. She suggests that the company drop its cost-plus-pricing strategy and replace it with a new approach called *target pricing*. **Target pricing** begins with the determination of a price at which a product will sell and then focuses on developing that product with a cost structure that will satisfy market demands. Since the target price leads to a target cost, this market-based pricing strategy is also called **target costing**. It focuses on the design stage of product development. Given the target price of $28 per

LO5
Understand the concept of target pricing.

bottle, the issue is how to design the product *at a cost* that will enable Bright Day to earn its desired profit of $40,000. Fortunately, the marketing manager had some suggestions.

■ Use of the Contribution Approach to Estimate the Effects of Changes in Variable Costs

LO4

Use the contribution-per-unit approach to assess the effects of changes in sales price, variable costs, and fixed costs.

LO6

Consider the ethical considerations associated with misleading advertising.

The manufacturer has agreed to provide Delatine to Bright Day in two additional packaging formats. The current cost is $24 for a bottle containing 100 capsules of 90 milligram (mg) strength. The two new alternatives are: (1) a bottle costing $12 that contains 100 capsules of 30 mg strength, and (2) a bottle costing $3 that contains 100 capsules of only 5 mg of Delatine mixed with a vitamin C compound. This dosage is the minimum allowable to support a packaging label indicating that the product contains Delatine. The marketing manager observes that both options would enable Bright Day to sell Delatine at a price that customers would be willing to pay.

The president vehemently rejected the second option. He called the proposal a blatant attempt to deceive customers by suggesting they were buying Delatine when, in fact, they were getting vitamin C. *He considered the idea to be unethical and dangerous.* He ended his tirade with the statement that he would not be seen on the six o'clock news trying to defend a fast-buck scheme while his company's reputation went up in smoke. After allowing himself a few minutes to calm down, he said that the first option appeared to have some merit. The appropriate dosage for Delatine was uncertain; customers who wanted to take 90 mg per day could take three capsules instead of one. He turned to the accountant and asked, "What's the effect on the bottom line?"

The change in the variable cost (cost per bottle) from $24 to $12 per bottle has a dramatic effect on the level of sales volume required to produce the target profit. The contribution margin per unit shifts from $4 per bottle ($28 sales price − $24 variable cost per bottle) to $16 per bottle ($28 sales price − $12 variable cost per bottle). The significant increase in contribution margin per unit results in a dramatic decrease in the sales volume necessary to attain the target profit. The appropriate computations are shown here:

$$\text{Sales volume in units} = \frac{\text{Fixed costs} + \text{Desired profit}}{\text{Contribution margin per unit}}$$

$$= \frac{\$60,000 + \$40,000}{\$16} = 6,250 \text{ units}$$

Healthy people or healthy profits? If you were president of a major drug manufacturing company, which would you choose? Long-term studies for the treatment of high blood pressure suggest that the cheapest medications available (beta blockers and diuretics) are more effective and safer than more expensive ones. Even so, a survey of drug ads in the *New England Journal of Medicine* reveals an advertising program that advocates the use of more expensive medications (calcium-channel blockers and ACE inhibitors). The most aggressively marketed are the high-priced, high-profit calcium channel blockers. This marketing effort persists despite the fact that studies have linked these drugs to an increased risk of heart attack, cancer, and suicide. Why are the drug companies interested in selling these drugs? Could it have something to do with the fact that calcium channel blockers have a price more than three times that of diuretics? The marketing campaign appears to be working. Between 1992 and 1995, sales of calcium channel blockers increased by approximately 15 percent while that of diuretics dropped by 50 percent. One study suggests that the shift to the more expensive drugs is adding approximately $3 billion in unnecessary expenditures to the national medical bill. Healthy people or healthy profits? Practising high ethical standards in business is not always an easy task. Keep in mind, however, that shortcuts to high profitability are filled with booby traps. A class action lawsuit could easily wipe out any benefit attained by unscrupulous business practices. The demise of the silicone breast implant industry stands as a clear example.

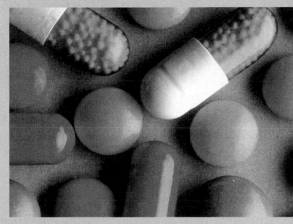

© SuperStock

Source: Catherine Arnst, "Is Good Marketing Bad Medicine?" *Business Week*, April 13, 1998, p. 62. The opinions regarding the ethical implications are those of the authors of this text. © SuperStock

The required sales volume expressed in sales dollars can be determined by multiplying this number of units by the sales price per unit. Accordingly, the level of sales *expressed in dollars* required to produce the desired profit is $175,000 (6,250 units × $28). The following income statement confirms these amounts:

Sales Revenue (6,250 units × $28)	$ 175,000
Total Variable Expenses (6,250 units × $12)	(75,000)
Total Contribution Margin (6,250 units × $16)	100,000
Fixed Expenses	(60,000)
Net Income	$ 40,000

Although the drop in required sales from 25,000 units to 6,250 was truly significant, the marketing manager still felt uneasy about the company's ability to sell 6,250 bottles of Delatine. She restated the argument that the company had no other product that produced sales of that magnitude. The accountant suggested that considerable savings could be obtained by using a series of radio, rather than television, commercials. While gathering cost data for the TV campaign, the accountant had conferred with account executives of radio companies who had assured him that they could equal the TV audience exposure at about half the cost of the televised ads. Even though the TV ads would likely be more effective, he argued that since radio advertising costs would be half those of TV, the desired profit could be attained at a significantly lower volume of sales. The company president was impressed with the possibilities. He asked the accountant to determine the required sales volume, assuming that advertising costs were cut from $60,000 to $30,000.

■ Using the Contribution Approach to Estimate the Effects of Changes in Fixed Costs

LO4

Use the contribution-per-unit approach to assess the effects of changes in sales price, variable costs, and fixed costs.

Changing the fixed costs from $60,000 to $30,000 will dramatically affect the sales level required to earn the target profit. Since the contribution margin will cover a lower amount of fixed costs, the sales volume required to reach the desired profit is significantly reduced. The appropriate computations are shown here:

$$\text{Sales volume in units} = \frac{\text{Fixed costs} + \text{Desired profit}}{\text{Contribution margin per unit}}$$

$$= \frac{\$30,000 + \$40,000}{\$16} = 4,375 \text{ units}$$

The required sales volume expressed in sales dollars can be determined by multiplying this number of units by the sales price per unit. Accordingly, the level of sales *expressed in dollars* required to produce the desired profit is $122,500 (4,375 units × $28). The following income statement confirms these amounts:

Sales Revenue (4,375 units × $28)	$122,500
Total Variable Expenses (4,375 units × $12)	(52,500)
Total Contribution Margin (4,375 units × $16)	70,000
Fixed Expenses	(30,000)
Net Income	$ 40,000

The marketing manager voiced her approval. Obviously, she could not guarantee any specific sales volume, but she felt confident that sales figures would fall within a range of 4,000 to 5,000 units.

■ Using the Cost-Volume-Profit Graph

LO7

Draw and interpret a cost-volume-profit graph.

To further analyze the revised expectations, the accountant had his staff prepare a chart to depict cost-volume-profit relationships over the range of sales activity from zero to 6,000 units. The accountant gave his staff the following instructions that were used to produce the CVP graph (sometimes called a *break-even chart*) shown in Exhibit 3–1:

1. *Draw the Axis:* The sales activity is expressed in units along the horizontal axis and in dollars along the vertical axis.
2. *Draw the Fixed Cost Line:* Fixed costs are constant for all levels of activity. To represent this relationship, a horizontal line is drawn across the graph at the dollar amount of fixed cost. In this case, the horizontal line is drawn at the $30,000 level.
3. *Draw the Total Cost Line:* A diagonal line representing total cost is drawn by selecting some arbitrary level of activity expressed in units and making the following computations: To determine the total variable cost, multiply the selected volume of activity by the variable cost per unit. Add the total variable cost to the total fixed cost. The result is the amount of total cost at the selected level of activity. This point is plotted on the graph. A line starting from the vertical axis at the level of fixed cost is drawn through this point. For example, using a volume of activity of 6,000 units, the total cost amounts to $102,000 ([6,000 units × $12] + $30,000 fixed cost). A point is plotted at the coordinates of $102,000 and 6,000 units. Another point is plotted at the level of fixed cost and the zero level of activity ($30,000 at zero units). A straight line representing total cost is drawn through these two points.

The number of bikes that must be sold to cover the cost of sponsoring the bike team can be determined by dividing the fixed cost of the promotional campaign by the contribution margin per bike. The contribution margin per bike is $300 ($900 − 600). In the first case, in which Cahaba Cycles acts as the sole sponsor, the number of bikes that must be sold to cover the cost of the promotional campaign is computed as follows:

Bicycle	$1,200
Clothing	200
Helmet	100
Travel and fees	2,000
Cost per biker	$3,500 × 2 = $ 7,000
Promotional items............................	5,000
Total fixed cost................................	$12,000 ÷ $300
	Contribution margin
	= 40 bikes

If the team is co-sponsored, Cahaba will save the fixed cost of two bicycles ($1,200 × 2 = $2,400). Accordingly, total fixed cost will drop to $9,600 ($12,000 − $2,400). Since the price and variable cost of bikes sold to customers do not change, the contribution margin remains constant at $300. The number of bikes that must be sold to cover the new level of fixed cost is as follows:

$$Total\ fixed\ cost\ =\ \$9,600 \div \$300\ Contribution\ margin$$
$$=\ 32\ bikes$$

4. ***Draw the Sales Line:*** Draw the revenue line by using a procedure similar to that described for drawing the total cost line. Select some arbitrary level of activity expressed in units and multiply that figure by the sales price per unit. Plot the result on the graph and draw a line from the zero origin through this point. For example, using a volume of activity of 6,000 units, the revenue point is $168,000 (6,000 units × $28). Plot a point at the coordinates of $168,000 and 6,000 units. Drawing a line from the zero origin to the plotted point establishes the revenue line that completes the graph.

You should trace these procedures to the graph shown in Exhibit 3–1 to ensure your understanding of how to construct a CVP chart.

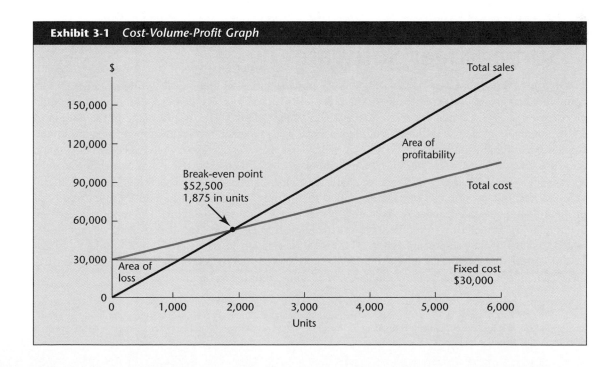

Exhibit 3-1   *Cost-Volume-Profit Graph*

▌Calculating the Margin of Safety

LO8

Calculate the margin of safety in units, dollars, and percentages.

The final meeting of the management team focused on a discussion of the reliability of the data used to construct the CVP chart. The accountant opened the discussion by calling attention to the sales volume figures under the area of profitability. Recall that 4,375 bottles of Delatine must be sold to earn the company's desired profit. Measured in dollars, budgeted sales amount to $122,500 (4,375 bottles × $28 per bottle). The accountant highlighted the wide gap between this level of budgeted sales and the break-even point. The amount of this gap, called the *margin of safety*, can be measured in number of units or in sales dollars. The appropriate computations are shown in the table below:

The **margin of safety** is defined as the number of units, or the amount of sales dollars, by which *actual sales* can fall below *budgeted sales* before a loss is incurred. If the margin of safety is high, as in this case, profitability can be expected even if actual sales fall significantly below expectations.

	In Units	In Dollars
Budgeted sales	4,375	$122,500
Break-even sales	(1,875)	(52,500)
Margin of safety	2,500	$ 70,000

To facilitate comparisons between products or companies of different sizes, the margin of safety can be expressed as a percentage by dividing the margin of safety by the amount of the budgeted sales volume.[1] The appropriate computations are shown here:

$$\text{Margin of safety} = \frac{\text{Budgeted sales} - \text{Break-even sales}}{\text{Budgeted sales}}$$

$$\text{Margin of safety} = \frac{\$122,500 - \$52,500 \times 100}{\$122,500} = 57.14\%$$

This analysis suggests that actual sales would have to fall short of expected sales by more than 57.14 percent before Bright Day would experience a loss. This large a margin of safety suggests that undertaking the proposed radio advertising program for bottles of the 30 mg Delatine capsules has minimal risk.

▌Performing Sensitivity Analysis Using Spreadsheet Software

LO9

Understand how spreadsheet software can be used to conduct sensitivity analysis for cost-volume-profit relationships.

The *margin of safety* focuses on the vulnerability of profits to a decline in sales volume. Other factors could threaten profitability as well. For example, profits decline if costs increase. Safety margins could be determined for fixed and variable costs as well as sales volume. The disadvantage of the margin of safety approach is that it constitutes a unidimensional analysis when profits are subject to multidimensional forces. What happens to profitability if the level of fixed cost is higher than expected but variable costs are lower than expected? What if sales volume is higher than expected as are costs? Fortunately, spreadsheet software is highly efficient for analyzing "what if" questions, such as these. Exhibit 3–2 provides an example of an *Excel* spreadsheet report that permits management to assess the sensitivity of profits to simultaneous changes in fixed cost, variable cost, and sales volume. The report is based on data regarding Bright Day's proposed project for marketing Delatine. Recall that the accountant estimated the cost of the radio campaign to be $30,000. The report provides profitability projections that permit considering conditions in which advertising costs fall to $20,000 or rise to $40,000. Likewise, the effects of potential changes in variable cost and sales volume can be investigated.

[1] The margin of safety percentage can be computed for existing as well as budgeted sales. For example, an analyst may want to compare the margins of safety of two companies under current operating conditions. In this case, existing sales would be substituted for budgeted sales. The formula for computing the margin of safety percentages would be ([Actual sales − Break-even sales] ÷ Actual sales).

The range of scenarios described in the report is impressive, but it represents only a few of the many alternatives that can be analyzed with a few quick keystrokes. The spreadsheet program recalculates profitability figures instantly when one of the variables changes. Suppose that someone asks, "What would happen if we sold 10,000 units?" The accountant merely replaces one of the sales volume figures with the new number, and revised profitability numbers appear instantly. By changing the variables, management can get a real feel for the sensitivity of profits to changes in cost and volume for the project that is under consideration. Investigating a multitude of what-if questions regarding simultaneous changes in fixed cost, variable cost, and volume is called **sensitivity analysis**.

Exhibit 3-2 *Spreadsheet Report to Facilitate "What-if" Analysis*

If Fixed Cost Is	While Variable Cost Is	And Sales Volume Is				
		2,000	3,000	4,000	5,000	6,000
		Then Profitability Will Be				
$20,000	11	14000	31000	48000	65000	82000
20,000	12	12000	28000	44000	60000	76000
20,000	13	10000	25000	40000	55000	70000
30,000	11	4000	21000	38000	55000	72000
30,000	12	2000	18000	34000	50000	66000
30,000	13	0	15000	30000	45000	60000
40,000	11	-6000	11000	28000	45000	62000
40,000	12	-8000	8000	24000	40000	56000
40,000	13	-10000	5000	20000	35000	50000

▍Assessing the Pricing Strategy

After reviewing the spreadsheet report, Bright Day's management team is convinced that it should proceed with the radio campaign for Delatine. Only under the most dire circumstances (i.e., if actual sales fall significantly below expectations while costs increase at rates well above expectations) will the company incur a loss. Indeed, the president feels uneasy because the figures simply look too good to be true. If Bright Day pays $12 per bottle for Delatine and sells it for $28 per bottle as projected, the effective markup on cost would be 133 percent ([$28 − $12] ÷ $12). Recall that the company's normal markup is only 50 percent of cost. The president asks the marketing manager, "Are you sure people will buy this stuff at that price?"

The marketing manager explains that the pricing practice she is advocating is a recognized strategy known as **prestige pricing**. According to this concept, many people are fascinated with new technologies. They are willing to pay a premium to be the first to obtain and use a new product, especially when its introduction receives widespread media attention, as is the case with Delatine. Similarly, people may be willing to pay more for a product because it carries a prestigious brand name. The marketing manager reminds the president that although the price spread for Delatine is unusually wide, the company has introduced other products at cost-plus margins that were considerably higher than the average 50 percent markup. Indeed, many of its current products sell at above average margins. Certainly, news coverage for Delatine will dissipate, competitors will offer alternatives, and customer interest will wane. That will be the time to reduce prices. The marketing manager is confident that the product will sell initially at the proposed price.

■ Using the Contribution Approach to Assess the Effect of Simultaneous Changes in CVP Variables

LO4

Use the contribution-per-unit approach to assess the effects of changes in sales price, variable costs, and fixed costs.

In a previous section of this chapter, we discussed the use of sensitivity analysis as a means to analyze the effects of simultaneous changes in CVP variables. On occasion, managers may desire to analyze the impact of simultaneous changes without the availability of computer technology. The contribution approach that has been illustrated to analyze unidimensional CVP relationships can also be used to study the effects of simultaneous changes in CVP variables. The approach offers simple and quick results in a low-technology environment. To illustrate several possible scenarios, assume that Bright Day has developed the following budgeted income statement:

Sales Revenue (4,375 units × $28 sales price)	$ 122,500
Total Variable Expenses (4,375 units × $12 cost per bottle)	(52,500)
Total Contribution Margin (4,375 units × $16)	70,000
Fixed Expenses	(30,000)
Net Income	$ 40,000

A Decrease in Sales Price Accompanied by an Increase in Sales Volume

Suppose that the marketing manager believes that sales will increase by 625 units if the price per bottle of Delatine is reduced to $25. Should Bright Day reduce the price? Under these circumstances, the per-unit contribution margin drops to $13 ($25 sales price − $12 cost per bottle). The expected number of units sold increases to 5,000 (4,375 + 625). On the basis of these figures, the expected profit is as follows:

Total Contribution Margin (5,000 units × $13)	$ 65,000
Less: Contribution Margin Used to Cover Fixed Expenses	(30,000)
Expected Profit	$ 35,000

The following revised income statement confirms these amounts:

Sales Revenue (5,000 units × $25 sales price)	$ 125,000
Total Variable Expenses (5,000 units × $12 cost per bottle)	(60,000)
Total Contribution Margin (5,000 units × $13)	65,000
Fixed Expenses	(30,000)
Net Income	$ 35,000

Since budgeted income falls from $40,000 to $35,000, the suggestion to reduce the sales price should be rejected.

An Increase in Fixed Cost Accompanied by an Increase in Sales Volume

Return to the original data set for the budgeted income statement. In summary, the company expects to sell 4,375 units of Delatine for $28 per bottle. Variable costs are expected to be $12 per bottle, and fixed costs are budgeted at $30,000. Suppose that the management team believes that sales can be increased to 6,000 units if the company pays an additional $12,000 to advertise its product. The contribution margin per unit will remain unchanged at $16 (i.e., $28 − $12). Should the company incur the additional advertising cost, thereby increasing fixed costs to $42,000? On the basis of these figures, the expected profit is as follows:

Total Contribution Margin (6,000 units × $16)	$ 96,000
Less: Contribution Margin Used to Cover Fixed Expenses	(42,000)
Expected Profit	$ 54,000

The following revised income statement confirms these amounts:

Sales Revenue (6,000 units × $28 sales price)	$ 168,000
Total Variable Expenses (6,000 units × $12 cost per bottle)	(72,000)
Total Contribution Margin (6,000 units × $16)	96,000
Fixed Expenses	(42,000)
Net Income	$ 54,000

Since budgeted income increases from $40,000 to $54,000, Bright Day should seek to increase sales through additional advertising.

A Simultaneous Reduction in Sales Price, Fixed Costs, Variable Costs, and Sales Volume

Return again to the data set for the original budget. Recall that the company expects to sell 4,375 units of Delatine for $28 per bottle, and variable cost are expected to be $12 per bottle. Fixed costs are budgeted at $30,000. Suppose that Bright Day is able to negotiate a $4 reduction in the cost of a bottle of Delatine. The management team wants to consider passing on some of the savings to its customers by reducing the sales price to $25 per bottle. Furthermore, the team believes that advertising costs can be reduced by $8,000 without seriously affecting sales volume. Sales are expected to fall to 4,200 units because of the reduction in advertising. Additional reductions in demand are not expected, however, because the decrease in the sales price is expected to increase demand by some customers. Should Bright Day proceed with the plan to reduce prices and advertising costs?

Under the revised operating scenario, sales volume would decline to 4,200 units. The contribution margin would increase to $17 per bottle ($25 new selling price − $8 new variable cost per bottle), and fixed cost would fall to $22,000 ($30,000 − $8,000). On the basis of these figures, the expected profit is as follows:

Total Contribution Margin (4,200 units × $17)	$ 71,400
Less: Contribution Margin Used to Cover Fixed Expenses	(22,000)
Expected Profit	$ 49,400

The following revised income statement confirms these amounts:

Sales Revenue (4,200 units × $25 sales price)	$ 105,000
Total Variable Expenses (4,200 units × $8 cost per bottle)	(33,600)
Total Contribution Margin (4,200 units × $17)	71,400
Fixed Expenses	(22,000)
Net Income	$ 49,400

Because budgeted income increases from $40,000 to $49,400, Bright Day should proceed with the new operating strategy.

Many other possible scenarios could be considered. However, it should be clear at this point that the contribution approach can be used to analyze independent or simultaneous changes in the CVP variables. Two alternative approaches to CVP analysis, the contribution margin ratio approach and the equation approach, will be introduced in the following sections of this chapter.

■ Calculating Cost-Volume-Profit (CVP) Analysis Using the Contribution Margin Ratio

LO10

Conduct cost-volume-profit analysis using the contribution margin ratio and the equation method.

When the contribution margin is expressed as a percentage of the sales price, the result is called the **contribution margin ratio**. To illustrate, assume that Bright Day is considering the possibility of selling a new product called Multi Minerals. The expected sales price, variable cost, and contribution margin per unit are shown here:

Sales revenue per unit	$20
Variable cost per unit	12
Contribution margin per unit	$ 8

On the basis of these data, the *contribution margin ratio* for Multi Minerals is 40 percent ($8 ÷ $20). This ratio suggests that every dollar of sales provides 40 cents ($1 × .40) to cover fixed costs. After fixed costs have been covered, each dollar of sales provides 40 cents of profit. Like the *per-unit contribution margin*, the *contribution margin ratio* can be used to analyze CVP relationships. The results are identical with the exception that the per-unit contribution margin produces a sales volume measured in units while the contribution margin ratio yields a sales volume figure measured in dollars. As such, the two approaches merely represent different means of arriving at the same conclusion. To demonstrate, we calculate the break-even point, assuming that the company expects to incur $24,000 of fixed expenses to market the product. The computations under the alternative approaches follow:

Per-Unit-Contribution Approach Break-Even in Units	Contribution-Ratio Approach Break-Even in Dollars
$\dfrac{\text{Fixed costs}}{\text{Contribution margin per unit}} = \text{Units}$	$\dfrac{\text{Fixed costs}}{\text{Contribution margin ratio}} = \text{Dollars}$
$\dfrac{\$24,000}{\$8} = 3,000 \text{ units}$	$\dfrac{\$24,000}{40\%} = \$60,000$

Converting the break-even point expressed in units to one expressed in sales dollars demonstrates that the two approaches lead to the same results. Mathematically, 3,000 units × $20 = $60,000. Likewise, the break-even point expressed in sales dollars can be converted to units ($60,000 ÷ $20 = 3,000). Accordingly, it should be clear that the two approaches represent different views of the same data set. The similarities and differences between the two approaches hold when other CVP variables are added or changed. For example, the sales volume necessary to reach a target profit of $8,000 under the two approaches is computed as follows:

Per-Unit-Contribution Approach Break-Even in Units	Contribution-Ratio Approach Break-Even in Dollars
$\dfrac{\text{Fixed costs + Desired profit}}{\text{Contribution margin per unit}}$ = Units	$\dfrac{\text{Fixed costs + Desired profit}}{\text{Contribution margin ratio}}$ = Dollars
$\dfrac{\$24,000 + \$8,000}{\$8}$ = 4,000 units	$\dfrac{\$24,000 + \$8,000}{40\%}$ = $80,000

Once again, multiplying the $20 sales price by the sales volume expressed in units equates to the sales volume expressed in dollars ($20 × 4,000 = $80,000). Because both approaches yield the same results, the method to use is a matter of personal preference. However, to ensure your ability to communicate in a variety of potential circumstances, we encourage you to experiment with both approaches. Indeed, you should also master a third alternative, the *equation method*, which is discussed in the following section.

Cost-Volume-Profit Analysis Using the Equation Method

The **equation method** begins with the expression of the break-even point in terms of an algebraic equation. This equation is shown here:[2]

$$\text{Sales} = \text{Variable cost} + \text{Fixed cost}$$

LO10

Conduct cost-volume-profit analysis using the contribution margin ratio and the equation method.

The break-even point expressed in terms of sales volume (i.e., number of units) can be determined by restating the formula as indicated here:

$$\text{Selling price per unit} \times \text{No. of units sold}$$
$$= (\text{Variable cost per unit} \times \text{No. of units sold}) + \text{Fixed cost}$$

Using the Multi Minerals $20 sales price, $12 variable cost, and $24,000 fixed cost, the *break-even point* computed *in number of units* is as follows:

$$\$20 \times \text{Units} = \$12 \times \text{Units} + \$24,000$$
$$\$8 \times \text{Units} = \$24,000$$
$$\text{Units} = 3,000$$

The break-even sales volume expressed in units can be converted into break-even sales volume expressed in dollars by multiplying the sales price per unit times the number of units sold. The *break-even point* for Bright Day expressed *in number of dollars* is as follows:

$$\text{Sales price per unit} \times \text{Number of units sold} = \text{Sales volume in dollars}$$
$$\$20 \quad \times \quad 3,000 \quad = \quad \$60,000$$

---

[2] The equation method results in the same computation as the per-unit-contribution-margin approach. As proof, consider the following: Under the per-unit-contribution-margin approach, the break-even point is determined as follows (X equals the break-even point in units):

X = Fixed cost ÷ Per unit contribution margin

Under the equation method, the break-even point is determined as follows (X equals the break-even point in units):

Unit sales price (X) = Variable cost per unit (X) + Fixed cost
(Unit sales price − Variable cost per unit) X = Fixed cost

Since:

Unit sales price − Variable cost per unit = Per unit contribution margin
Per unit contribution margin (X) = Fixed cost
X = Fixed cost ÷ Per unit contribution margin

The equation method can also be used to analyze additional CVP relationships. For example, the sales volume necessary to attain a target profit of $8,000 can be computed as follows:

$$\text{Selling price per unit} \times \text{No. of units sold}$$
$$= (\text{Variable cost per unit} \times \text{No. of units sold}) + \text{Fixed cost} + \text{Desired Profit}$$

The computations are shown here:

$$\$20 \times \text{Units} = \$12 \times \text{Units} + \$24,000 + \$8,000$$
$$\$8 \times \text{Units} = \$32,000$$
$$\text{Units} = 4,000$$

By comparing these results with those determined using the per-unit-contribution approach and the contribution margin ratio approach, it should be apparent that the equation method is simply another way to achieve the same result. Again, the method you use will depend on your personal preferences and those of the management team you encounter on the job. As a student seeking entry into an unknown work environment, you should familiarize yourself with as many of the alternatives as possible.

▌Recognizing Cost-Volume-Profit Limitations

LO11

Identify the limitations associated with cost-volume-profit analysis.

The accuracy of cost-volume-profit analysis is limited because it assumes a strictly *linear* relationship among the variables. True linearity among actual CVP variables is the exception rather than the norm. For example, suppose that a business receives a volume discount on materials that it purchases. The more material it purchases, the lower its cost per unit is. In this case, the cost varies but not in direct proportion to the amount of material purchased. The relationship is not linear. Similarly, fixed costs can change. A supervisor's salary that is thought to be fixed may change if the supervisor receives a raise. Likewise, amounts charged for telephone, rent, insurance, taxes, and so on may increase or decrease. In practice, fixed costs frequently fluctuate. Accordingly, the relationships are not strictly linear.

CVP assumes that such factors as worker efficiency are constant over the range of the activity analyzed. Businesses frequently are able to increase productivity, thereby reducing variable or fixed costs, but CVP formulas are not constructed to allow for such changes in efficiency.

Finally, the analytical techniques assume that the level of inventory does not change during the period. In other words, sales and production are assumed to be equal. CVP formulas are used to provide the estimated number of units that must be *produced and sold* to attain break-even status or to achieve some designated target profit. Producing or acquiring inventory that is not sold generates costs without producing corresponding revenue. This condition undoubtedly affects the CVP relationships. Accordingly, the assumptions associated with CVP are frequently violated in business practice. Within the relevant range of activity, however, violations of the basic assumptions are normally insignificant. A prudent business manager who exercises good judgment will certainly find the data generated by cost-volume-profit analysis to be useful, regardless of its limitations.

---

a look

back

Profitability is affected by changes in the sale price, costs, and the volume of activity. The relationship between these variables is known as *cost-volume-profit analysis*. One important variable in the analysis of these relationships is the *contribution margin*, which is determined by subtracting the variable costs from the sales price. The *contribution margin per unit* is the amount from each unit sold available to cover fixed costs. Once fixed costs have been covered, each additional unit sold increases net income by the amount of the per-unit contribution margin.

The *break-even point* (i.e., the point where total revenue equals total cost) in units can be determined by dividing fixed costs by the contribution margin per unit. The break-even point expressed in sales dollars can be determined by multiplying the number of break-even units by the sales price per unit. To determine sales in units to obtain a designated profit, the sum of fixed costs and desired profit is divided by the contribution margin per unit. The contribution margin per unit can also be used to assess the effects of changes in sales price, variable costs, and fixed costs on the company's profitability.

Many methods are available to determine the prices at which products should sell. In *cost-plus pricing*, the sales price per unit is determined by adding a percentage markup to the cost per unit. *Target pricing* (*target costing*) begins with an estimate of market price that customers would be willing to pay for the product and then develops the product at a cost that will enable the company to earn its desired profit.

A *break-even graph* can be drawn to depict cost-volume-profit relationships for a product over a range of sales activity. Units are expressed along the horizontal axis and sales along the vertical axis. Lines for fixed costs, total costs, and sales can be drawn on the basis of the sales price per unit, variable cost per unit, and fixed costs. The graph can be used to determine the break-even point in units and sales dollars.

The *margin of safety* is the number of units or the amount of sales dollars by which actual sales can fall below expected sales before a loss is incurred. The margin of safety can also be expressed as a percentage to permit comparison among companies of different sizes. The margin of safety can be computed as a percentage by dividing the difference between budgeted sales and break-even sales by the amount of budgeted sales.

Spreadsheet software as well as the contribution-margin approach can be used to conduct sensitivity analysis of cost-volume-profit relationships. *Sensitivity analysis* is used to determine the effect on profitability of different scenarios of fixed costs, variable costs, and sales volumes. The effects of simultaneous changes in all three variables can be assessed.

A *contribution margin ratio* can be used to determine the break-even point in sales dollars. The ratio is a percentage expression determined by dividing the contribution margin per unit by the sales price per unit. Once the contribution ratio has been determined, the break-even volume expressed in dollars can be determined by dividing the total fixed costs by the ratio. Cost-volume-profit relationships can also be examined by using the following algebraic equation:

$$Sales = Variable\ cost + Fixed\ cost$$

Assumptions are made in using cost-volume analysis. The analysis assumes true linearity among the CVP variables, a constant level of worker efficiency, and a constant level of inventory. Violating these assumptions compromises the accuracy of the analysis.

The next chapter will introduce a new concept known as *cost relevance*. Applying the concepts you have learned to real-world business problems can be challenging. Frequently, so much information is available that it is difficult to distinguish the important from the useless. The next chapter will help you learn to identify information that is relevant in a variety of short-term decision-making scenarios, including special offers, outsourcing, segment elimination, and asset replacement.

a look
forward

Multiple-Product Break-Even Analysis

When a company analyzes CVP relationships for multiple products that are sold simultaneously, the break-even point can be affected by the relative number (i.e., sales mix) of the products sold. For example, suppose that Bright Day decides to run a special sale on its two leading antioxidants, vitamins C and E. The income statements presented in Exhibit 3–1A illustrate these results.

LO12

Perform multiple-product break-even analysis.

Exhibit 3-1A *Budgeted Data for Antioxidant Special*

	Vitamin C			Vitamin E			Total	
	Budgeted Number	Per Unit	Budgeted Amount	Budgeted Number	Per Unit	Budgeted Amount	Budgeted Number	Budgeted Amount
Sales	2,100	7.20 =	$ 15,120	700	@ 11.00 =	$ 7,700	2,800	$ 22,820
Variable cost	2,100	6.00 =	(12,600)	700	@ 7.00 =	(4,900)	2,800	(17,500)
Contribution margin	2,100	1.20 =	2,520	700	@ 4.00 =	2,800	2,800	5,320
Fixed cost			(2,520)			(2,800)		(5,320)
Net income			$ 0			$ 0		$ 0

Recall that the break-even point is the point where total sales equal total costs. Accordingly, net income equals zero at that point. The data in Exhibit 3–1A indicate that the budgeted break-even sales volume for the antioxidant special is 2,800 bottles of vitamins with a sales mix consisting of 2,100 bottles of vitamin C and 700 bottles of vitamin E. What happens if the relative sales mix changes? Exhibit 3–2A depicts the expected condition if total sales remain at 2,800 units but the sales mix changes to 2,200 bottles of vitamin C and 600 bottles of vitamin E.

Exhibit 3-2A *Budgeted Data for Antioxidant Special*

	Vitamin C			Vitamin E			Total	
	Budgeted Number	Per Unit	Budgeted Amount	Budgeted Number	Per Unit	Budgeted Amount	Budgeted Number	Budgeted Amount
Sales	2,200	7.20 =	$ 15,840	600	@ 11.00 =	$ 6,600	2,800	$ 22,440
Variable cost	2,200	6.00 =	(13,200)	600	@ 7.00 =	(4,200)	2,800	(17,400)
Contribution margin	2,200	1.20 =	2,640	600	@ 4.00 =	2,400	2,800	5,040
Fixed cost			(2,520)			(2,800)		(5,320)
Net income			$ 120			$ (400)		$ (280)

Although the total number of bottles sold remains at 2,800 units, profitability shifts from breaking even to a $280 loss because of the change in the sales mix of the two products, that is, selling more vitamin C than expected and less vitamin E. Because vitamin C has a lower contribution margin (i.e., $1.20 per bottle) than vitamin E (i.e., $4.00 per bottle), selling more of C and less of E reduces profitability. The opposite impact occurs if Bright Day sells more E and less C. Exhibit 3–3A depicts the expected condition if total sales remain at 2,800 units but the sales mix changes to 1,400 bottles each of vitamin C and vitamin E.

Exhibit 3-3A *Budgeted Data for Antioxidant Special*

	Vitamin C			Vitamin E			Total	
	Budgeted Number	Per Unit	Budgeted Amount	Budgeted Number	Per Unit	Budgeted Amount	Budgeted Number	Budgeted Amount
Sales	1,400	7.20 =	$ 10,080	1,400	@ 11.00 =	$15,400	2,800	$ 25,480
Variable cost	1,400	6.00 =	(8,400)	1,400	@ 7.00 =	(9,800)	2,800	(18,200)
Contribution margin	1,400	1.20 =	1,680	1,400	@ 4.00 =	5,600	2,800	7,280
Fixed cost			(2,400)			(2,800)		(5,200)
Net income			$ (720)			$ 2,800		$ 2,080

Clearly, companies must consider sales mix when they perform break-even analysis for multi-product business ventures. The multiple product break-even point can be determined using the per-unit contribution margin approach. However, it is necessary to use a weighted average to determine the per unit contribution margin. The contribution margin of each product must be weighted by its proportionate share of units sold. For example, in the preceding case, the relative sales mix between the two products is 1:1 (one unit Vitamin C to one unit Vitamin E). What is the break-even point given a relative sales mix of 1:1? To answer this question, the companies must first determine the weighted average per-unit contribution margin by multiplying the contribution margin of each product by its weighting. The required computation is shown here:

Vitamin C ($1.20 × 1)	$1.20
Vitamin E ($4.00 × 1)	4.00
Weighted average per-unit contribution margin	$5.20

The break-even point in total units at a 1:1 sales mix is computed as follows:

$$\text{Break-even point} = \text{Fixed costs}$$
$$\div \text{ Weighted average per-unit contribution margin}$$
$$\text{Break-even point} = \$5,200 \div \$5.20 = 1,000 \text{ sales mixes}$$

Next, divide the total units to breakeven in proportion to the relative sales mix. In other words, the break-even point occurs at 1,000 bottles of vitamin C (1,000 × 1) and 1,000 bottles of vitamin E (1,000 × 1). The income statements presented in Exhibit 3–4A illustrate these results:

Exhibit 3-4A *Budgeted Data for Antioxidant Special*

	Vitamin C			Vitamin E			Total	
	Budgeted Number	Per Unit	Budgeted Amount	Budgeted Number	Per Unit	Budgeted Amount	Budgeted Number	Budgeted Amount
Sales	1,000	7.20 =	$ 7,200	1,000	@ 11.00 =	$11,000	2,000	$ 18,200
Variable cost	1,000	6.00 =	(6,000)	1,000	@ 7.00 =	(7,000)	2,000	(13,000)
Contribution margin	1,000	1.20 =	1,200	1,000	@ 4.00 =	4,000	2,000	5,200
Fixed cost			(2,400)			(2,800)		(5,200)
Net income			$ (1,200)			$ 1,200		$ 0

Break-even point The point where total revenue equals total cost; can be expressed in units or sales dollars. *(p. 87)*

Contribution margin per unit The difference between the sales price and the variable costs per unit; represents the amount available from each unit sold to cover fixed costs and to provide a profit. The per-unit contribution margin can be used in cost-volume-profit analysis to determine the amount of the break-even sales volume expressed in units or to determine the level of sales required to attain a desired profit. *(p. 86)*

Contribution margin ratio The result of dividing the contribution margin per unit by the sales price; can be used in cost-volume-profit analysis to determine the amount of the break-even sales volume expressed in dollars or to determine the dollar level of sales required to attain a desired profit. *(p. 98)*

Cost-plus-pricing strategy A pricing strategy that sets the price at cost plus a markup equal to a percentage of the cost. *(p. 86)*

Cost-volume-profit (CVP) analysis An analysis that shows the interrelationships among sales prices, volume, fixed, and variable costs; an important tool in determining the break-even point or the most profitable combination of these variables. *(p. 86)*

Equation method A cost-volume-profit analysis technique that uses a basic mathematical relationship among sales, variable costs, fixed costs, and desired net income before taxes and provides a solution in terms of units. *(p. 99)*

Margin of safety The difference between budgeted

sales and break-even sales expressed in units, dollars, or as a percentage; the amount by which actual sales can fall below budgeted sales before a loss is incurred. *(p. 94)*

Prestige pricing A pricing strategy that sets the price at a premium (above average markup above cost) under the assumption that people will pay more for the product because of its prestigious brand name, media attention, or some other reason that has piqued the interest of the public. *(p. 95)*

Sensitivity analysis A spreadsheet technique that analyzes "what-if" questions to assess the sensitivity of profits to simultaneous changes in fixed cost, variable cost, and sales volume. *(p. 95)*

Target pricing (target costing) A pricing strategy that begins with the determination of a price at which a product will sell and then focuses on the development of that product with a cost structure that will satisfy market demands. *(p. 89)*

QUESTIONS

1. What does the term *breakeven* mean? Name the two ways it can be measured.
2. How does a contribution margin income statement differ from the income statement used in financial reporting?
3. In what three ways can the contribution margin be useful in cost-volume-profit analysis?
4. If Company A has a projected margin of safety of 22 percent while Company B has a margin of safety of 52 percent, which company is at greater risk when actual sales are less than budgeted?
5. What variables affect profitability? Name two methods for determining profitability when simultaneous changes occur in these variables.
6. When would the customer be willing to pay a premium price for a product or service? What pricing strategy would be appropriate under these circumstances?
7. What are three alternative approaches to determine the break-even point? What do the results of these approaches show?
8. What is the equation method for determining breakeven? Explain how the results of this method differ from those of the contribution-margin approach.
9. Before the break-even point is reached, what strategy probably would be most effective in increasing profitability, and why? After breakeven, what strategies should be considered?

10. If a company is trying to find the break-even point for multiple products that sell simultaneously, what consideration must be taken into account?
11. What assumptions are necessary for cost-volume-profit analysis to be completely accurate? Since these assumptions are usually violated, why do managers still use the analysis in decision making?
12. Mary Hartwell and Jane Jamail are college roommates who are considering the joint purchase of a computer that they can share to prepare class assignments. Ms. Hartwell wants a particular model that costs $2,000; Ms. Jamail prefers a more economical model that costs $1,500. In fact, Ms. Jamail has become adamant about her position, stating that she refuses to contribute more than $750 toward the purchase. If Ms. Hartwell is also adamant about her position, should she accept Ms. Jamail's $750 offer and apply that amount toward the purchase of the more expensive computer?
13. How would the algebraic formula used to compute the break-even point under the equation method be changed to consider a desired target profit?
14. Setting the sales price is easy: Just enter cost information and the desired profit data into one of the cost-volume-profit formulas, and the appropriate sales price can be computed mathematically. Do you agree with this line of reasoning? Explain.
15. What is the relationship between cost-volume-profit analysis and the relevant range?

EXERCISES

L.O. 2 EXERCISE 3-1   *Per-Unit Contribution Margin Approach*

CLK Corporation sells a product for $6 each that has variable costs of $4.50 per unit. CLK's annual fixed cost amounts to $120,000.

Required
Use the per-unit-contribution-margin approach to determine the break-even point in units and dollars.

L.O. 2 EXERCISE 3-2   *Equation Method*

Saylor Corporation produces a product that it sells for $8 each. Its variable costs per unit are $5.50, and annual fixed costs are $125,000.

Required

Use the equation method to determine the break-even point in units and dollars.

EXERCISE 3-3　　*Contribution Margin Ratio*　　　　　　　　　　　　　**L.O. 3**

Sigma Company incurs annual fixed cost of $70,000, variable costs for its product amount to $3.20 per unit, and the sales price per unit is $8. Sigma desires to earn an annual profit of $26,000.

Required

Use the contribution-margin-ratio approach to determine the amount of the sales volume in dollars and units required to earn the desired profit.

EXERCISE 3-4　　*Equation Method*　　　　　　　　　　　　　　　　**L.O. 3**

Westside Company produces a product that sells for $12 per unit and has a variable cost of $4.20 per unit. Westside incurs annual fixed cost of $80,000. It desires to earn a target profit of $37,000.

Required

Use the equation method to determine the amount of the sales volume in units and dollars required to earn the desired profit.

EXERCISE 3-5　　*Fixed and Variable Cost per Unit*　　　　　　　　　**L.O. 3**

Toro-Blade Corporation produced and sold 24,000 units of product during September. It earned a contribution margin of $60,000 on sales of $180,000 and determined that cost per unit of product was $8.

Required

On the basis of this information, determine the variable and fixed cost per unit of the product.

EXERCISE 3-6　　*Determination of Variable Cost from Incomplete Cost Data*　　**L.O. 3**

Quartz Corporation produced 60,000 watches that it sold for $10 each during its 2006 accounting period. The company determined that fixed manufacturing cost per unit was $5 per watch. The company showed $120,000 of gross margin on its financial statements.

Required

Determine the total variable cost, the variable cost per unit, and the total amount of contribution margin.

EXERCISE 3-7　　*Contribution Margin per Unit Approach for Break-Even and Desired Profit*　　**L.O. 2, 3**

Information concerning a product produced by Drew Company appears here:

Sales price per unit	$160
Variable cost per unit	90
Total annual fixed manufacturing & operating costs	620,200

Required

Determine the following:
a. Contribution margin per unit.
b. Number of units that must be sold to break even.
c. Sales level in units that must be reached to earn a profit of $300,300.

EXERCISE 3-8　　*Change in Sales Price*　　　　　　　　　　　　　　**L.O. 4**

Kimberly Company produces a product that has a variable cost of $2 per unit; it sells for $3 per unit. The company's annual fixed costs total $250,000; it had net income of $80,000 during the previous year. In an effort to increase the company's market share, management is considering lowering the selling price to $2.75 per unit.

Required

If Kimberly desires to maintain its current income level, how many additional units must it sell to justify the price decline?

L.O. 4 EXERCISE 3-9   *Simultaneous Change in Sales Price and Desired Profit*

Use the same data as presented in Exercise 3–8 but assume that in addition to increasing its market share by lowering its selling price to $2.75, Kimberly desires to increase its net income by $7,500.

Required

Determine the number of units the company must sell to satisfy these requirements.

L.O. 2, 3, 7 EXERCISE 3-10   *Components of Break-Even Graph*

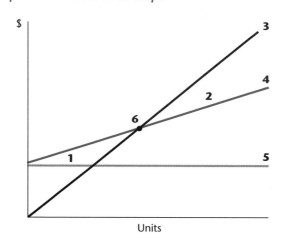

Required

Match the numbers shown in the graph with the following items:
a. Fixed cost line
b. Total cost line
c. Break-even point
d. Area of profit
e. Revenue line
f. Area of loss

L.O. 4 EXERCISE 3-11   *Evaluation of Simultaneous Changes in Fixed and Variable Costs*

Hancock Company currently produces and sells 5,000 units annually of a product that has a variable cost of $22 per unit and an annual fixed cost of $180,000. The company currently earns $20,000 annual profit. Assume that Hancock has the opportunity to invest in new labour-saving production equipment that will enable the company to reduce variable costs to $19 per unit. The investment would cause fixed costs to increase by $10,000 because of additional amortization cost.

Required

a. Use the equation method to determine the sales price per unit under existing conditions (i.e., current equipment is used).
b. Prepare a contribution margin income statement, assuming that Hancock invests in the new production equipment. Recommend whether Hancock should invest in the new equipment.

EXERCISE 3-12   *Margin of Safety*   **L.O. 8**

Firmin Company makes a product that sells for $5 per unit. The company pays $3 per unit for the variable costs of the product and incurs annual fixed costs of $50,000. Firmin expects to sell 30,000 units of product.

Required
Determine Firmin's margin of safety expressed as a percentage.

EXERCISE 3-13   *Cost-Volume-Profit Relationship*   **L.O. 1, 2, 3**

Bellview, Inc. is a manufacturing company that makes small electric motors it sells for $18 per unit. The variable costs of production amount to $12 per motor, and annual fixed costs of production amount to $36,000.

Required
a. How many units of product must Bellview make and sell to break even?
b. How many units of product must Bellview make and sell to earn a $12,000 profit?
c. The marketing manager believes that sales would increase dramatically if the price were reduced to $15 per unit. How many units of product must Bellview make and sell to earn a $12,000 profit, assuming that the sales price is set at $15 per unit?

EXERCISE 3-14   *Understanding of the Global Economy through CVP Relationships*   **L.O. 4**

An article published in the December 8, 1997, issue of *U.S. News & World Report* summarized several factors likely to support a continuing decline in the rate of inflation over the next decade. Specifically, the article stated that "global competition has…fostered an environment of cheap labor, cost cutting, and increased efficiency." The article notes that these developments in the global economy have led to a condition in which "the production of goods is outpacing the number of consumers able to buy them." Even so, the level of production is not likely to decline because factories have been built in the developing countries where labour is cheap. The recent decline in the strength of the Asian economies is likely to have a snowballing effect so that within the foreseeable future, there will "be too many goods chasing too few buyers."

Required
a. Identify the production cost factor(s) referred to that exhibit variable cost behaviour. Has (have) the cost factor(s) increased or decreased? Provide logical explanations as to why the variable costs have increased or decreased.
b. Identify the production cost factor(s) referred to that exhibit fixed cost behaviour. Has (have) the cost factor(s) increased or decreased? Provide logical explanations as to why the fixed costs have increased or decreased.
c. The article implies that production levels are likely to remain high even though demand is expected to be weak. Explain the logic behind this implication.
d. The article suggests that manufacturers will continue to produce goods even though they may have to sell goods at a price that is below the total cost of production. Considering what you know about fixed versus variable cost, speculate on how low manufacturers would permit prices to drop before they would stop production.

EXERCISE 3-15   *Target Costing*   **L.O. 5**

The marketing manager of TelCo., Inc. has determined that a market exists for a telephone with a sales price of $10 per unit. The production manager suggests that the fixed cost of producing between 10,000 and 30,000 telephones is $72,000.

Required
Assume that TelCo desires to earn a $40,000 profit from the phone sales. How much can TelCo afford to spend on variable cost per unit if production and sales equal 25,000 phones?

APPENDIX

L.O. 12 EXERCISE 3-16   *Multiple Product Break-Even Analysis*

Tracy Company makes two products. The budgeted per-unit contribution margin for each product follows:

	Product A	Product B
Sales price	$25	$45
Variable cost per unit	(15)	(25)
Contribution margin per unit	$10	$20

Tracy expects to incur fixed costs amounting to $10,000. The relative sales mix of the products is 3 Product A and 1 Product B.

Required
a. Determine the total number of products (units of A and B combined) that must be sold to break even.
b. How many units each of Product A and Product B must be sold to break even?

PROBLEMS—SERIES A

L.O. 2 PROBLEM 3-1A   *Determination of the Break-Even Point and Preparation of a Contribution Margin Income Statement*

Maletta Manufacturing Company makes a product that it sells for $30 per unit. The company incurred variable manufacturing costs of $14 per unit. Variable selling expenses totalled $4 per unit, annual fixed manufacturing costs were $87,000, and fixed selling and administrative costs totalled $45,000 per year.

Required
Determine the break-even point in units and dollars using each of the following approaches:
a. Contribution margin per unit.
b. Equation method.
c. Contribution margin ratio.
d. Confirm your results by preparing a contribution margin income statement when sales volume is at the break-even point.

L.O. 2, 7 PROBLEM 3-2A   *Determination of the Break-Even Point and Preparation of a Break-Even Graph*

Conduit Company is considering the production of a new product. The expected variable cost is $8 per unit. Annual fixed costs are expected to amount to $280,000. The anticipated sales price is $15 each.

Required
Determine the break-even point in units and dollars using each of the following:
a. Contribution-margin-per-unit approach.
b. Equation method.
c. Contribution margin ratio approach.
d. Prepare a break-even graph to visually demonstrate the cost-volume-profit relationships.

L.O. 2, 3, 4 PROBLEM 3-3A   *Effect of Converting Variable to Fixed Costs*

Highland Manufacturing Company reported the following data regarding a product it manufactures and sells. The sales price is $16.

Variable costs:	
Manufacturing	$7.50 per unit
Selling	4.50 per unit
Fixed costs:	
Manufacturing	$80,000 per year
Selling and administrative	50,000 per year

Required

a. Use the per-unit-contribution-margin approach to determine the break-even point in units and dollars.

b. Use the per-unit-contribution-margin approach to determine the level of sales in units and dollars required to obtain a profit of $62,000.

c. Suppose that variable selling costs could be eliminated by having a salaried sales force. If the company could sell 50,000 units, how much could it pay in salaries for salespeople and still have a profit of $62,000? (*Hint:* Use the equation method.)

PROBLEM 3-4A   *Analysis of Change in Sales Price Using the Contribution Margin Ratio*   **L.O. 2, 3, 4**

GDP Company reported the following data regarding the product it sells:

Sales price	$6.00
Contribution margin ratio	20%
Fixed costs	$8,400

Required

Use the contribution margin ratio approach and consider each requirement separately.

a. What is the break-even point in dollars? in units?

b. To obtain a profit of $1,800, what must the sales be in dollars? in units?

c. If the sales price increases to $6.40 and variable costs do not change, what will be the new break-even point in dollars? in units?

PROBLEM 3-5A   *Analysis of Sales Price and Fixed Cost Using the Equation Method*   **L.O. 2, 3, 4**

Shim Company is considering adding a new product. The cost accountant has provided the following data:

Expected variable cost of manufacturing	$10 per unit
Expected annual fixed manufacturing costs	$16,400

The administrative vice-president has provided the following estimates:

Expected sales commission	$2.50 per unit
Expected annual fixed administrative costs	$8,200

The manager has decided that any new product must at least break even in the first year.

Required

Use the equation method and consider each requirement separately.

a. If the sales price is set at $15, how many units must be sold to break even?

b. Shim has determined that sales will probably be 12,000 units. What sales price per unit will allow the company to break even?

c. Shim has decided to advertise the product heavily and has set the sales price at $16. If sales are 10,000 units, how much can the company spend on advertising and still break even?

L.O. 8 PROBLEM 3-6A   *Margin of Safety and Operating Leverage*

Ravon Company is considering the addition of a new product to its cosmetic line of products. The company has three distinctly different options: a skin cream, a bath oil, or a hair colouring gel. Relevant information and a budgeted income statement for each of the products follow:

	Relevant Information		
	Skin Cream	Bath Oil	Colour Gel
Budgeted Sales in Units (a)	25,000	45,000	15,000
Expected Sales Price (b)	$ 3.50	$ 2.00	$ 6.50
Variable Costs per Unit (c)	$ 2.00	$ 0.75	$ 4.50
Income Statements			
Sales Revenue (a × b)	$ 87,500	$ 90,000	$ 97,500
Variable Costs (a × c)	(50,000)	(33,750)	(67,500)
Contribution Margin	$ 37,500	$ 56,250	$ 30,000
Fixed Cost	(30,000)	(52,500)	(26,000)
Net Income	$ 7,500	$ 3,750	$ 4,000

Required

a. Determine the margin of safety as a percentage for each product.

b. Prepare a revised income statement for each product, assuming a 25 percent increase in the budgeted sales volume.

c. For each product, determine the percentage of change in net income that results from the 25 percent increase in sales. Which product has the highest operating leverage?

d. Assuming that management is pessimistic and risk averse, which product should the company add to its line of products? Support your answer with appropriate commentary.

e. Assuming that management is optimistic and risk aggressive, which product should the company add to its line of products? Support your answer with appropriate commentary.

L.O. 2, 3, 4, 7, 8 PROBLEM 3-7A   *Comprehensive CVP Analysis*

Kirk Company makes and sells a product with variable costs in the amount of $20 each. Kirk incurs annual fixed costs of $16,000. The current sales price is set at $30.

Required

The requirements listed here are interdependent. For example, the $4,000 desired profit introduced in Requirement *c* also applies to subsequent requirements. Likewise, the $25 sales price introduced in Requirement *d* applies to the subsequent requirements.

a. Determine the amount of the contribution margin per unit.

b. Determine the break-even point in units and in dollars. Confirm your answer by preparing an income statement using the contribution-margin format.

c. Suppose that Kirk desires to earn a $4,000 profit. Determine the sales volume expressed in units and dollars required to earn the desired profit. Confirm your answer by preparing an income statement using the contribution-margin format.

d. If the sales price drops to $25 per unit, how will reducing the sales price affect the level of sales required to earn the desired profit? Express your answer in units and dollars. Confirm your answer by preparing an income statement using the contribution-margin format.

e. If fixed cost drops to $12,000, how will the reduction affect the level of sales required to earn the desired profit? Express your answer in units and dollars. Confirm your answer by preparing an income statement using the contribution-margin format.

f. If variable cost drops to $15 per unit, how will the reduction affect the level of sales required to earn the desired profit? Express your answer in units and dollars. Confirm your answer by preparing an income statement using the contribution-margin format.

g. Assume that Kirk concludes that it can sell 1,600 units of product for $25 each. Recall that variable costs are $15 each and fixed costs amount to $12,000. Compute the margin of safety in terms of units and dollars and as a percentage.

h. Draw a break-even graph using the cost and price assumptions described in Requirement g.

PROBLEM 3-8A   *Assessment of Simultaneous Changes in CVP Relationships*   **L.O. 2, 3, 4, 7, 8**

Lazy Days, Inc. (LDI) sells hammocks; variable costs are $40 each, and the hammocks are sold for $60 each. LDI incurs $95,000 of fixed operating expenses annually.

Required

a. Determine the sales volume in units and dollars that would be required to attain a $25,000 profit. Verify your answer by preparing an income statement using the contribution-margin format.

b. LDI is considering the implementation of a quality improvement program. The program will require a $5 increase in the variable cost per unit. To inform its customers of the quality improvements, the company plans to spend an additional $10,000 for advertising. Assuming that the improvement program will increase sales to a level that is 3,000 units above the amount computed in Requirement *a*, should LDI proceed with plans to improve product quality? Support your answer by preparing a budgeted income statement.

c. Determine the new break-even point volume of units and sales dollars as well as the margin of safety percentage, assuming that the quality improvement program is initiated.

d. Prepare a break-even graph using the cost and price assumptions outlined in Requirement *b*.

APPENDIX

PROBLEM 3-9A   *Determination of the Break-Even Point and Margin of Safety for a Company with*   **L.O. 2, 8**
                   Multiple Products

Shank Company makes two products. Budgeted annual income statements for the two products are provided here:

	Product A			Product B			Total	
	Budgeted Number	Per Unit	Budgeted Amount	Budgeted Number	Per Unit	Budgeted Amount	Budgeted Number	Budgeted Amount
Sales	320	@ $580 =	$ 185,600	1,280	@ $430 =	$ 550,400	1,600	$ 736,000
Variable cost	320	@ $400 =	(128,000)	1,280	@ $320 =	(409,600)	1,600	(537,600)
Contribution Margin	320	@ $180 =	$ 57,600	1,280	@ $110 =	$ 140,800	1,600	$ 198,400
Fixed cost			(22,320)			(126,480)		(148,800)
Net income			$ 35,280			$ 14,320		$ 49,600

Required

a. On the basis of the budgeted sales, determine the relative sales mix between the two products.

b. Determine the weighted-average contribution margin per unit.

c. Calculate the break-even point in total number of units.

d. Determine the number of units of each product that must be sold to break even.

e. Verify the break-even point by preparing an income statement for each product as well as an income statement for the combined products.

f. Determine the margin of safety on the basis of the combined sales of the two products.

L.O. 2   PROBLEM 3-1B   *Determination of the Break-Even Point and Preparation of a Contribution Margin Income Statement*

Dandy Company manufactures radio and cassette players and sells them for $50 each. According to the company's records, the variable costs, including direct labour and direct materials, amounted to $25. Factory amortization and other fixed manufacturing costs were $96,000 per year. Dandy paid its salespeople a commission of $9 per unit. Annual fixed selling and administrative costs were $64,000.

Required

Determine the break-even point in units and dollars, using each of the following:
a. Contribution-margin-per-unit approach.
b. Equation method.
c. Contribution-margin-ratio approach.
d. Confirm your results by preparing a contribution margin income statement when sales volume is at the break-even point.

L.O. 2, 7   PROBLEM 3-2B   *Determination of the Break-Even Point and Preparation of a Break-Even Graph*

Executive officers of Homer Company are assessing the profitability of a potential new product. They expect that the variable cost of making the product is $24 per unit and fixed manufacturing cost will be $480,000. The executive officers plan to sell the product at the price of $48 each.

Required

Determine the break-even point in units and dollars using each of the following approaches:
a. Contribution margin per unit.
b. Equation.
c. Contribution margin ratio.
d. Prepare a break-even graph to visually demonstrate the cost-volume-profit relationships.

L.O. 2, 3, 4   PROBLEM 3-3B   *Effect of Converting Variable to Fixed Costs*

Phillips Company manufactures and sells its own brand of cameras. It sells each camera for $28. The company's accountant prepared the following data:

Manufacturing costs	
Variable	$12 per unit
Fixed	$100,000 per year
Selling and administrative expenses	
Variable	$4 per unit
Fixed	$44,000 per year

Required

a. Use the per-unit-contribution-margin approach to determine the break-even point in units and dollars.
b. Use the per-unit-contribution-margin approach to determine the level of sales in units and dollars required to obtain an $84,000 profit.
c. Suppose that variable selling and administrative costs could be eliminated by having a salaried sales force. If the company could sell 20,000 units, how much could it pay in salaries for the salespeople and still have a profit of $84,000? (*Hint:* Use the equation method.)

PROBLEM 3-4B   *Analysis of Change in Sales Price Using the Contribution Margin Ratio*   **L.O. 2, 3, 4**

Standard Company reported the following data regarding the one product it sells:

Sales price	$20
Contribution margin ratio	15%
Fixed costs	$72,000 per year

Required

Use the contribution-margin-ratio approach and consider each requirement separately.

a. What is the break-even point in dollars? in units?
b. To obtain an $18,000 profit, what must the sales be in dollars? in units?
c. If the sales price increases to $25 and variable costs do not change, what will be the new break-even point in units? in dollars?

PROBLEM 3-5B   *Analysis of Sales Price and Fixed Cost Using the Equation Method*   **L.O. 2, 3, 4**

Baxter Company is analyzing whether its new product will be profitable. The following data are provided for analysis:

Expected variable cost of manufacturing	$15 per unit
Expected fixed manufacturing costs	$24,000 per year
Expected sales commission	$3 per unit
Expected fixed administrative costs	$6,000 per year

The company has decided that any new product must at least break even in the first year.

Required

Use the equation method and consider each requirement separately.

a. If the sales price is set at $24, how many units must be sold to break even?
b. Baxter has determined that sales will probably be 6,000 units. What sales price per unit will allow the company to break even?
c. Baxter has decided to heavily advertise the product and has set the sales price at $27. If sales are 9,000 units, how much can the company spend on advertising and still break even?

PROBLEM 3-6B   *Margin of Safety and Operating Leverage*   **L.O. 8**

Chase Company has three distinctly different options when it considers adding a new product to its automotive division: engine oil, coolant, or windshield washer. Relevant information and a budgeted annual income statement for each product follow:

	Engine Oil	Coolant	Windshield Washer
	Relevant Information		
Budgeted Sales in Units (a)	35,000	57,000	225,000
Expected Sales Price (b)	$ 2.40	$ 2.85	$ 1.15
Variable Costs per Unit (c)	$1.00	$ 1.25	$ 0.35
Income Statements			
Sales Revenue (a × b)	$ 84,000	$162,450	$ 258,750
Variable Costs (a × c)	(35,000)	(71,250)	(78,750)
Contribution Margin	$ 49,000	$ 91,200	$180,000
Fixed Cost	(35,000)	(60,000)	(120,000)
Net Income	$ 14,000	$ 31,200	$ 60,000

Required

a. Determine the margin of safety as a percentage for each product.
b. Prepare a revised income statement for each product, assuming 20 percent growth in the budgeted sales volume.
c. For each product, determine the percentage of change in net income that results from the 20 percent increase in sales. Which product has the highest operating leverage?
d. Assuming that management is pessimistic and risk averse, which product should the company add? Support your answer with appropriate commentary.
e. Assuming that management is optimistic and risk aggressive, which product should the company add? Support your answer with appropriate commentary.

L.O. 2, 3, 4, 7, 8   PROBLEM 3-7B   *Comprehensive CVP Analysis*

Earl Company makes a product that it sells for $75. Earl incurs annual fixed costs of $80,000 and variable costs of $50 each.

Required

The following requirements are interdependent: (For example, the $20,000 desired profit introduced in Requirement *c* also applies to subsequent requirements. Likewise, the $70 sales price introduced in Requirement *d* applies to the subsequent requirements.)

a. Determine the amount of the contribution margin per unit.
b. Determine the break-even point in units and in dollars. Confirm your answer by preparing an income statement using the contribution-margin format.
c. Suppose that Earl desires to earn a $20,000 profit. Determine the sales volume in units and dollars required to earn the desired profit. Confirm your answer by preparing an income statement using the contribution-margin format.
d. If the sales price drops to $70 per unit, how will the reduction of sales price affect the level of sales required to earn the desired profit? Express your answer in units and dollars. Confirm your answer by preparing an income statement using the contribution-margin format.
e. If fixed cost drops to $70,000, how will the reduction affect the level of sales required to earn the desired profit? Express your answer in units and dollars. Confirm your answer by preparing an income statement using the contribution-margin format.
f. If variable cost drops to $40 per unit, how will reducing the sales price affect the level of sales required to earn the desired profit? Express your answer in units and dollars. Confirm your answer by preparing an income statement using the contribution-margin format.
g. Assume that Earl concludes that it can sell 4,800 units of product for $68 each. Recall that variable costs are $40 each and fixed costs amount to $70,000. Compute the margin of safety in terms of units, dollars, and as a percentage.
h. Draw a break-even graph using the cost and price assumptions described in Requirement *g*.

L.O. 2, 3, 4, 7, 8   PROBLEM 3-8B   *Assessment of Simultaneous Changes in CVP Relationships*

Floyd Company sells tennis racquets; variable costs for each are $75 and each is sold for $105. Floyd incurs $270,000 of fixed operating expenses annually.

Required

a. Determine the sales volume in units and dollars required to attain a $120,000 profit. Verify your answer by preparing an income statement using the contribution-margin format.
b. Floyd is considering the possibility of establishing a quality improvement program that will require a $10 increase in the variable cost per unit. To inform its customers of the quality improvements, the company plans to spend an additional $60,000 for advertising. Assuming that the improvement program will increase sales to a level that is 5,000 units above the amount computed in Requirement *a*, should Floyd proceed with plans to improve product quality? Support your answer by preparing a budgeted income statement.
c. Determine the new break-even point and the margin of safety percentage, assuming that the quality improvement program is initiated.
d. Prepare a break-even graph using the cost and price assumptions outlined in Requirement *b*.

APPENDIX

PROBLEM 3-9B   *Determination of the Break-Even Point and Margin of Safety for a Company with Multiple Products*

Executive officers of Gretal Company have prepared the annual budgets for its two products, X and Y, as follows:

	Product X			Product Y			Total	
	Budgeted Number	Per Unit	Budgeted Amount	Budgeted Number	Per Unit	Budgeted Amount	Budgeted Number	Budgeted Amount
Sales	500	@ $450 =	$ 225,000	1,500	@ $285 =	$ 427,500	2,000	$ 652,500
Variable cost	500	@ $250 =	(125,000)	1,500	@ $145 =	(217,500)	2,000	(342,500)
Contribution Margin	500	@ $200 =	$ 100,000	1,500	@ $140 =	$ 210,000	2,000	$ 310,000
Fixed cost			(31,000)			(124,000)		(155,000)
Net income			$ 69,000			$ 86,000		$ 155,000

Required

a. On the basis of the number of units sold, determine the relative sales mix between the two products.
b. Determine the weighted-average contribution margin per unit.
c. Calculate the break-even point in total number of units.
d. Determine the number of units of each product that must be sold to break even.
e. Verify the break-even point by preparing an income statement for each product as well as an income statement for the combined products.
f. Determine the margin of safety on the basis of the combined sales of the two products.

ANALYZE, THINK, COMMUNICATE

BUSINESS APPLICATIONS CASE   *Sales Required to Achieve a Desired Profit*   **ACT 3-1**

Peggy Grear just fulfilled a dream as she completed her first season as the owner of a rafting company. Unfortunately, her operation was not profitable. She has enough savings to get her through another season or two, but she realizes that she will have to start making a profit or give up the dream. Her company's income statement for the first year of operation follows.

Grear Rafting Company Income Statements For the Year Ended December 31, 2003	
Revenue	$1,048,000
Rental Cost of Rafts and Camping Equipment	(208,600)
Meals Provided to Rafters	(314,400)
Advertising Expenses	(50,000)
Compensation Paid to Guides	(471,600)
Salary of Office Manager	(16,500)
T-shirts and Hats Provided to Rafters	(31,440)
Office Utility Expense	(3,850)
Net Income (Loss)	$ (48,390)

Additional Information: Equipment is rented on an annual basis. Additional equipment is not available, nor is an allowance provided for early returns. Guides are paid on a commission basis. Ms. Grear's company served 1,048 rafters during the year.

Required
a. Identify the fixed and variable costs relative to the number of rafters.
b. Reconstruct the income statement using the contribution-margin approach.
c. How many rafters are required for Ms. Grear to earn a $50,000 profit?
d. In discussions with her accountant, Ms. Grear was told to expect a 10 percent increase in fixed cost during the following year. She responded with this question, "If these costs are fixed, why are they going to increase?" Assume that you are the accountant; respond to Ms. Grear's question.
e. In addition to the expected increase in fixed cost, the accountant told Ms. Grear to plan for a 20 percent increase in variable cost. On the basis of these increases, how many rafters would be required to earn the $50,000 desired profit if the price per rafter remains the same?
f. Assume that Ms. Grear believes that it is unlikely that she will be able to attract the number of rafters identified in Part *e*. Explain how *sensitivity analysis* could be used to investigate how to attain a $50,000 profit.

ACT 3-2   **GROUP ASSIGNMENT**   *The Effect of Changes in Fixed and Variable Costs on Profitability*

In a period when sales amounted to 100 units of product, King Manufacturing Company (KMC) produced the following internal income statement:

Revenue	$ 2,000
Variable Costs	(1,200)
Contribution Margin	$ 800
Fixed Cost	(600)
Net Income	$ 200

KMC has the opportunity to alter its operations in one of the following ways:
1. Increasing fixed advertising costs by $400, thereby increasing sales by 60 units.
2. Lowering commissions paid to the sales staff by $2 per unit, thereby reducing sales by 5 units.
3. Decreasing fixed inventory holding cost by $200, thereby decreasing sales by 10 units.

Required
a. The instructor will divide the class into groups and then organize the groups into two sections. For a large class (e.g., 12 or more groups), four sections may be necessary. At least three groups in each section are needed. Having more groups in one section than another section is acceptable because offsetting advantages and disadvantages exist. Having more groups is advantageous because more people will work on the task but has a disadvantage because having more people complicates communication.

Group Task
The sections are to compete with each other to see which section can determine the most profitable alternative in the shortest period of time. No instruction is provided regarding how the sections are to proceed with the task. In other words, each section is required to organize itself with respect to how to accomplish the task of selecting the best alternative. A total quality management (TQM) constraint is imposed requires zero defects. A section that turns in a wrong answer is disqualified. Once an answer is submitted to the instructor, it cannot be changed. Sections continue to turn in answers until all sections have submitted a response. The first section to submit the correct answer wins the competition.
b. If any section submits a wrong answer, the instructor or a spokesperson from the winning group should explain how the right answer was determined.
c. Discuss the dynamics of group interaction. How was the work organized? How was leadership established?

WRITING ASSIGNMENT *Operating Leverage, Margin of Safety, and Cost Behaviour*   **ACT 3-3**

The article "Up Front: More Condensing at the Digest?" in the October 19, 1998, issue of *Business Week* reported that Thomas Ryder, CEO of Reader's Digest Association, was considering a spinoff of Reader's Digest's direct-marketing operations into a joint venture with Time Warner. The article's author, Robert McNatt, noted that the direct marketing of books, music, and videos is a far larger part of the Reader's Digest business than is its namesake magazine. Further, the article stated that 1998 direct-marketing sales of $1.6 billion were down 11 percent from 1997. The decline in revenue caused the division's operating profits to decline by 58 percent. The article stated that the contemplated alliance with Time Warner could provide some fast help. Gerald Levin, Time Warner chairman, has said that his company's operations provide customer service and product fulfillment far better than other Web sellers do because of Time Warner's established 250 Web sites.

Required

a. Write a memo explaining how an 11 percent decrease in sales could result in a 58 percent decline in operating profits.
b. Provide a brief explanation as to how the decline in revenue will affect the company's margin of safety.
c. Provide a logical explanation as to why a joint venture between Reader's Digest's direct-marketing division and Time Warner could work to the advantage of both companies. (*Hint:* Consider the effects of fixed-cost behaviour in formulating your response).

ETHICAL DILEMMA   *Manipulation of Amount of Reported Earnings*   **ACT 3-4**

The article "Garbage In, Garbage Out" (*Fortune*, May 25, 1998, pp. 130–138) describes a litany of questionable accounting practices that ultimately led to the demise of Waste Management, Inc. Under pressure to retain its reputation on Wall Street as a growth company, Waste Management extended its estimates of the lives of its garbage trucks by two to four years beyond the standard used in the industry. It also began to use a $25,000 expected salvage value on each truck when the industry standard was to recognize a zero salvage value. Because Waste Management owned approximately 20,000 trucks, these moves had a significant impact on the company's earnings. Extended lives and exaggerated salvage values were also applied to the company's 1.5 million steel dumpsters and its landfill facilities. These accounting practices boosted reported earnings by approximately $110 million per year. The long-term effect on real earnings was disastrous, however; maintenance costs began to soar, and the company was forced to spend millions to keep broken-down trucks on the road. Overvalued assets failed to generate expected revenues. The failure to maintain earnings growth ultimately led to the replacement of management. When the new managers discovered the misstated accounting figures, the company was forced to recognize a pretax charge of $3.54 billion in its 1997 income statement. The stock price plummeted, and the company was ultimately merged out of existence.

Required

a. Did Waste Management manipulate the recognition of fixed or variable costs?
b. Explain how extending the life estimates of assets will increase earnings and the book values of assets.
c. Explain how inflating the salvage values of assets will increase earnings and the book values of assets.
d. Speculate as to what motive would cause executives to manipulate earnings.

ACT 3-5   SPREADSHEET ASSIGNMENT   *Using Excel*

Ferrell Company has provided the estimated data that appear in Rows 4 to 8 of the following spreadsheet.

Required

Construct a spreadsheet as below that would allow you to determine net income, break-even in units, and the operating leverage for the estimates at the top of the spreadsheet, and to see the effects of changes to the estimates. Set up this spreadsheet so that any change in the estimates will automatically be reflected in the calculation of net income, break-even, and operating leverage.

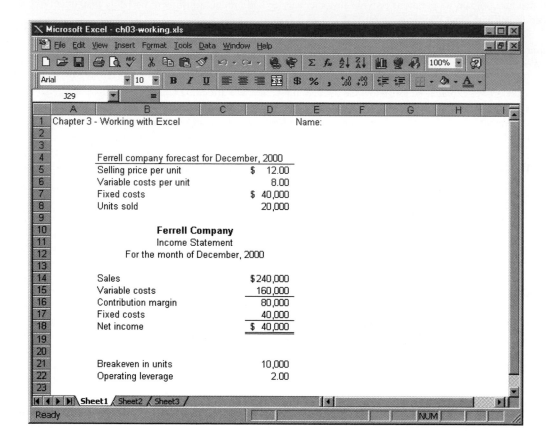

Spreadsheet Tip

To centre a heading across several columns, such as the Income Statement title, highlight the area to be centred (Columns B, C, and D), choose Format, then choose Cells, and click on the tab titled Alignment. Near the bottom of the alignment window, place a check mark in the box titled Merge cells. The shortcut method to merge cells is to click on the icon near the middle of the top icons that contains an a in a box.

SPREADSHEET ASSIGNMENT   *Mastering Excel*   **ACT 3-6**

Required

Build the spreadsheet pictured in Exhibit 3–2. Be sure to use formulas that will automatically calculate profitability if fixed cost, variable cost, or sales volume is changed.

Spreadsheet Tips

1. The shading in Column D and in Row 6 can be inserted by first highlighting a section to be shaded, choosing Format from the main menu, then Cells, then clicking on the tab titled Patterns, and then choosing a colour for the shading. The shortcut method to accomplish the shading is to click on the fill colour icon (it looks like a tipped bucket and is in the upper right area of the screen).

2. Similar to basic math rules, the order of calculation within a formula is multiplication and division before addition and subtraction. Therefore, if you wish to subtract variable cost from selling price and multiply the difference by units sold, the formula must be $= (28 - C7)*E7$.

3. The quickest way to get the correct formulas in the area of E7 to I15 is to place the proper formula in Cell E7 and then copy this formula to the entire block of E7:I15. However, the formulas must use the $ around the cell addresses to lock either the row or the column, or both. For example, the formula $= 2*\$B\$7$ can be copied to any other cell, and the cell reference will remain B7 because the $ symbol locks the row and column. Likewise, $\$B7$ indicates that only the column is locked, and $B\$7$ indicates that only the row is locked.

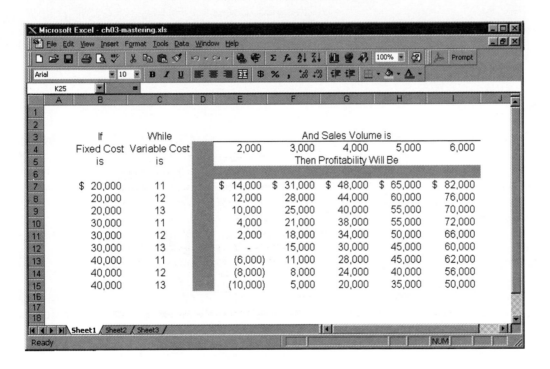

Relevant Information for Special Decisions

Learning Objectives

After completing this chapter, you should be able to:

1 Identify the characteristics of relevant information.

2 Recognize sunk costs and understand why these costs are not relevant in decision making.

3 Understand what the term *differential revenue* means.

4 Understand what the terms *avoidable cost* and *differential cost* mean.

5 Distinguish among unit-level, batch-level, product-level, and facility-level costs and understand how these costs are involved in decision making.

6 Understand that relevance is a unique concept and its application is context sensitive.

7 Identify opportunity costs and understand why these costs are relevant in decision making.

8 Distinguish between quantitative and qualitative characteristics of decision making.

9 Perform analysis leading to appropriate decisions for special order, outsourcing, segment elimination, and asset replacement decisions.

10 Understand the conflict between short- and long-term profitability.

11 Perform the analysis necessary to make decisions regarding the allocation of scarce resources.

the *curious* manager

© SuperStock

U.S. companies have frequently accused companies of other countries of dumping their products in the United States, selling many of these products below cost. Why would a company be willing to sell its products below cost?

Mary Daniels is a partner in a small investment company. Her research has led her to the conclusion that Secor, Inc. is a likely takeover target by a large multi-national corporation. She is certain that the price of Secor's shares will appreciate significantly in the immediate future and wants to buy some of the shares. Unfortunately, she is fully invested and short of cash. She thinks to herself, I wish I had known this last week when I bought 1,000 shares of Telstar Communications, Inc. at $24 per share. Telstar had recently launched a series of satellites that promised to enable true international phone service. With a small device not much larger than a thick credit card, customers could send and receive phone calls anywhere in the world. The day after Ms. Daniels bought the shares, Telstar announced technical difficulties with the satellites, and the price of its shares dropped to $20 per share. She told herself, These Telstar shares are going nowhere, but if I sell it now, I'll take a $4,000 loss ([$24 cost − $20 market] × 1,000 shares). Ms. Daniels decided to hold the Telstar shares instead of selling them and buying Secor. The Secor shares appeared to be a sure thing, but she did not want to incur a loss. Did Ms. Daniels make the right decision? The topics covered in this chapter will help you answer this question.

▌The Decision Environment

The decision environment is exciting and challenging. Decision makers almost always have incomplete information, and they must speculate, estimate, and anticipate because decisions are future oriented. It seems that the right kind of information is never available but useless information is always abundant. The road to the right decision is paved with thousands of useless facts and figures; decision makers need some way to cut to the core to isolate the useful data. Highly successful executives seem to possess an uncanny ability to identify the relevant revenue and cost data. They always seem to make the right choices. It is not merely a matter of luck; the tricks of the trade are revealed in the following pages.

▌Relevant Information

LO1

Identify the characteristics of relevant information.

What distinguishes relevant from useless information? *Relevant information* has two primary characteristics. First, relevant information *indicates differences* between the alternatives. In other words, **relevant information** makes a difference in a decision, but irrelevant information does not. Suppose that you have decided to become a Chartered Financial Analyst and two prestigious banks have offered you a job. You are now trying to decide which offer to accept. Both offers include identical salaries. Under these circumstances, salary is not a relevant factor in the decision-making process. In other words, because salary does not differ between the alternatives, it cannot be a factor in determining which offer to accept. This does not mean that salary is totally unimportant, but it is not *relevant* for this specific decision. If you receive a third offer that includes a significantly different salary, salary then becomes *relevant* because it would enable you to differentiate this offer from the other two. *The point to remember is that relevant information **differs** between the alternatives under consideration.*

A second characteristic of relevant information is that it is *future oriented.* "There is no use in crying over spilt milk." "It's water under the bridge." These aphorisms help people avoid the common mistake of trying to change the past. Applying the concept to business decisions, we note that *you cannot avoid a cost that has already been incurred.* To illustrate, return to the case presented in the opening paragraph of this chapter. Recall that Mary Daniels had purchased 1,000 shares of Telstar at $24 per share. She had an opportunity to sell Telstar at $20 per share and invest the proceeds in Secor, the price of which was expected to rise because the company was rumoured to be the target of a takeover attempt. She decided to hold the investment in Telstar because she did not want to take a loss. Was the decision to hold the shares a good one?

We cannot say whether Ms. Daniels will make more or less money by deciding to hold the Telstar shares. The price of the shares of either company could go up or down. However, we can say that the decision was based on *irrelevant* data. *Ms. Daniels incurred a loss at the time the price dropped.* She cannot *avoid* a loss that has already occurred. Past mistakes should not affect current decisions. Owning the Telstar shares is equivalent to having $20,000 cash today. The relevant question is whether the $20,000 should be invested in Telstar or Secor. If the answer is Secor, she should sell the Telstar shares and buy the Secor shares.

LO2

Recognize sunk costs and understand why these costs are not relevant in decision making.

The investment in the Telstar shares referred to is an example of what accountants call a *sunk cost.* A **sunk cost** is a cost that has been incurred in past transactions; it represents historical facts that cannot be changed by a current decision. *Since **sunk costs** have already been incurred in past transactions, they cannot be avoided and therefore are not relevant for decision-making purposes.*

You may be wondering why we even bother to gather historical information if it is not relevant. Historical information may provide insight into the future. A company that earned $5,000,000 last year is more likely to earn $5,000,000 this year than a company that earned $5,000 last year. Accordingly, the historical information's predictive capacity provides relevance. *Clearly, relevant information must be **future** oriented.*

Suppose that Ms. Daniels is not naive but fully understands the sunk cost concept and believes that she should sell the Telstar shares. Now, let us change the circumstances slightly. Assume that she is an investment counsellor and that she purchased the Telstar shares for one of her clients. If she advises her client to sell the shares now, he will know that she gave him bad advice when she told him to buy it. He may lose faith in her abilities and terminate his account. On the other hand, she knows that the client would be better served by knowing the truth. Should she tell him? There is no easy answer to this question. If the client is smart, however, he will appreciate the fact that Ms. Daniels has the courage to admit her mistakes; a person who can do so is in a position to take corrective action. Ms. Daniels hopes that the switch from Telstar to Secor will make money for the client and restore his confidence. Anyway, trying to hide the truth is likely to have its own set of adverse effects. The client will eventually realize that the Telstar investment is not performing and will know that he got bad investment advice. Discovering the condition is truly a matter of *when* rather than *if*. In addition, failing to perform at peak level tends to put a person on a cycle of decline; distinguishing what the person truly believes in from what she thinks will serve her immediate interests becomes increasingly more difficult. Gradually, the person loses the ability to think clearly, which impairs performance. In the long term, honesty is not only the right thing but also the most effective strategy for attaining success.

©VCG/FPG International

Relevant (Differential) Revenues

As the preceding discussion suggests, *relevant revenues are the expected future revenues that differ between the alternatives under consideration*. Accordingly, they may also be called *differential revenues*. The primary goal of a profit-oriented business is to maximize net income. When evaluating income opportunities, managers choose the option that will maximize revenues and/or minimize costs. All other things being equal, a profit-oriented business seeks to attain all the revenue that it can. When deciding between two alternative business opportunities, a manager selects the alternative that produces the highest revenue relative to its associated costs. If the two alternatives are expected to produce the same revenue relative to cost, revenue is not relevant because it would not make a *difference* in the amount of net income that could be *obtained in the future*.

LO3
Understand what the term *differential revenue* means.

Relevant (Avoidable) Costs

Profit-oriented businesses seek to minimize cost. In other words, managers try to *avoid* costs, whenever possible. Indeed, **relevant costs** are frequently called **avoidable costs**; they are the costs that can be eliminated by taking a specified course of action. For example, suppose that Pecks Department Stores sells men's, women's, and children's clothing and is considering the possibility of discontinuing the children's line. Some of the costs that could be avoided by the elimination include the cost of merchandise; the salaries of the buyers and the sales staff; the cost of interest on debt used to finance the inventory; packaging and transportation; insurance; lost, damaged, and stolen merchandise; bad debts; shopping bags, sales slips, price tags, and other supplies. Many other costs could not be avoided, however, and would stay the same, regardless of whether the children's line is eliminated. For example, the company president's salary cannot be avoided by closing down the children's line; it does not differ between the alternatives of keeping the children's line and eliminating it. Either way, the president's salary stays

LO4
Understand what the terms *avoidable cost* and *differential cost* mean.

the same. Other examples of costs that cannot be avoided include amortization on the buildings, rent, property taxes, general advertising, and storewide utilities. *Costs that do not differ between the alternative courses of action are not avoidable and therefore are not relevant to making a decision.*

Revenues as well as expenses are affected by a decision to discontinue the children's clothing line. Obviously, revenues will be less if the clothes are not sold. Before making a decision to eliminate a product line, management must compare the decline in revenue with the avoidable costs. If the avoidable costs (i.e., amount that can be saved) exceed the decline in revenue, the children's line should be eliminated. As discussed later, many qualitative (nonfinancial) factors must be considered when making decisions. From a quantitative perspective, however, the critical factors are the amount of the *relevant* (i.e., differential) *revenue* and the amount of the *relevant* (i.e., differential or avoidable) *cost*.

Relationship of Cost Avoidance to a Cost Hierarchy

LO5

Distinguish among unit-level, product-level, and facility-level costs and understand how these costs are related to decision making.

The identification of avoidable costs can be facilitated by classifying the costs in one of four hierarchical levels.[1] As indicated here, the costs associated with each level can be avoided by eliminating the services or products that compose the level.

1. *Unit-Level Costs.* The costs incurred each time a company generates a product are **unit-level costs**.[2] Examples include the cost of materials, labour, inspections, packaging, shipping, and handling. Incremental (i.e., additional) unit-level costs increase with *each additional unit of product generated. Unit-level costs can be avoided by eliminating the production of a single unit of product.* In other words, the elimination of a single product can avoid the cost of materials, labour, and so on that would have been used to make that product.

2. *Batch-Level Costs.* Products are frequently organized into batches of work, rather than in individual units. For example, a heating and air-conditioning technician may be assigned to service a batch of air conditioners in an apartment complex. Some costs incurred on the job relate to the entire batch of work, and other costs apply only to individual units. For instance, the labour expended on each air conditioner is classified as a unit-level cost, but the time spent planning the work and setting up the equipment to take to the job site are **batch-level costs**. Similarly, the parts used on each air conditioner are unit-level costs, but the gas used to drive the service truck to the complex is a batch-level cost.

    The classification of costs into unit- versus batch-level categories frequently depends on the context, rather than the type of cost. For example, shipping and handling costs to send 200 computers to a university are batch-level costs. In contrast, the shipping and handling cost to deliver a single computer to each of a number of individual customers is a unit-level cost. The elimination of a batch of work can avoid both batch-level and unit-level costs. Similarly, the addition of a batch of work increases batch-level and unit-level costs. Increasing the number of units made or serviced in a particular batch of work increases unit-level costs but not batch-level costs. Likewise, decreasing the number of units in a batch reduces unit-level costs but not batch-level costs.

3. *Product-Level Costs.* Costs that are incurred to support specific products or services are called **product-level costs**. Examples of product-level costs include quality inspection costs, the costs of engineering efforts necessary to maintain design specifications, the costs of obtaining and protecting patents, the costs of regulatory compliance, and inventory holding costs, including interest, insurance, maintenance, and storage. *Product-level costs can be avoided when a product line is discontinued.* For example, suppose that Snapper Company makes the engines used in its lawn mowers. A decision to buy from an outside supplier instead enables Snapper to avoid the associated

[1] R. Cooper and R. S. Kaplan, *The Design of Cost Management Systems* (Englewood Cliffs, NJ: Prentice-Hall, 1991). Our definitions are broader than those typically presented. Our classifications are designed to encompass service and merchandising companies as well as manufacturing businesses. The original cost hierarchy was developed as a platform for activity-based costing, a topic we will introduce later, but we have found these classifications are equally effective as a tool for identification of avoidable costs.

[2] Recall that we use the term *product* in a generic sense to represent the production of goods or services.

product-level costs, such as the legal cost of patents, the manufacturing supervisory costs of producing the engines, and the maintenance and inventory costs of holding engine parts.

4. *Facility-Level Costs*. **Facility-level costs** are incurred on behalf of the entire company and therefore are not related to any specific product, batch, or unit of production. Because these costs are incurred to maintain the facility as a whole, they are frequently called *facility-sustaining costs*. Examples of these costs include rent, amortization, personnel administration and training, property and real estate taxes, insurance, maintenance, administrative salaries, selling costs, landscaping, utilities, and security. Total facility-level costs cannot be avoided unless the entire company is dissolved. However, a decision to eliminate a segment of a business (i.e., a division, department, office) may enable the avoidance of some facility-level costs. For example, if a bank eliminates one of its branches, it can avoid the costs of building rental, maintenance, insurance, and so forth associated with the operation of that particular branch. In general, *segment-level facility costs* can be avoided when a segment is eliminated. In contrast, *corporate-level facility costs* cannot be avoided unless the corporation is eliminated.

In practice, the distinctions between the various categories are often blurred. One company may classify sales staff salaries as a facility-level cost, while another company may pay commissions that it could trace to product lines or even specific units of a product line. Accordingly, you cannot master the art of cost classification through memorization. Instead, you must exercise judgment when classifying specific cost items into the designated categories.

Relevance Is an Independent Concept

The concept of relevance is independent from the concept of cost behaviour. More specifically, a relevant cost can be fixed or variable. To illustrate the independent characteristics of relevant costs, consider the following scenario. Executives of Better Bakery Products are considering the addition of a new product to the company's line of goods. They are trying to decide whether the production of cakes or pies would be more profitable. The following costs have been accumulated for the two options:

LO6

Understand that relevance is a unique concept and its application is context sensitive.

Cost of Cakes			Cost of Pies		
Materials (per unit)	$	1.50	Materials (per unit)	$	2.00
Direct labour (per unit)		1.00	Direct labour (per unit)		1.00
Supervisor's salary*		25,000.00	Supervisor's salary*		25,000.00
Franchise fee†		50,000.00	Advertising‡		40,000.00

*It will be necessary to hire a new production supervisor at a cost of $25,000 per year.

†Cakes will be distributed under a nationally advertised label. Better Bakery pays an annual franchise fee for the right to use the product label. Because of the established brand name, Better Bakery will not be required to advertise the product.

‡Better Bakery will market the pies under its own name and will advertise the product in the local market in which the product is sold.

Which costs are relevant? Fifty cents per unit of the materials can be avoided by choosing to make cakes instead of pies. A portion of the materials cost is therefore relevant. One dollar per unit of labour will be incurred, regardless of whether cakes or pies are made. Accordingly, this cost is not relevant. Note that although both materials and direct labour are variable costs, one is relevant but the other is not. Since the supervisor's salary will be incurred regardless of which alternative is selected, it is not relevant. The franchise fee can be avoided if pies are made and advertising costs can be avoided if cakes are made. All three of these costs are fixed, but two are relevant and one is not. Indeed, all of the costs (fixed and variable) could be avoided if the bakery chooses to reject both products. Clearly, whether a cost is fixed or variable has no bearing on its relevance.

Relevance of Opportunity Costs

LO7

Identify
opportunity
costs and
understand
why these
costs are
relevant in
decision
making.

Suppose that you pay $50 to acquire a highly desirable ticket to an Olympic event. Just before entering the stadium, someone offers to buy your ticket for $500. If you refuse the offer, how much will it cost you to attend the event? From the perspective of managerial accounting, the answer is $500. The $50 original purchase price is a *sunk cost* and is not relevant to the decision at hand. The decision involves a choice between attending and not attending the Olympic event. The $500 offer differs between the alternatives and is future oriented; it is therefore relevant. If you enter the stadium, you give up the *opportunity* to obtain $500 cash. The sacrifice of a potential benefit associated with a lost opportunity is called an **opportunity cost**.

Suppose that you turn down the first offer to sell your ticket for $500. A few minutes later, another person offers you $600 for the ticket. If you refuse the second offer, does this mean that your opportunity cost has risen to $1,100 (the first $500 offer plus the second $600 offer)? The answer is, no; opportunity costs are not cumulative. If you had accepted the first offer, you could not have accepted the second. You may have many opportunities, but the acceptance of one of the alternatives eliminates the possibility of accepting the others. Normally, the opportunity cost is considered to be the highest value of the available alternative courses of action. In this case, the opportunity cost of attending the Olympic event is $600.

Opportunity costs are not recorded in the financial accounting records, but they represent an information factor used in decision making. Remember that financial accounting is historically based, but opportunity costs are future oriented. They affect the decisions that managers make. The financial results of those decisions appear in the financial statements, but the information used to make the decisions does not. The fact that opportunity costs are not recorded does not negate their importance, although they are not a part of the financial accounting system, they are an integral part of management accounting. You would not report the $600 opportunity cost as an expense on the income statement, but it will certainly affect your decision regarding whether you attend the Olympic event. *Opportunity costs are relevant costs.*

Context-Sensitive Relevance

The very same cost that is classified as relevant in one context may be identified as irrelevant in another context. Consider the salary of a manager of a store that carries men's, women's, and children's clothing. The store manager's salary could not be avoided by the elimination of the children's department, but it could be avoided if the entire store were closed. Accordingly, the salary is not relevant with respect to a decision regarding the elimination of the children's department but is relevant with respect to a decision regarding the closing of the store. In one context, the salary is not relevant. In the other context, it is relevant. As this example implies, there is no way to provide a list of all relevant costs. The classification of a particular cost as relevant or irrelevant depends on the unique set of circumstances applicable to the decision at hand. You must focus on understanding the concept, rather than trying to memorize some list of relevant costs.

Relationship between Relevance and Accuracy

Information does not have to be precisely accurate to be relevant. Knowing that the price of a piece of equipment is going to drop can delay a decision to purchase even if you do not know the exact amount of the expected decrease. In other words, you know that part of the cost can be avoided by waiting; you are just not sure of the exact amount. Obviously, the most useful information is highly relevant and precisely accurate. It is equally obvious that information that is totally inaccurate is useless. Likewise, information that is irrelevant is useless, regardless of how accurate it may be. What level of accuracy is required for information to be relevant? The degree of accuracy required differs among decision makers and for decisions made by the same person. The balance between accuracy and relevance is one more factor requiring judgment on the part of management accountants.

Quantitative versus Qualitative Characteristics of Decision Making

Relevant information can have both **quantitative** and **qualitative characteristics**. The previous discussion focused on quantitative data. Now, let us consider some qualitative issues. Suppose that you are trying to decide which of two computers to purchase. Computer A costs $300 more than Computer B. Both computers conform to the required performance standards; however, Computer A is housed in a more attractive case. On the basis of quantitative considerations, an argument could be made for selecting Computer B. You could avoid $300 of cost by purchasing this machine. Even so, the final selection may be affected by the qualitative features. If the machine will be used in instances when clients need to be impressed, appearance may be more important than cost minimization, so Computer A might be purchased even though the quantitative analysis suggested otherwise. Both qualitative and quantitative data are relevant to decision making. Both features must be evaluated to make the choice.

As with quantitative data, *relevant* qualitative features *differ* between the alternatives. If both computers were housed in the same type of case, attractiveness would not be relevant to a decision regarding the selection of one computer versus the other.

LO8
Distinguish between quantitative and qualitative characteristics of decision making

▮ Relevant Information and Special Decisions

Five types of special decisions are frequently encountered in business practice: (1) special order, (2) outsourcing, (3) segment elimination, (4) asset replacement, and (5) scarce resource allocation. The following sections discuss the use of relevant information in making the first four types of special decisions. The Appendix to this chapter discusses decisions involving scarce resources.

Special Order Decisions

Occasionally, a company receives an offer to sell its goods at a price significantly below its normal selling price. The company must evaluate this offer carefully before it makes a **special order decision** to accept or reject it. To illustrate, assume that Stoerner Office Products makes three types of office equipment, including copy machines, computers, and printers. Stoerner expects to make and sell 2,000 printers in 10 batches containing 200 units per batch during the coming year. The expected cost of production includes unit-level costs for materials, labour, and overhead. The batch-level costs include assembly setup and materials handling. The company expects to incur product-level costs for engineering design and the salary of a production manager. In addition, facility-level costs associated with the printer division include administrative salaries, amortization, and general operating expenses. The budgeted costs for the expected production of 2,000 units of product are summarized Exhibit 4–1.

After adding the normal markup to the total cost per unit, Stoerner set the selling price at $360 per printer. Suppose that Stoerner receives a *special order* for 200 printers that would require production above the expected level of production. In other words, if Stoerner accepts the order, the company's expected sales would increase from 2,000 units to 2,200 printers. It has *excess productive capacity* and is able to make the additional units without disrupting service to its regular customers. Unfortunately, the special order customer is willing to pay only $250 per printer. This price is well below not only

LO9
Perform analysis leading to appropriate decisions for special order, outsourcing, segment elimination, and asset replacement decisions.

Stoerner's normal selling price of $360 but also the company's expected per unit cost of $329.25. Should Stoerner accept or reject the special order? At first glance, it appears that it should reject the special order because the price is below the expected cost per unit. Analyzing relevant costs and revenue, however, leads to a different conclusion.

Analysis of Relevant Costs and Revenue

We begin by considering what happens to existing costs and revenue if Stoerner accepts the special order. Some of the costs shown in Exhibit 4–1 will not be affected by a decision to accept the special order. Specifically, the product-level and facility-level costs will be incurred, even if Stoerner rejects the special order. Because these costs are the same, regardless of whether the special order is accepted or rejected, they are not relevant to the decision at hand. The *relevant costs,* are the additional costs that will be incurred as a result of accepting the special order. These costs are the *unit-level costs*, including materials, labour, and overhead. Furthermore, *batch-level costs* are relevant because the company must produce an additional batch to fill the special order. The unit- and batch-level costs are relevant because they could be avoided if the special offer were rejected. In addition, the amount of revenue will change if Stoerner accepts the special order. Specifically, the amount of revenue will increase by $50,000 ($250 × 200 units) if Stoerner accepts the special order. The relevant information is shown in Exhibit 4–2.

Exhibit 4-1	Budgeted Cost for Expected Production of 2,000 Printers		
Unit-level costs			
Materials costs (2,000 units × $90)		$180,000	
Labour costs (2,000 units × $82.50)		165,000	
Overhead (2,000 units × $7.50)		15,000	
Total unit-level costs (2,000 × $180)			$360,000
Batch-level costs			
Assembly setup (10 batches × $1,700)		17,000	
Materials handling (10 batches × $500)		5,000	
Total batch-level costs (10 batches × $2,200)			22,000
Product-level costs			
Engineering design		14,000	
Production manager salary		63,300	
Total product-level costs			77,300
Facility level costs			
Segment-level costs			
Division manager's salary		85,000	
Administrative costs		12,700	
Corporate-level costs			
Company president's salary		43,200	
Amortization		27,300	
General expenses		31,000	
Total facility-level costs			199,200
Total expected cost			$658,500
Cost per unit: $658,500 ÷ 2,000 = $329.25			

Exhibit 4-2	*Relevant Information for Special Order of 200 Printers*	
Differential revenue ($250 × 200 units)		$50,000
Avoidable unit-level costs ($180 × 200 units)		(36,000)
Avoidable batch-level costs ($2,200 × 1 batch)		(2,200)
Contribution to income		$11,800

Because differential revenue exceeds the relevant avoidable costs, quantitative factors suggest that Stoerner should accept the offer. As indicated, accepting the offer will increase profitability by $11,800.

Opportunity Cost Consideration

Suppose that Stoerner has an opportunity to lease the equipment and buildings that constitute its excess capacity for $15,000. This would change the decision to accept the special order. Using the excess capacity to make printers would force Stoerner to give up the opportunity to lease the excess capacity to a third party. The sacrifice of the potential income from the lease is an opportunity cost that will be incurred if the special order is accepted. When the opportunity cost is added to the other relevant costs, the total cost becomes $53,200 ($38,200 unit-level and batch-level costs + $15,000 opportunity cost). Because the avoidable costs would then exceed the differential revenue, the result would be a projected loss of $3,200 ($50,000 differential revenue − $53,200 avoidable costs). Under these circumstances Stoerner should reject the special order but should lease the excess capacity. In other words, the company would be better off to lease the excess capacity than to produce and sell the 200 additional printers.

Relevance and the Decision Context

Return to the assumption that Stoerner does not have the opportunity to lease the excess capacity. Recall that the original data suggested that the company could earn an $11,800 contribution to profit by accepting the special order to sell printers at $250 per unit (see Exhibit 4–2). Because Stoerner can earn a contribution to profit at a price of $250 each, does this mean the company can lower its normal selling price (price charged to existing customers) to this amount? The answer is, no. The analysis shown in Exhibit 4–3 illustrates the reason.

Exhibit 4-3	*Projections Based on 2,200 Printers at a Sales Price of $250 per Unit*	
Revenue ($250 × 2,200)		$ 550,000
Unit-level supplies and inspection ($180 × 2,200 units)	$396,000	
Batch-level costs ($2,200 × 11 batches)	24,200	
Product-level costs	77,300	
Facility-level costs	199,200	
Total cost		(696,700)
Projected loss		$(146,700)

Clearly, the product-level and facility-level costs cannot be totally ignored. If a company is to be profitable, it must ultimately generate revenue in excess of total costs. Although the facility-level and product-level costs are not relevant to the special order, they are relevant to the operation of the business as a whole.

At this point, it should be clear that there is usually a difference between avoidable cost and total cost. When U.S. companies complain that businesses from other countries are selling their products in the United States at a price that is less than cost, they mean full cost (i.e., total cost). Since the avoidable cost may be considerably less than the full cost, products that are sold for less than full cost can still contribute to profitability. This phenomenon explains why products made in Mexico may sell for less in the United States than in Mexico.

Qualitative Characteristics

When should a company reject a special order? Obviously, it should reject it if the additional costs are higher than the additional revenue. Furthermore, rejecting a special order may be appropriate even if projected revenue exceeds relevant costs. Qualitative characteristics may be even more important than the quantitative factors. If Stoerner's regular customers learn that the company had sold printers to other buyers at $250 per unit, they may demand a similar price for the goods they buy. As demonstrated, Stoerner cannot afford to lower the price for all customers. Accordingly, special order customers should reside outside Stoerner's normal sales territory. In addition, the special order customers should be clearly advised that the special price does not apply to repetitive business. If the special order customer becomes a regular customer, conflicts may occur when Stoerner fills its idle capacity with orders from regular customers. At full capacity, Stoerner should reject special orders at reduced prices because filling those orders reduces its ability to satisfy the regular customers who are willing to pay the higher sales price. Cutting off a special order customer who has been permitted to establish a continuing relationship is likely to lead to ill-feelings and harsh words. A business's reputation can depend on how management handles such relationships.

Outsourcing Decisions

LO9

Perform analysis leading to appropriate decisions for special order, outsourcing, segment elimination, and asset replacement decisions.

For a variety of reasons, one company may produce a product or service for less than another company. Wage rates, economies of scale, specialization, level of bureaucracy, motivation, reward structure, technological competence, degree of automation, and many other cost-related factors differ among companies. As a result, a company may purchase a product or service at a price below its cost to make the product or provide it. This situation explains why automobile companies purchase rather than make many of the parts in their cars. The practice of buying goods and services from other companies is commonly known as **outsourcing**. Determining the relevant cost of buying goods or services is usually an easy task. First, what happens to existing cost if the product or service is outsourced must be determined. Some costs will be unaffected, and other costs will decrease. If the company buys the products, it will not have to pay to have them made. The firm then compares the potential decrease in existing costs with the cost of buying (outsourcing). Cost minimization is achieved by selecting the make-or-buy alternative with the lowest relevant costs.

To illustrate, assume that Stoerner is considering the purchase of the printers that it now makes. A supplier has offered to sell an unlimited supply of printers to Stoerner for $240 each. A quick review of Exhibit 4–1 indicates that Stoerner expects the cost of making printers to be $329.25 per unit. This information suggests that Stoerner could buy the printers for less than it can make them. Analysis of relevant costs proves this conclusion wrong, however.

Analysis of Relevant Costs

What happens to existing costs if Stoerner decides to outsource the printers? Begin by reviewing the information in Exhibit 4–1. A decision to outsource will not affect some costs, for example, the facility-level costs will be incurred, regardless of whether Stoerner outsources the printers. Accordingly, these costs are not relevant to the outsourcing decision. In contrast, the relevant costs are those costs that could be avoided if Stoerner purchases the printers. Clearly, purchasing would avoid unit-level and batch-level production costs. If Stoerner purchases the products, it would eliminate the cost of materials, labour, overhead, batch set-up costs, and the materials handling cost. Likewise, it could avoid the product-level costs. Stoerner could eliminate engineering design costs and could lay off the production supervisor, thereby eliminating her salary. Because these costs could be avoided if Stoerner buys the printers, they are relevant to the decision-making process. The relevant (avoidable) costs associated with a decision to outsource the printers are shown in Exhibit 4–4.

Because the relevant cost of production is lower than the purchase price of the printers ($229.65 per unit versus $240), the quantitative analysis suggests that Stoerner should continue to make the printers. Indeed, it can expect profit to decline by $20,700 ($459,300 − [$240 × 2,000]) if the printers are outsourced.

Suppose that Stoerner's accountant identified another cost item that had not been included in the original cost data. The space currently being used to manufacture printers could be converted to warehouse space for finished goods. By using this space for warehouse storage, Stoerner could save $40,000 per year that it currently spends to rent warehouse space. This information would change the decision to continue the production of printers. By using the space to manufacture printers, Stoerner is *forgoing the opportunity* to save $40,000 in warehouse

Exhibit 4-4	Relevant Cost for Expected Production for Outsourcing 2,000 Printers
Unit-level costs ($180 × 2,000)	$360,000
Batch-level costs ($2,200 × 10)	22,000
Product-level costs	77,300
Total relevant cost	$459,300
Cost per unit: $459,300 ÷ 2,000 = $229.65	

costs. Because the *opportunity cost* can be avoided by purchasing the printers, it is relevant to the outsourcing decision. When the opportunity cost is added to the other relevant costs, the total relevant cost increases to $499,300 ($459,300 + $40,000). Accordingly, the relevant cost per unit becomes $249.65 ($499,300 ÷ 2,000). Because this amount is higher than the purchase price of $240, Stoerner should outsource the printers. In other words, it would be better off buying the printers and using the warehouse space to store the finished goods than continuing producing the printers.

Evaluation of the Effect of Growth on the Level of Production

The decision to outsource would change if the level of production increased to 3,000 units. Because some of the avoidable costs are fixed relative to the level of production, cost per unit decreases as volume increases. For example, assume that the product-level costs, including the cost of engineering design, the production supervisor's salary, and the opportunity cost, are fixed relative to the level of production. On the basis of these assumptions, relevant cost per unit is computed as shown in Exhibit 4–5.

Exhibit 4-5	Relevant Cost for Expected Production for Outsourcing 3,000 Printers
Unit-level costs ($180 × 3,000)	$540,000
Batch-level costs ($2,200 × 15)	33,000
Product-level costs	77,300
Opportunity cost	40,000
Total relevant cost	$690,300
Cost per unit: $690,300 ÷ 3,000 = $230.10	

At 3,000 units of production, the relevant cost of making printers is less than the cost of outsourcing ($230.10 versus $240). If management believes that the company is likely to experience growth in the near future, it should reject the outsourcing option. This case demonstrates that managers must consider potential growth when making outsourcing decisions.

Qualitative Features

A company that controls the full range of activities from the acquisition of raw materials to the distribution of goods or services is said to be **vertically integrated**. Outsourcing reduces the level of vertical integration and thereby forces the company to relinquish its absolute control of the enterprise. Accordingly, the reliability of the supplier is a critical consideration in the outsourcing decision. An unscrupulous supplier may lure an unsuspecting manufacturer into an outsourcing decision through a practice known as **low-ball pricing**. Once the manufacturer comes to depend on the supplier, the supplier raises prices. Problems can also emerge with respect to quality issues and delivery commitments. Poor quality reflects on the seller's reputation. Stoerner's customers will be angry with it if the printers do not work and will not be content with an excuse that blames the supplier. Similarly, if a supplier fails to deliver printers on schedule, Stoerner's customers will blame it, not the supplier, for late deliveries. Stoerner depends on the supplier to deliver quality goods at the designated price, according to a specified schedule. Failures of the supplier become Stoerner's failures.

To protect themselves from unscrupulous or incompetent suppliers, many companies establish a select list of **certified suppliers** with whom they strive to develop mutually beneficial relationships. These companies offer incentives, such as guarantees to purchase mass quantities with rapid payment schedules. In essence, the companies seek to become the preferred customers of the suppliers, thereby motivating the suppliers to adhere to strict quality standards and delivery schedules. The buyers understand that prices depend on the suppliers' ability to control costs. Accordingly, the buyers and suppliers work together to minimize costs. For example, buyers might share confidential information about their production plans with suppliers if such information would enable the suppliers to better plan their activities to effectively control costs.

focus on International Issues

Outsourcing—How Do They Do It in Japan?

Many outsourcing opportunities suffer from a lack of long-term commitment. For example, a supplier may be able to attain economic efficiencies by redesigning its facilities to produce a product needed by a special order customer. Unfortunately, the redesign cost cannot be recovered on a small order quantity. The supplier needs assurances of a long-term relationship to justify a significant investment in the supply relationship. Japanese businesses have resolved this condition through what is sometimes called obligational contract relationships. While these contracts are renewable annually, most suppliers expect to form a supply relationship that will last more than five years. Indeed, Japanese custom establishes a commitment between the supplier and the buyer that includes the exchange of sensitive cost information. If deficiencies in price, delivery, or quality conformance occur, the buyer is likely to send production engineers to the offices of the supplier. The buyer's engineers will study the facilities of the supplier and give detailed advice as to how to achieve improved results. In the process of analyzing the supplier's operations, the buyer obtains detailed information regarding the supplier's costs. This information is used to negotiate prices that ensure reasonable, rather than excessive, profits for the supplier. Accordingly, costs are controlled for not only the supplier but the buyer as well.

Source: Miles B. Gietzmann, "Emerging Practices in Cost Accounting," *Management Accounting (UK)*, January 1995, pp. 24–25. ©SuperStock

Companies must approach the outsourcing decision with caution even when relationships with reliable suppliers are secure. These companies must direct attention to internal as well as external effects. Outsourcing usually involves employee displacement. Once a trained workforce has been dissolved, it cannot be easily replaced. If conditions with the supplier deteriorate, the reestablishment of internal production capacity will be expensive. Former employees may be reluctant to return to a company that had previously discharged them. Trust and loyalty are difficult to develop but easy to destroy. With this in mind, companies must consider not only the effects on the employees who are discharged but also the morale of those who remain. Increased efficiencies gained through outsourcing are of little benefit if they are acquired at the expense of internal productivity.

Having acknowledged the potential pitfalls associated with outsourcing, we must recognize that the vast majority of Canadian businesses engage in some form of the practice. This widespread acceptance suggests that most companies believe that the benefits available through outsourcing exceed the potential shortcomings.

Decisions to Eliminate Segments

Businesses frequently organize information to facilitate comparisons among different products, departments, or divisions. For example, in addition to a single companywide income statement, J. C. Penney may prepare a separate income statement for each store. It can then evaluate managerial performance by comparing profitability measures among stores. Similarly, Ford Motor Company may prepare income statements for each type of automobile it produces to determine, for example, whether it earned a higher return on its investment in the Taurus or the Explorer line. The component parts of an organization that are designated as reporting entities are called **segments**. *Segment reports* can be prepared for products, services, departments, branches, centres, offices, or divisions. These reports normally consist of revenue and cost data. The primary objective of segment analysis is to determine whether relevant revenues exceed the relevant costs.

LO9
Perform analysis leading to appropriate decisions for special order, outsourcing, segment elimination, and asset replacement decisions.

When accounting reports indicate that a particular segment is operating at a net loss, management should consider eliminating that segment. However, the decision should not be made hastily. Although it may seem that eliminating the segment would stop the loss, this is not necessarily the case. For example, company-level facility costs that have been allocated to the segment will continue to be incurred, even if the segment is eliminated. The subject of *allocation* will be discussed in Chapters 6 and 7. At this point, it is sufficient to note that the term means to divide a total into parts and to assign those parts to certain objects. For example, the $93,000 of general corporate-level facility expenses have been divided equally among the three segments, thereby assigning $31,000 to each segment. Because the $93,000 of cost is incurred, at the corporate level, it will continue to be incurred, even when the segment is eliminated. In other words, eliminating the segment does not eliminate the corporate-level activities that cause the $93,000 of cost to be incurred. Clearly, the other two corporate-level facility costs (i.e., division manager's salary and amortization) have not been allocated equally to the three segments. A total cost can be allocated between the three segments in many ways. A full discussion of these alternatives will be provided in the subsequent chapters.

Only the costs that can be avoided by eliminating the segment are relevant to the decision-making process. If the revenue generated by a segment is higher than the avoidable cost, that segment should not be eliminated. To illustrate, we analyze the information in the cost report for Stoerner Office Products that is shown in Exhibit 4–6. As the report indicates, Stoerner divides its operations into three divisions: copiers, computers, and printers.

It appears that Stoerner would be better off by eliminating the copiers segment. You may conclude that by eliminating the segment, the business could avoid the $22,250 loss, thereby increasing overall profitability to $257,750 ($136,250 + $121,500). Analysis of the relevant costs and revenue proves, however, that this conclusion is incorrect.

Exhibit 4-6	Projected Revenue and Costs by Segment			
	Copiers	**Computers**	**Printers**	**Total**
Projected revenue	$ 550,000	$ 850,000	$ 780,000	$ 2,180,000
Projected costs				
Unit-level costs				
Materials costs	(120,000)	(178,000)	(180,000)	(478,000)
Labour costs	(160,000)	(202,000)	(165,000)	(527,000)
Overhead	(30,800)	(20,000)	(15,000)	(65,800)
Batch- level costs				
Assembly setup	(15,000)	(26,000)	(17,000)	(58,000)
Materials-handling	(6,000)	(8,000)	(5,000)	(19,000)
Product-level costs				
Engineering design	(10,000)	(12,000)	(14,000)	(36,000)
Production manager's salary	(52,000)	(55,800)	(63,300)	(171,100)
Facility-level costs				
Segment level				
Division manager's salary	(82,000)	(92,000)	(85,000)	(259,000)
Administrative costs	(12,200)	(13,200)	(12,700)	(38,100)
Allocated—corporate level				
Company president's salary	(34,000)	(46,000)	(43,200)	(123,200)
Amortization	(19,250)	(29,750)	(27,300)	(76,300)
General expenses	(31,000)	(31,000)	(31,000)	(93,000)
Projected profit (loss)	$(22,250)	$136,250	$ 121,500	$ 235,500

Analysis of Relevant Costs and Revenue

Begin by asking what happens to existing costs if Stoerner eliminates the copiers division. The allocated portion of corporate-level facility costs would be incurred, even if Stoerner stopped making and selling copiers. Further, amortization cannot be avoided because it is a *sunk cost*. Accordingly, the corporate-level facility costs are not relevant. Many other costs, including the segment-level facility costs, the product-level costs, the batch-level costs, and the unit-level costs, could be avoided, however, if the copiers division were eliminated. If the revenue generated from the sale of copiers exceeds these avoidable costs, Stoerner should continue to operate the segment. The relevant revenue and cost items are summarized in Exhibit 4–7.

Because the operation of the segment is contributing $62,000 per year to the store's profitability, Stoerner should continue to operate the copiers division. Indeed, elimination of the segment would cause profitability to decline by $62,000. This point can be verified by reconstructing the revenue and cost data as if the computers and printers divisions were operated without the copiers division. The reconstructed data are shown in Exhibit 4–8. Note that the projected profit declines by $62,000 ($235,500 − $173,500) without the operation of the copiers segment, confirming the fact that the elimination of the copiers segment would be detrimental to Stoerner's profitability.

Exhibit 4-7	Relevant Revenue and Cost Data for Copiers Segment
Projected revenue	$550,000
Projected costs	
Unit-level costs	
Materials costs	(120,000)
Labour costs	(160,000)
Overhead	(30,800)
Batch-level costs	
Assembly setup	(15,000)
Materials handling	(6,000)
Product-level costs	
Engineering design	(10,000)
Production manager's salary	(52,000)
Facility-level costs	
Segment-level	
Division manager's salary	(82,000)
Administrative costs	(12,200)
Projected profit (loss)	$ 62,000

Exhibit 4-8	Projected Revenue and Costs without Copiers Division		
	Computers	**Printers**	**Total**
Projected revenue	$850,000	$780,000	$1,630,000
Unit-level costs			
Materials costs	(178,000)	(180,000)	(358,000)
Labour costs	(202,000)	(165,000)	(367,000)
Overhead	(20,000)	(15,000)	(35,000)
Batch-level costs			
Assembly setup	(26,000)	(17,000)	(43,000)
Materials handling	(8,000)	(5,000)	(13,000)
Product-level costs			
Engineering design	(12,000)	(14,000)	(26,000)
Production manager's salary	(55,800)	(63,300)	(119,100)
Facility-level costs			
Segment level			
Division manager's salary	(92,000)	(85,000)	(177,000)
Administrative costs	(13,200)	(12,700)	(25,900)
Corporate level*			
Company president's salary	(63,000)	(60,200)	(123,200)
Amortization	(39,375)	(36,925)	(76,300)
General expenses	(46,500)	(46,500)	(93,000)
Projected profit (loss)	$ 94,125	$ 79,375	$ 173,500

*The corporate-level facility costs that were previously *allocated* to the copiers division have been reassigned on the basis of one-half to the computer division and one-half to the printer division.

Qualitative Considerations in Decisions to Eliminate Segments

As with other special decisions, qualitative factors should be considered when determining whether to eliminate segments. For example, employees' services will be disrupted; some may be moved into other areas of the company, but others will be discharged. Once a trained work force is dissolved, reestablishing it is difficult if the company decides to resume the segment's operation later. Furthermore, employees in other segments, suppliers, customers, and investors may believe that the elimination of a segment implies that the company, as a whole, is experiencing financial difficulty. These individuals may lose faith in the company and seek business contacts with other companies they perceive to be more stable.

Finally, the sales of different product lines are interdependent. Some customers like one-stop shopping; they want to buy all their office equipment from one supplier. When Stoerner no longer sells copiers, customers may stop buying its computers and printers. Accordingly, the elimination of one segment may result in sales losses in other segments.

What will happen to the space that was used to make the copiers has not yet been asked. Suppose that Stoerner Office Products decides to make telephone systems in the space that it previously used for copiers. The contribution to profit associated with the telephone business would be an *opportunity cost* of operating the copiers segment. As demonstrated in previous examples, adding the opportunity cost to the avoidable costs of operating the copiers segment could change the decision that the previous analysis suggested.

As with outsourcing, changes in the volume can affect elimination decisions. Because many costs associated with operating a segment can be fixed, the cost per unit decreases as production increases. As a result, growth can transform a segment that is currently producing real losses into a segment that produces a real profit. Accordingly, managers must consider growth potential when making elimination decisions.

Summary of Relationships between Avoidable Costs and the Hierarchy of Business Activity

LO5

Distinguish among unit-level, product-level, and facility-level costs and understand how these costs are related to decision making.

You may have noticed a relationship between the cost hierarchy and the different types of special decisions just discussed. Avoidable costs are drawn from increasingly higher levels of the cost hierarchy as the type of decision moves from special order, to outsourcing, to segment elimination. A special order decision involves making additional units of an existing product. A decision to accept a special order affects unit-level and possibly batch-level costs. In contrast, a decision to outsource a product stops the production of that product. Because no products are made, outsourcing can avoid many product-level as well as unit-level and batch-level costs. Finally, if an entire business division is eliminated, some of the facility-level costs can be avoided. As you move up the scale of the decision hierarchy, more opportunities to avoid costs emerge. Moving to a new category does not mean, however, that all costs associated with the higher level of activity are automatically avoidable. For example, all product-level costs may not be avoidable if a company chooses to outsource a product. The company may incur inventory holding costs, regardless of whether it makes or buys the inventory. Understanding the relationship between decision type and level of cost hierarchy can improve your ability to identify avoidable costs. The relationships to look for are summarized in Exhibit 4–9. For each type of decision, look for avoidable costs in the categories marked with an X. Remember also that sunk costs cannot be avoided.

Exhibit 4-9	**Relationship between Decision Type and Level of Cost Hierarchy**			
Decision Type	**Unit Level**	**Batch Level**	**Product Level**	**Facility Level**
Special order	X	X		
Outsourcing	X	X	X	
Elimination	X	X	X	X

Equipment Replacement Decisions

LO9

Perform analysis leading to appropriate decisions for special order, outsourcing, segment elimination, and asset replacement decisions.

Equipment may become technologically deficient long before it deteriorates physically. Accordingly, **equipment replacement decisions** should be determined on the basis of profitability analysis, rather than physical deterioration. To illustrate, consider the replacement analysis performed by the accountant of Stoerner Office Products. Stoerner owns a machine that originally cost $90,000 and is currently being amortized at the rate of $11,000 per year and has accumulated amortization of $33,000. The book value of the machine is $57,000 ($90,000 − $33,000). The machine has a remaining estimated useful life of five years and an estimated salvage value of $2,000. Labour costs associated with operating the machine are $9,000 per year. Stoerner has an opportunity to replace the existing equipment with a new machine that offers efficiencies estimated to reduce labour costs by one-half ($4,500 per year). The old machine can be sold right now for $14,000; the new machine costs $29,000. The expected useful life of the new machine is five years, and its estimated salvage value is $4,000. These facts are summarized here:

Old Machine		**New Machine**	
Original cost	$90,000	Cost of the new machine	$29,000
Accumulated amortization	(33,000)	Salvage value (in 5 years)	4,000
Book value	$57,000	Operating expense	
		($4,500 × 5 years)	22,500
Market value (now)	$14,000		
Salvage value (in 5 years)	2,000		
Annual amortization expense	11,000		
Operating expenses			
($9,000 × 5 years)	45,000		

Analysis of Relevant Costs

The first step in the decision-making process is to determine what relevant costs will be incurred if the old machine is used.

1. The *original cost* ($90,000), *current book value* ($57,000), *accumulated amortization* ($33,000), and *annual amortization expense* ($11,000) are different measures of costs that were incurred in a prior period. As such, they represent sunk costs that are not relevant.
2. The $14,000 market value represents the current sacrifice that must be made to use the existing machine. In other words, if Stoerner does not use the machine, it can sell it for $14,000. From an economic perspective, *forgoing the opportunity* to sell the machine is the same thing as buying it. Accordingly, the *opportunity cost* is relevant to the replacement decision.
3. The salvage value of the old machine reduces the opportunity cost. In other words, Stoerner can sell the old machine today for $14,000 or can use it for five years and then sell it for $2,000. As a result, the opportunity cost of using the old machine for five years is $12,000 ($14,000 − $2,000). Note that the opportunity cost per year is $2,400 ([$14,000 − $2,000] ÷ 5). This computation is consistent with the computation for straight-line amortization. Indeed, the annualized opportunity cost can the thought of as opportunity cost amortization.
4. The $45,000 ($9,000 × 5) of operating expenses will be incurred if the old machine is used but can be avoided if it is replaced. Accordingly, the operating expenses are relevant costs.

Next, determine what relevant costs will be incurred if the new machine is purchased and used.

1. The cost of the new machine represents a future economic sacrifice that must be incurred if the new machine is purchased. Accordingly, it is a relevant cost.
2. The salvage reduces the cost of purchasing the new machine. Although the new machine costs $29,000, part of this amount ($4,000) will be recovered at the end of five years. Accordingly, the relevant cost of purchasing the new machine is $25,000 ($29,000 − $4,000).
3. The $22,500 ($4,500 × 5) of operating expenses will be incurred if the new machine is purchased; it can be avoided if the new machine is not purchased. Accordingly, the operating expenses are relevant costs.

The relevant costs for the two machines are summarized here:

Old Machine		New Machine	
Opportunity cost	$14,000	Cost of the new machine	$29,000
Salvage value	(2,000)	Salvage value	(4,000)
Operating expenses	45,000	Operating expenses	22,500
Total	$57,000	Total	$47,500

The analysis suggests that Stoerner should acquire the new machine because it produces the lowest relevant cost. Stated differently, the $57,000 cost of using the old machine can be *avoided* by incurring the $47,500 cost necessary to acquire and use the new machine. During the five-year period, the company would save $9,500 ($57,000 − $47,500) by purchasing the new machine. Note that the analysis ignores tax considerations and the time value of money. These subjects will be covered in Chapter 10. The present discussion focuses on identifying and using relevant costs in decision making.

a look
back

Decision making requires managers to make choices between alternative courses of action. Successful decision making depends on a manager's ability to identify and isolate the *relevant information*. Information that is relevant for decision making differs among the alternatives and is future oriented. Relevant revenues are sometimes referred to as *differential revenues* because they are the expected future revenues that differ among the alternatives. Relevant costs are sometimes referred to as *avoidable costs* because they are the future costs that can be eliminated or avoided by taking a specified alternative.

Costs that do not differ among the alternatives are not avoidable and therefore not relevant. *Sunk costs* are not relevant in decision making because they have already been incurred in past transactions and therefore cannot be avoided. *Opportunity costs* are relevant because they represent potential benefits that may or may not be realized, depending on the decision maker's action. In other words, future benefits that differ among the alternatives are relevant. Opportunity costs are not recorded in the financial accounting records.

Classifying costs into one of four hierarchical levels can facilitate the identification of relevant costs. *Unit-level* costs, such as materials and labour, are the costs incurred each time a single unit of product is made. These costs can be avoided by eliminating the production of a single unit of product. *Batch-level* costs are the costs associated with the production of a group of products. Examples include setup costs and inspection costs related to a batch (group) of work, rather than a single unit. Eliminating a batch would avoid both batch-level costs and unit-level costs. *Product-level* costs are incurred to support specific kinds of products or services (design and regulatory compliance costs). Product-level costs can be avoided when a product line is discontinued. *Facility-level* costs are incurred for the whole company or a segment of the company; the president's salary is an example. In segment elimination decisions, the facility-level costs related to a particular segment being considered for elimination are relevant and avoidable. Those applying to the company as a whole are not avoidable.

Cost behaviour (i.e., fixed or variable) is independent from the concept of relevance. Furthermore, a cost that is relevant in one decision context may be irrelevant in another context. Decision making depends on quantitative as well as qualitative information. *Quantitative information refers to numbers that can be mathematically manipulated. Qualitative information* is nonquantitative information, such as personal preferences or opportunities.

The four types of special decisions that are frequently encountered in business include (1) *special orders*, (2) *outsourcing*, (3) *elimination decisions*, and (4) *asset replacement*. The relevant costs in a special order decision are the unit-level and batch-level costs that will be incurred if the special order is accepted. If the differential revenue from the special order exceeds the relevant costs, the order should be accepted. Outsourcing decisions must determine whether goods and services should be purchased from other companies. The relevant costs are the unit-level, batch-level, and product-level costs that could be avoided if the company outsources the product or service. If these costs are more than the cost to buy and the qualitative characteristics are satisfactory, the company should outsource. Segment-related unit-level, batch-level, product-level, and facility-level costs that can be avoided when a segment is eliminated are relevant. If the segment's avoidable costs exceed its differential revenue, it should be eliminated, assuming favourable qualitative features. Asset replacement decisions compare the relevant costs of existing equipment with the relevant costs of new equipment to determine whether replacing the old equipment would be profitable.

a look
forward

The next chapter begins a two-chapter investigation of cost measurement. Accountants seek to determine the cost of certain objects. A cost object may be a product, a service, a department, a customer, or any other thing for which the cost is being determined. Some costs can be directly traced to a cost object, others are difficult to trace. Costs that are difficult to trace to cost objects are called *indirect costs* or *overhead*. Indirect costs are assigned to cost objects through a process known as *cost allocation*. The next chapter introduces the basic concepts and procedures associated with cost allocation.

Short-Term versus Long-Term Goals

Suppose that the final equipment replacement decision for Stoerner Office Products is made by a departmental supervisor who is under significant pressure to maximize profitability. She is told if profitability declines, she will lose her job. Under these circumstances, the supervisor may choose to keep the old machine even though it is to the company's advantage to purchase a new one. This occurs because the beneficial impact of the new machine is realized in years 2002 through 2005. Indeed, replacing the equipment will result in more expense/loss recognition in the first year. To illustrate, study the following information:

LO10
Understand the conflict between short- and long-term profitability.

	2001	2002	2003	2004	2005	Totals
Keep Old Machine						
Amortization expense*	$ 11,000	$11,000	$ 11,000	$ 11,000	$ 11,000	$ 55,000
Operating expense	9,000	9,000	9,000	9,000	9,000	45,000
Total	$ 20,000	$20,000	$ 20,000	$ 20,000	$ 20,000	$100,000
Replace Old Machine						
Loss on disposal†	$ 43,000	$ 0	$ 0	$ 0	$ 0	$ 43,000
Amortization expense‡	5,000	5,000	5,000	5,000	5,000	25,000
Operating expense	4,500	4,500	4,500	4,500	4,500	22,500
Total	$ 52,500	$ 9,500	$ 9,500	$ 9,500	$ 9,500	$ 90,500

*($57,000 book value − $2,000 salvage) ÷ 5 years
†($57,000 book value − $14,000 market value)
‡($29,000 cost − $4,000 salvage) ÷ 5 years

This analysis verifies fact that total cost at the end of the five-year period is $9,500 less if the equipment is replaced ($100,000 − $90,500). Note, however, that total costs at the end of the first year are higher by $32,500 ($52,500 − $20,000) if the old machine is replaced. A decision maker under significant pressure to report higher profitability may be willing to sacrifice tomorrow's profits to look better today. By emphasizing short-term profitability, she may secure a promotion before the long-term effects of her decision become apparent. Even if she stays in the same position, her boss may be replaced by someone not so demanding in terms of reported profitability. The department supervisor's intent is to survive the moment and let the future take care of itself. Misguided reward systems can be as detrimental as threats of punishment. For example, a manager may choose short-term profitability to obtain a bonus that is based on reported profitability. It is the responsibility of upper-level management to establish policies and procedures that motivate subordinates to perform in ways that maximize the company's long-term profitability.

Decisions Regarding the Allocation of Scarce Resources

Suppose that Stoerner Office Products makes two types of computers: a high-end network server and an inexpensive personal computer. The relevant sales and variable cost data for each unit follow:

LO11
Perform the analysis necessary to make decisions regarding the allocation of scarce resources.

Network Server		Personal Computer	
Sales price	$ 4,000	Sales price	$ 1,500
Less: Variable cost	(3,760)	Less: Variable cost	(1,370)
Contribution margin	$ 240	Contribution margin	$ 130

In many circumstances, variable costs act as proxies for *avoidable costs*. For example, by definition, unit-level costs increase and decrease in direct proportion with the number of units of product made and sold. As previously indicated, unit-level costs are avoidable with respect to many special decision scenarios. To the extent that variable costs are proxies for avoidable costs, the contribution margin can be used as a measure of profitability. Other things being equal, higher contribution margins translate into more profitable products. If Stoerner could sell 1,000 computers, the company would certainly prefer that they be network servers. The contribution to profitability on those machines is almost double the contribution margin on the personal computer.

Even though the contribution margin is higher for network servers, selling personal computers may be more profitable. Why? If Stoerner can sell considerably more of the personal computers, the volume of activity will make up for the lower margin. In other words, selling three personal computers produces more total margin (3 × $130 = $390) than selling one network server (1 × $240). Many factors could limit the sales of one or both of the products. Factors that limit a business's ability to satisfy the demand for its product are called **constraints**. Suppose that warehouse space is limited (i.e., the warehouse is a scarce resource that constrains sales). Accordingly, Stoerner cannot warehouse all the computers that it needs to satisfy its customer orders. If a network server requires considerably more warehouse space than a personal computer, stocking and selling personal computers may be more profitable than stocking and selling network servers. To illustrate, assume that it requires 5 square feet of warehouse space for a network server and 2 square feet for a personal computer. If only 2,100 square feet of warehouse space are available, which computer should Stoerner stock and sell?

In this case, the warehouse space is considered a scarce resource. The computer that produces the highest contribution margin per unit of scarce resource (i.e., per square foot) is the more profitable product. The per-unit computations for each product are shown here:

	Network Server	Personal Computer
Contribution margin per unit (a)	$240	$130
Divide by warehouse space needed to store one unit (b)	5 sq. ft.	2 sq. ft.
Contribution margin per unit of scarce resource (a ÷ b)	$ 48	$ 65

The data suggest that Stoerner should focus on the personal computer. Even though the personal computer produces a lower contribution margin per product, its contribution margin per scarce resource is higher. The effect on total profitability is shown as follows:

	Network Server	Personal Computer
Amount of available warehouse space (a)	2,100	2,100
Divide by warehouse space needed to store one unit (b)	5 sq. ft.	2 sq. ft.
Warehouse capacity in number of units (a ÷ b) = (c)	420	1,050
Times contribution margin per unit (d)	$240	$130
Total profit potential (c × d)	$100,800	$136,500

Although the quantitative data suggest that Stoerner will maximize profitability by limiting its inventory to personal computers, qualitative considerations may force the company to maintain a reasonable sales mix between the two products. For example, a business that buys several personal computers may also need a network server. A customer who cannot obtain both products from Stoerner may choose to buy nothing at all. Instead, the customer will find a supplier who will satisfy all his needs. In other words, Stoerner may still need to stock some servers to offer a competitive product line.

The chairman of the board of directors asked the president of Stoerner why company sales had remained level, while the company's chief competitor had experienced significant increases. The president replied, "You cannot sell what you do not have. Our warehouse is too small. We stop production when we fill up the warehouse. The products sell out rapidly, and then we have to wait around for the next batch of computers to be made. When we are out of stock, our customers turn to the competition. We are constrained by the size of the warehouse." In accounting terms, the warehouse is a **bottleneck**. Its size is limiting the company's ability to sell its products.

Many businesses use a management practice known as the **theory of constraints (TOC)** to increase profitability by managing bottlenecks or constrained resources. TOC's primary objective is to identify the bottlenecks restricting the operations of the business and then to open those bottlenecks through a practice known as **relaxing the constraints**. The effect of applying TOC to the Stoerner case is apparent via contribution margin analysis. According to the preceding computations, a new server and a new personal computer produce a contribution margin of $48 and $65 per square foot of storage space, respectively. So long as additional warehouse space can be purchased for less than these amounts, Stoerner can increase its profitability by acquiring the space.

Allocation of scarce resource decisions (Appendix) Decisions that consider scarce resources in determining which products to produce and sell, generally made by selecting the product that has the highest contribution margin per unit of scarce resource. *(p. 139)*

Avoidable costs Future costs that are relevant for decision making can be avoided by taking a specified course of action. To be avoidable in a decision-making context, costs must differ among the alternatives. For example, if the cost of material used to make two different products is the same for both products, that cost could not be avoided by choosing to produce one product over the other. Therefore, the material's cost is not an avoidable cost. *(p. 123)*

Batch-level costs Costs associated with producing a batch of products. For example, the cost of setting up machinery to produce 1,000 products is a batch-level cost. The classification of batch-level costs is context sensitive. Postage for one product is classified as a unit-level cost. In contrast, postage for a large number of products delivered in a single shipment is classified as a batch-level cost. *(p. 124)*

Bottleneck (Appendix) A constraint limiting the capacity of a company to produce or sell its products. An example is a

piece of equipment that cannot produce enough component parts to keep employees in the assembly department busy. *(p. 140)*

Certified suppliers Suppliers who have gained the confidence of the buyer by providing quality goods and services at desirable prices and usually in accordance with strict delivery specifications; frequently provide the buyer with preferred customer status in exchange for guaranteed purchase quantities and prompt payment schedules. *(p. 132)*

Constraints (Appendix) Factors that limit a business's ability to satisfy the demand for its product. *(p. 140)*

Differential Costs or revenues that differ among alternative business opportunities and are usually relevant for decision making. Note, however, that not all are relevant. For example, although amortization may differ among the alternatives, it is not avoidable because it is a sunk cost and therefore not relevant for decision making. *(p. 123)*

Equipment replacement decisions Decisions regarding whether existing equipment should be replaced with newer equipment on the basis of identification and comparison of the avoidable costs of the old and new equipment to determine which equipment is more profitable to operate. *(p. 136)*

Facility-level costs Costs incurred for the whole company or a segment of the company; not related to any specific product, batch, or unit of production or service and unavoidable unless the entire company or segment is eliminated. *(p. 125)*

Low-ball pricing Pricing a product below competitors' price to lure customers and then raising the price once customers depend on the supplier for the product. *(p. 132)*

Opportunity costs The revenue or cost savings sacrificed when one alternative is chosen over another in decision making; do not involve actual cash outlays but are relevant to decision making since they can be avoided by choosing the alternative that produces the revenue or cost savings. *(p. 126)*

Outsourcing The practice of buying goods and services from another company, rather than producing them internally. *(p. 130)*

Product-level costs Costs incurred to support different kinds of products or services; can be avoided by the elimination of a product line or a type of service. *(p. 124)*

Qualitative characteristics Nonquantifiable features, such as company reputation, welfare of employees, and customer satisfaction, that can be affected by certain decisions. *(p. 127)*

Quantitative characteristics Numbers in decision making subject to mathe-

matical manipulation, such as the dollar amounts of revenues and expenses. *(p. 127)*

Relaxing the constraints (Appendix) Opening a bottleneck to allow more products or services to be produced or sold. *(p. 140)*

Relevant costs Future-oriented costs that differ among business alternatives; also known as *avoidable costs*. *(p. 123)*

Relevant information Decision-making information about costs, cost savings, or revenues that have these features: (1) future-oriented information and (2) information that differs among the alternatives; decision-specific (i.e., information that is relevant in one decision may not be relevant in another decision). *Relevant costs* are referred to as *avoidable costs* and *relevant revenues* are referred to as *differential revenues*. *(p. 122)*

Segment A component part of an organization that is designated as a reporting entity. *(p. 133)*

Special order decisions Decisions regarding whether to accept orders from nonregular customers who want to buy goods or services significantly below the normal selling price. If the order's differential revenue exceeds its avoidable costs, the order should be accepted. Qualitative features, such as the order's effect on the existing customer base if accepted, must also be considered. *(p. 127)*

Sunk costs Costs that have been incurred in past transactions and therefore are not relevant for decision making. In an equipment replacement decision, the cost of the old machine presently used is a sunk cost and is not avoidable because it has already been incurred. *(p. 122)*

Theory of constraints (TOC) (Appendix) A practice used by many businesses to increase profitability by managing bottlenecks or constrained resources by identifying the bottlenecks restricting the business's operations and then opening them by relaxing the constraints. *(p. 140)*

Unit-level costs Costs incurred each time a company makes a single product or performs a single service and that can be avoided by eliminating a unit of product or service. Likewise, unit-level costs increase with each additional product produced or service provided. *(p. 124)*

Vertically integrated Having control over the entire spectrum of business activity from production to sales; as an example, a grocery store that owns farms. *(p. 132)*

QUESTIONS

1. What are the primary qualities of revenues and costs that are relevant for decision making?
2. Are variable costs always relevant? Explain.
3. What are the four hierarchical levels used to classify costs? When can each of these levels of costs be avoided?
4. What is the relationship between relevance and accuracy?
5. Carmon Company invests $300,000 in the equity securities of Mann Corporation. The current market value of Carmon's investment in Mann is $250,000. Carmon currently needs funds for operating purposes. Although interest rates are high, Carmon's president has decided to borrow the needed funds instead of selling the investment in Mann. He has explained his decision by stating that his company cannot afford to take a $50,000 loss on the Mann shares. Evaluate the president's decision on the basis of this information.
6. What is an opportunity cost? How does it differ from a sunk cost?
7. A local bank advertises that it offers a free noninterest-bearing chequing account if the depositor maintains a $500 minimum balance in the account. Is the chequing account truly free?
8. A manager is faced with the decision to replace machine A or machine B. The original cost of machine A was $20,000 and that of machine B was $30,000. Because the two cost figures differ, they should be included in the manager's decision. Do you agree? Explain your position.
9. Are all fixed costs unavoidable?
10. What are two qualitative considerations that could be associated with special order decisions?
11. Which of the following items would not be relevant to a make-or-buy decision?
    a. Allocated portion of amortization expense on existing facilities.
    b. Variable cost of labour used to produce products that are currently being purchased.
    c. Warehousing costs for inventory of completed products (inventory levels will be constant, regardless of whether products are purchased or produced).
    d. Cost of materials used to produce the items that are currently being purchased.
    e. Property taxes on the factory building.
12. What two factors should be considered in deciding how to allocate shelf space in a retail establishment?
13. What level(s) of costs is (are) relevant in special order decisions?
14. Why would a company consider outsourcing products or services?
15. Chris Sutter, the production manager of Satellite Computers, insists that the floppy drives used in the company's upper-end computers be outsourced, since they can be purchased from a supplier at a lower cost per unit than the company is presently incurring to produce the drives. Jane Meyers, his assistant, insists that if sales growth continues at the current levels, the company will be able to produce the drives in the near future at a lower cost because of the company's predominately fixed cost structure. Does Ms. Meyers have a legitimate argument? Explain.
16. What are some qualitative factors that should be considered in addition to quantitative costs in deciding whether to outsource?
17. The managers of Wilcox, Inc. are suggesting that the company president eliminate one of the company's segments that is operating at a loss. Why may this be a hasty decision?
18. Why would a supervisor choose to continue using a more costly old machine instead of replacing it with a less costly new machine?
19. What are some of the constraints that limit a business's ability to satisfy the demand for its products or services?

EXERCISE 4-1   *Distinction between Relevance and Cost Behaviour*   L.O. 1

Beth Davies is trying to decide which of two different kinds of candy to sell in her retail candy store. One type is a name brand candy that will practically sell itself. The other candy is cheaper to produce but does not carry an identifiable brand name. Ms. Davies believes that she will have to incur significant advertising costs to sell this candy. Several related cost items for the two types of candy are as follows:

Brandless Candy		Name Brand Candy	
Cost per box	$4.50	Cost per box	$7.00
Sales commissions per box	1.00	Sales commissions per box	1.00
Rent of display space	2,000.00	Rent of display space	2,000.00
Advertising	5,000.00	Advertising	1,000.00

Required

Identify each cost as being relevant or irrelevant to Ms. Davies' decision and indicate whether it is fixed or variable relative to the number of boxes sold.

EXERCISE 4-2   *Distinction between Relevance and Cost Behaviour*   L.O. 1, 2

Flores Company makes and sells a single product. The following costs were included in the company's most recent annual income statement:

Cost Items Appearing on the Income Statement	
Materials Cost ($3 per unit)	Sales Commissions (5% of sales)
Company President's Salary	Salaries of Administrative Personnel
Amortization on Manufacturing Equipment	Shipping and Handling ($0.25 per unit)
Customer Billing Costs (1% of sales)	Amortization on Office Furniture
Rental Cost of Manufacturing Facility	Manufacturing Supplies ($0.25 per unit)
Advertising Costs ($250,000 per year)	Production Supervisor's Salary
Labour Cost ($4 per unit)	

Flores has an opportunity to purchase the products that it currently makes. If it purchases the items, the company would continue to sell the products using its own logo, advertising program, and sales staff.

Required

Identify each cost as being relevant or irrelevant to the outsourcing decision and indicate whether the cost is fixed or variable relative to the number of products manufactured and sold.

EXERCISE 4-3   *Distinction between Avoidable Costs and Cost Behaviour*   L.O. 1

Just Jewels (JJ) makes fine jewellery that it sells to department stores throughout Canada. JJ is trying to decide which of two bracelets to manufacture. Cost data pertaining to the two choices follow:

	Bracelet A	Bracelet B
Cost of materials per unit	$38	$42
Cost of labour per unit	60	60
Advertising cost per year	6,000	5,000
Annual amortization on existing equip.	4,000	4,500

Required

a. Identify the fixed costs and determine the amount of fixed cost for each product.
b. Identify the variable costs and determine the amount of variable cost per unit for each product.
c. Identify the avoidable costs and determine the amount of avoidable cost for each product.

L.O. 1, 2, 9 EXERCISE 4-4   *Special Order Decision*

Belton Concrete Company pours concrete slabs for single-family dwellings. Clint Construction Company, which operates outside Belton's normal sales territory, asks Belton to pour 20 slabs for Clint's new development of homes. Belton has the capacity to build 200 slabs and is presently working on 150 of them. Clint explains that she is willing to pay only $2,200 per slab. Belton estimates the cost of a typical job to include unit-level materials, $1,200; unit-level labour, $800; and an allocated portion of facility-level overhead, $300.

Required

Should Belton accept or reject the special order to pour 20 slabs for $2,200 each? Support your answer with appropriate computations.

L.O. 1, 2, 9 EXERCISE 4-5   *Special Order Decision*

Glenntronics manufactures a personal computer designed for use in schools and markets it under its own label. Glenntronics has the capacity to produce 15,000 units a year but is currently producing and selling only 10,000 units a year. The computer's normal selling price is $2,000 per unit with no volume discounts. The unit-level costs associated with the computer's production include $700 for direct materials, $300 for direct labour, and $400 for indirect manufacturing costs. The total product- and facility-level costs incurred by Glenntronics during the year are expected to be $2,500,000 and $1,000,000, respectively. Assume that Glenntronics receives a special order to produce and sell 2,000 computers at $1,500 each.

Required

Should Glenntronics accept or reject the special order? Support your answer with appropriate computations.

L.O. 8 EXERCISE 4-6   *Identification of Qualitative Factors for a Special Order Decision*

Required

Describe the qualitative factors that Glenntronics should consider before accepting the special order described in Exercise 4-5.

L.O. 9 EXERCISE 4-7   *Use of the Contribution Margin Approach for a Special Order Decision*

Alpha Company, which produces and sells small digital clocks, bases its pricing strategy on a 20 percent markup on total cost. Based on annual production costs for 20,000 units of product, computations for the sales price per clock follow:

Unit-level costs	$170,000
Fixed costs	70,000
Total cost (a)	240,000
Markup (a $\times$ .20)	48,000
Total sales (b)	$288,000
Sales price per unit (b $\div$ 20,000)	$14.40

Required

a. Alpha has excess capacity and receives a special order for 5,000 clocks for $10 each. Calculate the contribution margin per unit; on the basis of it, should Alpha accept the special order?

b. Support your answer by preparing a contribution margin income statement for the special order.

L.O. 9 EXERCISE 4-8   *Outsourcing Decision*

Zaslow Bicycle Manufacturing Company currently produces the handlebars that are used in manufacturing its bicycles, which are high-quality racing bikes with limited sales. It produces and sells only 5,000 bikes each year. Due to the low volume of activity, Zaslow is unable to obtain the economies of scale that larger producers achieve. For example, the handlebars can be bought for $28 each, but they cost $31 each to make. The following is a detailed breakdown of current production costs:

Item	Unit Cost	Total
Unit-level costs		
Materials	$10	$50,000
Labour	14	70,000
Overhead	2	10,000
Allocated facility-level costs	5	25,000
Total	$31	$155,000

After seeing these figures, Zaslow's president remarked that it would be foolish for the company to continue to produce the handlebars at $31 each when it can buy them for $28 each.

Required

Do you agree with the president's conclusion? Support your answer with appropriate computations.

EXERCISE 4-9   *Price Establishment for an Outsourcing Decision*   L.O. 9

Clean Cut, Inc. makes and sells lawn mowers for which it currently makes the engines. It has an opportunity to purchase the engines from a reliable manufacturer. The annual costs associated with making the engines are shown here:

Cost of materials (12,000 Units × $15)	$180,000
Labour (12,000 Units × $20)	240,000
Amortization on manufacturing equipment*	6,000
Salary of supervisor of engine production	60,000
Rental cost of equipment used to make engines	12,000
Allocated portion of corporate-level facility-sustaining costs	15,000
Total cost to make 12,000 engines	$513,000

*The equipment has a book value of $28,000 but its market value is zero.

Required

a. Determine the maximum price per unit that Clean Cut would be willing to pay for the engines.
b. Would the price computed in Requirement *a* change if production increased to 20,000 units? Support your answer with appropriate computations.

EXERCISE 4-10   *Outsourcing Decision with Qualitative Factors*   L.O. 8, 9

Sound Products, Inc. (SPI), which makes and sells 10,000 radios annually, currently purchases the radio speakers it uses for $48 each. Each radio uses one speaker. The company has idle capacity and is considering the possibility of making the speakers that it needs. SPI believes that the cost of materials and labour needed to make each speaker would be $40 each. In addition, the costs of supervisor salaries, rent, and other manufacturing costs would be $100,000. Allocated facility-level costs will be $50,000.

Required

a. Determine the amount of the effect on net income that would occur if SPI decides to make the speakers.
b. Discuss the qualitative factors that SPI should consider.

EXERCISE 4-11   *Outsourcing Decision Affected by Opportunity Costs*   L.O. 7, 9

Gulf Shores Electronics currently produces the shipping containers it uses in the delivery of the electronics products it sells. The monthly cost of producing 6,000 containers follows:

Unit-level materials	$8,000
Unit-level labour	6,000
Unit-level overhead	4,000
Product-level costs*	12,000
Allocated facility-level costs	32,000

*Twenty-five percent of these costs can be avoided by purchasing the containers.

Pascal Container Company has offered to sell comparable containers to Gulf Shores for $4 each.

Required

a. Should Gulf Shores continue to make the containers? Support your answer with appropriate documentation.

b. Gulf Shores has the opportunity to lease the space currently being used in the manufacturing process. If the lease would produce $5,000 per month, would this affect your answer to Requirement *a*? Support your answer with appropriate commentary.

L.O. 7 EXERCISE 4-12   *Opportunity Cost*

Abbco Truck Lines, Inc. owns a truck that cost $100,000. Currently, its net book value is $60,000 and its expected remaining useful life is five years. Abbco has the opportunity to purchase for $80,000 a replacement truck that is extremely fuel efficient. Fuel cost for the old truck is expected to be $10,000 per year more than that for the new truck. The old truck is paid for but, in spite of being in good condition, can be sold for only $40,000.

Required

Should Abbco Truck Lines replace the old truck with the new fuel-efficient model, or should it continue to use the old truck until it wears out? Explain.

L.O. 7, 8 EXERCISE 4-13   *Opportunity Costs*

Jane Nottingham owns her own taxi, for which she bought a $12,000 permit to operate two years ago. Ms. Nottingham earns $22,000 a year operating as an independent but has the opportunity to sell the taxi and permit for $40,000 and take a position as dispatcher for Large Taxi Co. The new position will pay $20,000 a year, but she will have to work only a 40-hour week. Driving her own taxi, she works approximately 55 hours per week. If Ms. Nottingham sells the business, she will invest the funds and can earn a 10 percent return.

Required

a. Determine the opportunity cost of owning and operating the independent business.

b. Solely on the basis of financial considerations, should Ms. Nottingham sell the taxi and accept the position as dispatcher?

c. Discuss the qualitative as well as quantitative characteristics that Ms. Nottingham should consider.

L.O. 9 EXERCISE 4-14   *Segment Elimination Decision*

Reston Company operates three segments. Income statements for the segments imply that profitability could be improved if Segment A were eliminated.

RESTON COMPANY Financial Statements For the Year 2009			
Segment	A	B	C
Sales	$ 97,000	$ 220,000	$ 210,000
Cost of Goods Sold	(69,000)	(92,000)	(95,000)
Sales Commissions	(12,000)	(22,000)	(22,000)
Contribution Margin	$ 16,000	$ 106,000	$ 93,000
Amortization and Other General Fixed Overhead Cost	(32,000)	(42,000)	(34,000)
General Fixed Oper. Exp. (allocation of president's salary)	(10,000)	(10,000)	(10,000)
Advertising Expense	(2,000)	(10,000)	0
Net Income	$(28,000)	$44,000	$49,000

Required

a. Explain the effect on profitability if segment A is eliminated.

b. Prepare comparative income statements for the company as a whole under two alternatives: (1) the retention of Segment A, and (2) the elimination of Segment A.

EXERCISE 4-15   *Segment Elimination Decision*   **L.O. 9**

Toccoa Transport Company divides its operations into four divisions. A recent income statement for Southern Division follows:

TOCCOA TRANSPORT COMPANY Southern Division Financial Statements For the Year 2005	
Revenue	$ 550,000
Salaries for Drivers	(400,000)
Fuel Expenses	(100,000)
Insurance	(20,000)
Amortization Expense (sunk cost)	(50,000)
Division-Level Facility-Sustaining Costs	(40,000)
Companywide Facility-Sustaining Costs	(70,000)
Net Loss	$(130,000)

Required

a. Should Southern Division be eliminated? Support your answer by explaining how the division's elimination would affect the net income of the company as a whole. By how much would companywide income increase or decrease?

b. Assume that Southern Division is able to increase its revenue to $570,000 by raising its prices. Would this change the decision you made in Requirement *a*? Determine the amount of the increase or decrease that would occur in companywide net income if the segment were eliminated at a time when revenue was $570,000.

c. What is the minimum amount of revenue required to justify continuing the operation of Southern Division?

EXERCISE 4-16   *Identification of Avoidable Cost of a Segment*   **L.O. 4**

Data Corporation is considering the elimination of one of its segments. The segment incurs the following fixed costs. If the segment is eliminated, the building it uses will be sold.

Advertising expense	$120,000
Supervisory salaries	80,000
Allocation of companywide facility-level costs	7,500
Original cost of building	40,000
Book value of building	25,000
Market value of building	30,000
Amortization on building	5,000
Maintenance costs on equipment	25,000
Real estate taxes on building	2,000

Required

On the basis of this information, determine the amount of avoidable cost associated with the segment.

EXERCISE 4-17   *Asset Replacement Decision*   **L.O. 9**

A machine purchased three years ago for $65,000 has a current book value using straight-line amortization of $45,000; its operating expenses are $12,000 per year. A replacement machine would cost $100,000, have a useful life of nine years, and would require $4,000 per year in operating expenses. It has an expected salvage value of $8,000 after nine years. The current disposal value of the old machine is $30,000; if it is kept for nine more years, its residual value would be $5,000.

Required

On the basis of this information, should the old machine be replaced? Support your answer with appropriate documentation.

L.O. 9 EXERCISE 4-18   *Asset Replacement Decision*

J. Edgars Company is considering replacement of some of its manufacturing equipment. Information regarding the existing equipment and the potential replacement equipment follows:

Existing Equipment		Replacement Equipment	
Cost	$35,000	Cost	$40,000
Operating expenses*	50,000	Operating expenses*	8,000
Salvage value	5,000	Salvage value	7,000
Market value	25,000		
Book value	16,000		

*The amounts shown for operating expenses are the cumulative total of all such expected expenses to be incurred over the useful life of the equipment.

Required

On the basis of this information, make a recommendation regarding the replacement of the equipment. Support your recommendation with appropriate computations.

L.O. 9 EXERCISE 4-19   *Asset Replacement Decision*

Agarwal Company paid $40,000 to purchase a machine on January 1, 2004. During 2006, a technological break-through resulted in the development of a new machine that costs $75,000. The old machine costs $24,000 per year to operate, but the new machine could be operated for only $6,000 per year. The new machine, which will be available for delivery on January 1, 2007, has an expected useful life of four years. The old machine is more durable and is expected to have a remaining useful life of four years. The current market value of the old machine is $5,000. The expected salvage value of both machines is zero.

Required

On the basis of this information, make a recommendation regarding the replacement of the machine. Support your recommendation with appropriate computations.

L.O. 7, 9 EXERCISE 4-20   *Annual versus Cumulative Data for Replacement Decision*

Because of rapidly advancing technology, Perry Publications, Inc. is considering the replacement of its existing typesetting machine with leased equipment. The old machine, purchased two years ago, has an expected useful life of six years and is in good condition. Apparently, it will continue to perform as expected for the remaining four years of its expected useful life. A four-year lease for equipment with comparable productivity can be obtained for $8,000 per year. The following data apply to the old machine:

Original cost	$90,000
Accumulated amortization	30,000
Current market value	45,000
Estimated salvage value	5,000

Required

a. Determine the annual opportunity cost of using the old machine. On the basis of your computations, make a recommendation as to whether it should be replaced.
b. Determine the total cost of the lease over the four-year contract. On the basis of your computations, make a recommendation as to whether the old machine should be replaced.

L.O. 11 EXERCISE 4-21   *Scarce Resource Decision*

Ozark Funtime Novelties has the capacity to produce either 18,000 corncob pipes or 8,000 cornhusk dolls per year. The pipes cost $3 each to produce and can be sold for $6 each. The dolls sell for $10 each and cost only $4 to produce.

Required

Assuming that Ozark Funtime Novelties can sell all it produces of either product, should it produce the corncob pipes or the cornhusk dolls? Show computations to support your answer.

PROBLEM 4-1A   *Context-Sensitive Relevance*   **L.O. 1, 6**

Required

Respond to each requirement independently.

a. Describe two decision-making contexts, one in which unit-level materials costs are avoidable, and the other in which they are unavoidable.

b. Describe two decision-making contexts, one in which batch-level setup costs are avoidable, and the other in which they are unavoidable.

c. Describe two decision-making contexts, one in which advertising costs are avoidable, and the other in which they are unavoidable.

d. Describe two decision-making contexts, one in which rent paid for a building is avoidable, and the other in which it is unavoidable.

e. Describe two decision-making contexts, one in which amortization on manufacturing equipment is avoidable, and the other in which it is unavoidable.

PROBLEM 4-2A   *Context-Sensitive Relevance*   **L.O. 6**

Sun State Construction Company (SSCC) is a building contractor that specializes in small commercial buildings. The company has the opportunity to accept one of two jobs; it cannot accept both because they must be performed at the same time and SCSS does not have the necessary labour force for both jobs. Indeed, it will be necessary to hire a new supervisor if either job is accepted. Furthermore, additional insurance will be required if either job is accepted. The revenue and costs associated with each job follow:

Cost Category	Job A	Job B
Contract price	$320,000	$290,000
Unit-level materials	123,000	108,000
Unit-level labour	118,500	121,200
Unit-level overhead	8,200	6,600
Supervisor's salary	36,200	36,200
Rental equipment costs	12,400	14,100
Amortization on tools (zero market value)	10,000	10,000
Allocated portion of companywide facility-sustaining costs	3,200	2,900
Insurance coverage	8,000	8,000
Cost incurred to obtain and evaluate jobs	2,000	2,500

Required

a. Assume that SSCC has decided to accept one of the two jobs. Identify the relevant information to the selection of one job versus the other. Recommend which job should be accepted and support your answer with appropriate computations.

b. Assume that Job A is no longer available. SSCC's choice is to accept or reject Job B alone. Identify the relevant information to this decision. Recommend whether Job B should be accepted or rejected. Support your answer with appropriate computations.

PROBLEM 4-3A   *Special Order Decision with Operating Leverage Consideration*   **L.O. 8, 9**

Webber Quilting Company makes blankets that it markets through a variety of department stores. It makes the blankets in batches of 1,000 units. The company made 25,000 blankets during the prior accounting period. The cost of producing the blankets is summarized here:

Materials cost ($30 per unit × 25,000)	$ 750,000
Labour cost ($40 per unit × 25,000)	1,000,000
Manufacturing supplies ($3 × 25,000)	75,000
Batch-level costs (25 batches at $4,000 per batch)	100,000
Product-level costs	200,000
Facility-level costs	300,000
Total costs	$2,425,000

Cost per unit = $2,425,000 ÷ 25,000 = $97

Required

a. Best Night Motels has offered to buy a batch of 500 blankets for $80 each. Webber's normal selling price is $120 per unit. On the basis of the preceding quantitative data, should Webber accept the special order? Support your answer with appropriate computations.

b. Would your answer to Requirement *a* change if Best Night offered to buy a batch of 1,000 blankets for $80 per unit? Support your answer with appropriate computations.

c. Describe the qualitative factors that Webber Quilting Company should consider before accepting a special order to sell blankets to Best Night Motels.

L.O. 8, 9   PROBLEM 4-4A   *Effects of the Level of Production on an Outsourcing Decision*

Lajoie Chemical Company makes a variety of cosmetic products, one of which is a skin cream designed to reduce the signs of aging. Lajoie produces a relatively small amount (20,000 units) of the cream and is considering the purchase of the product from an outside supplier for $4.50 each. If Lajoie purchases from the outside supplier, it would continue to sell and distribute the cream under its own brand name. Lajoie's accountant constructed the following profitability analysis:

Revenue (20,000 units × $10)	$200,000
Unit-level materials costs (20,000 units × $1.40)	(28,000)
Unit-level labour costs (20,000 units × $0.50)	(10,000)
Unit-level overhead costs (20,000 × $0.10)	(2,000)
Unit-level selling expenses (20,000 × $0.25)	(5,000)
Contribution margin	$155,000
Skin cream production supervisor's salary	(60,000)
Allocated portion of facility-level costs	(15,000)
Product-level advertising cost	(50,000)
Contribution to companywide income	$30,000

Required

a. Identify the cost items relevant to the make-or-outsource decision.

b. Should Lajoie continue to make the product or buy it from the supplier? Support your answer by determining the amount of the effect on net income if Lajoie buys the cream instead of making it.

c. Suppose that Lajoie is able to increase sales by 10,000 units (i.e., sales will increase to 30,000 units). At this level of production, should Lajoie make or buy the cream? Support your answer by explaining how the increase in production affects the cost per unit.

d. Discuss the qualitative factors that Lajoie should consider before deciding to outsource the skin cream. How can Lajoie minimize the risk of establishing a relationship with an unreliable supplier?

L.O. 9   PROBLEM 4-5A   *Outsourcing Decision Affected by Equipment Replacement*

Euro Bike Company (EBC) makes the frames used to build its bicycles. During 2006, EBC made 10,000 frames; the costs incurred follow:

Unit-level materials costs (10,000 units × $180)	$1,800,000
Unit-level labour costs (10,000 units × $210)	2,100,000
Unit-level overhead costs (10,000 × $20)	200,000
Amortization expenses on manufacturing equipment	50,000
Bike frame production supervisor's salary	40,000
Inventory holding costs	240,000
Allocated portion of facility-level costs	600,000
Total costs	$5,030,000

Euro has an opportunity to purchase frames for $390 each.

Additional Information

1. The manufacturing equipment, which originally cost $250,000, has a book value of $200,000, a remaining useful life of four years, and a zero salvage value. If the equipment is not used in the production process, it can be leased for $30,000 per year.

2. Euro has the opportunity to purchase for $480,000 new manufacturing equipment that will have an expected useful life of four years and a salvage value of $40,000. This equipment will increase productivity substantially, thereby reducing unit-level labour costs by 15 percent. Assume that Euro will maintain its production and sales at 10,000 frames per year in the future.

3. If Euro outsources the frames, the company can eliminate 80 percent of the inventory holding costs.

Required

a. Determine the avoidable cost per bike frame under the assumption that the existing equipment is used to make the frames. On the basis of the quantitative data, should Euro outsource the bike frames? Support your answer with appropriate computations.

b. Assuming that the old equipment is replaced, determine the avoidable cost per unit of making the bike frames. Calculate the impact on profitability if the bike frames are made using the old versus the new equipment. On the basis of the per unit cost data computed in Requirements *a* and *b*, should Euro replace the equipment?

c. Assuming that the old equipment has been replaced, should Euro make or outsource the frames?

d. Discuss the qualitative factors that Euro should consider before making a decision to outsource the bike frames. How can Euro minimize the risk of establishing a relationship with an unreliable supplier?

PROBLEM 4-6A   *Elimination of a Segment*   **L.O. 9**

Wild West Boot Co. sells men's, women's, and children's boots. For each type of boot sold, it operates a separate department that has its own manager. The manager of the men's department has a sales staff of nine employees, the manager of the women's department has six employees, and the manager of the children's department has three employees. All departments are housed in a single store. In recent years, the children's department has operated at a net loss and is expected to continue to do so. Last year's income statements follow:

	Men's Department	Women's Department	Children's Department
Sales	$ 780,000	$590,000	$ 248,000
Cost of Goods Sold	(312,000)	(247,000)	(140,000)
Gross Margin	$ 468,000	$343,000	$ 108,000
Departmental Manager's Salary	(48,000)	(42,000)	(28,000)
Sales Commissions	(216,000)	(168,000)	(58,000)
Rent on Store Lease	(25,000)	(25,000)	(25,000)
Store Utilities	(5,000)	(5,000)	(5,000)
Net Income (loss)	$ 174,000	$103,000	$ (8,000)

Required

a. Determine whether the Children's Department should be eliminated.

b. Confirm the conclusion you reached in Requirement *a* by preparing income statements for the company as a whole with and without the Children's Department.

c. The elimination of the Children's Department would make more space available to display a wider variety of men's and women's boots. Suppose management estimates that a wider selection of adult boots would generate sales that would increase the store's net earnings by $32,000. Would this information affect the decision that you made in Requirement *a*? Explain your answer.

PROBLEM 4-7A   *Elimination of a Segment with Volume of Activity and Opportunity Cost*   **L.O. 7, 9**
                    Considerations

San Monica Manufacturing Co. produces and sells specialized equipment for use in the petroleum industry. The company is organized into three separate operating branches: Division A, which manufactures and sells heavy equipment; Division B, which manufactures and sells hand tools; and Division C, which makes and sells electric motors. Each division is housed in a separate manufacturing facility. Company headquarters is located in a separate building. In recent years, Division B has been operating at a net loss and is expected to continue to do so. Income statements for the three divisions for 2008 follow:

	Division A	Division B	Division C
Sales	$5,000,000	$1,200,000	$6,000,000
Less: Cost of Goods Sold			
Unit-Level Manufacturing Costs	(3,000,000)	(700,000)	(3,700,000)
Rent on Manufacturing Facility	(600,000)	(400,000)	(500,000)
Gross Margin	$1,400,000	$ 100,000	$1,800,000
Less: Operating Expenses			
Unit-Level Selling and Admin. Expenses	(200,000)	(50,000)	(300,000)
Division-Level Fixed Selling and Admin. Expenses	(400,000)	(150,000)	(500,000)
Headquarters Facility-Level Costs	(300,000)	(300,000)	(300,000)
Net Income (loss)	$ 500,000	$ (400,000)	$ 700,000

Required

a. On the basis of the preceding information, recommend whether Division B should be eliminated. Support your answer by preparing companywide income statements before and after eliminating Division B.

b. During 2008, Division B produced and sold 20,000 units of hand tools. Would your recommendation in response to Requirement *a* change if sales and production increase to 25,000 units in 2009? Support your answer by comparing differential revenue and avoidable costs for Division B, assuming that it sells 25,000 units.

c. Suppose that San Monica could sublease Division B's manufacturing facility for $450,000. Would you operate the division at a production and sales volume of 25,000 units, or would you close it? Support your answer with appropriate computations.

L.O. 9 PROBLEM 4-8A   *Comprehensive Problem, Including Special Order, Outsourcing, and Segment Elimination Decisions*

Techtronics, Inc. makes and sells state-of-the-art electronics products. One of its segments produces The Math Machine, an inexpensive four-function calculator. The company's chief accountant recently prepared the following income statement showing annual revenues and expenses associated with the segment's operating activities. The relevant range for the production and sale of the calculators is between 30,000 and 60,000 units per year.

Revenue (40,000 units × $8)	$320,000
Unit-Level Variable Costs	
Materials Cost (40,000 × $2)	(80,000)
Labour Cost (40,000 × $1)	(40,000)
Manufacturing Overhead (40,000 × $0.50)	(20,000)
Shipping and Handling (40,000 × $0.25)	(10,000)
Sales Commissions (40,000 × $1)	(40,000)
Contribution Margin	$130,000
Fixed Expenses	
Advertising Costs	(20,000)
Salary of Production Supervisor	(60,000)
Amortization on Production Equipment (zero market value)	(30,000)
Allocated Companywide Facility-Level Expenses	(50,000)
Net Loss	$ (30,000)

Required

Consider each of the requirements independently.

a. A large discount store has approached the owner of Techtronics about buying 5,000 calculators. It would replace The Math Machine's label with its own logo to avoid affecting Techtronics' existing customers. Because the offer was made directly to the owner, no sales commissions on the transaction would be involved, but the discount store is willing to pay only $4.50 per calculator. On the basis of quantitative factors alone, should Techtronics accept the special order? Support your answer with appropriate computations. Specifically, by what amount would the special order profitability increase or decrease?

b. Techtronics has an opportunity to buy the 40,000 calculators it currently makes from a reliable competing manufacturer for $4.90 each. The product meets Techtronics's quality standards. Techtronics could continue to use its own logo, advertising program, and sales force to distribute the products. Should Techtronics buy the calculators or continue to make them? Support your answer with appropriate computations. Specifically, how much more or less would it cost to buy the calculators than to make them? Would your answer change if the volume of sales were increased to 60,000 units?

c. Because the calculator division is currently operating at a loss, should it be eliminated from the company's operations? Support your answer with appropriate computations. Specifically, by what amount would the segment's elimination increase or decrease profitability?

APPENDIX

PROBLEM 4-9A   *Allocation of Scarce Resources*

L.O. 11

The following information applies to the products of Krivacek Company:

	Product A	Product B
Selling price per unit	$44	$40
Variable cost per unit	36	28

Required

Identify the product that should be produced or sold under each of the following constraints. Consider each constraint separately.

a. One unit of Product A requires 2 hours of labour to produce, and one unit of Product B requires 4 hours of labour to produce. Due to labour constraints, demand is higher than the company's capacity to make both products.

b. The products are sold to the public in retail stores. The company has limited floor space and cannot stock as many products as it would like. Display space is available for only one of the two products. Expected sales of Product A are 10,000 units and of Product B are 8,000 units.

c. The maximum number of machine hours available is 40,000. Product A uses two machine hours, and Product B uses five machine hours. The company can sell all the products it produces.

PROBLEM 4-10A   *Conflict between Short-Term and Long-Term Performance*

L.O. 10

James Arrington manages the cutting department of Smith Timber Company. He purchased a tree-cutting machine on January 1, 2001, for $200,000. The machine had an estimated useful life of five years and zero salvage value, and the cost to operate it is $45,000 per year. Technological developments resulted in the development of a more advanced machine available for purchase on January 1, 2002, that would allow a 25 percent reduction in operating costs. The new machine would cost $120,000 and have a four-year useful life and zero salvage value. The current market value of the old machine on January 1, 2002, is $100,000, and its book value is $160,000 on that date. Straight-line amortization is used for both machines. The company expects to generate $112,000 of revenue per year from the use of either machine.

Required

a. Make a recommendation regarding the replacement of the old machine on January 1, 2002. Support your answer with appropriate computations.

b. Prepare income statements for four years (i.e., 2002 through 2005) under the assumption that the old machine is retained.

c. Prepare income statements for four years (i.e., 2002 through 2005) under the assumption that the old machine is replaced.

d. Discuss the potential ethical conflicts that may result from the timing of the loss and expense recognition depicted in the two income statements.

PROBLEMS—SERIES B

PROBLEM 4-1B   *Context-Sensitive Relevance*

L.O. 1, 6

Required

Respond to each requirement independently.

a. Describe two decision-making contexts, one in which unit-level labour costs are avoidable, and the other in which they are unavoidable.

b. Describe two decision-making contexts, one in which batch-level shipping costs are avoidable, and the other in which they are unavoidable.

c. Describe two decision-making contexts, one in which administrative costs are avoidable, and the other in which they are unavoidable.

d. Describe two decision-making contexts, one in which the insurance premium paid on a building is avoidable, and the other in which it is unavoidable.

e. Describe two decision-making contexts, one in which amortization on a product patent is avoidable, and the other in which it is unavoidable.

L.O. 1, 6 PROBLEM 4-2B   *Context-Sensitive Relevance*

Jeremy Machines Company is evaluating two customer orders from which it can accept only one because of capacity limitations. The data associated with each job order follow:

Cost Category:	Order M	Order N
Contract price	$480,000	$440,000
Unit-level materials	180,000	158,000
Unit-level labour	167,000	172,400
Unit-level overhead	53,000	49,000
Supervisor's salary	40,000	40,000
Rental equipment costs	10,000	12,000
Amortization on tools (zero market value)	14,000	14,000
Allocated portion of companywide facility-sustaining costs	4,000	3,600
Insurance coverage	27,000	27,000
Cost incurred to obtain and evaluate orders	3,000	2,200

Required

a. Assume that Jeremy has decided to accept one of the two jobs. Identify the relevant information to the selection of one order versus the other. Recommend which job should be accepted, and support your answer with appropriate computations.

b. The customer presenting Order M has withdrawn it because of its financial hardship. Under this circumstance, Jeremy's choice is to accept or reject Order N alone. Identify the relevant information to this decision. Recommend whether Order N should be accepted or rejected. Support your answer with appropriate computations.

L.O. 8, 9 PROBLEM 4-3B   *Special Order Decision with Operating Leverage Consideration*

Gorman Company made 100,000 electric drills in batches of 2,000 units each during the prior accounting period. Normally, Gorman markets its products through a variety of hardware stores. The following is the summarized cost to produce electric drills:

Materials cost ($4.50 per unit × 100,000)	$ 450,000
Labour cost ($5.00 per unit × 100,000)	500,000
Manufacturing supplies ($0.50 × 100,000)	50,000
Batch-level costs (50 batches at $3,000 per batch)	150,000
Product-level costs	60,000
Facility-level costs	190,000
Total costs	$ 1,400,000
Cost per unit = $1,400,000 ÷ 100,000 = $14	

Required

a. Bypassing Gorman's regular distribution channel, Kelly Home Repair and Maintenance, Inc. has offered to buy a batch of 1,200 electric drills for $12 each directly from Gorman. Gorman's normal selling price is $18 per unit. On the basis of the preceding quantitative data, should Gorman accept the special order? Support your answer with appropriate computations.

b. Would your answer to Requirement *a* change if Kelly Home Repair and Maintenance offered to buy a batch of 2,000 electric drills for $12 each? Support your answer with appropriate computations.

c. Describe the qualitative factors that Gorman Company should consider before accepting a special order to sell electric drills to Kelly Home Repair and Maintenance.

PROBLEM 4-4B   *Effects of the Level of Production on an Outsourcing Decision*   L.O. 8, 9

One of Rivers Company's major products is a fuel additive designed to improve fuel efficiency and keep engines clean. Rivers, a petrol–chemical firm, makes and sells 50,000 units of the fuel additive per year. Its management is evaluating the possibility of having an outside supplier manufacture the product for Rivers for $2 each. Rivers would continue to sell and distribute the fuel additive under its own brand name if both parties accept the deal. Rivers's accountant constructed the following profitability analysis:

Revenue (50,000 units × $3.50)	$175,000
Unit-level materials costs (50,000 units × $0.80)	(40,000)
Unit-level labour costs (50,000 units × $0.12)	(6,000)
Unit-level overhead costs (50,000 × $0.38)	(19,000)
Unit-level selling expenses (50,000 × $0.20)	(10,000)
Contribution margin	$100,000
Fuel additive production supervisor's salary	(40,000)
Allocated portion of facility-level costs	(10,000)
Product-level advertising cost	(20,000)
Contribution to companywide income	$ 30,000

Required
a. Identify the cost items relevant to the make-or-outsource decision.
b. Should Rivers continue to make the fuel additive or buy it from the supplier? Support your answer by determining the amount of the effect on net income if Rivers buys the fuel additive instead of making it.
c. Suppose that Rivers is able to increase sales by 30,000 units (i.e., sales will increase to 80,000 units). At this level of sales, should Rivers make or buy the fuel additive? Support your answer by explaining how the increase in production affects the cost per unit.
d. Discuss the qualitative factors that Rivers should consider before deciding to outsource the fuel additive. How can Rivers minimize the risk of establishing a relationship with an unreliable supplier?

PROBLEM 4-5B   *Outsourcing Decision Affected by Equipment Replacement*   L.O. 9

During 2007, Juno Toy Company made 5,000 units of Model A, the costs of which follow:

Unit-level materials costs (5,000 units × $10)	$ 50,000
Unit-level labour costs (5,000 units × $40)	200,000
Unit-level overhead costs (5,000 × $4)	20,000
Amortization expenses on manufacturing equipment	30,000
Model A production supervisor's salary	30,000
Inventory holding costs	60,000
Allocated portion of facility-level costs	40,000
Total costs	$430,000

An independent contractor offered to make the same product for Juno for $50 each.

Additional Information
1. The manufacturing equipment originally cost $210,000 and has a book value of $120,000, a remaining useful life of four years, and a zero salvage value. If the equipment is not used in the production process, it can be leased for $20,000 per year.
2. Juno has the opportunity to purchase for $120,000 new manufacturing equipment that will have an expected useful life of four years and a salvage value of $40,000. This equipment will increase productivity substantially, thereby reducing unit-level labour costs by 20 percent.
3. If Juno discontinues the production of Model A, the company can eliminate 50 percent of its inventory holding cost.

Required
a. Determine the avoidable cost per unit of Model A under the assumption that the existing equipment is used to make the product. On the basis of the quantitative data, should Juno outsource Model A? Support your answer with appropriate computations.

b. Assuming that the old equipment is replaced, determine the avoidable cost per unit of making Model A. Calculate the impact on profitability if Model A were made using the old versus the new equipment. On the basis of the per unit cost data computed in Requirements *a* and *b*, should Juno replace the equipment?

c. Assuming that the old equipment has been replaced, should Juno make or outsource Model A?

d. Discuss the qualitative factors that Juno should consider before making a decision to outsource Model A. How can Juno minimize the risk of establishing a relationship with an unreliable supplier?

L.O. 9 PROBLEM 4-6B   *Elimination of a Segment*

Nguyen's Grocery Store has three departments, meat, canned food, and produce, each of which has its own manager. All departments are housed in a single store. Recently, the produce department has been suffering a net loss and is expected to continue doing so. Last year's income statements follow:

	Meat Department	Canned Food Department	Produce Department
Sales	$650,000	$580,000	$420,000
Cost of Goods Sold	(250,000)	(310,000)	(240,000)
Gross Margin	$400,000	$270,000	$180,000
Departmental Manager's Salary	(42,000)	(30,000)	(35,000)
Rent on Store Lease	(80,000)	(80,000)	(80,000)
Store Utilities	(20,000)	(20,000)	(20,000)
Other General Expenses	(98,000)	(98,000)	(98,000)
Net Income (loss)	$160,000	$42,000	$(53,000)

Required

a. Determine whether the produce department should be eliminated.

b. Confirm the conclusion you reached in Requirement *a* by preparing before and after income statements, assuming that the produce department is eliminated.

c. The elimination of the produce department would allow the meat department to utilize the available space to add seafood to its products. Suppose that management estimates that the availability of seafood would increase the store's net earnings by $160,000. Would this information affect the decision that you made in Requirement *a*? Explain your answer.

L.O. 7, 9 PROBLEM 4-7B   *Elimination of a Segment with Volume of Activity and Opportunity Cost Considerations*

Regent Company has three separate operating branches: Division X, which manufactures utensils; Division Y, which makes plates; and Division Z, which makes cooking pots. Each division operates its own facility. The company's administrative offices are located in a separate building. In recent years, Division Z has experienced a net loss and is expected to continue to do so. Income statements for 2008 follow:

	Division X	Division Y	Division Z
Sales	$1,780,000	$1,420,000	$1,500,000
Less: Cost of Goods Sold			
Unit-Level Manufacturing Costs	(1,080,000)	(600,000)	(900,000)
Rent on Manufacturing Facility	(240,000)	(220,000)	(360,000)
Gross Margin	$460,000	$600,000	$240,000
Less: Operating Expenses			
Unit-Level Selling and Admin. Expenses	(60,000)	(45,000)	(90,000)
Division-Level Fixed Selling and Admin. Expenses	(140,000)	(125,000)	(180,000)
Headquarters Facility-Level Costs	80,000)	(80,000)	(80,000)
Net Income (loss)	$180,000	$350,000	$(110,000)

Required

a. On the basis of the preceding information, recommend whether Division Z should be eliminated. Support your answer by preparing companywide income statements before and after eliminating Division Z.

b. During 2008, Division Z produced and sold 30,000 units of product. Would your recommendation in Requirement *a* change if sales and production increase to 45,000 units in 2009? Support your answer by comparing differential revenue and avoidable costs for Division Z, assuming that 45,000 units are sold.

c. Suppose that Regent could sublease Division Z's manufacturing facility for $740,000. Would you operate the division at a production and sales volume of 45,000 units, or would you close it? Support your answer with appropriate computations.

PROBLEM 4-8B   *Comprehensive Problem, Including Special Order, Outsourcing, and Segment*   **L.O. 9**
                   Elimination Decisions

Sunny Company's electronics division produces radio/cassette players. The vice-president in charge of the division is evaluating the income statement on the next page showing annual revenues and expenses associated with the division's operating activities. The relevant range for the production and sale of the radio/cassette players is between 25,000 and 75,000 units per year.

Required

Consider each of the requirements independently.

a. An international trading firm has approached top management about buying 15,000 radio/cassette players for $26.50 each. It would sell the product in a foreign country so that Sunny's existing customers would not be affected. Because the offer was made directly to top management, no sales commissions on the transaction would be involved. On the basis of quantitative features alone, should Sunny accept the special order? Support your answer with appropriate computations. Specifically, by what amount would profitability increase or decrease if the special order is accepted?

Income Statement	
Revenue (30,000 units × $30)	$900,000
Unit- Level Variable Costs	
Materials Cost (30,000 × $15)	(450,000)
Labour Cost (30,000 × $8)	(240,000)
Manufacturing Overhead (30,000 × $1.50)	(45,000
Shipping and Handling (30,000 × $0.50)	(15,000)
Sales Commissions (30,000 × $2)	(60,000)
Contribution Margin	$90,000
Fixed Expenses	
Advertising Costs	(15,000)
Salary of Production Supervisor	(63,000)
Amortization on Production Equipment (zero market value)	(40,000)
Allocated Companywide Facility- Level Expenses	(60,000)
Net Loss	$(88,000)

b. Sunny has an opportunity to buy the 30,000 radio/cassette players it currently makes from a foreign manufacturer for $26 each. The manufacturer has a good reputation for reliability and quality, and Sunny could continue to use its own logo, advertising program, and sales force to distribute the products. Should Sunny buy the radio/cassette players or continue to make them? Support your answer with appropriate computations. Specifically, how much more or less would it cost to buy the radio/cassette players than to make them? Would your answer change if the volume of sales were increased to 70,000 units?

c. Because the electronics division is currently operating at a loss, should it be eliminated from the company's operations? Support your answer with appropriate computations. Specifically, by what amount would the segment's elimination increase or decrease profitability?

APPENDIX

L.O. 11 **PROBLEM 4-9B**   *Allocation of Scarce Resources*

Hank Company makes two products, P and Q. Product information follows:

	Product P	Product Q
Selling price per unit	$65	$80
Variable cost per unit	41	50

Required

Identify the product that should be produced or sold under each of the following constraints. Consider each constraint separately.

a. One unit of Product P requires three hours of labour to produce, and one unit of Product Q requires five hours of labour to produce. Due to labour constraints, demand is greater than the company's capacity to make both products.

b. The products are sold to the public in retail stores. The company has limited floor space and cannot stock as many products as it would like. Display space is available for only one of the two products. Expected sales of Product P are 8,000 units and expected sales of Product Q are 7,000 units.

c. The maximum number of machine hours available is 24,000. Product P uses four machine hours, and Product Q uses six machine hours. The company can sell all the products it produces.

L.O. 10 **PROBLEM 4-10B**   *Conflict between Short-Term and Long-Term Performance*

Kucera Construction Components, Inc. purchased a machine on January 1, 2001, for $120,000. The chief engineer estimated the machine's useful life to be six years and its salvage value to be zero. The operating cost of this machine is $60,000 per year. By January 1, 2003, a new machine that requires 30 percent less operating cost than the existing machine becomes available for $90,000; it would have a four-year useful life with zero salvage. The current market value of the old machine on January 1, 2003, is $50,000, and its book value is $80,000 on that date. Straight-line amortization is used for both machines. The company expects to generate $160,000 of revenue per year from the use of either machine.

Required

a. Make a recommendation regarding the replacement of the old machine on January 1, 2003. Support your answer with appropriate computations.

b. Prepare income statements for four years (i.e., 2003 through 2006) under the assumption that the old machine is retained.

c. Prepare income statements for four years (i.e., 2003 through 2006) under the assumption that the old machine is replaced.

d. Discuss the potential ethical conflicts that may result from the timing of the loss and expense recognition depicted in the two income statements.

ANALYZE, THINK, COMMUNICATE

ACT 4-1   **BUSINESS APPLICATION CASE**   *Elimination of a Product Line*

The Japanese car maker [Mazda Motor Company] has accumulated nearly a billion dollars in operating losses in three years. Its market share in Japan fell from nearly 8 percent to below 5 percent in the first half of the decade, and its overall car production dropped by a stunning 46 percent. In fact, Mazda has been fighting for its life. To salvage the company, Ford Motor Co., Mazda's biggest shareholder, gambled $430 million [in 1996] and raised its equity stake in Mazda to 33.4 percent, which in practice gave it operating control. The U.S. car maker chose Henry Wallace, a Ford man for 25 years, to spearhead a turnaround. Mr. Wallace is the first foreigner to lead a big Japanese company. While the Japanese have a well-deserved reputation for insularity, they also have a tradition of welcoming foreign guidance when it suits their purposes. In this case, Mr. Wallace has been warmly embraced by the Japanese—both inside and outside Mazda. Wallace's first move was to retrench—cut out product lines, consolidate sales channels, reduce inventory, and in the United States, halt unprofitable fleet and car-rental sales. Wallace also took action to instill a profit motive among the board of directors. Wallace observed, "I don't think previously there was a strong profit motive within the company." Instead, Mazda was a club of engineers who turned out wonderful niche cars—some with exotic styling, others with superb performance—that few consumers wanted to buy. When drivers developed a taste for sport utility vehicles, Mazda's beautiful sedans collected dust on the lots.

Required

a. The article indicated that one action taken by Mr. Wallace was to cut product lines. Explain which level (i.e., unit, batch, product, and/or facility) costs could be avoided by eliminating product lines. What sacrifices will Mazda likely have to make to obtain the cost savings associated with eliminating product lines?

b. Suppose that the cost data in the table below apply to three sales channels that were eliminated through the consolidation program.

   Additional Information

   1. Sales are expected to drop by 10 percent because of the consolidation program. The remaining sales volume was absorbed by other sales channels.
   2. Half the sales staff accepted transfers that placed them in positions in other sales channels. The other half left the company.
   3. The supervisor of Channel 1 accepted a job transfer. The other two supervisors left the company.

Annual Costs of Operating Each Sales Channel	Channel 1	Channel 2	Channel 3
Unit-level selling costs			
Selling supplies cost	$25,000	$18,000	$32,000
Sales commissions	285,000	180,000	340,000
Shipping and handling	32,000	19,000	39,000
Miscellaneous	16,000	14,000	23,000
Facility-level selling costs			
Rent	196,000	189,000	192,000
Utilities	32,000	38,000	40,000
Staff salaries	720,000	684,000	870,000
Supervisory salaries	120,000	80,000	136,000
Amortization on equipment	240,000	246,000	242,000
Allocated companywide facility-level expenses	80,000	80,000	80,000

   4. The combined equipment with an expected remaining useful life of four years and a $100,000 salvage value, had a market value of $500,000.
   5. The offices operated by the eliminated channels were closed.
      Determine the amount of annual costs saved by consolidating the sales channels.

c. How will reducing inventory save costs?

d. Although the cost-cutting measures are impressive, Mr. Wallace was quoted as saying, "Obviously no one is going to succeed in our business just by reducing costs." Speculate as to some other measures that Mr. Wallace could take to improve Mazda's profitability.

GROUP ASSIGNMENT   *Relevance and Cost Behaviour*   **ACT 4-2**

Maccoa Soft, a division of Zayer Software Company, produces and distributes an automated payroll software system. A contribution margin format income statement for Maccoa Soft for the past year follows:

Revenue (12,000 units × $1,200)	$14,400,000
Unit-Level Variable Costs	
Product Materials Cost (12,000 × $60)	(720,000)
Installation Labour Cost (12,000 × $200)	(2,400,000)
Manufacturing Overhead (12,000 × $2)	(24,000)
Shipping and Handling (12,000 × $25)	(300,000)
Sales Commissions (12,000 × $300)	(3,600,000)

(Table continued on the following page)

Nonmanufacturing Miscellaneous Costs (12,000 × $5)	(60,000)
Contribution Margin (12,000 × $608)	$7,296,000
Fixed Expenses	
Research and Development	(2,700,000)
Legal Fees to Ensure Product Protection	(780,000)
Advertising Costs	(1,200,000)
Rental Cost of Manufacturing Facility	(600,000)
Amortization on Production Equipment (zero market value)	(300,000)
Other Manufacturing Cost (salaries, utilities, etc.)	(744,000)
Division-Level Facility Sustaining Expenses	(1,730,000)
Allocated Companywide Facility-Level Expenses	(1,650,000)
Net Loss	$ (2,408,000)

a. Divide the class into groups and then organize the groups into three sections. Assign Task 1 to the first section, Task 2 to the second section, and Task 3 to the third section. Each task should be considered independently of the others.

Group Tasks

1. Assume that Maccoa has excess capacity. The sales staff has identified a large franchise company with 200 outlets that is interested in Maccoa's software system but is willing to pay only $800 for each program. Ignoring qualitative considerations, should Maccoa accept the special order?
2. Maccoa has the opportunity to purchase a comparable payroll system from a competing vendor for $600 per program. Ignoring qualitative considerations, should Maccoa outsource the software? Maccoa would continue to sell and install the software if the manufacturing activities were outsourced.
3. Given that Maccoa is generating a loss, should Zayer eliminate it? Would your answer change if Maccoa could increase sales by 1,000 units?

b. Have a representative from each section explain its respective conclusions. Discuss the following:

(1) Representatives from Section 1 should respond to the following: The analysis related to the special order (i.e., Task 1) suggests that all variable costs are always relevant. Is this conclusion valid? Explain your answer.
(2) Representatives from Section 2 should respond to the following: With respect to the outsourcing decision, identify a relevant fixed cost and a nonrelevant fixed cost. Discuss the criteria for determining whether a cost is or is not relevant.
(3) Representatives from Section 3 should respond to the following: Why did the segment elimination decision change when the volume of production and sales increased?

ACT 4-3   **ETHICAL DILEMMA**   *Asset Replacement Clouded by Self-Interest*

John Dillworth is in charge of buying property used as building sites for branch offices of the National Bank of Commerce. Mr. Dillworth recently paid $110,000 for a site located in a growing section of the city. Shortly after purchasing this lot, Mr. Dillworth had the opportunity to purchase a more desirable lot at a significantly lower price. The traffic count at the new site is virtually twice that of the old site, but the price of the lot is only $80,000. It was immediately apparent that he had overpaid for the previous purchase. The current market value of the purchased property is only $75,000. Mr. Dillworth believes that it would be in the bank's best interests to buy the new lot, but he does not want to report a loss to his boss Kelly Fullerton. He knows that Ms. Fullerton will severely reprimand him, even though she has made her share of mistakes. In fact, he is aware of a significant bad loan that Ms. Fullerton recently approved. When confronted with the bad debt by the senior vice-president in charge of commercial lending, Ms. Fullerton blamed the decision on one of her former subordinates, Ira Sacks. Ms. Fullerton implied that Mr. Sacks had been dismissed for reckless lending activities when, in fact, he had been an excellent lending officer with an uncanny ability to assess the credit-worthiness of his customers. Indeed, Mr. Sacks had voluntarily resigned to accept a better position.

Required

a. Determine the amount of the loss to be recognized on the sale of the existing branch site.
b. Name the type of cost represented by the $110,000 original purchase price of the land. Also, name the type of cost represented by its current market value of $75,000. Indicate which cost is relevant to a decision as to whether the original site should be replaced the new site.

c. Is Mr. Dillworth's conclusion that the old site should be replaced supported by quantitative analysis? If not, what facts justify his conclusion?

d. Discuss the ethical dilemma that Mr. Dillworth faces within the context of Donald Cressey's common features of ethical misconduct that were outlined in Chapter 1.

SPREADSHEET ASSIGNMENT   *Using Excel*   ACT 4-4

Dorina Company makes cases of canned dog food in batches of 1,000 cases and sells each case for $15. The plant capacity is 50,000 cases; the company currently makes 40,000 cases. DoggieMart has offered to buy 1,500 cases for $12 per case. Because product-level and facility-level costs are unaffected by a special order, they are omitted.

Required

a. Prepare a spreadsheet like the following one to calculate the contribution to income if the special order is accepted. Construct formulas so that the number of cases or the price could be changed and the new contribution would be automatically calculated.

b. Try different order sizes (such as 2,000) or different prices to see the effect on contribution to profit.

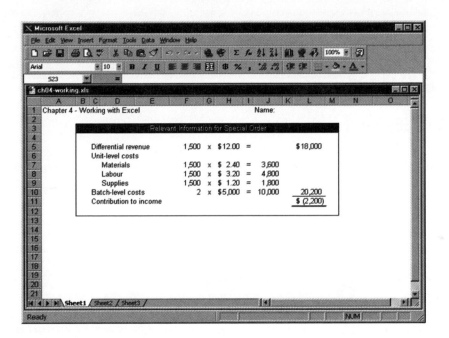

Spreadsheet Tips

1. The numbers in Cells F7 to F9 should be formulas that refer to F5. This allows the number of cases to be changed in Cell F5 with the other cells changing automatically.

2. The formula in Cell F10 uses a function named ROUNDUP to calculate the even number of batches. The formula should be =ROUNDUP(F5/1000,0), where the zero refers to rounding up to the nearest whole number.

SPREADSHEET ASSIGNMENT   *Mastering Excel*   ACT 4-5

Refer to the data in Problem 4-9A.

Required

a. Prepare a spreadsheet to solve Requirements *a*, *b*, and *c*.

b. While construcing formulas for Requirement *a*, include a formula to calculate contribution margin per labour hour.

c. While constructing formulas for Requirement *b*, include formulas to calculate total contribution margin for each product.

d. While constructing formulas for Requirement *c*, include formulas to calculate contribution margin per machine hour and total contribution margin for each product.

Cost Accumulation, Tracing, and Allocation

After completing this chapter, you should be able to:

1 Understand the relationships among cost objects, cost drivers, and cost allocation.

2 Distinguish between direct cost and indirect cost.

3 Appreciate the unique nature of the direct cost concept and understand the context-sensitive nature of cost classification.

4 Understand the mathematical procedures used to make allocations.

5 Select appropriate cost drivers for making allocations under a variety of circumstances.

6 Understand the implications of cost behaviour associated with making allocations.

7 Understand the need to establish cost pools.

8 Understand the allocation of common costs associated with joint products and byproducts.

9 Understand the association between cost allocation and relevance.

10 Understand the allocation of service centre costs to operating departments under the direct and step methods. (Appendix)

the *curious* manager

Andrea just finished "Barrista school" in preparation for her new job at a local Espresso shop. She was now quite expert at grinding beans, drawing espresso, steaming milk, and preparing coffee to satisfy the most demanding customer. During her schooling, she learned that the "cost" of a cappuccino was $0.30. The menu at her work listed a cappuccino for $3.75. What could Andrea's manager say to justify the charge of $3.75?

*"How much does it cost?" is one of the world's most frequently asked questions in business as well as in society in general. Business managers need cost information for a variety of reasons. Determining the cost to operate a department, branch office, or division of a business is important for performance evaluation. Did cost increase or decrease from last year's level? Who is responsible? Who should be rewarded? How can improvement be accomplished? Similarly, determining the cost of products is necessary for performance evaluation, decision making, and financial reporting. Were the actual costs incurred to make a product consistent with expected costs? Can we sell our products for a price that will cover our cost and provide adequate profitability? What amount of product cost should appear in the inventory accounts on the balance sheet? What is the **cost** of goods sold? As this discussion implies, managers need to know the cost of many different objects. These **cost objects** include the cost of products, processes, departments, services, activities, properties, and so on. This chapter focuses on the managerial accounting techniques used to determine the cost of a variety of objects.*

▮ Use of Cost Drivers to Accumulate Costs

LO1

Understand the relationships among cost objects, cost drivers, and cost allocation.

Determining the cost of a particular object is called **cost accumulation**. Unfortunately, determining the exact cost of most cost objects is impossible; cost accumulation is an imprecise practice that requires considerable judgment and estimation. Suppose that the advertising manager of the Toronto Blue Jays is considering a promotional campaign that would provide a free baseball cap to all children who attend a Tuesday night ball game. The manager wants to know the cost of the proposed campaign (i.e., the cost object). To determine the cost of the campaign, the team's accountant must accumulate several individual costs into a single total. Some of the costs are for the caps, the advertising necessary to announce the promotion, and the wages of the employees who would work on the campaign. For simplicity, we consider these items to be the only cost components used to determine the total campaign cost.

The first step in determining the amounts of the individual cost components is to identify the factors that *drive* the costs. A **cost driver** is any factor having a *cause-and-effect relationship* with a cost object. For example, children attending the promotional ball game will *cause* the incurrence of cap costs that, in turn, has an *effect* on the cost of the proposed campaign (i.e., cost object). Accordingly, the number of children is a *cost driver* of the proposed campaign. The more children attending, the higher the cost of the campaign will be. Fewer children will mean lower total cost. Assuming that caps cost $2.50 each and 4,000 children attend, the cost of caps would be $10,000 ($2.50 $\times$ 4,000). Similarly, the cost to announce the campaign is driven by the number of advertisements. If advertisements cost $100 each and 50 are used, the cost of announcing the campaign is $5,000 ($100 $\times$ 50). The cost of the employee is driven by the number of hours he spends working on the project. Assuming that the employee is paid $8 per hour and works 100 hours, the cost of employee compensation is $800 ($8 $\times$ 100). On the basis of this information, the *accumulated relevant cost* of the promotional campaign (i.e., cost object) is $15,800 ($10,000 + $5,000 + $800). A manager should weigh this cost against the benefit of the expected increase in sales revenue that the free-cap promotion would generate. If the incremental (i.e., relevant) revenue were higher than the expected relevant cost of the campaign, the manager should proceed with plans to implement the campaign.

Estimated versus Actual Cost

Obviously, the amount of the accumulated cost for the promotional campaign—$15,800—is an *estimate*. No one knows for sure how many children will attend or how many hours the employee will be required to work. Estimating these numbers and the level of expected sales requires a considerable amount of guesswork. Increased accuracy can be attained by measuring costs and benefits after the campaign has been conducted. At that time, the actual cost of caps, advertisements, and employee compensation can be measured precisely. While the *actual* information is more accurate, it is not relevant. Knowing that costs exceeded benefits after the fact is of no use. Managers need to know about costs and benefits before the activities that cause them have occurred; they need timely information. For this reason, managers are willing to accept the unavoidable inaccuracies associated with cost estimation to obtain relevant information. Remember that to be relevant, information must have a future orientation.

Cost estimates may be useful in many circumstances. For instance, estimates may be used to set prices, make bids, evaluate proposals, distribute resources, plan production, and set goals. Actual cost data are required in other circumstances. For example, actual cost data are used in public financial reports and to evaluate managerial performance. Indeed, both estimated and actual cost data are frequently accumulated for the same cost object. For example, it is common practice to use cost estimates to establish managerial goals and to use actual cost data to evaluate performance regarding the attainment of those goals. In the following paragraphs, you will encounter a number of business scenarios in which estimated data, actual data, or a combination of both are used.

▋ Assignment of Cost to Objects in a Retail Business

In Style, Inc. (ISI) is a retail clothing store that sells merchandise for women, men, and children. The company's income statement for the month of January 2009 is shown in Exhibit 5–1. ISI's operations are subdivided into three departments: women's, men's, and children's. ISI encourages the manager of each department to maximize sales by paying him a bonus based on a percentage of departmental sales dollars, a strategy that has been somewhat successful. Total sales in each department has definitely increased. Unfortunately, some negative side effects have also occurred. The managers have begun to fight among themselves over the availability of floor space; each manager wants more space in which to display merchandise. They argue with the store manager over the types of clothing they are permitted to carry. Each manager wants to offer customers a wider selection of goods. In some instances, managers have attempted to lower prices and to increase sales commissions. In the drive to maximize sales, the managers have lost sight of the need to control costs. In an effort to remedy the situation, the store manager has decided to base future bonuses on a department's contribution to profitability, rather than the amount of its sales.

Identification of Direct versus Indirect Costs

The first step in the development of the new bonus strategy is to determine the cost to operate each department. In this case, each department is classified as a separate *cost object*. The process of assigning costs to two or more objects requires **cost tracing** and **cost allocation**. Costs that are easily traceable to a cost object are called *direct costs*. Costs that cannot be easily traced to a cost object are labelled *indirect costs*. The measure of whether a cost is easily traceable or not depends on *cost/benefit analysis*.

Exhibit 5-1	*Income Statement*
IN STYLE, INC.	
Income Statement	
For the Month Ended January 31	
Sales	$ 360,000
Cost of Goods Sold	(216,000)
Gross Margin	$ 144,000
Sales Commissions	(18,000)
Depart. Managers' Salaries	(12,000)
Store Manager's Salary	(9,360)
Amortization	(16,000)
Rental Fee for Store	(18,400)
Utilities	(2,300)
Advertising	(7,200)
Supplies	(900)
Net Income	$ 59,840)

LO2

Distinguish between direct cost and indirect cost.

Some of ISI's costs can be easily traced to the cost objects (i.e., specific departments), but others cannot be. For example, the cost of goods sold can be easily traced to the specific departments. The price tags are coded so that the scanner that rings up sales reads both the sales price and a departmental code. Indeed, the specific type of merchandise, including size, colour, and so on, is coded so that inventory records can be maintained perpetually, thereby facilitating effective inventory management. Cost of goods sold data are not only easily traceable but also is useful in making many decisions. ISI's managers can gain significant insight into the company's purchasing and pricing strategies by analyzing its cost of goods sold history. Is a department currently paying more or less for its merchandise than it paid a year ago? Is it paying more or less than its competitors are paying? By analyzing the relationships between cost of goods sold and sales, departmental managers can determine whether they are charging more or less for goods than their competitors are charging. Because the sacrifice required to trace *cost of goods sold* is small in relation to the informational benefits attained, the cost would be classified as a *direct cost*.

In contrast, the cost of supplies (shopping bags, sales slips, pens, staples, price tags) used by each department are much more difficult to trace. How could the number of staples used to seal the shopping bags that contain customer purchases be determined? The sales staff could count the number of staples used, but this would require considerable effort for very little benefit. Staples are so inexpensive that no one really cares how many are used. Although tracing the cost of supplies to each department may be possible, it is not economically beneficial to do so. Accordingly, the cost of supplies would be classified as an *indirect cost.*

In summary, direct and indirect costs can be defined as follows:

Direct costs can be traced to objects in a *cost-effective*, economically beneficial manner.

Indirect costs cannot be traced to objects in a *cost-effective*, economically beneficial manner.

ISI's accountant reviewed the data in the income statement in Exhibit 5–1. Her analysis resulted in the classifications shown in Exhibit 5–2; her rationale for the classifications is discussed in the following paragraph:

All figures represent the amount of costs incurred during the month of January. Items 1 though 4 represent the direct costs, which are traceable to the cost objects in a cost-effective manner. Cost of goods sold is traced at the point of sale through a scanning system that identifies the department. Sales commissions are determined on the basis of a percentage of departmental sales and are therefore easy to trace to the departments. Because the departmental managers' duties are restricted to their designated departments, their salaries are easily traceable. Equipment, furniture, and fixtures are tagged with departmental codes that permit amortization charges to be traced directly to specific departments. Items 5 through 8 are incurred for the company as a whole and are therefore not directly traceable to any specific department. Although Item 9 could be traced to specific departments, the cost of doing so would exceed the benefits. Accordingly, the cost of supplies is also classified as an indirect cost.

Exhibit 5-2	Income Statement Classification of Costs			
	Direct Costs			**Indirect**
Cost Item	**Women's**	**Men's**	**Children's**	**Costs**
1. Cost of Goods Sold—$216,000	$120,000	$58,000	$38,000	
2. Sales Commissions—$18,000	9,500	5,500	3,000	
3. Dept. Managers' Salaries—$12,000	5,000	4,200	2,800	
4. Amortization—$16,000	7,000	5,000	4,000	
5. Store Manager's Salary				$ 9,360
6. Rental Fee for Store				18,400
7. Utilities				2,300
8. Advertising				7,200
9. Supplies				900
Totals	$141,500	$72,700	$47,800	$38,160

Cost Definitions—Independent and Context Sensitive

LO3

Appreciate the unique nature of the direct cost concept and understand the context-sensitive nature of cost classification.

It is important to note that the definitions for direct and indirect costs are independent of the definitions for fixed cost versus variable cost. For example, both the cost of goods sold and the cost of supplies vary in relation to the volume of sales (both are variable costs), but one is classified as direct and the other as indirect. Furthermore, the cost of rent and the cost of amortization are both fixed in relation to the volume of sales, but the cost of rent is classified as an indirect cost and the cost of amortization is classified as a direct cost. Indeed, the same exact cost can be classified as direct or indirect, depending on the cost object's designation. For example, the store manager's salary is not directly traceable to the cost of operating a specific department, but it is traceable to the operation of a particular store.

Similarly, the designations *direct* versus *indirect* are independent of the characteristics that determine relevance. For example, both the cost of goods sold and the cost of supplies for a particular department could be avoided if that department were eliminated. Accordingly, both costs are relevant to a segment elimination decision, yet one is classified as direct, and the other is classified as indirect. These examples emphasize the fact that you cannot memorize a list of costs as being direct or indirect, fixed or variable, relevant or not relevant. When trying to identify costs as to type or behaviour, you must consider the cost in relation to the context within which it resides.

Allocation of Indirect Costs to Objects

Allocation is the process of dividing a total cost into parts and distributing the parts among the relevant cost objects. Accordingly, *cost allocation* is sometimes called *cost distribution*. With respect to ISI, how much of the $38,160 of indirect costs should be allocated to each of the three departments? The first step in the allocation process is to identify the most appropriate cost driver for each cost. To the extent possible, costs should be distributed to reflect the way the departments consume resources. The cost driver enables the accountant to tie the consumption of resources to the cost objects. For example, the store rental fee is related to the size of the store space. Holding other factors constant, the larger the building, the higher is the rental fee. In other words, the size of the store is *driving* the rental cost. On the basis of this rationale, a department that occupies a larger portion of the floor space should be allocated a larger portion of the rental cost. Assume that the store capacity is 23,000 square feet with 12,000, 7,000, and 4,000 square feet being occupied by the women's, men's, and children's departments, respectively. A rational allocation can be accomplished according to the following two-step process.[1]

LO4
Understand the mathematical procedures used to make allocations.

Step 1.   Compute the *allocation rate* by dividing the *total cost to be allocated* ($18,400 rental fee) by the *cost driver* (23,000 square feet of store space). *Since the cost driver is the basis for the allocation process, it is sometimes called the **allocation base**.* The result of the process is called the **allocation rate**. The computation follows:

Total cost to be allocated	÷	Cost driver (i.e., allocation base)	=	Allocation rate
$18,400 rental fee	÷	23,000 square feet	=	$0.80 per square foot

Step 2.   Multiply the *allocation rate* by the *weight of the cost driver* (i.e., weight of the base) to determine the allocation *per cost object*. This computation follows:

Cost Object	Allocation Rate	×	Number of Square Feet	=	Allocation per Cost Object
Women's department	$0.80	×	12,000	=	$ 9,600
Men's department	0.80	×	7,000	=	5,600
Children's department	0.80	×	4,000	=	3,200
Total			23,000		$18,400

Cost of utilities can also be logically related to the amount of floor space occupied by each department. The more floor space used, the more heating, lighting, air conditioning, and so on will be consumed. Accordingly, floor space can be considered to be a reasonable cost driver for utility cost. On the basis of square footage, the cost allocated to each department is computed as follows:

---

[1] Note that other mathematical approaches can be used to determine the same result. However, to reduce confusion, this text consistently uses the two-step method described here. More specifically, the text consistently follows the practice of determining the amount of an allocation by (1) computing a *rate*, and (2) multiplying the *rate* by the *weight of the base* (i.e., cost driver).

How does Air Canada know the cost of flying a passenger from Montreal, Quebec to Vancouver, British Columbia? The fact is that Air Canada does not know the actual cost of flying particular passengers anywhere. There are many indirect costs associated with flying passengers. Some of these include the cost of planes, fuel, pilots, office buildings, and ground personnel. Indeed, besides insignificant food and beverage costs, there are few costs that could be traced directly to customers. Air Canada and other airlines are forced to use allocation and averaging to determine the estimated cost of providing transportation services to customers. It is estimated, rather than actual, cost that is used for decision-making purposes.

© Photodisc/PhotoLink

Step 1. Compute the *allocation rate* by dividing the *total cost to be allocated* ($2,300 utility cost) by the *cost driver* (23,000 square feet of store space). The computation of the allocation rate for utility cost follows:

Total cost to be allocated	÷	Cost driver	=	Allocation rate
$2,300 utility cost	÷	23,000 square feet	=	$0.10 per square foot

Step 2. Multiply the *allocation rate* by the *weight of the cost driver* to determine the *allocation per cost object*:

Cost Object	Allocation Rate	×	Number of Square Feet	=	Allocation per Cost Object
Women's department	$0.10	×	12,000	=	$1,200
Men's department	0.10	×	7,000	=	700
Children's department	0.10	×	4,000	=	400
Total			23,000		$2,300

Selection of a Cost Driver

LO5

Select appropriate cost drivers for making allocations under a variety of circumstances.

Frequently, more than one driver is associated with a particular indirect cost. For example, the use of supplies can be logically related to floor space. The more floor space a department occupies, the more merchandise it displays. Accordingly, a department that occupies more floor space is also likely to use more hangers, price tags, and shopping bags. This relationship may be weak, however, if the types of merchandise differ among departments. Suppose that one department is displaying men's coats in the same amount of space that another department uses to display boys' T-shirts. Because the store sells more T-shirts than men's coats, square footage would not constitute the best basis for the utilization of shopping bags; a more rational cost driver would be the number of sales transactions. The best cost driver is the one with the strongest cause-and-effect relationship. The more sales transactions that are completed, the more bags, cash register tape, and staples are consumed. Sales transactions cause supplies to be consumed; floor space does not.

The *availability of information* can also affect the selection of the allocation base (cost driver). Suppose that we decide that the number of sales transactions is the most logical cost driver for the assignment of supplies cost. Even so, we would not be able to use this base unless the company maintains records that show the number of sales transactions per department. If a store tracks the dollar volume of sales but not the number of transactions, we may accept the use of dollar volume as the cost driver even though we believe that the number of transactions has a stronger cause-and-effect relationship. On the basis of the information provided for the ISI illustration, sales volume expressed in dollars appears to be the most reasonable cost driver (allocation base) for the assignment of supplies cost. Assume that sales volume for the women's, men's and children's departments was $190,000, $110,000, and $60,000, respectively. The computations for the appropriate allocation of supplies cost follow:

Step 1.   Compute the *allocation rate* by dividing the *total cost to be allocated* ($900 supplies cost) by the *cost driver* ($360,000 total sales volume). The computation of the allocation rate for supply cost is as follows:

Total cost to be allocated	÷	Cost driver	=	Allocation rate
$900 supplies cost	÷	$360,000 sales volume	=	$0.0025 per sales dollar

Step 2.   Multiply the *allocation rate* by the *weight of the cost driver* to determine the *allocation per cost object*:

Cost Object	Allocation Rate	×	Sales Volume	=	Allocation per Cost Object
Women's department	$0.0025	×	190,000	=	$475
Men's department	0.0025	×	110,000	=	275
Children's department	0.0025	×	60,000	=	150
Total			360,000		$ 90

The advertising cost could also be related to the sales volume. It could be argued that the sales generated in each department were influenced by the general advertising campaign. The computations for the appropriate allocation of advertising cost follow:

Step 1.   Compute the *allocation rate* by dividing the *total cost to be allocated* ($7,200 advertising cost) by the *cost driver* ($360,000 total sales volume). The computation of the *allocation rate* for advertising cost follows:

Total cost to be allocated	÷	Cost driver	=	Allocation rate
$7,200 advertising cost	÷	$360,000 sales volume	=	$0.02 per sales dollar

Step 2.   Multiply the *allocation rate* by the *weight of the cost driver* to determine the *allocation per cost object*:

Cost Object	Allocation Rate	×	Sales Volume	=	Allocation per Cost Object
Women's department	$0.02	×	190,000	=	$3,800
Men's department	0.02	×	110,000	=	2,200
Children's department	0.02	×	60,000	=	1,200
Total			360,000		$7,200

The selection of the most appropriate cost driver for the store manager's salary requires considerable judgment. No strong cause-and-effect relationship exists between the manager's salary and the departments. In other words, no definitive cost driver exists. The manager is paid the same salary, regardless of the level of sales, the square footage of store space, the number of hours worked, or any other identifiable variable. Under these circumstances, making the arbitrary allocation of an equal portion of the total cost to each department may be necessary. The results of the allocation process should be used with great care, recognizing their imprecision when a weak relationship exists between cost drivers and costs to be allocated. So that you can verify the validity of the two-step allocation process, the computations follow:

Step 1. Compute the *allocation rate* by dividing the *total cost to be allocated* ($9,360 manager's monthly salary) by the *allocation base* (number of departments). The computation follows:

Total cost to be allocated	÷	Cost driver	=	Allocation rate
$9,360 store manager's salary	÷	3 departments	=	$3,120 per department

Step 2. Multiply the *allocation rate* by the *weight of the cost driver* to determine the *allocation per cost object*:

Cost Object	Allocation Rate	×	Number of Departments	=	Allocation per Cost Object
Women's department	$3,120	×	1	=	$3,120
Men's department	3,120	×	1	=	3,120
Children's department	3,120	×	1	=	3,120
Total			3		$9,360

Behavioural Implications

LO6

Understand the implications of cost behaviour associated with making allocations.

Exhibit 5–3 shows the profit generated by each department for January. The supervisors of the three departments were paid bonuses on the basis of their department's contributions to profitability. The store manager noticed an immediate change in the attitudes of the departmental managers. For example, the manager of the women's department offered to give up 1,000 square feet of floor space because she believed that she was carrying too many different lines of clothes and that reducing the selection of available products would not reduce sales significantly. Customers would simply buy a different brand. Although sales would not decline dramatically, her allocation of rental and utility cost would decrease, thereby increasing the profitability of her department.

In contrast, the manager of the children's department wanted the extra space. He believed that he was losing sales because his department did not have the floor space available to offer an adequate selection of merchandise. He believed that his department operated at a disadvantage. Customers came to the store to shop at the women's department, but they did not come to specifically shop at his department. He wanted the extra space to carry the items that would encourage customers to come to the store for the purpose of buying children's wear. He believed that he could generate enough additional sales to cover the additional allocation of rental and utility costs.

In summary, the store manager was pleased with the new emphasis on profitability that resulted from tracing and assigning costs to the specific departments.

Exhibit 5-3	*Profit Analysis by Department*			
	Department			
	Women's	**Men's**	**Children's**	**Total**
Sales	$190,000	$110,000	$ 60,000	$360,000
Cost of goods sold	(120,000)	(58,000)	(38,000)	(216,000)
Sales commissions	(9,500)	(5,500)	(3,000)	(18,000)
Supervisors' salary	(5,000)	(4,200)	(2,800)	(12,000)
Amortization	(7,000)	(5,000)	(4,000)	(16,000)
Store manager's salary	(3,120)	(3,120)	(3,120)	(9,360)
Rental fee for store	(9,600)	(5,600)	(3,200)	(18,400)
Utilities	(1,200)	(700)	(400)	(2,300)
Advertising	(3,800)	(2,200)	(1,200)	(7,200)
Supplies	(475)	(275)	(150)	(900)
Departmental profit	$ 30,305	$ 25,405	$ 4,130	$ 59,840

The manager would probably agree that the "cost" of a cappuccino was $0.30, if you only consider the coffee beans and milk. However, she would then explain that the menu price of $3.75 would have to recover the cost of Andrea's salary, the cost of the espresso machine, rent on the shop, cleaning, security, property taxes, payroll benefits, business taxes, tables, chairs, and so on. If there was anything left over, that would be the owner's return for his or her investment and time.

■ Effects of Cost Behaviour on the Selection of the Most Appropriate Cost Driver

As previously indicated, indirect costs may exhibit variable or fixed cost behaviour patterns. The failure to consider the effects of cost behaviour in the allocation process can lead to significant distortions in the measurement of product cost. Accordingly, we next examine the critical relationships between cost behaviour and cost allocation.

LO6

Understand the implications of cost behaviour associated with making allocations.

Using Volume Measures to Allocate Variable Overhead Costs

A *causal relationship* exists between the incurrence of variable overhead costs (e.g., indirect materials, inspection costs, utilities) and the volume of production. More specifically, increases in the volume of production cause variable overhead costs to increase. In other words, *volume drives the incurrence of the cost*. For example, the cost of indirect materials, such as glue, staples, screws, nails, and varnish, will increase or decrease in proportion to the number of units of furniture that a manufacturing company makes. For this reason, *volume measures serve as good cost drivers* for the allocation of variable overhead costs.

Volume can be expressed in a variety of ways. For example, number of units can be used to measure volume. Alternatively, volume could be expressed by the number of labour hours required to complete the production process. Furthermore, the amount of direct materials used in the production process could act as a measure of the volume of activity. Units, labour hours, and direct materials consumption are only three of many possible measures of volume. Given the variety of possible measures of volume, how does management select the most appropriate one to use as the cost driver (allocation base) for the assignment of particular overhead costs? Selecting the most appropriate measure of volume to use as the cost driver requires judgment and the exercise of logic. To illustrate, consider the case of Filmier Furniture Company.

Using Units as the Cost Driver

During its most recent accounting period, Filmier Furniture Company produced 5,000 items of furniture, including 4,000 chairs and 1,000 tables. It incurred $60,000 of *indirect materials* cost during the period. How much of this cost should be allocated to chairs versus tables? Using number of units as the cost driver produces the following allocation:

Step 1.　Compute the *allocation rate*.

Total cost to be allocated	÷	Cost driver	=	Allocation rate
$60,000 variable overhead cost	÷	5,000 units	=	$12 per unit

Step 2. Multiply the *allocation rate* times the *weight of the cost driver* to determine the *allocation per object.*

Product	Allocation Rate	×	Number of Units Produced	=	Allocation Cost
Tables	$12	×	1,000	=	$12,000
Chairs	12	×	4,000	=	48,000
Total	12	×	5,000	=	$60,000

Using Direct Labour Hours as the Cost Driver

When the number of units is used as the cost driver, an *equal amount* ($12) of indirect materials cost is assigned to each unit of furniture. This may be inappropriate if one type of furniture requires more indirect materials to make than the other type does. For example, assume that a table is larger and more complicated to make than a chair. Accordingly, making a table requires more labour and materials. To illustrate, assume that the following information applies to the chairs and tables made by the Filmier Furniture Company:

	Tables	Chairs	Total
Direct labour hours	3,500 hrs.	2,500 hrs.	6,000 hrs.
Direct materials cost	$1,000,000	$500,000	$1,500,000

Both these measures (direct labour hours, direct materials cost) are volume indicators that are logically linked to the consumption of indirect materials cost. For example, a logical relationship exists between the amount of labour consumed and the amount of indirect materials used. Because workers use materials to make furniture, it is logical to assume that the longer they work, the more materials they use. Following this line of reasoning, the indirect materials cost could be assigned to the chairs and tables as indicated here:

Step 1. Compute the *allocation rate.*

Total cost to be allocated	÷	Cost driver	=	Allocation rate
$60,000 variable overhead cost	÷	6,000 hours	=	$10 per hour

Step 2. Multiply the *allocation rate* by the *weight of the cost driver.*

Product	Allocation Rate	×	Number of Labour Hours	=	Allocation Cost
Tables	$10.00	×	3,500	=	$35,000
Chairs	10.00	×	2,500	=	25,000
Total	10.00		6,000		$60,000

Compared with the allocation based on the number of units, the allocation based on labour hours distributes a larger portion of the indirect materials cost to the tables ($35,000 versus $12,000). Indeed, the allocation is more than double. Is this increase too much? The preceding information suggests that it may be. Recall that tables are larger and more complicated to make than chairs. If the complication requires labour that is not related to the consumption of indirect materials, basing the allocation on labour hours is inappropriate. For example, if the additional labour needed to make a table is required for decorative carvings, the labour is not related to the consumption of indirect materials (glue, staples, screws, nails, and varnish). Under these circumstances, it would be inappropriate to use direct labour as the allocation base for indirect materials cost.

Using Direct Material Dollars as the Cost Driver

Assuming that the number of labour hours is an inappropriate allocation base, we now consider direct material usage as measured by material dollars. A logical link exists between the usage of direct and indirect materials. The more lumber (direct material) that is used, the more glue, nails, and so forth (indirect materials) are used. Accordingly, a case can be made that the use of direct materials drives the use of indirect materials. Using direct materials dollars as the cost driver for indirect materials produces the following allocation:

Step 1.   Compute the *allocation rate*.

Total cost to be allocated	÷	Cost driver	=	Allocation rate
$60,000 variable overhead cost	÷	$1,500,000 direct material dollars	=	$0.04 per material dollar

Step 2.   Multiply the *allocation rate* by the *weight of the cost driver*.

Product	Allocation Rate	×	Number of Material Dollars	=	Allocation Cost
Tables	$0.04	×	$1,000,000	=	$40,000
Chairs	0.04	×	500,000	=	20,000
Total	0.04		$1,500,000		$60,000

Selecting the Best Cost Driver

Which of the three volume-based cost drivers (units, labour hours, or material dollars) results in the most accurate distribution of the overhead cost? As indicated, the answer involves judgment and logical reasoning. Given that the consumption of direct materials is causing the incurrence of the indirect material costs, direct material dollars appears to be the best allocation base for the distribution of this overhead cost. If the cost to be allocated were fringe benefits, however, direct labour hours would be a more appropriate cost driver. Alternatively, if the cost to be allocated were machine maintenance cost, then a new cost driver, machine hours, would constitute a more appropriate base.

The best allocation base for the distribution of any indirect variable cost is the base that most accurately reflects the use of the resource. Products that consume more resources should be allocated a proportionately higher share of the cost of those resources. Attaining the highest degree of accuracy may require the use of multiple cost drivers. For example, using direct labour hours for allocating fringe benefits, material dollars for indirect materials, and machine hours for utilities may be necessary.

Allocating Fixed Overhead Costs

Fixed costs present a unique problem with respect to cost allocation. By definition, a fixed cost has no volume-based cost drivers. Suppose that Lednicky Bottling Company pays $28,000 per year to rent its manufacturing facility. The rental cost remains fixed, no matter how many units of product Lednicky makes. Accordingly, the volume of production does not drive the cost of rent. Even so, we may choose to use a volume-based cost driver as the allocation base. The objective of allocating fixed costs to products is to distribute a *fair share* of the overhead cost to each product. In many instances, a fair share distribution can be accomplished by selecting an allocation base that spreads the total overhead cost equally over the total volume of production. For example, assume that Lednicky produces 2,000,0000 units of bottled water during its 2003 accounting period. If the company sells 1,800,000 units of the bottled water during 2003, how much of the $28,000 of rental cost should be allocated to ending inventory versus the amount that should be allocated to cost of goods sold? The following allocation is a rational solution:

Step 1.   Compute the *allocation rate*.

Total cost to be allocated   ÷   Allocation base   =   Allocation rate
                                        (i.e., cost driver)
$28,000 rental cost   ÷   2,000,000 units   = $0.014 per bottle of water

Because the base (number of units) used to distribute the cost does not drive the cost, it is sometimes called an *allocation base* instead of a *cost driver*; it is common practice to use the terms interchangeably. Accordingly, the term *cost driver* may be used in conjunction with the term *fixed cost*, even though it is a semantic contradiction to do so. Likewise, the term *allocation base* is a common substitute for the term *cost driver*.

Step 2.   Multiply the *allocation rate* by the *weight of the cost driver*.

Financial Statement Item	Allocation Rate	×	Number of Bottles	=	Allocated Cost
Inventory	$0.014	×	200,000	=	$ 2,800
Cost of goods sold	0.014	×	1,800,000	=	25,200

Note that the allocation base (number of units) assigns an equal portion of the rental cost to each unit of product. This is appropriate so long as the units are homogeneous. If the units have independent characteristics, however, choosing a different allocation base to achieve a fair distribution of the rental cost may be necessary. For example, if some of the bottles are significantly larger than others, using some physical measure of direct material usage (e.g., litres) may be more appropriate as an allocation base. Regardless of whether a cost is fixed or variable, selecting the most appropriate allocation base requires logical reasoning and judgment.

■ Allocation of Costs to Solve Timing Problems

Obtaining a fair distribution of fixed costs can be complicated when the volume of production varies from month to month. To illustrate, assume that Grave Manufacturing pays its production supervisor a salary of $3,000 per month. Furthermore, assume that Grave makes 800 units of product in January and 1,875 in February. How much salary cost should be assigned to products made in January and February, respectively? At first glance, the solution appears to be simple. Just divide the $3,000 monthly salary cost by the number of units of product made each month. Specifically, the cost per unit for January and February is as follows:

January $3,000   ÷   800 units   = $3.75 cost per unit
February $3,000   ÷   1,875 units   = $1.60 cost per unit

If this information were used in a cost-plus-pricing decision, products made in January would be priced significantly higher than those made in February. Do you think customers would be willing to pay more for products simply because they happen to be made in January? Obviously not. What is needed is an *allocation base* that will spread the annual salary cost evenly over the annual production. A special timing problem exists, however, if we are attempting to make the allocation before the end of the accounting period. Specifically, the data are needed before the actual costs information is available. The problem is solved by using estimated costs, rather than actual costs.

Suppose that Grave Manufacturing uses a cost-plus-pricing strategy and cannot wait until the end of the year to price its products. On the basis of the preceding information, we can estimate the cost of the supervisor's annual salary (i.e., indirect labour) to be $36,000 ($3,000 × 12 months). Grave Manufacturing cannot be certain that this will be the actual cost of indirect labour because the supervisor may receive a pay raise or may be replaced by a person who is paid a lower salary. Even so, on the basis of the current information, $36,000 is a reasonable estimate of the annual indirect labour cost. Next, it is necessary to estimate the total annual volume of production. Suppose that last year's production was 18,000 units and the company expects no significant change. On the basis of this information, we can make the following allocation of indirect materials cost for January and February:

Step 1.   Compute the *allocation rate*.

Total cost to be allocated	÷	Allocation base (i.e., cost driver)	=	Allocation rate
$36,000	÷	18,000 units	=	$2.00 *per unit*

Step 2.   Multiply the *rate* by the *weight of the base* (number of units per month) to determine the portion of the salary cost to allocate to the monthly production.

Month	Allocation Rate	×	Number of Units Produced	=	Allocation per Month
January	$2.00	×	800	=	$1,600
February	2.00	×	1,875	=	3,750

These allocated costs are added to other product costs incurred during the month to determine the total estimated product cost. The estimated product cost is then used in cost-plus-pricing or other managerial decisions.

The use of estimated data is common with many overhead costs. An example is the allocation of indirect materials (i.e., supplies) cost. When production supplies are maintained under a periodic inventory system, the amount of actual supplies used cannot be determined until the end of the accounting period. Accordingly, estimated supply cost must be used for decisions made during the accounting period. Note that the allocation base (i.e., total expected annual production) is an estimate as well. The actual number of units produced will be unknown until the end of the accounting period. Because the overhead allocation rate is determined *before* the actual data are known, the rate is customarily called a **predetermined overhead rate**. The predetermined overhead rate may be used for product costing purposes during an accounting period, but actual cost data must be used in year-end public financial statements. Accordingly, it may be necessary to make year-end adjustments to the accounting records when estimated data are used on an interim basis. The procedures required to accomplish such adjustments are discussed in Chapter 8 of this text.

▍ Cost Allocation: The Human Factor

Anyone who has tried to divide a candy bar between two children has probably experienced the human side of the allocation process. In practice, allocations frequently have a significant impact on individuals. They may affect performance evaluation and the level of compensation that managers receive. Likewise, allocations may dictate the amount of resources made available to departments, divisions, and other organizational subunits. The manager who has control over resources usually has prestige and the opportunity to affect the organization's operations. The following scenario provides insight into fairness and the emotional aspect of allocation decisions.

LO6

Understand the implications of cost behaviour associated with making allocations.

Using Cost Allocation in a Budgeting Decision

A budget is a plan, and Sharon Southport is in dire need of a plan. Dr. Southport is the dean of the School of Business at a major Canadian university. Due to a cutback in provincial funding, the School of Business has been advised that it will receive a 40 percent reduction in the funds available for duplicating services. Four departments operate under Dean Southport's control: management, marketing,

finance, and accounting. Dean Southport is certain that significant waste exists in the school's use of copy equipment and that some departments are more wasteful than others. She is determined to cut the fat out of the budget, rather than simply take 40 percent from every department.

In an effort to analyze the situation, Dean Southport, reviewed last year's expenditures. She had discovered that total copy cost for that year was $36,000. Individual departmental expenditures were $12,000 for management, $10,000 for accounting, $8,000 for finance, and $6,000 for marketing.

Dean Southport wonder how these actual costs would compare with a distribution that divided the total amount of copy cost ($36,000) equally among the four departments. The computations for making the division under this alternative are as follows.

Total copying budget	÷	Number of departments	=	Amount per department
$36,000	÷	4	=	$9,000 *per department*

Dividing the total cost equally suggests that each department should have spent $9,000 for copying costs and implies that the management and accounting departments spent too much on copying costs ($3,000 and $1,000 too much, respectively).

Using Cost Drivers to Make Allocations

To ensure a fair allocation, Dean Southport decides to discuss the matter with the chairpersons of the departments. She presents her findings that the management and accounting departments are spending more than an equal share of the total copy cost and opens the discussion by asking whether the chairpersons agree with this conclusion. Bill Thompson, the chairperson of the management department, protests that an equal allotment is unfair because his department has more faculty members than each of the other three departments. He argues that copy costs are directly related to the size of the faculty; more faculty obviously make more copies. In accounting terms, Thompson is suggesting that the number of faculty members is an appropriate cost driver for the allocation of copy funds.

Thompson suggests the following allocation scheme: Because the School of Business has 72 faculty members (29 in management, 16 in accounting, 12 in finance and 15 in marketing), the allocation should be computed as follows:

Step 1.   Compute the *allocation rate*.

Total cost to be allocated	÷	Cost driver	=	Allocation rate
$36,000	÷	72	=	$500 *per faculty member*

Step 2.   Multiply the *rate* by the *weight of the driver* (the number of faculty per department) to determine the *allocation per object* (department).

Department	Allocation Rate	×	Number of Faculty	=	Allocation per Department	Actual Cost, Previous Year
Management	$500	×	29		$14,500	$12,000
Accounting	500	×	16		8,000	10,000
Finance	500	×	12		6,000	8,000
Marketing	500	×	15		7,500	6,000
Total					$36,000	$36,000

Recall that actual copy cost was $12,000 for management, $10,000 for accounting, $8,000 for finance, and $6,000 for marketing. Accordingly, accounting and finance are overspending when cost allocation is based on the size of the faculty. Seeing these figures, Beth Smethers, chairperson of the accounting department, questions the appropriateness of the use of the number of faculty as the cost driver. Smethers suggests that the *number of students*, rather than the *size of the faculty*, drives the cost of copying. She argues that most copying results from the duplication of syllabi, exams, and handouts and that her department teaches mass sections of introductory accounting in which the student/teacher ratio is extremely high. Because her department teaches more students, it should be expected to spend more on copying even though it has fewer faculty members. Smethers demonstrates her point by recomputing the allocation as follows:

Step 1.   The allocation rate is computed on the basis of number of students. University records indicate that the School of Business taught 1,200 students during the most recent academic year. Accordingly, she computed the allocation rate (i.e., copy cost per student) as follows:

Total cost to be allocated	÷	Cost driver	=	Allocation rate
$36,000	÷	1,200	=	$30 *per student*

Step 2.   Multiply the *rate* by the *weight of the driver* (number of students served by each department) to determine the *allocation per object* (department).

Department	Allocation Rate	×	Number of Students	=	Allocation per Department	Actual Cost, Previous Year
Management	$30	×	330		$ 9,900	$12,000
Accounting	30	×	360		10,800	10,000
Finance	30	×	290		8,700	8,000
Marketing	30	×	220		6,600	6,000
Total					$36,000	$36,000

Choosing the Best Cost Driver

Given the actual copy cost expenditures of $12,000 for management, $10,000 for accounting, $8,000 for finance, and $6,000 for marketing, the allocation based on the number of students suggests that the management department is overspending on copying. Thompson objects vigorously to the use of the number of students as the cost driver. He continues to argue that the size of the faculty is a more appropriate basis for allocation. The chairs of the finance and marketing departments side with Smethers, and the dean is forced to settle the dispute.

Dean Southport recognizes that the views of the chairpersons are clouded by self-interest. Clearly, it is to their advantage to identify the management department as the villain of waste. Further, she recognizes that some duplicating costs are, in fact, related to the size of the faculty. For example, the cost of copying manuscripts that faculty submit for publication relates to faculty size. When more faculty submit articles, the cost of duplication rises. Even so, the dean believes that the number of students, to a significant degree, drives the cost of duplication. Further, she desires to send a signal that encourages faculty to minimize the impact of funding cuts on student services. Accordingly, Dean Southport decides to allocate copying costs on the basis of the number of students served by each department. Thompson is incensed and storms out of the meeting in anger. The dean proceeds with the development of a budget by assigning the amount of available funds to each department via an allocation based on the number of students.

Controlling Emotions

Bill Thompson's behaviour deserves comment. Expressing anger may relieve frustration but is seldom a sign of clear thinking. Obviously, Dean Southport recognized some merit in Thompson's contention that copy costs were related to faculty size. Had Thompson offered a compromise, rather than an emotional outburst, he might have been able to increase his department's share of the allocated funds. Perhaps a portion of the funding base could have been allocated using number of faculty members with the other portion being allocated on the basis of number of students. If Thompson had acted appropriately, all parties might have agreed to the compromise. The technical ability to compute the numbers is of little use without the interpersonal skills necessary to sell ideas. Never forget the human factor.

▌ Establishment of Cost Pools

LO7

Understand the need to establish cost pools.

Allocating every single indirect cost that a company incurs would be a tedious and time-consuming task. To reduce the computational process, organizations frequently accumulate many individual costs into a single total called a **cost pool**. The total cost pool is then allocated to the cost objects. Accordingly, a single allocation can replace numerous allocations that would otherwise be required to distribute each individual cost to the relevant cost objects. For example, a company may accumulate the costs for phones, gas, water, and electricity into a single cost pool called *utilities cost*. The total cost in the utilities cost pool is then allocated to the cost objects, rather than making an individual allocation for each of the four types of utility cost.

How far should the pooling process go? Why not pool amortization on machinery with fringe benefits cost? *Remember that the primary objective of the allocation process is to assign costs to objects in a manner that accurately reflects the incurrence of those costs.* If Product A is made with human labour and Product B is made with machines, pooling fringe benefits with amortization charges will create a total cost pool with no rational cost driver. Because the human labour and machine hours are utilized differently by each product, no single cost driver matches both costs with the objects that cause the cost to be incurred. Different allocation bases (i.e., cost drivers) are necessary so that the different types of costs can be rationally linked to specific products. Accordingly, it is appropriate to limit pooling to costs that are rationally linked to a common cost driver.

▌ Allocation of Joint Costs

LO8

Understand the allocation of common costs associated with joint products and byproducts.

Joint costs are common costs incurred in the process of making two or more products. An example is the cost of raw milk (i.e., joint cost) that is used to make cream, whole milk, 2 percent milk, and skim milk. The products derived from joint costs are called **joint products**. Joint costs include not only materials costs but also the costs incurred to transform the materials into finished products. For example, the common costs incurred to refine crude oil into premium and regular gasoline are classified as joint costs. The point in the production process at which products become separate and identifiable is called the **split-off point**. For balance sheet valuation and income determination, all costs incurred up to the split-off point must be allocated to the joint products. Some products require additional processing after the split-off point. These separate and identifiable costs should be assigned to the specific products that cause their incurrence.

To illustrate, assume that the Westar Chemical Company uses a joint production process that produces two chemical compounds at the split-off point. The joint cost to produce the two compounds is $48,000, including $27,000 of materials cost and $21,000 of processing cost. The joint products consist of 12,000 litres of Compound AK and 4,000 litres of Compound AL. Westar allocates joint costs to the products on the basis of the number of litres of compound produced. After the split-off point, Compound AL requires further processing before it can be sold. In other words, it has a zero market value at the split-off point. The cost of additional processing is $8,000. The 12,000 litres of Compound AK sell for $50,000. The 4,000 litres of Compound AL sell for $13,000. The allocation rate for the *joint cost* is $3 per litre ($48,000 ÷ 16,000 litres). At the split-off point, $36,000 ($3 × 12,000 litres) of the joint cost is allocated to Compound AK and $12,000 ($3 × 4,000) of the joint cost is allocated to Compound AL. The $8,000 of additional processing cost is assigned to Compound AL, resulting in a total cost of $20,000 ($12,000 + $8,000) for that compound. The cost distribution and the determination of gross margin for the two products are shown in Exhibit 5–4.

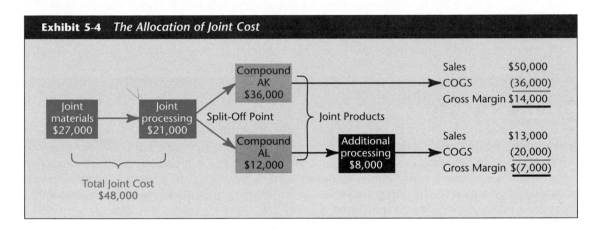

Exhibit 5-4 *The Allocation of Joint Cost*

Joint Costs and the Issue of Relevance

The $7,000 loss generated by Compound AL may lead a naive manager to the mistaken conclusion that the $8,000 of additional processing costs should not be incurred to bring this product to market. In fact, this product is contributing $5,000 ($13,000 sales revenue − $8,000 additional processing cost) to the company's overall profits. The allocated portion of the joint cost ($12,000) is *not relevant* to a decision regarding the further processing of Compound AL. This cost will be incurred, regardless of whether Compound AL is processed beyond the split-off point. Because the allocated cost does *not* differ between the alternatives (i.e., process further versus not process further), it is not a relevant cost. To validate this point, we calculate the total profit for the company under the two alternatives: (1) processing Compound AL beyond the split-off point, and (2) not processing Compound AL beyond the split-off point.

LO9
Understand the association between cost allocation and relevance.

	With Additional Processing	Without Additional Processing
Sales	$63,000	$50,000
Cost of goods sold	(56,000)	(48,000)
Gross margin	$ 7,000	$ 2,000

If Compound AL is processed beyond the split-off point, total revenue will equal the sales revenue of Compound AL and Compound AK ($50,000 + $13,000 = $63,000). Total cost equals the joint cost plus the cost of additional processing ($48,000 + $8,000 = $56,000). Without additional processing, Compound AL has a zero market value. Accordingly, total revenue equals the revenue generated by Compound AK ($50,000), and total cost is equal to the joint cost ($48,000).

Relative Sales Value as the Allocation Base

To distribute the earnings more meaningfully over all joint products, many companies allocate joint costs to products on the basis of the relative sales value of each product at the split-off point. In the case of Westar Chemical, all of the joint cost would be allocated to Compound AK because Compound AL has a zero market value at the split-off point. Accordingly, the gross margins of the two products are computed as follows:

	Compound AK	Compound AL
Sales	$50,000	$13,000
Cost of goods sold	(48,000)	(8,000)
Gross margin	$ 2,000	$ 5,000

Regardless of whether a physical measure (e.g., litres) or the relative sales value is used as the allocation base, joint costs are irrelevant to decisions regarding whether further processing should be pursued. Another way to view the relevance issue is to recognize that joint costs are *sunk costs* with respect to further processing decisions. Because joint costs are incurred before products are processed separately, they represent a historical fact that cannot be changed, regardless of whether further processing takes place.

Byproduct Costs

Like joint products, byproducts share common inputs. The difference between joint products and byproducts is that **byproducts** have a relatively insignificant market value relative to the joint products. An example of a byproduct is sawdust produced in the process of making lumber. Although the accounting treatment for byproducts will not be discussed in this text, you should be aware that the common costs associated with producing them are not relevant with respect to further processing decisions.

---

a look

back

Managers need to know how much it costs. The "it" could be the cost of products, processes, departments, activities, and so on. The item for which accountants attempt to determine the cost is called a *cost object*. Knowing the cost of specific objects enables management to control costs, evaluate performance, and price products. *Direct costs* can be traced to a cost object in a cost-effective manner. Costs that cannot be easily traced to designated objects are called *indirect costs*.

The same cost can be classified as either a direct or indirect cost, depending on the designation of the cost object. For example, the cost of the salary of a manager of a Burger King restaurant can be directly traced to a particular store but cannot be traced to particular products made and sold in the store. The definitions of direct and indirect are independent of the definitions of fixed and variable cost behaviour; they are also independent of the characteristics that determine relevance. A direct cost could be either fixed or variable or either relevant or nonrelevant, depending on the context within which the cost is used. In summary, one cost can be classified as direct/indirect, fixed/variable, or relevant/not relevant, depending on the designation of the cost object.

Indirect costs are assigned to objects through a process known as *cost allocation*. Allocation is the process of dividing an indirect cost into parts and distributing the parts among the relevant cost objects. Costs are frequently allocated to cost objects in proportion to the factors that cause the cost to be incurred. The factors that cause a cost to be incurred are called *cost drivers*. The first step in the allocation process is to determine the allocation rate by dividing the total cost to be allocated by the chosen cost driver. The next step is to multiply the amount of the cost driver for a particular object by the allocation rate. The product is the amount of the cost to be assigned to the cost object.

More than one driver may be associated with a particular indirect cost. The best cost driver is the one that most accurately reflects the use of the resource by the cost object. Objects that consume the highest resources should be allocated a proportionately higher share of the costs. If no strong cost driver exists, making an arbitrary allocation, such as assigning an equal portion of the total cost to each cost object, may be necessary.

Allocations have important behavioural implications. Choosing an inappropriate cost driver can distort allocations and motivate managers to act in ways that are detrimental to the company's profitability.

To avoid the time-consuming task of allocating every single indirect cost, managers accumulate many costs into a single total called a *cost pool*. The costs included in the pool should be those that can logically be allocated to the cost object by a single cost driver. Only one allocation can then be made for the entire cost pool.

The joint costs that are incurred in the process of making two or more products are allocated between the products at the *split-off point*, which is where the products become separate and identifiable. The allocation base can be the products' relative sales values or some measure of the amount of each product made. If one of the joint products requires additional processing costs to bring it to market, only these additional processing costs are relevant to a decision regarding further processing. The allocated joint costs are not relevant because they will be incurred, regardless of whether the byproduct is processed after being split off. Byproducts share common costs with other products but have an insignificant market value relative to their joint products.

a look
forward

The failure to accurately allocate indirect costs to cost objects can result in misinformation that impairs decision making. The next chapter explains how automation has caused distortions in allocations that are determined with traditional allocation approaches. The chapter introduces a new allocation approach known as *activity-based costing* and explains how it can improve efficiency and productivity through a practice known as *activity-based management*. Finally, the chapter introduces a practice known as *total quality management* that seeks to minimize the costs of conforming to a designated standard of quality.

APPENDIX

Allocating Service Centre Costs

Most organizations establish departments responsible for accomplishing specific tasks. Departments that are assigned tasks leading to the accomplishment of the primary objectives of the organization are called **operating departments**. Those that provide support to operating departments are called **service departments**. For example, the department of accounting at a university is classified as an operating department because its faculty perform the university's primary functions of teaching, research, and service. In contrast, the maintenance department is classified as a service department because its employees provide janitorial services that support primary university functions. Professors are more likely to be motivated to perform university functions when facilities are clean, but the university's primary purpose is not to clean buildings. Similarly, the lending department in a bank is an operating department, and the personnel department is a service department. The bank is in the business of making loans. Hiring employees is a secondary function that assists the lending activity.

The costs to produce a product (or a service) include both operating and service department costs. Therefore, service department costs must somehow be allocated to the products produced (or services provided). Service department costs are frequently distributed to products through a two-stage allocation process. First-stage allocations involve the distribution of costs from service centre cost pools to operating department cost pools. In the second stage, costs in the operating cost pools are allocated to products. Three different approaches can be used to allocate costs in the first stage of the two-stage costing process: the *direct method*, the *step method*, and the *reciprocal method*.

Direct Method

The **direct method** is the simplest allocation approach. It allocates service department costs directly to operating department cost pools. To illustrate, assume that Candler & Associates is a law firm that desires to determine the cost of handling each case. The firm has two operating departments; one that represents clients in civil suits and the other that defends clients in criminal cases. The two operating departments are supported by two service departments; personnel and secretarial support. Candler uses a two-stage allocation system to allocate the service centre's costs to the firm's legal cases. In the first stage, the costs to operate each service department are accumulated in separate cost pools. For example, the costs to operate the personnel department are $80,000 in salary, $18,000 in office rental, $12,000 in amortization, $3,000 in supplies, and $4,000 in miscellaneous costs. These costs are added

LO10
Understand the allocation of service centre costs to operating departments under the direct and step methods.

together in a single services department cost pool amounting to $117,000. Similarly, the costs incurred by the secretarial department are accumulated in a cost pool. We assume that this cost pool contains $156,800 of accumulated costs. The amounts in these cost pools are then allocated to the operating departments' cost pools. The appropriate allocations are described in the following paragraphs.

Assume that Candler's accountant decides that the number of attorneys working in the two operating departments constitutes a rational cost driver for the allocation of the personnel department cost pool and that the number of request forms submitted to the secretarial department constitutes a rational cost driver for the allocation of costs accumulated in the secretarial department cost pool. The total number of attorneys working in the two operating departments is 18, with 11 in the civil department and 7 in the criminal department. The secretarial department received 980 work request forms with 380 from the civil department and 600 from the criminal department. Using these cost drivers as the allocation bases, the accountant made the following first-stage allocations:

Determination of Allocation Rates

$$\text{Allocation rate for personnel department cost pool} \quad \frac{\$117,000}{18} \quad = \quad \$6,500 \text{ per attorney}$$

$$\text{Allocation rate for secretarial department cost pool} \quad \frac{\$156,800}{980} \quad = \quad \$160 \text{ per request form}$$

The accountant then multiplied these rates by the weight of the base to determine the amount of each service cost pool to allocate to each operating department cost pool. The appropriate computations are shown in Exhibit 5–1A.

Exhibit 5-1A   First-Stage Allocations for Candler & Associates—Direct Method

Allocated Service Department Overhead	Allocation Rate	×	Weight of Base	=	Civil Department	Criminal Department	Total Service Department Cost Pool
Personnel	$6,500	×	11 attorneys	=	$ 71,500		
	6,500	×	7 attorneys	=		$ 45,500	
Total cost of personnel department							$117,000
Secretarial	$160	×	380 requests	=	60,800		
	160	×	600 requests	=		96,000	
Total cost of secretarial department							156,800
Total of cost pools after allocation				=	132,300	141,500	$273,800
Other operating department overhead costs				=	785,100	464,788	
Total of operating department overhead cost pools				=	$ 917,400	$606,288	

As indicated, the allocated service department costs are pooled with other operating department overhead costs to form the operating department cost pools. In the second stage of the costing process, the costs in the operating department cost pools are allocated to the firm's products (cases). To illustrate second-stage allocations, assume that Candler allocates the operating department overhead cost pools on the basis of billable hours. Further, assume that the civil department expects to bill 30,580 hours to its clients and the criminal department expects to bill 25,262 hours. On the basis of this information, the following predetermined overhead rates are used to allocate operating department cost pools to particular cases:

$$\text{Predetermined overhead rate for the civil department} \quad \frac{\$917,400}{30,580} \quad = \quad \$30 \text{ per billable hour}$$

$$\text{Predetermined overhead rate for the criminal department} \quad \frac{\$606,288}{25,262} \quad = \quad \$24 \text{ per billable hour}$$

These rates are used to calculate the amount of operating department cost pools to include in the determination of the cost to litigate specific cases. For example, a case in the civil department that required 300 billable hours of legal service is allocated $9,000 (300 hours × $30 predetermined overhead rate) of overhead cost. Assuming that the other costs to litigate the case amounted to $25,000, the total cost of this particular case is $34,000 ($25,000 +

$9,000 allocated overhead). This accumulated cost figure could be used as a guide to determine the charge to the client or the profitability of the case.

Step Method

The direct method of allocating service centre costs fails to consider the fact that service departments render assistance to other service departments. A service that is performed by one service department for the benefit of another service department is called an **interdepartmental service**. To illustrate this, we return to the case of Candler & Associates. Suppose that Candler's personnel department works with the employees in the secretarial department as well as the attorneys in the civil and criminal operating departments. Under these circumstances, Candler needs a cost approach that recognizes the interdepartmental service activity. One such approach is known as the **step method**. The primary difference between the direct method and the step method is depicted graphically in Exhibit 5–2A. Focus your attention on the first stage of the allocation process. Note that the step method includes one additional allocation, specifically from the personnel department cost pool to the secretarial department cost pool. The direct method ignores this interdepartmental service cost allocation. Indeed, the direct method derives its name from the fact that it allocates costs only directly from service cost pools to operating cost pools.

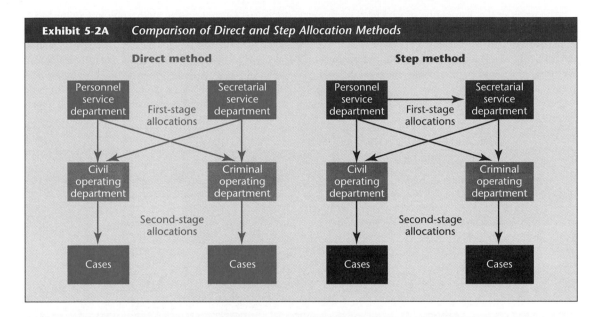

Exhibit 5-2A   *Comparison of Direct and Step Allocation Methods*

The fact that the direct method ignores the effect of interdepartmental services may cause distortions in the measurement of cost objects. The primary purpose of the step method is to avoid such distortions, thereby improving the accuracy of product costing. To illustrate this point, consider Candler & Associates. First, note that the interdepartmental portion of the personnel department cost is, in fact, a cost of providing secretarial services. In other words, the personnel service costs could be reduced if the personnel department did not provide service to the secretarial staff. Accordingly, the cost of providing personnel support to the secretarial staff should be included in the secretarial cost pool. Under the direct method, however, the interdepartmental service cost is allocated between the civil and criminal operating departments. This is not a problem in and of itself because the cost of secretarial service is also allocated between the civil and criminal operating departments. Unfortunately, the base used to allocate personnel costs to the operating departments (i.e., number of attorneys) distributes more cost to the civil department than to the criminal department. This is unfortunate because the criminal department uses more secretarial service than the civil department does. In other words, more secretarial cost (i.e., interdepartmental personnel cost) is being allocated to the civil department although the criminal department uses more secretarial services. This means that ultimately the cost to litigate civil cases will be overstated and the cost to litigate criminal cases will be understated.

The step method corrects this distortion by distributing the interdepartmental personnel department cost to the secretarial department cost pool before it is allocated to the operating departments. Because the secretarial cost pool is allocated on the basis of requests for secretarial services, more of the interdepartmental cost will be allocated to the criminal operating division. To validate this result, assume that the personnel department cost pool is allocated to the secretarial department cost pool and the two operating department cost pools on the basis of the number of employees in each department. In addition to the 18 attorneys in the firm, assume that two employees work in the secretarial department. Accordingly, the allocation rate for the personnel cost pool is calculated as follows:

$$\text{Allocation rate for personnel department cost pool} \quad \frac{\$117,000}{20} = \$5,850 \text{ per employee}$$

On the basis of this rate, the first step in the allocation process distributes the personnel department cost pool as indicated here:

Personnel Cost Pool Allocated to	Allocation Rate		Weight of Base		Allocated Cost
Secretarial	$5,850	×	2 employees	=	$ 11,700
Civil	5,850	×	11 employees	=	64,350
Criminal	5,850	×	7 employees	=	40,950
Total	5,850	×	20 employees		$117,000

The result of the distribution of personnel department costs is shown as the Step 1 allocation in Exhibit 5–3A. The $11,700 interdepartmental personnel department cost allocated to the secretarial department cost pool is added to the $156,800 existing balance in that cost pool (see Exhibit 5–3A). The result is the accumulation of secretarial cost of $168,500. The second step in the costing process allocates this cost pool to the operating departments. Recall that the secretarial cost pool is allocated on the basis of number of work request forms submitted. Furthermore, recall that 980 request forms were submitted to the secretarial department (380 from the civil department and 600 from the criminal department). Accordingly, the allocation rate for the secretarial department cost pool is computed as follows:

$$\text{Allocation rate for secretarial department cost pool} \quad \frac{\$168,500}{980} = \$171.93878 \text{ per request form}$$

On the basis of this rate, the second step in the allocation process distributes the secretarial cost pool as indicated here:

Secretarial Cost Pool Allocated to	Allocation Rate		Weight of Base		Allocated Cost
Civil	$171.93878	×	380 requests	=	$ 65,337
Criminal	171.93878	×	600 requests	=	103,163
Total	171.93878	×	980 requests		$168,500

Exhibit 5-3A *First-Stage Allocations for Candler & Associates—Step Method*

	Personnel Cost Pool	Secretarial Cost Pool	Civil Department	Criminal Department
Cost to be allocated	$ 117,000	$ 156,800		
Step 1 allocation	(117,000) =	$ 11,700 +	$ 64,350 +	$ 40,950
Step 2 allocation		(168,500) =	65,337 +	103,163
Total in cost pool after allocation	0	0	129,687	144,113
Other operating department overhead costs			785,100	464,788
Total of operating department overhead cost pool			$914,787	$608,901

The result of this allocation is shown as the Step 2 allocation in Exhibit 5–3A. Note that the final cost pools for the operating departments reflect the expected shift in the cost distribution between the two departments. Specifically, the cost pool in the criminal department is higher and the cost pool in the civil department is lower than the comparable cost pool amounts computed under the direct method (see Exhibit 5–3A for the appropriate comparison). This distribution of cost is consistent with the fact that more of the interdepartmental service cost should be assigned to the criminal department because it uses more secretarial services than does the civil department. Accordingly, the step method of allocation more accurately reflects the manner in which the two operating departments consume resources.

The preceding illustration considered a simple two-stage allocation process with only two service departments and two operating departments. In large organizations, the costing process may be significantly more complex. Interdepartmental cost allocations may involve several service departments. For example, the personnel department may provide service to the secretarial department that provides service to the engineering department that provides service to the accounting department that provides service to several operating departments. In addition, general overhead costs may be allocated to both service and operating departments before costs are allocated from service to operating departments. For example, general utility costs may be pooled together and allocated to service and operating departments on the basis of square footage of floor space. These allocated utility costs are then redistributed to other service departments and to operating departments in a sequence of step-down allocations. The step-down process usually begins with the cost pool that represents resources used by the largest number of departments. This constitutes the first step in the costing process. The second step proceeds with allocations from the cost pool that represents resources used by the second largest number of departments and so on, until all overhead costs have been allocated to the operating departments. Accordingly, the first stage of a two-stage costing process may include many allocations (steps) before all costs have been distributed to the operating departments. Regardless of how many allocations are included in the first stage, the second stage begins when costs are allocated from the operating departments to the organizations' products.

Reciprocal Method

Note that the step method is limited to one-way interdepartmental relationships. In practice, many departments have two-way working relationships. For example, the personnel department may provide services to the secretarial department and receive services from it. Two-way associations in which departments provide and receive services from one another are called **reciprocal relationships**. Allocations that recognize reciprocal relationships require complex mathematical manipulation involving the use of simultaneous linear equations. The resultant cost distributions are difficult to interpret. Furthermore, the results attained with the **reciprocal method** are not significantly different from those attained through the step method. As a result, the reciprocal method is rarely used in practice.

KEY TERMS

Allocation base The cost driver that constitutes the basis for the allocation process. *(p. 167)*

Allocation rate The factor used to allocate or assign costs to a cost object; determined by taking the total cost to be allocated and dividing it by the appropriate cost driver. *(p. 167)*

Byproducts Products that share common inputs with other joint products but have relatively insignificant market values relative to the other joint products. *(p. 180)*

Cost The amount of resources that must be sacrificed to obtain some benefit. *(p. 163)*

Cost accumulation The process of determining the cost of a particular object by accumulating many individual costs into a single total cost. *(p. 164)*

Cost allocation The process of dividing a total cost into parts and apportioning the parts among the relevant cost objects. *(p. 165)*

Cost driver Any factor, usually some measure of activity, that causes cost to be incurred; sometimes referred to as the *activity base* or the *allocation base*. Examples are labour hours, machine hours, or some other measure of activity whose change causes corresponding changes in the cost object. *(p. 164)*

Cost objects The objects for which managers need to know the cost; can be products, processes, departments, services, activities, and so on. *(p. 163)*

Cost pool Many individual costs that have been accumulated into a single total for the purposes of allocation. *(p. 178)*

Cost tracing Relating specific costs to the objects that cause their incurrence. *(p. 165)*

Direct cost Cost that is easily traceable to a cost object and for which the sacrifice to trace is small in relation to the information benefits attained. *(p. 166)*

Direct method (Appendix) A method that allocates service centre costs directly to operating department cost pools. *(p. 181)*

Indirect cost Cost that cannot be easily traced to a cost object and for which the economic sacrifice to trace is not worth the informational benefits. *(p. 166)*

Interdepartmental service (Appendix) A service performed by one service department for the benefit of another service department. *(p. 183)*

Joint costs Common costs incurred in the process of making two or more products. *(p. 178)*

Joint products The products derived from joint cost. *(p. 178)*

Operating departments (Appendix) Departments assigned tasks leading to the accomplishment of the organization's objectives. *(p. 181)*

Overhead costs Indirect costs of doing business that cannot be directly traced to a product, department, or process, such as amortization. *(p. 171)*

Predetermined overhead rate The overhead allocation rate determined before the actual overhead costs and actual cost driver are known. *(p. 175)*

Reciprocal method (Appendix) An allocation method that considers two-way associations between/among service centres (service centres provide services to as well as receive services from other service centres); uses simultaneous linear equations, but the resultant cost distributions are difficult to interpret. *(p. 185)*

Reciprocal relationships (Appendix) Two-way associations in which departments provide services to and receive services from one another. *(p. 185)*

Service departments (Appendix) Departments, such as quality control, repair and maintenance, personnel, and accounting, that provide support to the operating departments. *(p. 181)*

Split-off point The point in the production process where products become separate and identifiable. *(p. 178)*

Step method (Appendix) A two-step allocation method that considers one-way interdepartmental service centre relationships by allocating costs from service centres to service centres as well as from service centres to operating departments; does not consider reciprocal relationships between/among service centres. *(p. 183)*

QUESTIONS

1. What is a cost object? Name four different cost objects which a manager would be interested in knowing.
2. Why is cost accumulation an imprecise practice?
3. If the cost object is a manufactured product, what are the three major cost categories to accumulate?
4. What is a direct cost? What criteria are used to determine whether a cost is a direct cost?
5. Why are the terms *direct cost* and *indirect cost* independent of the terms *fixed cost* and *variable cost*? Give an example to illustrate.
6. Give an example of why the statement "All direct costs are avoidable costs" is incorrect.
7. What are the important factors in determining the appropriate cost driver to use in allocating a cost?
8. How is an allocation rate determined? How is an allocation made?
9. In a manufacturing environment, which costs are direct and which are indirect in product costing?
10. Why are some manufacturing costs not directly traceable to products?
11. What is the objective of allocating indirect manufacturing overhead costs to the product?
12. On January 31, the managers of Integra, Inc. seek to determine the cost of producing their product during January for product pricing and control purposes. The company can easily determine the costs of direct materials and direct labour used in January production, but many fixed indirect costs are

not affected by the level of production activity and have not yet been incurred. The managers can reasonably estimate the overhead costs for the year on the basis of the fixed indirect costs incurred in past periods. Assume the managers decide to allocate an equal amount of these estimated costs to the products produced each month. Explain why this practice may not provide a reasonable estimate of product costs in January.

13. Respond to the following statement: "The allocation base chosen is unimportant. What is important in product costing is that overhead costs be assigned to production in a specific period by an allocation process."
14. Larry Kwang insists that the costs of his school's fund-raising project should be determined after the project is completed. He argues that only after the project is completed can its costs be determined accurately and that it is a waste of time to try to estimate future costs. Georgia Sundum counters that waiting until the project is completed will not provide timely information for planning expenditures. How would you arbitrate this discussion? Explain the trade-offs between accuracy and timeliness.
15. Define the term *cost pool*. How are cost pools important in allocation?
16. What are the three methods used for allocating service centre costs? How do the methods differ?
17. What is the difference between a joint product and a byproduct?

EXERCISES

L.O. 1 EXERCISE 5-1   *Allocation of Costs between Divisions*

Western Services Company (WSC) has 20 employees, 14 of whom are assigned to Division A and 6 to Division B. WSC incurred $120,000 of fringe benefit cost during 2004.

Required

Determine the amount of the fringe benefit cost to be allocated to Division A and to Division B.

EXERCISE 5-2   *Allocation to Smooth Cost over Varying Levels of Production*   **L.O. 1**

Production workers of Kaminski Manufacturing Company provided 80 hours of labour in January and 140 hours in February. Kaminski expects to use 1,200 hours of labour during the year. The rental fee for the manufacturing facility is $2,000 per month.

Required

Explain why allocation is needed. On the basis of this information, how much of the rental cost should be allocated to the products made in January and to those made in February?

EXERCISE 5-3   *Allocation to Solve a Timing Problem*   **L.O. 1**

Production workers of Ditzel Manufacturing Company provided 1,600 hours of labour in January and 1,000 hours in February. The company, whose operation is labour intensive, expects to use 18,000 hours of labour during the year. Ditzel expects to pay a $22,500 annual premium on July 1 for an insurance policy that protects the manufacturing facility.

Required

Explain why allocation is needed. On the basis of this information, how much of the insurance cost should be allocated to the products made in January and to those made in February?

EXERCISE 5-4   *Allocation of a Fixed Cost*   **L.O. 1, 6**

World Wide Air is a large airline company that pays a customer relations representative $1,500 per month. The representative, who processed 900 customer complaints in January and 600 complaints in February, is expected to process 12,000 customer complaints during 2007.

Required

a. Determine the total cost of processing customer complaints in January and in February.

b. Explain why allocating the cost of the customer relations representative would or would not be relevant to decision making.

EXERCISE 5-5   *Allocation of Overhead Cost among Products*   **L.O. 1**

Julia Hats, Inc. manufactures three different models of hats: Vogue, Beauty, and Deluxe. Julia expects to incur $375,000 of overhead cost during the next fiscal year. Other budgetary information follows:

	Vogue	Beauty	Deluxe	Total
Direct labour hours	3,000	5,000	4,500	12,500
Machine hours	1,000	1,000	1,000	3,000

Required

a. Use direct labour hours as the cost driver to compute the allocation rate and the budgeted overhead cost for each product.

b. Use machine hours as the cost driver to compute the allocation rate and the budgeted overhead cost for each product.

EXERCISE 5-6   *Allocation of Overhead Costs among Products*   **L.O. 1**

Smith Company makes three products in its factory plastic cups, plastic tablecloths, and plastic bottles. The expected overhead costs of the next fiscal year include the following:

Factory manager's salary	$ 65,000
Factory utility costs	25,000
Factory supplies	10,000
Total overhead cost	$100,000

Smith uses machine hours as the cost driver to allocate the overhead cost. The budgeted machine hours for the products are as follows:

Cups	500 Hours
Tablecloths	800
Bottles	1,200
Total machine hours	2,500

Required

Allocate the budgeted overhead cost to the products.

L.O. 1 EXERCISE 5-7   *Allocation of Costs among Products*

Reid Construction Company expects to build three new homes during a specific accounting period. The estimated direct materials and labour costs are as follows:

Expected Costs	Home 1	Home 2	Home 3
Direct labour	$30,000	$45,000	$85,000
Direct materials	45,000	65,000	90,000

Assume that two major overhead costs ($20,000 of employee fringe benefits and $10,000 of indirect materials costs) need to be allocated among the three jobs.

Required

Choose an appropriate cost driver for each of the overhead costs and determine the total cost of each house.

L.O. 1 EXERCISE 5-8   *Allocation of Overhead Cost to Accomplish Smoothing*

West Coast Corporation expects to incur indirect overhead costs of $25,000 per month and direct manufacturing costs of $7 per unit. The expected production activity for the first four months of 2001 is as follows:

	January	February	March	April
Estimated production in units	2,000	3,500	1,500	3,000

Required

a. Calculate a predetermined overhead rate on the basis of the number of units of product expected to be made during the first four months of the year.
b. Allocate overhead costs to each month using the overhead rate computed in Requirement *a*.
c. Calculate the total cost per unit for each month using the overhead allocated in Requirement *b*.

L.O. 1 EXERCISE 5-9   *Allocation of Overhead for Product Costing*

Tillman Manufacturing Company produced 300 units of inventory in January 2001. It expects to produce an additional 2,100 units during the remaining 11 months of the year. In other words, total production for 2001 is estimated to be 2,400 units. Direct materials and direct labour costs are $64 and $52 per unit, respectively. Tillman Company expects to incur the following manufacturing overhead costs during the 2001 accounting period:

Production supplies	$ 1,200
Supervisor salary	48,000
Amortization on equipment	36,000
Utilities	9,000
Rental fee on manufacturing facilities	24,000
Total	$118,200

Required

a. Determine the estimated cost of the 300 units of product made in January.

b. Is the amount computed in Requirement *a* an actual cost or an estimated cost? Could accuracy be improved by waiting until December to determine the cost of products? Identify two reasons that a manager would want to know the cost of products in January. Discuss the relationship between accuracy and relevance as it pertains to this problem.

EXERCISE 5-10   *How the Allocation of Fixed Cost Affects a Pricing Decision*   **L.O. 1**

Dallas Manufacturing Co. expects to make 12,000 chairs during the 2003 accounting period. The company made 2,000 chairs in January. Materials and labour costs for January were $8,000 and $12,000, respectively. There were 1,000 chairs produced in February. Material and labour costs for February were $4,000 and $6,000, respectively. The company paid the $60,000 annual rental fee on its manufacturing facility on January 1, 2003.

Required
Assuming that Dallas desires to sell its chairs for cost plus 40% of cost, what price should be charged for the chairs produced in January and February?

EXERCISE 5-11   *Allocating Joint Product Cost*   **L.O. 8**

Moore Chemical Company makes three products, A123, H704, and L888, which are joint products from the same materials. In a standard batch of 300,000 kilograms of raw material, the company generates 70,000 kilograms of A123, 150,000 kilograms of H704, and 80,000 kilograms of L888. The production cost of a standard batch is $900,000. The sales prices per kilogram are $2, $4.80, and $8 for A123, H704, and L888, respectively.

Required
a. Allocate the joint product cost among the three final products using weight as the allocation base.
b. Allocate the joint product cost among the three final products using market value as the allocation base.

EXERCISE 5-12   *Allocation of a Service Department Cost to Operating Departments (Appendix)*   **L.O. 10**

Roesch Corporation's computer services department assists two operating departments to use the company's information system effectively. The annual cost of computer services is $250,000. The production department employs 18 employees, and the sales department employs 7 employees. Roesch uses the number of employees as the cost driver to allocate the cost of computer services to operating departments.

Required
Allocate the cost of computer services to operating departments.

EXERCISE 5-13   *Allocation of Costs of Service Departments to Operating Departments—Step Method (Appendix)*   **L.O. 10**

Charter Health Care Centre, Inc. has three clinics servicing the Ottawa-Hull metropolitan area. Supporting the clinics are the company's legal services department. Moreover, its computer services department supports all three clinics and the legal services department. The annual cost to operate the legal services department is $240,000. The annual cost to operate the computer services department is $320,000. The company uses the number of patients served as the cost driver to allocate the cost of legal services and the number of computer workstations as the cost driver to allocate the cost of computer services. Other relevant information follows:

	Number of Patients	Number of Workstations
Ottawa clinic	3,000	15
Ottawa-Downtown clinic	2,100	16
Hull clinic	2,900	12
Legal services		7
Computer services		10

Required
a. Allocate the cost of computer services to all three clinics and the legal services department.
b. After the cost of computer services has been allocated, allocate the cost of legal services to the three clinics.
c. Compute the total allocated cost of service centres for each clinic.

L.O. 10 EXERCISE 5-14   *Allocation of Costs of Service Departments to Operating Departments—Direct Method (Appendix)*

City Trust has two service departments: actuary and economic analysis. City also has three operating departments: annuity, fund management, and employee benefit services. The annual costs to operate the service departments are $260,000 for actuary and $320,000 for economic analysis. City uses the direct method to allocate service centre costs to operating departments. Other relevant data follow:

	Operating Cost*	Revenue
Annuity	$250,000	$420,000
Fund management	450,000	630,000
Employee benefit services	300,000	550,000

*The operating costs are measured before the allocation of service centre costs.

Required

a. Use operating cost as the cost driver to allocate service centre costs to operating departments.
b. Use revenue as the cost driver to allocate service centre costs to operating departments.

PROBLEMS—SERIES A

L.O. 1, 2, PROBLEM 5-1A   *Cost Accumulation and Allocation*
3, 5

Shackelford Manufacturing Company makes two different products, A and B. The company's two departments are named after the products; for example, Product A is made in Department A. Shackelford's accountant has identified the following annual costs associated with these two products:

Financial Data

Salary of vice-president of production division	$ 80,000
Salary of supervisor Department A	37,400
Salary of supervisor Department B	27,400
Direct materials cost Department A	150,000
Direct materials cost Department B	210,000
Direct labour cost Department A	120,000
Direct labour cost Department B	340,000
Direct utilities cost Department A	60,000
Direct utilities cost Department B	12,000
General factorywide utilities	14,400
Production supplies	18,000
Fringe benefits	64,400
Amortization	360,000

Nonfinancial data

Machine hours Department A	5,000
Machine hours Department B	1,000

Required

a. Identify the costs that are (1) direct costs of Department A, (2) direct costs of Department B, and (3) indirect costs.
b. Select the appropriate cost drivers for the indirect costs and allocate these costs to Departments A and B.
c. Determine the total estimated cost of the products made in Departments A and B. Assume that 1,000 units of Product A and 2,000 units of Product B were made during the accounting period. If Shackelford prices its products at cost plus 40 percent of cost, what price per unit must it charge for Product A and for Product B?

L.O. 1, 5 PROBLEM 5-2A   *Selection of an Appropriate Cost Driver (What Is the Base?)*

The administrative office of Finley School of Vocational Technology has organized the school training programs into three departments. Each department provides training in a different area as follows: nursing assistant, dental hygiene, and office technology. The school's owner, Sara Finley, wants to know how much it costs to operate each of the three departments. To accumulate the total cost for each department, the accountant has identified several indirect costs that must be allocated to each. These costs are $4,200 of phone expense, $840 of office supplies, $432,000 of office rent, $48,000 of janitorial services, and $36,000 of salary paid to the dean of students. To provide a reasonably accurate allocation of costs, the accountant has identified several cost drivers. These drivers and their association with each department follow:

Cost Driver	Department 1	Department 2	Department 3
Number of telephones	14	16	26
Number of faculty members	10	8	6
Square footage of office space	12,000	7,000	5,000
Number of secretaries	1	1	1

Required

a. Identify the appropriate cost objects.

b. Name the appropriate cost driver for each indirect cost component and compute the allocation rate for assigning each cost component to the cost objects.

c. Determine the amount of telephone expense that should be allocated to each of the three departments.

d. Determine the amount of supplies expense that should be allocated to Department 3.

e. Determine the amount of office rent that should be allocated to Department 2.

f. Determine the amount of cost for janitorial services that should be allocated to Department 1.

g. Name two cost drivers not listed here that could be used to allocate the cost of the dean's salary to the three departments.

PROBLEM 5-3A   *Cost Allocation in a Service Industry*   **L.O. 1, 2**

Southeast Airlines is a small airline that occasionally carries overload shipments for the overnight delivery company Never-Fail, Inc. Never-Fail is a multimillion-dollar company started by Peter Never immediately after he failed to finish his first accounting course. The company's motto is "We Never-Fail to Deliver Your Package on Time." When Never-Fail has more freight than it can deliver, it pays Southeast to carry the excess. Southeast contracts with independent pilots to fly its planes on a per-trip basis. Southeast recently purchased an airplane that cost the company $5,600,000. The plane has an estimated useful life of 8,000,000 kilometres and a zero salvage value. During the first week in January, Southeast flew two trips. The first trip was a round trip flight from Hamilton to Regina, for which Southeast paid the pilot $500 to fly the plane and $350 for fuel. The second flight was a round trip from Hamilton to Moncton. For this trip, it paid the pilot $300 and $150 for fuel. The round trip between Hamilton and Regina is approximately 3,200 kilometres and the round trip between Hamilton and Moncton is 2,200 kilometres.

Required

a. Identify the direct and indirect costs that would be used in determining the cost of each trip.

b. Determine the total cost of each trip.

c. In addition to depreciation, name three other indirect costs that may need to be allocated to determine the cost of the trip.

PROBLEM 5-4A   *Cost Allocation in a Manufacturing Company*   **L.O. 1, 5**

Campo Manufacturing Company makes tents that it sells directly to sport enthusiasts through a mail order marketing program. The company pays a quality control expert $36,000 per year to inspect completed tents before they are shipped to customers. Assume that the company completes 800 tents in January and 600 tents in February. For the entire year, the company expects to produce 6,000 tents.

Required

a. Explain how changes in the cost driver (i.e., number of tents inspected) affect the total amount of fixed cost.

b. Explain how changes in the cost driver (i.e., number of tents inspected) affect the fixed cost per unit.

c. If the cost objective is to determine the cost per tent, is the expert's salary a direct or an indirect cost?

d. How much of the expert's salary should be allocated to tents produced in January and February?

PROBLEM 5-5A   *Fairness in the Allocation Process*   **L.O. 1, 5**

Western Manufacturing Company uses two departments to make its products. Department I is a cutting department that is machine intensive and uses very few employees. Machines cut and form parts and then place the finished parts on a conveyor belt that carries them to Department II, where they are assembled into finished goods. The assembly department is labour intensive and requires a large number of workers to assemble parts into finished goods. The company incurs two significant overhead costs, employee fringe benefits and utility costs. For the manufacturing facility, the annual costs of fringe benefits are $126,000 and utility costs are $90,000. The typical consumption patterns for the two departments are as follows:

	Department I	Department II	Total
Machine hours used	16,000	4,000	20,000
Direct labour hours used	5,000	13,000	18,000

The supervisor of each department is given a bonus based on how well the department is able to control costs. The company's current policy requires that a single activity base (machine hours or labour hours) be used to allocate the total overhead cost of $216,000.

Required

a. Assume that you are the supervisor of Department I. Choose the allocation base that would minimize your department's share of the total overhead cost. Calculate the amount of overhead that would be allocated to both departments using the base that you selected.

b. Assume that you are the supervisor of Department II. Choose the allocation base that would minimize your department's share of the total overhead cost. Calculate the amount of overhead that would be allocated to both departments using the base that you selected.

c. Assume that you are the plant manager and have the authority to change the company's overhead allocation policy. Formulate an overhead allocation policy that would be fair to the supervisors of both Department I and Department II. Compute the overhead allocations for each department using your policy.

L.O. 1 PROBLEM 5-6A   *Allocation to Accomplish Smoothing*

Schacter Corporation estimates its overhead costs to be $12,000 per month, except for January when it pays the $36,000 annual insurance premium on the manufacturing facility. Accordingly, the January overhead costs are expected to be $48,000 ($36,000 + $12,000). The company expects to use 7,000 direct labour hours per month, except during July, August, and September when the company expects 9,000 hours of direct labour each month to build inventories for high demand that normally occurs during the Christmas season. The company's actual direct labour hours were the same as the estimated hours. The company made 3,500 units of product in each month, when except July, August, and September it produced 4,500 units each month. Direct labour costs were $12 per unit, and direct materials costs were $5 per unit.

Required

a. Calculate a predetermined overhead rate on the basis of direct labour hours.

b. Determine the total allocated overhead cost for January, March, and August.

c. Determine the cost per unit of product for January, March, and August.

d. Determine the price that the company should sell the product for, assuming that the company desires to earn a gross margin of $10 per unit.

L.O. 1, 5 PROBLEM 5-7A   *Allocation of Indirect Cost between Products*

Fiona Stark is considering expansion of her business. She plans to hire a salesperson to cover trade shows. Because of compensation, travel expenses, and booth rental, fixed costs for a trade show are expected to be $6,600. The booth will be open 30 hours during the trade show. Ms. Stark also plans to add a new product line, ProOffice, which will cost $90 per package. She will continue to sell the existing product, EZRecords, which costs $50 per package. Ms. Stark believes that the salesperson will spend approximately 20 hours selling EZRecords and 10 hours marketing ProOffice.

Required

a. Determine the estimated total cost and cost per unit of each product, assuming that the salesperson is able to sell 80 units of EZRecords and 60 units of ProOffice.

b. Determine the estimated total cost and cost per unit of each product, assuming that the salesperson is able to sell 120 units of EZRecords and 90 units of ProOffice.

c. Explain why the cost-per-unit figures calculated in Requirement *a* are different from the amounts calculated in Requirement *b*. Also explain how the differences in estimated cost per unit will affect pricing decisions.

PROBLEM 5-8A   *Allocating Joint-Product Cost*

Tryson Chicken, Inc. processes and packages chicken for grocery stores. It purchases chickens from farmers and processes chickens into two different products: chicken drumsticks and chicken steak. For a standard batch of 12,000 kilograms of raw chickens that cost $3,500, the company produces two parts: 2,800 kilograms of drumsticks and 4,200 kilograms of breast for a processing cost of $1,225. The chicken breast is further processed into 3,200 kilograms of steak for a processing cost of $1,000. The market prices of drumsticks per kilogram is $0.75 and the market price of chicken steak is $1.70. If Tryson decided to sell chicken breast instead of steak, the price per kilogram would be $1.00. The cost of processing chicken breast into chicken steak is $1,000.

Required
a. Allocate the joint product cost between the two final products using weight as the allocation base.
b. Allocate the joint product cost between the two final products using market value as the allocation base.
c. Assume that the company uses market value as the allocation base. Determine the company's gross margin per unit for steak if all chicken breast is processed into steak and sold.

PROBLEM 5-9A   *Allocation of Service Centre Costs—Step Method and Direct Method (Appendix)*

Culligan Information Services, Inc. has two service departments: employee benefits and billing. Culligan's operating departments, organized according to the special industry each department serves, include health care, retail, and legal services. The billing department supports only the three operating departments, but the employee benefits department supports all operating departments and the billing department. Other relevant information follows:

	Employee Benefits	Billing	Health Care	Retail	Legal Services
Number of employees	20	50	190	140	120
Annual cost*	$900,000	$1,710,000	$6,000,000	$4,800,000	$2,800,000
Annual revenue	—	—	$9,000,000	$6,200,000	$4,800,000

*This is the operating cost before the allocation of service department costs.

Required
a. Allocate service department costs to operating departments, assuming that Culligan adopts the step method. The company uses the number of employees as the base to allocate employee benefits department costs and departmental annual revenue as the base to allocate the billing department costs.
b. Allocate service department costs to operating departments, assuming that Culligan adopts the direct method. The company uses the number of employees as the base to allocate the employee benefits department costs and departmental annual revenue as the base to allocate the billing department costs.
c. Compute the total allocated cost of service centres for each operating department under each allocation method.

PROBLEMS—SERIES B

PROBLEM 5-1B   *Cost Accumulation and Allocation*

Simon Tools Company has two production departments in its manufacturing facilities. Home tools specializes in hand tools for individual home users, and professional tools makes sophisticated tools for professional maintenance workers. Simon's accountant has identified the following annual costs associated with these two products:

Financial Data	
Salary of vice-president of production	$ 90,000
Salary of manager, home tools	26,000
Salary of manager, professional tools	29,000
Direct materials cost, home tools	200,000
Direct materials cost, professional tools	250,000
Direct labour cost, home tools	224,000
Direct labour cost, professional tools	276,000
Direct utilities cost, home tools	50,000
Direct utilities cost, professional tools	20,000
General factorywide utilities	21,000
Production supplies	27,000

Fringe benefits	75,000
Amortization	240,000
Nonfinancial Data	
Machine hours, home tools	4,000
Machine hours, professional tools	2,000

Required

a. Identify the costs that are the (1) direct costs of home tools, (2) direct costs of professional tools, and (3) indirect costs.

b. Select the appropriate cost drivers and allocate the indirect costs to home tools and to professional tools.

c. Determine the total estimated cost of the products made in each department. Assume that each department has only a single product. Home tools produces its Deluxe Drill for home use and professional tools produces the Professional Drill. The company made 30,000 units of Deluxe Drill and 40,000 units of Professional Drill during the period. If Simon prices its products at cost plus 30 percent of cost, what is the price per unit that it must charge for the Deluxe Drill and the Professional Drill?

L.O. 1, 5 PROBLEM 5-2B   *Selection of an Appropriate Cost Driver (What Is the Base?)*

Kuani Research Institute has three departments: biology, chemistry, and physics. The controller of the institute wants to estimate the cost of operating each department. He has identified several indirect costs that must be allocated to each department, including $5,600 of phone expense, $1,200 of office supplies, $560,000 of office rent, $70,000 of janitorial services, and $75,000 of salary paid to the director. To provide a reasonably accurate allocation of costs the controller identified several cost drivers. These drivers and their association to each department follow:

Cost Driver	Biology	Chemistry	Physics
Number of telephones	10	14	16
Number of researchers	8	10	12
Square footage of office space	8,000	8,000	12,000
Number of secretaries	1	1	1

Required

a. Identify the appropriate cost objects.

b. Name the appropriate cost driver for each indirect cost component and compute the allocation rate to assign each cost component to the cost objects.

c. Determine the amount of telephone expense that should be allocated to each of the three departments.

d. Determine the amount of supplies expense that should be allocated to the physics department.

e. Determine the amount of office rent cost that should be allocated to the chemistry department.

f. Determine the amount of cost for janitorial services that should be allocated to the biology department.

g. Name two cost drivers not listed here that could be used to allocate the cost of the director's salary to the three departments.

L.O. 1, 2 PROBLEM 5-3B   *Cost Allocation in a Service Industry*

Perez, Fong, and Associates provides legal services for its local community. In addition to its regular lawyers, the firm hires some part-time lawyers to handle small cases. Two secretaries assist all part-time lawyers exclusively. In 2009, the firm paid $36,000 for the two secretaries who worked a total of 3,600 hours. Moreover, the firm paid Kate Czonka $60 per hour and Joe Tortelli $50 per hour for their part-time legal services.

In August 2009, Ms. Czonka completed a case that took 60 hours. Mr. Tortelli finished a case on which he had worked 20 hours. The firm also paid a private investigator to uncover relevant facts. The investigation fees cost $800 for Ms. Czonka's case and $500 for Mr. Tortelli's case. She used 30 hours of secretarial assistance, and he used 40 hours.

Required

a. Identify the direct and indirect costs that would be used in determining the cost of each case that occurred in August 2009.

b. Determine the total cost of each case.

c. In addition to secretaries' salaries, name three other indirect costs that may need to be allocated to determine the cost of the cases.

PROBLEM 5-4B   *Cost Allocation in a Manufacturing Company*   **L.O. 1, 5**

Sander's Doors, Inc. makes a particular type of door. The labour cost is $80 per door and the material cost is $150 per door. Sander's also rents a factory building for $60,000 a month. Sander's plans to produce 24,000 doors annually. In March and April, it made 2,000 and 3,000 doors, respectively.

Required
a. Explain how changes in the cost driver (number of doors made) affect the total amount of fixed cost.
b. Explain how changes in the cost driver (number of doors made) affect the fixed cost per unit.
c. If the cost objective is to determine the cost per door, is the factory rent a direct cost or an indirect cost?
d. How much of the factory rent should be allocated to doors produced in March and April?

PROBLEM 5-5B   *Fairness in the Allocation Process*   **L.O. 1, 5**

Hermosa Furniture Company has two production departments. The parts department uses automated machinery to make parts; as a result, it uses very few employees. The assembly department is labour intensive because it requires workers to assemble parts manually into finished furniture. Employee fringe benefits and utility costs are the two major overhead costs of the company's production division. The cost of fringe benefits and utility costs for the period are $150,000 and $72,000, respectively. The typical consumption patterns for the two departments follow:

	Parts	Assembly	Total
Machine hours used	26,000	4,000	30,000
Direct labour hours used	3,500	20,500	24,000

The supervisor of each department is given a bonus based on how well the department is able to control costs. The company's current policy requires that a single activity base (machine hours or labour hours) be used to allocate the total overhead cost of $222,000.

Required
a. Assume that you are the supervisor of the parts department. Choose the allocation base that would minimize your department's share of the total overhead cost. Calculate the amount of overhead that would be allocated to both departments using the base that you selected.
b. Assume that you are the supervisor of the assembly department. Choose the allocation base that would minimize your department's share of the total overhead cost. Calculate the amount of overhead that would be allocated to both departments using the base that you selected.
c. Assume that you are the plant manager and that you have the authority to change the company's overhead allocation policy. Formulate an overhead allocation policy that would be fair to the supervisors of both the parts and assembly departments. Compute the overhead allocation for each department using your policy.

PROBLEM 5-6B   *Allocation to Accomplish Smoothing*   **L.O. 1**

Yadzinski Corporation's estimated overhead costs are usually $20,000 per month. However, the company pays $48,000 of property tax on the factory facility in July. Thus, the overhead costs for July increase to $68,000. The company normally uses 5,000 direct labour hours per month except for August, September, and October, in which the company requires 9,000 hours of direct labour per month to build inventories for high demand in the Christmas season. Last year, the company's actual direct labour hours were the same as the estimated hours. The company made 5,000 units of product in each month, except August, September, and October when it produced 9,000 units per month. Direct labour costs were $8 per unit; direct materials costs were $7 per unit.

Required
a. Calculate a predetermined overhead rate on the basis of direct labour hours.
b. Determine the total allocated overhead cost for the months of March, August, and December.
c. Determine the cost per unit of product for the months of March, August, and December.
d. Determine the selling price for the product, assuming that the company desires to earn a gross margin of $7 per unit.

L.O. 1, 5 PROBLEM 5-7B   *Allocation of Indirect Cost between Products*

Kemp Corporation has hired a marketing representative to sell the company's two products, Whiz and Bang. The representative's total salary and fringe benefits are $5,000 monthly. The product cost is $45 per unit for Whiz and $72 per unit for Bang. Kemp expects the representative to spend 48 hours per month marketing Whiz and 112 hours promoting Bang.

Required
a. Determine the estimated total cost and cost per unit, assuming that the representative is able to sell 100 units of Whiz and 70 units of Bang in a month. Allocate indirect cost on the basis of labour hours.
b. Determine the estimated total cost and cost per unit, assuming that the representative is able to sell 250 units of Whiz and 140 units of Bang. Allocate indirect cost on the basis of labour hours.
c. Explain why the cost per unit figures calculated in Requirement *a* differ from the amounts calculated in Requirement *b*. Also explain how the differences in estimated cost per unit will affect pricing decisions.

L.O. 8 PROBLEM 5-8B   *Allocating Joint-Product Cost*

Manitoba Dairy Products produces three different products from whole milk: low-fat milk: cream, and butter. The production requires two steps of processing. In the first step, the company pasteurizes whole milk and separates it into cream and low-fat milk. In the second step, cream is churned into butter. In a regular batch of 40,000 litres of whole milk, Manitoba Dairy pays dairy farmers $5,000. The additional processing cost in the first step is $4,000. At the end of the first step, the company produces 28,000 litres of low-fat milk and 1,500 kilograms of cream. The weight of 28,000 litres of low fat milk is about 21,000 kilograms. Manitoba Dairy sells its low-fat milk at the price of $0.60 per litre. The cream is churned into 500 kilograms of butter. The cost of churning 1,500 kilograms of cream is $1,425. The company sells butter at the price of $27 per kilogram. The current market price of cream is $3.60 per kilogram.

Required
a. Allocate the joint product cost to the cream and low-fat milk products using weight as the allocation base.
b. Allocate the joint product cost to the cream and low-fat milk products using market value as the allocation base.
c. Assume that all cream is further processed to produce butter. Determine the final cost and the market value of butter if market value is used as the allocation base.

L.O. 10 PROBLEM 5-9B   *Allocation of Service Centre Costs—Step Method and Direct Method (Appendix)*

Bullington Corporation has three production departments: forming, assembly, and packaging. The maintenance department supports only the production departments, the computer services department supports all departments including maintenance. Other relevant information follows:

	Forming	Assembly	Packaging	Maintenance	Computer Services
Machine hours	6,000	2,500	1,500	400	
Number of computers	14	20	11	15	8
Annual cost*	$450,000	$800,000	$250,000	$100,000	$90,000

*This is the annual operating cost before the allocation of service department costs.

Required
a. Allocate service department costs to operating departments, assuming that Bullington adopts the step method. The company uses the number of computers as the base to allocate the computer services costs and machine hours as the base to allocate the maintenance costs.
b. Use machine hours as the base to allocate maintenance department costs and the number of computers as the base to allocate computer services cost. Allocate service department costs to operating departments, assuming that Bullington adopts the direct method.
c. Compute the total allocated cost of service centres for each operating department under each allocation method.

ANALYZE, THINK, COMMUNICATE

BUSINESS APPLICATIONS CASE *Allocation of Fixed Costs*   **ACT 5-1**

Hilyear Company pays $5,000 per month to rent its manufacturing facility. Hilyear estimates total production volume for 2003 to be 12,000 units of product. The company actually produced 800 units of product during January and 900 units in February.

Required

a. For each of the following items, indicate whether the rent charge is a
    (1) product or general, selling, and administrative (G,S&A) cost.
    (2) relevant cost with respect to a special order decision.
    (3) fixed or variable cost relative to the volume of production.
    (4) direct or indirect if the cost object is the cost of products made in January.
b. With respect to the rent charge, determine the total cost and the cost per unit of products made in January and February.
c. Assuming that actual production in 2003 is 10,000 units, indicate whether the cost of the January production determined in Requirement *b* is over- or understated.
d. Assume that the information computed in Requirement *b* was used to price Hilyear's product in 2003. Furthermore, assume that management used the price estimates to project income and that the income projections were used in public announcements to stock analysts. Finally, assume that actual production was 10,000 units. Indicate whether year-end net income is likely to be higher or lower than management forecasts. Describe the likely impact on Hilyear's share price and executive stock option incentive program.

GROUP ASSIGNMENT *Selection of the Cost Driver*   **ACT 5-2**

Millikin School of Business is divided into three departments: accounting, marketing, and management. Relevant information for each of the departments follows:

Cost Driver	Accounting	Marketing	Management
Number of students	700	400	200
Number of classes per semester	32	18	14
Number of professors	10	12	5

Millikin is a private school that expects each department to generate a profit. It rewards departments for profitability by assigning 20 percent of each department's profits back to that department. Departments have free rein as to how to use these funds. Some departments have used them to supply professors with computer technology. Others have expanded their travel budgets. The practice has been highly successful in motivating the faculty to control costs. The revenues and direct costs for the year 2000 follow:

	Accounting	Marketing	Management
Revenues	$14,800,000	$8,300,000	$4,150,000
Direct costs	12,300,000	6,900,000	3,300,000

The School of Business is allocated $2,246,400 of indirect overhead costs, such as administrative salaries and costs of operating the registrar's office and the bookstore.

Required

a. Divide the class into groups and organize the groups into three sections. Assign each section a department. For example, groups in Section 1 should assume they represent the Accounting Department. Groups in Sections 2 and 3 should represent the Marketing Department and Management Department, respectively. Assume that the dean of the school is planning to assign an equal amount of the overhead to each department. Have the students in each group prepare a response to the dean's plan. Each group should select a spokesperson who is prepared to answer the following questions:
    (1) Is your group in favour of or opposed to the allocation plan suggested by the dean?

(2) Does the plan suggested by the dean provide a fair allocation? Why?

The instructor should lead a discussion designed to assess the appropriateness of the dean's proposed allocation plan.

b. Have each group select the cost driver (i.e., allocation base) that best serves the self-interest of the department it represents.

c. Consensus on Requirement c should be achieved before completing Requirement d. Each group should determine the amount of the indirect cost to be allocated to each department using the cost driver that best serves the self-interest of the department it represents. Have a spokesperson from each section go to the board and show the income statement that would result for each department.

d. Discuss the development of a cost driver(s) that would promote fairness, rather than self-interest, in the allocation of the indirect cost.

ACT 5-3 WRITING ASSIGNMENT *Selection of the Appropriate Cost Driver*

Recognition Enterprises, Inc. (REI) makes gold, silver, and bronze medals used to recognize outstanding athletic performance in regional and national sporting events. The per-unit direct cost to produce the medals follows:

	Gold	Silver	Bronze
Direct materials	$297	$125	$ 30
Labour	100	100	100

During 2001, REI made 1,200 units of each type of medal. Accordingly, it made a total of 3,600 (1,200 × 3) medals. All medals are created through the same production process, and they are packaged and shipped in identical containers. Indirect overhead costs amounted to $313,200. REI currently uses the number of units as the cost driver for the allocation of overhead cost. As a result, REI allocated $87 ($313,200 ÷ 3,600 units) of overhead cost to each medal produced.

Required

The president of the company has questioned the wisdom of assigning the same amount of overhead to each type of medal. He believes that overhead should be assigned on the basis of the cost to produce the medals. In other words, more overhead should be charged to expensive gold medals, less to silver, and even less to bronze. Assume that you are REI's chief financial officer. Write a memo responding to the president's suggestion.

ACT 5-4 ETHICAL DILEMMA   *Allocation to Achieve Fairness*

The Canadian Insurance Association offers continuing professional education courses for its members at its annual meeting. Instructors are paid a fee for each student attending their courses but are charged a fee for overhead costs that is deducted from their compensation. Overhead costs include fees paid to rent instructional equipment, such as overhead projectors, provide supplies to participants, and offer refreshments during coffee breaks. The number of courses offered is used as the allocation base for determining the overhead charge. For example, if overhead costs amount to $10,000 and 50 courses are offered, each course is allocated an overhead charge of $200 ($10,000 ÷ 50 courses). Cindy Robinson, who taught one of the courses, received the following statement with her cheque in payment for her instructional services:

Instructional fees (20 students × $60 per student)	$1,200
Less: Overhead charge	(200)
Less: Charge of sign language assistant	(300)
Amount due instructor	$ 700

Although Ms. Robinson was well aware that one of her students was deaf and required a sign language assistant, she was surprised to find that she was required to absorb the cost of this service.

Required

a. Given that the Canadians with Disabilities Act stipulates that the deaf student cannot be charged for the cost of providing sign language, who should be required to pay the cost of sign language services?

b. Explain how allocation can be used to promote fairness in the distribution of service costs to the disabled. Describe two ways to treat the $300 cost of providing sign language services that improves fairness.

SPREADSHEET ASSIGNMENT   *Using Excel*

ACT 5-5

Refer to Exercise 5-13. In the following year, the annual cost of the Department of Legal Services was $340,000 and the annual cost of the Department of Computer Services was $250,000. Other relevant information for the second year follows:

	Number of Patients	Number of Workstations
Ottawa clinic	3,100	14
Ottawa Downtown clinic	2,300	17
Hull clinic	2,800	13
Legal services		6

Required

Construct a spreadsheet like the following one to allocate the service costs using the step method.

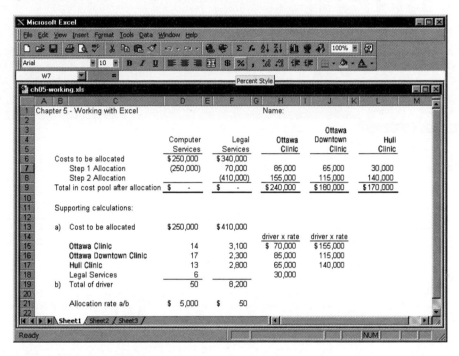

Spreadsheet Tips

1. The headings in Rows 4 and 5 are right aligned. To right align text, choose Format, then Cells and then click on the tab titled Alignment, and set the horizontal alignment to Right. The shortcut method to right align text is to click on the right align icon in the middle of the second tool bar.

2. The supporting calculation section must be completed simultaneously with the allocation table. However, most of the supporting calculations can be completed first. The exception is that the value in Cell F13 refers to the sum of Cells F6 and F7.

SPREADSHEET ASSIGNMENT   *Mastering Excel*

ACT 5-6

Specialty Paints manufactures three types of paint in a joint process: rubberized paint, rust-proofing paint, and aluminum paint. In a standard batch of 500,000 litres of raw material, the outputs are 240,000 litres of rubberized paint, 80,000 litres of rust-proofing paint, and 180,000 litres of aluminum paint. The production cost of a batch is $5,400,000. The sales prices per 4-litre tin are $15, $18, and $20 for rubberized, rust-proofing, and aluminum paint, respectively.

Required

a. Construct a spreadsheet to allocate joint costs to the three products using the number of litres as the allocation base.

b. Include formulas in your spreadsheet to calculate the gross margin of each paint.

Learning Objectives

After completing this chapter, you should be able to:

1 Understand the limitations associated with using direct labour hours as a single companywide overhead allocation rate.

2 Understand how automation has affected the selection of cost drivers.

3 Distinguish between volume-based and activity-based cost drivers.

4 Identify and use activity cost centres and related cost drivers in an activity-based cost system.

5 Classify activities into one of four hierarchical categories, including unit-level, batch-level, product-level, and facility-level activities.

6 Understand the effect that under- or overcosting can have on profitability.

7 Distinguish among manufacturing costs, upstream costs, and downstream costs.

8 Appreciate the limitations of activity-based costing, including the effects of employee attitudes and the availability of data.

9 Categorize quality costs into one of four categories, including prevention cost, appraisal cost, internal failure cost, and external failure cost.

10 Understand relationships among the components of quality costs.

11 Prepare and interpret information contained in quality cost reports.

the *curious* manager

© Photodisc/Phillip Spears

An ABC pilot project was undertaken in the die-cast engine parts area of the Volkswagen Canada Inc. plant in Barrie, Ontario, Volkswagen was ripe for ABC: it made about 25 engine parts, ranging from mass-produced gear housings to highly specialized camshaft-bearing caps. The cost analysis turned up numerous profit laggards. "A lot of them came out negative," says George Waddell, a cost accountant who led the project team. "The whole die-cast operation was profitable then, but that was because maybe only five or six of those parts were making a lot of money and covering for the ones that were losing money."

How can this happen?

Worldwide growth in capitalism has created a highly competitive, global business environment. Managers have responded by using technology to increase productivity. They employ sophisticated techniques to more accurately measure and control cost. Accordingly, they are able to identify and eliminate nonprofitable products and to promote those products that maximize profitability. Accounting managers work with engineers to develop designs to make the manufacturing process more efficient. Managers seek to identify and eliminate non–value-added activities, and they direct attention to the development of quality control procedures that reduce cost and enhance customer satisfaction. This chapter focuses on the new and emerging business practices employed by world-class companies.

▮ Development of a Single Companywide Cost Driver

LO1

Understand the limitations associated with using direct labour hours as a single company-wide overhead allocation rate.

Traditional cost systems were created when the manufacturing process was labour intensive. In most cases, indirect manufacturing costs were relatively small and highly correlated with the use of labour. In other words, products using a high level of labour consumed a high amount of overhead. Given this correlation, the number of labour hours constituted an effective cost driver for the allocation of overhead costs. To illustrate, suppose that production workers spent an eight-hour day working on two jobs. Job 1 required two hours to complete, and Job 2 required six hours. Now, suppose that $120 of utilities were consumed during the day. How much of the $120 should be assigned to each job? The utility cost cannot be directly traced to each specific job, but it is likely that the job that required more labour also consumed a larger part of the utility cost. For example, workers consume more heat, electricity, water, and so on the longer they work on a job. Using this line of reasoning, it is rational to allocate the utility cost to the two jobs on the basis of *direct labour hours*. Specifically, the utility cost could be allocated at the rate of $15 per hour ($120 ÷ 8 hours). Job 1 could be assigned $30 of the total cost ($15 per hour × 2 hours), and the remaining $90 of cost ($15 × 6 hours) could be assigned to Job 2.

Just as direct labour drives the cost of utilities, it also drives many other indirect costs. Consider the amortization charges on the tools used in the process of completing the jobs. The more time worked, the more the tools are used. Accordingly, direct labour hours could be an effective cost driver (i.e., allocation base) for the amortization expense associated with tool usage. Similar arguments could be made for supervisory salaries, supplies, manufacturing rent expense, and so forth. Indeed, many companies invoked this rationale to justify the use of direct labour hours as the *sole basis* for the establishment of a **companywide allocation rate**. These companies used the labour-based, companywide overhead rate to allocate all overhead costs to their products or other cost objects. Clearly, using one base for all overhead costs caused some degree of inaccuracy in the measurement of some cost objects. Remember, however, that in the labour-intensive environment that spawned the use of a companywide allocation rate, overhead costs were relatively small when compared with the costs of labour and materials. Accordingly, to the extent that inaccurate allocations did occur, they were relatively insignificant as to amount.

Automation has changed the nature of the manufacturing process to the extent that the number of direct labour hours no longer constitutes an effective allocation base in many modern manufacturing companies. Indeed, machines have largely replaced human labour. The workers who remain operate technically complex equipment. They are highly skilled and not easily replaced. As a result, workers are seldom laid off when production declines. Likewise, increasing the number of units produced does not require the addition of employees. Production control is accomplished by simply turning additional machines on or off. Under these circumstances, labour is not related to the volume of production and therefore loses its effectiveness as a rational basis for the allocation of overhead costs. Accordingly, labour-intensive companies that become automated usually find it necessary to develop more refined and sophisticated ways to allocate overhead costs.

As machines have replaced people, overhead costs have become a larger part of total manufacturing cost. In highly automated companies, overhead costs may be larger than the cost of labour or materials combined. Although the misallocation of an insignificant amount of overhead does little harm, inaccurate distributions of major costs can destroy the integrity of accounting information. Accordingly, understanding how automation affects the allocation of overhead costs is critical.

■ Effects of Automation on the Selection of a Cost Driver

In an automated manufacturing company, robots and sophisticated machinery have replaced the human labour that traditionally transformed raw materials into finished goods. To understand how these changes affect the selection of a cost driver, we will return to the previous example. Suppose the production process for Job 2 is automated. Now, instead of using six hours of labour, it requires only one hour of direct labour and four hours of mechanical processing. Assume that the use of the new machinery causes utility consumption to increase. Furthermore, total overhead costs increase as a result of the additional amortization charges on the new machinery. Suppose that these changes cause the amount of daily overhead to increase from $120 to $420. Because Job 1 requires two hours of direct labour and Job 2 requires one hour of direct labour, the allocation rate becomes $140 per direct labour hour ($420 ÷ 3 hours). As a result, $280 ($140 × 2 hours) of the total overhead cost is allocated to Job 1 and $140 ($140 × 1 hour) is allocated to Job 2. The pre- and postautomation allocations are compared here:

LO2
Understand how automation has affected the selection of cost drivers.

Product	Preautomation Cost Distribution	Postautomation Cost Distribution
Job 1	$ 30	$280
Job 2	90	140
Total	$120	$420

Clearly, the postautomation use of direct labour hours as the cost driver distorts the allocation of the overhead cost. Although the actual processing of Job 1 was not affected by the automation, it received a $250 ($280 − $30) increase in its share of the allocated overhead cost. This increase should have been assigned to Job 2 because the automation of that job caused overhead costs to increase. The problem results from the fact that the automation caused the consumption of labour for Job 2 to decrease. Note that prior to automation, Job 2 represented six of a total of eight hours of labour. Accordingly, Job 2 was allocated 75 percent (6 ÷ 8) of the overhead cost with the remaining 25 percent being allocated to Job 1. After automation, Job 2 consumed only one of a total of three hours of labour, thereby receiving only 33 percent of the allocated overhead, leaving 67 percent of the allocation for Job 1. These changes in the allocation base coupled with the increase in total overhead cost cause the postautomation cost of Job 1 to be significantly overstated and of Job 2 to be significantly understated.

One way to solve the misallocation problem is to select a more effective volume-based cost driver. For example, instead of using labour hours, machine hours could be used to allocate the utility cost. Indeed, we demonstrated the use of many different **volume-based cost drivers** (e.g., material dollars, material quantities, machine hours, labour dollars) in Chapter 5. Unfortunately, many of the automated processes generate costs that have no cause-and-effect relationship with volume-based cost drivers. To accomplish more meaningful allocations, many companies have begun to use **activity-based cost drivers** to improve the accuracy of product costing. To illustrate, consider the case of Carver Soup Company.

Activity-Based Cost Drivers

Carver Soup Company (CSC) makes vegetable and tomato soup in batches. Each time the company changes from a batch of vegetable soup to a batch of tomato soup or vice versa, it incurs certain costs. For example, the mixing, blending, and cooking equipment must be cleaned. Settings on the equipment must be changed to the specifications required for the particular soup being made. Quality testing must be conducted to ensure that the recipe has been applied correctly. Because these costs are incurred each time a new batch is started, they are called **start-up** or **setup costs**. CSC plans to make 180 batches of each type of soup during the accounting period. Expected production information is summarized in the following table:

LO3
Distinguish between volume-based and activity-based cost drivers.

	Vegetable	Tomato	Total
Number of cans	954,000	234,000	1,188,000
Number of setups	180	180	360

CSC expects that each setup will cost $264. Accordingly, the total expected setup cost is $95,040 ($264 × 360 setups). Using the number of cans as the cost driver (i.e., volume-based driver) produces an allocation rate of $0.08 per can ($95,040 ÷ 1,188,000 cans). Multiplying the allocation rate times the weight of the base (i.e., number of cans) produces the following allocation:

Product	Allocation Rate	×	Number of Cans Produced	=	Allocated Product Cost
Vegetable	$0.08	×	954,000	=	$76,320
Tomato	0.08	×	234,000	=	18,720

As expected, the volume-based allocation rate assigns more cost to the high-volume vegetable soup product; however, this allocation is misleading. Assigning more setup cost to the vegetable soup makes little sense because both products required the *same number of setups*. Given that the setup cost should be distributed equally between the two products, the volume-based cost driver is *overcosting the high-volume product* (vegetable soup) and undercosting the low-volume product (tomato soup). In other words, some of the cost that should be assigned to tomato soup is being allocated to vegetable soup.

The factor that is causing the setup cost to be incurred is the number of times the setup activity is conducted. The more the setups undertaken, the higher is the total setup cost. Accordingly, an *activity-based cost driver* (number of setups) is a more appropriate base for the allocation of the setup costs. Indeed, the activity-based cost driver does allocate an equal portion of the setup cost to both products. Specifically, the allocation rate is $264 ($95,040 ÷ 360 setups) per setup. Multiplying the allocation rate times the weight of the base (number of setups) produces the following allocation:

Product	Allocation Rate	×	Number of Setups	=	Allocated Product Cost
Vegetable	$264	×	180	=	$47,520
Tomato	264	×	180	=	47,520

Activity-Based Cost Drivers Enhance Relevance

The *activity-based cost driver* produces a better allocation because it distributes the *relevant costs* to the appropriate products. If CSC were to stop producing tomato soup, it could *avoid* 180 setups costing $47,520. We are, of course, assuming that the employees currently performing the setup activities could be discharged. Likewise, we assume that the supplies and other resources used in the setup process could be saved. This *avoidable cost is relevant* to decision making. Indeed, the volume-based product cost data provides misleading information for decision-making purposes. Suppose that CSC has an opportunity to outsource the setup activity for tomato soup. A company specializing in the performance of setup activities offers to provide 180 setups for $40,000. A manager considering the volume-based allocated cost of $18,720 would reject the offer because the cost of performing the setup activities appears to be less than the cost of outsourcing them. In fact, CSC should accept the offer because it could avoid $47,520 of cost if the outside company performs the setup activity. In a highly automated environment in which companies produce many different products with varying levels of production, it is little wonder that many companies have turned to activity-based costing to improve the accuracy of their allocations and the effectiveness of their decisions.

▌Activity-Based Costing

Activity-based costing (ABC) is a two-stage allocation process that employs a variety of cost drivers. In the first stage, ABC assigns costs to pools according to the activities that cause the costs to be incurred. In the second stage, the costs in the activity cost pools are allocated to products. Accordingly, the first step in developing an ABC system is to identify the essential activities and the costs required to perform those activities.

Activities are the actions taken by an organization to accomplish its mission. Typical activities include acquiring raw materials, transforming materials into completed products, and delivering products to customers. These general categories of activities can be subdivided into more detailed subclassifications. For example, the activity of acquiring raw materials can be separated into subcategory activities, such as identifying suppliers, obtaining price quotes, evaluating product specifications, completing purchase orders, confirming the receipt of goods purchased, and so on. Each of these categories can be subdivided into more detailed classifications. For instance, the identification of suppliers may include such activities as reviewing advertisements, making internet searches, and obtaining recommendations from business associates. Additional subdivisions are obviously possible. Indeed, companies typically perform thousands of activities in the process of accomplishing their goals.

Identification of Activity Centres

Maintaining the records necessary to determine the cost of performing thousands of activities is expensive. To reduce record-keeping costs, companies organize related activities into hubs called **activity centres**. Overhead costs associated with performing the related activities are combined into cost pools. Pooling costs according to activity centres reduces the number of allocations and the record-keeping required to make those allocations. Because the activities assigned to each centre are related, rational cost allocations can be accomplished through the use of a common cost driver. The number of activity centres used by a company depends on a *cost/benefit analysis*. Companies are willing to incur higher record-keeping costs only to the extent that such record keeping pays for itself through improved decision making. Accordingly, the number of cost centres established by a company depends on management's judgment as to whether the additional accuracy is worth the cost that must be incurred to attain that accuracy.

LO4

Identify and use activity cost centres and related cost drivers in an activity-based cost system.

Comparison of ABC with Traditional Two-Stage Cost Allocation

How does an ABC system differ from the traditional two-stage allocation systems discussed in the appendix of Chapter 5? Traditional two-stage allocation systems pool costs according to departments. Costs in the departmental cost pools are then allocated to cost objects by using some form of volume-based cost driver. In contrast, an ABC system pools costs by activity centres and then uses a variety of volume- and activity-based cost drivers to allocate costs to cost objects. Typically, an ABC system has many more activity centres than the number of departments in a traditional two-stage allocation system. Indeed, ABC improves cost tracing by increasing the number of cause-and-effect relationships employed in the assignment of indirect costs. Instead of assigning costs to a few departments, ABC assigns costs to numerous activity centres. The primary differences between a traditional two-stage allocation system and the ABC system are depicted graphically in Exhibit 6–1. Both allocation systems shown in the exhibit could be drawn with more costs pools. In other words, businesses can have more than two departments or three activity centres. The exhibit is designed to show the typical case in which an ABC system incorporates more cost pools than does a traditional two-stage allocation plan.

focus on International Issues

Eliminating Non–Value-Added Activities in a Sushi Bar

Identifying and eliminating activities that do not add value can lead to increased customer satisfaction and profitability. An emerging trend in Japanese sushi bars validates this point. Sushi delivered via conveyor belt leads to significant cost sav-

©Tom Wagner/SABA

ings that are passed on to customers. A moving belt, not a waiter, delivers sushi directly to the customers. Cooks fill the merry-go-round conveyor belt, instead of patron orders. The savings associated with the elimination of non–value-added activities, such as taking orders, delivering food, and avoiding waste, have enabled conveyor belt shops to offer customers quality sushi at economy prices—two pieces for $1 versus $3 to $4 at standard sushi shops. Customers are so wowed by the deal that they are braving waits of up to an hour. Owners are benefiting, too, because diners get their fill and move on faster, thereby increasing turnover and sales volume. The increased volume produced is highly profitable because fixed costs are not affected by the soaring sales. When insights gained through activity-based costing (ABC) lead to the changes in the way a business is managed, the process is known as activity-based management (ABM).

Source: Miki Tanikawa, "Sushi Bars: What Comes Around," *Business Week*, November 9, 1998, p. 8.

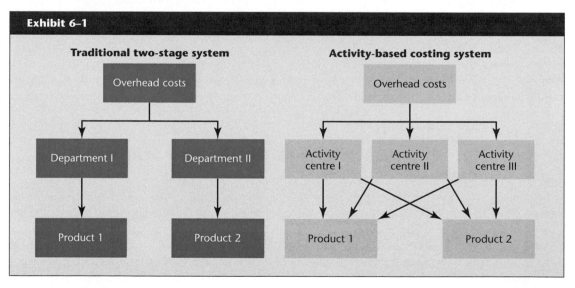

Exhibit 6–1

Traditional two-stage system

Overhead costs → Department I, Department II → Product 1, Product 2

Activity-based costing system

Overhead costs → Activity centre I, Activity centre II, Activity centre III → Product 1, Product 2

Types of Production Activities

LO5

Classify activities into one of four hierarchical categories, including unit-level, batch-level, product-level, and facility-level activities.

Many companies have found that organizing activities into four hierarchical categories facilitates cost tracing. These categories are (1) unit-level activities, (2) batch-level activities, (3) product-level activities, and (4) facility-level activities.[1] The overhead costs associated with each category are pooled together and allocated to products according to the way those products benefit from the activities. *The primary objective is to trace the cost of performing activities to the products that are causing the activities to be performed.* To illustrate, we discuss the classification of the overhead costs incurred by Unterman Shirt Company.

[1] The cost associated with these activities were discussed in Chapter 4. It may be helpful to review the definitions of these costs prior to continuing your study of this chapter.

Unterman has two different product lines: dress shirts and casual shirts. The company expects to produce 680,000 dress shirts and 120,000 casual shirts during 2003 and expects overhead costs to total $5,730,000. Currently, Unterman assigns an equal amount of overhead to each shirt. Under these conditions, determining the overhead cost per shirt is easily accomplished by dividing the total expected overhead cost by the total expected production ($5,730,000 ÷ 800,000 units = $7.16 per shirt rounded to the nearest whole cent). Dress shirts and casual shirts require approximately the same amount of direct materials and labour. Direct materials cost approximately $8.20 per shirt, and direct labour costs approximately $6.80. Accordingly, the total cost per shirt is $22.16 ($7.16 + $8.20 + $6.80). Unterman sells shirts for $31 each, thereby yielding a gross margin of $8.84 per shirt ($31 − $22.16).

Bob Unterman, president and owner of the company, is convinced that although the allocation computation is easy, it is also inaccurate. The direct materials and labour costs seem reasonable, but he is sure that the overhead costs are not the same for both product lines. Accordingly, Mr. Unterman decides to hire a consultant, Rebecca Lynch, to trace the overhead costs to the two product lines. Ms. Lynch decides to use an *activity-based cost* system. She begins by identifying the activities necessary to make shirts and categorizes the activities into the following four activity cost centres.

Unit-Level Activity Centre

Unit-level activities occur each time a unit of product is made. For example, every time a shirt is made, Unterman incurs inspection costs, machine-related utility costs, and costs for production supplies. Accordingly, total unit-level cost increases each time a product is made and decreases each time the volume of production is reduced. Some costs that are not purely unit-level costs exhibit behaviour patterns that justify treating them as such. For example, suppose that machinery is lubricated after every eight hours of continuous operation. Although the cost of lubrication is not incurred each time a shirt is produced, the cost behaviour pattern is so closely tied to the level of production that it may be treated as a unit-level cost even though it does not meet a strict interpretation of that categorization.

Ms. Lynch identifies the following unit-level overhead costs: (1) $300,000 for machine-related utilities, (2) $50,000 for machine maintenance, (3) $450,000 for indirect labour and materials, (4) $200,000 for inspection and quality control, and (5) $296,000 for miscellaneous unit-level costs. She combines these costs into a single cost pool containing $1,296,000 of overhead cost and assigns this cost to a *unit-level activity centre*. This assignment constitutes the first stage of the two-stage ABC allocation system. In other words, $1,296,000 of the total $5,730,000 overhead cost has now been allocated to one of the four activity centres. The remaining balance of the overhead cost will be allocated among the three other activity centres.

The second-stage cost assignment involves allocating the $1,296,000 unit-level cost pool between the two product lines. Because unit-level costs are incurred each time a shirt is produced, they should be allocated with a base that is correlated with the level of production. Assume that Ms. Lynch chooses to use direct labour hours as the allocation base. Past performance suggests that 272,000 direct labour hours are required to make the dress shirts and 48,000 direct labour hours are required to make the casual shirts. On the basis of this information, Ms. Lynch allocates the unit-level overhead costs and computes the cost per unit as indicated in Exhibit 6–2.

Exhibit 6–2　*Allocation of Unit-Level Overhead Costs*

	Product Lines		
	Dress Shirts	Casual Shirts	Total
Number of direct labour hours (a)	272,000	48,000	320,000
Cost per labour hour ($1,296,000 ÷ 320,000 hours)(b)	$4.05	$4.05	n/a
Total allocated overhead cost (c = a × b)	$1,101,600	$194,400	$1,296,000
Number of shirts (d)	680,000	120,000	800,000
Cost per shirt (c ÷ d)	$1.62	$1.62	

Note that the unit-level costs follow a variable cost behaviour pattern. Total cost changes in direct proportion to the number of units produced. Cost per unit is constant, regardless of the number of units produced. Because cost per unit is not affected by the volume of activity, the pricing structure of dress versus casual shirts should not be affected by the fact that the company makes more dress shirts than casual shirts.

Batch-Level Activity Centre

Batch-level activities are related to the production of groups of products. Costs associated with a batch of products are fixed, regardless of the number of units of product included in the batch of work. For example, the costs associated with setting up machinery to cut material for a certain size shirt are the same, regardless of how many are cut with that particular machine setting. Similarly, the cost of a first-item batch test is the same, regardless of whether 200 or 2,000 shirts are made in the batch. Another cost commonly classified as a batch-level cost is materials handling. This classification applies because materials are usually transferred from one department to another in batches. For example, all the small dress shirts are cut in the sizing department. Then the entire batch of cut material is transferred to the sewing department. Because the equipment used to transfer materials makes a single delivery of all the work-in-process inventory in any size batch, the cost of materials handling is the same, regardless of whether the batch load is large or small.

Because total batch costs depend on the number of batch runs performed, more costs should be allocated to products that require more batch runs. Assume that Ms. Lynch estimates total batch-level overhead costs to be $690,000. Accordingly, the first-stage allocation places this amount in a batch-level cost pool.

With respect to the second-stage allocation, Ms. Lynch determines that the casual shirt line requires considerably more setups than the dress shirt line because the casual shirts are subject to frequent style changes. Because customers are willing to buy only small amounts of items with limited shelf life, Unterman is forced to produce casual shirts in small batches. On the basis of this information, Ms. Lynch decides that more of the batch-level costs should be allocated to the casual shirt line than to the dress shirt line. She believes that the number of setups constitutes the most rational allocation base. Because 1,280 setups are performed for casual shirts and 1,020 setups are required to make the dress shirts, Ms. Lynch allocates the batch-level costs as indicated in Exhibit 6–3.

Exhibit 6–3   Allocation of Batch-Level Overhead Costs

	Product Lines		
	Dress Shirts	Casual Shirts	Total
Number of setups performed (a)	1,020	1,280	2,300
Cost per setup ($690,000 ÷ 2,300 setups)(b)	$300	$300	n/a
Total allocated overhead cost (c = a × b)	$306,000	$384,000	$690,000
Number of shirts (d)	680,000	120,000	800,000
Cost per shirt (c ÷ d)	$0.45	$3.20	

Note that the per shirt batch-level cost for casual shirts is considerably larger than the per shirt cost for dress shirts. This occurs for two reasons. First, as indicated, more batch-level costs are assigned to the casual shirt line ($384,000 versus $306,000). Second, the number of casual shirts made is significantly smaller than the number of dress shirts made (120,000 units versus 680,000). Recall that batch-level costs follow a fixed cost behaviour pattern relative to the number of units in a particular batch. This means that the cost per unit increases as the number of units in a batch decreases. For example, if setup costs amount to $300, the cost per unit for a batch of 100 units is $3 ($300 ÷ 100 units). The cost per unit rises to $30 if the batch contains only 10 units ($300 ÷ 10 units). This explains why the average batch cost per shirt is considerably higher for casual shirts ($3.20 per shirt) than for dress shirts ($0.45). Accordingly, when batch-level costs are significant, companies should pursue products with high volume. As demonstrated in this case, low-volume products are more expensive to make because the fixed costs must be spread over fewer shirts. To the extent that cost affects pricing, the casual shirts should be priced higher than the dress shirts.

Product-Level Activity Centre

Product-level activities support a specific product or product line made by a company. Examples include materials inventory holding costs, engineering development costs, and legal fees to obtain and protect patents, copyrights, trademarks, and brand names. Unterman Shirt Company prides itself on being the fashion leader with respect to contemporary trends in style. It incurs considerable fashion design costs to ensure that it remains the trend setter. The company also incurs engineering costs of continually improving the quality of materials used in its products. In addition, it incurs legal fees to protect the brand names of the company's products. After a careful review of Unterman's operations, Ms. Lynch concludes that $1,800,000 of the total overhead cost could be traced to the product-level activity centre.

The second-stage allocation requires assessing the extent to which these activities focus on sustaining the dress shirt line versus the casual shirt line. Interviews with fashion design personnel disclose that more of their time is spent on casual shirts because the styles of these shirts change so frequently. Similarly, the engineers spend more of their time developing new fabric, buttons, and zippers for casual shirts. The materials used in dress shirts are fairly stable. Although some work is performed to improve the quality of dress shirt materials, the time spent is significantly less than that spent on the more unusual materials used in the casual shirts. Similarly, the legal department spends more time developing and protecting the newer patents, trademarks, and brand names of the casual line of shirts. On the basis of these interviews, Ms. Lynch concludes that 70 percent of the product-level cost pool should be allocated to the casual line of shirts, leaving 30 percent of the pool to be allocated to the dress shirt line. On the basis of this information, she allocates product-level costs to the two product lines as indicated in Exhibit 6–4.

Exhibit 6–4	*Allocation of Product-Level Overhead Costs*		
		Product Lines	
	Dress Shirts	Casual Shirts	Total
Percent of product-level activity utilization (a)	30%	70%	100%
Total allocated overhead cost (b = a × $1,800,000)	$540,000	$1,260,000	$1,800,000
Total units produced (c)	680,000	120,000	800,000
Cost per unit (b ÷ c)	$0.79*	$10.50	

*Rounded to the nearest whole cent.

As indicated, product-level costs are frequently distributed unevenly for the different product lines. In the case of Unterman Shirts, considerably more costs are incurred to sustain the casual shirt line than the dress shirt line. If differential costs are distributed evenly over all products, as is the case using a single companywide overhead rate, distortions in cost measurement occur. These distortions can lead to negative consequences, such as irrational pricing policies and reward structures that motivate inappropriate behaviour. The use of ABC reduces the likelihood of measurement distortions by more accurately tracing costs to the products that cause their incurrence. In this case, more of the overhead cost is assigned to the casual shirt product line.

Facility-Level Activity Centre

Facility-level activities are performed to benefit the production process as a whole and therefore are not related to any specific product, batch, or unit of production. For example, the fire insurance on the manufacturing facility does not benefit any particular product or product line. Other examples of facility-level costs include amortization for the manufacturing facility and the costs of security, landscaping and plant maintenance, general utilities, and taxes. With respect to Unterman Shirt Company, Ms. Lynch identifies $1,944,000 of facility-level overhead costs. Because no logical relationship exists between these facility-level manufacturing costs and the two product lines, she is forced to allocate these costs on an arbitrary basis. Assuming that the facility-level costs are arbitrarily allocated equally over the total number of units produced, Ms. Lynch allocates 85 percent (680,000 ÷ 800,000) of the facility-level cost pool to the dress shirt product line and 15 percent (120,000 ÷ 800,000) to the casual shirt line. The allocation schedule and computation of cost per unit are shown in Exhibit 6–5.

Exhibit 6–5 Allocation of Facility-Level Overhead Costs			
	Product Lines		
	Dress Shirts	**Casual Shirts**	**Total**
Percent of total units (a)	85%	15%	100%
Total allocated overhead cost (b = a × $1,944,000)	$1,652,400	$291,600	$1,944,000
Total units produced (c)	680,000	120,000	800,000
Cost per unit (b ÷ c)	$2.43	$2.43	

Classification of Activities Not Limited to Four Categories

As previously indicated, the number of activity centres used in business practice depends on cost/benefit analysis. The four categories used here frequently constitute a starting point. Any of the four categories could be further subdivided into more detailed activity centres. For example, an activity cost centre for unit-level labour-related activities and a different centre for unit-level machine-related activities could be established. Indeed, identifying the list of activity centres to use in a real-world company can be quite tedious. Paulette Bennett describes the process used in the Material Control Department at Compumotor, Inc. as follows:

> Recognizing that ordinarily the two biggest problems with an ABC project are knowing where to start and how deep to go, we began by analyzing the activities that take place in our procurement process. As the old saying goes, to find the biggest alligators you usually have to wade into the weeds; therefore, we started by writing down all the procurement activities. Creating a real world picture of costs by activity was our aim. But had we used our initial list we would have designed a spreadsheet so large that no human could ever have emerged alive at the other end.[2]

Ms. Bennett's abbreviated list still contained 83 separate activities. Even so, this list represents the activity centres for only one department of a very large company. Although we limit our discussion for instructional purposes to four general categories, be aware that the real-world equivalent is far more complicated.

Context-Sensitive Classification of Activities

Note that a particular type of activity could be classified as belonging to any of the four hierarchical categories. For example, inspections conducted on a piecemeal basis is a unit-level activity. Inspecting the first item of each batch to determine whether the setup was accomplished properly is a batch-level activity. Inspections established for a specific product or product line are product-level activities. Finally,

---

[2] Paulette Bennett, "ABM and the Procurement Cost Model," *Management Accounting*, March 1996, pp. 28–32.

inspections of the factory building are facility-level activities. You cannot memorize a list of activities as belonging to any particular category. You must learn instead to analyze the context within which the activity takes place to classify it properly.

Cost Driver Selection

As noted, activity-based costing uses *volume-based cost drivers* and *activity-based cost drivers*. Volume-based drivers are appropriate for indirect costs that increase or decrease relative to the volume of activity. Accordingly, the use of such cost drivers as units, labour hours, or machine hours, is appropriate for unit-level activities. The problem with traditional costing systems is that they use a volume-based measure (usually labour hours) for the allocation of all indirect costs. In contrast, the more sophisticated ABC approach uses such activity drivers as number of setups or percentage of utilization for overhead costs that are not affected by volume. Accordingly, ABC improves the accuracy of allocations by using a combination of volume- and activity-based cost drivers.

Use of the Information to Trace Costs to Product Lines

A summary of the ABC allocation plan prepared by Ms. Lynch is shown in Exhibit 6–6. Mr. Unterman was shocked to see that the overhead costs for casual shirts line is virtually three times the cost for dress shirts. For comparative purposes, he asked Ms. Lynch to prepare the information shown in Exhibit 6–7.

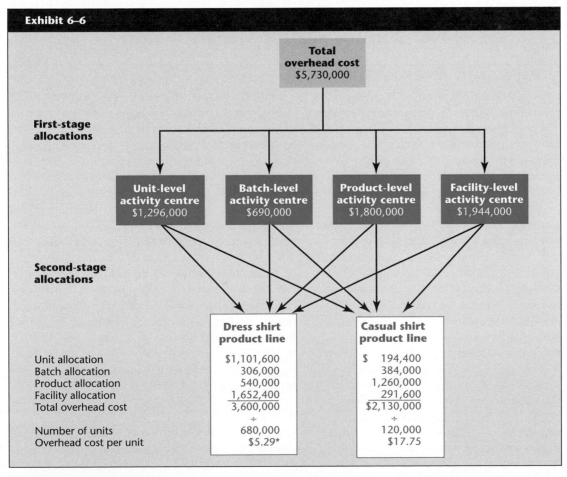

Exhibit 6–6

Total overhead cost
$5,730,000

First-stage allocations

| Unit-level activity centre $1,296,000 | Batch-level activity centre $690,000 | Product-level activity centre $1,800,000 | Facility-level activity centre $1,944,000 |

Second-stage allocations

	Dress shirt product line	Casual shirt product line
Unit allocation	$1,101,600	$ 194,400
Batch allocation	306,000	384,000
Product allocation	540,000	1,260,000
Facility allocation	1,652,400	291,600
Total overhead cost	3,600,000	$2,130,000
	÷	÷
Number of units	680,000	120,000
Overhead cost per unit	$5.29*	$17.75

*Rounded to the nearest whole cent.

Exhibit 6-7 *Allocation of Facility-Level Overhead Costs*

	Gross Margins Product Lines		ABC Margins Product Lines	
	Dress Shirts	**Casual Shirts**	**Dress Shirts**	**Casual Shirts**
Sales price	$31.00	$31.00	$31.00	$31.00
Cost of goods sold				
Materials cost	(8.20)	(8.20)	(8.20)	(8.20)
Labour cost	(6.80)	(6.80)	(6.80)	(6.80)
Overhead	(7.16)	(7.16)	(5.29)	(17.75)
Margin	$ 8.84	$ 8.84	$10.71	($ 1.75)

This table shows the computation of traditional per-unit gross margins versus the ABC margins for the two product lines. Recall that direct materials and direct labour costs for dress and casual shirts are $8.20 and $6.80, respectively. The difference in the margins is attributable to the overhead allocation. Using a traditional companywide overhead rate results in the allocation of an equal amount of overhead to each shirt ($5,730,000 ÷ 800,000 units = $7.16 per shirt). In contrast, the ABC approach assigns $5.29 to each dress shirt and $17.75 to each casual shirt. These differential rates reflect the cost of activities used to make the shirts. Total overhead cost is $5,730,000 under both approaches. It is the *assignment of* rather than the *amount of* the total cost that differs for the two approaches. ABC makes clear the fact that making a casual shirt costs more than making a dress shirt. After reviewing the data in Exhibit 6–7, Mr. Unterman remarked, "I knew that the overhead wasn't being allocated on a rational basis, but I had no idea we were incurring losses on the casual shirt line. Something must be done. What are our options?"

Under- and Overcosting

LO6

Understand
the effect that
under- or
overcosting can
have on
profitability.

Clearly, the single companywide overhead rate has resulted in undercosting Unterman Shirt Company's casual line. Indeed, the understated overhead cost has caused Unterman to price its product below cost. The most obvious response to the ABC margin data shown in Exhibit 6–7 is to raise the price of casual shirts. Unfortunately, the market may not be willing to cooperate. If other companies are selling casual shirts at prices near $31, Unterman's customers may buy from the company's competitors instead of paying a higher price for Unterman's shirts. In a market-driven economy, raising prices may not be a viable option. Accordingly, Unterman may be forced to establish a target-pricing strategy.

Target pricing requires management to determine the price that customers are willing to pay. The company then controls cost factors to produce the product at a cost that will enable it to sell at the price that customers demand. The data in Exhibits 6–3 and 6–4 indicate that batch-level and product-level costs are significantly higher for casual shirts than for dress shirts. Unterman may be too fashion conscious with respect to its casual shirt line. Perhaps the company would be better off to relinquish its trend-setting position. It could adopt the strategy of focusing on a few traditional styles. This would enable the company to reduce fashion design costs. Furthermore, because following established trends provides more security than setting new ones, the traditional designs may increase customer confidence in the marketability of the casual shirt line, which will likely lead them to place larger orders, which would enable Unterman to reduce its per-unit batch costs.

Note that the single companywide overhead rate not only undercosts the casual shirt line but also overcosts the dress shirt line. To the extent that price is affected by the overstated overhead cost, the dress shirt line is overpriced. Overpricing can place the dress shirt business at a competitive disadvantage, which can lead to the loss of market share, which, in turn, can have a snowballing effect. If volume declines, Unterman's fixed costs will be spread over fewer units, resulting in a higher cost per unit. Higher costs encourage price increases, which further aggravate the competitive disadvantage. To avoid this condition, it is as important for Unterman to consider lowering the price of its dress shirts as it is to consider raising the price of its casual shirts.

Examining the Relevance of Allocated Facility-Level Costs

If Unterman is unable to raise the price or lower the cost of its casual shirts, management should consider eliminating that product line. As indicated in Chapter 4, evaluating the elimination of a product line requires an assessment of the *relevant costs*. Recall that the relevant costs are those costs that can be *avoided* by eliminating a product line. So, which of the ABC-allocated overhead costs can be avoided by eliminating the casual shirt product line? Generally, the unit-level, batch-level, and product-level costs can be eliminated or substantially reduced when a product line is eliminated. On the other hand, *facility-level costs are usually not affected by product elimination and are therefore unavoidable.* Amortization on the manufacturing building and the cost of security, insurance, taxes, and so forth will remain the same, regardless of whether Unterman makes casual shirts. Indeed, *many companies do not allocate facility-level costs directly to products for decision-making purposes.* With respect to Unterman, the avoidable overhead costs amount to $15.32 (unit-level $1.62 + batch-level $3.20 + product-level $10.50). Assuming that direct labour and materials costs can be avoided, the total avoidable cost is $30.32 ($8.20 labour + $6.80 materials + $15.32 overhead). Because the avoidable cost is less than the sales price of $31, the analysis suggests the casual shirt product line should not be eliminated.

Downstream Costs and Upstream Costs

The analysis in the preceding paragraph is incomplete because it considers only product costs. Businesses incur **upstream costs** that occur before or **downstream costs** that occur after goods are manufactured. These costs may be relevant to decisions regarding the elimination of a product or product line. For example, suppose that Unterman pays sales personnel a $2 commission on each shirt sold. Although these commissions are selling and administrative costs, they are relevant to a decision regarding whether to eliminate the casual shirt line. Indeed, the commission expense could be avoided if Unterman sells no casual shirts. As a result, the total avoidable cost is $32.32 ($30.32 product costs + $2 sales commissions). Under these circumstances, the total avoidable cost ($32.32) is above the sales price of $31 per unit, leading to the conclusion that Unterman should abandon the casual shirt product line. Likewise, upstream costs, such as research and development, must be considered in decision making. Ultimately, products must be sold at a price that exceeds the total cost to develop, make and sell them. Anything less than this amount will lead to the eventual demise of the business.

LO7
Distinguish among manufacturing costs, upstream costs, and downstream costs.

Employee Attitudes and the Availability of Data

As the preceding scenarios indicate, ABC costing can bring insights that lead to the implementation of cost-cutting measures, including the elimination of products and product lines. Because these measures can result in the loss of jobs, it is little wonder that employees are sometimes reluctant to cooperate with the implementation of an ABC system. It is important to make employees aware that ABC and other *strategic cost management* techniques frequently result in a redirection of the workforce, rather than the displacement of workers. Ultimately, the benefits of employment depend on the employer's competitive health. Accordingly, actions that benefit a company usually benefit its employees as well. The implementation of an ABC system is more likely to succeed when key managers and their personnel are convinced that their fate as well as that of the company will be affected positively.

Even when employees are cooperative, data can be difficult to collect. Frequently, the necessary data are not being collected. For example, suppose that a manager wants to allocate inspection costs on the basis of the number of hours an inspector spends on each job. Unfortunately, the inspector may not maintain records regarding the time spent on individual jobs. Accordingly, making the allocation requires a policy change requiring inspectors to maintain records regarding time spent on individual jobs. The accuracy of the allocation then depends on how conscientious the inspectors were in maintaining their time reports. As this example indicates, gaining personnel support and obtaining accurate data are two of the more challenging obstacles to the implementation of a successful ABC system.

LO8
Appreciate the limitations of activity-based costing, including the effects of employee attitudes and the availability of data.

Consider one of the not-so-profitable parts: an engine-mounting bracket. Random samples of most parts pass through an X-ray machine to check for structural defects that could cause them to break. But a snapped engine-mounting bracket could be a safety hazard. So, Volkswagen was X-raying every single bracket to guard against a flawed one slipping through. In fact, X-raying these brackets took up about 80% of machine time. Under the ABC system, when the pool of inspection costs was divided up according to the proportion of X-ray inspections devoted to the various parts, engine brackets carried 80 percent of the load. This is appropriate; as a safety issue, VW is ensuring minimal risk due to failure and attaching the additional cost to the part being inspected—an excellent example of activity-based costing.

Source: Southerst, *Suddenly, it all makes sense* (business costs). Vol. 67, *Canadian Business*, March 1, 1994, pp 39(3).

■ Total Quality Management

LO9

Categorize quality costs into one of four categories including prevention cost, appraisal cost, internal failure cost, and external failure cost.

Quality is widely recognized as a key ingredient in a company's ability to obtain and retain customers. Even so, quality is an elusive term. It does not always mean "the very best." A silver spoon is of a higher quality than a plastic spoon, but customers are perfectly willing to accept plastic spoons when they eat at fast food restaurants. So, what do we mean when we say that a business must produce quality products to be competitive? **Quality** refers to the degree to which actual products or services *conform* to their design specifications. The costs that companies incur to ensure quality conformance can be classified into four categories: prevention, appraisal, internal failure, and external failure.

Prevention and appraisal costs are incurred because of the potential lack of conformance to quality standards. **Prevention costs** are incurred to avoid nonconforming products. **Appraisal costs** are incurred to identify nonconforming products that were not avoided via the prevention cost expenditures. **Failure costs** result from the actual occurrence of nonconforming products. **Internal failure costs** are incurred when defects are corrected before the goods reach the customer. **External failure costs** result from defective goods being delivered to customers.

The four components can be summarized into two broad categories. Because prevention and appraisal costs are a function of managerial discretion, they are often called **voluntary costs**. Management makes direct decisions as to the amount of funds to be expended for these voluntary costs. In contrast, failure costs are not directly controllable by management. For example, the cost of customer dissatisfaction may not be measurable, much less controllable. Even though failure costs may not be directly controllable, they are definitely related to voluntary costs. When additional funds are allocated for prevention and appraisal activities, failure costs tend to decline. The logic is obvious; as the level of control increases, quality conformance increases, thereby lowering failure costs. When control activities are reduced, quality conformance decreases and failure cost increases. Accordingly, *voluntary costs and failure costs move in opposite directions.*

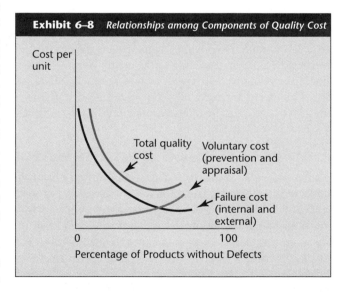

Exhibit 6–8 *Relationships among Components of Quality Cost*

Cost per unit

Total quality cost

Voluntary cost (prevention and appraisal)

Failure cost (internal and external)

0   100

Percentage of Products without Defects

Does quality pay? It definitely does, according to returns provided in the stock market. The Baldridge Index, which is composed of companies that have received the Malcolm Baldridge National Quality Award, outperformed the Standard & Poors (S&P) 500 stock index by almost 3 to 1. As indicated in Exhibit 6–9, the Baldridge Index provided a 362 percent four-year return as compared with a 148 percent return provided by S&P 500 index. Because stock prices reflect investor beliefs regarding companies' present and future earnings, these returns provide a clear indication that investors believe that quality enhances profitability.

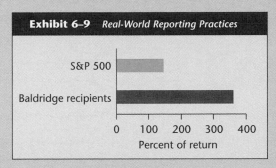

Exhibit 6–9 *Real-World Reporting Practices*

S&P 500

Baldridge recipients

0   100   200   300   400

Percent of return

©Jon Riley/ Tony Stone Images

Source: "Quality Claims Its Own Bull Market," *Business Week*, March 16, 1998, p. 113.

Minimization of Total Quality Cost

Total quality control cost is defined as the sum of voluntary costs plus failure costs. Because voluntary costs and failure costs are negatively correlated, the minimum amount of total quality cost is located at the point on a graph where the marginal voluntary expenditures equal the marginal savings on failure cost. This relationship is depicted in Exhibit 6–8.

The data in Exhibit 6–8 clearly indicate that the minimum total quality cost per unit is located at a level of quality assurance that is less than 100 percent. At very low levels of assurance, significant failure costs outweigh any cost savings that would be attained by avoiding voluntary costs. In contrast, extremely high levels of quality assurance result in voluntary cost expenditures that are not offset by failure cost savings. Although the "zero defects" concept sounds great, it does not represent a cost-effective strategy. Realistic managers seek to minimize total quality cost, rather than to eliminate all defects.

LO10
Understand relationships among the components of quality cost.

Quality Cost Reports

Management of quality costs in a manner that leads to the highest level of customer satisfaction is known as **total quality management (TQM)**. To facilitate TQM, accountants are frequently asked to prepare a **quality cost report**, which typically lists the company's quality costs and provides a horizontal analysis showing each item as a percentage of the total cost. Data are normally shown for two or more accounting periods to reveal the effects of changes over time. Exhibit 6–10 is a quality cost report for Unterman Shirt Company. The company's accountant prepared the report to assess the effects of a quality control campaign that the company recently initiated. Review the information in Exhibit 6–10 and attempt to determine Unterman's quality control strategy and the degree of the campaign's success or failure.

The data in Exhibit 6–9 suggest that Unterman is seeking to control quality by focusing on appraisal activities. The total expenditures for prevention activities remained unchanged, but expenditures for appraisal activities increased significantly. The results of this strategy are also apparent in the failure cost data. Note that internal failure costs increased significantly, while external failure cost decreased dramatically. The strategy was successful in lowering total quality costs. Even so, the data suggest that more

LO11
Prepare and interpret information contained in quality cost reports.

Exhibit 6-10	Quality Cost Report for Unterman Shirt Company			
	2002		**2001**	
	Amount	Percentage*	Amount	Percentage*
Prevention costs				
Product design	$ 50,000	6.54%	52,000	6.60%
Preventive equipment (amortization)	7,000	0.92	7,000	0.89
Training costs	27,000	3.53	25,000	3.17
Promotion and awards	22,000	2.88	22,000	2.79
Total prevention	$106,000	13.87%	$106,000	13.45%
Appraisal costs				
Inventory inspection	75,000	9.82	25,000	3.17
Reliability testing	43,000	5.63	15,000	1.90
Testing equipment (amortization)	20,000	2.62	12,000	1.52
Supplies	12,000	1.57	8,000	1.02
Total Appraisal	$150,000	19.63%	$ 60,000	7.61%
Internal failure costs				
Scrap	90,000	11.78	40,000	5.08
Repair and rework	140,000	18.32	110,000	13.96
Downtime	38,000	4.97	20,000	2.54
Reinspection	30,000	3.93	12,000	1.52
Total internal failure	$298,000	39.01%	$182,000	23.10%
External failure costs				
Warranty repairs and replacement	120,000	15.71	260,000	32.99
Freight	20,000	2.62	50,000	6.35
Customer relations	40,000	5.24	60,000	7.61
Restocking and packaging	30,000	3.93	70,000	8.88
Total external failure	$210,000	27.49%	$440,000	55.84%
Grand total	$764,000	100.00%	$788,000	100.00%

*Percentages do not add exactly because of rounding.

improvement is possible. Note that 86.13 percent (appraisal 19.63 percent + internal failure 39.01 percent + external failure 27.49 percent) of total quality cost is associated with finding and correcting mistakes. You have probably heard the adage that "an ounce of prevention is worth a pound of cure." If Unterman were to concentrate more on prevention, perhaps it could avoid many of the appraisal and failure costs.

a look

back

Many traditional cost systems used direct labour hours as the sole basis for the allocation of overhead costs. Labour hours served as an effective *companywide allocation base* because labour was highly correlated with the incurrence of overhead costs. In other words, more labour resulted in the production of more products and the incurrence of more overhead cost. Accordingly, it made sense to assign more overhead to cost objects that required more labour. Because labour was related to the volume of production, it was frequently called a volume-based cost driver. Other *volume-based cost drivers* included machine hours, number of units, and labour dollars. Companywide, volume-based cost drivers were never perfect measures of overhead consumption. However, misallocation was not a serious problem because overhead costs were relatively small. If a manager misallocates an insignificant cost, it does not matter.

Automation has changed the nature of the manufacturing process. This change may cause significant distortions in the allocation of overhead costs when a companywide, volume-based cost driver is used as the allocation base. There are two primary reasons for distortions. First, in an automated environment, the same amount of labour (i.e., a flip of a switch) may be required to produce a large or a small volume of products. Under these circumstances, labour use is not related to the incurrence of overhead and cannot be used as a rational allocation base. Second, the distortions may be significant because overhead costs are much higher relative to the cost of labour and materials. For example, when robots replace people in the production process, amortization becomes a larger portion of the total product cost and labour becomes a smaller portion of the total.

To improve the accuracy of allocations, managerial accountants began to study the wide array of activities required to make a product. Such activities may include acquiring raw materials, materials handling and storage activities, product design activities, legal activities, and traditional production labour activities. Various measures of theses activities can be used as a basis for making numerous allocations related to the determination of product cost. The process of using activity measures to allocate overhead costs has become known as *activity-based costing* (ABC). In an ABC system, costs are allocated in a two-stage process. First, activities are organized into *activity centres* and the related costs of performing these activities are combined into *cost pools*. Second, the pooled costs are allocated to designated cost objects through the use of activity-based cost drivers. The implementation of ABC is most likely to succeed when employees are made aware that it will positively affect their fate and that of the company. Without employee cooperation, collecting the necessary data for the system's success may be difficult.

Many ABC systems begin by organizing activities into one of four categories. Total *unit-level activity cost* increases each time a unit of product is made and decreases each time the volume of production is reduced. Unit-level activity costs can be allocated with a base that is correlated with the level of production (volume-based cost drivers). *Batch-level activities* are related to the production of groups of products. Their costs are fixed, regardless of the number of units in a batch. Batch-level costs are assigned so that the products requiring the most batches are assigned the most batch costs. *Product-level activities* support a specific product or specific product line. Product-level cost are frequently assigned to products on the basis of the product's percentage use of product level activities. *Facility-level activities* are performed for the benefit of the production process as a whole. The allocation of these costs is often arbitrary.

Accurate allocations are important because distortions can cause products to be over- or undercosted. Overcosting can cause a product line to be overpriced, and overpriced products may cause a company to lose market share, and the decline in sales revenue will cause profits to fall. When products are underpriced, revenue is less than it should be and profitability suffers.

Product costs are frequently distinguished from upstream and downstream costs. *Upstream costs* result from activities that occur *before* goods are manufactured. Examples include research and development, product design, and legal development. *Downstream costs* result from activities that occur *after* the goods are manufactured. Examples of downstream costs include selling and administrative expenses. The treatment of upstream and downstream costs is important in making pricing decisions and decisions regarding the elimination of a product or product line.

The next chapter introduces the topics of planning and cost control. You will learn how to prepare budgets and projected (i.e., pro forma) financial statements. Finally, you will learn the importance of considering human factors as well as the quantitative aspects of the budgeting process.

a look
forward

KEY TERMS

Activities Actions taken by an organization to accomplish its mission. *(p. 205)*

Activity-based cost drivers Measures of the use and consumption of such activities as number of setups, percentage of use, and pounds of material delivered; used as allocation bases, they can improve the accuracy of allocations in technical and automated business environments in which overhead is no longer driven by volume. *(p. 203)*

Activity-based costing (ABC) A two-stage allocation process that employs a variety of cost drivers. In the first stage, costs associated with specific business activities are allocated or assigned to activity cost pools. The second stage involves allocating these pooled costs to designated cost objects through the use of cost drivers. The cost drivers chosen for each cost pool are drivers that measure the demand placed on that cost pool by the cost object. *(p. 205)*

Activity centres Cost centres organized around operating activities that have similar characteristics; reduce the costs of record keeping by pooling indirect costs in a manner that enables allocations through the use of a common cost driver. *(p. 205)*

Appraisal costs Costs incurred to identify nonconforming products that were not avoided via the prevention cost expenditures. *(p. 214)*

Batch-level activities Activities (e.g., materials handling, production setups) related to the production of groups of products, the costs of which are fixed, regardless of the number of units produced; best allocated using cost drivers that measure activity consumption. *(p. 208)*

Companywide allocation rate The use of direct labour hours or some other measure of volume to allocate all overhead cost to the company's products or other cost objects. *(p. 202)*

Downstream costs The cost of activities (e.g., sales commissions and advertising) that occur after goods are manufactured but are still relevant for pricing the product. *(p. 213)*

External failure costs Costs incurred when defective goods are delivered to customers. *(p. 214)*

Facility-level activities Activities (e.g., insurance on the facility, plant maintenance, and taxes) performed for the benefit of the production process as a whole and whose allocation is arbitrary. *(p. 210)*

Failure costs Costs incurred from the actual occurrence of nonconforming events. *(p. 214)*

Internal failure costs Costs incurred when defects are corrected before the goods reach the customer. *(p. 214)*

Prevention costs Cost incurred to avoid nonconforming products. *(p. 214)*

Product-level activities Activities (e.g., inventory holding cost, engineering developmental) that support a specific product or product line and whose allocation is based on the extent to which the activities are used in sustaining the product or product line. *(p. 209)*

Quality The degree to which actual products or services conform to their design specifications. *(p. 214)*

Quality cost report An accountant's report that typically lists the company's quality costs and provides a horizontal analysis showing each item as a percentage of total cost. *(p. 215)*

Start-up (setup) costs The costs associated with the activities of changing machinery, the production configuration, inspection, and so on, to prepare for making a new product or a batch of a product. *(p. 203)*

Total quality management (TQM) Management of quality costs in a manner that leads to the highest level of customer satisfaction. *(p. 215)*

Target pricing A pricing plan by which management determines the price that customers are willing to pay for a product so that costs can be controlled to produce the product at a cost that will enable it to sell at a price in line with customer demand. *(p. 212)*

Unit-level activities Activities that occur each time a unit of product is made; the costs associated with these activities exhibit a variable cost behaviour pattern. *(p. 207)*

Upstream costs The cost of activities (e.g., research and development) that occur before goods are manufactured and whose cost should be considered in a cost-plus-pricing decision. *(p. 213)*

Volume-based cost drivers Measures of volume such as labour hours, machine hours, or amounts of materials that have a strong correlation with unit-level overhead cost and that make appropriate allocation bases for the allocation of unit-level overhead costs. *(p. 203)*

Voluntary costs Prevention and appraisal costs that are a function of managerial discretion. *(p. 214)*

QUESTIONS

1. Why did the traditional cost system base allocations on a single companywide cost driver?
2. Why are labour hours ineffective as a companywide allocation base in many industries today?
3. What is the difference between volume-based cost drivers and activity-based cost drivers?
4. Why do activity-based cost drivers provide more accurate allocations of overhead in an automated manufacturing environment?
5. When would it be appropriate to use volume-based cost drivers in an activity-based cost system?
6. Martinez Manufacturing makes two products, one of which is produced at a significantly higher volume than the other. The low-volume product consumes more of the company's engineering resources because it is technologically complex. Even so, the company's cost accountant chose to allocate engineering departmental costs on the basis of the number of units produced. How could the selection of this allocation base affect a decision regarding the outsourcing of engineering services for the low-volume product?
7. What is the allocation process under activity-based costing? Briefly describe it.
8. Tom Rehr made the following comment: "Facility-level costs should not be allocated to products because they are irrelevant for decision-making purposes." Do you agree or disagree with this statement? Justify your response with appropriate commentary.
9. To facilitate cost tracing, a company's activities can be subdivided into four hierarchical categories. What are these four categories? Describe them and give at least two examples of each category.
10. If each patient in a hospital is considered a cost object, what are examples of unit-, batch-, product-, and facility-level costs that would be allocated to this object under an activity-based cost system?
11. Milken Manufacturing has three product lines. The company's new accountant, Marvin LaSance, has the responsibility of allocating facility-level costs to these product lines. Mr. LaSance is finding the allocation assignment a daunting task. He knows there have been disagreements among the product managers over the allocation of facility costs, and he fears being asked to defend his method of allocation. Why would you expect the allocation of facility-level costs to be subject to disagreements?
12. Why would machine hours be an inappropriate allocation base for batch-level costs?
13. Alisa Kamuf's company has shown a loss on income from operations for several years. Industry standards indicate that prices are normally set at 30 percent above manufacturing cost, which Ms. Kamuf has done. Assuming that her other costs are in line with industry norms, how could she continue to lose money, while her competitors earn a profit?
14. Issacs Corporation produces two lines of pocket knives. The Arrowsmith product line involves very complex engineering designs; the Starscore product line involves relatively simple designs. Since its introduction, the low-volume Arrowsmith products have gained market share at the expense of the high-volume Starscore products. This pattern of sales has been accompanied by an overall decline in company profits. Why may the existing cost system be inadequate?
15. What is the relationship between activity-based management and just-in-time inventory?

EXERCISES

EXERCISE 6-1   *Classification of the Costs of Unit-, Batch-, Product-, or Facility-Level Activities*   **L.O. 5**

Cahaba Valley Manufacturing is developing an activity-based costing system to improve overhead cost allocation. One of the first steps in developing the system is to classify the cost of performing operating activities into activity cost pools.

Required
Using your knowledge of the four categories of operating activities, classify the cost of each activity in the following list into unit-, batch-, product-, or facility-level cost pools.

Cost Activity	Cost Pool
a. Wages of workers moving units of work between workstations	
b. Factorywide electricity	
c. Salary of a manager in charge of a product line	
d. Sales commissions	
e. Engineering product design	
f. Supplies	
g. Wages of maintenance staff	
h. Labelling and packaging	
i. Plant security	
j. Ordering materials for a specific type of product	

L.O. 5 EXERCISE 6-2   *Identification of Appropriate Cost Drivers*

Required

Give at least one example of an appropriate cost driver (i.e., allocation base) for each of the following activities:
a. Production equipment is set up for new production runs.
b. Engineering drawings are produced for design changes.
c. Purchase orders are issued.
d. Products are labelled, packaged, and shipped.
e. Machinists are trained on new computer-controlled machinery.
f. Lighting is used for production facilities.
g. Materials are unloaded and stored for production.
h. Maintenance is performed on manufacturing equipment.
i. Sales commissions are paid.
j. Direct labour is used to change machine configurations.

L.O. 4, 5 EXERCISE 6-3   *Classification of Costs and Identification of the Appropriate Cost Driver*

Vassolo Manufacturing incurred the following costs during 2005 in the production of its high-quality precision instruments. The company uses an activity-based costing system and identified the following activities:
1. Setup for each batch produced.
2. Insurance on production facilities.
3. Amortization on manufacturing equipment.
4. Materials handling.
5. Inventory storage.
6. Inspection of each batch produced.
7. Salaries of receiving clerks.

Required

a. Classify each activity as a unit-level, batch-level, product-level, or facility-level activity.
b. Identify an appropriate cost driver (i.e., allocation base) for each activity.

L.O. 5 EXERCISE 6-4   *Context-Sensitive Nature of Activity Classification*

Required

Describe a set of circumstances under which the cost of painting could be classified as a unit-level, a batch-level, a product-level, and a facility-level cost.

L.O. 5 EXERCISE 6-5   *Context-Sensitive Nature of Activity Classification*

Rummler Company makes two types of circuit boards. One is a high-calibre board designed to accomplish the most demanding tasks; the other is a low-calibre board designed to provide limited service at an affordable price. During its most recent accounting period, Rummler incurred $40,000 of inspection cost. When Rummler recently established an activity-based costing system, its activities were classified into four categories. Each of the categories and appropriate cost drivers follow:

	Direct Labour Hours	Number of Batches	Number of Inspectors	Number of Square Metres
High calibre	4,000	25	3	40,000
Low calibre	16,000	15	2	60,000
Totals	20,000	40	5	100,000

Required

Allocate the inspection cost between the two products assuming that the cost is related to (a) unit-level activities, (b) batch-level activities, (c) product-level activities, and (d) facility-level activities.

EXERCISE 6-6   *Computing Overhead Rates on the Basis of Different Cost Drivers*   **L.O. 4**

Jacob Industries produces two electronic decoders: A and B. Decoder A is more sophisticated and requires more programming and testing than does Decoder B. Because of these product differences, the company wants to use activity-based costing to allocate overhead costs. It has identified four activity centres and their related information as follows:

Activity Centres	Cost Pool Total	Cost Driver
Repair and maintenance on assembly machine	$90,000	Number of units produced
Programming cost	199,500	Number of programming hours
Software inspections	15,000	Number of inspections
Product testing	20,000	Number of tests
Total overhead cost	$324,500	

Expected activity for each product follows:

	Number of Units	Number of Programming Hours	Number of Inspections	Number of Tests
Decoder A	20,000	2,000	190	1,400
Decoder B	30,000	1,500	60	1,100
Totals	50,000	3,500	250	2,500

Required
a. Compute the overhead rate for each activity centre.
b. Determine the overhead cost that would be allocated to each product.

EXERCISE 6-7   *Comparison of an ABC System and a Traditional Costing System*   **L.O. 1, 3**

Use the information in Exercise 6-6 to complete the following requirements. Assume that before shifting to activity-based costing, Jacob Industries allocated all overhead costs on the basis of direct labour hours. Direct labour data regarding the two decoders follow:

	Direct Labour Hours
Decoder A	10,000
Decoder B	15,000
Total	25,000

Required
a. Compute the amount of overhead cost that is allocated to each decoder when direct labour hours is used as the allocation base.
b. Determine the cost per-unit for overhead when direct labour is used as the allocation base and when ABC is used.
c. Explain why the overhead cost expressed on a per-unit basis is lower for the high-volume product under ABC.

EXERCISE 6-8   *Allocation of Costs with Different Cost Drivers*   **L.O. 1, 3**

Outdoor Living Company produces gardening equipment for commercial use. Being highly automated, the company allocates its overhead cost to product lines under an activity-based costing system. The cost and cost drivers associated with the four overhead activity cost pools follow:

	Activities			
	Unit Level	Batch Level	Product Level	Facility Level
Cost	$25,000	$10,000	$5,000	$60,000
Cost driver	2,000 labour hrs.	40 setups	Percentage of use	12,000 units

Production of 800 units of cutting shears, one of the company's 20 products, took 200 labour hours and six setups and consumed 15 percent of the product sustaining activities.

Required

a. Had the company used labour hours as a companywide allocation base, how much overhead would have been allocated to the cutting shears?

b. How much overhead should be allocated to the cutting shears if the company uses activity-based costing?

c. Compute the cost per unit for cutting shears under activity-based costing and under direct labour hours if 800 units are produced. If direct product cost is $25 and the product is priced at 30 percent above cost (rounded to the nearest whole dollar), for what price would the product sell under each allocation system?

d. Assuming that activity-based costing provides a more accurate estimate of cost, indicate whether the cutting shears would be over- or underpriced if direct labour hours are used as an allocation base. Explain how over- or undercosting can affect Outdoor's profitability.

e. Comment on the validity of using the allocated facility-level cost in the pricing decision. Should other costs be considered in a cost-plus-pricing decision? If so, name them. What costs would you include if you were trying to decide whether to accept a special offer?

L.O. 1, 3 EXERCISE 6-9   *Allocation of Costs with Different Cost Drivers*

Sharp Publishing identified the following activities as well as their respective costs and cost drivers for the production of the three types of textbooks the company publishes:

		Type of Textbook		
Activity (Cost)	Cost Driver	Deluxe	Moderate	Economy
Machine maintenance ($200,000)	Number of machine hours	250	750	1,000
Setups ($350,000)	Number of setups	30	15	5
Packing ($90,000)	Number of cartons	10	30	50
Photo development ($280,000)	Number of pictures	4,000	2,000	1,000

Deluxe textbooks are made with the finest-quality paper, six-colour printing, and many photographs. Moderate texts are made with three colours and a few photographs spread throughout each chapter. Economy books are printed in black and white and include pictures only in chapter openings.

Required

a. Sharp currently allocates all overhead costs on the basis of machine hours. The company produced the following number of books during the accounting period:

Deluxe	Moderate	Economy
50,000	150,000	200,000

Determine the cost per book for each book type.

b. Determine the cost per book, assuming that the volume-based allocation system described in Requirement *a* is replaced with an activity-based costing system.

c. Explain why the per-unit costs determined in Requirements *a* and *b* differ.

L.O. 4 EXERCISE 6-10   *Computation of Product Cost with Given Activity Allocation Rates*

Messina Manufacturing produces two modems, one that is used in laptop computers and the other that is used in desktop computers. The production process is automated, and the company has found it useful to use activity-based costing in assigning overhead costs to its products. The company has identified five major activities needed for the production of the modems.

Activity	Allocation Base	Allocation Rate
Materials receiving & handling	Cost of material	2% of material cost
Production setup	Number of setups	$150 per setup
Assembly	Number of parts	$6 per part
Quality inspection	Inspection time	$1.50 per minute
Packing and shipping	Number of orders	$10 per order

Activity measures for the two kinds of modems follow:

	Labour Cost	Material Cost	Number of Setups	Number of Parts	Inspection Time	Number of Orders
Laptops	$2,398	$10,000	30	42	7,200 min.	65
Desktops	$2,206	$15,000	12	24	5,100 min.	20

Required

a. Compute the cost per unit of laptop and desktop modems, assuming that 300 units of each type of modem were made.
b. Explain why laptop modems are more costly to make even though they have less material cost and are smaller in size than desktop modems.

EXERCISE 6-11   *Allocation of Facility-Level Cost and a Product Elimination Decision*   **L.O. 4**

Kitz Boards produces two kinds of skate boards. Selected unit data for the two boards for the last quarter follow:

	Basco Boards	Shimano Boards
Production Costs		
Direct material	$45	$60
Direct labour	$65	$85
Allocated overhead	$25	$30
Total units produced and sold	4,000	8,000
Total sales revenue	$560,000	$1,480,000

Kitz allocates production overhead using activity-based costing. However, the quarterly delivery expense and sales commissions, which amount to $90,000, are allocated to the two products equally.

Required

a. Compute the net profit for each product.
b. Assuming that the overhead allocation for Basco boards includes $20,000 of facility-level cost, would you advise Kitz to eliminate these boards? (*Hint*: Give reasonable consideration to the method used to allocate the delivery and selling expense.)

EXERCISE 6-12   *Recognition of the Components of Quality Cost and Their Relationship*   **L.O. 10**

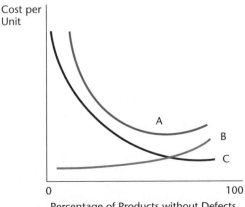

Percentage of Products without Defects

Required

The preceding graph depicts the relationships among the components of total quality cost.

a. Name the lines labelled A, B, and C.

b. Explain the relationships depicted in the graph.

PROBLEMS—SERIES A

L.O. 1, 3   PROBLEM 6-1A   *Comparison of an ABC System and a Traditional Costing Systeme*

Hot Express produces video games in three market categories: commercial, home, and miniature. Hot Express has traditionally allocated overhead costs to the three product categories using direct labour hours as a companywide allocation base. The company recently implemented an ABC system when it installed computer-controlled assembly stations that rendered the traditional costing system ineffective. In the implementation of the ABC system, the company identified the following activity cost pools and drivers:

Category	Total Pooled Cost	Types of Cost	Cost Driver
Unit	$600,000	Indirect labour wages, supplies, amortization, machine maintenance	Machine hours
Batch	$324,000	Materials handling, inventory storage, labour for setups, packaging, labelling and shipping, scheduling	Number of production orders
Product	$176,000	Research and development	Time spent by research department
Facility	$500,000	Rent, utilities, maintenance, admin. salaries, security	Square footage

Additional data for each of the product lines follow:

	Commercial	Home	Miniature	Total
Direct materials cost	$30/unit	$20/unit	$25/unit	—
Direct labour cost	$12/hour	$12/hour	$15/hour	—
Number of labour hours	6,000	12,000	2,000	20,000
Number of machine hours	10,000	45,000	25,000	80,000
Number of production orders	200	2,000	800	3,000
Research and development time	10%	20%	70%	100%
Number of units	15,000	45,000	14,000	74,000
Square footage	20,000	50,000	30,000	100,000

Required

a. Determine the total cost and cost per unit for each product line assuming that overhead costs are allocated to each product line using direct labour hours as a companywide allocation base. Also determine the combined cost of all three product lines.

b. Determine the total cost and cost per unit for each product line, assuming that an ABC system is used to allocate overhead costs. Determine the combined cost of all three product lines.

c. Explain why the combined total cost computed in Requirements *a* and *b* is the same amount. Given that the combined cost is the same under both, why is using an ABC system with many different allocation rates better than using a traditional system with a single companywide overhead rate?

L.O. 2   PROBLEM 6-2A   *Effect of Automation on Overhead Allocation*

Randon Rug Company makes two types of rugs, seasonal and all purpose. Both types of rugs are handmade, but the seasonal rugs require significantly more labour because of their decorative designs. The annual number of rugs made and the labour hours required to make each type of rug follow:

	Seasonal	All Purpose	Totals
Number of rugs	600	1,400	2,000
Number of direct labour hours	60,000	84,000	144,000

Required

a. Assume that annual overhead costs total $72,000. Select the appropriate cost driver and determine the amount of overhead to allocate to each type of rug.

b. Randon automates the seasonal rug line causing a dramatic decline in labour usage, making the 600 rugs in only 6,000 hours. The all purpose rugs continue to be made in the same manner that they had been made. The number of rugs made and the labour hours required to make them after automation follow:

	Seasonal	All Purpose	Totals
Number of rugs	600	1,400	2,000
Number of direct labour hours	60,000	84,000	90,000

Overhead costs are expected to increase to $90,000 as a result of the automation. Allocate the new overhead cost to the two types of rugs using direct labour hours as the allocation base and comment on the appropriateness of the allocation.

PROBLEM 6-3A   *Use of Activity-Based Costing to Improve Allocation Accuracy*   **L.O. 3, 4**

This problem is an extension of Problem 6-2A and should not be attempted until that problem has been completed. Randon's accounting staff has disaggregated the $90,000 of overhead into the following items:

(1)	Inspection costs	$8,000
(2)	Setup cost	5,400
(3)	Engineering cost	8,000
(4)	Legal cost related to products	3,000
(5)	Materials movement cost per batch	1,200
(6)	Salaries of production supervisors	20,000
(7)	Fringe benefit costs	4,000
(8)	Utilities costs	2,000
(9)	Plant manager's salary	12,000
(10)	Amortization on production equipment	18,000
(11)	Amortization on building	4,000
(12)	Miscellaneous costs	2,500
(13)	Indirect material cost	1,400
(14)	Production employee incentive cost	500
	Total	$90,000

Required

a. Each of Randon's rug lines operates as a department. The all-purpose department occupies 3,000 square feet of floor space, and the seasonal department occupies 6,000 square feet of space. Comment on the validity of allocating the overhead costs by square footage.

b. Assume that the following additional information is available:

(1) Rugs are inspected on an individual basis.

(2) Randon incurs setup cost each time a new style of seasonal rug is established. The seasonal rugs were altered nine times during the accounting period. The manual equipment for all-purpose rugs is reset twice per year to ensure accuracy in the weaving process. The setup for the technical equipment used on the seasonal rugs requires more highly skilled workers, but the all-purpose rugs require more manual equipment items, thereby resulting in a *per-setup* charge that is roughly equal for both types of setup. In summary, 11 setups were conducted during the year, nine of which applied to seasonal rugs and two that applied to all-purpose rugs.

(3) Ninety percent of the product-level cost can be traced to the production of seasonal rugs.

(4) Three supervisors oversee the production of all-purpose rugs. Because seasonal rugs are made in an automated department, only one production supervisor is needed.

(5) Each rug requires an equal amount of indirect materials.

(6) Costs associated with production activities are pooled into six activity cost centres: (1) labour-related activities, (2) unit-level activities, (3) batch-level activities, (4) product-level supervisory activities, (5) product-level other activities, and (6) facility-level activities.

Organize the $90,000 of overhead into activity centre cost pools and allocate the cost to the two types of rugs.

c. Assuming that 45 seasonal and 120 all-purpose rugs were made in January, determine the overhead costs that would be assigned to each of the two rug types for the month of January.

L.O. 4 PROBLEM 6-4A   *Use of Activity-Based Costing to Improve Allocation Accuracy*

The Learning Place, Inc. (LPI) is a profit-oriented education business. LPI provides remedial training for high school students who have fallen behind in their classroom studies. It charges its students $300 per course. During the previous year, LPI provided instruction for 1,000 students. The income statement for the company follows:

Revenue	$300,000
Cost of Instructors	(119,000)
Overhead Costs	(85,000)
Net Income	$ 96,000

The company president, Beth Sanderson, indicated in a discussion with the accountant, John Ganzi, that she was extremely pleased with the growth in the area of computer-assisted instruction. She said that this department served 200 students and required only one part-time instructor. In contrast, the classroom-based instructional department required 16 instructors to teach 800 students. Ms. Sanderson noted that the cost of instruction per student was dramatically lower for the computer-assisted department. She offered the following information to support her conclusion.

LPI pays its part-time instructors $7,000 per year on average. Accordingly, the total cost of instruction and the cost per student are computed as follows:

Type of Instruction	Computer-Assisted	Classroom
Number of instructors (a)	1	16
Number of students (b)	200	800
Total cost (c = a × $7,000)	$7,000	$112,000
Cost per student (c ÷ b)	$35	$140

Assuming that overhead cost was distributed equally across the student population, Ms. Sanderson concluded that the cost of instructors was the critical variable in the company's capacity to generate profits. On the basis of her analysis, her strategic plan called for a heavy emphasis on increased use of computer-assisted instruction.

Mr. Ganzi responded that he was not so sure that computer-assisted instruction should be stressed. After attending a seminar on activity-based costing (ABC), he believed that the allocation of overhead cost could be more closely traced to the different types of learning activities. To facilitate the activity-based analysis, he developed the following information about the costs associated with computer-assisted versus classroom instructional activities. He identified $48,000 of overhead costs that were directly traceable to computer-assisted activities, including the costs of computer hardware, software, and technical assistance. He believed the remaining $37,000 of overhead costs should be allocated to the two instructional activities on the basis of the number of students enrolled in each program.

Required

a. On the basis of the preceding information, determine the total cost and the cost per unit to provide courses through computer-assisted activities versus classroom activities.
b. Comment on the validity of stressing growth in the area of computer-assisted instruction.

L.O. 6 PROBLEM 6-5A   *Key Concepts of Activity-Based Costing*

Colourbrite Paint Company makes paint in many different colours; it charges the same price for all of its paint, regardless of the colour. Recently, Colourbrite's chief competitor cut the price of its white paint, which normally outsells any other color by a margin of 4 to 1. Colourbrite's marketing manager requested permission to match the competitor's price. When Horace Jacobs, Colourbrite's president, discussed the matter with Charlene Thompson, the chief accountant, he was told that the competitor's price was below Colourbrite's cost. Mr. Jacobs responded, "If that's the case, then there is something wrong with our accounting system. I know the competition wouldn't sell below cost. Prepare a report showing me how you determine our cost of paint and get back to me as soon as possible."

The next day, Ms. Thompson returned to Mr. Jacobs' office and began by saying, "Determining the cost per litre is a pretty simple computation. It includes $0.80 of labour, $3.20 of materials, and $4.10 of overhead cost. Accordingly, our total cost is $8.10 per 4-litre tin. The problem is that the competition is selling the stuff for $7.99 per 4-litre tin. They've got to be losing money."

Mr. Jacobs then asked Ms. Thompson how she determined the cost of the overhead. She replied, "We take the total overhead cost and divide it by the total labour hours and then assign it to the products on the basis of the direct labour hours required to make the paint." Mr. Jacobs then asked what kinds of costs are included in the total overhead cost. Ms. Thompson said, "It includes the depreciation on the building and equipment, the cost of utilities, supervisory salaries, interest. Just how detailed do you want me to go with this list?"

Mr. Jacobs responded, "Keep going, I'll tell you when I've heard enough."

Ms. Thompson continued, "There is the cost of setups. Every time a colour is changed, the machines have to be cleaned, the colour release valves reset, a trial batch prepared, and colour quality tested. Sometimes mistakes occur and the machines must be reset. In addition, purchasing and handling the colour ingredients must be accounted for as well as adjustments in the packaging department to change the paint cans and to mark the boxes to show the colour change. Then. . . . "

Mr. Jacobs interrupted, "I think I've heard enough. We sell so much white paint that it is run through a separate production process. White paint is produced continuously. There are no shutdowns and setups. White uses no colour ingredients. So, why are these costs being assigned to our white paint production?"

Ms. Thompson replied, "Well, sir, these costs are just a part of the big total that is allocated to all of the paint, no matter what colour it happens to be."

Mr. Jacobs looked disgusted and said, "As I told you yesterday, Ms. Thompson, something is wrong with our accounting system!"

Required

a. Explain what the terms *overcost* and *undercost* mean. Is Colourbrite's white paint over- or undercost?
b. Explain what the term *companywide overhead rate* means. Is Colourbrite using a companywide overhead rate?
c. Explain how Colourbrite could improve the accuracy of its cost-allocating process.

PROBLEM 6-6A   *Pricing Decisions Made with ABC System Cost Data*   L.O. 4, 7

Nestor Sporting Goods Corporation makes two types of racquets: tennis and badminton. The company uses the same facility to make both products, even though the processes are quite different. The company has recently converted its cost accounting system to activity-based costing. The following are the cost data that Jay Scanon, the cost accountant, prepared for the third quarter of 2002 (during which Nestor made 70,000 tennis racquets and 30,000 badminton racquets):

Direct Cost/Unit	Tennis Racquet (TR)	Badminton Racquet (BR)
Direct materials	$12	$ 8
Direct labour	40	30

Category	Estimated Cost	Cost Driver	Use of Cost Driver
Unit level	$ 750,000	Number of inspection hours	TR: 1,500 hours; BR: 10,000 hours
Batch level	250,000	Number of setups	TR: 80 setups; BR: 45 setups
Product level	150,000	Number of TV commercials	TR: 4; BR: 1
Facility level	650,000	Number of machine hours	TR: 30,000 hours; BR: 35,000 hours
Total	$1,800,000		

Inspectors are paid according to number of actual hours they work, which is determined by the number of racquets inspected. Engineers who set up equipment for both productions are paid monthly salaries. TV commercials are paid at the beginning of the quarter. Facility-level cost includes amortization of all production equipment.

Required

a. Compute the cost per unit for each product.
b. If management wants to price badminton racquets 30 percent above its cost, what price should the company set?
c. The market price of tennis racquets has declined substantially because of new competitors entering the market. Management asks you to determine the minimum price for which the company can continue producing tennis racquets in the short term. Provide that information.

L.O. 4, 7 PROBLEM 6-7A   *Target Pricing and Target Costing with ABC*

Laurel Cameras, manufactures two models of cameras. Model ZM has a zoom lens; Model DS has a fixed lens. Laurel uses an activity-based costing system. The following are the related cost data for the previous month:

Direct Cost/Unit	Model ZM	Model DS
Direct materials	$20	$10
Direct labour	22	8

Category	Estimated Cost	Cost Driver	Use of Cost Driver
Unit level	$ 27,000	Number of units	ZM: 2,400 units; DS: 9,600 units
Batch level	50,000	Number of setups	ZM: 25 setups; DS: 25 setups
Product level	90,000	Number of TV commercials	ZM: 15; DS: 10
Facility level	300,000	Number of machine hours	ZM: 500 hours; DS: 1,000 hours
Total	$467,000		

Laurel's facility has the capacity to operate 4,500 machine hours per month.

Required

a. Compute the cost per unit for each product.
b. The current market price for products comparable with Model ZM is $125 and for DS is $45. If Laurel had sold all its products at the market prices, what was its profit or loss for the previous month?
c. A market expert believes that Laurel can sell as many cameras as it can produce by pricing Model ZM at $120 and Model DS at $42. Laurel would like to use those estimates as its target prices and have a profit margin of 20 percent. What is the target cost for each product?
d. Is there any way for the company to reach its target costs?

L.O. 4 PROBLEM 6-8A   *Cost Management with an ABC System*

Judith Chairs, makes two types of chairs. Model Diamond is a high-end product designed for professional offices. Model Gold is an economical product designed for family use. Judith Lundquist, the president, has been very worried about cut-throat price competition in the market. In fact, the company suffered a loss in the last quarter, an unprecedented event in the company's history. The company's accountant prepared the following cost data for Ms. Lundquist:

Direct Cost/Unit	Model Diamond (D)	Model Gold (G)
Direct material	$18/unit	$9/unit
Direct labour	$24/hour × 2 hours production time	$24/hour × 1 hour production time

Category	Estimated Cost	Cost Driver	Use of Cost Driver
Unit level	$ 300,000	Number of units	D: 15,000 units; G: 35,000 units
Batch level	750,000	Number of setups	D: 104 setups; G: 146 setups
Product level	450,000	Number of TV commercials	D: 5; G: 10
Facility level	500,000	Number of machine hours	D: 1,500 hours; G: 3,500 hours
Total	$2,000,000		

The market price for office chairs comparable with Model Diamond is $110 and to Model Gold is $67.

Required

a. Compute the cost per unit for both products.
b. Ron Dorman, the chief engineer, told Ms. Lundquist that the company is currently making about 150 units of Model Diamond per batch and about 245 units of Model Gold per batch. He suggests that the factory double the batch sizes to cut number of setups in half. Mr. Dorman argues that he can reduce the setup cost by 50 percent. What will the cost per unit for each product be if Ms. Lundquist adopts his suggestion?
c. Is there any side effect if Ms. Lundquist increases the production batch size by 100 percent?

PROBLEM 6-9A   *Assessment of a Quality Control Strategy*   **L.O. 10, 11**

The following quality cost report came from the records of KoMo Company:

	2006		2005	
	Amount	Percentage	Amount	Percentage
Prevention costs				
Engineering and design	$ 68,000	13.74%	$ 29,000	3.86%
Training and education	17,000	3.43	6,000	0.80
Amortization on prevention equipment	29,000	5.86	15,000	1.99
Incentives and awards	44,000	8.89	20,000	2.66
Total prevention	$158,000	31.92%	$ 70,000	9.31%
Appraisal costs				
Inventory inspection	25,000	5.05	25,000	3.32
Reliability testing	16,000	3.23	15,000	1.99
Testing equipment (amortization)	11,000	2.22	12,000	1.60
Supplies	7,000	1.41	8,000	1.06
Total appraisal	$ 59,000	11.92%	$ 60,000	7.98%
Internal failure costs				
Scrap	24,000	4.85	40,000	5.32
Repair and rework	49,000	9.90	110,000	14.63
Downtime	12,000	2.42	20,000	2.66
Reinspection	4,000	0.81	12,000	1.60
Total internal failure	$ 89,000	17.98%	$182,000	24.20%
External failure cost				
Warranty repairs and replacement	110,000	22.22	260,000	34.57
Freight	24,000	4.85	50,000	6.65
Customer relations	28,000	5.66	60,000	7.98
Restocking and packaging	27,000	5.45	70,000	9.31
Total external failure	$189,000	38.18%	$440,000	58.51%
Grand total	$495,000	100.00%	$752,000	100.00%

Required

a. Provide a logical explanation concerning the strategy that KoMo Company initiated to control its quality costs.
b. Indicate whether the strategy was successful or unsuccessful in reducing quality costs.
c. Provide a logical explanation as to how the strategy affected customer satisfaction.

PROBLEMS—SERIES B

PROBLEM 6-1B   *Comparison of an ABC System and a Traditional Costing System*   **L.O. 1, 3**

Since its inception, BioGraphics has produced a single product, Product X. With the advent of automation, the company had the technological capability to begin producing a second product, Product Z. Because of the success of the new product, manufacturing has been shifting toward its production. Sales of Product Z are now 50 percent of the total annual sales of 10,000 units, and the company is optimistic about the new product's future sales growth. One reason the company is so excited about the sales potential of its new product is that the new product's gross profit margin is higher than that of Product X. Management is thrilled with the new product's initial success, but management is concerned about the company's declining profits since the product's introduction. Suspecting a problem with the company's costing system, management hires you to investigate:

In reviewing the company's records, product specifications, and manufacturing processes, you discover the following information:

1. The company is in an extremely competitive industry in which markups are low and accurate estimates of cost are critical to success.
2. Product Z has more complex parts that require more labour, machine time, setups, and inspections.
3. Cost for direct material and labour as budgeted follow:

Direct Cost/Unit	Product X	Product Z
Direct material	$20	$20
Direct labour	$12/hour × 2 hours production time	$12/hour × 8 hours production time

4. The company presently allocates overhead cost to its products using direct labour hours. After carefully studying the company's overhead, you discover four different categories of overhead costs. Using your knowledge of this company and similar companies in the same industry, you estimate the total costs for each of these categories and identify the most appropriate cost driver for measuring the product's use of each cost category. Detailed information for each cost category follows:

Category	Estimated Cost	Cost Driver	Use of Cost Driver
Unit level	$450,000	Number of machine hours	X: 20,000 hours; Z: 60,000 hours
Batch level	190,000	Number of machine setups	X: 1,500; Z: 3,500
Product level	150,000	Number of inspections	X: 200; Z: 600
Facility level	50,000	Equal percentage for products	X: $25,000; Z: $25,000
Total	$840,000		

Required

a. Determine the predetermined overhead rate the company is using.
b. Compute the amount of overhead that would be assigned to each product using this rate.
c. Determine the cost per unit and total cost of each product when overhead is assigned using direct labour hours.
d. To remain competitive, the company prices its products at only 20 percent above cost. Compute the price for each product with this markup.
e. Compute the overhead rate for each category of activity.
f. Determine the amount of overhead cost, including the total cost and per-unit cost, that would be assigned to each product if you chose to use an activity-based cost system.
g. Assuming that prices are adjusted to reflect an activity-based cost system, determine the price for each product under such a cost system.
h. On the basis of your results in Requirements *f* and *g*, explain why Product Z is more costly to make and why sales prices need to be adjusted to reflect this reality.

L.O. 1, 3 PROBLEM 6-2B   *Use of Activity-Based Costing to Improve Allocation Accuracy*

Commemorative Collectibles makes and sells two types of decorative plates. One plate displays a hand-painted image of Princess Diana; the other plate displays a machine-pressed image of Marilyn Monroe. The Diana plates require 50,000 hours of direct labour to make; the Monroe plates require only 10,000 hours of direct labour. Overhead costs are composed of (1) $70,000 machine-related activity costs including, indirect labour, utilities, and amortization, and (2) $50,000 labour-related activity costs including overtime pay, fringe benefits, and payroll taxes.

Required

a. Assuming that direct labour hours are used as an allocation base, determine the amount of the total $120,000 overhead cost that should be allocated to the Diana plates and to the Monroe plates.
b. Provide a logical explanation as to why using direct labour hours may distort the allocation of overhead cost to the two products.
c. Explain how activity-based costing could be used to improve the accuracy of the allocation of overhead costs to the two products.

L.O. 4 PROBLEM 6-3B   *Use of Activity-Based Costing to Improve Allocation Accuracy*

This problem is an extension of Problem 6-2B and should not be attempted until that problem has been completed. Assume the same data as in Problem 6-2B with the following additional information. Processing the Diana plates requires 2,000 hours of machine time; processing the Monroe plates requires 5,000 hours of machine time.

Required

a. Establish two activity centres, one for machine-related activities and the second for labour-related activities. Assign the total overhead costs to the two activity centres.
b. Allocate the machine-related activity overhead costs to each product on the basis of machine hours.
c. Allocate the labour-related activity overhead costs to each product on the basis of direct labour hours.

d. Draw a diagram that compares the one-stage allocation method used in Problem 6-2B with the two-stage activity-based costing approach used in this problem.

PROBLEM 6-4B   *Key Concepts of Activity-Based Costing*

Alberta Boot and Shoe Company makes hand-sewn boots and shoes. Alberta uses a companywide overhead rate based on direct labour hours to allocate indirect manufacturing costs to its products. Making a pair of boots normally requires two hours of direct labour and making a pair of shoes requires 1.5 hours. The company's shoe division has been faced with increased competition from international companies that have access to cheap labour. Alberta has responded to the competition by automating its shoe production. The reengineering process was expensive, requiring the purchase of manufacturing equipment and the restructuring of the plant layout. In addition, utility costs and maintenance costs associated with the operation of the new equipment increased significantly. Even so, labour costs decreased significantly. Now making a pair of shoes requires only 15 minutes of direct labour. As predicted, the labour savings more than offset the increase in overhead cost, thereby reducing the total cost to make a pair of shoes. The company experienced an unexpected side effect, however; according to the company's accounting records, the cost to make a pair of boots increased even though the manufacturing process in the boot division was not affected by the reengineering of the shoe division. In other words, the cost of boots increased even though Alberta did not change anything about the way it makes them.

Required

a. Explain why the accounting records reflected an increase in the cost to make a pair of boots.
b. Explain how the companywide overhead rate could result in the underpricing of shoes.
c. Explain how activity-based costing could be used to improve the accuracy of overhead cost allocations.

PROBLEM 6-5B   *Decisions Made with ABC System Cost Data*   **L.O. 4**

Burleson Furniture Corporation makes two types of dining tables—Elegance for formal dining and Comfort for casual dining—at its single factory. With the economy beginning to experience a recession, Jimmy Burleson, the president, is concerned about whether the company can stay in business while the market price keeps falling. Following Mr. Burleson's request, Jenny Wu, the controller, prepared cost data for further analysis.

Inspectors are paid according to the number of actual hours they worked, which is determined by the number of tables inspected. Engineers who set up equipment for both productions are paid monthly salaries. TV commercials are paid at the beginning of the quarter.

Direct Cost	Elegance (E)	Comfort (C)
Direct material	$40/unit	$22/unit
Direct labour	$24/hour × 1.5 hours production time	$24/hour × 1 hour production time

Category	Estimated Cost	Cost Driver	Use of Cost Driver
Product inspection	$ 80,000	Number of units	E: 2,500 units; C: 7,500 units
Machine setups	50,000	Number of setups	E: 23 setups; C: 27 setups
Product advertisement	140,000	Number of TV commercials	E: 5; C: 9
Facility amortization	270,000	Number of machine hours	E: 5,000 hours; C: 5,000 hours
Total	$540,000		

Required

a. Compute the cost per unit for each product.
b. If management wants to make a 30 percent profit margin for Elegance, what price should the company set?
c. The market price of tables in the Comfort class has declined because of the recession. Management asks you to determine the minimum price for which the company can continue producing Comfort tables in the short term. Provide that information.

PROBLEM 6-6B   *Target Pricing and Target Costing with ABC*   **L.O. 4, 7**

Alvarez Corporation manufactures two models of watches. Model Wonder has cartoon characters with simple features designed for kids. Model Marvel has sophisticated features, such as dual time zones and an attached calculator. Alvarez's product design team has worked with a cost accountant to prepare a budget for the two products for the next fiscal year as follows:

Direct Cost	Wonder (W)	Marvel (M)
Direct material	$4/unit	$10/unit
Direct labour	$20/hour × 0.2 hour production time	$20/hour × 0.6 hour production time

Category	Estimated Cost	Cost Driver	Use of Cost Driver
Materials handling	$183,000	Number of parts	W: 700,000; M: 520,000
Machine setups	90,000	Number of setups	W: 50; M: 40
Product testing	14,000	Number of units tested	W: 1,000; M: 400
Facility amortization	180,000	Number of machine hours	W: 3,200; M: 4,000
Total	$467,000		

Wonder watches contain 35 parts, and Marvel watches contain 65 parts. The budget plans for the production of 20,000 units of Wonder and 8,000 units of Marvel. Alvarez tests 5 percent of its product for quality assurance. It sells all its products at market prices.

Required

a. Compute the cost per unit for each product.
b. The current market price for products comparable with Wonder is $18 and for products comparable with Marvel is $55. What will Alvarez's profit or loss for the next year be?
c. Alvarez likes to have a 25 percent profit margin based on the current market price for each product. What is the target cost for each product? What is the total target profit?
d. The president of Alvarez has asked the design team to refine the production design to bring down the product cost. After a series of redesigns, the team recommends a new process that requires the purchase of a new machine for $200,000 with five years of useful life and no salvage value. With the new process and the new machine, Alvarez can decrease the number of machine setups to four for each product and cut the cost of materials handling in half. The machine hours used will be 4,500 for Wonder and 6,500 for Marvel. Does this new process enable Alvarez to achieve its target costs?

L.O. 4, 7 PROBLEM 6-7B   *Cost Management with an ABC System*

Shelby Corporation manufactures two different coffee makers: Professional for commercial use and Home for family use. Michael Danon, the president, recently received complaints from some members of the board of directors about the company's failure to reach the expected profit of $200,000 per month. Mr. Danon is, therefore, under great pressure to improve the company's bottom line. Under his direction, Amy Magid, the controller, prepared the following monthly cost data for Mr. Danon:

Direct Cost	Professional (P)	Home (H)
Direct material	$21/unit	$7/unit
Direct labour	$18/hour × 0.8 hours production time	$18/hour × 0.3 hour production time

Category	Estimated Cost	Cost Driver	Use of Cost Driver
Product inspection	$ 60,000	Number of units	P: 15,000 units; H: 45,000 units
Machine setups	15,000	Number of setups	P: 30 setups; H: 45 setups
Product promotion	200,000	Number of TV commercials	P: 10; H: 10
Facility amortization	295,000	Number of machine hours	P: 7,160 hours; H: 4,640 hours
Total	$570,000		

The market price for coffee makers comparable with Professional is $65 and with Home is $22. The company's administrative expenses amount to $195,000.

Required

a. Compute the cost per unit for both products.
b. Determine the company's profit or loss.
c. Rose Angelini, marketing manager, recommends that the company implement a focused marketing strategy. She argues that for the commercial market advertisements in trade journals are more effective than are TV commercials. Besides, the cost of journal advertisements is only $21,000. She also argues that sending discount coupons

to targeted households will reach a broad market base. The coupons program will cost $72,000. Compute the new cost of each product, assuming that Mr. Danon replaces the original product promotion with this proposal.

d. Determine the company's profit or loss following the information in Requirement *c*.

PROBLEM 6-8B   *Assessment of a Quality Control Strategy*   **L.O. 10, 11**

Kenaba Kolby, the president of Burton Plastic Company, is a famous cost cutter in the plastics industry. Two years ago, he accepted the offer from Burton's board of directors to help the company implement its mission to cut the company's costs quickly. In fact, his compensation package included a year-end bonus tied to the percentage of cost decrease over the preceding year. On February 12, 2004, Mr. Kolby received the comparative financial statements for the two preceding years. He was especially interested in the results of his cost-cutting measures on quality control. The quality report, shown below, was extracted from the company's financial statements.

Required

a. Provide a logical explanation concerning the strategy that Mr. Kolby initiated to control its Burton's costs.
b. Indicate whether the strategy was successful or unsuccessful in reducing quality costs.
c. Provide a logical explanation as to how the strategy affected the company's business in the long term.

	2003		2002	
	Amount	Percentage	Amount	Percentage
Prevention costs				
Engineering and design	$ 65,000	6.57%	$ 69,000	7.39%
Training and education	26,000	2.63	76,000	8.14
Amortization on prevention equipment	15,000	1.51	15,000	1.60
Incentives and awards	20,000	2.02	20,000	2.14
Total prevention	$126,000	12.73%	$180,000	19.27%
Appraisal costs				
Product & materials inspection	33,000	3.33	73,000	7.82
Reliability testing	27,000	2.73	67,000	7.17
Testing equipment (amortization)	38,000	3.83	38,000	4.07
Supplies	10,000	1.01	16,000	1.71
Total appraisal	$108,000	10.90%	$194,000	20.77%
Internal failure costs				
Scrap	52,000	5.25	120,000	12.85
Repair and rework	46,000	4.65	150,000	16.06
Downtime	64,000	6.46	40,000	4.28
Reinspection	8,000	0.81	24,000	2.57
Total internal failure	$170,000	17.17%	$334,000	35.76%
External failure cost				
Warranty repairs and replacement	347,000	35.05	125,000	13.38
Freight	75,000	7.58	31,000	3.32
Customer Relations	45,000	4.55	28,000	3.00
Restocking and packaging	119,000	12.02	42,000	4.50
Total external failure	$586,000	59.20%	$226,000	24.20%
Grand total	$990,000	100.00%	$934,000	100.00%

ANALYZE, THINK, COMMUNICATE

BUSINESS APPLICATION CASE   *Use of ABC to Improve Product Costing*   **ACT 6-1**

London Technologies produces component parts for vinyl window manufacturers. The component parts consist of strips of material priced and sold by square footage. The material comes in different grades and colours. London recently implemented an ABC system. In an effort to evaluate the effectiveness of the new system, London's managerial accountants prepared reports to permit comparisons between cost data based on ABC allocations and cost data based on traditional costing. The traditional costing approach uses a single driver (material dollars) as the basis for making allocations for product costing. The ABC system uses a variety of cost drivers related to the activities required to produce the vinyl materials. The following data regarding three specific products were included in the reports:

Product	Selling Price per Metre	Metres Produced	ABC Cost per Metre	Traditional Cost per Metre
X	$3.75	1,275,000	$3.30	$2.43
Y	2.85	1,200,000	2.61	2.01
Z	2.67	1,050,000	2.22	1.59

Required

a. Determine the ABC margin ([selling price − ABC cost] × metres produced) for each product.
b. Determine the traditional margin ([selling price − traditional cost] × metres produced) for each product.
c. Provide a logical explanation as to why the ABC margins are lower than the traditional margins.
d. On the basis of the information provided, has traditional costing resulted in over- or undercosting of products X, Y, and Z? Speculate as to how the over- or undercosting is affecting London's profitability.
e. Speculate as to what action should be taken with respect to the discoveries brought to light by the ABC cost analysis. Assume that London normally expects a product to produce a margin of at least 25 percent of the sales price.

ACT 6-2 GROUP ASSIGNMENT *Use of ABC in a Service Business*

A dialysis clinic provides two types of treatment for its patients. Hemodialysis (HD) is an in-house treatment that requires patients to visit the clinic three times each week for dialysis treatments. Peritoneal dialysis (PD) permits patients to self-administer their treatments at home on a daily basis. On average, the clinic serves 102 HD patients and 62 PD patients. A recent development caused clinic administrators to develop a keen interest in cost measurement for the two separate services. Provincial Insurance plans began to pay treatment providers a fixed payment per insured participant, regardless of the level of services provided by the clinic. With fixed fee revenues, the clinic was forced to control costs to ensure profitability. As a result, knowing the cost to provide HD versus PD services was critically important for the clinic. It needed accurate cost measurements to answer the following questions: Were both services profitable, or was one service carrying the burden of the other service? Should advertising be directed toward the acquisition of HD or PD patients?

Unfortunately, the existing cost allocation system was believed to be inaccurate in the measurement of the true cost to provide the respective services; it had been developed in response to provincial insurance reporting requirements. It allocated costs between HD and PD on the basis of the ratio of cost to charges (RCC). In other words, RRC allocates indirect costs in proportion to revenues. To illustrate, consider the allocation of $1,766,560 of indirect nursing service costs, which are allocated to the two treatment groups in relation to the revenue generated by each group. Given that the clinic generated total revenue of $6,013,550, an allocation rate of $0.2937633 per revenue dollar was established ($1,766,560 ÷ $6,013,550). This rate was multiplied by the proportionate share of the revenue generated by each service category to produce the following allocation:

Type of Service	Service Revenue	×	Allocation Rate	=	Allocated Cost
HD	$3,720,574	×	0.2937633	=	$1,092,968
PD	2,292,976	×	0.2937633	=	673,592
Total	6,013,550	×	0.2937633	=	$1,766,560

To better assess the cost to provide each type of service, the clinic initiated an activity-based costing (ABC) system. The ABC approach divided the nursing service cost into four separate cost pools. A separate cost driver (allocation base) was identified for each cost pool. The cost pools and their respective cost drivers follow:

	Total	HD	PD
Nursing services cost pool categories		?	?
RNs (Registered Nurses)	$ 478,240	?	?
LPNs (Licensed Practical Nurses)	808,128	?	?
Nursing administration and support staff	230,336	?	?
Dialysis machine operations (tech. salaries)	249,856	?	?
Total	$1,766,560	?	?

	Total	HD	PD
Activity cost drivers (corresponding to cost pools)			
Number of RNs (Registered Nurses)	14	10	4
Number of LPNs (Licensed Practical Nurses)	38	30	8
Number of treatments (nursing administration)	69,934	28,686	41,248
Number of dialyzer treatments (machine operations)	28,686	28,686	
Total	$1,766,560	?	?

Required

a. Organize the class into four sections and divide the sections into groups of four or five students each. Assign Task 1 to the first section of groups, Task 2 to the second section, Task 3 to the third section, and Task 4 to the fourth section.

Group Tasks

1. Allocate the RN cost pool between the HD and PD service centres.
2. Allocate the LPN cost pool between the HD and PD service centres.
3. Allocate the nursing administration and support staff cost pool between the HD and PD service centres.
4. Allocate the dialysis machine operations cost pool between the HD and PD service centres.

b. Have the class determine the total cost to allocate to the two service centres in the following manner. Select a spokesperson from each section and have the selected representatives go to the board. Each spokesperson should supply the allocated cost for the cost pool assigned by her respective section. The instructor should total the amounts and compare the ABC cost allocations with those developed through the traditional RCC system.

c. The instructor should lead the class in a discussion that addresses the following questions:

(1) Assuming that the ABC system provides a more accurate measure of cost, which service centre (HD or PD) is overcosted by the traditional allocation system and which is undercosted?

(2) What is the potential impact on pricing and profitability for both service centres?

(3) How could management respond to the conditions described in the problem?

WRITING ASSIGNMENT *Assessment of a Strategy to Control Quality Cost*   **ACT 6-3**

Ingrid Braxton, who owns and operates Braxton Toy Company, is a perfectionist. She believes literally in the "zero defects" approach to quality control. Her favourite saying is, "You can't spend too much on quality." Even so, in 2002, her company experienced an embarrassing breach of quality that required the national recall of a defective product. She vowed never to repeat the experience and instructed her staff to spend whatever it takes to ensure that products are delivered free of defects in 2003. She was somewhat disappointed with the 2003 year-end quality cost report shown here:

	2002	2003
Prevention costs	$120,000	$ 80,000
Appraisal costs	240,000	430,000
Internal failure costs	140,000	560,000
External failure cost	320,000	210,000
Grand Total	$820,000	$1,280,000

Although external failure costs had declined, they remained much higher than expected. The increased inspections had identified defects that were corrected, thereby avoiding another recall; however, the external failure costs were still too high. Ms. Braxton responded by saying, "We will have to double our efforts." She authorized the hiring of additional inspectors and instructed her production supervisors to become more vigilant in the identification and correction of errors.

Required

Assume that you are the chief financial officer (CFO) of Braxton Company. Ms. Braxton has asked you to review the company's approach to quality control. Prepare a memo to Ms. Braxton that evaluates the existing approach and recommend changes in expenditure patterns that can improve profitability as well as increase the effectiveness of the quality control system.

ACT 6-4 ETHICAL DILEMMA

Conflicts between Controlling Cost and Providing Social Responsibility to Patients

This case examines potential ethical issues related to the dialysis clinic used in ACT 6-2. It is, however, an independent case that can be studied in conjunction with or separately from ACT 6-2. The dialysis clinic provides two types of treatment to its patients. Hemodialysis (HD) is an in-house treatment that requires patients to visit the clinic three times each week. Alternatively, peritoneal dialysis (PD) permits patients to self-administer their treatments at home on a daily basis. The clinic serves a number of patients under a contract that limits collections from the Provincial insurer to a fixed amount per patient. As a result, the clinic's profitability is directly related to its ability to control cost. To illustrate, assume that the clinic is paid a fixed annual fee of $15,000 per contract patient served. Also assume that the current cost to provide health care averages $14,000 a year per patient, resulting in an average profitability of $1,000 per patient ($15,000 − $14,000). Because the revenue base is fixed, the only way the clinic can increase profitability is to lower its average cost of providing services. If the clinic fails to control costs and the average cost of patient care increases, profitability will decline. A recent ABC study suggests that the cost to provide HD service exceeds the amount of revenue generated from providing that service. The clinic remains profitable because PD services carry a disproportionate share of the cost burden.

Required

Respond to each potential scenario described here. Each scenario is independent of the others.

a. Suppose that as a result of the ABC analysis, the chief accountant who is a certified management accountant (CMA) recommends that the clinic discontinue service to HD patients. On the basis of this assumption, answer the following questions:

Assume that the clinic is located in a small town. If it discontinues service for the HD patients, they will be forced to drive 50 miles to the nearest alternative treatment centre. Does the clinic have a moral obligation to society to continue to provide HD service, even though it is not profitable to do so?

b. Assume that the clinic continues to provide service to HD patients. However, to compensate for the loss incurred on these patients, the clinic raises prices charged to noninsured patients (out of province). Is this fair?

c. Suppose that the clinic administrators respond to the ABC data by cutting costs. The clinic overbooks HMO patients to ensure that downtime is avoided when cancellations occur. It reduces the RN nursing staff and assigns some of the technical work to less qualified assistants. Ultimately, an overworked, underqualified nurse's assistant makes a mistake, and a patient dies. Who is at fault—the provincial insurance company, the accountant who conducted the ABC analysis, or the clinic administrators who responded to the ABC information?

ACT 6-5 SPREADSHEET ASSIGNMENT   *Using Excel*

Refer to Problem 6-1A. In the following year, the activity in each of the three lines is shown in Rows 3 to 9 of the following spreadsheet. The pooled costs are shown in Cells E11 to E15.

Required

Construct a spreadsheet like the following one to answer Requirement *b*. Cells K4 to K9, G12 to I15, E19 to E28, G19 to G28, I19 to I28, and K26 should all be formulas.

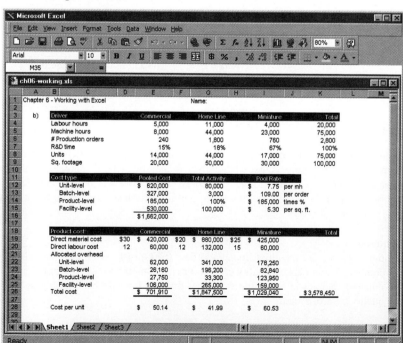

SPREADSHEET ASSIGNMENT   *Mastering Excel*   **ACT 6-6**

Beasley Company makes three types of exercise machines. Data have been accumulated for four possible drivers of overhead. Data for these four possible drivers are shown in Rows 3 to 7 of the following spreadsheet.

Required
Construct a spreadsheet that will allocate overhead and calculate unit cost for each of these alternative drivers. A screen capture of the spreadsheet and data follows:

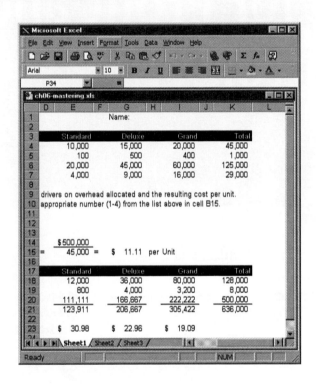

Spreadsheet Tips
1. This spreadsheet uses a function called *vertical lookup*. This function can pull the appropriate values from a table. The form of this function is =VLOOKUP (value, table, column#). In this example, the table is in Cells B4 to K7. Three examples of the use of VLOOKUP follow.
2. Cell C15 is =VLOOKUP (B15, B4:K7, 2). This function operates by using the one (1) in Cell B15 to look up a value in the table. Note that the table is defined as B4:K7 and that the function is looking up the value in the second column, which is Unit.
3. Cell E15 is =VLOOKUP (B15, B4:K7, 10). In this case, the function is looking up the value in the tenth column, which is 45,000. Be sure to count empty columns.
4. Cell E20 is =VLOOKUP (B15, B4:K7, 4)*G15. In this case, the function is looking up the value in the fourth column, which is $10,000. Be sure to count empty columns.
5. Cells I15, G20, and I20 also use the VLOOKUP function.
6. After completing the spreadsheet, you can change the value in Cell B15 (1-4) to see the effect of choosing a different driver for overhead.

Planning for Profit and Cost Control

Learning Objectives

After completing this chapter, you should be able to:

1 Understand budgeting as a planning process.

2 Identify and describe the three levels of planning for business activity.

3 Understand the advantages of budgeting.

4 Appreciate the human factor in the budget process.

5 Identify the primary components of a master budget.

6 Prepare a sales budget and associated schedule of cash receipts.

7 Prepare a purchases budget and associated schedule of cash payments.

8 Prepare a selling and administrative expense budget and associated schedule of cash payments.

9 Prepare a cash budget.

10 Prepare a set of pro forma financial statements, including an income statement, a balance sheet, and a cash flow statement.

the *curious* manager

Randi Anglin/The Image Works

How much money will you need next week, next month, or next year? How will you get that money? Will you need to borrow, or will your earnings cover your needs? These questions apply to companies as well as individuals. Indeed, think about trying to determine how much money Capital Records will need next year. Will cash flows from sales of records by stars, such as Garth Brooks, cover the costs of promoting artists who do not sell? How much money will be needed to pay the back-up studio artists, cover designers, lawyers, executives, and other employees? Will money be available for ordinary expenses, such as rent, utilities, and postage? How do really large companies know what the future will bring?

*Planning is critical to the operation of a profitable business. The area of planning that is associated with financial matters is commonly called **budgeting**, which is a process that involves coordinating the finances of all areas of the business. For example, the production department cannot formulate its manufacturing plan until it knows how many units of product to produce. The level of production depends on the sales projection, which the marketing department normally develops. The marketing department cannot project sales volume until it knows the type of products that the company will sell. This information comes from the research and development department. The scenario could be continued, but the point should be clear now. A company's **master budget** results from the combination of numerous specific budgets that have been prepared by different departments within the business.*

*The responsibility for the coordination of budgeting activities normally rests with a **budgeting committee**. This committee supervises the preparation of the master budget and is responsible for settling disputes among various departments over budget matters. The committee also receives reports* *on how various segments are progressing toward the attainment of their budget standards. The budgeting committee is not an accounting committee. Indeed, its membership—the president; vice-presidents of marketing, production, purchasing, finance; and the controller—attests to the importance and comprehensive nature of the budgeting process.*

∎ The Planning Process

LO1

Understand budgeting as a planning process.

The nature of planning changes according to the length of the time period being considered. Generally, the shorter the time period, the more specific are the plans. Consider your decision to enter community college as an example. A well-organized decision could be subdivided into three distinct planning phases. First, there are the long-range plans. To make these plans, a student must consider a number of questions. Should he go to college? What does he intend to gain from the experience? Does he want a broader base of understanding, or is he seeking to attain specific job skills? In what area does he want to concentrate his studies? Unfortunately, many students go to college to find answers to these questions, rather than to accomplish preplanned goals, and many of them learn the misfortunes of poor planning the hard way. While their friends are graduating, they find themselves starting over with a new major.

The second planning phase involves planning for time periods of intermediate length, usually defined as three to five years. In this stage, the potential student must decide which school to attend, how to support herself while in school, and whether to live on or off campus. In the final phase, the student plans for the short term. The student decides which courses to take in the coming year, which instructors to choose, how to schedule part-time employment, and whether to join a study group. At this stage, the plans become specific, and details are important. The work may seem tedious, but careful planning generally leads to the efficient use of resources and to high levels of productivity. A word of caution is in order, however; plans are only as good as the intentions that support them. Making a careful plan for entering dental school is a waste of time for the individual who truly desires to build homes.

∎ Three Levels of Planning for Business Activity

LO2

Identify and describe the three levels of planning for business activity.

When applied to business activity, the three levels of planning are called *strategic planning*, *capital budgeting*, and *operations budgeting*. **Strategic planning** involves making long-term decisions, such as defining the scope of the business, determining which products to develop, deciding whether to discontinue a product, and determining which market niche should be most profitable. Upper-level management is responsible for these decisions. Strategic plans are stated in descriptive, rather than quantified, terms. Objectives, such as "to be the largest firm" or "to be the best quality producer," result from strategic planning. Although strategic planning is an interesting area, an in-depth discussion of the subject is beyond the scope of this text.

Capital budgeting deals with intermediate-range planning. It involves making such decisions as whether to buy or lease equipment, to stimulate sales, or to increase the company's asset base. Capital budgeting will be discussed in detail in a later chapter.

The **operating budget** constitutes the central focus of this chapter. It involves the establishment of a master budget that will direct the firm's activities over the short term. The master budget states objectives in specific quantities and includes sales targets, production objectives, and financing plans. The master budget constitutes a specific statement of management's short-term plans and represents a description of how management intends to achieve its objectives.

The master budget normally covers a one-year time span. It is frequently subdivided into quarterly projections and often includes quarterly data subdivided by month. Obviously, management does not want to wait until year end to know whether it will meet its budget. Monthly data provide the timely feedback necessary to take corrective action.

Many companies use a technique known as **perpetual** or **continuous budgeting** that utilizes a 12-month reporting period. At the completion of the current month, a new month is added to the end of the budget period, resulting in a continuous 12-month budget. The advantage of the perpetual budget is that it keeps management involved in the budget process. The traditional approach too often leads to a frenzied stop-and-go mentality. The annual budget is prepared in a year-end rush, and the assumptions underlying its formation are forgotten shortly thereafter. Changing conditions are not likely to be discussed until the next year-end review cycle. The perpetual budget corrects these shortcomings by keeping management continuously involved with the budget. Adding a new monthly budget each month to replace the preceding month's budget forces management into a constant 12-month think-ahead process.

▌Advantages of Budgeting

Budgeting is a costly, time-consuming activity; however, the sacrifices are more than offset by the benefits. Budgeting encourages planning, coordination, performance measurement, and corrective action.

LO3
Understand the advantages of budgeting.

Planning

Almost everyone makes plans. Shortly after waking up each morning, most people think about what they will do during the day. This thinking ahead is a form of planning. Likewise, most business managers naturally think ahead about how they will conduct their business. Unfortunately, the planning is frequently as informal as making a few mental notes. The problem with this type of planning is that it lacks the capacity for effective communication. The business manager knows what she wants to accomplish, but her superiors and subordinates have no knowledge of these objectives. If a manager's plans are inconsistent with her superior's plans, considerable amounts of time and effort will likely be wasted before the disagreement is discovered. Similarly, subordinates must wait until the manager tells them what to do; they have no way to exercise self-initiative because they do not know what is expected of them. Budgeting attempts to solve these problems by acting as a communication vehicle. The budget formalizes the manager's plans in a document that clearly communicates objectives to both superiors and subordinates.

Coordination

In certain situations, an action that is beneficial to one department may be detrimental to another department. For example, the purchasing agent may desire to order large amounts of raw materials to obtain discounts from suppliers. In doing so, the purchasing agent poses a storage problem for the inventory manager that may lead to excessive warehousing costs. The budgeting process forces departments to coordinate their activities to ensure the attainment of the objectives of the firm as a whole.

Performance Measurement

Budgets represent a specific, quantitative statement of management's objectives. As such, budgets represent standards that can be used to evaluate performance. For example, if a company budgets for $10 million in sales volume, this figure can be treated as a benchmark for measuring the performance of the sales department. If actual sales exceed the budgeted figure, the sales department should be recognized for superior performance. If the actual figure falls below the budgeted amount, the sales manager should be called on to explain the unsatisfactory sales volume.

Corrective Action

Budgeting provides advance notice of shortages, bottlenecks, or other weaknesses in operating plans. For example, a cash flow budget advises management when the company can expect to experience cash shortages during the coming year. On the basis of this information, the company can establish an organized borrowing plan with its creditors. Without such information, management would be forced to rush to the bank at the last minute to cover shortages as they arise. If the shortages occur during periods of tight credit, the company may be unable to find the necessary financing, or it may have to pay excessively high rates of interest to obtain the funds it needs. Budgeting provides an early warning system that advises managers of potential trouble spots in time for them to react in a calm and rational manner.

▐ Consideration of the Human Factor

LO4

Appreciate the human factor in the budget process.

Proper handling of human relations is essential to the establishment of an effective budget system. People have a natural tendency to be uncomfortable with budgets because budgets often have a constraining effect. The freedom to follow an individual's own whim is certainly more appealing than the rigor of sticking to an established plan. Further, evaluation related to budgeted expectations frightens many people. Most students experience a similar fear about being tested. As with an examination, the budget represents a standard by which performance is evaluated. Employees are put in the position of wondering whether they will be able to attain the expected level of performance. For many people, this is an unsettling experience.

The attitudes of upper-level management have a significant impact on the effectiveness of a budget. Subordinates develop a keen awareness of management's expectations; if upper-level managers degrade, make fun of, or ignore the budget, subordinates will follow suit. If management uses budgets to humiliate or embarrass subordinates, they will resent the treatment and the budgeting process. To be effective, upper-level management must consider the budget as a sincere effort to express realistic goals that employees will be expected to accomplish, and their behaviour must demonstrate this. The proper atmosphere is essential to budgeting success.

One technique, which has frequently proven successful in creating a healthy atmosphere, is known as **participative budgeting**. As the name implies, this technique encourages participation in the budget process by all levels of the business, not just upper-level managers. Information flows from the bottom up as well as from the top down during the preparation of the budget. Because they are directly responsible for accomplishing the budget objectives, subordinates are able to make more realistic estimates of what can be attained. Their participation in budget preparation is likely to result in the development of a team mentality. Participation encourages subordinates to be more cooperative, less fearful, and more highly motivated. They tend to look at budgets as representations of self-imposed constraints. They have no one to blame but themselves if they fail to accomplish the budget objectives.

Upper management participates in the process by ensuring that the employee-generated objectives are consistent with the company's objectives. Furthermore, if subordinates were granted complete freedom to establish budget standards, they might be tempted to set lax standards to ensure that they will meet the budget goals. A sincere effort is required by both managers and subordinates if the participatory process is to generate an effective budget.

If handled properly, budgets can help motivate employees to achieve superior performance. Natural human fears must be overcome, and management must strive to create an effective budget atmosphere. If these conditions are satisfied, the budget will represent realistic goals that employees will be encouraged to attain.

▮ The Master Budget

The master budget consists of a series of detailed schedules and budgets that describe the company's overall financial plans for the coming accounting period. The three major budget categories are (1) *operating budgets*, (2) *capital budgets*, (3) *financial statement budgets*. The budgeting process normally begins with the preparation of the operating budgets. An *operating budget* is prepared by individual sections within a company and becomes part of the company's master budget. The number of operating budgets depends on the nature of the business entity. For example, budgeting for the inventory needs of a manufacturing entity requires the preparation of a raw materials budget, a labour budget, and an overhead budget. In contrast, a retail company needs only an inventory purchases budget. The next section of this chapter focuses on Hamilton Hams Company, a retail sales company that uses four operating budgets: (1) a sales budget, (2) an inventory purchases budget, (3) a selling and administrative (S&A) budget, and (4) a cash budget.

The sales, inventory, and S&A budgets contain schedules that identify the cash consequences associated with the various business activities. For example, the sales budget includes a schedule of cash receipts from customers. Similarly, the inventory and S&A budgets contain schedules of cash payments associated with acquiring inventory and paying expenses. Preparation of the master budget begins with the sales forecast. The detailed budgets for inventory purchases and operating expenses are developed on the basis of projected sales. The information in the schedules of cash receipts and payments is used in the preparation of the cash budget.

The **capital budget** describes the company's long-term plans regarding investments in facilities, equipment, new products, store outlets, and lines of business. The information from the capital budget is input to several operating budgets. For example, acquisitions of equipment result in the recognition of amortization expense that appears on the S&A budget. In addition, the cash flows associated with capital investment appear on the cash budget.

Information contained in the operating budgets is used to prepare the **financial statement budgets**. Again, the number of financial statement budgets, also called **pro forma statements**, depends on the nature and needs of the budget entity. The company analyzed in this chapter, Hamilton Hams, prepares three pro forma statements including an income statement, a balance sheet, and a cash flow statement. Specific operating budgets provide data related to particular financial statements; for example, the sales, inventory, and S&A budgets contain information used to prepare the income statement and balance sheet. The sales budget, for example, contains information regarding the amount of sales revenue shown in the income statement and accounts receivable balances. Similarly, the inventory and the S&A expense budgets contain expense and liability information that appears on the income statement and balance sheet. The cash budget contains (1) the amount of interest expense appearing on the income statement, (2) the ending cash balance and capital acquisitions that appear on the balance sheet, and (3) the bulk of information that is included in the cash flow statement. Exhibit 7–1 is a graphic presentation of the information flows in a master budget.

LO5
Identify the primary components of a master budget.

▮ Hamilton Hams Budgeting Illustration

To illustrate the budgeting process, we describe the budgeting activities of the Hamilton Hams Company. Hamilton Hams (HH) is a major corporation with retail outlets located in shopping malls throughout Eastern Canada. As its name implies, the company sells cured hams. By focusing on a single product, the company has been able to standardize its operations, and the high degree of standardization has enabled the company to exercise stringent cost control procedures, which have allowed it to offer high-quality hams at competitive prices.

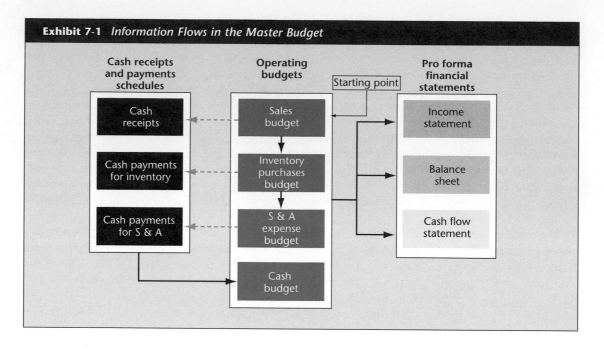

Exhibit 7-1 *Information Flows in the Master Budget*

Hamilton Hams has experienced phenomenal growth during the past five years, adding an average of five new stores each month. Within the past month, HH has opened two new stores in Ontario and plans to open a third in the near future. It finances new stores with debt. The company has a line of credit with the Bank of Montreal, whose lending officer has asked for a monthly budget for each of the first three months of the new store's operations. HH plans to open the store in October, and the accountant began to prepare a master budget for the months of October, November, and December. The first step in the budgeting process was to develop a sales budget.

Sales Budget

LO6

Prepare a sales budget and associated schedule of cash receipts.

The preparation of the master budget begins with the sales forecast. The accuracy of the sales forecast is critical because it acts as the data source for all the other budgets. If the sales figures are unreliable, the entire budgeting process is a waste of time. Thus, it is easy to understand why every available effort is made to obtain reliable estimates of projected sales.

The marketing department normally coordinates the effort to establish the sales forecast. Frequently, the information flows from the bottom up to the higher management levels. Sales personnel are asked to prepare estimates of sales projections for their designated products and territories and then to pass these estimates up the line, where they are combined with the estimates of other sales personnel to form the regional and national estimates. Using a variety of information sources, upper-level sales managers make appropriate adjustments to the estimates generated by the salespersons. Some of the more common inputs to the adjustment process include information gathered from industry periodicals and trade journals, analysis of general economic conditions, marketing surveys, historical sales figures, and assessments of changes in competitive forces. The information may be assimilated through a sophisticated system of computer programs, statistical techniques, and quantitative methods, or it may simply be subjected to the professional judgment of the upper-level sales managers. Regardless of the technique, the senior vice-president of sales ultimately formulates a sales forecast for which she is held responsible.

To initiate the budgeting process for HH's new store, the sales manager reviewed the sales history of stores operating in locations similar to the proposed site. He then made adjustments for startup conditions. October was considered an opportune time to start a new store because customers would have time to become familiar with the store's location during October before the holiday season. He expected significant sales growth in November and December and envisioned the company's hams as the centrepiece of many Thanksgiving and Christmas dinner tables. Specifically, he expected the new store's sales to start in October at $160,000. Cash versus credit sales (i.e., sales on account) were projected at $40,000 and $120,000, respectively, and sales were expected to increase 20 percent per month during November and December. On the basis of these estimates, the sales manager prepared the sales budget (Exhibit 7–2).

Note that the sales budget is subdivided into two panels, the first of which describes the projected sales for each month. The sales forecast for November is computed by adding a 20 percent increase to the amount of October sales. For example, *cash sales* for November are calculated as $48,000 ($40,000 + [$40,000 × 0.20]) and for December as $57,600 ($48,000 + [$48,000 × 0.20]). *Sales on account* are computed using the same mathematical procedures.

Schedule of Cash Receipts

Panel 2 in Exhibit 7–2 contains a schedule of the cash receipts associated with the expected sales. This information is used to prepare the cash budget in a later section of this chapter. The accountant has prepared the schedule under the assumption that accounts receivable from credit sales are collected *in full* in the month following the sale. In practice, collections may be somewhat more complicated, perhaps spread over several months, and some receivables may become bad debts that are never collected. Service charges for credit card sales may also reduce the amount collected. Regardless of the level of complication associated with making the estimates, the objective is to determine the amount and timing of expected cash collections. In the HH case, *total cash receipts* are determined by adding the *accounts receivable balance* from the previous month's *credit sales* to the current month's *cash sales*. Because the business will begin in October, no accounts receivable balance from September (i.e., previous month's credit sales) is available. Accordingly, cash receipts for October equal the amount of October's *cash sales*. November collections equal November's *cash sales* plus the *accounts receivable balance* generated from October's *credit sales* ($48,000 + $120,000 = $168,000). December's receipts

Exhibit 7-2				

HAMILTON HAMS
Sales Budget and Schedule of Cash Receipts
For the Quarter Ended December 31, 2006

Budget Line	October	November	December	Pro Forma Statement Data
Panel 1: Sales Budget				
1 Budgeted cash sales	$ 40,000	$ 48,000	$ 57,600	
2 Budgeted sales on account	120,000 →	144,000 →	172,800	→ $ 172,800*
3 Total budgeted sales	$160,000	$192,000	$230,400	$ 582,400†
Panel 2: Schedule of Cash Receipts				
4 Current month's cash sales	$40,000	$48,000	$57,600	
5 Accounts receivable from previous month's credit sales	0	→ 120,000	→ 144,000	
6 Total budgeted collections	$ 40,000	$168,000	$201,600	

*Ending accounts receivable balance appearing on the balance sheet.
†Sales revenue appearing on income statement (i.e., $160,000 + $192,000 + $230,400).

equal December's *cash sales* and the *accounts receivable balance* generated from November's *credit sales* ($57,600 + $144,000 = $201,600). The amounts in the Pro Forma Statement Data column are discussed next.

Pro Forma Financial Statement Data

The column Pro Forma Statement Data contains two items that will appear on the end-of-quarter (i.e., December 31) budgeted financial statements. The first item ($172,800) represents the amount of the ending *accounts receivable balance* on the pro forma balance sheet. Since December's credit sales will be collected in January, the receivables account will have a $172,800 balance as of December 31, 2006. The pro forma balance sheet is shown in Exhibit 7–7. We suggest you trace the accounts receivable balance from the sales budget to the pro forma statements before continuing.

The second item in the Pro Forma Statement Data column ($582,400) is the amount of sales revenue reported on the company's budgeted income statement. This amount was determined by summing the amounts of the monthly sales. In other words, sales for the quarter equal the total sales for each month of the quarter ($160,000 + $192,000 + $230,400 = $582,400). The pro forma income statement is shown in Exhibit 7–6. Again, we encourage you to trace the data from the operating budget to the financial statement budget.

Inventory Purchases Budget

LO7

Prepare a purchases budget and associated schedule of cash payments.

After the amount of projected sales has been established, HH's accountant focuses on the amount of inventory that will be needed to satisfy the sales demand. Meeting the sales demand requires having enough inventory to cover expected sales and future sales between reorder points. Accordingly, the *total amount of inventory needed* for each month equals the amount of *budgeted sales* plus the desired *ending inventory*. The total amount of inventory needed can be obtained from two sources. First, the company can use existing stock. In other words, customer demand can be satisfied with goods that are in *beginning inventory*. The difference between the amount of *goods needed* and the *beginning inventory* is the amount of *goods to be purchased*. Accordingly, the purchases budget follows a logical format that is summarized on the next page:

focus on International Issues

Buyer Beware: An Appropriate Caveat in International Markets

What happens when budget preparers cross the line to become fraud perpetrators? Perhaps nothing happens when international boundaries are interjected into the equation. Take the case of Bre-X Minerals as an example. The value of Bre-X's stock, which trades on the Vancouver Stock Exchange, soared when the company announced a gold find in Indonesia said to be worth billions. The company's estimates of the size of the find increased steadily from 40 million ounces to 57 million to 71 million. The final estimate announced by Bre-X's vice-chairman suggested that the real size of the find might be 200 million ounces, making it one of the largest in recent history. The stock price followed the upward spiral, ultimately reaching a market capitalization of $4.5 billion. When an independent review concluded that the original tests had been falsified, Bre-X's stock collapsed.

Another example of reporting using questionable practices recently occurred with the Texas-based energy marketing company Enron. Enron, using questionable reporting methods, questionable statements by its auditors, and questionable management practices, filed for bankruptcy creating billions of dollars of losses in savings and pension funds. It truly is "buyer beware" when investing your savings. Even "well-managed and well-financed companies" can fail, with no apparent warning.

Source: Kevin Whitlaw, "Fool's Gold and Other Goodies from Canada," *U.S. News and World Report* (May 19, 1997), pp. 50–51.

Cost of budgeted sales	XXX
Plus: Desired ending inventory	XXX
Inventory needed	XXX
Less: Beginning inventory	(XXX)
Amount to purchase	XXX

HH's *cost of budgeted sales* equals 70 percent of *total budgeted sales* (see Line 3 in Exhibit 7–2). In addition, HH has the policy of maintaining an ending inventory that equals 20 percent of the current month's *cost of budgeted sales*. On the basis of this information and the data contained in the sales budget, the accountant prepared the purchases budget shown in Panel 1 of Exhibit 7–3. The *budgeted cost of sales* for October was determined by multiplying October's *budgeted sales* times 70 percent ($160,000 × 0.70 = $112,000). *Budgeted cost of sales* for November and December were computed in a similar fashion. The *desired ending inventory* for October was computed by multiplying October's *budgeted cost of goods sold* times 20 percent ($112,000 × 0.20 = $22,400). Desired ending inventory for November and December is computed in a similar fashion.

Exhibit 7-3

HAMILTON HAMS
Inventory Purchases Budget and Schedule of Cash Payments for Inventory
For the Quarter Ended December 31, 2006

Budget Line		October	November	December	Pro Forma Statement Data
Panel 1: Sales Budget					
1	Budgeted cost of goods sold	$112,000	$134,400	$161,280	407,680*
2	Plus: Desired end inventory (line 1 × 0.20)	22,400	26,880	32,256	32,256†
3	Inventory needed	$134,400	161,280	$193,536	
4	Less: Beginning inventory	0	(22,400)	(26,880)	20%
5	Total required purchases	$134,400	$138,880	$166,656	33,331‡
Panel 2: Schedule of Cash Receipts					
6	Current purchases at 80%	$107,520	$111,104	$133,325	
7	Prior month's purchases at 20%	0	26,880	27,776	
8	Total budgeted payments for inventory	$107,520	$137,984	$161,101	

*Cost of goods sold appearing on pro forma income statement (sum of monthly amounts $112,000 + $134,400 + $161,280).
†Ending inventory balance appearing on pro forma balance sheet.
‡Ending accounts payable balance appearing on pro forma balance sheet ($166,656 × .20).

Schedule of Cash Payments for Inventory Purchases

Panel 2 of Exhibit 7–3 contains the cash payments budget. All merchandise is purchased on account. Because the hams are perishable, the supplier demands that a significant portion of the accounts payable be settled within the month of purchase. Specifically, 80 percent of the current payables balance must be paid in the month goods are purchased. The remaining 20 percent is paid during the following month. Because the store opens in October, no September balance exists. Accordingly, *cash payments* for October are 80 percent of October's *required purchases* ($134,400 × 0.80 = $107,520). *Cash payments* for November amount to 80 percent of November purchases plus 20 percent of October purchases ([$138,880 × 0.80 = 111,104] + [$134,400 × 0.20 = $26,880] = $137,984). Similarly, *cash payments* for December amount to 80 percent of December purchases plus 20 percent of November purchases ([$166,656 × 0.80 = 133,325] + [$138,880 × 0.20 = $27,776] = $161,101).

Pro Forma Financial Statement Data

The purchases budget contains three items that are relevant to the preparation of the pro forma financial statements. First, the amount of cost of goods sold (see Exhibit 7–3, Budget Line 1) will be shown on the budgeted income statements. The amount of the *cost of goods sold* for the quarter equals the total of the monthly amounts ($112,000 + $134,400 + $161,280). The *ending inventory* balance for December 31 also represents the ending inventory balance for the quarter. Accordingly, the $32,256 ending inventory balance is shown in the pro forma balance sheet. Finally, the assumed payments schedule results in a year-end balance in the *accounts payable account*. Because 20 percent of December credit purchases will be collected in January, the payables account will have a balance of $33,331 (from Line 5, December column, $166,656 × 0.20 = $33,331) as of December 31, 2006. In the previous and all future computations, we round the numbers to the nearest whole dollar amount. We suggest that you trace these amounts to the pro forma statements shown in Exhibits 7–6 and 7–7.

Selling and Administrative Expense Budget

LO8

Prepare a selling and administrative expense budget and associated schedule of cash payments.

The selling and administrative (S&A) expense budget for Hamilton Hams' new store is shown in Exhibit 7–4. Most of the items in Panel 1 are self-explanatory; however, two of the items merit some explanation. The amortization expense (see Line 5 in Exhibit 7–4) was based on information contained in the *capital expenditures budget*. Although detailed capital budgets are not presented in this chapter, you can assume that the budget indicates that opening the new store will require a significant investment in store fixtures, including refrigeration equipment. Each of HH's stores is furnished with an identical equipment package. Total investment in fixtures, which are expected to have an average useful life of 10 years and a $10,000 salvage value, is expected to be $130,000. Amortization expense is determined on a straight-line basis, resulting in an annual charge of $12,000 ([$130,000 − $10,000] ÷ 10). Monthly amortization expense is $1,000 ($12,000 annual charge ÷ 12 months). Note that the S&A expense budget does

---

Exhibit 7-4

HAMILTON HAMS
S&A Expense Budget and Schedule of Cash Payments for S&A Expense
For the Quarter Ended December 31, 2006

Budget Line		October	November	December	Pro Forma Statement Data
Panel 1: Selling and Administrative Expense Budget					
1	Salary expense	$24,000	$24,000	$24,000	
2	Sales commissions (2 percent of sales)	3,200	3,840	4,608 ⟶	$ 4,608*
3	Supplies expense (1 percent of sales)	1,600	1,920	2,304	
4	Utilities	1,400	1,400	1,400 ⟶	1,400†
5	Amortization on store equipment	1,000	1,000	1,000	3,000‡
6	Rent	3,600	3,600	3,600	
7	Miscellaneous	900	900	900	
8	Total S&A expenses before interest	$35,700	$36,660	$37,812	$ 110,172§
Panel 2: Schedule of Cash Payments for Selling and Administrative Expenses					
9	Salary expense paid monthly as incurred	$24,000	$24,000	$24,000	
10	Prior month's sales commisions, 100 percent	0	3,200	3,840	
11	Supplies expense paid monthly as incurred	1,600	1,920	2,304	
12	Prior month's utilities, 100 percent	0	1,400	1,400	
13	Rent paid monthly as incurred	3,600	3,600	3,600	
14	Miscellaneous paid monthly as incurred	900	900	900	
15	Total cash payments for S&A expenses	$30,100	$35,020	$36,044	

*Ending sales commissions payable account balance shown on pro forma balance sheet.
†Ending utilities payable account balance shown on pro forma balance sheet.
‡Accumulated amortization appears on the pro forma balance sheet (sum of monthly amounts: $1,000 + $1,000 + $1,000).
§S&A expense appearing on pro forma income statement (sum of monthly amounts: $35,700 + $36,660 + $37,812).

not contain a provision for interest expense; the amount of interest expense cannot be determined until the amount of expected borrowing has been established through the preparation of the *cash budget*. Accordingly, the interest component will be determined at a later point in the budgeting process.

Schedule of Cash Payments for Selling and Administrative Expenses

Panel 2 of Exhibit 7–4 contains the schedule of cash payments associated with S&A expenses. Differences between expense recognition and cash flow result from several conditions. First, cash payments for sales commissions and utilities are expected to be paid in the month following their incurrence. Note that amortization expense is not included in the cash payments budget. Recall that the cash outflow for equipment is shown as an investing activity at the time cash is paid to purchase the equipment. Accordingly, this item will be shown as a separate line item on the cash budget.

Pro Forma Financial Statement Data

The assumed payments schedule results in a year-end *balance in the sales commissions and utilities payable accounts*. Because December's payments for commissions and utilities will be paid in January, the commissions and utilities payable accounts will have balances of $4,608 and $1,400, respectively, as of December 31 (see Pro Forma Statement Data column amounts for Budget Lines 2 and 4, Exhibit 7–4). The items will appear on the pro forma balance sheet. The total amount of S&A expenses before interest is determined by summing the monthly amounts ($35,700 + $36,660 + 37,812 = $110,172). This amount appears on Budget Line 8 under the Pro Forma Statement column. The S&A expense is shown on the pro forma income statement. We suggest that you trace the utilities and commissions payable and the total S&A expense to the pro forma statements shown in Exhibits 7–6 and 7–7.

LO9

Prepare a cash budget.

Cash Budget

Few things are more important to the success of a company than the effective management of cash. If excess cash is permitted to accumulate, the business will lose the opportunity to earn investment income or to repay debt, thereby reducing interest costs. On the other hand, if cash shortages occur, the business will be unable to pay its debts and may be forced into bankruptcy. A **cash budget** is prepared to advise management of anticipated cash shortages or excessive cash balances. Management uses this information to plan its financing activities. It makes arrangements with creditors to ensure that anticipated shortages can be covered by borrowing. It also plans to repay past borrowings and to make appropriate investments in the periods in which excess amounts of cash are expected.

The cash budget is composed of three major components: (1) a cash receipts section, (2) a cash payments section, and (3) a financing section. Most of the raw data needed to prepare the cash budget are included in the cash receipts and payments schedules that were discussed earlier; however, further refinements of these data are sometimes necessary. The complete cash budget is shown in Exhibit 7–5.

Cash Receipts Section

The cash receipts for HH is shown in the *schedule of cash receipts* (refer to Budget Line 6 in Panel 2 of Exhibit 7–2). The amounts in this schedule are transferred to Budget Line 2 of the cash budget (see Exhibit 7–5). The expected cash receipts are added to the beginning cash balance to determine the amount of cash available for use (Budget Line 3 in Exhibit 7–5).

Cash Payments Section

Cash payments include expected cash outflows for inventory purchases, S&A expenses, and investments. The cash payments for inventory purchases are shown in the *schedule of cash payments for inventory purchases* (Budget Line 8 in Panel 2 of Exhibit 7–3). The amounts in the inventory payments

Exhibit 7-5

HAMILTON HAMS
Cash Budget
For the Quarter Ended December 31, 2006

Budget Line		October	November	December	Pro Forma Statement Data
Cash Receipts					
1	Beginning cash balance	$ 0	$ 7,624	$ 7,550	
2	Add cash receipts (Exhibit 7–2)	40,000	168,000	201,600	$409,600*
3	Total cash available	40,000	175,624	209,150	
Less: Cash Payments					
4	For inventory purchases (Exhibit 7–3)	107,520	137,984	161,101	406,605†
5	For S&A expenses (Exhibit 7–4)	30,100	35,020	36,044	101,164‡
6	To purchase store fixtures	130,000	0	0	130,000§
7	Total cash payments	267,620	173,004	197,145	
Cash Needs					
8	Shortage (surplus) of cash: (Line 7 Line 3)	227,620	(2,620)	(12,005)	
9	Plus desired cash cushion	10,000	10,000	10,000	
Financing Activity					
10	Amount borrowed (repaid)	237,620	7,380	(2,005)	242,995**
11	Interest expense at 1 percent per month	(2,376)	(2,450)	(2,430)	7,256††
12	Ending cash balance (Line 3 − 7 + 10 + 11)	$ 7,624	$ 7,550	$ 7,570 ⟶	$7,570‡‡

*Operating Activities section of pro forma cash flow statement (sum of monthly amounts $40,000 + $168,000 + $201,600).
†Operating Activities section of pro forma cash flow statement (sum of monthly amounts $107,520 + $137,984 + $161,101).
‡Operating Activities section of pro forma cash flow statement (sum of monthly amounts $30,100 + $35,020 + $36,044).
§Investing Activities section of pro forma cash flow statement (sum of monthly amounts $130,000 + $0 + $0). The investment in store fixtures also appears on the pro forma balance sheet.
**Financing Activities section of pro forma cash flow statement (sum of monthly amounts $237,620 + $7,380 − $2,005).
††Operating Activities section of pro forma cash flow statement (sum of monthly amounts $2,376 + $2,450 + $2,430).
‡‡The ending cash balance appears on the pro forma balance sheet (Exhibit 7–7) and as the last item in the cash flow statement (Exhibit 7–8).

schedule have been transferred to Budget Line 4 of the cash budget (see Exhibit 7–5). The cash payments for S&A expenses shown in the schedule of cash payments for S&A expenses (Budget Line 15 in Panel 2 of Exhibit 7–4). The amounts in the receipts schedule are transferred to Budget Line 5 of the cash budget (see Exhibit 7–5). Also recall that the *capital expenditures budget* (the detail of which is not shown in this chapter) indicated that HH would spend $130,000 to equip the new store with the standard fixtures package. This amount is shown on Budget Line 6 on the cash budget (see Exhibit 7–5), and the total expected cash payments is displayed on Budget Line 7.

Financing Section

In October, HH expects to have a cash deficit of $227,620 (Budget Line 8, October column, Exhibit 7–5). Accordingly, HH will need to borrow money to finance the establishment and operation of the new store. If the company were to borrow only $227,620, it would have an insufficient amount of funds available to pay interest and to maintain a reasonable minimum ending cash balance. For this reason, HH decided to borrow a *cash cushion* amounting to $10,000 more than the amount of the expected cash shortage. This amount is shown on Budget Line 9 of Exhibit 7–5. The total amount borrowed is $237,620 ($227,620 cash shortage + $10,000 cash cushion), shown on Budget Line 10.

In practice, borrowing and repayment activities occur on a daily basis. For firms managing millions of dollars, one day's interest is a large amount of money. However, for illustrative purposes, the computation of daily interest is too cumbersome. As a result, for the purpose of computing interest, we assume that HH borrows and repays on the first day of each month. Furthermore, we assume that it pays

Six Reasons to Budget

1. **Control:** Money makes a good slave but a poor master. When it comes to money, you want to be in control. If you let your finances rule your life, you will always fall short of reaching your financial goals.

2. **Knowledge:** You know how much money you have and where it is going, right down to the last penny.

3. **Opportunity:** Having your financial life in order enables you to see opportunities that you might have otherwise missed.

4. **Organization:** Even the simplest of budgets systematizes and organizes your finances. Budgets also provide you with records of all your monetary transactions and form the basis of a filing system to organize bills, receipts, and financial statements.

5. **Stress Reduction:** Money issues are the most common cause of marital discord and family tensions. By communicating openly about money, as budgets forces one to do, there is less chance of money issues complicating human relationships.

6. **Time:** All your financial transactions are automatically organized well in advance of the tax season, or in the event of a tax audit, saving you precious time hunting down receipts and statements at the last minute.

Source: Anne Papmehl, M.A., "In Praise of Budgeting," *CMA Management*, February 2002.

---

interest in cash on the last day of each month. The interest rate on the line of credit is 1 percent per month. Accordingly, interest expense (Budget Line 11, Exhibit 7–5) for October is $2,376 ($237,620 amount borrowed × 0.01). The ending cash balance is determined by adding the cash available (Budget Line 3) plus the funds borrowed (Budget Line 10) minus total cash payments for S&A expense (Budget Line 7) minus cash paid for interest expense (Budget Line 11). The result appears on Budget Line 12. The ending cash balance becomes the beginning cash balance for the following month.

The computation for the amount borrowed in November begins with the cash surplus of $2,620 (Budget Line 8). This surplus is insufficient to maintain the $10,000 desired cash cushion. Accordingly, HH must borrow an additional $7,380 ($10,000 − $2,620). Interest expense is calculated as 1 percent of the outstanding debt ([$237,620 October borrowings + $7,380 November borrowings] × 0.01 = $2,450).

In December, the company produces enough surplus cash to make a partial repayment of the principal balance. The amount available for repayment is $2,005 ($12,005 surplus − $10,000 cash cushion). The interest expense for December is $2,430 ([$237,620 + $7,380 − $2,005] × 0.01).

Pro Forma Financial Statement Data

The *pro forma cash flow statement* is shown in Exhibit 7–8. The total of the cash receipts and the totals of the cash payments for inventory and S&A expenses are shown in the Cash Flow from Operating Activities section of the pro forma cash flow statement. The totals of the cash receipts and payments are determined by summing the monthly amounts. For example, the total cash receipts ($409,600) shown on the cash budget (Exhibit 7–5, Budget Line 2) is computed by adding the amounts for October, November, and December. Totals for the cash payment items on Budget Lines 4 and 5 are computed in a similar fashion. The $130,000 purchase price of the store fixtures appears in the Cash Flow from Investing Activities section of the cash flow statement and in the Assets section of the pro forma balance sheet. The amount borrowed ($242,995, Budget Line 10) is determined by adding the borrowings in October and November minus the repayment made in December ($237,620 + $7,380 − $2,005 = $242,995) and is shown in the Cash Flow from Financing Activities section of the pro forma cash flow statement (see Exhibit 7–8) and in the Liabilities section of the pro forma balance sheet (see Exhibit 7–7). The total amount of interest expense shown in Exhibit 7–6 is also determined by summing the monthly amounts on Line 11 of Exhibit 7–5 ($2,376 + $2,450 + $2,430 = $7,256). Because the interest is paid in cash, the interest expense is shown in the Cash Flow from Operating Activities section of the pro forma cash flow statement (see Exhibit 7–8) and on the pro forma income statement (see Exhibit 7–6). Finally, the ending cash balance ($7,570) for December also constitutes the ending balance for the quarter. This amount is shown on the pro forma balance sheet and as the last item on the pro forma cash flow statement.

Pro Forma Income Statement

LO10

Prepare a set of pro forma financial statements.

The budgeted income statement for Hamilton Hams is shown in Exhibit 7–6. The information needed to prepare this statement is contained in Exhibits 7–1, 7–2, 7–3, and 7–4. The budgeted income statement provides insight into the new store's expected profitability. If expected profitability is unsatisfactory, management may decide to abandon the project or to alter planned activity. Perhaps the owners of the shopping centre would be willing to lease space for less, employees might accept lower pay or the number of employees could be reduced. Likewise, the pricing strategy could be scrutinized for possible changes. Indeed, budgets are usually prepared on spreadsheets or computerized mathematical models that enable managers to easily perform "what-if" analysis. Managers change some variable on the spreadsheet, and the software instantly presents a revised set of budgets. Although computer technology can provide instant access to a wide array of budgeted data, the manager remains responsible for data analysis and decision making. The proper interpretation of budget data requires an understanding of the origins and limitations of the budget amounts. For this reason, we recommend that you retrace the data in the financial statements back to the source data in the referenced exhibits.

Exhibit 7-6

HAMILTON HAMS
Pro Forma Income Statement
For the Quarter Ended December 31, 2006

		Data Source
Sales Revenue	$582,400	Exhibit 7–2
Cost of Goods Sold	(407,680)	Exhibit 7–3
Gross Margin	174,720	
Selling and Administrative Expenses	(110,172)	Exhibit 7–4
Operating Income	64,548	
Interest Expense	(7,256)	Exhibit 7–5
Net Income	$57,292	

Pro Forma Balance Sheet

Most of the items shown on the pro forma balance sheet in Exhibit 7–7 have been explained in the previous exhibits. The new store has no contributed capital because its operations are fully financed through debt and retained earnings. The amount of the retained earnings equals the amount of net income because no distributions were made and because no earnings from prior periods exist. Again, you are encouraged to trace the amounts shown in the financial statement to the source data contained in Exhibits 7–1 through 7–5.

Pro Forma Cash Flow Statement

The pro forma cash flow statement is shown in Exhibit 7–8. All the information used to prepare this statement was drawn from the cash budget shown in Exhibit 7–5. The individual items have been discussed in previous sections of the chapter. However, to reinforce your understanding, we suggest that you trace the amounts shown in the cash flow statement to their source in the cash budget. If you have trouble tracing any of the information, you should reread the section Pro Forma Financial Statement Data in the discussion of the cash budget.

Capital Records, like almost all companies, engages in a sophisticated budgeting process. Complications due merely to the size of today's major companies require extensive planning to ensure that they remain solvent.

Exhibit 7-7

HAMILTON HAMS
Pro Forma Balance Sheet
For the Quarter Ended December 31, 2006

			Data Source
Assets			
Cash		$ 7,570	Exhibit 7–5
Accounts Receivable		172,800	Exhibit 7–2
Inventory		32,256	Exhibit 7–3
Store Fixtures and Equipment $130,000	130,000		Exhibit 7–4 Discussion
Accumulated Amortization (3,000)	$ (3,000)		Exhibit 7–4 Discussion
Book Value of Equipment		127,000	
Total Assets		$339,626	
Liabilities			
Accounts Payable		$ 33,331	Exhibit 7–3
Utilities Payable		1,400	Exhibit 7–4
Sales Commissions Payable		4,608	Exhibit 7–4
Line of Credit Borrowings		242,995	Exhibit 7–5
Equity			
Retained Earnings		57,292	
Total Liabilities and Equity		$339,626	

Exhibit 7-8

HAMILTON HAMS
Pro Forma Cash Flow Statement
For the Quarter Ended December 31, 2006

Cash Flow from Operating Activities		
Cash Receipts from Customers	$409,600	
Cash Payments for Inventory	(406,605)	
Cash Payments for S&A Expenses	(101,164)	
Cash Payments for Interest Expense	(7,256)	
Net Cash Flow from Operations		$(105,425)
Cash Flow from Investing Activities		
Cash Outflow to Purchase Fixtures		(130,000)
Cash Flow from Financing Activities		
Inflow from Borrowing on Line of Credit		242,995
Net Change in Cash		7,570
Plus Beginning Cash Balance		0
Ending Cash Balance		$ 7,570

---

a look
back

The planning of financial matters is called *budgeting*. The degree of detail included in a company's budget depends on the time period considered. Generally, the shorter the time period, the more specific the plans. *Strategic planning* involves long-term plans, such as the overall objectives of the business. Examples of strategic planning include which products to manufacture and sell and which market niches to pursue. Strategic plans are stated in descriptive terms and are very broad. Capital budgeting deals with intermediate investment planning. *Operations budgeting* deals with short-term plans and is used in creating the master budget.

The budgeting committee has the responsibility of incorporating numerous departmental budgets into a master budget for the whole company. The *master budget* is very detailed with objectives stated in specific amounts; it represents a description of how management intends to achieve its objectives. It usually covers a one-year period of time. Budgeting encourages planning, coordination, performance measurement, and corrective action.

Employees may feel uncomfortable with budgets, which can have constraining effects and can serve as standards by which performance is evaluated. Therefore, the human factor should be considered in establishing an effective budget system. Upper-level management must set the proper atmosphere by taking budgets seriously and avoiding using them to humiliate subordinates. One way to create the proper atmosphere is to encourage subordinates' participation in the budgeting process; *participative budgeting* can help set goals that are more realistic about what can be accomplished and to establish a team mentality in trying to reach those goals.

The primary components of the master budget are the *operating budgets*, the *capital budgets*, and the *financial statement budgets*. The budgeting process begins with the preparation of the operating budgets, which consist of detailed schedules and budgets prepared by the company's departments. The first operating budget to be prepared is the sales budget. The detailed operating budgets for inventory purchases and S&A expenses are based on the projected sales indicated in the sales budget. The information in the schedules of cash receipts (prepared in conjunction with the sales budget) and of cash payments (prepared in conjunction with the inventory and S&A budgets) is used in preparing the cash budget. The cash budget subtracts cash receipts from cash payments; the resultant cash surplus or shortage determines the company's financing activities.

The capital budget describes the company's long-term plans regarding investments in facilities, equipment, new products, or other lines of business. The information from the capital budget is used as input to several of the operating budgets.

The financial statements budgets (pro forma financial statements) are prepared from information contained in the operating budgets. The operating budgets for sales, inventory, and S&A expenses contain information that is used to prepare the income statement and balance sheet. The cash budget includes the amount of interest expense appearing on the income statement, the ending cash balance, the capital acquisitions that appear on the balance sheet, and most of the information included in the statement of cash flows.

a look
forward

Once a company has completed its budget, it has determined what it plans to do. Then the plan must be followed. The next chapter investigates the techniques associated with performance evaluation. You will learn to compare actual results with budgets, to calculate variances, and to identify the parties who are normally held accountable for creating the deviations from expectations. Finally, you will learn to appreciate the human factors that must be considered in taking corrective action when employees fail to accomplish budget goals.

Budget committee The group of individuals responsible for coordinating budgeting activities, normally consisting of upper-level managers including the president; the vice-presidents of marketing, production, purchasing, and finance; and the controller. *(p. 239)*

Budgeting A form of planning that formalizes a company's goals and objectives in financial terms. *(p. 239)*

Capital budget A budget that describes the company's plans regarding investments, new products, or lines of business for the coming year; is used as input to prepare many of the operating budgets and becomes a formal part of the master budget. *(p. 243)*

Capital budgeting The financial planning activities that cover the intermediate

range of time, such as whether to buy or lease equipment, whether to purchase a particular investment, or whether to increase operating expenses to stimulate sales. *(p. 240)*

Cash budget A budget that shows the expected cash inflows and outflows, including cash receipts from revenues, cash payments for inventories and general selling and administrative expenses, and the anticipated financing activities. *(p. 249)*

Financial statement budgets (pro forma statements) Projected financial statements found in the master budget that are based on information contained in the operating budgets. *(p. 243)*

Master budget The composition of the numerous separate but interdependent departmental budgets

that cover a wide range of operating and financial factors, such as sales, production, manufacturing expenses, and administrative expenses. *(p. 239)*

Operating budgets Budgets prepared by different departments within a company that will become a part of the company's master budget; typically include a sales budget, an inventory purchases budget, a selling and administrative budget, and a cash budget. *(p. 240)*

Participative budgeting A budget technique that allows subordinates to participate with upper-level managers in setting budget objectives, thereby encouraging cooperation and support in the attainment of the company's goals. *(p. 242)*

Perpetual (continuous) budgeting A continuous

budgeting activity normally covering a 12-month time span by replacing the current month's budget at the end of each month with a new budget; keeps management constantly involved in the budget process so that changing conditions can be incorporated on a timely basis. *(p. 241)*

Pro forma statements Budgeted financial statements prepared from the information in the master budget. *(p. 243)*

Strategic planning The planning activities associated with long-range decisions, such as defining the scope of the business, determining which products to develop, deciding whether to discontinue a business segment, and determining which market niche would be most profitable. *(p. 240)*

1. Budgets are useful only for small companies that can estimate sales with accuracy. Do you agree with this statement?
2. Why is it necessary to have a committee responsible for the preparation of the master budget?
3. What are the three levels of planning? Explain each briefly.
4. What is the primary factor that distinguishes the three different levels of planning from each other?
5. What is the advantage of using a perpetual budget instead of the traditional annually revised budget?
6. What are the advantages associated with budgeting?
7. How may budgets be used as a measure of performance?
8. Ken Shilov, manager of the marketing department, tells you that "budgeting simply does not work." He says that he made budgets for his employees and when he reprimanded them for failing to accomplish budget goals, he got unfounded excuses. Suggest how Mr. Shilov could encourage employee cooperation.

9. What is a master budget?
10. What is the normal starting point in the development of the master budget?
11. How does the level of inventory affect the production budget? Why is it important to manage the level of inventory?
12. What are the components of the cash budget? Describe each.
13. The primary reason for preparing a cash budget is to determine the amount of cash to include on the budgeted balance sheet. Do you agree or disagree with this statement? Support your position with appropriate commentary.
14. What information does the pro forma income statement provide? How does its preparation depend on the operating budgets?
15. How does the pro forma cash flow statement differ from the cash budget?

EXERCISES

L.O. 1, 4 EXERCISE 7-1   *Budget Responsibility*

Alice Moore, the accountant, is a perfectionist. No one can do the job as she can. Indeed, she has found the budget information provided by the departments to be worthless. She must change everything they give her. She has to admit that her estimates have not always been accurate, but she shudders to think of what would happen if she used the information supplied by marketing and the operating departments. No one seems to care about accuracy. Indeed, some of the marketing staff have even become insulting. When Ms. Moore confronted one of the salesmen with the fact that he was behind in meeting his budgeted sales forecast, he responded by saying, "They're your numbers. Why don't you go out and make the sales? It's a heck of a lot easier to sit there in your office and make up numbers than it is to get out and get the real work done." Ms. Moore reported the incident, but, of course, nothing was done about it.

Required

Write a brief memo suggesting how the budgeting process could be improved.

L.O. 6, 10 EXERCISE 7-2   *Preparation of Sales Budget*

Magic Feet, which expects to start operations on January 1, 2006, will sell sports shoes in shopping malls. Magic Feet has budgeted sales as indicated in the following table. The company expects a 20 percent increase in sales per month for November and December.

Sales	October	November	December
Cash sales	$15,000	?	?
Sales on account	45,000	?	?
Total budgeted sales	$60,000	?	?

Required

a. Complete the sales budget by filling in the missing amounts.
b. Determine the amount of sales revenue that will appear on the company's fourth quarter pro forma income statement.

L.O. 6, 10 EXERCISE 7-3   *Preparation of Schedule of Cash Receipts*

Vintage Beds Co. sells brass beds. Its budget director has prepared the sales budget that follows. The company had a beginning balance of $60,000 in accounts receivable on October 1. Vinatge Beds normally collects 100 percent of accounts receivable in the month following the month of sale.

Sales Budget			
Sales	October	November	December
Cash sales	$20,000	$22,000	$24,200
Sales on account	45,000	49,500	54,450
Total budgeted sales	$65,000	$71,500	$78,650
Schedule of Cash Receipts			
Current cash sales	?	?	?
Plus collections from accounts receivable	?	?	?
Total budgeted collections	$80,000	$67,000	$73,700

Required

a. Complete the schedule of cash receipts by filling in the missing amounts.
b. Determine the amount of accounts receivable that will appear on the company's fourth quarter pro forma balance sheet.

L.O. 6 EXERCISE 7-4   *Preparation of Sales Budgets with Different Assumptions*

Pakula Corporation, which has three divisions, is preparing its sales budget. However, each division expects a different growth rate because the economic conditions vary in different regions of the country. The growth expectations per quarter are 2 percent for East Division, 3 percent for West Division, and 5 percent for South Division.

Current Quarter	First Quarter	Second Quarter	Third Quarter	Fourth Quarter
East Division	$520,000			
West Division	740,000			
South Division	340,000			

Required

a. Complete the sales budget by filling in the missing amounts. (Round the figures to the nearest dollar.)
b. Determine the amount of sales revenue that will appear on the company's quarterly pro forma income statements.

EXERCISE 7-5   *Determination of Cash Receipts from Accounts Receivable*   **L.O. 6**

Travel Lite operates a mail-order business that sells clothes designed for people who travel frequently. It had sales of $290,000 in December. Because Travel Lite is in the mail-order business, all sales are made on account. The company expects a 30 percent drop in sales for January. The balance in the Accounts Receivable account on December 31 was $45,200 and is budgeted to be $33,800 as of January 31. Travel Lite normally collects accounts receivable in the month following the month of sale.

Required

a. Determine the amount of cash expected to be collected from accounts receivable during January.
b. Is it reasonable to assume that sales will decline in January for this type of business? Why, or why not?

EXERCISE 7-6   *Use of Judgment in Making a Sales Forecast*   **L.O. 6**

Old Tyme Sweets, is a candy store located in a large shopping mall.

Required

Write a brief memo describing the sales pattern that you would expect Old Tyme Sweets to experience during the year. In which months will sales be high? In which months will sales be low? Explain why.

EXERCISE 7-7   *Preparation of Inventory Purchases Budget*   **L.O. 7**

Mayer Lighting Company sells lamps and other lighting fixtures. The director of the purchasing department prepared the following inventory purchases budget. Mayer desires to maintain an ending inventory balance equal to 10 percent of that month's cost of goods sold.

	April	May	June
Budgeted cost of goods sold	$42,250	$46,475	$51,123
Plus: Desired ending inventory	4,225	?	?
Inventory needed	46,475	?	?
Less: Beginning inventory	10,000	?	?
Required purchases (on account)	$36,475	$46,898	$51,587

Required

a. Complete the inventory purchases budget by filling in the missing amounts.
b. Determine the amount of cost of goods sold that will appear on the company's second quarter pro forma income statement.
c. Determine the amount of ending inventory that will appear on the company's second quarter pro forma balance sheet at the end of the second quarter.

EXERCISE 7-8   *Preparation of Schedule of Cash Payments for Inventory Purchases*   **L.O. 7**

Boyd Wholesale Books buys books and magazines directly from publishers and distributes them to grocery stores. The wholesaler expects to purchase the following inventory:

	April	May	June
Required purchases (on account)	$40,000	$50,000	$60,000

Boyd's accountant prepared the following schedule of cash payments for inventory purchases. Boyd's suppliers require that 95 percent of purchases on account be paid in the month of purchase; the remaining 5 percent are paid in the month following the month of purchase.

Schedule of Cash Payments for Inventory Purchases			
	April	May	June
Payment for current accounts payable	$38,000	?	?
Payment for previous accounts payable	2,400	?	?
Total budgeted payments for inventory	$40,400	$49,500	$59,500

Required

a. Complete the schedule of cash payments for inventory purchases by filling in the missing amounts.
b. Determine the amount of accounts payable that will appear on the company's pro forma balance sheet at the end of the second quarter.

L.O. 7 EXERCISE 7-9   *Determination of Amount of Expected Inventory Purchases and Cash Payments*

Reco Company, which sells electric razors, had $178,000 of cost of goods sold during the month of June. The company projects a 5 percent increase in cost of goods sold during July. The inventory balance as of June 30 is $18,400, and the desired ending inventory balance for July is $15,900. Reco pays cash to settle 80 percent of its purchases on account during the month of purchase and pays the remaining 20 percent in the month following the purchase. The accounts payable balance as of June 30 was $22,000.

Required

a. Determine the amount of budgeted purchases required for July.
b. Determine the amount of budgeted cash payment for inventory purchases in July.

L.O. 8 EXERCISE 7-10   *Preparation of Schedule of Cash Payments for Selling and Administrative Expenses*

The budget director for Watson Window Cleaning Services prepared the following list of expected operating expenses. All items that must be paid are paid when incurred except salary expense and insurance. Salary is paid in the month following the month in which it is incurred. The insurance premium is paid in on October 1 for six months. October is the first month of operations; accordingly, there are no beginning account balances.

Budgeted Operating Expenses	October	November	December
Equipment lease expense	$ 4,000	$ 4,000	$ 4,000
Salary expense	3,250	3,575	3,933
Cleaning supplies	1,300	1,430	1,573
Insurance expense	500	500	500
Amortization on computer	800	800	800
Rent	900	900	900
Miscellaneous expenses	250	250	250
Total Operating expenses	$11,000	$11,455	$11,956
Schedule of Cash Payments for Operating Expenses			
Equipment lease expense	?	?	?
Prior month's salary expense, 100 percent	?	?	?
Cleaning supplies	?	?	?
Insurance premium	?	?	?
Amortization on computer	?	?	?
Rent	?	?	?
Miscellaneous expenses	?	?	?
Total disbursements for operating expenses	$ 9,450	$ 9,830	$10,298

Required

a. Complete the schedule of cash payments for operating expenses by filling in the missing amounts.
b. Determine the amount of salaries payable that will appear on the company's pro forma balance sheet at the end of the fourth quarter.

c. Determine the amount of prepaid insurance that will appear on the company's pro forma balance sheet at the end of the fourth quarter.

EXERCISE 7-11   *Preparation of Inventory Purchases Budgets with Different Assumptions*   **L.O. 7**

Executive officers of Pizitz Company are wrestling with their budget for the next year. The following are two different sales estimates provided from two different sources:

Sources of Estimate	First Quarter	Second Quarter	Third Quarter	Fourth Quarter
Sales manager	$250,000	$200,000	$180,000	$320,000
Marketing consultant	$275,000	$240,000	$200,000	$300,000

Pizitz's past experience indicates that cost of goods sold is about 70 percent of sales revenue. The company tries to maintain 10 percent of the next quarter's expected cost of goods sold as the current quarter's ending inventory. This year's ending inventory is $15,000. For budgeting, next year's ending inventory is determined to be $16,000.

Required
a. Prepare an inventory purchases budget using the sales manager's estimate.
b. Prepare an inventory purchases budget using the marketing consultant's estimate.

EXERCISE 7-12   *Determination of Amount of Cash Payments and Pro Forma Statement Data for Selling and Administrative Expenses*   **L.O. 8, 10**

Budgeted selling and administrative expenses for the retail shoe store that Lin Ho Ding plans to open on January 1, 2001, are as follows: sales commissions, $6,500; rent, $5,000; utilities, $3,000; amortization, $2,400; and miscellaneous, $800. Utilities are paid in the month following their incursion. Other expenses are expected to be paid in cash in the month in which they are incurred.

Required
a. Determine the amount of budgeted cash payments for selling and administrative expenses for January.
b. Determine the amount of utilities payable that will appear on the January 31 pro forma balance sheet.
c. Determine the amount of amortization expense that would appear on the income statement for the year 2001.

EXERCISE 7-13   *Preparation of Cash Budget*   **L.O. 9, 10**

The accountant for Della's Dress Shop prepared the following cash budget. Della's desires to maintain a cash cushion of $7,000 before the interest payment at the end of each month. Funds are assumed to be borrowed and repaid on the first day of each month. Interest is charged at the rate of 2 percent per month. The company had a beginning balance in its line-of-credit loan of $20,000.

Cash Budget	July	August	September
Beginning cash balance	$ 9,000	?	?
Add: Cash receipts	80,000	$94,000	$112,800
Cash available before current financing activity (a)	$89,000	?	?
Less: Disbursements			
For inventory purchases	$76,763	$67,115	$ 82,076
For S&A expenses	22,250	27,280	28,216
Total budgeted disbursements (b)	$99,013	?	?
Payments minus receipts			
Shortage (surplus)	$10,013	?	?
Plus: Cash cushion	7,000	?	?
Financing activity			
Borrowing (repayment) (c)	17,013	?	?
Interest expense at 2 percent per month (d)	(740)	?	?
Ending cash balance (a − b + c − d)	$ 6,260	$ 6,237	$ 6,272

Required

a. Complete the cash budget by filling in the missing amounts. (Round all computations to the nearest whole dollar.)

b. Determine the amount of net cash flows from operating activities that will appear on the company's third quarter pro forma cash flow statement.

c. Determine the amount of net cash flows from financing activities that will appear on the company's third quarter pro forma cash flow statement.

L.O. 9, 10 EXERCISE 7-14   *Determination of Amount to Borrow and Pro Forma Statement Balances*

Camilla Castelluccio owns a small restaurant in Calgary, Alberta. Ms. Castelluccio provided her accountant with the following summary information regarding expectations for the month of June. The balance in accounts receivable as of May 31 is $24,000. Budgeted cash and credit sales for June are $44,000 and $230,000, respectively. Credit sales are made through Visa and MasterCard and are collected rapidly. Ninety percent of credit sales are collected in the month of sale, and the remainder is collected in the following month. Ms. Castelluccio's suppliers do not extend credit. Cash payments for June are expected to be $310,000. Ms. Castelluccio has a line of credit that enables the restaurant to borrow funds on demand; however, they must be borrowed on the first day of the month. Interest is paid in cash on the last day of the month. Ms. Castelluccio desires to maintain a $10,000 cash balance before consideration is given to the payment of interest. Her annual interest rate is 9 percent.

Required

a. Compute the amount of funds that needs to be borrowed.

b. Determine the amount of interest expense that will appear on the June pro forma income statement.

c. What amount will be shown as interest payable on the June 30 pro forma balance sheet?

L.O. 10 EXERCISE 7-15   *Preparation of Pro Forma Income Statement with Different Assumptions*

Steve Martin, the controller of Quick Corporation, is trying to prepare a sales budget for the next year. His staff has prepared the income statements of the last four quarters as follows:

	First Quarter	Second Quarter	Third Quarter	Fourth Quarter	Total
Sales revenue	$125,000	$120,000	$132,000	$223,000	$600,000
Cost of goods sold	75,000	72,000	79,200	133,800	360,000
Gross profit	50,000	48,000	52,800	89,200	240,000
Selling & admin. expense	25,000	24,000	26,400	44,600	120,000
Net income	$ 25,000	$ 24,000	$ 26,400	$ 44,600	$120,000

From experience, the cost of goods sold is about 60 percent of the sales revenue. The selling and administrative expenses are about 20 percent of the sales revenue.

Jack Quick, chief executive officer, told Mr. Martin that he expected the sales next year to be 10 percent above last year's level. However, June Kessler, vice-president of sales, told Mr. Martin that she believed the sales growth would be only 5 percent.

Required

a. Prepare a pro forma income statement for the next year using Mr. Quick's estimate.

b. Prepare a pro forma income statement for the next year using Ms. Kessler's estimate.

c. Explain why two executive officers in the same company could have different opinions as to future growth.

PROBLEMS—SERIES A

L.O. 6 PROBLEM 7-1A   *Preparation of Sales Budget and Schedule of Cash Receipts*

Penson Pointers, Co. expects to begin operations on January 1, 2006; it will operate as a specialty sales company that sells laser pointers over the Internet. Penson expects sales in January 2006 to total $25,000 and to increase 10 percent per month in February and March. All sales are on account. Penson expects to collect 60 percent of accounts receivable in the month of sale, 30 percent in the month following the sale, and 10 percent in the second month following the sale.

Required

a. Prepare a sales budget for the first quarter of 2006.
b. Determine the amount of sales revenue that would appear on the March 31, 2006, quarterly pro forma income statement.
c. Prepare a cash receipts schedule for the first quarter of 2006.
d. Determine the amount of accounts receivable as of March 31, 2006.

PROBLEM 7-2A   *Preparation of Inventory Purchases Budget and Schedule of Cash Payments*   **L.O. 7, 10**

Dyn-O-Mite, sells fire works. The company's marketing director developed the following budget of cost of goods sold for April, May, and June:

	April	May	June
Budgeted cost of goods sold	$20,000	$25,000	$40,000

Dyn-O-Mite had a beginning inventory balance of $1,800 on April 1 and a beginning balance in accounts payable of $7,400. The company desires to maintain an ending inventory balance equal to 10 percent of the current period's cost of goods sold. Dyn-O-Mite makes all purchases on account. The company pays 60 percent of the accounts payable in the month of purchase and the remaining 40 percent in the month following the purchase.

Required

a. Prepare an inventory purchases budget for April, May, and June.
b. Determine the amount of ending inventory that will appear on the end-of-quarter pro forma balance sheet.
c. Prepare a schedule of cash payments for inventory for April, May, and June.
d. Determine the balance in accounts payable that will appear on the end-of-quarter pro forma balance sheet.

PROBLEM 7-3A   *Preparation of Pro Forma Income Statements with Different Assumptions*   **L.O. 10**

Top executive officers of Newell Company, a merchandising firm, are preparing the next year's budget. The controller has provided everyone with the current year's estimated income statement.

	Current Year
Sales revenue	$ 800,000
Cost of goods sold	480,000
Gross profit	320,000
Selling & admin. expenses	260,000
Net Income	$ 60,000

Cost of goods sold is usually 60 percent of sales revenue, and selling and administrative expenses are usually 20 percent of sales plus a fixed cost of $100,000. The president has announced that the company's goal is to increase the net income by 15 percent.

Required

Consider the following items to be independent of each other:

a. What percentage of increase in sales would enable to company to reach its goal? Prepare a pro forma income statement that achieves the company's goal.
b. The market may become stagnant next year, and the company does not expect an increase in sales revenue. The production manager believes that under an improved production procedure, the cost of goods sold can be cut by 2 percent. What else can the company do to reach its goal? Prepare a pro forma income statement under your proposal.
c. The company decides to escalate its advertising campaign to boost its consumer recognition, which will increase selling and administrative expenses to $320,000. With the increased advertising, the company expects sales revenue to increase by 15 percent. Assume that cost of goods sold remains a constant proportion to sales. Can the company reach its goal?

L.O. 8, 9   PROBLEM 7-4A   *Preparation of Schedule of Cash Payments for Selling and Administrative Expenses*

On Top is a retail company specializing in men's hats. Its budget director prepared the list of expected operating expenses that follows. All items are paid when incurred except sales commissions and utilities, which are paid in the month following their incursion. July is the first month of operations. Accordingly, there are no beginning account balances.

	July	August	September
Salary expense	$5,000	$5,000	$5,000
Sales commissions (4 percent of sales)	720	800	880
Supplies expense	180	200	220
Utilities	600	600	600
Amortization on store equipment	1,300	1,300	1,300
Rent	3,300	3,300	3,300
Miscellaneous	360	360	360
Total S&A expenses before interest	$11,460	$11,560	$11,660

Required

a. Prepare a schedule of cash payments for selling and administrative expenses.
b. Determine the amount of utilities payable as of September 30.
c. Determine the amount of sales commissions payable as of September 30.

L.O. 9   PROBLEM 7-5A   *Preparation of Cash Budget*

Scarborough Medical has budgeted the following cash flows:

	January	February	March
Cash receipts	$80,000	$94,000	$112,800
Cash payments			
For inventory purchases	76,763	67,115	82,076
For S&A expenses	21,400	26,280	27,216

Scarborough Medical had a cash balance of $9,000 on January 1. The company desires to maintain a cash cushion of $5,000 before making a monthly interest payment. Funds are assumed to be borrowed on the first day of each month and repaid on the last day of each month; the interest rate is 1 percent per month. The company had a $35,000 beginning balance in its line of credit liability account.

Required

Prepare a cash budget. (Round all computations to the nearest whole dollar.)

L.O. 6, 7, 8   PROBLEM 7-6A   *Preparation of Budgets with Multiple Products*

Jenkins Fruits Corporation wholesales peaches and oranges. Julia Jenkins is working with the company's accountant to prepare next year's budget. Ms. Jenkins estimates that sales will increase 5 percent annually for peaches and 10 percent for oranges. The following is the current year's data of sales revenue:

	First Quarter	Second Quarter	Third Quarter	Fourth Quarter	Total
Peaches	$120,000	$125,000	$150,000	$125,000	$520,000
Oranges	200,000	225,000	285,000	190,000	900,000
Total	$320,000	$350,000	$435,000	$315,000	$1,420,000

According to the company's past experience, cost of goods sold is usually 60 percent of sales revenue. Company policy is to keep 20 percent of the next period's estimated cost of goods sold as the current period's ending inventory. (*Hint:* Use the cost of goods sold of the first quarter to determine the beginning inventory.)

Required

a. Prepare the company's sales budget for the next year for each quarter and according to individual products.

b. If the selling and administrative expenses are estimated to be $350,000, prepare the company's budgeted annual income statement.

c. Ms. Jenkins estimates next year's ending inventory will be $17,000 for peaches and $28,000 for oranges. Prepare the company's inventory purchases budgets of the next year showing quarterly figures by product.

PROBLEM 7-7A *Preparation of Master Budget for Retail Company with No Beginning Account Balances* **L.O. 6, 7, 8**

Red Rock Mountain Company is a retail company that specializes in the sale of outdoor camping equipment. The company is considering opening a new store on October 1, 2003. The planning committee has been given the task of preparing a master budget for the first three months of operation. Assume that you are the budget coordinator and have been asked to compile the budget using the following information.

Required

a. October sales are estimated to be $50,000 of which 40 percent will be cash and 60 percent will be credit. The company expects sales to increase at the rate of 25 percent per month. Prepare a sales budget.

b. The company expects to collect 100 percent of the accounts receivable generated by credit sales in the month following the sale. Prepare a schedule of cash receipts.

c. The cost of goods sold is 60 percent of sales. The company desires to maintain a minimum ending inventory equal to 10 percent of the current month's cost of goods sold. Assume that all purchases are made on account. Prepare an inventory purchases budget.

d. The company pays 70 percent of accounts payable in the month of purchase and the remaining 30 percent in the following month. Prepare a cash payments budget for inventory purchases.

e. Budgeted selling and administrative expenses per month follow:

Salary expense (fixed)	$8,000
Sales commissions	5 percent of Sales
Supplies expense	2 percent of Sales
Utilities (fixed)	$ 700
Amortization on store equipment (fixed)*	$2,000
Rent (fixed)	$2,400
Miscellaneous (fixed)	$600

*The capital expenditures budget indicates that Red Rock will be required to spend $82,000 on October 1 for store fixtures, which are expected to have a $10,000 salvage value and a three-year (36-month) useful life.

Use this information to prepare a selling and administrative expense budget.

f. Utilities and sales commissions are paid the month after they are incurred; all other expenses are paid in the month in which they are incurred. Prepare a cash payments budget for selling and administrative expense.

g. Red Rock borrows funds and repays them on the first day of the month. It pays interest of 1 percent per month in cash on the last day of the month. The company desires to maintain a $12,000 cash cushion to maintain a reasonable cash balance before paying interest. Prepare a cash budget.

h. Prepare a pro forma income statement for the quarter.

i. Prepare a pro forma balance sheet at the end of the quarter.

j. Prepare a pro forma cash flow statement for the quarter.

PROBLEM 7-8A *Behavioural Considerations of Budgeting* **L.O. 4**

Cedar Ridge Corporation has three divisions, each operating as a responsibility centre. To provide an incentive for divisional executive officers, the company gives divisional management a bonus equal to 20 percent of the excess of the actual net income over its budget. The following is North Shore Division's current year's performance:

	Current Year
Sales revenue	$1,800,000
Cost of goods sold	1,080,000
Gross profit	$ 720,000
Selling & admin. expenses	360,000
Net income	$ 360,000

The president has just received a budget proposal from the vice-president in charge of North Shore Division. The proposal includes a 5 percent increase of sales revenue and an extensive explanation about stiff market competition. The president is puzzled. North Shore has enjoyed an increase of around 10 percent for each of the past five years. The president had consistently approved the division's budget proposal of 5 percent growth in the past. This time, the president is unhappy. He wants to show that he is not a fool. "I will impose a 15 percent increase to teach them a lesson!" the president says to himself triumphantly.

Assume that cost of goods sold and selling and administrative expenses remain stable in proportion to sales.

Required

a. Prepare the budgeted income statement according to North Shore Division's proposal containing a 5 percent increase.
b. If growth is actually 10 percent as usual, how much bonus would North Shore Division's executive officers receive, assuming that the president eventually approves the division's proposal?
c. Prepare the budgeted income statement according to the 15 percent increase the president contemplates.
d. If the actual results turn out to be a 10 percent increase as usual, how much bonus would North Shore Division's executive officers receive, assuming that the president eventually imposes a 15 percent increase?
e. Propose a better procedure of budgeting for Cedar Ridge.

PROBLEMS—SERIES B

L.O. 6 PROBLEM 7-1B   *Preparation of Sales Budget and Schedule of Cash Receipts*

Albeiz Corporation sells computers through mail order. In December 2003, Albeiz has generated $350,000 of sales revenue, the company expects a 20 percent increase in sales in January and 10 percent in February. All sales are on account. Albeiz normally collects 80 percent of accounts receivable in the month of sale and 20 percent in the next month.

Required

a. Prepare a sales budget for January and February 2004.
b. Determine the amount of sales revenue that would appear on the February 29, 2004, bimonthly pro forma income statement.
c. Prepare a cash receipts schedule for January and February 2004.
d. Determine the amount of accounts receivable as of February 29, 2004.

L.O. 7, 10 PROBLEM 7-2B   *Preparation of Inventory Purchases Budget and Schedule of Cash Payments*

Swanson Company's purchasing manager, Ken Specter, is preparing a proposed purchases budget for the next quarter. On his request, Betsy Feazell, the manager of the sales department, forwarded him the following preliminary sales budget:

	October	November	December
Budgeted sales	$320,000	$384,000	$480,000

For budgeting purposes, Swanson estimates that cost of goods sold is 75 percent of sales. The company desires to maintain an ending inventory balance equal to 20 percent of the current period's cost of goods sold. The September ending inventory is $60,000. Swanson makes all purchases on account and pays 70 percent of the accounts payable in the month of purchase and the remaining 30 percent in the following month. The balance of accounts payable at the end of September is $45,000.

Required

a. Prepare an inventory purchases budget for October, November, and December.
b. Determine the amount of ending inventory that will appear on the end-of-quarter pro forma balance sheet.
c. Prepare a schedule of cash payments for inventory for October, November, and December.
d. Determine the balance in accounts payable that will appear on the end-of-quarter pro forma balance sheet.

PROBLEM 7-3B   Preparation of Pro Forma Income Statements with Different Assumptions   L.O. 10

Sammy Rohling, a successful entrepreneur, is reviewing the result of his first year of business. The following is the income statement that his accountant delivered just five minutes ago:

	Current Year
Sales revenue	$500,000
Cost of goods sold	320,000
Gross profit	$180,000
Selling & admin. expenses	110,000
Net income	$ 70,000

Mr. Rohling would like to have a 20 percent increase in net income in the next year. For this first year, selling and administrative expenses are 10 percent of the sales revenue plus $60,000 of fixed expenses.

Required

Consider the following questions to be independent of each other:

a. Mr. Rohling expects that cost of goods sold and variable selling and administrative expenses will remain stable in proportion to sales in the next year. The fixed selling and administrative expenses will increase to $72,000. What percentage of increase in sales would enable to company to reach its goal? Prepare a pro forma income statement for Mr. Rohling.
b. Market competition may become serious next year, and Mr. Rohling does not expect an increase in sales revenue. However, he has developed a good relationship with the supplier, who is willing to give him a volume discount that will decrease cost of goods sold by 3 percent. What else can the company do to reach its goal? Prepare a pro forma income statement under your proposal.
c. If the company decides to escalate its advertising campaign to boost its consumer recognition, the selling and administrative expenses will increase to $200,000. With the increased advertising, the company expects sales revenue to increase by 25 percent. Assume that cost of goods sold remains constant in proportion to sales. Can the company reach its goal?

PROBLEM 7-4B   Preparation of Schedule of Cash Payments for Selling and Administrative Expense   L.O. 8

Hamilton Travel Services, Inc. has prepared its selling and administrative expense budget for the next quarter. It pays all items when they are incurred except sales commissions, advertising expense, and telephone expense. These three items are paid in the month following the one in which they are incurred. January is the first month of operations. Accordingly, there are no beginning account balances.

	January	February	March
Salary expense	$ 4,000	$ 4,000	$ 4,000
Sales commissions	300	320	400
Advertising expense	250	250	300
Telephone expense	500	540	550
Amortization on store equipment	2,000	2,000	2,000
Rent	5,000	5,000	5,000
Miscellaneous	400	400	400
Total S&A expenses before interest	$12,450	$12,510	$12,650

Required

a. Prepare a schedule of cash payments for selling and administrative expense.
b. Determine the amount of telephone payable as of March 31.
c. Determine the amount of sales commissions payable as of February 28.

L.O. 9 PROBLEM 7-5B   *Preparation of Cash Budget*

Z-Mart has budgeted the following cash flows:

	April	May	June
Cash receipts	$150,000	$225,000	$302,000
Cash payments			
For inventory purchases	195,000	200,000	220,000
For S&A expenses	40,000	53,000	66,000

Z-Mart had an $18,000 cash balance on April 1. The company desires to maintain a $30,000 cash cushion before paying interest. Funds are assumed to be borrowed on the first day of each month and repaid on the last day of each month; the interest rate is 1.5 percent per month. The company had a $75,000 beginning balance in its line-of-credit liability account.

Required

Prepare a cash budget. (Round all computations to the nearest whole dollar.)

L.O. 6, 7, 8 PROBLEM 7-6B   *Preparation of Budgets with Multiple Products*

Khades Enterprises, has two products: palm-size computers and programmable calculators. Janice Walls, the chief executive officer, is working with her staff to prepare next year's budget. Ms. Walls estimates that sales will increase at an annual rate of 20 percent for palm-size computers and 5 percent for programmable calculators. The following are the current year's data of sales revenue:

	First Quarter	Second Quarter	Third Quarter	Fourth Quarter	Total
Palm-size computers	$500,000	$550,000	$620,000	$ 730,000	$2,400,000
Programmable calculators	250,000	275,000	290,000	325,000	1,140,000
Total	$750,000	$825,000	$910,000	$1,055,000	$3,540,000

According to the company's past experience, cost of goods sold is usually 75 percent of sales revenue. The company policy is to keep 10 percent of the next period's estimated cost of goods sold as the current period's ending inventory.

Required

a. Prepare the company's sales budget for the next year for each quarter and according to individual products.
b. If the selling and administrative expenses are estimated to be $600,000, prepare the company's budgeted annual income statement for the next year.
c. Ms. Walls estimates the current year's ending inventory will be $78,000 for computers and $32,000 for calculators and the ending inventory of the next year will be $88,000 for computers and $42,000 for calculators. Prepare the company's inventory purchases budget of the next year showing quarterly figures by product.

L.O. 6, 7, 8 PROBLEM 7-7B   *Preparation of Master Budget for Retail Company with No Beginning Account Balances*

New World Gifts Corporation begins business today, December 31, 2001. Judy Sestak, the president, is trying to prepare the company's master budget for the first three months (January, February, and March) of 2002. As her good friend and a business student, Ms. Sestak asks you to prepare the budget in accordance with the following specifications.

Required

a. January sales are estimated to be $100,000, of which 30 percent will be cash and 70 percent will be credit. The company expects sales to increase at the rate of 10 percent per month. Prepare a sales budget.
b. The company expects to collect 100 percent of the accounts receivable generated by credit sales in the month following the sale. Prepare a schedule of cash receipts.
c. The cost of goods sold is 50 percent of sales. The company desires to maintain a minimum ending inventory equal to 20 percent of the current month's cost of goods sold. Assume that all purchases are made on account. Prepare an inventory purchases budget.

d. The company pays 60 percent of accounts payable in the month of purchase and the remaining 40 percent in the following month. Prepare a cash payments budget for inventory purchases.

e. Budgeted selling and administrative expense per month follows:

Salary expense (fixed)	$10,000
Sales commissions	8 percent of Sales
Supplies expense	4 percent of Sales
Utilities (fixed)	$ 900
Amortizarion on store equipment (fixed)*	$ 2,500
Rent (fixed)	$ 3,600
Miscellaneous (fixed)	$ 1,000

*The capital expenditures budget indicates that New World will be required to spend $175,000 on January 1 for store fixtures. The fixtures are expected to have a $25,000 salvage value and a five-year (60-month) useful life.

Use this information to prepare a selling and administrative expense budget.

f. Utilities and sales commissions are paid the month after they are incurred; all other expenses are paid in the month in which they are incurred. Prepare a cash payments budget for selling and administrative expense.

g. The company borrows funds and repays them on the first day of the month. It pays interest of 1.5 percent per month in cash on the last day of the month. The company desires to maintain a $25,000 cash cushion to maintain a reasonable cash balance before paying interest. Prepare a cash budget.

h. Prepare a pro forma income statement for the quarter.

i. Prepare a pro forma balance sheet at the end of the quarter.

j. Prepare a pro forma cash flow statement for the quarter.

PROBLEM 7-8B   *Behavioural Considerations of Budgeting*   **L.O. 4**

Jennifer Roozen, the director of Summit Corporation's Mail Order Division, is in the process of preparing the division's budget proposal for the next year. The company's president will review the proposal for approval. Ms. Roozen estimates the current year's operating results to be the following:

	Current Year
Sales revenue	$4,800,000
Cost of goods sold	2,640,000
Gross profit	2,160,000
Selling & admin. expenses	960,000
Net income	$1,200,000

Ms. Roozen believes that the cost of goods sold as well as selling and administrative expense will continue to be stable in proportion to sales revenue.

Summit has an incentive policy to reward divisional managers whose performance exceeds their budget. Divisional directors are given a 10 percent bonus based on the excess of actual net income over the division's budget. For the last two years, Ms. Roozen has proposed a 4 percent rate of increase, which was proven accurate. However, her honesty and accuracy in forecasting caused her to receive no year-end bonus at all. She is pondering whether she should do something differently this time. If she continues to be honest, she should propose an 8 percent growth rate because of robust market demand. Alternatively, she can propose a 4 percent growth rate as usual and thereby could expect to receive some bonus at year end.

Required

a. Prepare the proposed pro forma income statement, assuming a 4 percent estimated increase.

b. Prepare the proposed pro forma income statement, assuming an 8 percent increase.

c. If growth actually is 8 percent, how much bonus would Ms. Roozen receive, assuming that the president eventually approves the division's proposal with the 4 percent growth rate.

d. Propose a better budgeting procedure for Summit Corporation.

ANALYZE, THINK, COMMUNICATE

ACT 7-1 BUSINESS APPLICATIONS CASE *Preparation and Use of Pro Forma Statements*

Bill Davis is a student enrolled at The University of Alberta and plans to subsidize his education by starting a company that rents computer equipment to his fellow students. He has negotiated a line of credit with the Bank of Montreal. The credit line permits Mr. Davis to borrow up to $2,000 at 10 percent interest, which is payable in cash on December 31 of each year. Mr. Davis plans to borrow the entire $2,000 amount on January 1, 2001. He plans to use the money to purchase a computer expected to have a useful life of two years and a $500 salvage value. Rent revenue is projected to be $100 cash per month. At December 31, 2002, Mr. Davis plans to sell the computer and repay the bank loan.

Required

a. On the basis of the information provided, prepare a pro forma income statement, balance sheet, and cash flow statement for 2001 and 2002.

b. Review the pro forma statements and recommend how Mr. Davis could improve profitability. Your recommendation(s) should result in real profit improvement. Accounting manipulation, such as extending the life of the asset or increasing its salvage value, is not acceptable. Furthermore, you are not permitted to increase the amount borrowed, reduce the interest rate, or raise revenues.

ACT 7-2 GROUP ASSIGNMENT *Master Budget and Pro Forma Statements*

The following trial balance was drawn from the records of Zimmerman Company as of October 1, 2002:

Cash	8,000	
Accounts receivable	30,000	
Inventory	20,000	
Equipment	100,000	
Accumulated amortization		38,400
Accounts payable		36,000
Line-of-credit loan		50,000
Common stock		25,000
Retained earnings		8,600
Totals	158,000	158,000

Required

a. Divide the class into groups, each with 4 or 5 students. Organize the groups into three sections. Assign Task 1 to the first section, Task 2 to the second section, and Task 3 to the third section.

Group Tasks

1. On the basis of the following information, prepare a sales budget and a schedule of cash receipts for October, November, and December. Sales for October are expected to be $90,000, of which $20,000 is cash and $70,000 is credit. The company expects sales to increase at the rate of 10 percent per month. All of accounts receivable is collected in the month following the sale.

2. On the basis of the following information, prepare a purchases budget and a schedule of cash payments for inventory purchases for October, November, and December. The inventory balance as of October 1 was $20,000. The amount of cost of goods sold for October is expected to be $36,000. Cost of goods sold is expected to increase by 10 percent per month. The company desires to maintain a minimum ending inventory equal to 20 percent of the current month's cost of goods sold. Seventy-five percent of accounts payable is paid in the month that the purchase occurs, the remaining 25 percent is paid in the following month.

3. On the basis of the following selling and administrative expense budgeted for October, prepare a selling and administrative expense budget for October, November, and December.

Sales commissions (10% increase per month)	$3,600
Supplies expense (10% increase per month)	900
Utilities (fixed)	1,100
Amortization on store equipment (fixed)	800
Salary expense (fixed)	17,000
Rent (fixed)	3,000
Miscellaneous (fixed)	500

Cash payments for sales commissions and utilities are made in the month following the one in which the expense is incurred. Supplies and other operating expenses are paid in cash in the month in which they are incurred.

b. Select a representative from each section. Have the representatives supply the missing information in the following pro forma income statement and balance sheet for the fourth quarter of 2002. The statements are prepared as of December 31, 2002.

Income Statement

Sales Revenue	$?
Cost of Goods Sold	?
Gross Margin	178,740
Operating Expenses	?
Operating Income	96,645
Interest Expense	(1,265)
Net Income	$ 95,380

Balance Sheet

Assets		
Cash		$ 4,880
Accounts Receivable		?
Inventory		?
Store Equipment	$100,000	
Accumulated Amortization Store Equipment	?	
Book Value of Equipment		59,200
Total Assets		$157,492
Liabilities		
Accounts Payable		?
Utilities Payable		?
Sales Commissions Payable		?
Line of Credit		11,968
Equity		
Common Stock		25,000
Retained Earnings		?
Total Liabilities and Equity		$157,492

c. Indicate whether Zimmerman will need to borrow money during October.

WRITING ASSIGNMENT *Continuous Budgeting*

ACT 7-3

HON Company is the largest maker of midpriced office furniture in the United States and Canada. Its management has expressed dissatisfaction with its *annual* budget system. Fierce competition requires businesses to be flexible and innovative. Unfortunately, building the effects of innovation into an annual budget is difficult because actions and outcomes often are evolutionary. Innovation unfolds as the year progresses. Consequently, HON's management team reached the conclusion that "when production processes undergo continuous change, standards developed annually for static conditions no longer offer meaningful targets for gauging their success."

Required

Assume that you are HON Company's budget director. Write a memo to the management team explaining how the practice of continuous budgeting could be used to overcome the shortcomings of an annual budget process.

ACT 7-4 ETHICAL DILEMMA   *Bad Budget System or Unethical Behaviour?*

Clarence Cleaver is the budget director for the Harris School District. Mr. Cleaver recently sent out an urgent e-mail message to Sally Simmons, principal of West Harris High. The message severely reprimanded Ms. Simmons for failing to spend the funds allocated to her for the purchase of computer equipment. Ms. Simmons responded that her school already had a sufficient supply of computers; indeed, the computer lab is never filled to capacity and usually was less than half filled. Ms. Simmons suggested that she would rather use the funds for teacher training. She argued that the reason the existing computers were not being used was that the teachers did not have a level of computer literacy necessary to make assignments for their students.

Mr. Cleaver responded that it was not Ms. Simmons' job to decide how the money was to be spent; this was the job of the board of education. It was the principal's job to spend the money as the board directed. He informed Ms. Simmons that if the money was not spent by the fiscal closing date, the board of education would likely reduce next year's budget allotment. To avoid a potential budget cut, Mr. Cleaver re-allocated Ms. Simmons' computer funds to Jules Carrington, principal of East Harris High. Mr. Carrington knew how to buy computers, regardless of whether they were needed or not. Mr. Cleaver's final words were, "Don't blame me if parents of West High students complain that East High has more equipment. If anybody comes to me, I'm telling them that you turned down the money."

Required

Explain how participative budgeting could improve the allocation of resources for the Harris School District.

ACT 7-5 SPREADSHEET ASSIGNMENT   *Using Excel*

Refer to Exercise 7-13. In the fourth quarter of the same year, the cash budget for Della's Dress Shop appears in the following spreadsheet:

		October	November	December
Desired Cash Cushion		$ 7,000		
Interest rate per month		2%		
Beginning loan balance		$36,403	$51,531	$54,262
Beginning Cash Balance		$ 6,272	$ 5,969	$ 5,915
Add Cash Receipts		82,000	96,000	115,000
Cash Available before Current Financing Activity (a)		88,272	101,969	120,915
Less Disbursements				
For Inventory Purchases		75,400	69,500	81,400
For S&A Expenses		21,000	28,200	29,200
Total Budgeted Disbursements (b)		96,400	97,700	110,600
Payments Minus Receipts				
Shortage (Surplus)		8,128	(4,269)	(10,315)
Plus Cash Cushion		7,000	7,000	7,000
Financing Activity				
Borrowing (Repayment)		15,128	2,731	(3,315)
Interest Expense		(1,031)	(1,085)	(1,019)
Ending Cash Balance		$ 5,969	$ 5,915	$ 5,981
Loan Balance		$51,531	$54,262	$50,947

Chapter 7 - Working with Excel   Name:

Required

Construct a spreadsheet to model the cash budget as in the following screen capture. Be sure to use formulas where possible so that any changes to the estimates will be automatically reflected in the spreadsheet.

Spreadsheet Tips
1. Rows 11, 15, 17, 18, 20 to 22, and 24 should be based on formulas.
2. Cells F6, H6, F9, and H9 should be based on formulas also. For example, Cell F6 should be =D24.

SPREADSHEET ASSIGNMENT   *Mastering Excel*   ACT 7-6

Spitzer Company has collected sales forecasts for next year from three people.

Sources of Sales Estimate	First Quarter	Second Quarter	Third Quarter	Fourth Quarter
a. Sales manager	$520,000	$410,000	$370,000	$610,000
b. Marketing consultant	540,000	480,000	400,000	630,000
c. Production manager	460,000	360,000	350,000	580,000

They have estimated that the cost of goods sold is 70 percent of sales. The company tries to maintain 10 percent of next quarter's expected cost of goods sold as the current quarter's ending inventory. The ending inventory of this year is $25,000. For budgeting, the ending inventory this year is expected to be $28,000.

Required

Construct a spreadsheet that allows the inventory purchases budget to be prepared for each of the preceding estimates.

Spreadsheet Tip
The VLOOKUP function can be used to choose one line of the preceding estimates. See the spreadsheet tips in Chapter 6 for an explanation of VLOOKUP.

Performance Evaluation

After completing this chapter, you should be able to:

1 Distinguish between flexible and static budgets.

2 Understand how spreadsheet software can be used to prepare flexible budgets.

3 Compute revenue and cost variances and interpret those variances as indicating favourable or unfavourable performance.

4 Compute sales activity variances (differences between static and flexible budgets) and explain how the volume variance affects fixed and variable costs.

5 Compute and interpret flexible budget variances (differences between a flexible budget and actual results).

6 Appreciate the human response to flexible budget variances.

7 Appreciate the process of setting standards.

8 Understand the criteria for selecting the most appropriate variances for investigation.

9 Calculate price and usage variances.

10 Identify the responsible parties for price and usage variances.

11 Understand the basic procedures for recording variances in a general ledger.

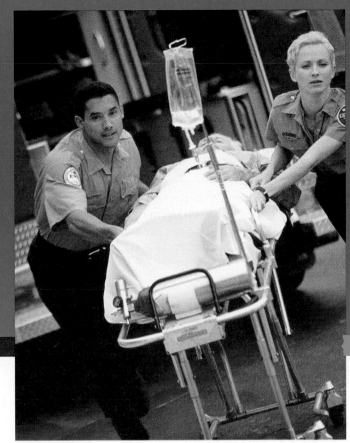

© Superstock

Memorial Hospital spent significantly more than it budgeted in serving its patients. Even so, the hospital administrators were congratulated for a job well done. What phenomenon could explain this apparent contradiction?

Suppose that you are a carpenter who makes picnic tables. You are normally expected to make 200 tables per year (i.e., the planned volume of activity*), but because of unexpected customer demand, you have been asked to make 225 tables (i.e., the* actual volume of activity*). You work hard and make the tables. Should you be criticized for using more materials, labour, or overhead than you normally use? Should the sales staff be criticized for selling more tables than expected? Obviously, the answer to both of these questions is, an emphatic no! Performance evaluation must be based on the* actual volume *of activity rather than the* planned volume *of activity. To facilitate planning and performance evaluation, managerial accountants frequently prepare budgets that are based on different levels of activity. These budgets are called flexible budgets. Their name is derived from the fact that the budget flexes or changes when the volume of activity changes.*

▮ Preparation of Flexible Budgets

LO1
Distinguish
between flexible
and static
budgets.

A **flexible budget** can be seen as an extension of the *master budget* that we discussed in Chapter 7. Recall that the master budget is based solely on the level of planned activity. Because of its rigid dependency on a single estimate of volume, the master budget is frequently called a **static budget**. In other words, the master budget remains static or stays the same when the volume of activity changes. Flexible budgets differ from static budgets in that they show the estimated amount of revenues and costs that are expected at a variety of levels of activity.

To illustrate the differences between static and flexible budgets, assume that Melrose Manufacturing Company makes small, high-quality statues that are used in award ceremonies. Melrose plans to make and sell 18,000 statues during its 2001 accounting period. Management's best estimates of the expected sales price and per unit costs for the statues are called *standard prices and costs*. The standard price and costs for the 18,000 statues follow:

Per-unit-sales price and variable costs	
Expected sales price	$ 80.00
Standard materials cost	12.00
Standard labour cost	16.80
Standard overhead cost	5.60
Standard general, selling, and administrative cost	15.00
Fixed costs	
Manufacturing cost	$201,600
General, selling, and administrative cost	90,000

LO2
Understand how
spreadsheet
software can be
used to prepare
flexible budgets.

Static and flexible budgets are based on the same per-unit *standard* amounts and the same fixed costs. The difference between the two budgets stems solely from the different volumes used to compute the budget amounts. Melrose Manufacturing's static budget is shown in Column D of the *Excel* spreadsheet in Exhibit 8–1. The amount of sales revenue and the amounts of the variable costs in Column D are determined by multiplying the per-unit standards shown in Column C by the number of units shown in Cell D4 (planned activity). For example, the amount of sales revenue shown in Cell D7 is determined by multiplying the per unit sales price in Cell C7 by the number of units shown in Cell D4 ($80 × 18,000 units = $1,440,000). The variable cost amounts are computed in a similar fashion. In each case, the cost-per-unit amount shown in Column C is multiplied by the planned activity shown in Cell D4.

Suppose that management wants to know what will happen to net income *if* actual volume is 16,000, 17,000, 18,000, 19,000, or 20,000 units. In other words, management wants to see a series of *flexible budgets*. This *what-if* information can be easily determined by using the computational power of the *Excel* spreadsheet. The formulas used to determine the static budget amounts in Column D can simply be copied to Columns F through J. Then, by changing the input variable to reflect the alternative levels of activity shown in Row 4, the appropriate amounts are calculated instantaneously. The result is the series of flexible budgets shown in Columns F through J.

The flexible budgets can be used for planning and performance evaluation. For example, managers may be able to evaluate the adequacy of the company's cash position by assuming different levels of activity. Similarly, the number of employees, the amounts of materials, and the necessary equipment and storage facilities can be evaluated for a variety of different potential activity levels. In addition to facilitating the planning activities, flexible budgets are critical to the implementation of an effective performance evaluation system.

Exhibit 8-1 *Static and Flexible Budgets in Excel Spreadsheet*

	Per-Unit Standards	Static Budget	Flexible Budgets				
Number of Units		18,000	16,000	17,000	18,000	19,000	20,000
Sales Revenue	$80.00	$1,440,000	$1,280,000	$1,360,000	$1,440,000	$1,520,000	$1,600,000
Variable Manuf. Costs							
Materials	$12.00	216000	192000	204000	216000	228000	240000
Labour	$16.80	302400	268800	285600	302400	319200	336000
Overhead	$5.60	100800	89600	95200	100800	106400	112000
Variable G,S,&A	$15.00	270000	240000	255000	270000	285000	300000
Contribution Margin		550,800	489,600	520,200	550,800	581,400	612,000
Fixed Costs							
Manufacturing		201,600	201,600	201,600	201,600	201,600	201,600
G,S,&A		90,000	90,000	90,000	90,000	90,000	90,000
Net Income		$259,200	$198,000	$228,600	$259,200	$289,800	$320,400

Determination of Variances for Performance Evaluation

LO3
Compute revenue and cost variances and interpret those variances as indicating favourable or unfavourable performance.

One means of evaluating managerial performance is to compare *standard* amounts with the *actual* results. The differences between the standard and actual amounts are called **variances**; they can be either *favourable* or *unfavourable*. Because managers seek to maximize revenue, a *favourable sales variance* occurs when actual sales revenue is higher than expected (i.e., standard) revenue. An *unfavourable sales variance* occurs when actual sales are lower than expected. Because managers try to minimize costs, *favourable cost variances* occur when actual costs are *lower than* standard costs. *Unfavourable cost variances* occur when actual costs are *higher* than standard costs. These relationships are summarized on the following page.

- When actual sales are higher than expected sales, variances are favourable.
- When actual sales are lower than expected sales, variances are unfavourable.
- When actual costs are higher than standard costs, variances are unfavourable.
- When actual costs are lower than standard costs, variances are favourable.

Sales Activity (Volume) Variances

LO4
Compute sales activity variances and explain how the volume variance affects fixed and variable costs.

The amount of a sales activity variance is calculated by determining the difference between the static budget, which is based on the planned volume, and a flexible budget prepared for the actual volume. This variance provides a measure of how effective managers have been in attaining the planned volume of activity. To illustrate, we assume that Melrose Manufacturing Company actually makes and sells

19,000 statues during 2001. Recall that the planned volume of activity was 18,000 statues. Melrose's static budget, flexible budget, and activity variances are shown in Exhibit 8–2.

Interpretation of the Sales and Variable Cost Variances

LO5

Compute and interpret flexible budget variances.

Because the static and flexible budgets are based on the same standard sales price and per-unit variable costs, the variances are solely attributable to the differences between the planned and actual volumes of activity. Marketing managers are usually held responsible for the volume variance. Because the volume of sales drives the level of production, production managers have little control over volume, although exceptions do occur. For example, the production manager is responsible for poor quality control in the production process that could lead to goods of low quality that are difficult to sell. Likewise, the production manager is responsible for delays in the production process that could affect the availability of products, which may restrict the volume of sales activity. Under normal circumstances, however, the marketing campaign controls the volume of sales. Upper-level marketing managers are on the front lines of the promotional program; they create the sales plan and are in the best position to explain why sales goals are or are not attained. When marketing managers talk about **making the numbers**, they are usually referring to their ability to attain the sales volume indicated in the master budget.

Exhibit 8-2

Melrose Manufacturing Company 's
Sales Volume Variances

	Static Budget	Flexible Budget	Activity Variances	
Number of units	18,000	19,000	1,000	Favourable
Sales revenue	$1,440,000	$1,520,000	$80,000	Favourable
Variable manufacturing costs				
Materials	216,000	228,000	12,000	Unfavourable
Labour	302,400	319,200	16,800	Unfavourable
Overhead	100,800	106,400	5,600	Unfavourable
Variable G,S,&A	270,000	285,000	15,000	Unfavourable
Contribution margin	550,800	581,400	30,600	Favourable
Fixed costs				
Manufacturing	201,600	201,600	0	
G,S,&A	90,000	90,000	0	
Net income	$ 259,200	$ 289,800	$30,600	Favourable

In the case of Melrose Manufacturing Company, the marketing manager not only made his numbers but also exceeded the planned volume of sales by 1,000 units. At the standard price, the additional volume produces a favourable revenue variance of $80,000 (1,000 units × $80 per unit). The increase in volume also produces unfavourable variable cost variances as indicated in Exhibit 8–2. The net result of producing and selling the additional 1,000 units is an increase of $30,600 in the contribution margin, indeed a favourable condition. These preliminary results suggest that the marketing manager is to be congratulated for a job well done. In practice, however, more analysis is necessary. For example, a closer look at market share could reveal whether the manager was able to win customers from the company's competitors or whether the manager simply reaped the benefit of a wave of unexpected industry-wide consumer demand. Furthermore, the increase in sales volume could have been attained by lowering the sales price, the success of which depends on the relationship between the magnitude of the change in the sales price versus the magnitude of the increase in sales volume. This possibility will be analyzed further in a later section of this chapter.

The unfavourable variable cost variances in Exhibit 8–2 are somewhat misleading because variable costs are, by definition, expected to increase as volume increases. Indeed, as previously stated, the unfavourable cost variances are more than offset by the favourable revenue variance, thereby resulting in a higher contribution margin. As a result, the variable cost volume variances could be more appropriately considered expected, rather than unfavourable.

Fixed Cost Considerations

Note that the total amount of fixed costs is the same in both the static and flexible budgets. By definition, the budgeted amount of fixed costs remains the same, regardless of the volume of activity. Because fixed costs are the same in both budgets, what can be gained by analyzing these costs? To answer this question, consider what you have learned about fixed cost behaviour. On the basis of our previous discussions regarding *operating leverage*, you should recall that a small increase in sales volume can have a dramatic impact on profitability. Indeed, note that although the 1,000 unit activity variance produces a 5.6 percent increase in revenue ($80,000 variance ÷ $1,440,000 static budget sales base), it results in an 11.8 percent increase in profitability ($30,600 variance ÷ $259,200 static budget net income base). In this case, the favourable sales activity variance has an even larger beneficial effect on profitability. If management is trying to understand why profitability increased so dramatically, it should consider the higher-than-expected sales volume.

Companies using a cost-plus-pricing strategy must be concerned with differences between the planned and actual volume of activity. Because actual activity is unknown until the end of the accounting period, prices that must be maintained currently are based on planned (estimated) activity. At the *planned volume* of activity of 18,000 units, Melrose's total fixed cost per unit is expected to be as follows:

Fixed manufacturing cost	$201,600	
Fixed G, S, & A cost	90,000	
Total fixed cost	$291,600	÷ 18,000 units = $16.20 per statue

At the *actual volume* of 19,000 units, the fixed cost per unit drops to $15.35 per statue ($291,600 ÷ 19,000 units). Because Melrose's prices were established on the $16.20 budgeted cost, rather than the actual cost of $15.35, the statues would have been overpriced. This condition could provide a price advantage for competitors that may limit Melrose's sales growth. Do not be deceived by the increase in sales volume. Perhaps sales volume could have been even higher if the statues had been competitively priced.

Although it appears that Melrose did not encounter this problem, you should note that underpricing can also have detrimental consequences. If planned activity is overstated, the estimated cost per unit will be understated and prices will be set too low. When the higher amount of actual costs is subtracted from revenues, actual profits will be lower than expected. To avoid these negative consequences, companies that consider unit cost in pricing decisions must monitor activity variances closely.

The activity variance is considered unfavourable if actual volume is less than planned because this produces a higher cost per unit than expected. A **favourable variance** occurs if the actual volume is higher than planned because this produces a lower cost per unit than expected. As this discussion implies, however, both favourable and unfavourable variances can lead to negative consequences. The ideal condition is to achieve the greatest possible degree of accuracy.

Flexible Budget Variances

For purposes of performance evaluation, a flexible budget prepared at the actual volume of activity is compared with actual results. Because the volume of activity is the same for the flexible budget and the actual results, any reported variances result from differences between the standard and actual per-unit amounts. To illustrate the determination and analysis of flexible budget variances, we assume that

Melrose Manufacturing Company experienced the following *actual* per unit amounts during its 2001 accounting period. The 2001 per-unit *standard* amounts that were listed earlier are repeated here for your convenience:

	Standard	Actual
Sales price	$80.00	$78.00
Variable materials cost	12.00	11.78
Variable labour cost	16.80	17.25
Variable overhead cost	5.60	5.75
Variable general, selling, and administrative (G, S, & A) cost	15.00	14.90
Actual and budgeted fixed costs are shown in Exhibit 8–3.		

The flexible budget, actual results, and flexible budget variances for Melrose Manufacturing Company's 2001 accounting period are shown in Exhibit 8–3. The flexible budget data are the same as those shown in Exhibit 8–2. Recall that the flexible budget amounts are determined by multiplying the standard per unit amounts by the actual volume of production. For example, the sales revenue in the *flexible budget is determined by multiplying the standard sales price by the actual volume* ($80 × 19,000). The variable cost data are computed in a similar manner. The *actual results are calculated by multiplying the actual per-unit sales price and cost figures shown in the preceding table by the actual volume of activity.* For example, the sales revenue in the Actual column is determined by multiplying the actual sales price by the actual volume ($78 × 19,000 = $1,482,000). The actual cost figures are computed in a similar manner. The **flexible budget variances** represent the difference between the flexible budget amounts and the actual results.

Exhibit 8-3

**Flexible Budget Variances
for Melrose Manufacturing Company**

	Static Budget	Flexible Budget	Activity Variances	
Number of units	19,000	19,000	0	Unfavourable
Sales revenue	$1,520,000	$1,482,000	$38,000	Unfavourable
Variable manufacturing costs				
Materials	228,000	223,820	4,180	Favourable
Labour	319,200	327,750	8,550	Unfavourable
Overhead	106,400	109,250	2,850	Unfavourable
Variable G,S,&A	285,000	283,100	1,900	Favourable
Contribution margin	581,400	538,080	43,320	Unfavourable
Fixed costs				
Manufacturing	201,600	210,000	8,400	Unfavourable
G,S,&A	90,000	85,000	5,000	Favourable
Net income	$ 289,900	$ 243,080	$46,720	Unfavourable

Calculating Sales Price Variance

Because the volume of activity used in the flexible budget equals the level of activity actually experienced, the price variance must be attributable to the sales price, rather than to the sales volume. In this case, the actual sales price of $78 per unit is less than the standard price of $80 per unit. Because Melrose sold its product for less than the standard sales price, the **sales price variance** is classified as *unfavourable*. The unfavourable designation in this case is misleading, however; recall that sales volume was 1,000 units higher than expected. The additional volume may have been attributable to the fact that Melrose's marketing manager lowered the sales price. Whether the combination of factors (lower sales price and higher sales volume) is favourable or unfavourable depends on the magnitude of the sales price variance versus the magnitude of the volume variance. In this case, the total sales variance (i.e., price and volume) can be computed as follows:

Actual sales (19,000 units × $78 per unit)	$1,482,000	
Expected sales (18,000 units × $80 per unit)	1,440,000	
Total sales variance	$ 42,000	Favourable

Alternatively,

Activity variance (i.e., volume)	$80,000	Favourable
Sales price variance	(38,000)	Unfavourable
Total sales variance	$42,000	Favourable

This analysis suggests that lowering prices had a favourable impact on the generation of total revenue. Accordingly, the unfavourable label on the sales price variance is, indeed, misleading. This condition highlights the fact that favourable variances cannot automatically be interpreted as good and unfavourable variances as bad. All variances should be considered signals for the need to conduct a rational investigation as to their cause.

∎ The Human Factor Associated with Flexible Budget Variances

The flexible budget cost variances provide insight into how efficiently managers have operated the business. For example, Melrose Manufacturing Company's favourable materials variance may indicate that managers were shrewd in negotiating price concessions, discounts, or delivery terms that reduced the price the company paid for materials. Similarly, managers may have used materials efficiently, thereby reducing the amount used. In contrast, the unfavourable labour variance may indicate that managers have been lax in controlling employee wages or have failed to motivate their employees to work hard. As with sales variances, cost variances must be analyzed carefully. What appears to be favourable on the surface may, in fact, be unfavourable. For example, the favourable materials variance may have been obtained by paying low prices for inferior goods. The substandard materials may have required additional labour in the production process, which would explain the unfavourable labour variance. Again, we caution that variances, whether favourable or unfavourable, should be treated as signals for the need for investigation.

LO6
Appreciate the human response to flexible budget variances.

In general, variances should not be used to single out managers for praise or punishment. The purpose of variances is to provide information that facilitates efficiency and improves productivity. If they are misused as a means of assigning rewards and punishment, managers are likely to respond by withholding or manipulating information. For example, a manager may manipulate the determination of the standard cost by deliberately overstating the amount of materials and/or labour that is expected to be required to complete a job. Later, the manager's performance will be evaluated as positive when the actual cost of materials and/or labour is lower than the inflated standard. Indeed, this practice has become so common that it has been given a name. The difference between inflated and realistic standards is called **budget slack**. A similar game played with respect to revenue is called *lowballing*. In this case, the sales staff deliberately underestimates the amount of expected sales. Later, when actual sales exceed expected sales, personnel are rewarded for exceeding the budget.

The motive for gamesmanship can be reduced by having superiors and subordinates participate in the standard setting process with a sincere intent to attain agreed-upon, reasonable expectations. Once standards have been established, they must be incorporated into an evaluation system that promotes long-term respect among superiors and their subordinates. If standards are used solely for punitive purposes, gamesmanship will rapidly degrade the standard costing system.

▌ Establishment of Standards

Establishing standards is probably the most difficult task required in the development of a standard cost system. A **standard** represents what *should be* on the basis of a certain set of anticipated circumstances. Think for a moment of the complexity of the standard setting task. Suppose that you are charged with establishing the standard cost of a pair of blue jeans. A partial list of the things you would need to know would include where you can get the best price for materials, who will pay transportation costs, whether cash or volume discounts are available, whether the suppliers with the lowest price are reliable, and whether they can supply the amount needed on a timely basis, how the material should be cut to conserve time and labour, in what order the pieces of material should be sewn together, what the wage rates of the persons who will provide the labour are, whether overtime will be necessary, and how many pairs of jeans need to be produced. Obtaining this information is obviously too large a task for one person. Effective standard setting requires the combined experience, judgment, and predictive capacity of all personnel who have responsibility for price and quantity decisions. Even when a multitalented group of experienced persons is involved in standard setting, the process requires significant amounts of trial and error. Revising standards is a common occurrence even in established systems.

Historical data provide a good starting point for the establishment of standards. These data must be updated for changes in technology, plant layout, new methods of production, worker productivity, and so on. Indeed, changes of this nature frequently result from the initiation of a standard cost system. Remember that a *standard* represents what *should be,* rather than what *is* or *was.* Frequently, engineers are consulted to establish standards, which represent the most efficient way to perform the required tasks. The engineers perform time and motion studies and review material utilization in the process of developing standards. Established practices and policies are frequently changed in response to the engineers' reports.

Behavioural implications must also be considered when developing standards. Managers, supervisors, purchasing agents, and other associated personnel should be consulted for two reasons: (1) their experience and expertise enable them to provide invaluable input to standard development, and (2) persons who are involved in the standard-setting process are more likely to accept the resulting standards and to be motivated by them.

Management should also consider the desired level of difficulty necessary to achieve standard performance. The ranges of difficulty can be subdivided into three logical categories: (1) ideal standards, (2) practical standards, and (3) lax standards.

Ideal standards represent perfection; they show what costs should be under ideal circumstances. They ignore allowances for normal materials waste and spoilage. They do not consider ordinary labour inefficiencies due to machine down time, cleanup, breaks, or personal needs. Ideal standards are beyond the capabilities of most, if not all, employees. Such standards may motivate some individuals to constantly strive for improvement, but unattainable standards tend to discourage the majority of people. When confronted with consistent failure, most people will become demotivated and reduce their efforts to succeed. In addition, the variances associated with ideal standards lose significance. They tend to reflect deviations that are largely beyond the control of the participants, and they obscure true measures of superior or inferior performance, thereby reducing the capacity for control.

Practical standards can be accomplished with a reasonable degree of effort; they constitute attainable goals for employees. They allow for normal levels of inefficiency in materials and labour usage. An average worker performing in a diligent manner would be able to achieve standard performance. Practical standards have motivational appeal for most employees; the feeling of accomplishment that they attain through earnest effort tends to encourage workers to do their best. Practical standards also produce meaningful variances. Deviations from the standard usually result from factors that the worker controls. Positive variances normally represent superior performance, and negative variances indicate inferior performance.

The administrators of Memorial Hospital may deserve to be congratulated, even if actual costs exceed the expected (i.e., standard) costs of serving patients. Perhaps the number of patients served is considerably higher than expected. Under these circumstances, variable costs are expected to increase because the volume of activity has increased. If the increase in cost is less than the standard necessary to serve the additional customers, the flexible budget variances are favourable. This indicates that the administrators were diligent in the use of the resources required to serve the unexpected patient load. In this case, the administrators would, in fact, deserve to be congratulated.

Lax standards represent easily attainable goals. Standard performance can be accomplished with minimal effort. Lax standards lack motivational appeal for most people; constant success attained by minimal effort tends to create boredom and low performance. In addition, variances lose meaningful content. Deviations caused by superior or inferior performance are obscured by the built-in slack.

The worker's level of ability must be considered when establishing standards. Standards that are attainable for a seasoned workforce may represent ideal standards to an inexperienced workforce. To be effective, standards should be constantly monitored and adjusted appropriately as the need arises.

Need for Standard Costs

As the previous discussion suggests, standard costs constitute the building blocks for the preparation of the master and flexible budgets. Accordingly, they facilitate the planning process. Standard costs also establish benchmarks by which actual performance can be judged. By highlighting differences between expected (i.e., standard) and actual performances, standard costing permits management to focus attention on the areas of greatest need. Because management talent is a valuable and expensive resource, businesses cannot afford to have managers devote large amounts of time to operations that are functioning normally. Instead, managers should concentrate on areas that are not performing in accordance with expectations. In other words, management should attend to the exceptions; indeed, this management philosophy has become known as the **management by exception** doctrine.

Standard costing facilitates the use of the exception principle. By reviewing performance reports that show differences between actual and standard costs, management is able to concentrate on the items that show significant variances. Areas that show only minor variances are subject to a cursory review or are ignored as management deems appropriate.

▌Selecting Variances to Investigate

Judgment, based on experience, plays a significant role in deciding which variances merit investigation. However, we can identify several factors that influence the decision. These include the *materiality concept*, *frequency of occurrence*, *capacity to control*, and the *characteristics of the item being considered*.

Standard costs are by nature estimated figures and therefore cannot be perfect predictors of actual costs. Slight variances will emerge in the normal course of business. These slight variances should not be investigated because they are not likely to produce useful information. In recognition of this fact, many companies follow the materiality concept by establishing guidelines for selecting variances to analyze. For example, a company may set a dollar or a percentage limit and instruct managers to ignore variances that fall below these limits. Only variances that qualify as material will be investigated. A **material variance** is one that would affect decision making. The need to analyze material variances applies to favourable as well as unfavourable variances. As mentioned earlier, purchasing substandard materials can create favourable variances, resulting in what may seem to be a positive price variance; however, the company's products will ultimately reflect the fact that they were constructed with substandard materials and sales will fall.

LO8

Understand the criteria for selecting the most appropriate variances to investigate.

The concept of *frequency of occurrence* is closely related to the materiality concept. An immaterial variance that amounts to $20,000 during one month can become a material variance amounting to $240,000 if the monthly performance is repeated throughout the year. Variance reports should highlight frequent as well as large variations.

The *capacity to control* refers to management's ability to take corrective action. If utility rates cause variances between actual and standard overhead cost, management has little control over these variances. Conversely, if actual labour costs exceed standard costs because a supervisor is unable to motivate employees, management can control this variance. Managers should concentrate on controllable variances to maximize their utility to the firm.

The *characteristics of the items being considered* may permit management abuse. For example, managers can reduce actual costs in the short term by delaying expenditures for maintenance, research and development, advertising, and so on. Although cost reductions in these areas may produce favourable variances and immediate gratification, they will have a long-term detrimental impact on profitability. Unfortunately, managers under stress may yield to the temptations of the short-term benefits. As a result, variances associated with these critical items should be closely scrutinized.

As previously indicated, the primary advantage of using a standard cost system is that it efficiently uses management talent to control costs. Secondary benefits include the following:

1. Standard cost systems provide immediate feedback that permits rapid response to troubled areas. For example, a standard amount of materials may be issued for a particular job. Requisitions of additional materials may require supervisory approval indicated by the use of specially marked requisition forms. Each time a supervisor is forced to use one of these forms, she is immediately aware that excess materials are being used and has time to act before the excessive material usage becomes unmanageable.

2. If established and maintained properly, standard cost systems can boost morale and motivate employees. Reward systems can be linked to accomplishments that exceed the established performance standards. Under such circumstances, employees become extremely conscious of the time and materials they use, minimizing waste and reducing costs.

3. Standard cost systems encourage proper planning. The failure to plan properly results in overbuying, excessive inventory, wasted time, and so on. A standard cost system forces planning, resulting in a more efficient operation with less waste.

❙ Manufacturing Cost Variances

The *manufacturing costs* incurred by Melrose Manufacturing Company are summarized here for your convenience:

	Standard	Actual
Variable materials cost per unit	$ 12.00	$ 11.78
Variable labour cost per unit	16.80	17.25
Variable overhead cost per unit	5.60	5.75
Total per unit variable manufacturing cost (a)	$34.40	$34.78
Total units produced (b)	19,000	19,000
Total variable manufacturing cost (a × b)	$653,600	$660,820
Fixed manufacturing cost	201,600	210,000
Total manufacturing cost	$855,200	$870,820

On the basis of this information, we can determine that the total manufacturing cost variance is $15,620 ($870,820 − $855,200), which is unfavourable because Melrose actually incurred more cost than expected.

What caused Melrose to spend more money than expected? Did it spend more or less than expected on materials, labour, or overhead? Did it spend more or less than expected for fixed costs? To answer these questions, it is necessary to subdivide the total manufacturing cost variance into four logical subcomponents. Specifically, the total manufacturing cost variance ($15,620) can be subdivided into three variable cost variances (materials, labour, and overhead) and one fixed cost variance. Indeed, these individual variances were listed in Exhibit 8–3. Recall that the standard variable cost amounts in Exhibit 8–3 were determined by multiplying the standard cost per unit by the actual number of units produced. Similarly, the actual variable cost amounts were determined by multiplying the actual cost per unit by the actual number of units produced. These relationships can be expressed as follows:

Algebraically, the variance can be expressed as follows:

$$\left| \begin{array}{cc} \text{Actual variable} & \text{Standard variable} \\ \text{cost per unit} & \text{cost per unit} \end{array} \right| \times \begin{array}{c} \text{Actual number} \\ \text{of units} \end{array} = \begin{array}{c} \text{Variable cost} \\ \text{variance} \end{array}$$

Note that the differences between actual and standard amounts are shown as an absolute value. This indicates that the mathematical sign is not useful in interpreting the condition of the variance. To determine the condition of the variance, use the same rules as previously discussed, which are repeated here for your convenience:

- When actual costs are higher than standard costs, variances are unfavourable.
- When actual costs are lower than standard costs, variances are favourable.

Using the algebraic equations and the classification rules, we can reconstruct the product cost variances in Exhibit 8–3. The formulas and their results are shown in Exhibit 8–4. To confirm your understanding that the algebraic formulas are merely an alternative way to accomplish the same result, you should compare the manufacturing cost variances in Exhibit 8–3 with those in Exhibit 8–4.

The information in Exhibit 8–4 suggests that Melrose spent less than expected for materials and more than expected for labour and overhead. Fixed manufacturing costs were also higher than expected. This information is useful, but more detailed information is necessary to facilitate cost control. For example, we know that Melrose paid more for labour than expected, but we do not know whether the employees were paid higher wages or worked more hours. To obtain this information, analyzing the price and amount of each resource used in the production process is necessary.

Price and Usage Variances

The resources used in the manufacturing process are frequently called **inputs** (i.e., materials, labour, and overhead). The purpose of the manufacturing process is to transform the set of *inputs* into **outputs** (i.e., products). As previously indicated, managers establish standards to exercise control over the consumption of the inputs. A *standard* represents the amount of input that management *expects* to be consumed in the manufacturing process. The **cost per unit of input** is composed of two factors; price and usage. A *favourable variance* occurs when production costs less than expected (i.e., the standard price). An **unfavourable variance** occurs when production costs more than expected. Likewise, favourable and unfavourable usage variances occur when production consumes more or less of an input than the standard amount. Price and usage variances are computed for each input factor in the production process including materials, labour, and variable overhead. The specific names of the variances change to reflect

LO9

Calculate price and usage variances.

the nature of the input being analyzed. For example, a variance for materials may be called a **materials price variance** and a **materials quantity variance**; the equivalent labour variances are called a **labour rate variance** and a **labour efficiency variance**. Regardless of the names used, the underlying concepts and computational procedures are the same for all variable price and usage variances.

Exhibit 8-4		
Total Manufacturing Cost Variances for Melrose Manufacturing Company		
Variable manufacturing costs		
Materials cost variance		
IActual cost Standard − costl × Actual units = I$11.78 − $12.00I × 19,000 = $ 4,180		Favourable
Total labour cost variance		
IActual cost − Standard costl × Actual units = I$17.25 − $16.80I × 19,000 = 8,550		Unfavourable
Total overhead cost variance		
IActual cost − Standard costl × Actual units = I$5.75 − $5.60I × 19,000 = 2,850		Unfavourable
Total variable costs variances	$ 7,220	Unfavourable
Fixed manufacturing cost	8,400	Unfavourable
Total manufacturing cost variance	$15,620	Unfavourable

Calculating Materials Price and Usage Variances

LO9

Calculate price and usage variances.

To illustrate the determination of the materials price and usage variances, return to the case of Melrose Manufacturing Company. Recall that performance evaluation is based on a flexible budget. Accordingly, the total materials variance is computed on the basis of the actual level of production of 19,000 statues. As shown in Exhibit 8–4, the total materials variance is computed as follows:

$$\left| \frac{\text{Actual}}{\text{cost}} - \frac{\text{Standard}}{\text{cost}} \right| \times \frac{\text{Actual}}{\text{units}} = \left| \$11.78 - \$12.00 \right| \times 19,000 = \$4,180 \text{ Favourable}$$

Why is the variance favourable? Because *actual cost* is lower than *standard cost*. In other words, Melrose spent less on materials than it expected to pay to make 19,000 statues. What caused the company to spend less than expected? The price of the materials may have been less than expected, or the company may have used fewer materials than expected. To determine which or what combination of these two components caused the total favourable variance, we must first separate the cost per unit data into quantity and price components. To illustrate, assume that the materials cost per unit data are composed of the following amounts:

	Actual Data	Standard Data
Quantity of materials per unit	6.2 pounds	6.0 pounds
Price per pound	× $1.90	× $2.00
Cost per unit	$11.78	$12.00

On the basis of this breakdown, we can determine the total quantity of materials as follows:

	Actual Data	Standard Data
Actual production volume	19,000 units	19,000 units
Quantity of materials per unit	× 6.2 pounds	× 6.0 pounds
Total quantity of materials	117,800 pounds	114,000 pounds

We can now validate the fact that the total variance is composed of price and quantity components. Specifically, the total variance can be recalculated as follows:

Exhibit 8-5

**Materials Price and Usage Variances
for Melrose Manufacturing Company**

Actual Cost		Variance-Dividing Data		Standard Cost	
Actual quantity	117,800	Actual quantity	117,800	Standard quantity	114,000
×	×	×	×	×	×
Actual price	$1.90	Standard price	$2.00	Standard price	$2.00
	$223,820		$235,600		$228,000
		Price variance		Quantity variance	
		$11,780 Favourable		$7,600 Unfavourable	
		Total variance: $4,180 Favourable			

Actual Costs		Standard Costs	
Actual quantity	117,800	Standard quantity	114,000
×	×	×	×
Actual price	$1.90	Standard price	$2.00
	$223,820		$228,000
	Total variance: $4,180 Favourable		

To isolate the price and usage variances, we insert a Variance-Dividing Data column between the Actual Cost and Standard Cost columns. The Variance-Dividing Data column is composed of a combination of standard and actual data. Specifically, the *standard price* is multiplied by the *actual quantity* of materials purchased and used.[1] The result is shown in Exhibit 8–5.

Algebraic Notation The amount of the price variance (i.e., difference between the *Actual Cost column* and the *Variance-Dividing Data column*) can be determined by multiplying the difference between the actual and standard prices by the actual quantity. This relationship can be written algebraically as follows:

$$\text{Price variance} = |\text{Actual price} - \text{Standard price}| \times \text{Actual quantity}$$
$$= |\$1.90 - \$2| \times 117{,}800$$
$$= \$0.10 \times 117{,}800$$
$$= \$11{,}780 \text{ Favourable}$$

As with the previous variance formulas, the difference between the actual price and the standard amounts is expressed as an *absolute value*. This mathematical notation suggests that the mathematical sign is not useful in interpreting the condition of the variance. To assess the condition of the variance, you must consider the type of variance being analyzed. With respect to cost variances, managers seek to attain actual prices that are lower than expected (standard) prices. In the case of Melrose Manufacturing Company, the actual price ($1.90) is less than the standard price ($2). Accordingly, the price variance is classified as favourable.

The materials usage variance also can be expressed in an algebraic formula. Specifically, the amount of the usage variance (difference between the *Variance-Dividing Data column* and the *Standard Cost column*) can be determined by multiplying the difference between the actual and standard quantity by the standard price. This relationship can be written algebraically as follows:

---

[1] In practice, raw materials are frequently stored in inventory prior to being used. Accordingly, differences may exist between the amount of materials purchased and the amount of materials used. When this condition occurs, the price variance is determined on the basis of the quantity of materials *purchased*, and the quantity variance is determined on the basis of the quantity of materials *used*. This text makes the simplifying assumption that the amount of materials purchased equals the amount of materials used during the period.

$$\begin{aligned}
\text{Quantity variance} &= |\text{Actual quantity} - \text{Standard quantity}| \times \text{Standard price} \\
&= |117{,}800 - 114{,}000| \times \$2 \\
&= 3{,}800 \times \$2 \\
&= \$7{,}600 \text{ Unfavourable}
\end{aligned}$$

LO10

Identify the responsible parties for price and usage variances.

Responsibility for Materials Variances Purchasing agent is normally considered to be responsible for a *favourable price variance*. The standard materials price is established for a particular grade of material. The standard assumes that the material will be purchased in a manner that will give the company favourable trade terms, including volume discounts, cash discounts, transportation savings, and supplier services. Due diligence in placing orders enables the purchasing agent to take advantage of positive trading terms. Under these circumstances, the company pays less than standard prices, which is reflected in the form of a favourable price variance. An investigation of the favourable price variance could result in the identification of purchasing strategies that can be shared with other purchasing agents. The analysis of favourable as well as unfavourable variances can result in the development of efficiencies that benefit the entire production process.

Certain factors limit the purchasing agent's control of the price variance. The agent may exercise his duties with diligence and still be confronted with an unfavourable price variance for many reasons. Suppliers may raise prices, rush orders may be necessary because of poor scheduling by the production department, or a truckers' strike may force the use of a more expensive delivery system. These and other factors are beyond the control of the purchasing agent. Care must be taken to ensure the identification of the proper causes of unfavourable variances. False accusations and overreactions lead only to resentment that will ultimately destroy the productive potential of the standard costing system.

The condition of the *materials usage variance* can be determined by simply looking at the quantity data. Because the actual quantity used is higher than the standard quantity, the variance is unfavourable. In other words, using more materials than expected increases the cost of production. If management is trying to minimize cost, using more materials than expected is an unfavourable condition. The materials quantity variance is largely under the control of the production department. Unfavourable variances reflect materials waste that may be caused by inexperienced workers, faulty machinery, negligent application, or poor planning. Unfavourable variances may also be caused by factors that are beyond the control of the production department, such as the purchasing agent's purchase of substandard materials. The lower-quality material may result in more scrap (waste) in the production process that would be reflected in an unfavourable usage variance.

Calculating Labour Variances

LO9

Calculate price and usage variances.

Labour variances are calculated using the same general formulas as those used to compute the materials price and usage variances. Accordingly, the total labour variance shown in Exhibit 8–4 is computed as follows:

$$\left| \frac{\text{Actual}}{\text{cost}} - \frac{\text{Standard}}{\text{cost}} \right| \times \frac{\text{Actual}}{\text{units}} = \left| \$17.25 - \$16.80 \right| \times 19{,}000 = \$8{,}550$$

Assume that Melrose's accountant determined that the labour cost per unit data are composed of the following amounts:

	Actual Data	Standard Data
Quantity of labour per unit	1.5 hours	1.4 hours
Price per hour	× $11.50	× $12.00
Cost per unit	$17.25	$16.80

© Superstock

Do purchasing agents really make a difference? They certainly do—at least that is the opinion of Inspector General Eleanor Hill, who is in charge of policing waste and fraud at the U.S. Department of Defense. Explaining preposterous costs, such as a $76 screw and a $714 electric bell, Ms. Hill told a Senate Armed Services subcommittee that Pentagon buyers failed to obtain volume discounts, neglected to compare prices with competitors, or otherwise failed to pursue aggressive purchasing strategies. Specifically, Ms. Hill said, "Department of Defense procurement approaches were poorly conceived, badly coordinated, and did not result in the government getting good value for the prices paid both for commercial and noncommercial items. We found considerable evidence that the Department of Defense had not yet learned how to be an astute buyer in the commercial marketplace."

Source: John Diamond, "Audits Say Pentagon Continues to Overpay," *USA Today*, March 19, 1998, p. 2A.

On the basis of this breakdown, we can determine the total quantity of labour as follows:

	Actual Data	Standard Data
Actual production volume	19,000 units	19,000 units
Quantity of labour per unit	× 1.5 hours	× 1.4 hours
Total quantity of labour	28,500 hours	26,600 hours

Using the price and quantity information described here, the labour price and usage variances can be computed as shown in Exhibit 8–6.

Responsibility for Labour Variances A quick glance at the price of labour indicates that the *labour price variance* is favourable because the actual amount paid for labour is less than the standard rate. The production supervisor is usually responsible for the labour price variance because price variances normally result from the use of labour, rather than from an underpayment or overpayment of the hourly rate. Labour price rates are frequently fixed by contracts. Accordingly, rates below or above established rates are not likely; however, the use of semiskilled labour to perform highly skilled tasks or vice versa will produce rate variances. Similarly, the use of unanticipated overtime will cause unfavourable variances. Production department supervisors are in the best position to control the assignment of labour and are therefore held accountable for the resultant labour price variances.

LO10
Identify the responsible parties for price and usage variances.

Labour usage variances measure the productive use of the labour force. Because Melrose used more labour than expected, the labour usage variance will be unfavourable. Unsatisfactory labour performance has many causes, low morale or poor supervision are possibilities. Furthermore, machine breakdowns, inferior materials, and poor planning can cause interruptions that waste labour and reduce productivity. Because these factors are generally under the control of the production department supervisors, these individuals are normally held responsible for labour usage variances.

Price and usage variances may be interrelated. The favourable labour price variance may have been obtained by using less skilled employees who may require more time to do the job, thereby causing an unfavourable labour usage variance. Once again, the variances must be investigated with due diligence before drawing conclusions as to who should be held responsible for them.

Exhibit 8-6						
Labour Price and Usage Variances for Melrose Manufacturing Company						
Actual Cost		**Variance-Dividing Data**			**Standard Cost**	
Actual hours	28,500	Actual hours	28,500		Standard hours	26,600
×	×	×	×		×	×
Actual price	$11.50	Standard price	$12.00		Standard price	$12.00
	$327,750		$342,000			$319,200
		Labour price variance			Labour usage variance	
		$14,250 Favourable			$22,800 Unfavourable	
		Algebraic solutions: IAP − SPI × AHrs			Algebraic solutions: IAHrs − SHrsl = SP	
		I$11.50 − $12.00I × 28,500 − $14,250			I28,500 − 26,600I × $12.00 − $22,800	
			Total variance: $4,180 Favourable			

Variable Overhead Variances

Variable overhead variances utilize the same general formulas as used to compute the other price and usage variances. However, unique characteristics that require special attention are associated with variable overhead costs. First, variable overhead is composed of a variety of inputs including supplies, utilities, indirect labour, and so on. The variable overhead cost pool is normally assigned to products on the basis of a predetermined variable overhead allocation rate. The use of a single rate to represent a mixture of different costs complicates the interpretation of variances. Suppose the actual overhead rate is higher than the predetermined rate. Does this mean that the company paid more than it should have paid for supplies, utilities, maintenance, or some other input variable? Indeed, the cost of some overhead inputs may have been higher than expected, while others were lower than expected. Similarly, an overall usage variance provides no clue as to which overhead inputs were over- or underused. Due to the difficulty of interpreting the results, many companies do not calculate price and usage variances for variable overhead costs. For this reason, we limit our coverage of this subject to the total flexible budget variances shown in Exhibit 8–3.

Fixed Overhead Variances

It should be clear from the previous discussion that *variable costs* have price and usage variances and that *fixed overhead costs* can also have price variances. Remember that *fixed* means that it stays the same relative to changes in the volume of production; it does not mean that it stays the same as expected. You may certainly pay more or less than you expected to pay for a fixed cost. For example, a supervisor may receive an unexpected raise, thereby causing actual salary costs to be higher than expected. Similarly, a manager may be able to negotiate a reduction in the rental cost for the manufacturing equipment, causing the actual rental costs to be lower than expected. The difference between the *actual fixed overhead costs* and the *budgeted fixed overhead costs* is called a **spending variance**. The spending variance is favourable if the amount spent is less than that expected (i.e., actual cost is less than the budgeted cost). The variance is unfavourable if more than expected is spent (i.e., actual is more than budgeted).

The analysis of fixed overhead costs differs from that of variable costs because no potential usage variance exists. If Melrose pays $25,000 to rent its manufacturing facility; the company cannot use more or less of this rent, no matter how many units of product it makes. Because the rent cost is fixed, however, the *cost per unit* of product will differ depending on the number of units of product made. The more the products made, the lower is the cost per unit. The fewer the products made, the higher is the cost per unit. Because the volume of activity affects the cost per unit, a variance between the expected and actual volume of activity is important. Accordingly, it is common practice to calculate a volume variance for fixed overhead costs. The **volume variance** is the difference between the *budgeted fixed cost* and the *amount of fixed costs allocated to production*. The amount of *allocated cost* is frequently called the *applied fixed cost*.

To illustrate the computation of the fixed overhead variances, we return to the case of Melrose Manufacturing Company. First, the overhead spending variance is shown in Exhibit 8–3. Specifically, the spending variance is the difference between the budgeted fixed overhead and the actual fixed overhead (|$201,600 budgeted − $210,000 actual| = $8,400 spending variance). The variance is considered unfavourable because Melrose actually spent more than it expected to spend for fixed overhead costs. Recall that there is no fixed overhead usage variance.

Calculation of the overhead volume variance involves first calculating the fixed cost predetermined overhead rate. Given budgeted fixed costs of $201,600 and planned activity of 18,000 statues, the predetermined fixed overhead rate is $11.20 per statue ($201,600 ÷ 18,000 statues). On the basis of actual production of 19,000 statues, $212,800 ($11.20 × 19,000 units) of fixed overhead costs would be applied (i.e., allocated) to production. The difference between the budgeted fixed overhead and the applied fixed overhead produces a volume variance of $11,200 (|$201,600 budgeted − $212,800 applied| = $11,200 variance). A summary of the fixed overhead variances is shown in Exhibit 8–7.

Responsibility for Fixed Overhead Cost Variances There is no way to know who is responsible for the unfavourable fixed overhead spending variance because all the fixed overhead costs have been pooled together. To improve accountability, significant fixed overhead costs that are controllable, such as supervisory salaries, should be tagged for individual analysis. Fixed overhead costs that are not controllable may still be reported as informational items for management. Fixed costs that are not controllable in the short term may be manageable in the long term. Accordingly, staying abreast of differences between the expected and actual costs of fixed overhead is important for management.

LO10

Identify the responsible parties for price and usage variances.

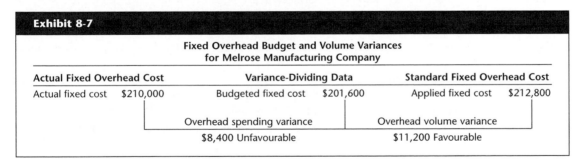

Exhibit 8-7

**Fixed Overhead Budget and Volume Variances
for Melrose Manufacturing Company**

Actual Fixed Overhead Cost	Variance-Dividing Data	Standard Fixed Overhead Cost
Actual fixed cost $210,000	Budgeted fixed cost $201,600	Applied fixed cost $212,800
	Overhead spending variance	Overhead volume variance
	$8,400 Unfavourable	$11,200 Favourable

The fixed overhead volume variance is favourable because the actual volume of production was higher than the planned volume. This condition caused a decrease in the cost per unit of product. Note that the lower cost per unit does not result from a reduction in spending. Indeed, as indicated earlier, Melrose actually spent more than it expected to spend on fixed overhead costs. The variance is caused by a higher utilization of the company's manufacturing facilities. Specifically, Melrose has taken greater advantage of the *economies of scale*. Because the overhead costs are fixed, a higher volume of production results in a lower cost per unit of product. As a rule, a company with high fixed costs should utilize its facilities to produce as high a volume as possible, thereby lowering its cost per unit of production. Of course, this rule assumes that products produced can be sold at prevailing prices. The under-utilization of manufacturing facilities causes a higher cost per unit; an unfavourable volume variance should alert management to this condition. In summary, a volume variance signifies the over- or under-utilization of facilities rather than over- or underspending.

As previously discussed, production managers are not usually responsible for volume variances. The level of production is normally determined by the sales volume that is under the control of upper-level marketing managers. Although the volume variance does provide a measure of the effective utilization of facilities, the marketing department is primarily responsible for establishing the volume of activity. Accordingly, marketing managers should be held accountable for volume variances.

Summary of Manufacturing Cost Variances

As indicated, the total variable manufacturing cost variance can be subdivided into materials, labour, and overhead variances. These variances can be further subdivided into price and usage variances. Manufacturing fixed cost can be subdivided into spending and volume variances. As its name implies, *volume variance* is not a cost variance, volume variance shows how volume affects fixed cost *per unit*, but it does not provide any indication of a difference between the *total* amount of actual and expected costs. The relationships between the cost variances computed for Melrose Manufacturing Company are summarized in Exhibit 8–8.

We have discussed a number of variable and fixed manufacturing cost variances. The algebraic formulas used to compute these variances are summarized in Exhibit 8–9.

▌ General, Selling, and Administrative Cost Variances

LO9

Calculate price and usage variances.

Variable general, selling, and administrative (G, S, & A) costs can have *price and usage variances*. For example, suppose that Melrose decides to attach a promotional advertising brochure to each statue it sells. Melrose may pay more or less for each brochure (i.e., incur a price variance). Melrose also could use more or less of the brochures than it expected to use (i.e., incur a usage variance). Indeed, businesses frequently compute variances for many G, S, & A costs, such as sales commissions, food and entertainment, postage, and supplies. The algebraic formulas used to compute variances for variable manufacturing costs apply equally to the computation of variable G, S, & A cost variances.

Fixed G, S, & A costs are also subject to variance analysis. As indicated in Exhibit 8–3, Melrose Manufacturing incurred a favourable $5,000 G, S, & A fixed cost *spending variance*. This means that Melrose actually had spent lower fixed G, S, & A costs than was expected. A fixed cost *volume variance* could also be computed. Certainly, changes in the volume of sales activity affect the per-unit amounts of fixed G, S, & A costs.

A number of individuals are responsible for G, S, & A cost variances. For example, lower-level sales personnel can be responsible for controlling the price and usage of promotional items. In contrast, upper-level administrative officers are responsible for fixed salary expenses. Due to the variety of personnel and types of costs involved, a full discussion of G, S& A cost variances is beyond the scope of this text.

---

focus on International Issues

Getting Better All the Time: The Japanese Way of Continuous Improvement

*K*aizen, pronounced "k-eye-ZIN," translates literally as "continuous improvement." The Japanese philosophy of work is rooted in *kaizen* style improvement.

One *kaizen* characteristic is a fixation on finding and rooting out mistakes. *Kaizen* practitioners revel in discovering errors, including their own. Each problem is seen as an opportunity for an improvement.

Kaizen focuses on improving processes instead of results. A *kaizen* practitioner may, for example, aim to improve the company's decision-making tools without necessarily trying to make a better decision on a matter at hand that day.

Similarly, *kaizen* aims to improve systems, not people. In a *kaizen* company, making a mistake is not an occasion to blame the person who erred. Instead, it is considered a chance to find out what is wrong with a process.

Source: Henricks, M, "Step by Step. (Management principle of continuous improvement)". Vol. 24, *Entrepreneur Magazine*, March 1, page 70(3).

Exhibit 8-8 *Relationship between Manufacturing Cost Variances for Melrose Manufacturing Company*

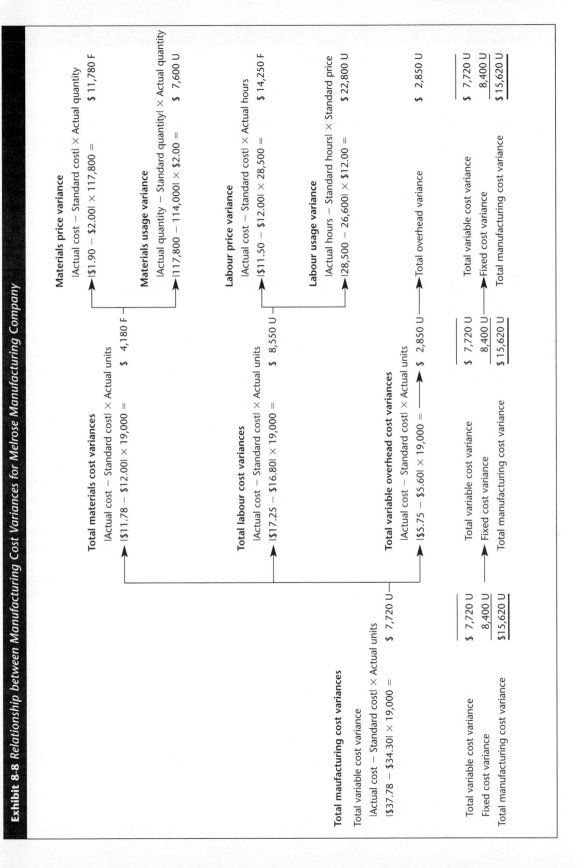

Exhibit 8-9   *Algebraic Formulas for Variances*

1. Variable cost variances (materials, labour, and overhead)
   a. Price variance
      |Actual price − Standard price| × Actual quantity
   b. Usage variance
      |Actual quantity − Standard quantity| × Standard price

2. Fixed overhead variances
   a. Fixed overhead spending variance
      |Actual fixed overhead costs − Budgeted fixed overhead costs|
   b. Fixed overhead volume variance
      |Applied fixed overhead costs − Budgeted fixed overhead costs|

▌ Standard Costs Recorded in Ledger Accounts

LO11

Understand the basic procedures for recording variances in a general ledger.

Under a **manufacturing standard cost system**, standard costs are recorded in the Inventory and Cost of Goods Sold accounts. The differences between the actual cost and the standard cost are recorded in the variance accounts. The variance accounts are then closed to the Cost of Goods Sold account at the end of the period. Accordingly, standard costs are available to management during the accounting period for decision-making purposes, and actual costs are reported on the company's published financial statements.

To illustrate the recording procedures associated with a standard costing system, assume that Tallchief Manufacturing Company began the accounting period with $6,000 cash acquired from the company's owners. Tallchief Manufacturing engaged in two transactions during the accounting period. In Transaction 1, the company spent $4,200 (actual cost) to produce wooden benches. The standard manufacturing cost of making the benches was $4,000. Suppose that Tallchief Manufacturing priced the benches at $1,000 above standard cost. In Transaction 2, all the benches that were made were sold during the accounting period. The effect of these transactions is shown in Exhibit 8–10. The two transaction numbers are shown in parentheses for easy reference. The letters CL in parentheses refer to the closing entries.

Note that the standard cost data are available for managerial decision making during the accounting period. For example, a cost-plus-pricing model was used during the period to determine the sales price of the benches ($4,000 standard cost + $1,000 desired profit = $5,000). Likewise, financial forecasts could be developed on the basis of the standard cost data. For example, projected profits would be $1,000 ($5,000 sales − $4,000 expected cost of goods sold). Even so, the ledger accounts will contain actual cost data at the end of the accounting period because each variance account is closed to the Cost of Goods Sold account. As a result, the year-end published financial statements would show a gross margin based on actual cost ($5,000 sales − $4,200 cost of goods sold = $800 gross margin).

oes variance analysis apply to service companies as well as manufacturers? The answer is, a definite yes! Canadian Tire could establish standard rates and times for the labour required to perform specific auto maintenance functions. Similarly, it could establish standards for materials, such as oil, filters, and transmission fluid. Also, fixed overhead costs and measures of volume (i.e., number of vehicles serviced) exist. Accordingly, a full range of variances could be computed for the services provided.

© Bob Daemmrich Photos/Stock Boston

Exhibit 8-10   *Examples of Variances Recorded in Ledger Accounts*

| Asset | = | Equity |

Cash

Bal. 6,000	4,200 (1)
(2) 5,000	
Bal. 6,800	

Inventory

| (1) 4,000 | 4,000 (2) |

Variance

| (cl) 200 | 200 (cl) |

Contributed Capital

| | 6,000 Bal. |

Sales Revenue

| | 5,000 (2) |

Cost of Goods Sold

| (2) 4,000 | |
| (cl)   200 | |

The essential topics in this chapter included the master budget, flexible budgets, and variance analysis. The *master budget* is determined by multiplying the standard sales price and per unit variable costs times the planned volume of activity. The master budget is prepared at the beginning of the accounting period and is used for planning purposes. The master budget is not adjusted to reflect differences between the planned and the actual volume of activity. Since this budget stays the same, regardless of the level of actual activity, it is sometimes called a *static budget*. *Flexible budgets* differ from static budgets in that they show the estimated amount of revenue and costs that are expected at different levels of activity. Both static and flexible budgets are based on the same per-unit standard amounts and the same fixed costs. The total amounts of revenue and costs shown in a master budget differ from those shown in a flexible budget because they are based on different levels of activity. Flexible budgets are used for planning, cost control, and performance evaluation.

The differences between standard (sometimes called expected or estimated) and actual amounts are called *variances*. Variances are used to evaluate managerial performance and can be either favourable or unfavourable. *Favourable sales variances* occur when actual sales are greater than expected sales.

a look

back

Unfavourable sales variances occur when actual sales are less than expected sales. *Favourable cost variances* occur when actual costs are less than expected costs. *Unfavourable cost variances* occur when actual costs are more than expected costs.

Activity variances are determined by the difference between the static budget and a flexible budget. Since both static and flexible budgets are based on the same standard sales price and costs per unit, the activity variances are attributable solely to differences between the planned and the actual volume of activity. Favourable sales activity variances suggest that the marketing manager has performed positively by selling more than was expected. Unfavourable sales activity variances suggest the inverse. Favourable or unfavourable variable cost activity variances are not meaningful for performance evaluation because variable costs are expected to change in proportion to changes in the volume of activity.

Flexible budget variances are computed by taking the difference between the amounts of revenue and variable costs that are expected at the actual volume of activity and the actual amounts of revenue and variable costs incurred at the actual volume of activity. Since the volume of activity is the same for the flexible budget and the actual results, variances are caused by the differences between the standard and actual sales prices and per-unit costs. Flexible budget variances are used for cost control and performance evaluation.

Flexible budget variances can be subdivided into *price and usage variances*. Price and usage variances for materials and labour can be computed with the formulas shown below. Variable overhead variances are calculated with the same general formulas, however the interpretation of the results is more difficult due to the variety of inputs in variable overhead.

$$\text{Price Variance} = |\text{Actual Price} - \text{Standard Price}| \times \text{Actual Quantity}$$

$$\text{Quantity Variance} = |\text{Actual Quantity} - \text{Standard Quantity}| \times \text{Standard Price}$$

The purchasing agent is normally held accountable for the material price variance. The production department supervisor is usually held responsible for the materials usage variance and the labour price and usage variances.

The fixed overhead cost variance is made up of a spending variance and a volume variance computed as follows:

$$\text{Spending Overhead Variance} = \text{Actual Fixed Overhead Costs} - \text{Budgeted Fixed Overhead Costs}$$

$$\text{Overhead Volume Variance} = \text{Budgeted Fixed Cost} - \text{Applied (Allocated) Fixed Costs}$$

The overhead spending variance is similar to a price variance. While fixed costs stay the same relative to changes in production volume, they may be more or less than they are expected to be. For example, a production supervisor's salary will stay the same, regardless of the level of activity, but the supervisor may receive a raise resulting in higher than expected fixed costs. The fixed overhead volume variance is favourable if the actual volume of production is higher than the expected volume. A higher volume of production results in a lower cost per unit. The volume variance measures how effectively production facilities are being utilized.

Care must be taken when interpreting variances. For example, a purchasing agent may produce a favourable price variance by buying low quality materials at a cheap price. However, an unfavourable labour usage variance may occur because the workers have difficulty using the substandard materials. In this case, the production supervisor is faced with an unfavourable usage variance for which she is not responsible. In addition, the purchasing agent's undesirable behaviour produced a favourable price variance. Accordingly, favourable variance cannot be assumed to indicate favourable performance. Likewise, unfavourable variances do not always suggest poor performance. All variances must be carefully investigated before responsibility is assigned.

Chapter 9 introduces other techniques that are used to evaluate managerial performance. The concept of decentralization and its relationship to responsibility accounting will be covered. You will learn how to calculate and interpret the return on investment and residual income. Finally, you will study the approaches used to establish the price of products that are transferred between divisions of the same company.

a look
forward

Budget slack The difference between inflated and realistic standards. *(p. 279)*

Cost per unit of input The cost of one unit of material, labour, or overhead determined by multiplying the price paid for one unit of material, labour, or overhead input by the usage of input for one unit of material, labour, or overhead. *(p. 283)*

Favourable variance A variance that occurs when actual costs are lower than standard costs or when actual sales are higher than standard sales. *(p. 277)*

Flexible budgets Budgets that show expected revenues and expected costs at a variety of different levels of activity. *(p. 274)*

Flexible budget variances Differences between budgets based on standard amounts at the actual level of activity and actual results; caused by differences in standard and actual unit cost since the volume of activity is the same. *(p. 278)*

Ideal standard The highest level of efficiency attainable, based on all input factors interacting perfectly under ideal or optimum conditions. *(p. 280)*

Inputs Materials, labour, and overhead used to produce outputs. *(p. 283)*

Labour efficiency variance A variance occurring in a standard cost accounting system when the actual amount or quantity of direct labour used differs from the standard amount required. *(p. 284)*

Labour rate variance A variance that occurs when the actual pay rate differs from the standard pay rate for direct labour. *(p. 284)*

Lax standards Easily attainable goals that can be accomplished with minimal effort. *(p. 281)*

Making the numbers An expression that indicates that marketing managers attained the sales volume indicated in the master budget. *(p. 276)*

Management by exception The use of management resources on areas that are not performing in accordance with expectations; a philosophy that directs management to concentrate on areas with significant variances. *(p. 281)*

Manufacturing standard cost system A cost system in which standard costs are used in accounting for the factors of production and that records standard costs in the inventory and cost of goods sold accounts and the differences between actual costs and the standard costs in variance accounts. *(p. 292)*

Material variance A variance that would affect decision making. *(p. 281)*

Materials price variance A variance that occurs when actual prices paid for raw materials differ from the standard prices. *(p. 284)*

Materials quantity variance A variance that occurs when the actual amounts of raw materials used to produce a good differ from the standard amounts required to produce that good. *(p. 284)*

Outputs The products that result from processing inputs. *(p. 283)*

Practical standard A level of efficiency in which the ideal standard has been modified to allow for normal tolerable inefficiencies. *(p. 280)*

Sales price variance The difference between actual sales and expected sales based on the standard sales price per unit times the actual level of activity. *(p. 278)*

Sales volume variance The difference between sales based on a static budget (standard sales price times standard level of activity) and sales based on a flexible budget (standard sales price times actual level of activity). *(p. 275)*

Spending variance The difference between actual fixed overhead costs and budgeted fixed overhead costs. *(p. 288)*

Standards The per-unit price or cost that "should be" based on a certain set of anticipated circumstances; per-unit cost standards are composed of price and quantity standards that together provide the per-unit cost standard. *(p. 280)*

Static budgets Budgets such as the master budget based solely on the level of planned activity; remain constant even when volume of activity changes. *(p. 274)*

Unfavourable variance A variance that occurs when actual costs exceed standard costs or when actual sales are less than standard sales. *(p. 283)*

Variances Differences between standard and actual amounts. *(p. 275)*

Volume variance The difference between the budgeted fixed cost and the amount of fixed costs allocated to production. *(p. 289)*

QUESTIONS

1. What is the difference between a static budget and a flexible budget? Explain when each would be used.

2. When the operating costs for Bill Smith's production department were released, he was sure that he would be getting a raise. His costs were $20,000 less than the planned cost in the master budget. His supervisor informs him that the results look good but that a more in-depth analysis is necessary before raises can be assigned. What other considerations could Mr. Smith's supervisor be interested in before she rates his performance?

3. When are sales and cost variances favourable and unfavourable?

4. Joan Mason, the marketing manager for a large manufacturing company, believes her unfavourable sales volume variance is the responsibility of the production department. What production circumstances that she does not control could have been responsible for her poor performance?

5. When would variable cost volume variances be expected to be unfavourable? How should unfavourable variable cost volume variances be interpreted?

6. What factors could lead to an increase in sales revenues that would not merit congratulations to the marketing manager?

7. Giving consideration to fixed costs, what are the consequences of actual volume of activity being larger than planned volume?

8. How are flexible budget variances determined? What are the causes of these variances?

9. Minnie Divers, the manager of the marketing department for one of the industry's leading retail businesses, has been notified by the accounting department that her department experienced an unfavourable sales volume variance in the preceding period but a favourable sales price variance. On the basis of these contradictory results, how would you interpret her overall performance solely on the basis of the numerical results of her variances?

10. What are three attributes necessary for establishing the best standards? What information and considerations should be taken into account when establishing standards?

11. What are the three ranges of difficulty in standard setting? What level of difficulty normally results in superior motivation of employees?

12. "So many variances," exclaimed Carl, a production manager with Bonnyville Manufacturing. "How do I determine the variances that need investigation? I can't possibly investigate all of them." Which variances will lead to useful information?

13. What is the primary benefit associated with the employment of a standard cost system?

14. A processing department of Carmine Corporation experienced a high unfavourable materials quantity variance. The plant manager initially commented, "The best way to solve this problem is to fire the supervisor of the processing department." Do you agree? Explain.

15. Sara Anderson says that she is a busy woman with no time to look at favourable variances. Instead, she concentrates solely on the unfavourable ones. She says that the favourable variances imply that employees are doing better than expected and need only a quick congratulation. In contrast, the unfavourable variances indicate that work is needed to get the substandard performance up to par. Do you agree? Explain.

16. What are two factors that affect the total materials and labour variances?

17. What individual is normally held responsible for a materials price variance? Name two factors that may be beyond this individual's control that could cause an unfavourable price variance.

18. John Jamail says that he does not understand why companies have labour price variances because most union contracts or other binding agreements set wage rates that do not normally change in the short term. How could rate variances occur even when binding commitments hold the dollar per-hour rate constant?

19. What individuals are normally held responsible for labour efficiency variances?

20. What is the primary cause of an unfavourable overhead volume variance?

21. What is the primary cause of a favourable overhead spending variance?

22. Explain how to record an unfavourable material price variance in the ledger accounts, assuming the variance is immaterial. How is this variance account closed at the end of the accounting period? What would be the effect on net income if the closing entry were not completed?

EXERCISES

L.O. 3 EXERCISE 8-1   *Variances Classified as Favourable or Unfavourable*

Required

For each of the following items, indicate whether the variance is favourable or unfavourable. The first item has been identified as an example.

Item to Classify	Standard	Actual	Type of Variance
Sale volume	25,400 units	25,200 units	Unfavourable
Sales price	$3.59 per unit	$3.60 per unit	
Materials cost	$2.68 per pound	$2.72 per pound	
Materials usage	92,400 pounds	91,900 pounds	
Labour cost	$9.25 per hour	$9.10 per hour	
Labour usage	45,600 hours	45,790 hours	
Fixed cost spending	$219,000	$214,000	
Fixed cost per unit (volume)	$2.51 per unit	$2.22 per unit	

EXERCISE 8-2   *Amount and Type (Favourable vs. Unfavourable) of Variance Determined*   **L.O. 3**

Compute variances for the following items and indicate whether each variance is favourable (F) or unfavourable (U):

Item	Budget	Actual	Variance	F or U
Sales revenue	$440,000	$425,000		
Cost of goods sold	$325,000	$300,000		
Material purchases at 5,000 pounds	$250,000	$265,000		
Materials usage	$175,000	$170,000		
Sales price	$550	$500		
Production volume	950 units	900 units		
Wages at 4,000 hours	$ 60,000	$ 58,700		
Labour usage at $16 per hour	$ 96,000	$ 97,000		
Research and development expense	$ 22,000	$ 25,000		
Selling and administrative expenses	$ 49,000	$ 40,000		
Service revenue	$125,000	$130,000		

EXERCISE 8-3   *Preparation of Master and Flexible Budgets*   **L.O. 1**

Papadopolis Manufacturing Company established the following standard price and cost data:

Sales price	$5 per unit
Variable manufacturing cost	$2 per unit
Fixed manufacturing cost	$2,000 total
Fixed selling and administrative cost	$800 total

Papadopolis planned to produce and sell 1,100 units. Actual production and sales amounted to 1,200 units.

Required
a. Prepare a pro forma income statement in contribution format that would appear in a master budget.
b. Prepare a pro forma income statement in contribution format that would appear in a flexible budget.

EXERCISE 8-4   *Determination of Sales Activity (Volume) Variances*   **L.O. 4**

Required
Use the information provided in Exercise 8-3.
a. Determine the sales activity variances.
b. Classify the variances as favourable or unfavourable.
c. Comment on the usefulness of the variances with respect to performance evaluation and identify the member of the management team who is most likely to be responsible for these variances.
d. Explain why the fixed cost variances are zero.
e. Determine the fixed cost per unit under planned activity and the fixed cost per unit under actual activity. Assuming that information in the master budget is used to price the company's product, comment on how the activity (volume) variance could affect the company's profitability.

L.O. 5 EXERCISE 8-5   *Determination of Flexible Budget Variances*

Use the standard price and cost data provided in Exercise 8-3. Assume that the actual sales price is $4.80 per unit and that the actual variable cost per unit is $2.05. The actual fixed manufacturing cost is $1,900 and the actual selling and administrative expenses are $850.

Required
a. Determine the flexible budget variances.
b. Classify the variances as favourable or unfavourable.
c. Comment on the usefulness of the variances with respect to performance evaluation and identify the member(s) of the management team who is (are) most likely to be responsible for these variances.

L.O. 5 EXERCISE 8-6   *Flexible Budget Used to Evaluate Market Uncertainty*

According to its original plan, Quinn Consulting Services Company would charge its customers for a service at $90 per hour in 2003. The company president expects the consulting services provided to customers to reach 40,000 hours at that rate. The marketing manager, however, argues that the actual result may range from 35,000 hours to 45,000 hours because of market uncertainty. Quinn's standard variable cost is $35 per hour, and its standard fixed cost is $1,500,000.

Required
Develop flexible budgets on the basis of the assumptions of service levels at 35,000 hours, 40,000 hours, and 45,000 hours.

L.O. 4, 5 EXERCISE 8-7   *Evaluation of Decision to Increase Sales Volume by Lowering Sales Price*

Executive Educational Services had budgeted its training service charge at $90 per hour. The company planned to provide 40,000 hours of training services during 2004. By lowering the service charge to $80 per hour, the company was able to increase the actual number of hours to 42,000.

Required
a. Determine the sales activity variance and indicate whether it is favourable or unfavourable.
b. Determine the flexible budget variance and indicate whether it is favourable or unfavourable.
c. Indicate whether lowering the price of training services proved to be profitable.

L.O. 4 EXERCISE 8-8   *Responsibility for Sales Volume (Activity) Variance*

Cuban Company expected to sell 350,000 of its four-function calculators during 2002. It set the standard sales price for the calculators at $8.50 each. During June, it became obvious that the company would be unable to attain the expected volume of sales. Cuban's chief competitor Stencil Co. had lowered prices and was pulling market share from Cuban. To be competitive, Cuban matched Stencil's price, thereby lowering its sales price to $8 per calculator. Stencil responded by lowering its price even further to $6 per calculator. In an emergency meeting of key personnel, Cuban's accountant, Justin Abdullah, stated, "We simply do not have a cost structure that will enable us to support a sales price in the $6 range." The production manager, Leslie Engles, said, "I don't understand why I'm here. The only unfavourable variance on my report is a fixed cost volume variance and that one is not my fault. We can't be making a product if the marketing department isn't selling it."

Required
a. Describe a scenario in which the production manager is responsible for the fixed cost volume variance.
b. Describe a scenario in which the marketing manager is responsible for the fixed cost volume variance.
c. Explain how a decline in sales volume would affect Cuban's ability to lower its sales price.

L.O. 5 EXERCISE 8-9   *Responsibility for Variable Manufacturing Cost Variance*

Sotak Manufacturing Company set its standard variable manufacturing cost at $12 per unit of product. The company planned to make and sell 4,000 units of product during 2002. More specifically, the master budget suggested that total variable manufacturing cost would be $48,000. Actual production during 2002 was 4,200 units and actual variable manufacturing costs amounted to $50,820. The production supervisor was asked to explain the variance between the budgeted and actual cost ($50,820 − $48,000 = $2,820). The supervisor responded that she was not responsible for the variance that was caused solely by the increase in sales volume controlled by the marketing department.

Required

Do you agree with the production supervisor's explanation? Support your answer with appropriate commentary.

EXERCISE 8-10   *Calculation of Materials Usage Variance*   **L.O. 9, 10**

Sara Culver is the manager of the South Point New York Bagel Shop. The corporate office had budgeted her store to sell 5,400 ham sandwiches during the week beginning July 17. Each sandwich was expected to contain 20 grams of ham. During the week of July 17, the store actually sold 5,842 sandwiches and used 118,775 grams of ham. The standard cost of ham is $0.1866 per 100 grams. The variance report from the company headquarters showed an unfavourable materials usage variance of $1,812.16. Ms. Culver thought the variance was too high, but she had no accounting background and did not know how to register a proper objection.

Required

a. Is the variance calculated properly? If not, recalculate it.
b. Provide three independent explanations as to what could have caused the materials price variance that you determined in Requirement *a*.

EXERCISE 8-11   *Calculation of Total Materials Variance: Two Different Ways*   **L.O. 9**

Soft Treats sells ice cream in 20 litre containers to retail ice cream parlours. The standard cost of sugar used to make one container of ice cream is $0.64. The company planned to make 200,000 containers of ice cream. Actual production amounted to 98,000 containers. The actual cost of sugar per container was $0.627.

Required

a. Determine the total flexible budget materials variance for sugar and indicate whether the variance is favourable or unfavourable.
b. The standard and actual costs of sugar per container of ice cream follow:

	Standard	Actual
Quantity of materials per container	1 kilo	1.1 kilo
Price per kilo	× $0.64	× $0.57
Cost per unit	$0.64	$0.63

Determine the actual and standard kilos of sugar required to make the 98,000 containers of ice cream.
c. Use the information computed in Requirement *b* to calculate the total materials variance for sugar.

EXERCISE 8-12   *Determination of Materials Price and Usage Variance*   **L.O. 9**

Flowers for All Occasions (FLO) produced a special Mother's Day arrangement that included six roses. The standard and actual costs of the roses used in each arrangement follow:

	Standard	Actual
Average number of roses per arrangement	6.0	6.1
Price per rose	× $0.32	× $0.30
Cost of roses per arrangement	$1.92	$1.83

FLO planned to make 380 arrangements but actually made 400.

Required

a. Determine the total flexible budget materials variance and indicate whether it is favourable or unfavourable.
b. Determine the materials price variance and indicate whether it is favourable or unfavourable.
c. Determine the materials usage variance and indicate whether it is favourable or unfavourable.
d. Confirm the accuracy of Requirements *a*, *b*, and *c* by showing that the sum of the price and usage variances equals the total variance.

L.O. 9, 10 EXERCISE 8-13   *Responsibility for Materials Usage Variance*

Niagara Fruit Basket Company makes baskets of assorted fruit. The standard and actual costs of oranges used in each basket of fruit follow:

	Standard	Actual
Average number of oranges per basket	3.00	3.90
Price per orange	× $0.25	× $0.20
Cost of oranges per basket	$0.75	$0.78

The actual volume of production was 25,000 baskets.

Required
a. Determine the materials price variance and indicate whether it is favourable or unfavourable.
b. Determine the materials usage variance and indicate whether it is favourable or unfavourable.
c. Provide a logical explanation as to why the purchasing agent may have been responsible for the usage variance.

L.O. 10   EXERCISE 8-14   *Responsibility for Labour Rate and Usage Variance*

Regions Manufacturing Company incurred a favourable labour rate variance and an unfavourable labour usage variance.

Required
a. Describe a scenario in which the personnel manager is responsible for the unfavourable usage variance.
b. Describe a scenario in which the production manager is responsible for the unfavourable usage variance.

L.O. 9, 10   EXERCISE 8-15   *Labour Price and Usage Variance Calculated and Explained*

Milton and Sons, a public accounting firm, established the following standard labour cost data for completing what the firm referred to as a Class 2 tax return. Milton expected each Class 2 return to require 3 hours of labour at a cost of $35 per hour. The firm actually completed 500 returns. Actual labour hours averaged 3.25 hours per return and actual labour cost amounted to $32 per hour.

Required
a. Determine the total labour variance and indicate whether it is favourable or unfavourable.
b. Determine the labour price variance and indicate whether it is favourable or unfavourable.
c. Determine the labour usage variance and indicate whether it is favourable or unfavourable.
d. Provide a logical explanation as to what could have caused these variances.

L.O. 9   EXERCISE 8-16   *Determination of Standard Labour Rate*

Devine Car Wash expected to wash 600 cars during the month of August. Washing each car was expected to require 0.25 hours of labour. The company actually used 168 hours of labour to wash 560 cars. The labour usage variance was $224 favourable.

Required
a. Determine the standard labour rate.
b. Indicate whether the variance was favourable or unfavourable.

L.O. 9, 10   EXERCISE 8-17   *Calculation of Variable Overhead Variance*

Pfeifer Company established a predetermined variable overhead cost rate at $6.20 per direct labour hour. The actual variable cost overhead rate was $5.80 per hour. The planned level of labour activity was 80,000 hours of labour. The company actually used 82,000 hours of labour.

Required
a. Determine the total flexible budget variable overhead cost variance.
b. Like many real-world companies, Pfeifer has decided not to desegregate the total variable overhead cost variance into price and usage components. Provide a logical explanation as to why Pfeifer may have decided not to do so.

EXERCISE 8-18   *Determination and Interpretation of Fixed Overhead Variances*   **L.O. 9, 10**

Heideman Company established a predetermined fixed cost overhead rate of $27 per unit of product. The company planned to make 9,000 units of product but actually produced only 8,000 units. Actual fixed overhead costs amounted to $255,000.

Required

a. Determine the fixed overhead cost spending variance and indicate whether it is favourable or unfavourable. In common terms, explain what this variance means. Identify the manager(s) who is (are) responsible for the variance.

b. Determine the fixed overhead cost volume variance and indicate whether it is favourable or unfavourable. In common terms, explain why this variance is important. Identify the manager(s) who is (are) responsible for the variance.

PROBLEMS—SERIES A

PROBLEM 8-1A   *Determination of Sales Activity Variances*   **L.O. 1, 4**

Bookout Publications established the following standard price and costs for a hard cover picture book that the company produces:

Standard price and variable costs	
Sales price	$40.00
Materials cost	10.00
Labour cost	5.00
Overhead cost	7.00
General, selling, and administrative costs	8.00
Expected fixed costs	
Manufacturing costs	$150,000
General, selling, and administrative costs	60,000

Bookout planned to make and sell 25,000 copies of the book.

Required

a. Prepare a pro forma income statement that would appear in the master budget.

b. Prepare flexible budget income statements, assuming production volume to be 24,000 and 26,000 units.

c. Determine the sales activity variances, assuming production and sales volume actually to be 26,000 units.

d. Indicate whether the variances are favourable or unfavourable.

e. Comment on how the variances could be used to evaluate performance.

PROBLEM 8-2A   *Determination and Interpretation of Flexible Budget Variances*   **L.O. 5**

Use the standard price and cost data supplied in Problem 8-1A. Assume that Bookout actually produced and sold 26,000 books. The actual sales price and costs incurred follow:

Actual price and variable costs	
Sales price	$39.00
Materials cost	10.20
Labour cost	4.90
Overhead cost	7.05
General, selling, and administrative costs	7.92
Actual fixed costs	
Manufacturing cost	$140,000
General, selling, and administrative costs	64,000

Required

a. Determine the flexible budget variances.

b. Indicate whether each variance is favourable or unfavourable.

c. For each variance, identify the management position responsible for it. Provide a logical explanation as to what could have caused the variance.

L.O. 1 PROBLEM 8-3A   *Flexible Budget Planning*

Cary Choi, the president of Sarnia Computer Services, needs your help. He wonders about the potential effects on the firm's net income if he changes the service rate that the firm charges its customers. The following are basic data for fiscal year 2005:

Standard rate and variable costs	
Service rate per hour	$60.00
Labour cost	32.00
Overhead cost	5.00
General, selling, and administrative cost	3.00
Expected fixed costs	
Repair facility cost	$350,000.00
General, selling, and administrative costs	100,000.00

Required

a. Prepare a pro forma income statement that would appear in the master budget if the firm expects 25,000 hours of repair services in 2005.

b. A marketing consultant suggests to Mr. Choi that the service rate may affect the number of service hours that the firm can achieve. According to the consultant's analysis, if Sarnia charges customers $55 per hour, the firm can achieve 32,000 hours of repair services. Prepare a flexible budget following the consultant's assumption.

c. The same consultant also suggests that if the firm raises its rate to $65 per hour, the number of service hours will decline to 21,000. Prepare a flexible budget with the new assumption.

d. Evaluate the three possible outcomes you determined in Requirements *a*, *b*, and *c* and recommend a pricing strategy.

L.O. 9 PROBLEM 8-4A   *Determination of Materials Price and Usage Variances*

Cowart Fruit Drink Company planned to make 200,000 containers of apple juice. It expected to use 500 ml of frozen apple concentrate to make one container of juice. Accordingly, Cowart planned to use 100,000 litres (200,000 containers × 500 ml) of frozen concentrate. The standard price of 250 ml of apple concentrate is $0.25. Cowart actually paid $110,168.10 to purchase 102,007.5 litres of concentrate, which was used to make 201,000 containers of apple juice.

Required

a. Are the flexible budget materials variances based on the planned volume of activity (200,000 containers) or actual volume of activity (201,000 containers)?

b. Compute the actual price per 250 ml of concentrate.

c. Compute the standard quantity (litres of concentrate) required to produce the containers.

d. Compute the materials price variance and indicate whether it is favourable or unfavourable.

e. Compute the materials usage variance and indicate whether it is favourable or unfavourable.

L.O. 9 PROBLEM 8-5A   *Determination of Labour Price and Efficiency Variances*

Della's Doll Company produces handmade dolls. The standard amount of time spent on each doll is 1.5 hours. The standard cost of labour is $8 per hour. The company planned to make 10,000 dolls during the accounting period but actually used 15,400 hours of labour to make 11,000 dolls. The payroll amounted to $123,816.

Required

a. Should the labour variances be based on the planned volume of 10,000 dolls or on the actual volume of 11,000 dolls?

b. Prepare a table that includes the standard labour price, the actual labour price, the standard labour hours, and the actual labour hours.

c. Compute the labour price variance and indicate whether it is favourable or unfavourable.
d. Compute the labour efficiency variance and indicate whether it is favourable or unfavourable.

PROBLEM 8-6A   *Fixed Overhead Variances Computed*

L.O. 9

In addition to other costs, Tindal Phone Company planned to incur $527,000 of fixed manufacturing overhead costs in making 340,000 telephones. Tindal actually produced 348,000 telephones and had actual overhead costs of $529,000. Tindal establishes its predetermined overhead rate on the basis of the planned volume of production (expected number of telephones).

Required
a. Calculate the predetermined overhead rate.
b. Determine the overhead spending variance and indicate whether it is favourable or unfavourable.
c. Determine the overhead volume variance and indicate whether it is favourable or unfavourable.

PROBLEM 8-7A   *Materials, Labour, and Overhead Variances Computed*

L.O. 9

The following data were drawn from the records of Norris Corporation:

Planned volume for year (static budget)	4,000 units
Standard direct materials cost per unit	1.25 kg. @ $4.50 per kg
Standard direct labour cost per unit	2 hours @ $8 per hour
Total expected fixed overhead costs	$18,000
Actual volume for the year (flexible budget)	4,200 units
Actual direct materials cost per unit	1.2 kg. @ $4.60 per kg
Actual direct labour cost per unit	2.2 hrs. @ $7.60 per hour
Total actual fixed overhead costs	$17,600

Required
a. Prepare a materials variance information table, including the standard price, the actual price, the standard quantity, and the actual quantity.
b. Calculate the materials price and quantity variances. Indicate whether the variances are favourable or unfavourable.
c. Prepare a labour variance information table, including the standard rate, the actual rate, the standard hours, and the actual hours.
d. Calculate the labour price and efficiency variances. Indicate whether the variances are favourable or unfavourable.
e. Calculate the predetermined overhead rate, assuming that Norris uses the number of units as the allocation base.
f. Calculate the overhead spending variance. Indicate whether the variances are favourable or unfavourable.
g. Calculate the overhead volume variance. Indicate whether the variances are favourable or unfavourable.

PROBLEM 8-8A   *Materials, Labour, and Overhead Variances Computed*

L.O. 9

Gem Manufacturing Company produces a component part of a top secret military communication device. The part, Product X, is expected to be produced at the following standard variable costs per unit:

Planned production	20,000 units
Per unit direct materials	800 grams @ $4.32 per kg
Per unit direct labour	3 hrs. @ $8 per hr.
Total estimated fixed overhead costs	$468,000

Gem purchased and used 17,600 kg of material at an average cost of $4.44 per kg. Labour usage amounted to 59,740 hours at an average of $8.10 per hour. Actual production amounted to 20,600 units. Actual fixed overhead costs amounted to $492,000. The company completed and sold all inventory for $1,200,000.

Required
a. Prepare a materials variance information table, including the standard price, the actual price, the standard quantity, and the actual quantity.

b. Calculate the materials price and usage variances. Indicate whether the variances are favourable or unfavourable.

c. Prepare a labour variance information table, including the standard rate, the actual rate, the standard hours, and the actual hours.

d. Calculate the labour price and usage variances. Indicate whether the variances are favourable or unfavourable.

e. Calculate the predetermined overhead rate, assuming that Gem uses the number of units as the allocation base.

f. Calculate the overhead spending and volume variances and indicate whether they are favourable or unfavourable.

g. Determine the amount of the gross margin that would appear on the company's year-end income statement.

L.O. 9 PROBLEM 8-9A   *Computation of Variances*

Nakase Manufacturing Company produces a single product. The following data apply to the standard cost of materials and labour associated with making the product:

Material quantity per unit	1 kilogram
Material price	$2.50 per kilogram
Labour quantity per unit	2 hours
Labour price	$9.00 per hour

During the accounting period, the company made 900 units of product. At the end of the accounting period, the variance accounts carried the following balances:

Materials Usage Variance Account	$50 Favourable
Materials Price Variance Account	$44 Unfavourable
Labour Usage Variance Account	$450 Unfavourable
Labour Price Variance Account	$740 Favourable

Required

a. Determine the actual amount of materials used.

b. Determine the actual price paid per kilogram for materials.

c. Determine the labour efficiency variance.

d. Determine the actual labour price per hour.

L.O. 9 PROBLEM 8-10A   *Standard Cost Computation and Variance Analysis*

Changing Times Company manufactures candles that are moulded and finished by hand. The company developed the following standards for a new line of drip candles:

Amount of direct material per unit	675 grams
Price of direct material per kg	$1.80
Quantity of labour per unit	2 hours
Price of direct labour per hour	$6/hour
Total budgeted fixed overhead	$63,000

During 2003, Changing Times expected to produce 15,000 drip candles. Production lagged behind expectations, and it only actually produced 12,000 drip candles. At year-end, direct materials purchased and used amounted to 8,400 kg at a unit price of $1.32 per kilogram. Direct labour costs were actually $5.75 per hour and 23,000 actual hours were worked to produce the drip candles. Overhead for the year actually amounted to $65,000. Overhead is applied to products using a predetermined overhead rate based on estimated units.

Required

(Round all computations to two decimal places.)

a. Compute the standard cost per candle for direct material, direct labour, and overhead.

b. Determine the total standard cost for one drip candle.

c. Compute the actual cost per candle for direct material, direct labour, and overhead.

d. Compute the total actual cost per unit.

e. Compute the price and usage variances for direct material and direct labour. Name any variances that need to be investigated. Comment as to the possible cause(s) for the variances.

f. Compute the fixed overhead spending and volume variances. Explain your findings.

g. Although the individual variances (price, usage, and overhead) were large, the standard cost per unit and the actual cost per unit differed by only a few cents. Explain this phenomenon.

PROBLEM 8-11A *Variance Analysis in a Not-for-Profit Entity*

The Women's Accounting Association held its annual public relations luncheon in April 2008. On the basis of the previous year's results, the organization allocated $10,515 of its operating budget to be available to cover the cost of the luncheon. To ensure that costs would be appropriately controlled, Sue Lyons, the treasurer, prepared the following budget for the 2008 luncheon. The budget for the luncheon was based on the following expectations:

1. The meal cost per person is expected to be $11.80. The cost driver for meals is based on the attendance number, which was expected to be 700 individuals.

2. Postage is based on $0.33 per invitation and 1,500 invitations are expected to be mailed. The cost driver for postage is number of invitations mailed.

3. The facility charge is $500 for a room that will accommodate up to 800 people; the charge for one to hold more than 800 people is $750.

4. A fixed amount was designated for printing, decorations, speaker's gift, and publicity.

Women's Accounting Association Public Relations Luncheon Budget April 2008	
Operating funds available	$10,515
Expenses	
Variable costs	
Meals (700 × $11.80)	$ 8,260
Postage (1,500 × 0.33)	495
Fixed costs	
Facility	500
Printing	475
Decorations	420
Speaker's gift	65
Publicity	300
Total expenses	10,515
Budget surplus (deficit)	$ 0

Actual results for the luncheon follow:

Women's Accounting Association Actual Results for Public Relations Luncheon April 2008	
Operating funds available	$10,515
Expenses	
Variable costs	
Meals (810 × $12.50)	$10,125
Postage (2,000 × $0.33)	660
Fixed costs	
Facility	750
Printing	475
Decorations	420
Speaker's gift	65
Publicity	300
Total expenses	12,795
Budget deficit	($ 2,280)

The following are the reasons for the differences between the budgeted and actual data:

1. The president of the organization, Paula Mercado, increased the invitation list to include 500 former members. As a result, 2,000 invitations were mailed.
2. Attendance was 810 individuals. Because of the higher-than-expected attendance, the luncheon was moved to a larger room, thereby increasing the facility charge to $750.
3. At the last minute, Ms. Lyons decided to add a dessert to the menu that increased the meal cost to $12.50 per person.
4. Printing, decorations, speaker's gift, and publicity costs were as budgeted.

Required

a. Prepare a flexible budget and compute the activity variances on the basis of a comparison between the master budget and the flexible budget.
b. Compute flexible budget variances by comparing the flexible budget with the actual results.
c. Ms. Mercado was extremely upset with the budget deficit. She immediately called Ms. Lyons to complain about the budget variance for the meal cost. She told Ms. Lyons that the added dessert caused the meal cost to be $1,865 ($10,125 − $8,260) over budget. She added, "I could expect a couple of hundred dollars one way or the other, but a couple of thousand is totally unacceptable. At the next meeting of the budget committee, I want you to explain what happened." Assume that you are Ms. Lyons. What would you tell the members of the budget committee?
d. Since this is a not-for-profit organization, why should anyone be concerned whether the budget is met?

PROBLEMS—SERIES B

L.O. 1, 4   **PROBLEM 8-1B**   *Determination of Sales Activity Variances*

Lohman Food Corporation has created the following standard price and costs for a refrigerated TV dinner that the company produces:

Standard price and variable costs	
Sales price	$6.49
Materials cost	2.25
Labour cost	0.65
Overhead cost	0.14
General, selling, and administrative costs	1.05
Expected fixed costs	
Manufacturing cost	$125,000
General, selling, and administrative costs	90,000

Lohman plans to make and sell 200,000 units of this dinner meal.

Required

a. Prepare a pro forma income statement that would appear in the master budget.
b. Prepare flexible budget income statements, assuming production and sales volume to be 180,000 and 220,000 units.
c. Determine the sales activity variances, assuming production and sales volume actually to be 190,000 units.
d. Indicate whether the variances are favourable or unfavourable.
e. Comment on how the variances are used to evaluate performance.

L.O. 5   **PROBLEM 8-2B**   *Determination and Interpretation of Flexible Budget Variances*

Use the standard price and cost data supplied in Problem 8-1B. Assume that Lohman actually produces and sells 216,000 units. The actual sales price and costs incurred follow:

Actual price and variable costs

Sales price	$6.45
Materials cost	2.20
Labour cost	0.67
Overhead cost	0.14
General, selling, and administrative costs	1.10

Actual fixed costs

Manufacturing cost	$128,000.00
General, selling, and administrative costs	89,000.00

Required

a. Determine the flexible budget variances.

b. Indicate whether each variance is favourable or unfavourable.

c. For each variance, identify the management position responsible for the variance. Provide a logical explanation as to what could have caused the variance.

PROBLEM 8-3B   *Flexible Budget Planning*   L.O. 1

Executive officers of Balden Seafood Processing Company are holding a planning session for fiscal year 2003. They have already established the following standard price and costs for their product:

Standard price and variable costs

Price per can	$3.00
Materials cost	1.05
Labour cost	0.64
Overhead cost	0.10
General, selling, and administrative costs	0.25

Expected fixed costs

Production facility costs	$215,000.00
General, selling, and administrative costs	180,000.00

Required

a. Prepare a pro forma income statement expected to appear in the master budget if the company expects to produce 600,000 cans of seafood in 2003.

b. A marketing consultant suggests to Balden's president that the product's price may affect the number of cans that the company can sell. According to the consultant's analysis, if the firm sets its price at $2.70, the company can sell 810,000 cans of seafood. Prepare a flexible budget on the basis of the consultant's suggestion.

c. The same consultant also suggests that if the company raises its price to $3.25 per can, the volume of sales will decline to 400,000. Prepare a flexible budget on the basis of this suggestion.

d. Evaluate the three possible outcomes you determined in Requirements *a*, *b*, and *c* and recommend a pricing strategy.

PROBLEM 8-4B   *Determination of Materials Price and Usage Variances*   L.O. 9

Bross Swimsuit Specialties, Inc. makes fashionable women's swimsuits. Its most popular swimsuit, with the Sarong trade name, uses fabric at a standard amount of 2 square metres of raw material with a standard price of $7.50 per square metre. The company planned to produce 100,000 Sarong swimsuits in 2004. At the end of 2004, the company's cost accountant discovered that Bross had used 212,000 square metres of fabric to make 102,000 swimsuits. Actual cost for the raw material was $1,653,600.

Required

a. Are the flexible budget material variances based on the planned volume of 100,000 swimsuits or actual volume of 102,000 swimsuits?

b. Compute the actual price per square metre of fabric.

c. Compute the standard quantity (square metres of fabric) required to produce the swimsuits.

d. Compute the materials price variance and indicate whether it is favourable or unfavourable.

e. Compute the materials usage variance and indicate whether it is favourable or unfavourable.

L.O. 9 PROBLEM 8-5B   *Determination of Labour Price and Efficiency Variances*

As noted in Problem 8-4B, Bross Swimsuit makes swimsuits. In 2004, Bross produced its most popular swimsuit, the Sarong, for a standard labour price of $15 per hour. The standard amount of labour was one hour per swimsuit. The company had planned to produce 100,000 Sarong swimsuits. At the end of 2004, the company's cost account- ant discovered that Bross had used 107,000 hours of labour to make 102,000 swimsuits. The total labour cost was $1,647,800.

Required
a. Should the labour variances be based on the planned volume of 100,000 swimsuits or on the actual volume of 102,000 swimsuits?
b. Prepare a table that includes the standard labour price, the actual labour price, the standard labour hours, and the actual labour hours.
c. Compute the labour price variance and indicate whether it is favourable or unfavourable.
d. Compute the labour efficiency variance and indicate whether it is favourable or unfavourable.

L.O. 9 PROBLEM 8-6B   *Fixed Overhead Variances Computed*

McGwire Sporting Goods Co. manufactures baseballs. According to McGwire's 2002 budget, the company planned to incur $300,000 of fixed manufacturing overhead costs to make 200,000 baseballs. McGwire actually produced 187,000 balls, incurring $296,000 of actual fixed manufacturing overhead costs. McGwire establishes its predeter- mined overhead rate on the basis of the planned volume of production (expected number of baseballs).

Required
a. Calculate the predetermined overhead rate.
b. Determine the overhead spending variance and indicate whether it is favourable or unfavourable.
c. Determine the overhead volume variance and indicate whether it is favourable or unfavourable.

L.O. 9 PROBLEM 8-7B   *Materials, Labour, and Overhead Variances Computed*

Andrew Jensen was a new cost accountant at Samuel Plastics, Inc. He was assigned to analyze the following data that his predecessor left him:

Planned volume for year (static budget)	2,500 units
Standard direct materials cost per unit	800 grams @ $3.60 per kg
Standard direct labour cost per unit	0.5 hours @ $10 per hour
Total expected fixed overhead costs	$3,000
Actual volume for the year (flexible budget)	2,700 units
Actual direct materials cost per unit	750 grams @ $3.84 per kg
Actual direct labour cost per unit	0.6 hrs. @ $8 per hour
Total actual fixed overhead costs	$3,100

Required
a. Prepare a materials variance information table, including the standard price, the actual price, the standard quan- tity, and the actual quantity.
b. Calculate the materials price and quantity variances and indicate whether they are favourable or unfavourable.
c. Prepare a labour variance information table, including the standard price, the actual price, the standard hours, and the actual hours.
d. Calculate the labour price and efficiency variances and indicate whether they are favourable or unfavourable.
e. Calculate the predetermined overhead rate, assuming that Samuel Plastics uses the number of units as the allo- cation base.
f. Calculate the overhead spending variance and indicate whether it is favourable or unfavourable.
g. Calculate the overhead volume variance and indicate whether it is favourable or unfavourable.

L.O. 9 PROBLEM 8-8B   *Materials, Labour, and Overhead Variances Computed*

Weber Corporation makes mouse pads for computer users. After the first year of operation, Brittany Weber, the pres- ident and chief executive officer, was eager to determine the efficiency of the company's operation. In her analysis, she used the following standards provided by her assistant:

Units of planned production	100,000
Per unit direct materials	250 square cm. @ $1 per square metre
Per unit direct labour	0.2 hrs. @ $7 per hr.
Total estimated fixed overhead costs	$50,000

Weber purchased and used 28,750 square metres of material at an average cost of $0.96 per square metre. Labour usage amounted to 19,800 hours at an average of $6.90 per hour. Actual production amounted to 104,000 units. Actual fixed overhead costs amounted to $51,000. The company completed and sold all inventory for $353,600.

Required

a. Prepare a materials variance information table, including the standard price, the actual price, the standard quantity, and the actual quantity.
b. Calculate the materials price and usage variances and indicate whether they are favourable.
c. Prepare a labour variance information table, including the standard price, the actual price, the standard hours, and the actual hours.
d. Calculate the labour price and usage variances and indicate whether they are favourable or unfavourable.
e. Calculate the predetermined overhead rate, assuming that Weber uses the number of units as the allocation base.
f. Calculate the overhead spending and volume variances and indicate whether they are favourable or unfavourable.
g. Determine the amount of the gross margin that would appear on the company's year-end income statement.

PROBLEM 8-9B *Computation of Variances* L.O. 9

A fire destroyed most of Hassein Products Corporation's records. Ginger Jacobson, the company's accountant, is trying to piece together the company's operating results from salvaged documents. She discovered the following data:

Standard material quantity per unit	1 kg
Standard material price	$5 per kg
Standard labour quantity per unit	0.6 hour
Standard labour price	$12 per hour
Actual number of products produced	2,000 units
Materials price variance	$198 favourable
Materials quantity variance	$100 favourable
Labour price variance	$488 unfavourable
Labour usage variance	$240 unfavourable

Required

a. Determine the actual amount of materials used.
b. Determine the actual price paid per pound for materials.
c. Determine the actual labour hours.
d. Determine the actual labour price per hour.

PROBLEM 8-10B *Standard Cost Computation and Variance Analysis* L.O. 9

Princeton Manufacturing Company, which makes aluminum alloy wheels for automobiles, recently introduced a new luxury wheel that fits small sports cars. The company developed the following standards for its new product:

Amount of direct material per wheel	800 grams
Price of direct material per kg	$12.10
Quantity of labour per wheel	2.5 hours
Price of direct labour per hour	$8/hour
Total budgeted fixed overhead	$84,000

In its first year of production, Princeton expected to produce 1,500 sets of wheels (4 wheels per set). Because of unexpected demand, it actually produced 1,800 sets of wheels. At year-end direct materials purchased and used amounted to 7,000 kg of aluminum metal at a cost of $87,750. Direct labour costs were actually $8.40 per hour. Actual hours worked were 2.20 hours per wheel. Overhead for the year actually amounted to $90,000. Overhead is applied to products using a predetermined overhead rate on the basis of the total estimated number of wheels to be produced.

Required

(Round all computations to two decimal places.)

a. Compute the standard cost per wheel for direct material, direct labour, and overhead.

b. Determine the standard cost per wheel.

c. Compute the actual cost per wheel for direct material, direct labour, and overhead.

d. Compute the actual cost per wheel.

e. Compute the price and usage variances for direct material and direct labour. Name any variances that need to be investigated. On the basis of your results, give a possible explanation for the labour usage variance.

f. Compute the fixed overhead spending and volume variances. Explain your findings.

L.O. 3, 4, 5   PROBLEM 8-11B *Variance Analysis for a Not-for-Profit Organization*

The Accounting Department of University of Saskatchewan planned its annual distinguished visiting lecturer (DVL) presentation to be held in October 2005. The secretary of the department prepared the following budget on the basis of costs that had been incurred in the past for the DVL presentation:

Accounting Department Distinguished Visiting Lecturer Budget October 2005	
Variable costs	
Beverages at break	$ 281.25
Postage	264.00
Step costs*	
Printing	500.00
Facility	250.00
Fixed costs	
Dinner	200.00
Speaker's gift	100.00
Publicity	50.00
Total costs	$1,645.25

*Step costs are costs that change abruptly after a defined range of volume (attendance). They do not change proportionately with unit volume increases (i.e., the cost is fixed within a range of activity but changes to a different fixed cost when the volume changes to a new range). For instance, the facility charge is $250 for from 1 to 400 attendees. From 401 to 500 attendees, the next larger room is needed, and the charge is $350. If more than 500 attended, the room size and cost would increase again.

The budget for the luncheon was based on the following expectations:

1. Attendance was estimated at 50 faculty from University of Saskatchewan and neighbouring Universities, 125 invited guest from the business community, and 200 students. Beverage charge per attendee would be $0.75. The cost driver for the beverages is the number of attendees.

2. Postage was based on $0.33 per invitation; 800 invitations were expected to be mailed to faculty and accounting business executives. The cost driver for postage was the number of invitations mailed.

3. Printing cost was expected to be $500 for 800 invitations and envelopes. Additional invitations and envelopes could be purchased in batches of 100 units with each batch costing $50.

4. The DVL presentation was held at a downtown convention centre. The facility charge was $250 for a room that has a capacity of 400 persons; the charge for one to hold more than 400 people rents for $350. The convention centre provided refreshments at break except beverages.

5. After the presentation, three University of Saskatchewan faculty members planned to take the speaker to dinner. The three-course dinner had been prearranged at a local restaurant for $200.

6. A gift for the speaker was budgeted at $100.
7. Publicity would consist of flyers and posters placed at strategic locations around campus and business offices, articles in the business section of the local newspapers, and announcements made in business classes and school newspapers. Printing for the posters and flyers had been prearranged for $50.
8. The speaker lives in Manitoba and had agreed to drive to the presentation at his own expense.

The actual results of the dinner follow:
1. Attendance consisted of 450 faculty, business executives, and students.
2. An additional 100 invitations were mailed when it was decided that selected alumni should also be invited.
3. On the basis of RSVP responses, the department rented the next size larger room at a cost of $350 for the presentation.
4. Postage, decorations, speaker's gift, printing, and publicity costs were as budgeted.
5. The department chairperson decided to have a four-course dinner, which cost $230.
6. Due to poor planning, the posters and flyers were not distributed as widely as expected. It was decided at the last minute to motivate student attendance by giving extra credit in accounting classes for attendance. The actual publicity cost was $75.

Required
a. Prepare a flexible budget and compute activity variances on the basis of a comparison between the master budget and the flexible budget. Provide a brief explanation as to the meaning of the activity variances.
b. Compute flexible budget variances by comparing the flexible budget with the actual results. Provide a brief explanation as to the meaning of the variable cost flexible budget variances. Discuss the fixed cost variances.
c. Calculate the expected and actual fixed cost per attendee. Discuss the significance of the difference in these amounts.
d. Since the department is a not-for-profit entity, why is it important for it to control the cost of sponsoring the distinguished visiting lecturer presentation?

ANALYZE, THINK, COMMUNICATE

BUSINESS APPLICATIONS CASE   *Static versus Flexible Budget Variances*   **ACT 8-1**

Larry Parker is the manufacturing production supervisor for Stained Glass Lamp Company. Trying to explain why he did not get the year-end bonus that he had expected, he told his wife, "This is the dumbest place I ever worked in. Last year the company set up this budget assuming we would sell 150,000 lamps. Well, they sold only 140,000. The company is losing money, and they give me a bonus for not using as much materials and labour as was called for in the budget. This year, the company has the same 150,000 goal and we sell 160,000. The company's making all kinds of money. You'd think I'd get this big fat bonus. Instead, they tell me I used more materials and labour than was budgeted. They say the company would have made a lot more money if I'd stayed within my budget. I guess I gotta wait for another bad year before I get a bonus. Like I said, this is the dumbest place I ever worked in."

Stained Glass Lamp Company's master budget and the actual results for the most recent year of operating activity follow:

Item	Master Budget	Actual Results	Variance	F or UF
Number of units	150,000	160,000	10,000	
Sales revenue	$33,000,000	$35,520,000	$2,520,000	F
Variable manufacturing costs				
Materials	4,800,000	5,300,000	500,000	UF
Labour	4,200,000	4,400,000	200,000	UF
Overhead	2,100,000	2,290,000	190,000	UF
Variable G, S, & A	5,250,000	6,180,000	930,000	UF
Contribution margin	$16,650,000	$17,350,000	$ 700,000	F
Fixed costs				
Manufacturing	7,830,000	7,830,000	0	
G, S, & A	6,980,000	6,980,000	0	
Net income	$ 1,840,000	$ 2,540,000	$ 700,000	F

Required

a. Did the marketing department increase sales by lowering prices or by using some other strategy?
b. Is Mr. Parker correct in his conclusion that something is wrong with Stained Glass Lamp Company's performance evaluation system? If so, make suggestions for improving the system.
c. Prepare a flexible budget and determine the amount of the flexible budget variances.
d. With respect to the flexible budget variances, assume that the materials price variance was favourable and the usage variance was unfavourable. Provide a rational explanation as to why Mr. Parker may not have been responsible for the usage variance. Provide a rational explanation as to why he may have been responsible for the usage variance.
e. With respect to the flexible budget variances, assume that the labour price variance is unfavourable. Was the labour usage variance favourable or unfavourable?
f. Is the fixed cost volume variance favourable or unfavourable? Explain how the cost per lamp will be affected.

ACT 8-2 GROUP ASSIGNMENT   *Variable Price and Usage Variances and Fixed Cost Variances*

Outdoor Tables, Inc. (OTI) makes picnic tables of 2 × 4 planks of treated pinewood. It sells the tables to large retail discount stores, such as Wal-Mart. After reviewing the following data generated by OTI's chief accountant, Arianne Schwartz, the company president, expressed concern that the total manufacturing cost was more than $0.5 million above budget ($7,084,800 − $6,520,000 = $564,800).

	Actual Results	Master Budget
Cost of planks per table	$ 44.10	$ 40.00
Cost of labour per table	26.10	25.50
Total variable manufacturing cost per table (a)	$70.20	$65.50
Total number of tables produced (b)	82,000	80,000
Total variable manufacturing cost (a × b)	$ 5,756,400	$ 5,240,000
Total fixed manufacturing cost	1,328,400	1,280,000
Total manufacturing cost	$ 7,084,800	$ 6,520,000

Ms. Schwartz asked Conrad Pearson, OTI's chief accountant, to explain what caused the increase in cost. Mr. Pearson responded that things were not as bad as they seemed. He noted that part of the cost variance resulted from making and selling more tables than had been expected. Making more tables naturally causes the cost of materials and labour to be higher. He explained that the flexible budget cost variance was less than $0.5 million. Specifically, he provided the following comparison:

	Actual Results	Flexible Budget
Cost of planks per table	$ 44.10	$ 40.00
Cost of labour per table	26.10	25.50
Total variable manufacturing cost per table (a)	$ 70.20	$ 65.50
Total number of tables produced (b)	82,000	82,000
Total variable manufacturing cost (a × b)	$ 5,756,400	$ 5,371,000
Total fixed manufacturing cost	1,328,400	1,280,000
Total manufacturing cost	$ 7,084,800	$ 6,651,000

On the basis of this information, he argued that the relevant variance for performance evaluation was only $433,800 ($7,084,800 − $6,651,000). Ms. Schwartz responded, "*Only* $433,800! I consider that a very significant number. By the end of the day, I want a full explanation as to what is causing our costs to increase."

Required

a. Divide the class into groups of four or five students and divide the groups into three sections. Assign Task 1 to the first section, Task 2 to the second section, and Task 3 to the third section.

Group Tasks

1. On the basis of the following information, determine the total materials cost variance and the price and usage variances. Assuming that the variances are an appropriate indicator of cause, provide a logical explanation as to what could have caused the variances. Identify the management position responsible.

	Actual Data	Standard Data
Number of planks per table	21	20
Price per plank	× $2.10	× $2.00
Material cost per table	$44.10	$40.00

2. On the basis of the following information, determine the total labour cost variance and the price and usage variances. Assuming that the variances are an appropriate indicator of cause, explain what could have caused each variance. Identify the management position responsible.

	Actual Data	Standard Data
Number of hours per table	2.9	3.0
Price per hour	× $9.00	× $8.50
Labour cost per table	$26.10	$25.50

3. Determine the amount of the fixed cost spending and volume variances. Explain what could have caused these variances. On the basis of the volume variance, indicate whether the actual fixed cost per unit would be higher or lower than the budgeted fixed cost per unit.

b. Select a spokesperson from each section to report the amount of the variances computed by the group. Reconcile any differences in the variances reported by the sections. Reconcile the individual variances with the total variance. Specifically, show that the total of the materials, labour, and overhead variances equals the total flexible budget variance ($433,800).

c. Discuss how Ms. Schwartz should react to the variance information.

WRITING ASSIGNMENT *Standard Costing—The Human Factor*

ACT 8-3

Supplex Corporation makes a protein supplement called Power Punch™. Its principal competitor for Power Punch is the protein supplement Superior Strength™, made by Paul Bryant Company (PBC). Mr. Bryant, a world-renowned weight-lifting champion, founded PBC. The primary market for both products is athletes. Supplex sells Power Punch to wellness stores, which sell it and other supplements and health foods to the public. In contrast, Superior Strength is advertised in sports magazines and sold through orders generated by the ads.

Mr. Bryant's fame is an essential factor in his company's advertising program. He is a dynamic character whose personality motivates people to strive for superior achievement. His demeanour not only stimulates sales but also provides a strong inspirational force for the employees of his company. He is a kind, understanding individual with high expectations who is fond of saying that "mistakes are just opportunities for improvement." Mr. Bryant is strong believer in total quality management.

Mr. Miller, president of Supplex Corporation, is a stern disciplinarian who believes in teamwork. He takes pride in his company's standard costing system. Managers work as a team to establish standards and then are held accountable for meeting them. Managers who fail to meet expectations are severely chastised, and continued failure leads to dismissal. After several years of rigorous enforcement, managers have fallen in line. Indeed, during the last two years, all managers have met their budget goals.

Even so, costs have risen steadily. These cost increases have been passed on to customers through higher prices. As a result, Power Punch is now priced significantly higher than Superior Strength. In fact, Superior Strength is selling directly to the public at a price that is below the wholesale price that Supplex is charging the wellness stores. The situation has reached a critical juncture. Sales of Power Punch are falling, while Superior Strength is experiencing significant growth. Given that industry sales have remained relatively stable, it is obvious that customers are shifting from Power Punch to Superior Strength. Mr. Miller is perplexed. He wonders how a company with direct market expenses can price its products so low.

Required

a. Provide a logical explanation as to why PBC has been able to gain a pricing advantage over Supplex.

b. Assume that you are a consultant who has been asked by the board of directors of Supplex to recommend how the decline in sales of Power Punch can be halted. Provide appropriate recommendations.

ACT 8-4 ETHICAL DILEMMA   *Budget Games*

Mildred Mosley is the most highly rewarded sales representative at Holt Corporation. Her secret to success is always to understate her abilities. Ms. Mosley is assigned to a territory in which her customer base is increasing at approximately 25 percent per year. Each year she estimates that her budgeted sales will be 10 percent higher than her previous year's sales. With little effort, she is able to double her budgeted sales growth. At Holt's annual sales meeting, she receives an award and a large bonus. Of course, Ms. Mosley does not disclose her secret to her colleagues. Indeed, she always talks about how hard it is to continue to top her previous performance. She tells herself, if they are dumb enough to fall for this rubbish, I'll milk it for all it's worth.

Required

a. What is the name commonly given to the budget game Ms. Mosley is playing?
b. Recommend how Ms. Mosley's budget game could be stopped.

ACT 8-5 SPREADSHEET ASSIGNMENT   *Using Excel*

Refer to the data in Problem 8-1A.

Required

Construct a spreadsheet to match the one shown in Exhibit 8–1 to answer Requirements *a* and *b*. However, build the spreadsheet flexible budget to show the results for production volume of 23,000, 24,000, 25,000, 26,000, and 27,000.

ACT 8-6 SPREADSHEET ASSIGNMENT   *Mastering Excel*

Refer to Problem 8-4A. In the following year, the standards remained the same, but the actual data are as follows: Cowart produced 202,000 containers of apple juice and purchased and used 102,500 litres of concentrate at $1.04 per litre.

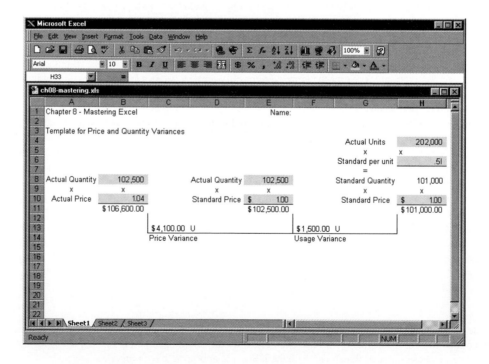

Required

Construct a spreadsheet template that could be used to calculate price and usage variances. The template should be constructed so that it could be used for any problem in the chapter that refers to price and usage variances by changing the data in the spreadsheet. The proceding screen capture represents a template for price and usage variances.

Spreadsheet Tip

1. The shaded cells can be changed according to the data in each problem. All other cells are formulas based on the numbers in the shaded cells.

2. The cells that label the variances as F or U (favourable or unfavourable) are based on a function called IF. The IF function is needed because the variance can be either favourable or unfavourable. The formula must determine whether actual expenditures exceed budgeted expenditures to determine whether the variance is unfavourable or favourable. As an example, the formula in Cell D13 is =IF(B11>E11,"U","F"). The formula evaluates the expression B11>E11. If this expression is true (B11 is less than E11), the text F is inserted in Cell D13. The IF function can also be used to place formulas or numbers in a cell on the basis of an expression is true or false. For example, the formula =IF(B11>E11,B11−E11,E11−B11) would calculate the amount of the variance as a positive number regardless of which amount is larger.

3. An easier way to make the variance a positive number, regardless of whether it is favourable, or unfavourable is to use the absolute value function. The format of the formula in Cells C13 and F13 would be =ABS(left number − right number).

4. The lines around the variances are produced by using the borders in *Excel* (Format, Cells, Border).

Responsibility Accounting

Learning Objectives

After completing this chapter, you should be able to:

1 Understand the concept of decentralization and describe its relationship to responsibility accounting.

2 Prepare and use responsibility reports.

3 Understand the controllability concept.

4 Explain how the management by exception doctrine relates to responsibility reports.

5 Understand the differences in cost, profit, and investment centres.

6 Evaluate investment opportunities by using the return on investment technique.

7 Evaluate investment opportunities by using the residual income technique.

8 Understand the three common approaches used to establish transfer prices.

the *curious* manager

Tony Freeman/PhotoEdit

Donald V. Fites is the chief executive officer of Caterpillar Inc. (Cat), a giant corporation with worldwide operations. Indeed, in 1998, more than 51 percent of its sales came from overseas. Mr. Fites hopes to increase that percentage to more than 75 percent by the end of the next decade. Accordingly, he spends a considerable amount of time analyzing the impact of foreign economies on Cat sales. When not involved in international issues, Mr. Fites is speaking to improve the company's fragile relationship with the United Autoworkers. In the 1990s, Mr. Fites spearheaded a $2 billion investment to modernize his company's U.S. plants. With such things on his agenda, how does Mr. Fites know that the company's purchasing agent is not paying too much for the paint used to colour and protect its equipment?

Walter Keller is a production manager for Evans Corporation. His budget includes a monthly allowance of $20,000 for labour costs. During April, his employees became unusually lethargic, everyone just seemed to slow down. They spoke of spring fever, beautiful weather, and a desire to be outside. The result was a decline in productivity, higher labour costs, and an unfavourable budget variance. Does this mean that the budget failed to control the labor costs? The answer is, no. People, not budgets, control costs. *In this case, Mr. Keller is responsible for the cost overrun.*

    Budgeting is merely a tool that is used in the process of cost control. The actual control of cost is the responsibility *of management.* **Responsibility accounting** *focuses reporting on individual managers; its objective is to increase productivity by providing information that is helpful in evaluating* *managerial performance. For example, expense items that the production department manager controls are presented in one report and the items that the marketing department manager controls are presented in a different report. This chapter discusses the development and utilization of a responsibility accounting system.*

▍Decentralization Concept

LO1

Understand the concept of decentralization and describe its relationship to responsibility accounting.

Clear lines of authority and responsibility are essential in establishing a responsibility accounting system. Divisions of authority and responsibility normally occur as a natural consequence of the management function. In a small business, it is possible for one person to control the entire operation. This person is able to perform all the necessary functions, such as marketing, management, production, and accounting, because of the simplicity of the business structure. In contrast, the level of complexity in large corporations is so great that it precludes using a single decision maker.

Consider as an example the decision to hire employees. In a small business, the owner/operator works in the business and is familiar with the job requirements, level of skill required, and local wage rates. She is, therefore, in a position to make a decision as to whom to offer a job. A major corporation, however, may have thousands of different jobs that require different skill levels. These jobs must be performed in a variety of locations that have different wage rate structures. Obviously, the president of the corporation cannot know all that is necessary to make informed hiring decisions for the entire company. Instead, he delegates that responsibility to individuals who are knowledgeable about the particular circumstances associated with the hiring decisions. Accordingly, a human resources department may be established to handle employment practices and policies.

Similarly, other departments or divisions will be established to delegate the decision-making authority to the individuals who are best suited to making the decision. The practice of delegating authority and responsibility is referred to as decentralization. Some of the advantages of **decentralization** include the following:

1. *Encourages upper-level management to concentrate on strategic decisions.* Because local management makes routine decisions, upper-level management has more time to concentrate on long-term planning, goal setting, and performance evaluation.
2. *Promotes improvements in decision making.* Local managers are usually better informed about local issues. Furthermore, their proximity to these issues permits them to react more rapidly to developing events. As a result, local managers are generally able to make better decisions.
3. *Motivates managers to improve productivity.* The freedom to act, coupled with responsibility for the actions taken, results in an environment that encourages most individuals to perform at high levels.
4. *Trains lower-level managers to accept greater responsibilities.* Decision making is a general skill. Managers who are accustomed to making decisions regarding local issues are generally able to apply their decision-making skills to broader issues when they are promoted to upper management positions.
5. *Improves performance evaluation.* When lines of authority and responsibility are clearly drawn, credit or blame can be more easily assigned on the basis of the results achieved.

Decentralization can also have detrimental effects. If authority is too widely disbursed, the cohesiveness of the overall organization may suffer. Five people working independently on a project will accomplish less than five people who put forth a team effort. For example, if each player on a basketball team were interested only in maximizing the number of points she scored personally, the total team score would suffer. Instead of passing the ball to a teammate who was in a good position to score, players would take poor shots to improve their personal scores. Managers in decentralized organizations must be encouraged to develop a team mentality; the benefit to the firm as a whole must take priority over personal successes or failures of any particular manager. Authority and responsibility should be delegated in a manner that promotes achieving the goals of the total firm.

▊ Organization Chart

Exhibit 9–1 is a partial organization chart showing the lines of authority and responsibility of a decentralized business. The chart includes five levels of responsibility. Other companies may have more or fewer responsibility levels, depending on their respective needs to decentralize. The responsibility levels are arranged in a hierarchical order with responsibility reports moving from the bottom upward. The information contained in the responsibility reports is cumulative; in other words, each manager receives detailed information about his or her particular responsibility level plus summary information about all responsibility centres that are under his chain of authority.

▊ Responsibility Reports

LO2
Prepare and use responsibility reports.

A **responsibility report** is prepared for each individual who has control over revenue or expense items. It normally includes a list of the items under that person's control, the budgeted amount for each item, the actual amount spent for each item, and the difference between the budgeted and actual amounts (i.e., the variance). The report shows the manager what was expected of her and how her actual performance compared with those expectations.

LO3
Understand the controllability concept.

Controllability Concept

The **controllability concept** is crucial to an effective responsibility accounting system. Each manager's evaluation should be based on only the revenue or cost items that he controls. Motivation is lost when a manager is rewarded or punished for actions that are beyond the scope of his control. Unfortunately, control may be shared rather than absolute. An actual case may serve to illustrate this point.

Dorothy Pasework, a buyer for a large department store chain, was held responsible for the retail sales of the goods that she purchased from wholesalers because it is the buyer's responsibility to purchase goods that can be resold. She purchased a large inventory of copper cookware that she thought would sell rapidly during the Christmas season. The expected sales failed to materialize, and upper management criticized Ms. Pasework's purchase. She complained that she was not at fault because the sales staff had not marketed the cookware properly, citing two instances in which she had personally visited stores that were not displaying the cookware in accordance with her instructions. The

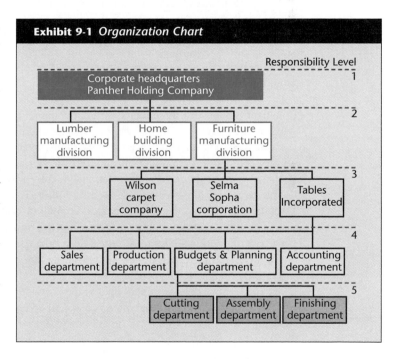

Exhibit 9-1 *Organization Chart*

Responsibility Level
1 — Corporate headquarters Panther Holding Company
2 — Lumber manufacturing division | Home building division | Furniture manufacturing division
3 — Wilson carpet company | Selma Sopha corporation | Tables Incorporated
4 — Sales department | Production department | Budgets & Planning department | Accounting department
5 — Cutting department | Assembly department | Finishing department

sales staff charged that the potential for selling the cookware was insufficient to merit the effort necessary to set up a proper display.

The exercise of control is frequently clouded as the preceding case illustrates. Accordingly, managers are usually held responsible for items over which they exercise *predominant* rather than *absolute* control. This practice can lead to motivational problems. Business operates in an imperfect world, however, and certain compromises must be accepted to continue operating activity. At times, responsibility accounting may not be completely fair, but it has proven to be an effective means of motivation in most situations. It is management's job to ensure that the numbers generated in a responsibility accounting system are properly interpreted and that rewards and punishments are administered fairly.

Management by Exception and Degree of Summarization

LO4

Explain how the management by exception doctrine relates to responsibility reports.

Responsibility reports are arranged in a manner that promotes the use of the **management by exception** doctrine. As noted earlier, the reports of a particular manager contain detailed information about revenue and cost items that are directly under his control, as well as summary data with regard to the activities of the responsibility centres that fall under his authority. We will use the chain of command as shown in Exhibit 9–1 as an example.

Starting with the Finishing Department at the fifth level of responsibility, the supervisor's report would contain all the cost and revenue items under her control. For example, the report would include the salary expenses of the employees who work in the Finishing Department; the expenses associated with the direct materials, such as paint, supplies, and small tools, used in the department; and any other expenses over which the supervisor had control. The report for the manager of the Production Department (i.e., the fourth level) would include the *total* of the items shown in the Finishing Department's report. It would also include the report *totals* of the other departments under the production manager's chain of authority (i.e., Cutting and Assembly Departments). In addition, the production manager's report would include a detailed account of the individual items for which he was personally responsible. These items may include administrative staff expenses and supervisory salaries.

The responsibility report for the manager of Tables Incorporated (i.e., third level) would include summary totals from the reports of the fourth-level managers (i.e., Sales, Production, Planning, and Accounting Departments) and a detailed analysis of the items under her direct control. This method of summarization continues up the chain of command.

Ultimately, headquarters personnel would receive summary data from the division managers and would add their particular revenue and expense items to those data. The data at headquarters level (i.e., first level) would include all revenue and expense items because full responsibility rests at the top of the organization. Accordingly, headquarters personnel usually prepare year-to-date financial statements to gain an understanding of the current financial condition.

Note that each manager receives only *summary* information regarding the performance of the responsibility centres that are under his supervision. For example, the production manager will be advised as to the amount of the *total* budget variance incurred by the Finishing Department but is not informed as to the cause of the variance. That information is reported only to the supervisor of the Finishing Department. At first glance, the lack of detailed information may appear to hinder the production manager's ability to control costs. In fact, it has the opposite effect. Be aware that managers are normally very busy individuals who must ration their time carefully. The supervisor of the Finishing Department should look at her responsibility report and take the necessary corrective action without bothering the production manager. The production manager should become concerned only when one of his supervisors loses control. The summary data in the production manager's report will be sufficient to advise him of such situations. Accordingly, managers will concentrate only on the exceptional items (i.e., management by exception), which will be automatically highlighted in their responsibility reports.

Qualitative Reporting Features

Responsibility reports should be stated in simple terms. If they are too complex, managers will ignore them. The reports should show clearly the budgeted and actual amounts of controllable revenue and expense items. Variances should be highlighted to promote the management by exception doctrine. Regular communication between the report preparer and the report user should be maintained to ensure the relevance of the information. Furthermore, reports must be issued on a timely basis. A report that describes yesterday's problem is not nearly as useful as one that reports today's problem. The utility of information tends to decrease with the passage of time.

Responsibility Reports Illustrated

Exhibit 9–2 is a partial set of responsibility reports for the third through fifth levels of Panther Holding Company. Before analyzing these reports, you may find it useful to review Panther's organization chart in Exhibit 9–1. From the lower level upward, each successive report contains summary data from the

Exhibit 9-2 *Responsibility Reports*

Panther Holding Company
Second Level: Furniture Manufacturing Division
For the Month Ended January 31, 2004

	Budget	Actual	Variance
Controllable expenses			
Administrative Division expense	$ 20,400	$ 31,100	$ (10,700) U
Company president's salary	9,600	9,200	400 F
Wilson Carpet Company	82,100	78,400	3,700 F
Selma Sopha Corporation	87,200	116,700	(29,500) U
Tables Incorporated	48,600	51,250	(2,650) U
Total	$247,900	$286,650	$ (38,750) U

Panther Holding Company
Third Level: Tables Incorporated
For the Month Ended January 31, 2004

	Budget	Actual	Variance
Controllable expenses			
Administrative Division expense	$ 3,000	$ 2,800	$ 200 F
Department managers' salaries	10,000	11,200	(1,200) U
Sales Department costs	9,100	8,600	500 F
Production Department costs	(13,500)	13,750	(250) U
Planning Department costs	(4,800)	7,000	(2,200) U
Accounting Department costs	8,200	7,900	300 F
Total	$ (48,600)	$ 51,250	$ (2,650) U

Panther Holding Company
Fourth Level: Production Department
For the Month Ended January 31, 2004

	Budget	Actual	Variance
Controllable expenses			
Administrative Staff expense	$ (900)	$ 1,100	$ (200) U
Supervisory salaries	2,800	2,800	0
Cutting Department costs	1,400	1,200	200 F
Assembly Department costs	(2,800)	2,900	(100) U
Finishing Department costs	(5,600)	5,750	(150) U
Total	$ (13,500)	$ 13,750	$ (250) U

Panther Holding Company
Fifth Level: Finishing Department
For the Month Ended January 31, 2004

	Budget	Actual	Variance
Controllable expenses			
Wages expenses	$ 3,200	$ 3,000	$ 200 F
Direct materials	(1,100)	1,400	(300) U
Supplies	(40)	500	(100) U
Small tools	(600)	650	(50) U
Other expenses	300	200	100 F
Total	$ (5,600)	$ 5,750	$ (150) U

preceding report. For example, the total $150 unfavourable variance in the Finishing Department's report is a single line item in the Production Department's report.

The illustration demonstrates how the summary data are useful in employing the management by exception doctrine. For example, a cursory review of the Furniture Manufacturing Division's report indicates that the division manager should concentrate her efforts on two areas. First, Selma Sopha Corporation's expenditures are out of line, as evidenced by the $29,500 unfavourable variance. Furthermore, the Furniture Manufacturing Division manager's administrative expenses are well above the budget expectations. On the basis of this information, the manager should ask for detailed reports covering these two areas. Management's attention is automatically directed to the areas that need the most supervision. The other areas seem to be operating within reasonable bounds and can be left to the direction of their respective managers.

A responsibility report would also be prepared for the first responsibility level, corporate headquarters. The report would be similar to those shown in Exhibit 9–2. Furthermore, at least at the headquarters level, year-to-date earnings statements would be prepared to inform management of the company's overall performance. Many times, divisions or companies operating within divisions also prepare year-to-date earnings statements that are used for managerial purposes and therefore are normally prepared in a contribution margin format. The January 2004 earnings statement for the Panther Holding Company is shown in Exhibit 9–3.

Exhibit 9-3 *Panther Earnings Statement*

Panther Holding Company
Earnings Statement for Internal Use
For the Month Ended January 31, 2004

	Budget	Actual	Variance
Sales	$984,300	$962,300	$ (22,000) U
Variable expenses			
Variable product costs	343,100	352,250	(9,150) U
Variable selling expenses	105,000	98,000	7,000 F
Other variable expenses	42,200	51,100	(8,900) U
Total variable expenses	490,300	501,350	(11,050) U
Contribution margin	494,000	460,950	(33,050) U
Fixed expenses			
Fixed product cost	54,100	62,050	(7,950) U
Fixed selling expense	148,000	146,100	1,900 F
Other fixed expenses	23,000	25,250	(2,250) U
Total fixed expenses	225,100	233,400	(8,300) U
Net income	$268,900	$227,550	$ (41,350) U

▌ Responsibility Centres

LO5

Understand the differences in cost, profit, and investment centres.

A **responsibility centre** is the point in an organization where the control over revenue or expense items is located. The point of control may be a division, a department, a subdepartment, or even a single machine. For example, a transportation company may identify a semitrailer truck as a responsibility centre. The company holds the driver of the truck responsible for the revenue and expense items associated with operating the truck. Responsibility centres may be divided into three categories: cost, profit, and investment.

A **cost centre** is a business segment that incurs expenses but does not generate revenue. Managers of cost centres can only influence costs; they cannot control them. In the Panther organization chart (see Exhibit 9–1), the Finishing Department and the Production Department are representative cost centres. As the illustration implies, cost centres normally exist at the lower levels of the organization chart.

A **profit centre** differs from a cost centre in that it not only incurs costs but also generates income. In other words, this responsibility centre can influence both revenue and expense items. The manager of a cost centre is judged on his ability to control costs within a budget range, but the manager of a profit centre is judged on her ability to produce revenue in excess of expenses. In the Panther organization chart, the companies in the third-level segments (i.e., Wilson Carpet Company, Selma Sopha Corporation, and Tables Incorporated) are considered profit centres.

Investment centre managers are responsible for revenue and expense items and for the investment of capital. Accordingly, these managers are held accountable for assets and liabilities as well as earnings. Investment centres are normally located at the upper-levels of the organization chart. The second-level division managers in the Panther organization are in charge of investment centres (i.e., managers of the lumber, home, and furniture divisions).

▮ Managerial Performance Measurement

One of the primary purposes of a responsibility accounting system is to facilitate the measurement of managerial performance. Managers are assigned responsibility for certain cost, profit, or investment centres. Managerial performance can be measured by comparing the operating results of the assigned responsibility centre with established standards or with the results of other responsibility centres within the organization.

In general, managers of cost centres are evaluated on the basis of their ability to attain preestablished standards by comparing actual costs with standard costs. Favourable variances indicate what is good performance and unfavourable variances suggest what is poor performance. In contrast, the results of profit centres are normally evaluated on the basis of earnings that are reported in a contribution format. The actual earnings may be compared with budgeted amounts, previous results, or the earnings of other profit centres. The results of investment centres must be evaluated on the basis of assets invested as well as revenue and expense measures. The measurement techniques (i.e., standard cost and contribution margin format income reporting) used for cost and profit centres have been discussed in previous chapters. The remainder of this chapter is devoted to discussing performance measures that are applicable to investment centres.

Return on Investment

Businesses use assets to obtain more assets. For example, a grocery store uses cash to purchase inventory. The inventory is converted to cash when it is sold to customers. If the business is profitable, the amount of cash received from the sale of the inventory will exceed the amount of cash that was used to purchase the inventory. Performance can be measured by the ability to increase the ratio of the assets returned to the amount of assets used. This measure is commonly referred to as the **return on investment** (ROI). It can be expressed in a simple equation.

$$\text{ROI} = \frac{\text{Net income}}{\text{Investment}}$$

To illustrate the use of ROI as an evaluation technique, assume that two managers are given $1,000 each to invest. The first manager invests in a certificate of deposit that earns $110 per year. The second manager invests in inventory that is sold at a $120 profit. The two managers' respective ROIs are computed as follows:

LO6

Evaluate investment opportunities by using the return on investment technique.

First Manager

$$\text{ROI} = \frac{\text{Net income}}{\text{Investment}} = \frac{\$110}{\$1,000} = 11\%$$

Second Manager

$$\text{ROI} = \frac{\text{Net income}}{\text{Investment}} = \frac{\$120}{\$1,000} = 12\%$$

On the basis of *quantitative* information alone, the second manager's performance is superior to the performance of the first manager. In other words, a higher ROI indicates better performance.

Qualitative Considerations

Using ROI as an evaluation technique may be complicated by certain qualitative characteristics. For example, assume that Panther Holding Company decides to use ROI to evaluate the performance of Renata Zupanic, the manager of the Furniture Manufacturing Division. What items should be included in the earnings and investment figures? Suppose that one year ago, Panther decided to close a furniture plant because recessionary conditions had caused a decline in the demand for furniture. Panther considered the situation to be temporary and planned to reopen the plant when demand returned to normal levels. Should this plant be included in Ms. Zupanic's investment base when computing the ROI for her division? It would be unfair to hold her responsible for such nonoperating assets. Accordingly, most companies do not use net income and total assets in the ROI formula. Instead, they normally use *operating income* divided by *operating assets*.

Some companies refine the computation even further by using only *controllable items* in the formula. This practice has appeal for motivational purposes, but it is usually difficult at the investment centre level to segregate controllable from noncontrollable items. As discussed earlier, when controllable versus noncontrollable criteria are used, the concept of predominant control, as opposed to absolute control, must be employed. Regardless of the definition used for earnings and investment, management must exercise judgment in deciding which specific items to include in the computation.

Measurement Basis

The ROI computation is further complicated by the question of what *value* to use for the assets included in the investment base. Suppose that three machines, A, B and C, are assigned to different investment centres. Each machine originally cost $5,000 and is currently rented to customers by its respective investment centre. Net rental income for each machine is approximately $1,000. Machine A was purchased first and has a current book value (i.e., cost minus accumulated amortization) of $2,000. Machine B was purchased second and has a book value of $4,000. Machine C was purchased last but was amortization on an accelerated basis that resulted in a more rapid decline in book value. Machine C's current book value is $2,500. See Exhibit 9–4 for the computation of ROI for each machine using book value as the valuation basis.

Do the data in Exhibit 9–4 imply that the manager of the investment centre to which Machine A is assigned is outperforming the managers of the other investment centres? Obviously, the answer is, no. The only difference is that Machine A is older and therefore has a lower book value. Machine C is newer, but it still has a reduced book value because it was amortized on an accelerated basis.

Clearly, when book value is used as the valuation basis, the ROI is affected by the age of the asset and the method of amortization. Accordingly, the use of book value can cause severe motivational problems. Managers will feel that comparisons of the ROIs of different investment centres are unfair because the numbers do not accurately reflect performance. Furthermore, managers may be tempted to use obsolete equipment because its replacement would increase the amount of their investment base for the ROI computation.

The problems described here may be reduced by using original cost instead of book value in the denominator of the ROI formula. In this example, each of the machines had an original cost of $5,000. Accordingly, the ROI for each machine is 20 percent ($1,000 ÷ $5,000). Note, however, that this practice may not entirely solve the valuation problem. As a result of inflation and technological advances, comparable equipment purchased at different times will have different costs. To counter this problem, some accountants advocate the use of *replacement cost*, rather than *historical cost*, as the valuation base. Although this practice is frequently suggested, it is seldom used because of the difficulty of determining the amount that it would cost to replace particular assets. For example, imagine the difficulty of determining the replacement cost of all the assets in a factory, such as a steel mill that has been operating for years.

As this discussion implies, the selection of the valuation basis is a complicated matter. In spite of its shortcomings, most companies continue to use book value as the valuation basis. Accordingly, it is important for management to consider those shortcomings when using ROI as a technique for performance evaluation.

Exhibit 9-4 *Comparison of ROIs*

$$ROI = \frac{Net\ income}{Investment}$$

$$Machine\ A = \frac{1,000}{2,000} = 50\%$$

$$Machine\ B = \frac{1,000}{4,000} = 25\%$$

$$Machine\ C = \frac{1,000}{2,500} = 40\%$$

Factors Affecting Return on Investment

The ROI formula can be subdivided into two ratios. It is often helpful to make this subdivision to encourage managers to further analyze factors that affect the firm's profitability. Profitability is affected by the *margin earned* on sales and by the number of times that the margin is collected during the accounting period (i.e., the *turnover rate*). For example, an item that can be purchased for $1 and sold for $1.20 may be more profitable than an item that is purchased for $1 and sold for $1.50. Perhaps during the accounting period, 75 units of the item with the $0.20 margin could be sold but only 25 units of the item with the $0.50 margin could be sold. Under these circumstances, the first item would produce $15 (75 × $0.20) of profit during the accounting period, while the second item would produce only $12.50 (25 × $0.50) of profit. Clearly, both margin and turnover affect profitability. If we express both the factors as separate ratios, the following expanded version of the ROI formula can be developed:

Step 1

$$Margin = \frac{Net\ Income}{Sales}$$

Step 2

$$\text{Turnover} = \frac{\text{Sales}}{\text{Investment}}$$

Step 3

$$\text{ROI} = \text{Margin} \times \text{Turnover}$$

Step 4

$$\text{ROI} = \frac{\text{Net Income}}{\text{Sales}} \times \frac{\text{Sales}}{\text{Investment}}$$

To illustrate, assume that Gamma Company produced $15,000 of net earnings from $200,000 of sales. Furthermore, Gamma had invested $100,000 in assets to produce the sales. On the basis of this information, Gamma's ROI can be computed as follows:

$$
\begin{aligned}
\text{ROI} &= \quad \text{Margin} \quad \times \quad \text{Turnover} \\
&= \frac{\$15,000}{\$200,000} \times \frac{\$200,000}{\$100,000} \\
&= 7.5\% \times 2 \\
&= 15\%
\end{aligned}
$$

It may be helpful to verify that this is the same ROI figure that would result from using our original ROI formula. Recall that the original formula was as follows:

$$\text{ROI} = \frac{\text{Net income}}{\text{Investment}}$$

In this case,

$$\text{ROI} = \frac{\$15,000}{\$100,000} = 15\%$$

Although the expanded formula looks more complicated, it is generally more useful because it encourages managers to concentrate on all the factors that affect ROI. By analyzing the expanded formula, we can see that profitability and the resultant ROI can be improved in one of three ways. Specifically, *increased sales*, *lowered expenses*, or *reduced investment base* will increase ROI. Each of these possibilities is demonstrated using the Gamma Company illustration.

1. *Increase ROI by increasing sales.* Suppose that Gamma Company increases sales from $200,000 to $240,000, thereby resulting in an increase in net income from $15,000 to $19,500. The ROI becomes

$$
\begin{aligned}
\text{ROI} &= \quad \text{Margin} \quad \times \quad \text{Turnover} \\
&= \frac{\$19,500}{\$200,000} \times \frac{\$240,000}{\$100,000} \\
&= 8.125\% \times 2.4 \\
&= 19.5\%
\end{aligned}
$$

2. *Increase ROI by reducing expenses.* Assume that Gamma Company embarks on a campaign to lower expenses without affecting sales or the investment base. It is successful in its effort to control expenses to the point that earnings increase from $15,000 to $20,000. Accordingly, ROI becomes

$$
\begin{aligned}
\text{ROI} &= \quad \text{Margin} \quad \times \quad \text{Turnover} \\
&= \frac{\$15,000}{\$200,000} \times \frac{\$200,000}{\$100,000} \\
&= 10\% \times 2 \\
&= 20\%
\end{aligned}
$$

3. *Increase ROI by reducing the investment base.* Managers who become too income oriented frequently overlook this possibility. By reducing the amount of funds invested in operating assets, such as inventory or accounts receivable, they can increase profitability because the funds released from current operations can be reinvested in other assets that produce new earnings. This effect is reflected in the ROI computation. For example, assume that through efficient operations, Gamma Company is able to reduce the carrying value of its inventory so that the required investment to produce the same amount of sales drops from $100,000 to $80,000. As a result, ROI becomes

$$
\begin{aligned}
ROI &= \quad \text{Margin} \quad \times \quad \text{Turnover} \\
&= \frac{\$15,000}{\$200,000} \times \frac{\$200,000}{\$80,000} \\
&= 7.5\% \times 2.5 \\
&= 18.75\%
\end{aligned}
$$

In each case, the ROI increased from the original 15 percent to some higher percentage. The use of the expanded ROI formula and the Gamma illustration emphasize that ROI is affected by sales, net earnings, and the level of investment. The prudent manager will consider all three components when trying to improve the company's profitability.

Residual Income

Suppose that you are the manager of an investment centre that operates within a large corporation. You are evaluated on the basis of your ability to maximize your ROI. The corporation's overall ROI is 15 percent. However, your particular investment centre has consistently outperformed other investment centres. Its current ROI is 20 percent. You have an opportunity to invest funds in a project that promises to earn an 18 percent ROI. Would you accept the investment opportunity?

LO7

Evaluate investment opportunities by using the residual income technique.

These circumstances place you in an awkward position. The corporation would benefit from having you accept the project because the expected ROI of 18 percent is higher than the corporate average ROI of 15 percent. However, you personally would suffer from a decision to accept the project because it would result in a decline in the level of your investment centre's current ROI of 20 percent. Accordingly, you are forced to choose between your personal benefit and that of the corporation. When faced with such decisions, many managers choose to benefit themselves at the expense of their corporations. The term used to describe this situation is **suboptimization**.

To avoid *suboptimization*, many businesses use an evaluation technique known as **residual income**. This approach evaluates a manager on his ability to maximize the dollar value of earnings above some targeted level of earnings. The targeted level of earnings is established by multiplying the amount of investment by a desired ROI. Expressed as a formula, *residual income* is defined as follows:

$$\text{Residual income} = \text{Earned income} - (\text{Investment} \times \text{Desired ROI})$$

To illustrate, assume that Bender Division is defined as an investment centre of Amcom Corporation. Noel Ducote, Bender's manager, controls $5,000,000 of assets that were used to produce net income of $900,000. Amcom has established a desired ROI of 12 percent on the basis of the corporation's average ROI. On the basis of this information, the residual income associated with the Bender Division is computed in Exhibit 9–5.

Note that Bender Division's current ROI is 18 percent ($900,000 ÷ $5,000,000). If Mr. Ducote discovers an opportunity to invest an additional $1,000,000 in a project that is expected to provide a 14 percent ROI, would he be motivated to accept it under a residual income evaluation system? The answer is, yes because the new investment would result in an increase in the total dollar value of the residual income. This fact is verified by the computations in Exhibit 9–6. Note that the amount of investment is increased by the $1,000,000 additional funding and earned income is increased by $140,000 ($1,000,000 × 0.14).

Accepting the new project would add $20,000 to Bender's residual income ($320,000 − $300,000). Because Mr. Ducote is evaluated on his ability to maximize residual income, he would benefit by the decision to accept any investment projects that return an ROI in excess of the desired 12 percent. The fact that Bender's ROI will fall does not enter into the decision. Accordingly, the residual income approach eliminates the problem of goal incongruence between management and the company.

Numerous comparisons are possible when using the residual income approach. The level of residual income in the current year can be compared with the level earned in previous years, with some target level, or with the amount generated by other investment centres. When making comparisons among different investment centres, however, care must be taken to ensure that the managers have equal access to investment funds because managers with larger investment bases would produce higher levels of residual income simply as a result of the size of their operations but not of superior performance. Here, as with any other evaluation techniques, fair and accurate assessments are possible only if upper management exercises due care when interpreting the results.

Exhibit 9-5 *Computation of Residual Income*

$$
\begin{aligned}
\text{Residual income} &= \text{Earned income} - (\text{Investment} \times \text{Desired ROI}) \\
&= \$900,000 - (\$5,000,000 \times 0.12) \\
&= \$900,000 - \$600,000 \\
&= \$300,000
\end{aligned}
$$

Exhibit 9-6 *Computation of Residual Income After Additional Investment*

$$
\begin{aligned}
\text{Residual income} &= \text{Earned income} - (\text{Investment} \times \text{Desired ROI}) \\
&= \$1,040,000^* - (\$6,000,000\dagger \times 0.12) \\
&= \$1,040,000 - \$720,000 \\
&= \$320,000
\end{aligned}
$$

*Earned income: $900,000 + $140,000 = $1,040,000
†Investment: $5,000,000 + $1,000,000 = $6,000,000

focus on International Issues

Transfer Pricing More Important Than Ever

Transfer pricing has become a hot topic in many multinational organizations. Management should be going to great lengths to document comprehensive transfer pricing policies and find "compromise" solutions that will survive a review by competing revenue authorities and, at the same time, accommodate the business deal reached between the two parties.

What is Canada doing in the transfer pricing area?

Through the auspices of the Organization for Economic Cooperation and Development (OECD), the taxing authorities of member countries (including Canada and the United States) have agreed to the basic objectives and principles underlying a review of transfer pricing. The basic principle reflected in the OECD guidelines is that "arm's-length" prices should be used in all intercompany transactions. Another common thread is that "reasonableness" should be used as a standard of measurement.

There are three recognized transfer-pricing methodologies that are considered to comply with the arm's-length principle:

1. *Comparable uncontrolled price.* Under this method, prices should be based on those used in similar transactions between arm's-length parties. If you are lucky enough to find such a transaction, you may adjust it for such things as volume, terms of credit, terms of sale, or warranty provisions, to arrive at a price on which you can rely.

2. *Cost-plus.* This method starts with the vendor's cost of goods or services and adds an arm's-length markup.

3. *Resale price.* The resale price is used as a starting point to determine an arm's-length margin for the functions performed by the selling company (which is netted off the third-party selling price to determine the price to be paid to the related supplying party).

Source: Humphreys, "International transfer pricing more important than ever before"! Vol. 68, *CMA Magazine*, May 1, 1994, p. 24(3).

The Volkswagen Beetle assembly plant purchases some of the parts used to make the car from independent third-party companies. Other parts are produced internally. Determining the cost of the parts purchased from outsiders is fairly easy by locating the price paid listed on the invoice. Determining the price of the goods that are transferred from one division to another division of the same company is a bit more difficult. To maintain motivation, Volkswagen's managers are required to establish transfer prices that are deemed to be fair to both the division sending and the division receiving the transferred parts.

Michael Newman/PhotoEdit

Transfer Pricing

In vertically integrated companies, one division commonly sells goods or services to another division. For example, in the case of Panther Holding Company in Exhibit 9–1, the Lumber Manufacturing Division may sell lumber to the Home Building and Furniture Manufacturing Divisions. When such intercompany sales occur, the price to charge is likely to become a heated issue.

In a decentralized organization, each division is likely to be defined as an investment centre with the division manager being held responsible for profitability. When goods are transferred internally, the sales price of one division becomes a cost to the other division. Accordingly, the amount of profit included in the **transfer price** will increase the selling division's earnings and decrease the purchasing division's earnings (via increased expenses). It is to the advantage of the selling division to obtain the highest price while the purchasing division seeks the lowest price possible. When a competitive evaluation system based on profitability measures is imposed on this situation, it is easy to understand why the transfer price is subject to considerable controversy.

Three common approaches are used to establish transfer prices. They are (1) price based on market forces, (2) price based on negotiation, and (3) price based on cost.

LO8
Understand the three common approaches used to establish transfer prices.

Market-Based Transfer Prices

The preferred method for establishing transfer prices is to base them on some form of competitive market price. Ideally, the selling division should have the authority to sell its merchandise to outsiders as well as or in preference to its other divisions. Likewise, the purchasing divisions should have the option to buy goods from outsiders if they are able to obtain favourable prices. However, both selling and purchasing divisions would be motivated to deal with each other because of savings in selling, administrative, and transportation costs that arise as a natural result of internal transactions.

Market-based transfer prices are preferred because they promote efficiency and fairness. Market forces coupled with the responsibility for profitability motivate managers to utilize their resources effectively. For example, Jerry Lowe, the manager of the lumber division, may stop producing high-quality woods that the furniture division uses if he finds that it is more profitable to produce low-quality lumber. The furniture division can buy its needed material from outside companies that have chosen to operate in the less-profitable, high-quality market sector. Accordingly, the company as a whole benefits from

Mr. Lowe's insight. An additional advantage of using market prices is the sense of fairness associated with them. It is difficult for a manager to complain that the price that she is being charged is too high when she has the opportunity to seek a lower price elsewhere. The natural justice of the competitive marketplace is firmly implanted in the psyche of most modern managers.

Negotiated Transfer Prices

Unfortunately, in many instances, a necessary product may not be available elsewhere or the market price may not be in the best interest of the company as a whole. Sometimes, a division makes a unique product that only one of its company's other divisions uses. When this occurs, the external market cannot be used as a deciding factor in determining the transfer price. At other times, market-based transfer prices may lead to suboptomization, discussed earlier.

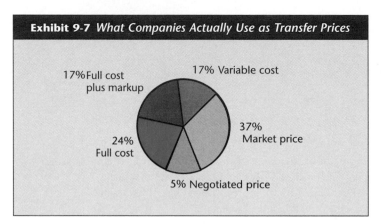

Exhibit 9-7 *What Companies Actually Use as Transfer Prices*

17% Full cost plus markup

17% Variable cost

24% Full cost

37% Market price

5% Negotiated price

Source: R. Tang, "Transfer Pricing in the 1990s," *Management Accounting,* pp. 22–26.

Consider the case of TrueTrust Vacuum Cleaner, Corp. TrueTrust's Engine Division (ED) has excess plant capacity. It can produce engines for the company's vacuum cleaning machines at a *full cost* of $80 per unit. The *avoidable cost* of producing the engines is only $60 per unit. To generate a reasonable divisional profit, Larry Lutz, the ED manager, wishes to sell the engines to the Assembly Division (AD) for $90. However, Laura Everhart, the AD manager, is able to buy the products from an outside source at a current market price of $70. If Ms. Everhart exercises her option to purchase from the outsider, her divisional profitability will benefit, but the company as a whole will lose $10 per engine, that is, the difference between the price to purchase and the avoidable cost of production ($70 − $60 = $10).

In such situations, it is advantageous to seek a **negotiated transfer price**. When the managers involved agree to a negotiated price, the concept of fairness is preserved. Furthermore, the element of profit remains intact; and the evaluation concepts discussed in this chapter can be applied. Although negotiated prices are not as good as market prices, they are able to offer many of the same advantages. Accordingly, they should act as the first possible alternative when a company is unable to use market-based transfer prices.

Suppose that Mr. Lutz and Ms. Everhart are unable to agree on a negotiated transfer price. Should the president of TrueTrust establish a reasonable price and force the managers to accept it? There is no definitive answer to this question. However, most senior-level executives recognize the motivational importance of maintaining autonomy in a decentralized organization. So long as the negative consequences are not significant, divisional managers are usually permitted to exercise their own judgment. In other words, the long-term benefits derived from autonomous management outweigh the short-term detriments of suboptimization.

Cost-Based Transfer Prices

The least desirable strategy is a **cost-based transfer price**. When cost is used, the amount of cost must first be determined. Some companies base the transfer price on *variable cost* (i.e., proxy for avoidable cost). Other companies use the *full cost* (i.e., variable cost plus an allocated portion of fixed cost) as the transfer price. In either case, using cost as the basis for transfer prices acts to remove the profit motive.

Without profitability as a guide, the incentive to control cost is diminished. One department's inefficiency is simply passed on to the next department. The result is low companywide profitability. Despite this potential detrimental effect, many companies continue to use cost as the basis for transfer prices because cost represents an objective number that is easy to compute. When a company chooses to use cost-based transfer prices, *it should use standard costs, rather than actual costs*. With this approach, departments are at least held responsible for the variances that they generate, and some degree of cost control is encouraged.

The practice of delegating authority and responsibility is referred to as *decentralization*. Clear lines of authority and responsibility are essential in establishing a responsibility accounting system. In a responsibility accounting system, segment managers are held accountable for profits on the basis of the amount of control they have over the profits in their segment.

a look
back

   Responsibility reports are used to compare actual results with budgets. The reports should be simple with variances highlighted to promote the *management by exception* doctrine. Individual managers should be held responsible only for those revenue or cost items that they control. Each manager should receive only summary information regarding the performance of the responsibility centres that are under her supervision.

   A *responsibility centre* is the point in an organization where control over revenue or expense is located. *Cost centres* are segments that incur costs but do not generate revenues. *Profit centres* generate revenues as well as incur costs, thus allowing for the calculation of profit. *Investment centres* generate revenues and incur expenses and can influence capital investment items.

   One of the primary purposes of responsibility accounting is to evaluate managerial performance. Comparison of results with standards and budgets and calculation of return on investment are used for this purpose. Because *return on investment* uses revenues, expenses, and investment, problems of measuring these parameters must be considered. The return on investment can be analyzed in terms of the margin earned on sales as well as the turnover (number of times the margin is collected) during the period. The *residual income approach* is sometimes used to avoid *suboptomization*, which occurs when managers choose to reject investment projects that would benefit their company's ROI but would reduce their investment centre's ROI. The residual income approach evaluates managers on their ability to generate earnings above some targeted level of earnings.

   Transfer pricing can affect a division's profitability. A transfer price must be determined when one division sells goods or services to another division within the same company. It is to the advantage of the selling division to obtain the highest price while the purchasing division seeks the lowest price possible. The three most common bases used to establish transfer prices are *market forces*, *negotiation*, and *cost*.

The next chapter expands on the concepts you learned in this chapter. You will see how managers select investment opportunities that will affect their future ROIs. You will learn to use present value techniques that consider the time value of money; specifically, you will learn to compute the net present value and the internal rate of return for potential investment opportunities. You will also learn to use less-sophisticated analytical techniques, such as payback and the unadjusted rate of return.

a look
forward

KEY TERMS

Controllability concept
The practice of holding a manager responsible for revenue and expense items over which he or she exercises predominant control. *(p. 319)*

Cost-based transfer price
A transfer price based on the historical or standard cost incurred by the supplying segment. *(p. 330)*

Cost centre A type of responsibility centre in which the manager influences only costs and is held accountable for a specific output at a given level of cost. *(p. 323)*

Decentralization The practice of delegating authority and responsibility for the operation of business segments. *(p. 318)*

Investment centre A type of responsibility centre in which the manager can

influence revenues, expenses, and capital investments. *(p. 323)*

Management by exception
When variances from the budgets are emphasized in reporting procedures so that management concentrates its attention predominantly on the exceptions from the budget. *(p. 320)*

Market-based transfer price A transfer price based on the external market price less any savings in cost; the closest approximation to an arm's-length transaction that segments can achieve. *(p. 329)*

Negotiated transfer price
A transfer price established by agreement of both the selling and buying segments of the firm. *(p. 330)*

Profit centre A type of responsibility centre in

which the manager can influence both revenues and expenses for the centre. *(p. 323)*

Residual income An approach that evaluates managers on their ability to maximize the dollar value of earnings above some targeted level of earnings. *(p. 327)*

Responsibility accounting
An accounting system in which the accountability for results is assigned to a segment manager of the firm on the basis of the amount of control or influence the manager possesses over those results. *(p. 317)*

Responsibility centre The point in an organization where the control over revenue or expense items is located. *(p. 322)*

Responsibility reports
Reports of the perform-

ance of various responsibility centres of the firm with respect to controllable costs; the report shows the variances that result from comparing budgeted and actual controllable costs. *(p. 319)*

Return on investment A measure of the ability of a firm or segment within a firm to utilize available resources effectively by expressing profit or income as a percentage of invested assets. *(p. 323)*

Suboptimization A situation where managers act in their own best interests, even though the organization as a whole suffers. *(p. 327)*

Transfer price The price at which products or services are transferred between divisions or other subunits of an organization. *(p. 329)*

QUESTIONS

1. Pam Kelly says that she has no faith in budgets. Her company, Kelly Manufacturing Corporation, spent thousands of dollars to install a sophisticated budget system. One year later, the company's expenses are still out of control. She believes that budgets simply do not work. How would you respond to Ms. Kelly's comments?

2. All travel expenses incurred by Pure Water Pump Corporation are reported only to John Daniels, the company president. Pure Water is a multinational company with five divisions. Are travel expenses reported in accordance with the responsibility accounting concept? Explain.

3. What are five potential advantages associated with decentralization?

4. Who receives responsibility reports? What do the reports include?

5. How does the concept of predominant as opposed to that of absolute control apply to responsibility accounting?

6. How do responsibility reports promote the management by exception doctrine?

7. What is a responsibility centre?

8. What are the three types of responsibility centres? Explain how each differs from the others.

9. Carmen Douglas claims that her company's performance evaluation system is unfair. Her company uses return on investment (ROI) to evaluate performance. Ms. Douglas says that even though her ROI is lower than another manager's, her performance is far superior. Is it possible that Ms. Douglas is correct? Explain your position.

10. What are the two factors that affect the computation of return on investment?

11. What are three ways that a manager can increase the return on investment?

12. How can a residual income approach to performance evaluation reduce the likelihood of suboptimization?

13. Is it true that the manager with the highest residual income is always the best performer?

14. Why are transfer prices important to managers who are evaluated on profitability criteria?

15. What are three approaches to establishing transfer prices? List the most desirable approach first and the least desirable last.

16. If cost is the basis for transfer pricing, should actual or standard cost be used? Why?

EXERCISE 9-1   *Organization Chart and Responsibilities*   **L.O. 1**

The production manager is responsible for the assembly, cleaning, and finishing departments. The executive vice-president reports directly to the president but is responsible for the activities of the production department, the finance department, and the sales department. The sales manager is responsible for the advertising department.

Required
Arrange this information into an organization chart and indicate the responsibility levels involved.

EXERCISE 9-2   *Responsibility Report*   **L.O. 3**

Sakowise Department Store is divided into three major departments: Men's Clothing, Women's Clothing, and Home Furnishings. Each of these three departments is supervised by a manager who reports to the general manager. The departments are subdivided into different sections managed by floor supervisors. The Home Furnishings Department has three floor supervisors, one for furniture, one for lamps, and one for housewares. The following items were included in the company's most recent responsibility report:

   Salary of general manager
   Salary of the Mens's Clothing Department manager
   Allocated companywide advertising expense
   Amortization on the facility
   Travel expenses for the buyer of the housewares section
   Seasonal decorations for the furniture section
   Revenues for the Home Furnishings Department
   Administrative expenses for the Men's Clothing Department
   Allocated utility cost for the Home Furnishings Department
   Cost of part-time Christmas help for the Women's Department
   Delivery expenses for furniture purchases
   Salaries for the sales staff in the lamp section
   Storewide revenues

Required
Which of the items are likely to be considered to be the responsibility of the Home Furnishings Department manager?

EXERCISE 9-3   *Organization Chart and Controllable Cost*   **L.O. 1, 3**

Cracker Company has employees with the following job titles:
   Vice-president of administration
   Sales office manager
   President of company
   Vice-president of marketing
   Product manager
   Controller
   Vice-president of manufacturing
   Treasurer
   Regional sales manager
   Human Resources manager
   Cashier
   Vice-president of finance
   Fringe benefits manager
   Board of directors
   Production supervisors

Required

a. Design an organization chart using these job titles.

b. Name some possible controllable costs for the person holding each job title.

L.O. 1, 2 EXERCISE 9-4   *Income Statement for Internal Use*

Graham Company has provided the following data of 2001:

Budget	
Sales	$102,000
Variable product costs	41,000
Variable selling expense	12,000
Other variable expenses	1,000
Fixed product costs	4,200
Fixed selling expense	6,300
Other fixed expenses	600
Variances	
Sales	2,200 U
Variable product costs	1,000 F
Variable selling expense	600 U
Other variable expense	300 U
Fixed product costs	60 F
Fixed selling expense	100 F
Other fixed expenses	40 U

Required

Prepare a budgeted and actual income statement in good form for internal use.

L.O. 1, 2 EXERCISE 9-5   *Evaluation of a Cost Centre (Flexible Budgeting Concepts Included)*

Overton Medical Equipment Company makes a blood pressure measuring kit. Ken Sampson is the production manager. The following is the production department's static budget and actual results for 2003:

	Static Budget	Actual Results
	10,000 kits	*10,500 kits*
Direct materials	$150,000	$161,700
Direct labour	135,000	138,600
Variable manufacturing overhead	35,000	44,600
Total variable costs	320,000	344,900
Fixed manufacturing cost	180,000	178,000
Total manufacturing cost	$500,000	$522,900

Required

a. Convert the static budget into a flexible budget.

b. Use the flexible budget to evaluate Mr. Sampson's performance.

c. Explain why Mr. Sampson's performance evaluation does not include sales revenue and net income.

L.O. 3, 5 EXERCISE 9-6   *Evaluation of a Profit Centre*

Michelle Woods, the president of Toy World Corporation, is trying to determine this year's pay raises for the store managers. Toy World has seven stores in western Canada. Corporate headquarters purchases all toys from different manufacturers globally and distributes them to individual stores. Additionally, headquarters makes decisions regarding location and size of stores. This practice allows Toy World to gain volume discounts from vendors and to implement coherent marketing strategies. Under a set of general guidelines, store managers have the flexibility to adjust product prices and hire local employees. Ms. Woods is considering three possible performance measures for evaluating the individual stores: cost of goods sold, return on sales (i.e., net income divided by sales), and return on investment.

Required

Advise Ms. Woods about the best performance measure using the concept of controllability.

EXERCISE 9-7   *Return on Investment*   **L.O. 6**

An investment centre of Bradford Corporation shows a net income of $2,400 on an investment of $12,000.

Required

Compute the return on investment.

EXERCISE 9-8   *Return on Investment*   **L.O. 6**

Panhandle Company calculated its return on investment as 12 percent. Sales are now $60,000, and the investment base is $100,000.

Required

a. If expenses are reduced by $6,000 and sales remain unchanged, what return on investment will result?
b. If both sales and expenses cannot be changed, what change in the investment base is required to achieve the same result?

EXERCISE 9-9   *Residual Income*   **L.O. 7**

Bellaire Corporation has a desired rate of return of 12 percent. Adam Wucetich is in charge of one of Bellaire's three investment centres. His centre controlled $8,000,000 of operational assets that were used to earn $1,120,000.

Required

Compute Mr. Wucetich's residual income.

EXERCISE 9-10   *Residual Income*   **L.O. 7**

Franklin Cough Drops operates two divisions. The following information is made available for each division for 2003:

	Division A	Division B
Sales	$60,000	$20,000
Operating income	$ 6,000	$ 3,200
Average operating assets	$24,000	$16,000
Company's desired rate of return	20%	20%

Required

a. Compute each division's residual income.
b. Which division increased the company's profitability the most?

EXERCISE 9-11   *Return on Investment and Residual Income*   **L.O. 6, 7**

Required

Supply the missing information in the following table for Mako Company:

Sales	$300,000
ROI	?
Investment in operating assets	?
Operating income	?
Turnover	2
Residual income	?
Margin	0.10
Desired rate of return	18%

L.O. 6, 7 EXERCISE 9-12   *Comparison of Return on Investment and Residual Income*

The Flour Division of Cakes, Co. has a current ROI of 15 percent. The company target ROI is 12 percent. The Flour Division has an opportunity to invest $1,000,000 at 13 percent but is reluctant to do so because its ROI will fall to 14.5 percent. The present investment base for the division is $3,000,000.

Required

Demonstrate how the Flour Division can be motivated to make the investment by using the residual income method.

L.O. 8 EXERCISE 9-13   *Transfer Pricing*

Marginal Company has two divisions: A and B. Division A manufactures 3,000 units of product per month. The cost per unit is calculated as follows:

Variable costs	$ 3
Fixed costs	10
Total cost	$13

Division B uses the product created by Division A. No outside market for Division A's product exists. The fixed costs incurred by Division A are allocated headquarters-level facility-sustaining costs. The manager of Division A suggests that the product be transferred to Division B at a price of at least $13 per unit. The manager of Division B argues that the same product can be purchased from another firm for $8 per unit and requests permission to do so.

Required

a. Should the manager of Division B be allowed to purchase the product from the outside firm for $8 per unit? Explain your response.

b. Assume that you are the president of the company. Write a brief paragraph recommending a resolution of the conflict between the two divisional managers.

L.O. 8 EXERCISE 9-14   *Transfer Pricing and Avoidable Cost*

The Tire Division of Independent Road Company (IRC) produces radial all-purpose tires for trucks that sold whole-sale to automotive manufacturers. Per-unit sales and cost data for the tires follow:

Selling price	$90
Unit-level variable cost	$60
Corporate-level fixed cost	$25
Manufacturing capacity	30,000 units
Average sales	25,000 units

IRC also has a Trucking Division that provides delivery service for outside independent businesses as well as divisions of IRC. The Trucking Division, which uses approximately 4,000 tires a year, presently buys tires for its trucks from an outside supplier for $85 per tire.

Required

Recommend a transfer price range for the truck tires that would be profitable for both divisions if it were decided that the Trucking Division would purchase the tires internally. Assume that both divisions operate as investment centres.

L.O. 8 EXERCISE 9-15   *Transfer Pricing and Fixed Cost per Unit*

The Small Parts Division of Sizemore Company plans to set up a facility with the capacity to make 5,000 units of an electronic computer part. The avoidable cost of making the part is as follows:

Costs	Total	Cost per Unit
Variable cost	$150,000	$ 30
Fixed cost	$ 40,000	$ 8 (at capacity)

Required

a. Assume that Sizemore's Assembly Division is currently purchasing 3,000 of the electronic parts from an outside supplier at a market price of $50. What would be the financial consequence to Sizemore if the Small Parts Division makes the part and sells it to the Assembly Division? What is the range of the transfer price that would increase the financial performance of both divisions?

b. Suppose that the Assembly Division increases production so that 5,000 units of the part made by the Small Parts Division could be used. How would the change in volume affect the range of the transfer price that would provide financial benefit to both divisions?

PROBLEMS—SERIES A

PROBLEM 9-1A *Determination of Controllable Costs* **L.O. 3**

Sam Ross is the manager of the production department of Consolidated Corporation. Consolidated incurred the following expenditures during 2005:

Production department supplies	$ 3,800
Administrative salaries	140,000
Production wages	326,000
Materials used	264,600
Amortization of manufacturing equipment	180,800
Corporate-level rental expense	120,000
Property taxes	34,300
Sales salaries	143,400

Required

Prepare a list of expenditures that Mr. Ross controls.

PROBLEM 9-2A *Comparison of Controllability and Responsibility* **L.O. 2, 3**

Susan Silversmith manages the production division of Thermo Corporation. Ms. Silversmith's responsibility report for the month of August follows:

	Budget	Actual	Variance	
Controllable costs				
Raw materials	$15,000	$18,750	$3,750	U
Labour	7,500	10,350	2,850	U
Maintenance	1,500	1,800	300	U
Supplies	1,275	900	375	F
Total	$25,275	$31,800	$6,525	U

The budget had called for 3,700 kilograms of raw materials at $4.40 per kilogram, and 3,700 kilograms were used during August; however, the purchasing department paid $5.50 per kilogram for the materials. The wage rate used to establish the budget was $7.50 per hour. On August 1, however, it increased to $9 as the result of an inflation index provision in the union contract. Furthermore, the purchasing department did not provide the materials needed in accordance with the production schedule, which forced Ms. Silversmith to use 100 hours of overtime at a $13.50 rate. The projected 1,000 hours of labour in the budget would have been sufficient had it not been for the 100 hours of overtime. In other words, 1,100 hours of labour were used in August.

Required

a. When confronted with the unfavourable variances in her responsibility report, Ms. Silversmith argued that the report was unfair because it held her accountable for materials and price variances that she did *not* control. Is she correct? Comment specifically on the materials and labour variances.

b. Prepare a responsibility report that reflects the cost items that Ms. Silversmith controlled during August.

c. Will the changes in the revised responsibility report require corresponding changes in the financial statements? Explain.

L.O. 2, 4 PROBLEM 9-3A   *Performance Reports and Evaluation*

Carter Corporation has four divisions: the assembly division, the processing division, the machining division, and the packing division. All four divisions are under the control of the vice-president of manufacturing. A manager operates each division, which is composed of several departments that are directed by supervisors. Accordingly, the chain of command runs downward from vice-president to division manager to supervisor. The processing division is composed of the paint and finishing departments. The responsibility reports for the supervisors of these departments for May follow:

	Budgeted*	Actual	Variance	
Paint Department				
Controllable costs				
Raw materials	$18,000	$18,750	$ 750	U
Labour	37,500	41,250	3,750	U
Repairs	3,000	2,400	600	F
Maintenance	1,500	1,425	75	F
Total	$60,000	$63,825	$3,825	U
Finishing Department				
Controllable costs				
Raw materials	$14,250	$14,100	$ 150	F
Labour	27,000	24,750	2,250	F
Repairs	1,800	2,025	225	U
Maintenance	1,050	1,275	225	U
Total	$44,100	$42,150	$1,950	F

*A flexible budget is used for performance evaluation.

Other pertinent cost data for May 2005 follow:

	Budgeted*	Actual
Cost data of other divisions		
Assembly	$202,500	$198,900
Machining	176,250	180,300
Packing	263,400	258,075
Other costs associated with		
Processing Division Manager	150,000	148,500
Vice-President of Manufacturing	82,500	85,650

*A flexible budget is used for performance evaluation.

Required

a. Prepare a responsibility report for the manager of the processing division.
b. Prepare a responsibility report for the vice-president of manufacturing.
c. Explain where the $3,750 unfavourable labour variance in the paint department supervisor's report is included in the vice-president's report.
d. On the basis of the responsibility report prepared in Requirement *a*, comment on where the processing division manager should concentrate his attention.

L.O. 5 PROBLEM 9-4A   *Different Types of Responsibility Centres*

Elwood Credit Union is a large municipal Credit Union with several branch offices. The Credit Unions computer department handles all data processing for its operations. In addition, the Credit Union acts as a service bureau by selling its expertise in systems development and its excess machine time to several small business firms.

The Credit Union currently treats the computer department as a cost centre. The manager of the computer department prepares a cost budget annually for senior Credit Union officials to approve. Monthly operating reports compare actual and budgeted expenses. Revenues from the department's service bureau activities are treated as other income by the Credit Union and are not reflected on the computer department's operating reports. The costs of serving these clients are included in the computer department reports, however.

The manager of the computer department has proposed that the Credit Union management convert the computer department to a profit or investment centre.

Required

a. Describe the characteristics that differentiate a cost centre, a profit centre, and an investment centre from each other.
b. Would the manager of the computer department be likely to conduct the operations of the department differently if the department were classified as a profit centre or an investment centre, rather than as a cost centre? Explain your answer.

PROBLEM 9-5A   *Evaluation of a Profit Centre*   L.O. 5

Renfro, Peterson, and Company is a firm specializing in custom parts assembly services. The firm has five branch offices in various communities. Jeff Renfro, the managing partner, makes all decisions regarding personnel and facility acquisitions for the entire firm. Each branch manager determines employee work hours and compensation. Mr. Renfro emphasized to his branch managers that profit is their number one responsibility. Wendy Daniels manages the Hoover Branch, which has the following static budget and actual results for 2002:

	Static Budget 5,000 Service Hours @$50 per Hour	Actual Results 4,800 Service Hours @$56 per Hour
Service revenue	$ 250,000	$ 268,800
Less: Variable costs		
Direct labour	(120,000)	(134,400)
Variable office overhead	(20,000)	(20,160)
Contribution margin	$110,000	$114,240
Less: Fixed costs		
Office rent	(20,000)	(20,000)
Other administrative expenses	(60,000)	(58,000)
Net income for the branch	$ 30,000	$ 36,240

Required

a. Convert the static budget into a flexible budget.
b. Determine the activity variances between the static budget and the flexible budget.
c. Compute the flexible budget variances.
d. Did Ms. Daniels do a good job as a branch manager? Support your answer with the information derived from Requirements *a*, *b*, and *c*.
e. Would you use return on investment to evaluate Ms. Daniels's performance? Explain your answer.

PROBLEM 9-6A   *Return on Investment*   L.O. 6

Hillyard Corporation's balance sheet indicates that the company has $200,000 invested in operating assets. During 2005, Hillyard earned income of $30,000 on $400,000 of sales.

Required

a. Compute Hillyard's margin for 2005.
b. Compute Hillyard's turnover for 2005.
c. Compute Hillyard's return on investment for 2005.
d. Recompute Hillyard's ROI under each of the following independent assumptions:
   1. Sales increase from $400,000 to $500,000, thereby resulting in an increase in income from $30,000 to $40,000.
   2. Sales remain constant, but Hillyard reduces expenses resulting in an increase in income from $30,000 to $32,000.
   3. Hillyard is able to reduce its invested capital from $200,000 to $160,000 without affecting income.

L.O. 6, 7 PROBLEM 9-7A   *Comparison of Return on Investment and Residual Income*

The manager of the Eastern Division of National Manufacturing Corporation has produced a 22 percent return on invested capital. National's desired rate of return is 18 percent. The Eastern Division has $16,000,000 of capital invested and access to additional funds as needed. The manager is considering a new investment that will require a $4,000,000 capital commitment and promises a 20 percent return.

Required

a. Would it be advantageous for National Manufacturing Corporation if the Eastern Division accepts the investment under consideration?
b. What effect will the acceptance of the proposed investment have on the Eastern Division's return on investment? Show computations.
c. What effect will the acceptance of the proposed investment have on the Eastern Division's residual income? Show computations.
d. Would return on investment or residual income be the best performance measure for the manager of the Eastern Division? Explain your position.

L.O. 8 PROBLEM 9-8A   *Transfer Pricing*

Mobile Radio Corporation is a subsidiary of Dalton Companies. Mobile makes car radios that are sold to retail outlets. Speakers for the radios are purchased from outside suppliers for $14 each. Recently, Dalton acquired the Sonic Speaker Corporation, which makes car radio speakers that are sold to manufacturers. Sonic produces and sells approximately 200,000 speakers per year which represents 70 percent of its operating capacity. At the present volume of activity, each speaker costs $12 to produce. The total cost is composed of an $8 variable cost component and a $4 fixed cost component. Sonic sells the speakers for $15 each. The managers of Mobile and Sonic have been asked to consider the use of Sonic's excess capacity to supply Mobile with some of the speakers that it currently purchases from unrelated companies. Both managers are evaluated on the basis of return on investment. Sonic's manager suggests that the speakers be supplied at a transfer price of $15 each (i.e., the current selling price). On the other hand, Mobile's manager suggests a $12 transfer price, noting that this amount covers total cost and provides Sonic a healthy contribution margin.

Required

a. What transfer price would you recommend?
b. Discuss the effect of the intercompany sales on each manager's return on investment.
c. Should Sonic be required to use more than excess capacity to provide speakers to Mobile? In other words, should it sell to Mobile some of the 200,000 units that it is currently selling to unrelated companies?

PROBLEMS—SERIES B

L.O. 3 PROBLEM 9-1B   *Determination of Controllable Costs*

In a professional conference just a few days ago, Anthony Perez, the president of Silverado Corporation, learned how the concept of controllability relates to performance evaluation. Trying to practise this new knowledge, he reviewed the financial data of the company's sales department.

Salaries of salespeople	$ 225,000
Cost of goods sold	24,000,000
Facility-level corporate costs	410,000
Travel expenses	32,000
Amortization of equipment	100,000
Salary of the sales manager	60,000
Property taxes	4,000
Telephone expenses	39,000

Required

Help Mr. Perez prepare a list of expenditures that the sales manager controls.

PROBLEM 9-2B   *Controllability and Responsibility*

George Wendham, president of Henman Corporation, evaluated the performance report of the company's production department. Mr. Wendham was confused by some arguments presented by Joan Ruberstein, the production manager. The following are some related data:

Variances	Amount
Materials quantity variance	$200,000 U
Materials price variance	120,000 F
Labour rate variance	38,000 F
Labour efficiency variance	138,000 U
Volume variance	300,000 U

Ms. Ruberstein argues that she had done a great job as indicated by the favourable materials price variance and labour rate variance. Regarding the unfavourable variances, she argued that she had had no control over those factors. For example, she argued that the unfavourable materials quantity variance was caused by the purchasing department's decision to buy substandard materials that caused a substantial amount of spoilage. Moreover, she argued that the unfavourable labour efficiency variance was caused by substantial materials spoilage causing many wasted labour hours and the hiring of underqualified workers by the manager of the personnel department. Finally, she said that the sales department's failure to obtain a sufficient number of customer orders really caused the unfavourable volume variance.

Required

a. What would you do first if you were George Wendham?
b. Did Ms. Ruberstein deserve the credit she claimed on the favourable variances? Explain.
c. Was Ms. Ruberstein responsible for the unfavourable variances? Explain.

PROBLEM 9-3B   *Performance Reports and Evaluation*

The mortgage division of Howell Financial Services, Inc. is managed by a vice-president who supervises three regional operations. Each regional office has a general manager and is composed of several branches directed by branch managers.

The eastern region has two branches, Hamilton and Oshawa. The responsibility reports for the managers of these branches for March follow:

	Budgeted*	Actual	Variance	
Hamilton Branch				
Controllable costs				
Employee compensation	$ 72,000	$ 75,200	$ 3,200	U
Office supplies	18,000	17,500	500	F
Promotions	38,000	32,000	6,000	F
Maintenance	4,000	5,300	1,300	U
Total	$132,000	$130,000	$2,000	F
Oshawa Branch				
Controllable costs				
Employee compensation	$ 65,000	$ 62,500	$2,500	F
Office supplies	19,000	21,000	2,000	U
Promotions	36,000	37,500	1,500	U
Maintenance	5,000	4,800	200	F
Total	$125,000	$125,800	$ 800	U

*A flexible budget is used for performance evaluation.

Other pertinent cost data for March 2002 follow:

	Budgeted*	Actual
Cost data of other regions		
Southern	$350,000	$363,000
Western	430,000	422,000
Other costs controllable by		
Eastern region general manager	70,000	73,000
Vice-president of mortgage	96,000	98,000

*A flexible budget is used for performance evaluation.

Required

a. Prepare a responsibility report for the general manager of the eastern region.
b. Prepare a responsibility report for the vice-president of the mortgage division.
c. Explain where the $6,000 favourable promotions variance in the Hamilton branch manager's report is included in the vice-president's report.
d. On the basis of the responsibility report prepared in Requirement *a*, comment on where the eastern region's general manager should concentrate her attention.

L.O. 5 PROBLEM 9-4B   *Different Types of Responsibility Centre*

Columbia Industries has five different divisions; each is responsible for the production and marketing of a particular product line. The electronic division makes cellular telephones, pagers, and modems. The division also buys and sells other electronic products made by outside companies. Each division maintains sufficient working capital for its own operations. The corporate headquarters, however, makes decisions about long-term capital investments.

Required

a. For purposes of performance evaluation, should Columbia classify its electronic division as a cost centre, a profit centre, or an investment centre? Why?
b. Would the manager of the electronic division be likely to conduct the operations of the division differently if the division were classified as a different type of responsibility centre the one you designated in Requirement *a*? Explain your answer.

L.O. 2 PROBLEM 9-5B   *Evaluation of Profit Centre*

Keeland Fruits Corporation, a wholesaler of fruits, has four divisions, each specializing in the wholesale operation of a particular type of fruit. Although the four divisions negotiate with their suppliers about price and quantity of their goods, the corporate office retains the power to make decisions on long-term investments. The following data reflect the Peach Division's budgeted and actual operations in 2003:

	Static Budget 2,000,000 Boxes @$15 per Box	Actual Results 1,860,000 Boxes @$14.50 per Box
Sales revenue	$30,000,000	$26,970,000
Less: Variable costs		
Cost of goods sold	(22,000,000)	(19,623,000)
Shipping expenses	(260,000)	(245,000)
Selling expenses	(500,000)	(400,000)
Contribution margin	7,240,000	6,702,000
Less: Fixed costs		
Personnel expenses	(1,200,000)	(1,280,000)
Other administrative expenses	(600,000)	(590,000)
Net income for the division	$ 5,440,000	$ 4,832,000

Required

a. Convert the static budget into a flexible budget.
b. Determine the activity variances between the static budget and the flexible budget.

c. Compute the flexible budget variances.

d. Did the manager of the Peach Division do a good job as a branch manager? Support your answer with the information derived from Requirements *a*, *b*, and *c*.

e. Would you use return on investment to evaluate the division's performance? Explain your answer.

PROBLEM 9-6B   *Return on Investment*

L.O. 6

Roca Corporation's balance sheet indicates that the company has $500,000 invested in operating assets. During 2003, Roca earned $80,000 of income on $1,600,000 of sales.

Required

a. Compute Roca's margin for 2003.

b. Compute Roca's turnover for 2003.

c. Compute Roca's return on investment for 2003.

d. Recompute Roca's ROI under each of the following independent assumptions.

   1. Sales increase from $1,600,000 to $1,800,000, thereby resulting in an increase in income from $80,000 to $94,500.

   2. Sales remain constant, but Roca reduces expenses, thereby resulting in an increase in income from $80,000 to $84,000.

   3. Roca is able to reduce its invested capital from $500,000 to $480,000 without affecting income.

PROBLEM 9-7B   *Comparison of Return on Investment and Residual Income*

L.O. 6, 7

Jenny Lofton, the manager of Winnipeg Division, Prairie Corporation, has enjoyed success. Her division's return on investment (ROI) has consistently been 18 percent on a total investment of $25,000,000. Prairie evaluates its divisional managers on the basis of ROI. The company's desired ROI is 14 percent. Ms. Lofton is evaluating an investment opportunity that will require a $5,000,000 capital investment and is expected to result in a 15 percent return.

Required

a. Would it be advantageous for Prairie Corporation if Ms. Lofton accepts the investment under consideration?

b. What effect will the acceptance of the proposed investment have on Winnipeg Division's ROI? Show computations.

c. What effect will the acceptance of the proposed investment have on Winnipeg Division's residual income (RI)? Show computations.

d. Would ROI or RI act as the best performance measure for Ms. Lofton? Explain your position.

PROBLEM 9-8B   *Transfer Pricing*

L.O. 8

Spring Electronics Corporation makes modems that it sells to retail stores for $75 each. The variable cost to produce a modem is $35 each; the total fixed cost is $5,000,000. Spring is operating at 80 percent capacity and is producing 200,000 modems. Spring's parent company, New Century Corporation, notified Spring's president that another subsidiary company, Valley Technologies, Inc., has begun making computers and can use Spring's modem as a part. Valley needs 40,000 modems and is able to acquire similar modems in the market for $72 each.

Under instruction from the parent company, the presidents of Spring and Valley meet to negotiate a price for the modem. Spring insists that its market price is $75 each and will stand firm on that price. Valley, on the other hand, wonders why it should even talk to Spring when Valley can get modems at a lower price.

Required

a. What transfer price would you recommend?

b. Discuss the effect of the intercompany sales on each president's return on investment.

c. Should Spring be required to use more than excess capacity to provide modems to Valley? In other words, should it sell some of the 200,000 modems that it currently sells to unrelated companies to Valley instead?

ANALYZE, THINK, COMMUNICATE

ACT 9-1 BUSINESS APPLICATIONS CASE   *Responsibility Accounting*

Tedesco Brothers Metal Products produces fabricated steel products on a contract basis. Profits based on annual sales volume averaging about $10,000,000 have been modest as compared with industry averages for the past several years. The firm has operated with decentralized management for many years with the president, Nick Tedesco, being able to keep a fairly good sense of all aspects of the business.

Two project managers work with Mr. Tedesco in supervising each project from the bidding stage through production and delivery. However, they do not have complete authority with respect to production decisions, materials purchases, or labour negotiations. Many of these tasks are frequently accomplished by individuals who have had experience in these fields. For instance, Freida Fowler, the purchasing agent, makes many independent buying decisions. She analyzes some of the signed contracts and production schedules and orders the necessary materials. Indirect materials are ordered from time to time by Tom Stovlen, the part-time production supervisor. Mr. Stovlen is frequently in charge of production to the extent that he schedules some projects and often assigns the workers to the various jobs. He also has many years of experience as a welder and often works in this capacity.

Joy Chan, the accountant, has suggested to Mr. Tedesco that some reorganization might be in order since continued efforts to control costs and improve profits under the present organization have not been effective. Mr. Tedesco does not see much advantage to reorganization, especially if it involves more administrative people; he is proud of the relatively low general and administrative expenses that his firm incurs. He admits that factory overhead could use some monitoring; this is evident from the fact that the predetermined overhead rate has increased rather steadily over time.

The sales manager, Bert Scott, is very much interested in what the accountant is saying. He believes that lower bids would result in more contracts, which should help profits since the company is operating at less than 75 percent capacity, but lower bids are possible only by reducing costs.

Mr. Tedesco has conceded that the accountant may have a point and asks: "Joy, do you believe that a change in organization could improve profits?"

Required

If you were Ms. Chan, how would you organize this company? Is it possible to apply the principles of responsibility accounting?

ACT 9-2 GROUP ASSIGNMENT   *Return on Investment versus Residual Income*

WolCo, a division of TransMark Corporation, is operated under the direction of Larry Anton. WolCo is an independent investment centre with approximately $48,000,000 of assets that generate approximately $5,760,000 in annual net income. TransMark has additional investment capital of $8,000,000 that is available for investment by the division managers. Mr. Anton is aware of an investment opportunity that will provide an 11 percent annual net return. TransMark's desired rate of return is 9 percent.

Required

Divide the class into groups of four or five students and then organize the groups into two sections. Assign Task 1 to the first section and Task 2 to the second section.

Group Tasks

1. Assume that Mr. Anton's performance is evaluated on the basis of his ability to maximize return on investment (ROI). Compute the ROI under the following two assumptions: WolCo retains its current asset size, and WolCo accepts and invests the additional $8,000,000 of assets. Determine whether Mr. Anton should accept the opportunity to invest additional funds. Select a spokesperson to present the decision made by the section.

2. Assume that Mr. Anton's performance is evaluated on the basis of his ability to maximize residual income. Compute the residual income under the following two assumptions: WolCo retains its current asset base, and WolCo accepts and invests the additional $8,000,000 of assets. Determine whether Mr. Anton should accept the opportunity to invest additional funds. Select a spokesperson to present the decision made by the section.

3. Have a spokesperson from the first section of one of the groups report the two ROIs and the section's recommendation for Mr. Anton. Have the groups in this section reach consensus on the ROI and the recommendation.

4. Have a spokesperson from the second section report the two amounts of residual income and disclose the group's recommendation for Mr. Anton. Have this section reach consensus on amounts of residual income.

5. Which technique (ROI or residual income) is more likely to result in suboptimization?

WRITING ASSIGNMENT *Transfer Pricing*

ACT 9-3

Clean Cut Lawn Mower, Inc. recently acquired Dawson Engines, a small engine manufacturing company. Clean Cut's president believes in the power of decentralization and intends to permit Dawson to continue to operate as an independent entity. However, she has instructed the manager of Clean Cut's lawn mower assembly division to investigate the possibility of purchasing engines from Dawson instead of using the third-party supplier currently being used. Dawson has excess capacity. The current full cost to produce each engine is $80. The avoidable cost of making engines is $65 per unit. The assembly division, which currently pays the third-party supplier $75 per engine, offers to purchase engines from Dawson at the $75 price. Dawson's president refuses the offer, stating that his company's engines are superior to those the third-party supplier provides. Dawson's president believes that the transfer price should be based on the market price for independent customers which is $110 per engine. The manager of the assembly division agrees that Dawson's engines are of a higher quality than those currently being used but notes that Clean Cut's customer base is in the low-end, discount market. Putting more expensive engines on Clean Cut mowers would raise the price above the competition and would hurt sales. Clean Cut's president tries to negotiate a settlement between the assembly manager and Dawson's president, but the parties are unable to agree on a transfer price.

Required

a. Assuming that Clean Cut makes and sells 40,000 lawn mowers per year, what is the cost of suboptimization resulting from the failure to establish a transfer price?

b. Assume that you are a consultant asked by the president of Clean Cut to recommend whether a transfer price should be arbitrarily imposed. Write a brief memo that includes your recommendation and your justification for making it.

SPREADSHEET ASSIGNMENT *Using Excel*

ACT 9-4

Bravo Corporation's balance sheet shows that the company has $500,000 invested in operating assets. During 2000, Bravo earned $100,000 on $800,000 of sales. The company's desired return on investment (ROI) is 12 percent.

Required

Construct a spreadsheet to calculate ROI and residual income for these data. Build the spreadsheet using formulas so that the spreadsheet could be used as a template for any ROI or residual income problem. The following screen capture shows how to construct the template:

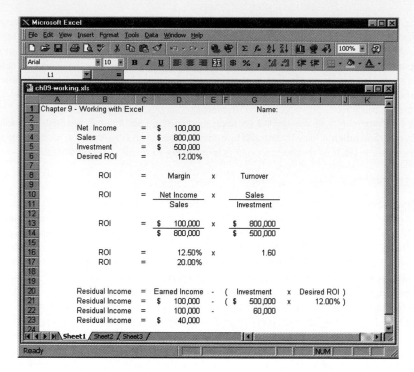

Spreadsheet Tips

1. The cells below Row 12 that show numbers should all be based on formulas. This allows changes in the data Rows 3 to 6 to be automatically recalculated.
2. The parentheses in Columns F and J have been entered as text in columns that have a column width of 1.

ACT 9-5 SPREADSHEET ASSIGNMENT   *Mastering Excel*

The Cohen Manufacturing Company has three identified levels of authority and responsibility. The organization chart as of December 31, 2007, appears as follows:

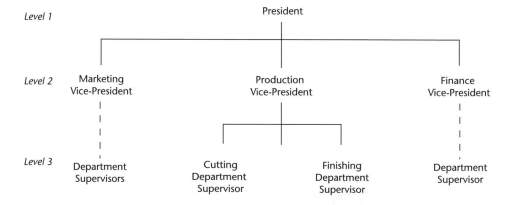

Pertinent expenses regarding Level 3 appear as follows:

	Budget	Actual
Finishing Department		
Wage expense	$6,240	$6,000
Direct materials	2,300	2,400
Supplies	840	980
Small tools	1,300	1,140
Other	700	820

Pertinent expenses regarding Level 2 appear as follows:

	Budget	Actual
Production Department		
Administrative expenses	$1,200	$1,400
Supervisory salaries	5,800	5,200
Cutting department	6,800	6,420
Finishing department	11,380	11,340

Pertinent expenses regarding Level 1 appear as follows:

	Budget	Actual
Presidential Office Expense		
Supervisory salaries	$4,900	$5,100
Clerical staff	800	400
Other expenses	600	700
Production department	25,180	24,360
Marketing department	8,850	8,300
Finance department	5,900	6,220

Required

a. Construct a spreadsheet that includes responsibility reports for the finishing department supervisor, the production department manager, and the president.

b. Include formulas in the responsibility reports that illustrate the interrelationships between these reports. For example, changes in the finishing department report should be automatically reflected in the production department report.

Spreadsheet Tip

Use the absolute value function [=ABS(value)] in the formulas that calculate the variances.

Planning for Capital Investments

After completing this chapter, you should be able to:

1 Distinguish between capital investments and investments in stocks and bonds.

2 Understand and apply the concept of time value of money to capital investment decisions.

3 Distinguish between return on investment and recovery of investment.

4 Explain why the cost of capital constitutes the minimum acceptable rate of return for a capital investment.

5 Use present value tables to determine the present value of future cash flows.

6 Distinguish between lump-sum payments and ordinary annuities.

7 Appreciate the power of computer software in determining present values.

8 Understand the reinvestment assumption implicit in the interest tables and computer software.

9 Determine and interpret the net present value of an investment opportunity.

10 Determine the internal rate of return of an investment opportunity.

11 Identify the typical cash inflows and outflows associated with capital investments.

12 Determine the payback period for an investment opportunity.

13 Determine the unadjusted rate of return for an investment opportunity.

14 Conduct a postaudit of an investment that has been exercised.

the *curious* manager

© Superstock

Universal Studios in Florida unveiled plans to build Islands of Adventure, a $1.5 billion theme park. Universal believes it can attract customers with high-technology, futuristic thrill rides. The company's chief rival, Disney World, has opted out of the high-tech option. Just how many visitors will be needed to recover a $1.5 billion investment? How long will it take Universal to recover its investment? What techniques do companies use to help them justify such vast investments?

The president of EZ Rentals (EZ) is considering the possibility of expanding the company's rental service business. EZ's customers have made numerous requests for LCD projectors that can be used with notebook computers. Indeed, forecasts based on a recent marketing study indicate that the rental of projectors could generate revenue of approximately $200,000 per year. The possibility of increasing revenue is alluring, but EZ's president has a number of unanswered questions. How much do the projectors cost? What is their expected useful life? Will they have a salvage value? Do we have the money it takes to buy them? Do we have the technical expertise to support the product? How much will training cost? How long can we expect customer demand to last? What if we buy the projectors and they become technologically obsolete? How quickly will we be able to recover our investment? Are there other more profitable ways to invest our funds?

Most managers get a bit nervous about making decisions to spend large sums of money that will have long-term effects on their company's profitability. What if Company A spends millions of dollars to build a factory in Canada, while its competitors locate their manufacturing facilities in countries *that provide cheap labour? Company A's products will become overpriced, but it cannot move the facility because it cannot find a buyer for the factory. What if a pharmaceutical company spends millions of dollars to develop a drug that fails to obtain FDA approval? What if another company installs underground cable wire but satellite transmission steals its market? What if a company buys computer equipment that rapidly becomes technologically obsolete? Although these possibilities may be considered remote, they can be very expensive when they do occur. For example, Wachovia Bank's 1997 annual report shows a $70 million dollar write-off of computer equipment. This chapter discusses some of the analytical techniques companies use to evaluate major investment opportunities.*

▌ Capital Investment Decisions

LO1

Distinguish between capital investments and investments in stocks and bonds.

The purchases of long-term operational assets are **capital investments**. Capital investments differ from investments in stocks and bonds in one important respect. Investments in stocks and bonds can be sold in organized free markets, such as the Toronto Stock Exchange. In contrast, investments in capital assets normally can be recovered only by using those assets. Once a company purchases a capital asset, it is committed to that investment for a time. If its market turns sour, it is stuck with the consequences. Likewise, the company may be unable to take advantage of new opportunities because its capital is committed. The ultimate profitability of an enterprise hinges, to a large extent, on the quality of a few critically important capital investment decisions.

A capital investment decision is essentially a decision to exchange current cash outflows for the promise of receiving future cash inflows. In the case of EZ Rentals, investing in projection equipment, a cash outflow today, provides an opportunity to collect $200,000 per year in rental revenue, a future cash inflow. Assuming that the projectors have a useful life of four years and no salvage value, how much should EZ be willing to pay for the future cash inflows? If you were EZ's president, would you spend $700,000 today to receive $200,000 per year for the next four years? You would be giving up $700,000 today for the opportunity to receive $800,000 (4 × $200,000) in the future. What happens if the future expectation fails to materialize? What if you collect less than $200,000 per year? If revenue is only $160,000 per year, you would lose $60,000 ($700,000 − [4 × $160,000]). Is $700,000 too much to pay for an opportunity to get $200,000 per year for four years? If $700,000 were too high, would you spend $600,000? If this figure is still too high, how about $500,000? There is no correct answer to these questions. However, an understanding of the *time value of money* concept can help you formulate a rational response.

Time Value of Money

LO2

Understand and apply the concept of time value of money to capital investment decisions.

The **time value of money** concept recognizes the fact that *the present value of a dollar received in the future is less than a dollar*. For example, you may be willing to pay only $0.90 today to receive a promise to collect $1 one year from today. The further into the future the receipt is expected to occur, the smaller is its present value. In other words, one dollar to be received two years from today is worth less than one dollar to be received one year from today. Likewise, one dollar to be received three years from today is less valuable than one dollar to be received two years from today, and so on.

The present value of cash inflows diminishes as the time until expected receipt increases for several reasons. First, today's dollar could be deposited in a savings account to earn *interest* that increases its total value. If you wait for your money, you lose the opportunity to earn *interest*. Second, an element of *risk* is associated with the future dollar. Conditions may change and the promise to pay the future dollar may be broken, thereby resulting in the failure to collect. Finally, *inflation* diminishes the buying power of the dollar. In other words, the longer you must wait to receive a dollar, the less you will be able to buy with it.

When a company invests in capital assets, it gives present dollars in exchange for the opportunity to receive future dollars. Given the negative consequences associated with trading current dollars for future dollars, companies must be compensated to encourage them to invest in capital assets. The compensation a company receives is called a *return on investment*, which, as discussed in Chapter 9, is normally expressed as a percentage of the amount of the investment. For example, a $1,000 investment that earns annual income of $100 provides a 10 percent rate of return ($100 ÷ $1,000 = 10%).

LO3
Distinguish between return on investment and recovery of investment.

Determining the Minimum Rate of Return

What is the minimum *return on investment* that will persuade a company to accept an investment opportunity? To answer this question, most companies consider their cost of capital. To attract capital, a company must provide a benefit to its creditors and owners. For example, the company pays interest to creditors and dividends to owners. Companies that earn a return that is lower than their cost of capital eventually go bankrupt. In other words, they cannot continuously pay out more than they collect. Accordingly, *the* **cost of capital** *represents the* **minimum rate of return** *on investments*. Calculating the cost of capital is a relatively complicated task covered in finance courses. Accordingly, we will not attempt to cover that topic in this text. Instead, we proceed to the subject of how management accounting uses the cost of capital to evaluate investment opportunities.

LO4
Explain why the cost of capital constitutes the minimum acceptable rate of return for a capital investment.

Capital budgeting decisions tend to fall into two broad categories: preference decisions and screening decisions. In a preference decision, a firm may have to select between a couple of alternatives when there is a decision to replace or acquire a piece of equipment. In this case, a company will select the alternative that provides the highest net present value using discount rates based on the required (or desired) rate of return. In screening decisions, a project must meet a minimum or hurdle rate of return before proceeding to the preference stage of the decision process.

Converting Future Cash Inflows into Their Equivalent Present Values

Simple algebra is used to determine the present value of future cash inflows. To illustrate, we examine the $200,000 that EZ expects to earn during the first year that it leases the projectors. Assuming that EZ desires to earn a 12 percent rate of return, what amount of cash should it invest today (i.e., present value outflow) to obtain the $200,000 cash inflow at the end of the year (i.e., future value)? The answer can be determined as follows:[1]

$$\text{Investment} + (0.12 \times \text{Investment}) = \text{Future cash inflow}$$
$$1.12 \text{ Investment} = \$200,000$$
$$\text{Investment} = \$200,000 \div 1.12$$
$$\text{Investment} = \$178,571$$

The computations indicate that if EZ invests $178,571 cash on January 1 and earns a 12 percent return on the investment, it will have $200,000 on December 31. Stated differently, an investor who is able to earn a 12 percent return on investment is indifferent as to the choice of having $178,571 now or receiving $200,000 one year from now. The investor views the two options as being equal. The following mathematical proof supports this equality:

$$\text{Investment} + (0.12 \times \text{Investment}) = \$200,000$$
$$\$178,571 + (0.12 \times \$178,571) = \$200,000$$
$$\$178,571 + 21,429 = \$200,000$$
$$\$200,000 = \$200,000$$

Present Value Table for Single-Amount Cash Inflows   Because EZ desires to earn a 12 percent rate of return, the previous computations suggest that the present value of the first cash inflow is $178,571.

[1] All computations in this chapter are rounded to the nearest whole dollar.

LO5

Use present value tables to determine the present value of future cash flows.

We now determine the present value of receiving a single amount (i.e., lump-sum) of $200,000 in the second, third, and fourth years. Using algebra to convert these future values into their present value equivalents requires a considerable amount of mathematical manipulation. To simplify such computation, financial analysts frequently use tables that contain factors to use to convert future values into their present value equivalents. The table of conversion factors is used to transform future values into present values; therefore, it is commonly called a **present value table**.[2] A present value table is normally composed of columns that represent different return rates and rows that represent different periods of time. A typical present value table is shown as Table 1 in Appendix A.

To illustrate the use of the present value table, locate the conversion factor in Table 1 at the intersection of the 12% column and the row representing one period. At this location, you will find the conversion factor 0.892857. Multiplying this factor by the $200,000 expected cash inflow yields the result $178,571 ($200,000 × 0.892857). Note that this is the same value that was determined algebraically in the previous section of this chapter. The conversion factors in the present value tables reduce the mathematical manipulation required to convert future values to present values.

The conversion factors for the second, third, and fourth periods are 0.797194, 0.711780, and 0.635518, respectively. These factors are located under the 12% column at rows 2, 3, and 4, respectively. Validate your understanding of the present value table by locating these factors in Table 1 of Appendix A. Multiplying the conversion factors by the future cash inflow for each period produces their present value equivalents. The conversion process is shown in Exhibit 10–1.

The information in Exhibit 10–1 indicates that investing $607,470 today at a 12 percent rate of return is equivalent to receiving $200,000 per year for four years. Stated differently, because EZ Rentals desires to earn a 12 percent rate of return, the company should be willing to pay $607,470 to purchase the projectors.

Exhibit 10-1				*Present Value of a $200,000 Cash Inflow to be Received for Four Years*			
	PV	=	FV	×	Present Value Table Factor	=	Present Value Equivalent
Period 1	PV	=	$200,000	×	0.892857	=	$178,571
Period 2	PV	=	200,000	×	0.797194	=	159,439
Period 3	PV	=	200,000	×	0.711780	=	142,356
Period 4	PV	=	200,000	×	0.635518	=	127,104
						Total	$607,470

LO6

Distinguish between lump-sum payments and ordinary annuities.

Present Value Table for Annuities   The mathematical manipulation required to convert the lump-sum cash inflows just described into their present value equivalents can be simplified even further by accumulating the present value table factors prior to multiplying them by the cash inflows. For example, the total of the present value table factors shown in Exhibit 10–1 is 3.037349 (0.892857 + 0.797194 + 0.711780 + 0.635518). By multiplying this **accumulated conversion factor** by the expected annual cash inflow, we determine the present value equivalent of $607,470 ($200,000 × 3.037349). As with lump-sum conversion factors, accumulated conversion factors can be precalculated and organized in a table format with *columns* that represent different rates of return and *rows* that represent different periods of time. A present value table showing accumulated conversion factors is shown in Table 2 of Appendix A. To confirm your understanding of this present value table, locate the conversion factor at the intersection of the 12% column and the row representing the fourth time period. At this intersection, you will find the value 3.037349, confirming that the accumulated conversion factors are merely the sum of the individual conversion factors.

The conversion factors shown in Table 2 apply to an **annuity**, which is a series of cash flows that meets three criteria: (1) equal payment amounts, (2) equal time intervals, and (3) a constant rate of return. In the case of EZ Rentals, all cash inflows were for equivalent amounts ($200,000); the interval between cash inflows was an equal length of time (one year); and the rate of return applied to each inflow was held constant at 12 percent. Accordingly, the series of expected cash inflows from renting the projectors is classified as an annuity. The present value annuity table cannot be used if any of these conditions is not satisfied.

---

[2]The present value table is constructed from the mathematical formula $(1 \div [1 + r]n)$ where r equals the rate of return and n equals the number of periods.

The purpose of the present value annuity tables is to reduce the amount of mathematical computations necessary to convert future cash inflows into their present value equivalents. In the case of EZ Rentals, you can convert the cash inflows as shown in Exhibit 10–1. This process requires you to locate four conversion factors, to multiply each conversion factor by the annual cash inflow (i.e., four multiplications), and to sum the products of the multiplications. In contrast, you can treat the series of payments as an annuity. This requires a single multiplication of a conversion factor drawn from Table 2 by the amount of the annuity payment. Regardless of which conversion approach you choose to use, you obtain the same result (a present value of $607,470). Recall also that the conversion can be accomplished by applying an algebraic formula. Indeed, the table values are derivations of algebraic formulas. The purpose of the present value tables is to reduce the computations necessary to convert future values to present values.

Software Programs That Determine Present Values Software programs offer an even more efficient means of converting future values into present value equivalents. These programs are frequently built into handheld calculators and computer spreadsheet programs. Different software developers use a variety of input formats. As an example, we demonstrate the procedures used in a Microsoft *Excel* spreadsheet.

An *Excel* spreadsheet contains a variety of financial functions, one of which is designed to convert a future value annuity into its present value equivalent. This present value function uses the syntax *PV(rate,nper,pmt)* in which *rate* is the desired rate of return, *nper* is the number of periods, and *pmt* is the amount of the payment (i.e., periodic cash inflow). To convert a future value annuity into its present

LO7

Appreciate the power of computer software in determining present values.

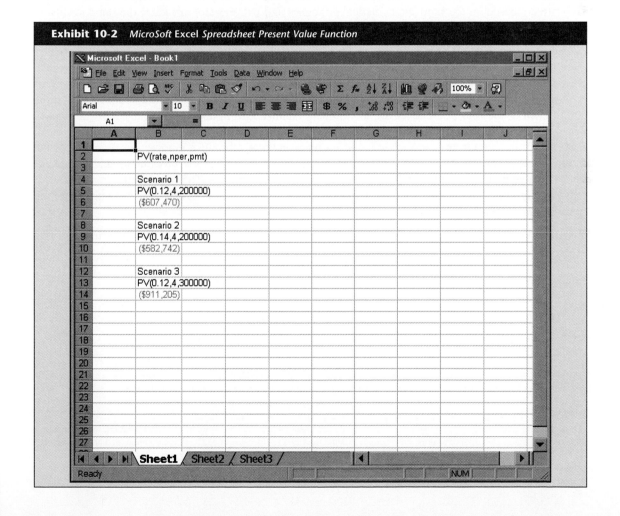

Exhibit 10-2 *MicroSoft* Excel *Spreadsheet Present Value Function*

value equivalent, you provide the function with the appropriate amounts for the rate, number of periods, and amount of the annuity (i.e., cash inflows) into a spreadsheet cell. When you press the Enter key, the present value equivalent appears in the spreadsheet cell.

The instantaneous conversion power of the spreadsheet is extremely useful for answering what-if questions. Exhibit 10–2 demonstrates this power by providing spreadsheet conversions for three different scenarios. The first scenario includes the cash flow annuity assumptions used in the EZ Rentals case. Specifically, the spreadsheet provides the present value equivalent ($607,470) for an annuity at a 12 percent rate of interest with a four-year term and a $200,000 per year cash inflow. Note that the present value is shown as a *negative* number. This format is used to indicate that a $607,470 *cash outflow* would be required to obtain the cash inflow annuity. The present value equivalent shown under Scenario 2 answers the question, "What if we change the annuity assumptions under Scenario 1 to reflect a 14 percent desired rate of return?" The present value equivalent shown under Scenario 3 answers the question, "What if we change the annuity assumptions under Scenario 1 to reflect a $300,000 annual cash inflow?" Similarly, a wide range of scenarios could be examined rapidly by changing the variables included in the spreadsheet function. In each case, the computer would do the calculations, leaving the manager more time to spend on the analysis of the data, rather than their mathematical manipulation.

Although the software approach is widely used in business practice, the diversity of interfaces used in different calculators and spreadsheet programs makes it an inappropriate approach for textbook presentations. Accordingly, this text uses the present value tables in Appendix A in the demonstration problems in the text and in the end-of-chapter exercises and problems. If you use software to solve these problems, you will obtain the same answers. All approaches including formulas, conversion tables, and software are based on the same mathematical principles and will therefore produce the same results.

Ordinary Annuity Assumption   You may have noticed that all the conversion methods we have described assumed that the cash inflows occurred at the end of each accounting period. This distribution pattern is called an **ordinary annuity**.[3] In practice, cash inflows are likely to be spread evenly over the period. For example, EZ Rentals is likely to collect cash revenue from the rental of its projectors evenly throughout the useful life of the investment, rather than collecting a single lump-sum receipt at the end of each of the four years. Even so, the ordinary annuity assumption is frequently used in practice because it simplifies the computations associated with accounting for the time value of money. Recall that capital investment projections are based on many estimates because pinpoint accuracy about the future is impossible to obtain. The anticipated cash inflows, the life of the investment, and the rate of return involve future expectations that are subject to many uncertainties. The compromise between accuracy and simplicity associated with the ordinary annuity assumption is just one more factor requiring human judgment in the decision-making process.

LO8
Understand the reinvestment assumption implicit in the interest tables and computer software.

Reinvestment Assumption   The present value computations in the previous sections indicate that investing $607,470 today at a 12 percent rate of return is equivalent to receiving $200,000 per year for four years. Stated differently, a $200,000 cash inflow per year is equivalent to earning a 12 percent rate of return on a $607,470 investment. Exhibit 10–3 illustrates this relationship.[4]

The information in Exhibit 10–3 indicates that an investment in the projection equipment does yield a 12 percent return. It is customary practice to assume that the desired rate of return includes the effects of *compounding*.[5] Accordingly, when we say an investment is "earning the desired rate of return," we

---

[3] When cash inflows occur at the beginning of each accounting period the distribution is called an *annuity due*. Although this distribution pattern is applicable to some business transactions, its application is less common than the ordinary annuity. This text focuses on the more common practice of using an ordinary annuity assumption.

[4] Exhibit 10–3 is analogous to an amortization table for a long-term note with equal payments.

[5] *Compounding* refers to reinvesting the proceeds from an investment so that the total amount of invested capital increases, thereby resulting in even higher returns. For example, assume that $100 is invested at a 10 percent compounded annual rate of return. At the end of the first year, the investment yields a $10 return ($100 × 0.10). The $10 return plus any recovered investment is reinvested so that the total amount of invested capital at the beginning of the second year is $110. The return for the second year is $11 ($110 × 0.10). All funds are reinvested so that the return for the third year is $12.10 ([$110 × $11] × 0.10).

Exhibit 10-3 *Cash Flow Classifications for EZ 's Investment in Projectors*

Time Period	(a) Investment Balance during the Year	(b) Annual Cash Inflow	(c) Return on Investment (a × 0.12)	(d) Recovered Investment (b − c)	(e) Year-End Investment Balance (a − d)
1	$607,470	$200,000	$ 72,896	$127,104	$480,366
2	480,366	200,000	57,644	142,356	338,010
3	338,010	200,000	40,561	159,439	178,571
4	178,571	200,000	21,429	178,571	(0)
Totals		$800,000	$192,530	$607,470	

are making the assumption that the cash inflows generated by the investment are reinvested at the desired rate of return. In this case, we are assuming that EZ will reinvest the $200,000 annual cash inflows in other investments that will earn a 12 percent return.

Techniques for Analyzing Capital Investment Proposals

Numerous analytical tools and techniques may be used to facilitate capital investment decisions. Each of the procedures has certain advantages and disadvantages. Management may choose to apply more than one technique to a particular proposal to take full advantage of the information at its disposal. Although it may seem that the application of different techniques to the same proposal is expensive, this is not the case. Most companies have access to computer facilities that include a variety of standard capital budgeting programs. Accordingly, applying different techniques to the same proposal normally requires little extra effort. In contrast, the benefits of obtaining a perspective that is not biased by selecting only one particular analytical procedure are substantial.

Net Present Value

By using the present value conversion techniques just described, EZ Rentals management was able to determine that it would be willing make a $607,470 present value investment to obtain a four-year, $200,000 future value annuity cash inflow. Note carefully that the $607,470 investment is *not* the cost of the projection equipment but is the amount that EZ is willing to pay for the equipment. The cost of the equipment may be more or less than its present value to EZ Rentals. To determine whether EZ should invest in the equipment, the present value of the future cash inflows ($607,470) must be compared with the cost of the equipment (the current cash outflow required to purchase the equipment). Specifically, the cost of the investment is subtracted from the present value of the future cash inflows to determine the **net present value** of the investment opportunity. A positive net present value indicates that the investment will yield a rate of return that is higher than 12 percent. In contrast, a negative net present value suggests the return is less than 12 percent.

To illustrate, assume that the projection equipment can be purchased for $582,742. Should EZ accept the capital investment opportunity? On the basis of the assumption of a desired rate of return of 12 percent, the answer is, yes. The net present value of the investment opportunity is computed as follows:

LO9
Determine and interpret the net present value of an investment opportunity.

Present value of future cash inflows	$607,470
Cost of investment (required cash outflow)	(582,742)
Net present value	$ 24,728

The positive net present value suggests that the investment will earn a rate of return in excess of 12 percent. Because the projected rate of return is higher than the desired rate of return, the analysis suggests that the investment opportunity should be accepted.

Internal Rate of Return

LO10
Determine the internal rate of return of an investment opportunity.

The net present value method indicates that the investment in the projection equipment will provide a return in excess of the desired rate, but it does not compute the actual rate of return to expect from the investment. If EZ's management team wants to know the rate of return to expect from the investment in the projections, it must use the *internal rate of return* method.

The **internal rate of return** is defined as the rate that equates the present value of cash inflows and outflows. In other words, it is the rate that will produce a zero net present value. In the case of EZ Rentals, the internal rate of return can be determined as follows. First, compute the *present value table factor* for a $200,000 annuity that would yield a $582,742 present value cash outflow (i.e., cost of investment).

$$\text{Present value table factor} \times \$200,000 = \$582,742$$
$$\text{Present value table factor} = \$582,742 \div \$200,000$$
$$\text{Present value table factor} = 2.91371$$

Second, since the expected annual cash inflows constitute a four-year annuity, scan Table 2 in Appendix A at period $n = 4$. Try to locate the table factor just computed. The rate that is listed at the top of the column in which the factor is located is the internal rate of return. We suggest that you turn to Table 2 and determine the internal rate of return for this case before you read further. The correct answer is located in the 14% column. The difference in the table value (2.913712) and the value computed here (2.91371) is due to rounding. Accordingly, if EZ invests $582,742 in the projectors and the equipment produces a $200,000 annual cash flow for four years, EZ will earn a 14 percent rate of return on its investment.

The *internal rate* of return may be compared with a *desired rate of return* to determine whether to accept or reject a particular investment project. Assuming that EZ desires to earn a minimum rate of return of 12 percent, the preceding analysis suggests that it should accept the investment opportunity. More specifically, because the internal rate of return (14 percent) is higher than the desired rate of return (12 percent), the investment alternative should be accepted. An internal rate of return that is below the desired rate would suggest that a particular proposal should be rejected. Because the desired rate of return constitutes the line of demarcation for the acceptance or rejection of investment alternatives, it is sometimes called the *cutoff rate* or the *hurdle rate*. In other words, to be accepted, an investment proposal must provide an internal rate of return that is higher than the hurdle rate, cutoff rate, or desired rate of return. Recall that these terms are merely alternative expressions for the firm's *cost of capital*. Ultimately, to be accepted, an investment must provide an internal rate of return that is higher than the company's cost of capital.

▌Techniques for Measuring Investment Cash Flows

LO11
Identify the typical cash inflows and outflows associated with capital investments.

EZ Rentals' analysis of the option to purchase projection equipment represents a simple capital investment scenario. The project included only one cash outflow and a single annuity inflow. Many investment decisions involve a variety of cash outflows and inflows. The following section of this chapter discusses the different types of cash flows encountered in business practice.

Cash Inflows

Cash inflows generated from capital investments come from *four basic sources*. As suggested in the case of EZ Rentals, the most common source of cash inflows is incremental revenue. **Incremental revenue** refers to the *additional* cash inflows from operations generated by using an additional capital asset. For example, a taxi company expects revenues from taxi fares to increase if it purchases additional automobiles. Similarly, investments in new apartments should result in rent revenue; the opening of a new store should result in incremental sales revenue.

The second type of cash inflow results from *cost savings*. More specifically, decreases in cash outflows have the same overall effect as increases in cash inflows. Either way, the firm's cash position is improved. For example, purchasing an automated computer system may enable a company to reduce cash outflows associated with salaries. Similarly, relocating a manufacturing facility near the source of its raw materials can reduce cash outflows associated with transportation costs. Ben Franklin recognized the value of cost savings in his famous observation, "A penny saved is a penny earned."

An investment's *salvage value*—a term used many times previously in this text—is a third source of cash inflow. Even when one company has fully used an asset, it may still be useful to another company. Accordingly, many assets are sold after some company no longer considers them to be useful. The salvage value represents a one-time cash inflow obtained at the termination of the investment.

A cash inflow can also be obtained through a *reduction in the amount of* **working capital** that is necessary to support an investment. A certain level of working capital is required to support most business investments. For example, a new retail outlet store requires cash, inventory, receivables, and so on to accomplish its sales function. When an investment is terminated, the decrease in the working capital commitment associated with the investment normally results in a cash inflow.

Cash Outflows

Cash outflows can be categorized into *three primary groups*. The first group includes the outflows associated with the *initial investment*. Care must be taken to identify all cash outflows that are connected with the purchase of a capital asset. The purchase price, transportation costs, installation costs, and training costs are examples of typical cash outflows related to the initial investment.

Second, cash outflows may result from *increases in operating expenses*. If a company increases its output capacity by investing in additional equipment, it may experience higher utility bills, labour costs, maintenance expenses, and so on when the machinery is placed into service. These expenditures cause cash outflows to increase.

Third, *increases in working capital* commitments result in cash outflows. Frequently, investments in new assets must be supported by a certain level of working capital. For example, investing in a copy machine requires that cash be spent to buy and maintain a supply of paper, toner, and other supplies. An increase in the amount of working capital commitment should be treated as a cash outflow in the period that the commitment is required.

Exhibit 10-4	*Typical Cash Flows Associated with Capital Investments*
Inflow Items	**Outflow Items**
1. Incremental revenue	1. Initial investment
2. Cost savings	2. Incremental expenses
3. Salvage values	3. Working capital commitments
4. Recovery of working capital	

Exhibit 10–4 summarizes the cash inflow and outflow items discussed. The illustration does not contain an exhaustive list but provides a summary of the most common items found in business practice.

■ Techniques for Comparing Alternative Capital Investment Opportunities

The management of Torres Transfer Company is considering two investment opportunities. The first opportunity, which would enable Torres to modernize its maintenance facility, would require the purchase of $80,000 of new equipment. The equipment would have an expected useful life of five years and a $4,000 salvage value and would replace existing equipment that had originally cost $45,000. The old equipment has a current book value of $15,000 and a trade-in value of $5,000. The old equipment is technologically obsolete, but it can operate for an additional five years. Torres expects to incur $3,000 of training cost to teach employees to operate the new equipment. Training is provided by the manufacturer of the equipment and must be paid for on the day the equipment is purchased. Two primary advantages are associated with the modernization. First, it will permit the company to better manage its inventory of small parts. Indeed, the company's accountant believes that by the end of the first year after its implementation, the carrying value of small parts inventory can be reduced by $12,000. Second, the modernization is expected to increase efficiency, resulting in a $21,500 reduction in annual operating expenses.

The second investment alternative available to Torres is the purchase of a truck that would enable Torres to expand its delivery area and thereby increase revenue. The truck is expected to cost $115,000. It will have a useful life of five years and a $30,000 salvage value. Operating the truck will require the company to increase its inventory of supplies, its petty cash account, and its accounts receivable and payable balances. As a result of these changes, an investment in the truck is expected to add $5,000 to the company's working capital base immediately and to be recovered at the end of the truck's useful life. The truck is expected to produce $69,000 per year in additional revenues. The driver's salary and other operating expenses are expected to be $32,000 per year. A major overhaul costing $20,000 is expected to be required at the end of the third year of operation. Assuming that Torres desires to earn a rate of return of 14 percent, which of the two investment alternatives should it choose?

Net Present Value

LO9

Determine and interpret the net present value of an investment opportunity.

We begin our analysis by calculating the net present value of the two investment alternatives. The results of these computations are shown in Exhibit 10–5. Study this exhibit carefully before reading further. Note the three-step approach used to determine the net present value of each investment alternative. Step 1 requires the identification of all cash inflows; some may be annuities; and others may be lump-sum receipts. In the case of Alternative 1, the cost saving is an annuity, and the inflow from the salvage value is a lump-sum receipt. Once the cash flows have been identified, the appropriate conversion factors are identified and the cash flows are converted to their equivalent present values. Step 2 follows the same process to determine the present value of the cash outflows. Step 3 subtracts the present value of the outflows from the present value of the inflows to determine the net present value. The same three-step approach is used to determine the net present value of Alternative 2.

Most of the items in Exhibit 10–5 are self-explanatory. However, note that with respect to Alternative 1, the original cost and the book value of the old equipment have been ignored. As indicated in a previous chapter, these cost measures represent *sunk costs* and are not relevant to the decision-making process. The concept of relevance applies to long-term capital investment decisions just as it applies to the short-term special decisions that were discussed in Chapter 4. To be relevant to a capital investment decision, costs or revenues must involve a different present and future cash flow for each alternative. The historical cost of the old equipment does not affect the cash flows of future periods. Because the cash flows are the same, regardless of the amount of the original cost and book value of the old equipment, these items are not relevant to the capital investment decision.

The fact that both investment alternatives produce a *positive net present value* indicates that both investments will generate a return in excess of 14 percent. Although this information is useful, it does

Exhibit 10-5   *Net Present Value Analysis*

	Amount	×	Conversion Factor	=	Present Value
Alternative 1: Modernize maintenance facility					
Step 1: Cash inflows					
1. Cost savings	$21,500.00	×	3.433081*	=	$73,811.24
2. Salvage value	4,000.00	×	0.519369†	=	2,077.48
3. Working capital recovery	12,000.00	×	0.877193‡	=	10,526.32
Total					$86,415.04
Step 2: Cash outflows					
1. Cost of equipment					
($80,000 cost − $5,000 trade-in)	$75,000.00	×	1.000000§	=	$75,000.00
2. Training costs	3,000.00	×	1.000000§	=	3,000.00
Total					$78,000.00
Step 3: Net present value					
Total present value of cash inflows	$86,415.04				
Total present value of cash outflows	(78,000.00)				
Net present value	$ 8,415.04				
Alternative 2: Purchase delivery truck					
Step 1: Cash inflows					
1. Incremental revenue	$69,000.00	×	3.433081*	=	$236,882.59
2. Salvage value	30,000.00	×	0.519369†	=	15,581.07
3. Working capital recovery	5,000.00	×	0.519369†	=	2,596.85
Total					$255,060.51
Step 2: Cash outflows					
1. Cost of truck	$115,000.00	×	1.000000§	=	$115,000.00
2. Working capital increase	5,000.00	×	1.000000§	=	5,000.00
3. Increased operating expense	32,000.00	×	3.433081*	=	109,858.59
4. Major overhaul	20,000.00	×	0.674972≠	=	13,499.44
Total					$243,358.03
Step 3: Net present value					
Total present value of cash inflows	$255,060.51				
Total present value of cash outflows	(243,358.03)				
Net present value	$ 11,702.48				

*Present Value of Annuity Table 2, $n = 5$, $r = 14\%$.
†Present Value of Single payment Table 1, $n = 5$, $r = 14\%$.
‡Present Value of Single payment Table 1, $n = 1$, $r = 14\%$.
§Present Value at Beginning of period 1.
≠Present Value of Single payment Table 1, $n = 3$, $r = 14\%$.

not indicate which investment is the more favourable. Indeed, the data may even mislead an uninformed manager. One is tempted to identify Alternative 2 as the better choice because its present value ($11,702.48) is higher than that produced by Alternative 1 ($8,415.04). However, net present value is expressed in *absolute dollar* amounts. This means that a large investment project can have a net present value that is higher than that of a small project even though the smaller project is earning a higher rate of return.

To make reasonable comparisons among investment alternatives, management should consider the size of the investment in the present value analysis. This can be accomplished by computing a **present value index**. This index is computed by dividing the present value of cash inflows by the present value of cash outflows. *The higher the ratio, the higher is the rate of return per dollar invested in the proposed project.* The present value index for the two alternatives available to Torres Transfer Company are as follows:

$$\frac{\text{Present value index}}{\text{for Alternative 1}} = \frac{\text{Present value of cash inflows}}{\text{Present value of cash outflows}} = \frac{\$86,415.04}{\$78,000.00} = 1.108$$

$$\frac{\text{Present value index}}{\text{for Alternative 2}} = \frac{\text{Present value of cash inflows}}{\text{Present value of cash outflows}} = \frac{\$255,060.51}{\$243,358.03} = 1.048$$

The present value index can be used to rank order investment alternatives. In this case, the indices reveal that Alternative 1 would yield a higher return than Alternative 2.

Internal Rate of Return

LO10

Determine the internal rate of return of an investment opportunity.

Investment alternatives can also be rank ordered by calculating the internal rate of return for each investment. Generally, *the higher the rate, the better is the investment.* We previously demonstrated the calculation of the internal rate of return for an investment that generates a simple cash inflow annuity. Unfortunately, the computations are significantly more complicated for investments with uneven cash flows. Recall that the internal rate of return is the rate that produces a zero net present value. The manual computation of the rate that produces a zero net present value may require a tedious trial-and-error process. First, estimate the rate of return for a particular investment and proceed by calculating the net present value. If the calculation produces a negative net present value, reduce the estimated rate of return and recalculate. If this calculation produces a positive net present value, the actual internal rate of return lies between the first and second estimates. Proceed by making a third estimate and once again recalculate the net present value. Continue in this fashion until you locate the rate of return that produces a net present value of zero. Fortunately, many calculators and spreadsheet programs are designed to make these computations. To illustrate, we show the process used in a Microsoft *Excel* spreadsheet. *Excel* uses the syntax *IRR(values, guess)* in which *values* is a reference to cells that contain the cash flows for which you want to calculate the internal rate of return and guess is a number that you *guess* is close to the internal rate of return (IRR) result. The IRRs for the two investment alternatives available to Torres Transfer Company are shown in Exhibit 10–6. When reviewing this exhibit, be aware that the *Excel* approach requires you to net cash outflows against cash inflows for any period that contains both. We have labelled the net cash flows in the spreadsheet for your convenience. This labelling process is not necessary to execute the IRR function. Indeed, the entire function, including values and guess, can be entered into a single cell of the spreadsheet. Accordingly, for a person who is familiar with spreadsheet programs, the input required can be significantly simplified.

The IRR results in Exhibit 10–6 validate the rank ordering that was accomplished through the present value index. Again, Alternative 1 (modernize maintenance facility) with an internal rate of return of 18.69 percent ranks above Alternative 2 (purchase a truck) with an internal rate of return of 17.61 percent. Recall that this result occurs even though Alternative 2 produced a higher net present value (see Exhibit 10–5). However, it must also be noted that Alternative 2 still may be the better investment option, depending on the amount of funds available for investment. Suppose that Torres has $120,000

McDonalds knows that some locations are better than others. Locations in high-traffic areas bring more customers with more cash than those in low-traffic areas. Unfortunately, high-traffic locations usually cost more. Rent is higher, and demand for employees increases salaries, taxes, and other charges in highly populated areas. Accordingly, cash flows vary for McDonalds' restaurants located in different types of areas. Fortunately, McDonalds can use discounted cash flow techniques, such as net present value and internal rate of return, to compare investment opportunities at different locations. These techniques enable the company to select the most profitable locations for new restaurants.

© McLaughlin/The Image Works

Exhibit 10-6 *Microsoft Excel spreadsheet Internal Rate of Return Function*

Internal Rate of Return for Alternative 1	
IRR (Values, Guess)	
IRR (B6:B11, 10%) = 18.6932%	
-78000	($80,000 Cost of Equipment - $5,000 Trade-In + $3,000 Training Cost)
33500	($21,500 Cost Savings + $12,000 Working Capital Recovery)
21500	(Cost Savings)
21500	(Cost Savings)
21500	(Cost Savings)
25500	($21,500 Cost Savings + $4,000 Salvage Value)
Internal Rate of Return for Alternative 2	
IRR (Values, Guess)	
IRR (B18:B23, 10%) = 17.6083%	
-120000	($115,000 Cost of Truck + $5,000 Working Capital Increase)
37000	($69,000 Revenue - $32,000 Operating Expense)
37000	($69,000 Revenue - $32,000 Operating Expense)
17000	($69,000 Revenue - $32,000 Operating Expense - $20,000 Overhaul)
37000	($69,000 Revenue - $32,000 Operating Expense)
72000	($69,000 Revenue - $32,000 Operating Expense + $30,000 Salvage + 5,000 Working Capital Recovery)

---

of available funds to invest. Because Alternative 1 requires only a $78,000 initial investment, $42,000 ($120,000 − $78,000) of capital will not be invested. If Torres has no other investment opportunities for this $42,000, the company would be better off to invest the entire $120,000 in Alternative 2 (i.e., $115,000 cost of truck + $5,000 working capital increase). In other words, earning 17.61 percent on a $120,000 investment is better than earning 18.69 percent on a $78,000 investment with no return on the remaining $42,000. Again, this discussion emphasizes the fact that management accounting requires the exercise of judgment in the decision-making process.

▌ Relevance and the Time Value of Money

Suppose that you have the opportunity to invest in one of two capital projects. Both projects require an immediate cash outflow of $6,000 and will produce future cash inflows of $8,000. The only difference between the two projects is the timing of the receipt of the inflows. The receipt schedule for both projects follows:

	Project 1	Project 2
2001	$3,500	$2,000
2002	3,000	2,000
2003	1,000	2,000
2004	500	2,000
Total	$8,000	$8,000

Because both projects cost the same and produce the same total cash inflows, they may appear to be equal. In other words, regardless of whether you select Project 1 or Project 2, you pay $6,000 and receive $8,000. When consideration is given to the time value of money, however, Project 1 is clearly preferable to Project 2. To validate this point, we determine the net present value of both projects, assuming a 10 percent desired rate of return.

Net Present Value for Project 1

Period	Cash Inflow	×	Conversion Factor Table 1, $r = 10\%$	=	Present Value
1	$3,500	×	0.909091	=	$3,181.82
2	3,000	×	0.826446	=	2,479.34
3	1,000	×	0.751315	=	751.32
4	500	×	0.683013	=	341.51
Present value of future cash inflows					$6,753.99
Present value of cash outflow					(6,000.00)
Net present value Project 1					$ 753.99

Net Present Value for Project 2

	Cash Inflow Annuity	×	Conversion Factor Table 2, $r = 10\%$, $n = 4$	
	$2,000	×	3.037349	$6,074.70
Present value of cash outflow				(6,000.00)
Net present value Project 2 $				74.70

Clearly, the net present value of Project 1 ($753.99) is preferable to the net present value of Project 2 ($74.70). As this case illustrates, it is important to recognize that the timing as well as the amount of cash flows has a significant impact on capital investment decisions. Recall that costs or revenues must be different for the alternatives to be considered relevant. Cash flows that differ with respect to the timing of payment or receipt are relevant for decision-making purposes.

Tax Considerations

To this point, we have ignored the effect of taxes on capital investment decisions. Taxes are important because they affect the amount of cash flows generated by investments. To illustrate, assume that Wu Company purchases an asset that costs $240,000. The asset has a four-year useful life and no salvage value and is depreciated on a straight-line basis. The asset generates cash revenue of $90,000 per year. Finally, assume that Wu's income tax rate is 40 percent. What is the net present value of the asset, assuming that Wu's management desires to earn a 10 percent rate of return after taxes? The first step in answering this question is to calculate the amount of annual cash flow generated by the asset. The appropriate computations are shown in Exhibit 10–7.

Because the amortization did not require a cash payment (i.e., cash is paid at the time of purchase, rather than when amortization is recognized), it must be added back to after-tax income to determine the amount of annual cash inflow. Once the amount of the cash flow has been determined, the net present value can be determined as indicated here:

Exhibit 10-7 *Determining Cash Flow from Investment*

	Period 1	Period 2	Period 3	Period 4
Cash revenue	$90,000	$90,000	$90,000	$90,000
Amortization expense (noncash)	(60,000)	(60,000)	(60,000)	(60,000)
Income before taxes	$30,000	$30,000	$30,000	$30,000
Income tax at 40%	(12,000)	(12,000)	(12,000)	(12,000)
Income after tax	$18,000	$18,000	$18,000	$18,000
Amortization add back	60,000	60,000	60,000	60,000
Annual cash inflow	$78,000	$78,000	$78,000	$78,000

$$\begin{array}{c} \text{Cash flow} \\ \text{annuity} \end{array} \times \begin{array}{c} \text{Conversion factor} \\ \text{Table 2, } r = 10\%, n = 4 \end{array} = \begin{array}{c} \text{Present Value} \\ \text{Cash inflows} \end{array} - \begin{array}{c} \text{Present Value} \\ \text{Cash Outflows} \end{array} = \begin{array}{c} \text{Net Present} \\ \text{Value} \end{array}$$

$$\$78,000 \times 3.169865 = \$247,249.47 - \$240,000 = \$7,249.47$$

Note that the amortization sheltered some of the income from taxation. In other words, the tax rate is applied to income after amortization has been deducted. Without amortization, the income tax would have been $36,000 ($90,000 × 0.40) instead of $12,000 ($30,000 × 0.40). The $24,000 differential ($36,000 − $12,000) is known as a *amortization tax shield*. The amount of the amortization tax shield can also be computed by multiplying the tax rate by the amortization expense ($60,000 × 0.40 = $24,000).

Because of the time value of money concept, companies desire to maximize the amortization tax shield early in the life of an asset. In other words, companies want to delay paying taxes as long as possible. Canada Customs and Revenue Agency does not allow amortization for tax reporting purposes. Instead, they use something called CCA or Capital Cost Allowance. The result is a method that allows for recovery of the capital cost of an asset (amortization) in an accelerated fashion. Each type of asset is placed into a "pool" of costs, and a prescribed fixed rate is applied to a declining balance in the pool (very similar to double declining amortization.)

For example, assume an asset with a capital cost of $100,000 and a prescribed rate of 20%. The result would be calculations of CCA (amortization) over the first five years as follows:

Year	UCC beginning of year	CCA allowed	UCC end of year
1	$100,000	$20,000 *	$80,000
2	80,000	16,000	64,000
3	64,000	12,800	51,200
4	51,200	10,240	40,940
5	40,940	8,188	32,752

UCC – Unamortized Capital Cost
* This example is to illustrate the principle. The reality is that there is something called a *half-year rule* that affects the CCA in the first year. We will leave this to a tax course to avoid unnecessary complication.

The higher CCA in the earlier years results in lower taxable income, resulting in lower income tax payable. As the years go by, the CCA becomes smaller, resulting in higher income tax payable. The company does not avoid paying tax; it delays the payment until later years. The result is that the company has more cash available in the earlier years to reinvest and longer time for that money to grow. Given your understanding of the time value of money, you can see why an accelerated method of capital recovery is desirable.

Techniques That Ignore the Time Value of Money

Several techniques for evaluating capital investment proposals ignore the time value of money. Although these techniques sacrifice accuracy, they provide a quick and simple means of evaluation. When investments are small or the returns are realized within a short time frame, these techniques are likely to lead to the same decisions that would result if more sophisticated techniques were employed.

Payback Method

LO12

Determine the payback period for an investment opportunity.

The **payback method** is simple to apply and easy to understand. It provides information regarding how long it will take to recover the initial cash outflow (i.e., the cost) of the investment. The formula for computing the payback period, measured in years, is as follows:

$$\text{Payback period} = \text{Net cost of investment} \div \text{Annual net cash inflow}$$

To illustrate, assume that Winston Cleaners can purchase a new machine that will press shirts in half the time of the one currently used. The new machine costs $100,000 and will reduce labour cost by $40,000 per year over a four-year useful life. The payback period is computed as follows:

$$\text{Payback period} = \$100,000 \div \$40,000 = 2.5 \text{ years}$$

Interpreting Payback   Generally, investments with shorter payback periods are considered to be better. However, this conclusion can be invalid because the method considers only the recovery of the investment. It provides no measurement of the profitability of different investment alternatives. To illustrate, assume that we extend the Winston Cleaners illustration to include an opportunity to purchase a different machine that also costs $100,000 and provides an annual labour savings of $40,000. However, the second machine will last for five years instead of four years. The payback period remains at 2.5 years ($100,000 ÷ $40,000), but the second machine is obviously a better investment because it improves profitability by providing an additional year of cost savings. The payback analysis does not reflect this fact.

Unequal Cash Flows   The preceding illustration assumed that the cash savings accrued equally over the life of the asset. The payback method may be complicated when cash inflows are collected on an unequal basis. Suppose that a company purchases a machine for $6,000. The machine will be used erratically and is expected to provide incremental income over the next five years as follows:

2001	2002	2003	2004	2005
$3,000	$1,000	$2,000	$1,000	$500

On the basis of this cash inflow pattern, what is the payback period? The problem can be solved in two acceptable ways. First, the incremental revenue can be accumulated to the point at which the sum equals the amount of the original investment.

Year	Annual Amount	Cumulative Total
2001	$3,000	$3,000
2002	1,000	4,000
2003	2,000	6,000

Companies, such as Universal Studios, use a variety of sophisticated analytical techniques to help them evaluate the worthiness of different investment opportunities. Two of these include net present value and internal rate of return. However, it is important to recognize that these techniques are merely mathematical manipulations of estimated cash flows. The adage "garbage in, garbage out" applies here. The appearance of mathematical precision must not be permitted to obscure the underlying economic uncertainty. The final result—no matter how precise it looks—is still just a rough estimate.

This approach reveals that payback would be accomplished at the end of three years.

The second alternative uses an averaging concept. The specific payments are used to determine an average annual cash inflow. This figure is then used in the denominator of the payback equation. Using the preceding data, the payback period is computed as follows:

1. Compute the average annual cash inflow.

    $$2001 \quad + \quad 2002 \quad + \quad 2003 \quad + \quad 2004 \quad + \quad 2005 \quad = \quad \text{Total} \quad \div \quad 5 \quad = \quad \text{Average}$$
    $$\$3,000 \quad + \quad \$1,000 \quad + \quad \$2,000 \quad + \quad \$1,000 \quad + \quad \$500 \quad = \quad \$7,500 \quad \div \quad 5 \quad = \quad \$1,500$$

2. Compute the payback period.

    $$\frac{\text{Net cost of}}{\text{investment}} \div \frac{\text{Average annual}}{\text{net cash inflow}} = 6,000 \div 1,500 = 4 \text{ years}$$

The average method is useful when a company purchases a number of similar assets with differing cash return patterns.

Unadjusted Rate of Return

The **unadjusted rate of return** method is another commonly used evaluation technique. It derives its name from the fact that it does not adjust the cash flows to reflect the time value of money. It is sometimes called the *simple rate of return*. This method represents an improvement over the payback method because it considers profitability as well as the recovery of the investment. The unadjusted rate of return is computed as follows:

LO13

Determine the unadjusted rate of return for an investment opportunity.

$$\frac{\text{Unadjusted}}{\text{rate of return}} = \frac{\text{Average incremental increase in annual net income}}{\text{Net cost of original investment}}$$

To illustrate the computation of the unadjusted rate of return, assume that The Dining Table, Inc. is considering the establishment of a new restaurant that will require a $2,000,000 original investment. Management anticipates operating the restaurant for 10 years before significant renovations will be required. The restaurant is expected to provide an average after-tax return of $280,000 per year. The unadjusted rate of return is computed as follows:

$$\text{Unadjusted rate of return} = \frac{\$280,000}{\$2,000,000} = 14\% \text{ per year}$$

The accuracy of the unadjusted rate of return suffers from its failure to recognize the recovery of invested capital. With respect to a amortizable asset, the capital investment is normally recovered through revenue over the life of the asset. To illustrate, assume that we purchase a $1,000 asset with a two-year life and a zero salvage value. For simplicity, we ignore income taxes. We assume that the asset produces $600 of cash revenue per year. The income statement for the first year of operation appears as follows:

Revenue	$600
Amortization Expense	(500)
Net Income	$100

On the basis of this information, what is the amount of invested capital during the first year? To answer this question, let us examine the cash flows. First, $1,000 in cash outflow was used to purchase the asset (i.e., the original investment). Next, we collected $600 of cash revenue of which $100 was a *return on investment* (i.e., net income) and $500 of which was a **recovery of investment**. As a result, $1,000 was invested in the asset at the beginning of the year and $500 was invested at the end of the year ($500 was recovered during the year). Similarly, we will recover an additional $500 of capital during the second year of operation, thereby leaving a zero balance of invested capital at the end of the second year. Given that the cash inflows from revenue are distributed somewhat evenly over the life of the investment, the amount of invested capital will range from a beginning balance of $1,000 to an ending balance of zero. On average, we will have $500 invested in the asset (i.e., the midpoint between $1,000 and zero). As this discussion implies, the average investment can be determined by dividing the total original investment by 2 (i.e., $1,000 ÷ 2 = $500). The unadjusted rate of return based on average invested capital can be calculated as follows:

$$\text{Unadusted rate of return (Based on average investment)} = \frac{\text{Average incremental increase in annual net income}}{\text{Net cost of original investment} \div 2}$$

$$= \frac{\$100}{\$1,000 \div 2} = 20\%$$

To avoid distortions caused by the failure to recognize the recovery of invested capital, it is recommended that you use the unadjusted rate of return based on the *average investment* when working with investments in amortizable assets.

▮ Real-World Reporting Practices

In a recent study, researchers found that companies in the forestry industry use discounted cash flow techniques more frequently when the investment being considered is in long-term timber investments. The use of techniques that ignore the time value of money increased when other shorter-term capital investment projects were being considered. The researchers' findings are summarized in Exhibit 10–8.

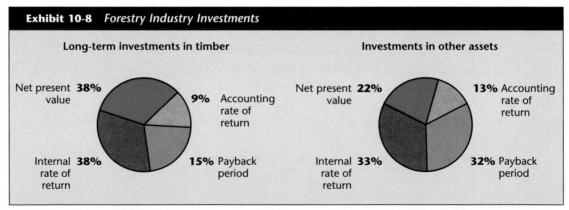

Exhibit 10-8 *Forestry Industry Investments*

Long-term investments in timber
Net present value **38%**   **9%** Accounting rate of return
Internal rate of return **38%**   **15%** Payback period

Investments in other assets
Net present value **22%**   **13%** Accounting rate of return
Internal rate of return **33%**   **32%** Payback period

Data Source: J. Bailes, J. Nielsen, and S. Lawton, "How Forest Product Companies Analyze Capital Budgets," *Management Accounting*, October 1998, pp. 24–30.

Lo**14**

Conduct a postaudit of an investment that has been exercised.

▮ Postaudits

The analytical techniques for evaluating capital investment proposals are highly dependent on the estimates of future cash flows. Although no one can be expected to predict the future with perfect accuracy, gross errors can lead to the demise of an organization. For example, optimistic projections of future cash inflows that do not materialize will lead to investments that do not return the cost of capital. Accordingly, managers must take their projections seriously. A postaudit is one way to ensure that managers closely scrutinize their capital investment decisions. A **postaudit** is conducted at the end of a capital investment project; it repeats the analytical technique that was used to justify the original investment. For example, if an internal rate of return was used as the basis for approving an investment project, an internal rate of return computation should be used in the postaudit. The difference between the original computation and the postaudit computation is that *actual,* rather than estimated, cash flows are used in the postaudit. This practice provides an opportunity to determine whether the expected results were actually accomplished.

The purpose of the postaudit should be continuous improvement, rather than punishment. Managers who are chastised for failing to attain expected results might become overly cautious when asked to provide estimates for future projects. Being overly conservative can create problems as serious as those caused by being too optimistic. Two types of errors can be made with respect to a capital investment decision. First, a manager might accept a project that should have been rejected. This result usually stems from being too optimistic in the projection of future cash flows. Second, the manager might reject a project that should have been accepted. These missed opportunities are usually the result of underestimating future cash flows. Indeed, a manager can become so cautious that she is unable to locate enough projects to fully invest the firm's funds. Remember that idle cash earns no return. If projects continue to outperform expectations, managers are probably being too conservative in their estimations of future cash flows. If projects consistently fail to live up to their expectations, managers are probably being too optimistic in their projections of future cash flows. Either way, the company suffers. The goal of a postaudit is to provide feedback that enables managers to improve the accuracy of the projections of future cash flows, thereby maximizing the quality of the firm's capital investments.

---

a look **back**

Capital expenditures have a significant, long-term effect on profitability. They usually involve major cash outflows that are recovered through future cash inflows. The most common cash inflow items include incremental revenue, savings of operating cost, salvage value, and working capital releases. The most common outflow items are the initial investment, increases in operating expenses, and working capital commitments.

Several techniques for analyzing the cash flow items associated with capital investments are available. The techniques can be divided into two categories: (1) techniques that include time value of money considerations, and (2) techniques that ignore time value of money considerations. Generally, the techniques that ignore time value of money considerations are less accurate but offer the benefits of simplicity and ease of understanding. These techniques include the *payback method* and the *unadjusted rate of return method.*

The techniques that include time value of money considerations are the *net present value method* and the *internal rate of return method.* These methods offer significant improvements in accuracy but are more difficult to understand. They may involve tedious computations and require exercising of experienced judgment. Fortunately, computer software and programmed calculators that ease the tedious computational burden are available to most managers. Furthermore, the superiority of the techniques justifies the effort of learning how to use them. Indeed, these methods should be used when investment expenditures are larger or when cash flow items extend over a prolonged time period.

a look **forward**

The next chapter moves into unexplored territory. It introduces the concept of inventory cost flow. It discusses how costs move through a series of inventory accounts, including raw materials, work in process, and finished goods. It presents techniques that enable overhead costs to be assigned to inventory as it is being produced. It identifies the differences in product costing for service and manufacturing companies. Finally, it introduces two approaches used to value inventory, variable versus full-absorption costing.

APPENDIX A

Table 1   Present Value of $1

n	4%	5%	6%	7%	8%	9%	10%	12%	14%	16%	20%
1	0.961538	0.952381	0.943396	0.934579	0.925926	0.917431	0.909091	0.892857	0.877193	0.862069	0.833333
2	0.924556	0.907029	0.889996	0.873439	0.857339	0.841680	0.826446	0.797194	0.769468	0.743163	0.694444
3	0.888996	0.863838	0.839619	0.816298	0.793832	0.772183	0.751315	0.711780	0.674972	0.640658	0.578704
4	0.854804	0.822702	0.792094	0.762895	0.735030	0.708425	0.683013	0.635518	0.592080	0.552291	0.482253
5	0.821927	0.783526	0.747258	0.712986	0.680583	0.649931	0.620921	0.567427	0.519369	0.476113	0.401878
6	0.790315	0.746215	0.704961	0.666342	0.630170	0.596267	0.564474	0.506631	0.455587	0.410442	0.334898
7	0.759918	0.710681	0.665057	0.622750	0.583490	0.547034	0.513158	0.452349	0.399637	0.353830	0.279082
8	0.730690	0.676839	0.627412	0.582009	0.540269	0.501866	0.466507	0.403883	0.350559	0.305025	0.232568
9	0.702587	0.644609	0.591898	0.543934	0.500249	0.460428	0.424098	0.360610	0.307508	0.262953	0.193807
10	0.675564	0.613913	0.558395	0.508349	0.463193	0.422411	0.385543	0.321973	0.269744	0.226684	0.161506
11	0.649581	0.584679	0.526788	0.475093	0.428883	0.387533	0.350494	0.287476	0.236617	0.195417	0.134588
12	0.624597	0.556837	0.496969	0.444012	0.397114	0.355535	0.318631	0.256675	0.207559	0.168463	0.112157
13	0.600574	0.530321	0.468839	0.414964	0.367698	0.326179	0.289664	0.229174	0.182069	0.145227	0.093464
14	0.577475	0.505068	0.442301	0.387817	0.340461	0.299246	0.263331	0.204620	0.159710	0.125195	0.077887
15	0.555265	0.481017	0.417265	0.362446	0.315242	0.274538	0.239392	0.182696	0.140096	0.107927	0.064905
16	0.533908	0.458112	0.393646	0.338735	0.291890	0.251870	0.217629	0.163122	0.122892	0.093041	0.054088
17	0.513373	0.436297	0.371364	0.316574	0.270269	0.231073	0.197845	0.145644	0.107800	0.080207	0.045073
18	0.493628	0.415521	0.350344	0.295864	0.250249	0.211994	0.179859	0.130040	0.094561	0.069144	0.037561
19	0.474642	0.395734	0.330513	0.276508	0.231712	0.194490	0.163508	0.116107	0.082948	0.059607	0.031301
20	0.456387	0.376889	0.311805	0.258419	0.214548	0.178431	0.148644	0.103667	0.072762	0.051385	0.026084

Table 2   Present Value of Annuity of $1

n	4%	5%	6%	7%	8%	9%	10%	12%	14%	16%	20%
1	0.961538	0.952381	0.943396	0.934579	0.925926	0.917431	0.909091	0.892857	0.877193	0.862069	0.833333
2	1.886095	1.859410	1.833393	1.808018	1.783265	1.759111	1.735537	1.690051	1.646661	1.605232	1.527778
3	2.775091	2.723248	2.673012	2.624316	2.577097	2.531295	2.486852	2.401831	2.321632	2.245890	2.106481
4	3.629895	3.545951	3.465106	3.387211	3.312127	3.239720	3.169865	3.037349	2.913712	2.798181	2.588735
5	4.451822	4.329477	4.212364	4.100197	3.992710	3.889651	3.790787	3.604776	3.433081	3.274294	2.990612
6	5.242137	5.075692	4.917324	4.766540	4.622880	4.485919	4.355261	4.111407	3.888668	3.684736	3.325510
7	6.002055	5.786373	5.582381	5.389289	5.206370	5.032953	4.868419	4.563757	4.288305	4.038565	3.604592
8	6.732745	6.463213	6.209794	5.971299	5.746639	5.534819	5.334926	4.967640	4.638864	4.343591	3.837160
9	7.435332	7.107822	6.801692	6.515232	6.246888	5.995247	5.759024	5.328250	4.946372	4.606544	4.030967
10	8.110896	7.721735	7.360087	7.023582	6.710081	6.417658	6.144567	5.650223	5.216116	4.833227	4.192472
11	8.760477	8.306414	7.886875	7.498674	7.138964	6.805191	6.495061	5.937699	5.452733	5.028644	4.327060
12	9.385074	8.863252	8.383844	7.942686	7.536078	7.160725	6.813692	6.194374	5.660292	5.197107	4.439217
13	9.985648	9.393573	8.852683	8.357651	7.903776	7.486904	7.103356	6.423548	5.842362	5.342334	4.532681
14	10.563123	9.898641	9.294984	8.745468	8.244237	7.786150	7.366687	6.628168	6.002072	5.467529	4.610567
15	11.118387	10.379658	9.712249	9.107914	8.559479	8.060688	7.606080	6.810864	6.142168	5.575456	4.675473
16	11.652296	10.837770	10.105895	9.446649	8.851369	8.312558	7.823709	6.973986	6.265060	5.668497	4.729561
17	12.165669	11.274066	10.477260	9.763223	9.121638	8.543631	8.021553	7.119630	6.372859	5.748704	4.774634
18	12.659297	11.689587	10.827603	10.059087	9.371887	8.755625	8.201412	7.249670	6.467420	5.817848	4.812195
19	13.133939	12.085321	11.158116	10.335595	9.603599	8.905115	8.364920	7.365777	6.550369	5.877455	4.843496
20	13.590326	12.462210	11.469921	10.594014	9.818147	9.128546	8.513564	7.469444	6.623131	5.928841	4.869580

Inflation and Net Present Value Analysis

In recent years, the inflation rate in Canada has been relatively modest, so the need to adjust cash flows for inflation may not be as critical. However, firms that operate in the international environment may face different circumstances: inflation can be very high in some countries, and its effect on capital investment decisions can be dramatic. Thus, it is important to know how to adjust the capital investment models for inflationary effects—particularly given the fact that many Canadian firms make capital investment decisions within many different national environments. In an inflationary environment, financial markets react by increasing the cost of capital to reflect inflation. Thus, the *cost of capital* is composed of two elements:

1. The real rate
2. The inflationary element (investors demand a premium to compensate for the loss in general purchasing power of the dollar or local currency)

Since the required rate of return used in capital investment analysis reflects an inflationary component at the time that the net present value (NPV) analysis is performed, inflation must also be considered in predicting the operating cash flows. If the operating cash flows are not adjusted to account for inflation, an erroneous decision may result. In adjusting predicted cash flows, specific price change indices should be used, if possible. If that is not possible, a general price index should be used.

Note, however, that cash inflows due to the tax effects of amortization, need *not* be adjusted for inflation as long as the national tax law for the country in question requires that amortization (or its equivalent) be based on the *original* dollar investment.

To illustrate, assume that a subsidiary of a Canadian company operating in Kazakhstan is considering a project that requires an investment of 5,000,000 tenge (the Kazakhstan currency) and is expected to produce annual cash inflows of 2,900,000 tenge for the coming two years. The required rate of return is 20 percent, which includes an inflationary component. The general inflation rate is expected to average 15 percent for the next two years. Net present value analysis with and without the adjustment of predicted cash flows for inflation is given in Exhibit 10-9. As the analysis shows, not adjusting predicted cash flows for inflation leads to a decision to reject the project, whereas adjusting for inflation leads to a decision to accept it. Thus, failure to adjust the predicted cash flows for inflationary effects can lead to an incorrect conclusion.

Exhibit 10-9   Net Present Value Analysis

Without Inflationary Adjustment

Year	Cash Flow	Discount Factor *	Present Value
0	(5,000,000)	1.000	5,000,000
1–2	2,900,000	1.528	4,431,200
Net Present Value			(568,800)

With Inflationary Adjustment

Year	Cash Flow†	Discount Factor‡	Present Value
0	(5,000,000)	1.000	(5,000,000)
1	3,335,000	.833	2,778,055
2	3,835,250	.694	2,661,663
Net Present Value			439,718

* From Table 2 p. 425
†Adjustment for inflation: 2,900,000 x 1.15; yr. 2: 3,335,000 × 1.15
Note: all cash flow in tenge.
‡From Table 1 p. 424

KEY TERMS

Accumulated conversion factors Factors that are used to convert a series of future cash inflows into their present value equivalent, that are applicable to cash inflows of equal amounts that are spread over equal interval time periods, and that can be determined by computing the sum of the individual single factors that are used for each period. *(p. 352)*

Annuity An equal series of cash flows received over equal intervals of time at a constant rate of return. *(p. 352)*

Capital investments Expenditures for the purchase of operational assets that involve a long-term commitment of funds that can be critically important to the company's ultimate success; normally recovered through the use of the assets. *(p. 350)*

Cost of capital The return paid to investors and creditors for the use of their assets (capital); usually represents a company's minimum rate of return. *(p. 351)*

Incremental revenue Additional cash inflows from operations generated by using an additional capital asset. *(p. 357)*

Internal rate of return The rate that will produce a present value of an investment's future cash inflows that equals cash outflows required to acquire the investments. Alternatively, the rate that produces a net present value of zero. *(p. 356)*

Minimum rate of return The minimum amount of profitability required to persuade a company to accept an investment opportunity; also known as *desired rate of return*, *required rate of return*, *hurdle rate*, *cutoff rate*, and *discount rate*. *(p. 351)*

Net present value An evaluation technique that uses a desired rate of return to discount future cash flows back to their present value equivalents and then subtracts the cost of the investment from the present value equivalents to determine the net present value. A zero or positive net present value (i.e., present value of cash inflows equals or exceeds the present value of cash outflows) implies that the investment opportunity provides an acceptable rate of return. *(p. 355)*

Ordinary annuity An annuity whose cash inflows occur at the end of each accounting period. *(p. 354)*

Payback method A technique that evaluates investment opportunities by determining the length of time necessary to recover the initial net investment through incremental revenue or cost savings; the shorter the period, the better is the investment opportunity. *(p. 364)*

Postaudit Repeated calculation using the techniques originally employed to analyze an investment project; accomplished with the use of actual data available at the completion of the investment project so that the actual results can be compared with expected results on the basis of estimated data at the beginning of the project. The purpose of the postaudit is to provide feedback as to whether the expected results were actually accomplished in order to improve the accuracy of future analysis. *(p. 367)*

Present value index The present value of cash inflows divided by the present value of cash outflows. Higher index numbers indicate higher rates of return. *(p. 360)*

Present value table A table that consists of a list of factors to use in converting future values into their present value equivalents; composed of columns that represent different return rates and rows that depict different periods of time. *(p. 352)*

Recovery of investment A recovery of the funds used to acquire the original investment. *(p. 366)*

Time value of money The concept that recognizes the fact that the present value of an opportunity to receive one dollar in the future is less than one dollar because of the factors of inflation. *(p. 350)*

Unadjusted rate of return A measure of profitability computed by dividing the average incremental increase in annual net income by the average cost of the original investment (i.e., original cost ÷ 2). *(p. 365)*

Working capital Current assets minus current liabilities. *(p. 357)*

QUESTIONS

1. What is a capital investment? How does it differ from an investment in stocks or bonds?
2. What are three reasons that cash is worth more today than cash to be received in the future?
3. "A dollar today is worth more than a dollar in the future." "The present value of a future dollar is worth less than one dollar." Are these two statements synonymous? Explain.
4. Define the term *return on investment*. How is the return normally expressed? Give an example of a capital investment return.
5. How does a company establish its minimum acceptable rate of return on investments?
6. If you wanted to have $500,000 one year from today and desired to earn a 10 percent return, what amount would you

need to invest today? Which amount has more value, the amount today or the $500,000 a year from today?

7. Why are present value tables frequently used to convert future values to present values?

8. Define the term *annuity*. What is one example of an annuity receipt?

9. How can present value "what-if" analysis be enhanced by the use of software programs?

10. What amount invested today at 14 percent is equivalent to receiving $100,000 per year for five years? Write a mathematical formula to solve this problem, assuming that a present value annuity table is used to convert the future cash flows to their present value equivalents. Write the expression for the *Excel* spreadsheet function that would accomplish the present value conversion.

11. Maria Espinosa borrowed $15,000 from the bank and agreed to repay the loan at 8 percent annual interest over four years, making payments of $4,529 per year. Because part of the bank's payment from Ms. Espinosa is a recovery of the original investment, what assumption must the bank make to earn its desired 8 percent compounded annual return?

12. Two investment opportunities have a positive net present value. Investment A's net present value amounts to $40,000 while B's is only $30,000. Does this mean that A is the better investment opportunity? Explain.

13. What are the criteria to determine whether a project is acceptable under the net present value method?

14. Does the net present value method provide a measure of the rate of return on capital investments?

15. Which is the best capital investment evaluation technique for ranking investment opportunities?

16. Paul Henderson is a manager for Maple Leaf Company. He tells you that his company always maximizes profitability by accepting the investment opportunity with the highest internal rate of return. Explain to Mr. Henderson how his company may improve profitability by sometimes selecting investment opportunities with lower internal rates of return.

17. What is the relationship between desired rate of return and internal rate of return?

18. What are the typical cash inflow and outflow items that are associated with capital investments?

19. "I always go for the investment with the shortest payback period." Is this a sound strategy? Why, or why not?

20. "The payback method cannot be used if the cash inflows occur in unequal patterns." Do you agree or disagree? Explain.

21. What are the advantages and disadvantages associated with the unadjusted rate of return method for evaluating capital investments?

22. How do capital investments affect profitability?

23. What is a postaudit? How is it useful in capital budgeting?

EXERCISES

EXERCISE 10-1   *Identification of Cash Inflows and Outflows*   **L.O. 2**

Required
In the right-hand column of the following table, indicate which of the items will result in cash inflows and which will result in cash outflows. The first item has been identified as an example.

Item	Type of Cash Flow
a. Incremental revenue	Inflow
b. Working capital commitments	
c. Cost savings	
d. Initial investment	
e. Salvage values	
f. Recovery of working capital	
g. Incremental expenses	

EXERCISE 10-2   *Determination of Present Value of Lump-Sum Future Cash Receipt*   **L.O. 2, 5**

Ed Maynard turned 20 years old today. His grandfather established a trust fund that will pay Mr. Maynard $30,000 on his next birthday. Unfortunately, Mr. Maynard needs money today to start his college education, and his father is willing to help. He has agreed to give Mr. Maynard the present value of the future cash inflow, assuming a 10 percent rate of return.

Required

a. Use a present value table to determine the amount of cash that Mr. Maynard's father should give him.
b. Use an algebraic formula to prove that the present value of the trust fund (i.e., the amount of cash computed in Requirement *a*) is equal to its $30,000 future value.

L.O. 2, 5 EXERCISE 10-3   *Determination of Present Value of Lump-Sum Future Cash Receipt*

Penny Grover expects to receive a $500,000 cash benefit when she retires five years from today. Ms. Grover's employer has offered an early retirement incentive by agreeing to pay her $300,000 today if she agrees to retire immediately. Ms. Grover desires to earn a rate of return of 12 percent.

Required

a. Assuming that the retirement benefit is the only consideration in making the retirement decision, should Ms. Grover accept her employer's offer?
b. Identify the factors that cause the present value of the retirement benefit to be less than $500,000.

L.O. 2, 5 EXERCISE 10-4   *Determination of Present Value of Annuity*

The dean of the School of Business is trying to decide whether to purchase a copy machine to be placed in the lobby of the building. The machine would add to student convenience, but the dean feels compelled to earn an 8 percent return on the investment of funds. Estimates of cash inflows from copy machines that have been placed in other university buildings indicate that the copy machine would probably produce incremental cash inflows of approximately $4,000 per year. The machine is expected to have a three-year useful life with a zero salvage value.

Required

a. Use Present Value Table 1 in Appendix A to determine the maximum amount of cash the dean should be willing to pay for a copy machine.
b. Use Present Value Table 2 in Appendix A to determine the maximum amount of cash the dean should be willing to pay for a copy machine.
c. Explain the consistency or lack of consistency in the answers to Requirements *a* and *b*.

L.O. 2, 5, 9 EXERCISE 10-5   *Determination of Net Present Value*

Rent-Your-Ride is considering an investment in a new van that is expected to generate a cash inflow of $8,000 per year. The van's purchase price is $26,000; it is expected to have a useful life of four years and a $6,000 salvage value. Rent-Your-Ride has an average cost of capital of 14 percent.

Required

a. Calculate the net present value of the investment opportunity.
b. Indicate whether the investment opportunity is expected to earn a return that is above or below the cost of capital and whether it should be accepted.

L.O. 2, 5, 9 EXERCISE 10-6   *Determination of Net Present Value*

William Thelen is looking for part-time employment while he attends school. He is considering the possibility of purchasing technical equipment that will enable him to start a small training services company that will offer tutorial services over the Internet. Demand for the service is expected to grow rapidly in the first two years of operation as customers learn about the availability of the Internet assistance. Thereafter, demand is expected to stabilize. The expected operating cash inflows and outflows are shown in the following table:

Year of Operation	Cash Inflow	Cash Outflow
2001	$4,500	$3,000
2002	6,500	4,000
2003	7,000	4,200
2004	7,000	4,200

In addition to these items, the equipment is expected to cost $7,000. Mr. Thelen expects to pay $1,200 for a major overhaul and updating of the equipment at the end of the second year of operation. The equipment is expected to have a $500 salvage value and a four-year useful life. Mr. Thelen desires to earn a rate of return of 8 percent.

Required

(Round computations to the nearest whole penny.)

a. Calculate the net present value of the investment opportunity.

b. Indicate whether the investment opportunity is expected to earn a return that is above or below the desired rate of return and whether it should be accepted.

EXERCISE 10-7   *Use of Present Value Index*   **L.O. 2, 5, 9**

Braxton Company has a choice of two investment alternatives. The first alternative has a present value of cash inflows and outflows of $45,000 and 42,000, respectively. The second alternative has a present value of cash inflows and outflows of $110,000 and $106,500, respectively.

Required

a. Calculate the net present value of each investment opportunity.

b. Calculate the present value index for each investment opportunity.

c. Indicate which investment will produce the higher rate of return.

EXERCISE 10-8   *Determination of Internal Rate of Return*   **L.O. 2, 10**

Cortez Manufacturing Company has an opportunity to purchase some technologically advanced equipment that will reduce the company's cash outflow for operating expenses by $320,000 per year. The cost of the equipment is $1,546,632.64; it is expected to have a 10-year useful life and a zero salvage value. Cortez has established an investment opportunity hurdle rate of 20 percent and uses the straight-line method for amortization.

Required

a. Calculate the internal rate of return of the investment opportunity.

b. Indicate whether the investment opportunity should be accepted.

EXERCISE 10-9   *Use of Internal Rate of Return to Compare Investment Opportunities*   **L.O. 2, 10**

Gillett and Petravick (G&P) is a partnership that owns a small company. It is considering two alternative investment opportunities. The first investment opportunity will have a five-year useful life, will cost $18,670.32, and will generate expected cash inflows of $4,800 per year. The second investment is expected to have a useful life of three years, will cost $12,434.26, and will generate expected cash inflows of $5,000 per year. Assume that G&P has the funds available to accept only one of the opportunities.

Required

a. Calculate the internal rate of return of each investment opportunity.

b. On the basis of the internal rate of return criteria, which opportunity should be selected?

c. Discuss other factors that should be considered in the investment decision.

EXERCISE 10-10   *Determination of Cash Flow Annuity with Income Tax Considerations*   **L.O. 2, 11**

Sampson Tire Company is planning to open a new store and the equipment needed to operate it is expected to cost $160,000, to have a useful life of four years, and to have no salvage value. The store will generate cash revenues of $210,000 per year, and cash operating expenses are expected to be $130,000 per year. Sampson's income is subject to a 30 percent tax rate. The company uses the straight-line method for amortization.

Required

Determine the amount of the annual net cash inflow from operations for the first four years of operating the store.

L.O. 11 EXERCISE 10-11 *Evaluation of Discounted Cash Flow Techniques*

Zina Craft is angry with Craig Brooks. He is behind schedule on the development of supporting material that will be used in tomorrow's capital budget committee meeting. When she approached him about his apparent lack-adaisical attitude in general and his tardiness in particular, he responded by saying: "I don't see why we do this stuff in the first place. It's all a bunch of estimates. Who knows what future cash flows will really be? I certainly don't. I've been doing this job for five years, and no one has ever checked to see if I even came close at these guesses. I've been waiting for marketing to provide the estimated cash inflows on the projects being considered tomorrow. But if you want my report now, I'll have it in a couple of hours. I can make up the marketing data as well as they can."

Required

Does Mr. Brooks have a point? Is there something wrong with the company's capital budgeting system? Write a brief memo explaining how to improve the investment evaluation system.

L.O. 12 EXERCISE 10-12 *Determination of Payback Period*

Air Cargo Company is considering the expansion of its territory. The company has the opportunity to purchase one of two different used airplanes. The first airplane is expected to cost $600,000; it will enable the company to increase its annual cash inflow by $200,000 per year. The plane is expected to have a useful life of five years and no salvage value. The second plane costs $1,200,000; it will enable the company to increase annual cash flow by $300,000 per year. This plane has an eight-year useful life and a zero salvage value.

Required

a. Determine the payback period for each investment alternative and identify the alternative that should be accepted if the decision is based on the payback approach.
b. Discuss the shortcomings of using the payback method to evaluate investment opportunities.

L.O. 12 EXERCISE 10-13 *Determination of Payback Period with Uneven Cash Flows*

Doremus Company has an opportunity to purchase a forklift that will be used in its heavy equipment rental business. The forklift will be leased on an annual basis during its first two years of operation. Thereafter, it will be leased to the general public on demand. Doremus will sell it at the end of the fifth year of its useful life. The expected cash inflows and outflows follow:

Year	Nature of Item	Cash Inflow	Cash Outflow
2001	Purchase price		$12,000
2001	Revenue	$5,000	
2002	Revenue	5,000	
2003	Revenue	3,500	
2003	Major overhaul		1,500
2004	Revenue	3,000	
2005	Revenue	2,400	
2005	Salvage value	1,600	

Required

a. Determine the payback period using the accumulated cash flows approach.
b. Determine the payback period using the average cash flows approach.

L.O. 13 EXERCISE 10-14 *Determination of Unadjusted Rate of Return*

Porter Paint Company is considering the purchase of a new spray paint machine that costs $4,000. The equipment is expected to save labour, thereby increasing net income by $600 per year. The effective life of the equipment is 15 years according to the manufacturer's estimation.

Required

a. Determine the unadjusted rate of return on the basis of the original cost of investment.
b. Discuss the shortcomings of using the unadjusted rate of return to evaluate investment opportunities.

EXERCISE 10-15   *Computation of Payback Period and Unadjusted Rate of Return for One Investment* **L.O. 12, 13**
Opportunity

Yee Rentals can purchase a van that costs $24,000; it has an expected useful life of three years and no salvage value. Yee uses straight-line amortization. Expected revenue is $12,000 per year.

Required
a. Determine the payback period.
b. Determine the unadjusted rate of return.

PROBLEMS—SERIES A

PROBLEM 10-1A   *Use of Present Value Techniques to Evaluate Alternative Investment Opportunities*   **L.O. 5, 9**

Speedy Delivery is a small company that transports business packages between Calgary and Edmonton. It operates a fleet of small vans that moves packages to and from a central depot within each city and uses a common carrier to deliver the packages between the depots in the two cities. Speedy recently acquired approximately $2 million of cash capital from its owners, and its president, Frank Church, is trying to identify the most profitable way to invest these funds.

Jim Waterson, the company's operations manager, believes that the money should be used to expand the fleet of city vans at a cost of $1,800,000. He argues that more vans would enable the company to expand its services into new markets, thereby increasing the revenue base. More specifically, he expects cash inflows to increase by $700,000 per year. The vans are expected to have an average useful life of four years and a combined salvage value of $250,000. Operating the vans will require additional working capital of $100,000, which will be recovered at the end of the fourth year.

In contrast, Marie Mendez, the company's chief accountant, believes that the funds should be used to purchase large trucks to deliver the packages between the depots in the two cities. The conversion process would produce continuing improvement in operating savings with reductions in cash outflows as indicated here:

Year 1	Year 2	Year 3	Year 4
$400,000	$800,000	$1,000,000	$1,100,000

The trucks are expected to cost $2,000,000 and to have a four-year useful life and a $200,000 salvage value. In addition to the purchase price of the trucks, up-front training costs are expected to amount to $40,000. Speedy Delivery's management has established a 16 percent desired rate of return.

Required
a. Determine the net present value of the two investment alternatives.
b. Calculate the present value index for each alternative.
c. Indicate which investment alternative you would recommend. Justify your choice with an appropriate explanation.

PROBLEM 10-2A   *Use of Payback Period and Unadjusted Rate of Return to Evaluate Alternative*   **L.O. 12, 13**
Investment Opportunities

Charles White owns a small retail ice cream parlour and White is considering the possible expansion of the business. He has identified two attractive alternatives; the first involves the purchase of a machine that would enable Mr. White to offer frozen yogurt to his customers. It would cost $4,500 and has an expected useful life of three years with no salvage value. Additional annual cash revenues and cash operating expenses associated with the sale of yogurt are expected to be $3,300 and $500, respectively.

Alternatively, Mr. White could purchase for $5,600 the equipment necessary to serve cappuccino. It has an expected useful life of four years and no salvage value. Additional annual cash revenues and cash operating expenses associated with the sale of cappuccino are expected to be $4,600 and $1,350, respectively.

The net income earned from the ice cream parlour is taxed at an effective rate of 20 percent.

Required

a. Determine the payback period and unadjusted rate of return for each alternative.

b. Indicate which investment alternative you would recommend. Justify your choice with an appropriate explanation.

L.O. 9, 10   **PROBLEM 10-3A**   *Use of Net Present Value and Internal Rate of Return to Evaluate Investment Opportunities*

Allison Sachetti, the president of Sachetti Enterprises, is considering two investment opportunities. Due to limited resources, she will be able to invest in only one project. Project A involves the purchase of a machine that will enable factory automation; it is expected to have a useful life of four years with no salvage value at the end. Project B supports a training program that will improve the skills of employees operating the current equipment. At the beginning, cash expenditures for Project A are $100,000 and for Project B $40,000. The annual expected cash inflows are $31,547 for Project A and $13,169 for Project B. Both investments are expected to provide cash flow benefits for the next four years. Sachetti Enterprise's cost of capital is 8 percent.

Required

a. Compute the net present value of each project. Which project should be adopted on the basis of the net present value approach?

b. Compute the approximate internal rate of return of each project. Which project should be adopted on the basis of the internal rate of return approach?

c. Compare the net present value approach and the internal rate of return approach. Which method is better under the given circumstances?

L.O. 9, 12   **PROBLEM 10-4A**   *Use of Net Present Value and Payback Period to Evaluate Investment Opportunities*

Ben Bennett saved $200,000 during the 25 years that he worked for a major corporation. Now he has retired at the age of 50 years from that job and has begun to draw a comfortable pension cheque every month. He wants to ensure the financial security of his retirement by investing his savings wisely and is currently considering two investment opportunities. Both investments require an initial payment of $150,000. The following table indicates the estimated cash inflows for the two alternatives:

	Year 1	Year 2	Year 3	Year 4
Project X	$44,500	$47,000	$63,000	$81,000
Project Y	82,000	87,000	14,000	12,000

Mr. Bennett decides to use his past average return on mutual fund investments as the discount rate; it is 8 percent.

Required

a. Compute the net present value of each project. Which project should be adopted on the basis of the net present value approach?

b. Compute the payback period of each project. Which project should be adopted on the basis of the payback approach?

c. Compare the net present value approach and the payback approach. Which method is better under the given circumstances?

L.O. 9, 11,   **PROBLEM 10-5A**   *Effects of Straight-Line versus Accelerated Amortization on Investment Decision*
12, 13

Wasserman Electronics is considering the possibility of investing in manufacturing equipment expected to cost $46,000. The equipment has an estimated useful life of four years and a salvage value of $6,000. It is expected to produce incremental cash revenues of $24,000 per year. Wasserman has an effective income tax rate of 30 percent and a desired rate of return of 12 percent.

Required

a. Determine the net present value and the present value index of the investment, assuming that Wasserman uses straight-line amortization for financial reporting.

b. Determine the net present value and the present value index of the investment, assuming that Wasserman uses double-declining-balance amortization for financial reporting.

c. Why are there differences in the net present values computed in Requirements *a* and *b*?

d. Determine the payback period and unadjusted rate of return, assuming that Wasserman uses straight-line amortization.

e. Determine the payback period and unadjusted rate of return, assuming that Wasserman uses double-declining-balance amortization. (Note: It is necessary to use average annual cash flow when computing the payback period and the average annual income when determining the unadjusted rate of return.)

f. Explain why no differences exist in the payback period or unadjusted rate of return computed in Requirements *d* and *e*.

PROBLEM 10-6A *Application of Net Present Value Approach with and without Tax Considerations*   **L.O. 9**

Dan Humble, the chief executive officer of Humble Corporation, has assembled his top advisers to evaluate an investment opportunity. The advisers expect the company to pay $100,000 cash at the beginning of the investment and the cash inflow each of the subsequent four years to be the following:

Year 1	Year 2	Year 3	Year 4
$21,000	$24,000	$30,000	$46,000

Mr. Humble agrees with his advisers that the company should use the discount rate (required rate of return) of 12 percent to compute net present value to evaluate the viability of the proposed project.

Required

a. Compute the net present value of the proposed project. Should Mr. Humble approve the project?

b. May Jentry, one of the advisers, is wary of the cash flow forecast, and she points out that the advisers failed to consider that the amortization on equipment used in this project will be tax deductible. The amortization is expected to be $20,000 per year for the four-year period. The company's income tax rate is 30 percent per year. Revise the company's expected cash flow from this project.

c. Compute the net present value of the project on the basis of the revised cash flow forecast. Should Mr. Humble approve the project?

PROBLEM 10-7A *Comparison of Internal Rate of Return with Unadjusted Rate of Return*   **L.O. 10, 13**

Eisner Auto Repair is evaluating a project to purchase a piece of equipment that will not only expand the company's capacity but also improve the quality of its repair services. The board of directors requires all capital investments to meet or exceed the minimum requirement of a 10 percent rate of return. However, the board has not clearly defined the rate of return. The president and controller are pondering two different rates of return: unadjusted rate of return and internal rate of return. The equipment, which costs $100,000, has a life expectancy of five years. The increased net profit per year will be approximately $7,000, and the increased cash inflow per year will be approximately $27,700.

Required

a. If it uses the unadjusted rate of return to evaluate this project, should the company invest in the project?

b. If it uses the internal rate of return to evaluate this project, should the company invest in the project?

c. Which method is better for this capital investment decision?

PROBLEM 10-8A *Postaudit Evaluation*   **L.O. 14**

Jason Cook is reviewing his company's investment in a cement plant. The company paid $25,000,000 five years ago to acquire the plant. Now, top management is considering an opportunity to sell it. The president wants to know whether the plant has met the original expectation before he decides its fate. The company's discount rate for present value computations is 8 percent. The following are the expected and actual cash flows:

	Year 1	Year 2	Year 3	Year 4	Year 5
Expected	$5,500,000	$8,200,000	$7,600,000	$8,300,000	$7,000,000
Actual	4,500,000	5,100,000	8,200,000	6,500,000	6,000,000

Required

a. Compute the net present value of the expected cash flows as of the beginning of the investment.

b. Compute the net present value of the actual cash flows as of the beginning of the investment.

c. What do you conclude from this postaudit?

PROBLEMS—SERIES B

L.O. 9   PROBLEM 10-1B *Use of Present Value Techniques to Evaluate Alternative Investment Opportunities*

Jensen Automobile Repair currently has three repair shops in Vancouver. Julius Jensen, the president and chief executive officer, is facing a pleasant dilemma: the business has continued to grow rapidly, and major shareholders are arguing about different ways to capture more business opportunities. The company requires a 12 percent rate of return for its investment projects and uses the straight-line method of amortization for all fixed assets.

The first group of shareholders wants to open another shop in a newly developed suburban community. This project will require an investment of $300,000 at the beginning to acquire all the necessary equipment, which has a useful life of five years with a salvage value of $100,000. Once the shop begins to operate, another $75,000 of working capital will be necessary; it will be recovered at the end of the fifth year. The following is the expected net cash inflow of the new shop:

Year 1	Year 2	Year 3	Year 4	Year 5
$30,000	$60,000	$95,000	$120,000	$150,000

The second group of shareholders prefers to invest $250,000 to acquire new computerized diagnostic equipment for the existing shops. The equipment is expected to have a useful life of five years with a salvage value of $50,000. Using this new state-of-the-art equipment, mechanics will be able to pinpoint automobile problems more quickly and accurately. Consequently, it would allow the existing shops to increase their service capacity and revenue by $75,000 per year. The company would need to train mechanics to use the equipment, which would cost $25,000 at the beginning of the first year.

Required
a. Determine the net present value of the two investment alternatives.
b. Calculate the present value index for each alternative.
c. Indicate which investment alternative you would recommend. Justify your choice with an appropriate explanation.

L.O. 12, 13   PROBLEM 10-2B *Use of Payback Period and Unadjusted Rate of Return to Evaluate Alternative Investment Opportunities*

Jacques and Yvonne Services is planning for a new business venture. With $100,000 of available funds for investment, it is investigating two possible options. The first is to acquire an exclusive contract to operate vending machines in civic and recreation centres of a small suburban city for four years. The contract requires the firm to pay the city $40,000 cash at the beginning. The firm expects the cash revenue of the operation to be $50,000 per year and the cash expenses to be $28,000 per year.

The second option is to operate a printing shop in an office complex. This option would require the company to spend $72,000 for printing equipment that has a useful life of four years with a zero salvage value. The cash revenue is expected to be $85,000 per year, and cash expenses are expected to be $47,000 per year.

The firm uses the straight-line method of amortization. Its effective income tax rate is expected to be 20 percent.

Required
a. Determine the payback period and unadjusted rate of return for each alternative.
b. Indicate which investment alternative you would recommend. Justify your choice with an appropriate explanation.

L.O. 9, 10   PROBLEM 10-3B *Use of Net Present Value and Internal Rate of Return to Evaluate Investment Opportunities*

Thor Thorsen's rich uncle gave him $250,000 cash as a birthday gift for his 40th birthday. Unlike his spoiled cousins who spend money carelessly, Mr. Thorsen wants to invest the money for his future retirement. After an extensive search, he has found only two investment opportunities. Project 1 would require an immediate cash payment of $220,000; Project 2 needs only a $100,000 cash payment at the beginning. The expected cash inflows are $72,000 per year for Project 1 and $35,000 per year for Project 2. Both projects are expected to provide cash flow benefits for the next four years. Mr. Thorsen found that the interest rate for a four-year certificate of deposit is about 7 percent. He decided that this is his required rate of return.

Required

a. Compute the net present value of each project. Which project should be adopted on the basis of the net present value approach?

b. Compute the approximate internal rate of return of each project. Which project should be adopted on the basis of the the internal rate of return approach?

c. Compare the net present value approach and the internal rate of return approach. Which method is better under the given circumstances?

PROBLEM 10-4B *Use of Net Present Value and Payback Period to Evaluate Investment Opportunities*   **L.O. 9, 12**

Ashley Tulane just won a lottery and received a cash award of $500,000. Ms. Tulane is 61 years old and would like to retire in four years. Weighing this important fact, she has found two possible investments, both of which require an immediate cash payment of $400,000. The expected cash inflows of the two investment opportunities are as follows:

	Year 1	Year 2	Year 3	Year 4
Project 101	$228,000	$130,000	$74,000	$84,000
Project 102	57,000	67,000	148,000	338,000

Ms. Tulane has decided that her required rate of return should be 10 percent.

Required

a. Compute the net present value of each project. Which should Ms. Tulane choose on the basis of the net present value approach?

b. Compute the payback period of each project. Which project should Ms. Tulane choose on the basis of the payback approach?

c. Compare the net present value approach and the payback approach. Which method is better under the given circumstances?

PROBLEM 10-5B *Effects of Straight-Line versus Accelerated Amortization on Investment Decision*   **L.O. 9, 12, 13**

Birmingham Pipe, decided to spend $20,000 to purchase new state-of-the-art equipment for its manufacturing plant. The equipment has a five-year useful life and a salvage value of $5,000. It is expected to generate additional cash revenue of $8,000 per year. Birmingham Pipe's required rate of return is 10 percent; its effective income tax rate is 25 percent.

Required

a. Determine the net present value and the present value index of the investment, assuming that Birmingham Pipe uses straight-line amortization for financial reporting.

b. Determine the net present value and the present value index of the investment, assuming that Birmingham Pipe uses double-declining-balance amortization for financial reporting.

c. Why are there differences in the net present values computed in Requirements *a* and *b*?

d. Determine the payback period and unadjusted rate of return, assuming that Birmingham Pipe uses straight-line amortization.

e. Determine the payback period and unadjusted rate of return, assuming that Birmingham Pipe uses double-declining-balance amortization. (*Note:* It is necessary to use average annual cash flow when computing the payback period and the average annual income when computing the unadjusted rate of return.)

f. Explain why no differences exist in the payback period or unadjusted rate of return computed in Requirements *d* and *e*.

PROBLEM 10-6B *Application of Net Present Value Approach with and without Tax Considerations*   **L.O. 9**

Joseph Kendall, the president of Joey's Moving Services, is planning to spend $125,000 for new trucks. He expects them to increase the company's cash inflow as follows:

Year 1	Year 2	Year 3	Year 4
$32,700	$35,643	$38,851	$42,347

The company's policy stipulates that all investments must earn a minimum rate of return of 10 percent.

Required

a. Compute the net present value of the proposed purchase. Should Mr. Kendall approve the purchase?
b. Julie Mensah, the controller, is wary of the cash flow forecast and she points out that Mr. Kendall failed to consider that the amortization on trucks used in this project will be tax deductible. The amortization is expected to be $30,000 per year for the four-year period. The company's income tax rate is 30 percent per year. Revise the company's expected cash flow of this purchase.
c. Compute the net present value of the purchase on the basis of the new cash flow forecast. Should Mr. Kendall approve the purchase?

L.O. 10, 13 PROBLEM 10-7B *Comparison of Internal Rate of Return with Unadjusted Rate of Return*

Vulcan Computers, Inc. faces stiff competition in the market. Top management is considering the replacement of its current production facility. The board of directors requires all capital investments to meet or exceed the minimum requirement of 9 percent rate of return. However, the board has not clearly defined the rate of return. The president and controller are pondering two different rates of return: unadjusted rate of return and internal rate of return. To purchase a new facility, the company must pay $900,000. Its life expectancy is four years. The increased net profit per year resulting from improved conditions will be approximately $100,000; the increased cash inflow per year will be approximately $275,000.

Required

a. If it uses the unadjusted rate of return to evaluate this project, should the company invest in the project?
b. If it uses the internal rate of return to evaluate this project, should the company invest in the project?
c. Which method is better for this capital investment decision?

L.O. 14 PROBLEM 10-8B *Postaudit Evaluation*

Michael Ancient is wondering whether he made the right decision four years ago. As the president of Ancient Health Care Services, he acquired a long-term care facility specializing in geriatic care with an initial cash investment of $7,000,000. Mr. Ancient would like to know whether the facility's financial performance has met the original investment objective. The company's discount rate (required rate of return) for present value computations is 14 percent. The following are the expected and actual cash flows:

	Year 1	Year 2	Year 3	Year 4
Expected	$2,300,000	$2,400,000	$2,500,000	$3,000,000
Actual	2,000,000	1,900,000	3,200,000	3,500,000

Required

a. Compute the net present value of the expected cash flows as of the beginning of the investment.
b. Compute the net present value of the actual cash flows as of the beginning of the investment.
c. What do you conclude from this postaudit?

ANALYZE, THINK, COMMUNICATE

ACT 10-1 BUSINESS APPLICATIONS CASE *Payback and Net Present Value*

Pitts Steel Company (PSC) is a steel-processing firm with sales approximating 30,000 tons per year. It purchases large coils of hot rolled prime steel from several steel mills. Each coil weighs between 30 and 35 thousand pounds. PSC flattens or levels the coils into rectangular pieces (sheets) in sizes ranging up to 144 inches by 36 inches. Customers then use these sheets in stamping machines to punch out various steel parts.

A number of PSC's customers need steel sheets with a width of 48 inches, but as indicated, its current levelling machines have the capability to cut pieces only up to 36 inches wide. The marketing department predicts that PSC can increase its sales by 5,000 tonnes in the first year if it purchases a new 48-inch levelling machine. The new steel would sale at an average price of $415 per tonne in the first two years. The following is a five-year sales volume and price forecast for the new steel:

Year	Volume in Tonnes	Sales Price
1	5,000	$415
2	5,200	415
3	5,500	455
4	6,000	455
5	6,400	460

PSC can purchase a machine to produce 48-inch wide sheets for $575,000. The machine has an expected useful life of five years and a salvage value of $100,000. In addition to amortization, the expected operating expenses for the machine are as follows:

	Years	
	1, 2	3, 4, 5
Expected operating expenses		
Variable cost per tonne of output		
Material cost	$240	$270
Labour cost	60	75
Overhead	45	50
Fixed cost per year		
Supervision	125,000	140,000
Maintenance	55,000	60,000
Miscellaneous (excluding amortization)	20,000	25,000

These costs are paid in cash in the year in which they are incurred. The cost of capital has been determined to be 10 percent. Amortization is computed using the straight-line method. The effective income tax rate is 35 percent. Tax expense is paid in cash in the year in which it is incurred. All revenues are collected in cash in the year in which revenue is recognized.

Required
a. Prepare an income statement using the contribution margin approach for each of the five years.
b. Compute the payback period for the investment. Use the incremental accumulation method.
c. Determine the net present value of the investment opportunity.
d. Indicate whether you would recommend acceptance or rejection of the investment.
e. Comment on the factors that involve uncertainty.

GROUP ASSIGNMENT   *Net Present Value*   **ACT 10-2**

Gunlley Real Estate Investment Company (GREIC) purchases new apartment complexes, establishes a stable group of residents, and then sells the complexes to apartment management companies. The average holding time is three years. GREIC is currently investigating two alternatives.

1. GREIC can purchase Branchwater Properties for $6,000,000. The property is expected to produce a net cash inflow of $480,000, $670,000, and $1,140,000 for the first, second, and third years of operations, respectively. The market value of the complex at the end of the third year is expected to be $6,900,000.
2. Mountain Top Apartments can be purchased for $4,600,000. The property is expected to produce a net cash inflow of $320,000, $580,000, and $800,000 for the first, second, and third years of operations, respectively. The market value of the complex at the end of the third year is expected to be $5,400,000.

GREIC has a desired rate of return of 12 percent.

Required
a. Divide the class into groups containing four or five students per group and then divide the groups into two sections. Assign Task 1 to the first section and Task 2 to the second section.

   Group Tasks
   1. Calculate the net present value and the present value index for Branchwater Properties.
   2. Calculate the net present value and the present value index for Mountain Top Apartments.

b. Have a spokesperson from one of the groups in the first section report the amounts calculated by the group. Make sure that all groups in the section have the same result. Repeat the process for the second section. Have the class as a whole select the investment opportunity that GREIC should accept, given that the objective is to produce the higher rate of return.

c. Assume that GREIC has $6,000,000 to invest and that any funds not invested in real estate properties must be invested in a certificate of deposit earning a 5 percent return. Would this information alter the decision made in Requirement *b*?

d. This requirement is independent of Requirement *c*. Assume that there is a 10 percent chance that the Branchwater project will be annexed into the city of Kranston, which has an outstanding school district. The annexation would likely increase net cash flows by $50,000 per year and would increase the market value at the end of year 3 by $400,000. Would this information change the decision reached in Requirement *b*?

ACT 10-3 WRITING ASSIGNMENT *Limitations of Capital Investment Techniques*

Grimaldi Publishing Company is evaluating two investment opportunities. One is to purchase an Internet company with the capacity to open new marketing channels through which Grimaldi can sell its books. This opportunity offers a high potential for growth but involves significant risk. Indeed, losses are projected for the first three years of operation. The second opportunity is to purchase a printing company that would enable Grimaldi to better control costs by printing its own books. The potential savings are clearly predictable but would make a significant change in the company's long-term profitability.

Required

Write a memo discussing the usefulness of capital investment techniques (i.e., net present value, internal rate of return, payback, and unadjusted rate of return) in making a choice between these two alternative investment opportunities. Your memo should discuss the strengths and weaknesses of capital budgeting techniques in general. Furthermore, your memo should include a comparison between techniques that consider the time value of money versus those that do not.

ACT 10-4 ETHICAL DILEMMA *Postaudit*

Cole Company recently initiated a postaudit program. To motivate employees to take the program seriously, Cole established a bonus program. Managers were given a bonus equal to 10 percent of the amount by which actual net present value exceeded the projected net present value. John Vickers, manager of the North Western Division, had an investment proposal on his desk when the new system was implemented. The investment opportunity required a $250,000 initial cash outflow and was expected to return cash inflows of $90,000 per year for the next five years. Cole's desired rate of return is 10 percent. Mr. Vickers immediately lowered the estimated cash inflows to $70,000 per year and recommended acceptance of the project.

Required

a. Assume that actual cash inflows turn out to be $91,000 per year. Determine the amount of Mr. Vickers's bonus if the original computation of net present value were based on $90,000 versus $70,000.

b. Speculate as to the long-term effect that the bonus plan is likely to have on the company.

c. Recommend how to compensate managers in a way that discourages gamesmanship.

ACT 10-5 SPREADSHEET ASSIGNMENT *Using Excel*

Fontaine Company is considering the purchase of new automated manufacturing equipment that will cost $120,000. The equipment will save $34,000 in labour costs per year over its six-year life. At the end of the fourth year, the equipment will require an overhaul that will cost $20,000. The equipment will have a $6,000 salvage value at the end of its life. Fontaine's cost of capital is 12 percent.

Required

Prepare a spreadsheet similar to the one following to calculate net present value, the present value index, and the internal rate of return.

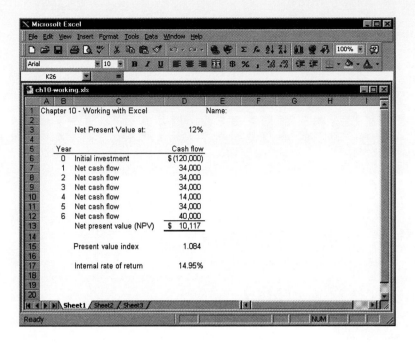

Spreadsheet Tips

Spreadsheets have built-in financial functions that make net present value and internal rate of return calculations very easy. The formats of these formulas are as follows:

1. *Net Present Value:* =NPV(rate,value1,value2,value3, … value29), where up to 29 values are allowed. The values must be at the end of the period, and each period must be equal in time (at year-end, for example). The formula is = NPV(D3,D7,D8,D9,D10,D11,D12) + D6.
2. *Internal Rate of Return:* 5IRR(values,guess), where *values* is the range that includes the cash flows (D6 to D12) and guess is an estimate of the rate. Use the cost of capital as the guess.
3. *Percentage:* Rather than entering 12% in the formulas, refer to Cell D3. This will allow you to change the rate and see the effect on the NPV and present value index.
4. *Present Value Index:* You must construct a formula because no built-in function calculates it.

SPREADSHEET ASSIGNMENT   *Mastering Excel*

ACT 10-6

Refer to the data in Problem 10-1A.

Required

a. Prepare a spreadsheet similar to the preceding one that calculates the net present value and the present value index for the two investments in Problem 10-1A.
b. Include formulas in your spreadsheet to calculate the internal rate of return for each investment alternative.

Product Costing in Service and Manufacturing Entities

Learning Objectives

After completing this chapter, you should be able to:

1 Understand the need for service and product cost information.

2 Understand how product costs flow from the Raw Materials, to Work in Process, to Finished Goods, and ultimately to Cost of Goods Sold accounts.

3 Distinguish between costing for service and manufacturing entities.

4 Demonstrate how product cost flow affects financial statements through a horizontal financial statements model.

5 Understand the necessity of assigning estimated overhead costs to the inventory and cost of goods sold accounts during an accounting period.

6 Record applied and actual overhead costs in a manufacturing overhead account.

7 Record product costs in T-accounts.

8 Understand the cyclical nature of product cost flows.

9 Comprehend the relationship between over- or underapplied overhead and variance analysis.

10 Prepare a schedule of cost of goods manufactured and sold.

11 Prepare a set of financial statements for a manufacturing entity.

12 Distinguish between absorption and variable costing.

the *curious* manager

Many of the costs of providing services to a client of a consulting firm are unknown when the client is being served. For example, the cost of the salaries of the consultant and assistants may not be known until year end. Similarly, the actual cost of rental fees, janitorial services, billing charges, bad debts, and many other items will not be known until long after the client has been served. How can consultants know what to charge a client today if they do not know the cost of providing services until later?

The purpose of service- and product-costing systems *is to supply information regarding the cost of providing services or making products. Product and service cost information is used in financial reporting, managerial accounting, and contract negotiations. Indeed, it is difficult to imagine an organization that could effectively conduct its operations without knowing the cost of providing services or making products.*

Generally accepted accounting principles (GAAP) require companies to show service and product costs in their public financial reports. For example, product costs for manufacturing companies must be allocated between inventory (shown on the balance sheet) and cost of goods sold (shown on the income statement). Similarly, service companies must match the costs of providing services with the revenues generated from the services provided on their income statements. Accordingly, product and service costing is required for financial reporting.

Product and service cost information is used for managerial accounting *purposes. Companies need to know the cost of providing services or making products so that they can plan their operations. For example, the budgeting process could not be accomplished without knowing the cost of services or products. Service and product costing is also needed for cost control. Corrective action may be taken if expected costs are inconsistent with actual costs. Finally, service and product cost information may be used in pricing and other short-term decision making. For example, the cost of a service or product may be used in special order, outsourcing, or product elimination decisions.*

Service and product costing information may be used by governmental agencies to regulate rates for public service entities, such as utility companies or transportation. Service and product costs are also used in determining the amount due on contracts that compensate companies for the costs they incur plus a reasonable profit (i.e., cost-plus contracts). For example, many governmental service contracts are established on a cost-plus basis. Cost-plus pricing may also be used in private companies; for example, many builders of custom homes are compensated on the basis of cost-plus contracts. Thus, costing information is necessary for contract negotiations.

▌ Cost Flow in Manufacturing Companies

LO1

Understand the need for service and product cost information.

In the previous chapters, we assumed that all inventory started during an accounting period was also completed during that accounting period. Accordingly, all product costs were included in the account Finished Goods Inventory or were expensed as Cost of Goods Sold. Most real-world companies have raw materials on hand at the end of the accounting period, and most manufacturing companies are likely to have inventory items that have been started but have not been completed. Indeed, most manufacturing companies accumulate their product costs in three distinct inventory accounts: (1) **Raw Materials Inventory**, which includes lumber, metals, paints, and chemicals that will be used to make the company's products; (2) **Work in Process Inventory**, which includes partially completed products; and (3) **Finished Goods Inventory**, which includes fully processed products that are ready for sale.

LO2

Understand how product costs flow from the Raw Materials, to Work in Process, to Finished Goods, and ultimately to Cost of Goods Sold accounts.

The cost of materials is first recorded in the Raw Materials Inventory account. The cost of materials placed in production is then transferred from the Raw Materials Inventory account to the Work in Process Inventory account. The cost of labour and overhead are added to the Work in Process Inventory account. The cost of goods completed during the period is transferred from the Work in Process Inventory account to the Finished Goods Inventory account. The cost of the goods that are sold during the accounting period is transferred from the Finished Goods Inventory account to the Cost of Goods Sold account. The balances that remain in the Raw Materials, Work in Process, and Finished Goods Inventory accounts appear on the balance sheet. The amount of product cost transferred to the Cost of Goods Sold account is expensed on the income statement. The flow of manufacturing costs is shown in Exhibit 11–1.

▌ Cost Flow in Service Companies

LO3

Distinguish between costing for service and manufacturing entities.

Like manufacturing companies, many service companies have costs that begin with raw materials and pass through production stages, such as work in process, finished goods, and cost of goods sold. For example, a hamburger from McDonalds starts with raw materials (meat, bun, and condiments), goes through work in process (is cooked, assembled, and wrapped), becomes a finished product, and is sold to a customer. Given this scenario, why is McDonalds classified as a *service* company, rather than a *manufacturing* company? The distinguishing feature is that the product from McDonalds is consumed immediately. In general, services cannot be stored and sold at a later time. As a result, service companies do not have Work in Process and Finished Goods Inventory accounts in which to store costs before transferring them to a Cost of Goods Sold account. At the end of the day, McDonalds has no work in process or finished goods inventory.

Is a retail company, such as Toys-R-Us, a service or manufacturing company? Because wholesale and retail companies have large inventory accounts, it may seem odd to think of them as service companies.

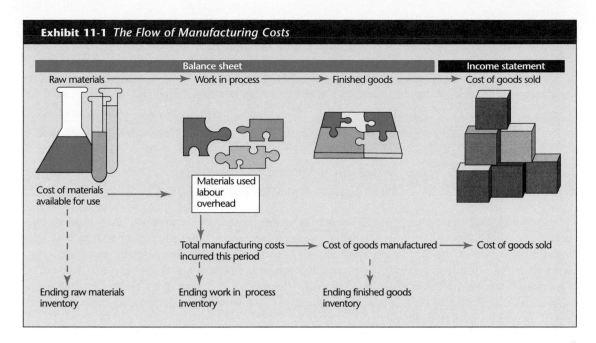

Exhibit 11-1 *The Flow of Manufacturing Costs*

Even so, wholesale and retail companies are traditionally classified this way. To understand this classification, think about what the employees of a wholesale or retail company do. Clearly, the actions of the employees cannot be stored and used at a later time. The services of a salesperson are consumed as the customer is being assisted. Other organizations that provide services include insurance companies, banks, cleaning establishments, airlines, law firms, hospitals, hotels, and governmental agencies.

Even though service companies do not store their costs in inventory accounts for financial reporting purposes, they do accumulate cost information to facilitate decision making. For example, a hotel needs to know the cost of providing a room to assess whether its pricing policy is appropriate. A private school may compare the expected and actual cost of offering a course to ensure that costs are controlled. An airline needs to know the cost of providing service for a specific route to decide whether to maintain or eliminate the route. Understanding the cost of providing services is just as important as knowing the cost of making a product, regardless of whether the cost is stored in an inventory balance sheet account or charged directly to the income statement.

■ Manufacturing Cost Flow Illustrated

To illustrate how manufacturing costs flow through ledger accounts, we consider the case of Ventra Manufacturing Company, which makes mahogany jewellery boxes that it sells to department stores. The account balances shown in Exhibit 11–2 were drawn from the company's accounting records as of January 1, 2002.

Ventra Manufacturing's 2002 accounting events are introduced here. The effects of the events are summarized in the T-accounts shown in Exhibit 11–4 on page 394. We strongly suggest that you study Exhibit 11–4 carefully as you read the description of the events provided in the following section of this chapter. The illustration assumes that Ventra determines the cost of making its product on a monthly basis. Accounting events for January are described here.

Exhibit 11-2 *Trial Balance as of January 1, 2002*

Cash	$ 64,500	
Raw Materials Inventory	500	
Work in Process Inventory	0	
Finished Goods Inventory	836	
Manufacturing Equipment	40,000	
Accumulated Amortization		$ 10,000
Common Stock		76,000
Retained Earnings		19,836
Totals	$105,836	$105,836

Events Affecting Manufacturing Cost Flow in January

LO4

Demonstrate how product cost flow affects financial statements through a horizontal financial statements model.

Ventra Manufacturing pays $26,500 cash to purchase raw materials. For the sake of simplicity, we assume that all raw materials are purchased one time at the beginning of the accounting period. In practice, materials are usually purchased on a more frequent basis. The effects of the materials purchase on the company's financial statements are shown in the following horizontal financial statements model:[1]

Event 1
Raw Materials Purchased

Assets		=	Liabilities	+	Equity	Revenue	−	Expenses	=	Net Income	Cash flow
Cash	+ Raw Materials Inventory										
(26,500) +	26,500	=	n/a	+	n/a	n/a	−	n/a	=	n/a	(26,500) OA

This event is an asset exchange event; neither the income statement nor the total assets shown on the balance sheet are affected. One asset account, Cash, decreases, and another asset account, Raw Materials Inventory, increases. Costs of raw materials are only one component of the company's total manufacturing costs. The materials costs will be included as part of the cost of goods sold expense that will be recognized when the inventory is sold to customers. Because cash is spent for a current asset that will be used in the operation of the business, the cash outflow is shown in the operating activities (OA) section of the statement of cash flows.

Event 2
Raw Materials Placed into Production

Ventra places $1,100 of raw materials into production in the process of making jewellery boxes. This event is also an asset exchange event; total assets shown on the balance sheet are not affected. One asset account, Raw Materials Inventory, decreases, and another asset account, Work in Process Inventory, increases. Neither the income statement nor the statement of cash flows is affected. The effects of the material usage on the company's financial statements follow:

Assets		=	Liabilities	+	Equity	Revenue	−	Expenses	=	Net Income	Cash flow
Raw Materials Inventory	+ Work in Process Inventory										
(1,100)	+ 1,100	=	n/a	+	n/a	n/a	−	n/a	=	n/a	n/a

Raw materials represent *direct* inputs to the production process that are accounted for under the *perpetual inventory method*. Because the materials are traced directly to products, it is easy to match the cost flow with the physical flow. Every time direct materials are moved from storage to work in process, the cost of materials is transferred in the accounting records as well.

Event 3
Production Supplies Purchased

Ventra pays $2,000 cash to purchase production supplies. This event is also an asset exchange event; total assets shown on the balance sheet are not affected. One asset account, Cash, decreases, and another asset account, Production Supplies, increases. Net income is not affected. However, the cash flow associated with the purchase of supplies is shown in the operating section of the cash flow statement. The effects of this event on the company's financial statements follow:

Assets		=	Liabilities	+	Equity	Revenue	−	Expenses	=	Net Income	Cash flow
Cash	+ Production Supplies										
(2,000) +	2,000	=	n/a	+	n/a	n/a	−	n/a	=	n/a	(2,000) OA

The production supplies are recorded in a separate asset account because practicality dictates that they be maintained under the *periodic inventory method*. Production supplies are *indirect* inputs. Such

---

[1]The horizontal model derives its name from the fact that it arranges the major elements from the financial statements horizontally across a single page. Reading from left to right, elements of the balance sheet are presented first, followed by those of the income statement, and then the cash flow statement. The types of activities recognized in the cash statement are identified by the letters "OA" for operating activities, "IA" for investing activities, and "FA" for financing activities.

small quantities are used on each unit that it is not worth the trouble to track the actual costs as the materials are being used. Nobody wants to stop to make a journal entry every time several drops of glue are used. *Instead of recognizing supply usage as it occurs (i.e., perpetually), the amount of usage is determined at the end of the accounting period (i.e., periodically).* The record-keeping procedures used to include the cost of production supplies in the flow of manufacturing costs are described in the explanation of the treatment of overhead costs (see Event 5).

Ventra pays production workers $1,400 cash. Note carefully that these wages are *not* treated as salary expense. Because the labour was used to make jewellery boxes, the cost is included in the Work in Process Inventory account. In other words, this is an asset exchange event. *Cash* was exchanged for the value added by making the inventory. Accordingly, one asset, Cash, decreases, and another asset, *Work in Process Inventory*, increases. Total assets as shown on the balance sheet are not affected nor is the income statement. Because cash was spent for a current asset that is used in the operation of the business, however, the cash outflow is shown in the operating activities section of the cash flow statement. The effects of the labour usage on the company's financial statements follow:

Event 4
Production
Worker Paid

Assets			=	Liabilities	+	Equity	Revenue	−	Expenses	=	Net Income	Cash flow
Cash	+	**Work in Process Inventory**										
(1,400)	+	1,400	=	n/a	+	n/a	n/a	−	n/a	=	n/a	(1,400) OA

Flow of Overhead Costs

Assume that Ventra made 500 jewellery boxes during January. What is the cost per jewellery box? Why does management need this information? First, we address the need-to-know issue. To the extent that Ventra uses a cost-plus-pricing strategy, it is necessary to know the cost per jewellery box to determine the price to charge for each one. Product cost information is also needed to accomplish control and performance evaluation. By comparing the current cost of production with historical or standard cost data, management can evaluate performance and take appropriate action to ensure that the company will accomplish its goals. Accordingly, Ventra has an immediate need to know the cost of products made in January for many reasons.

The *direct costs* of making the 500 jewellery boxes in January include $1,100 for materials and $1,400 for labour. The *actual indirect overhead costs* are unknown. Indeed, some of these costs will not be known until the end of the year. For example, Ventra uses the periodic inventory method to determine the cost of production supplies. Accordingly, the amount of supplies used will not be known until the year-end count of supplies is completed. Similarly, the actual cost of taxes, insurance, landscaping, supervisory bonuses, and other indirect costs may be unknown in January. Even so, Ventra cannot delay important managerial decisions until actual cost data become available. In summary, Ventra needs information on January 31 that will not be available until December 31. This condition is depicted in the following graphic:

LO5
Understand the necessity of assigning estimated overhead costs to the inventory and cost of goods sold accounts during an accounting period.

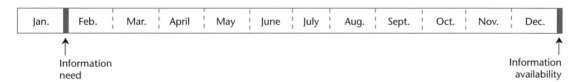

| Jan. | Feb. | Mar. | April | May | June | July | Aug. | Sept. | Oct. | Nov. | Dec. |

↑ Information need   ↑ Information availability

To resolve the conflict between the need for information and the availability of information, Ventra is forced to use *estimated costs* in its accounting system *during the accounting period*. To illustrate, assume that Ventra's accountant estimates that $40,320 of indirect overhead costs will be incurred during the entire year. This *estimate* of overhead cost includes $1,600 for the cost of production supplies,

© Griffin/The Image Works

Like manufacturing companies, service companies use predetermined overhead rates to obtain timely information for decision-making purposes. For example, the Marriott Corporation cannot wait until the end of the year to price its rooms or banquet services. Customers want price information before actual cost data can be determined. Accordingly, Marriott's management team must base decisions on estimated (predetermined) costs, rather than actual costs.

$10,000 of amortization cost, and $28,720 of other costs, such as supervisory salaries, rent on the manufacturing facility, utilities, and maintenance. How much of the $40,320 *estimated* overhead cost should be allocated to the units produced in January? To answer this question, it is necessary to identify the most appropriate allocation base. Assuming that the goods (i.e., jewellery boxes) are homogeneous (i.e., each box is exactly the same as every other box), it makes sense to assign the same amount of overhead cost to each box. This assignment is accomplished by using the number of units as the allocation base.

Suppose that Ventra's accountant expects that 12,000 jewellery boxes will be made during the year. On the basis of this estimate, the allocation rate is $3.36 per unit ($40,320 expected cost ÷ 12,000 units). Because the overhead allocation rate is determined before the actual overhead costs are known, it is called a **predetermined overhead rate**. On the basis of a $3.36 predetermined overhead rate, $1,680 of overhead cost is allocated to the 500 jewellery boxes made in January ($3.36 × 500 boxes).

Manufacturing Overhead Account

LO6

Record applied and actual overhead costs in a manufacturing overhead account.

How are overhead costs recorded in the accounting records? **Estimated overhead** costs are *applied* (i.e. assigned) to work in process inventory *at the time goods are produced*. In the case of Ventra Manufacturing, $1,680 of overhead cost would be applied (i.e., transferred) to the Work in Process account during the month of January. However, actual overhead costs may be incurred at a different time from the time when goods are being made. For example, Ventra may recognize amortization or the use of supplies at the end of the year. As a result, actual and estimated overhead costs are recorded at different times during the accounting period.

At the time estimated overhead is transferred (i.e., applied) to the Work in Process Inventory account, a corresponding amount of estimated overhead is accumulated in a *temporary* account called *Manufacturing Overhead*. It may be helpful to think of the **Manufacturing Overhead account** as a temporary asset account. The recognition of estimated overhead can then be viewed as an asset exchange transaction. At the time estimated overhead is recognized, the temporary account, Manufacturing Overhead, decreases and the Work in Process Inventory account increases. Actual overhead costs are recorded as increases in the Manufacturing Overhead account at the time they are incurred. For example, at the end of the accounting period, the amount of supplies used is removed from the Supplies account and placed into the Manufacturing Overhead account. In this case, the balance in the Supplies account decreases and the balance in the Manufacturing Overhead account increases.

Because differences normally exist between estimated and actual overhead costs, the Manufacturing Overhead account is likely to contain a balance at the end of the accounting period. If more overhead has been applied than was actually incurred, the account balance represents the amount of **overapplied overhead**. If less overhead was applied than was incurred, the account balance will be classified as **underapplied overhead**. Overapplied overhead means that the amount of estimated overhead cost recorded in the Work in Process Inventory account was more than the amount of actual overhead cost incurred. Underapplied overhead means that the amount of estimated overhead cost recorded in the Work in Process Inventory account was less than the amount of actual overhead cost incurred. Because costs flow from Work in Process Inventory to Finished Goods Inventory and then to Cost of Goods Sold, these accounts will also be overstated or understated relative to actual costs. If the amount of the overapplied or underapplied overhead is significant, it must be allocated proportionately to the Work in Process Inventory, Finished Goods Inventory, and **Cost of Goods Sold** accounts.

In most cases, over- or underapplied overhead is not significant. When the amounts are insignificant, companies may correct the misapplied overhead in any manner they deem expedient. Under these circumstances, companies normally avoid the complication associated with allocating the over- or underapplied overhead among the inventory accounts and cost of goods sold. Instead, the total amount of the overhead correction is assigned directly to cost of goods sold. We have adopted this simplifying practice throughout the text and in the end-of-chapter exercises and problems. The flow of product cost including actual and applied overhead is shown in Exhibit 11–3. To illustrate the use of a manufacturing overhead account, we return to the case of Ventra Manufacturing Company.

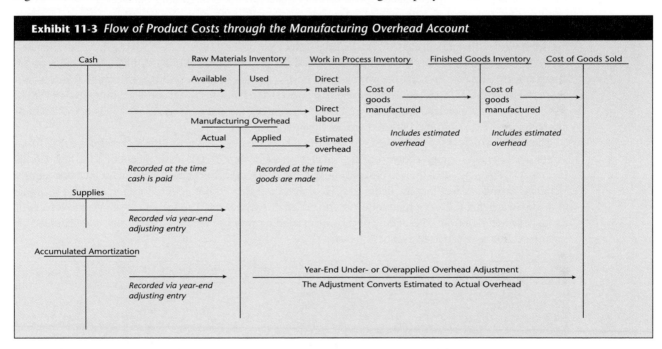

Exhibit 11-3 *Flow of Product Costs through the Manufacturing Overhead Account*

Ventra recognizes $1,680 of estimated manufacturing overhead costs at the end of January (see previous section entitled Flow of Overhead Costs to review the computation of this amount). This event is another asset exchange event. Total assets shown on the balance sheet, net income, and cash flow are not affected. The temporary asset account Manufacturing Overhead decreases, and the asset account Work in Process Inventory increases. The effects of this event on the company's financial statements follow:

Event 5
Overhead Costs Recognized

Assets			= Liabilities + Equity		Revenue − Expenses = Net Income			Cash flow
Manufacturing Overhead	+	Work in Process Inventory						
(1,680)	+	1,680 =	n/a	+ n/a	n/a −	n/a =	n/a	n/a

Event 6
Work in Process
Completed
and Cost
Transferred to
Finished Goods

Ventra transfers the total cost of the 500 jewellery boxes made in January ($1,100 materials + $1,400 labour + $1,680 estimated overhead 5 $4,180 cost of goods manufactured) from Work in Process to Finished Goods. This event is an asset exchange event. Total assets shown on the balance sheet, net income, and cash flow are not affected. The asset account Work in Process Inventory decreases, and the asset account Finished Goods Inventory increases. The effects of this event on the company's financial statements follow:

Assets			= Liabilities	+ Equity	Revenue	− Expenses	= Net Income	Cash flow
Work in Process Inventory	+	Finished Goods Inventory						
(4,180)	+	4,180	= n/a	+ n/a	n/a	− n/a	= n/a	n/a

Event 7
Cost of Goods
Sold Expense
Recognized

Ventra transfers the cost of 400 jewellery boxes from the Finished Goods Inventory account to the Cost of Goods Sold account. Remember that a total of 500 jewellery boxes costing $4,180 were made during January. Also, the Finished Goods Inventory account had a beginning balance of $836. Assume that this cost represented 100 units of inventory. As a result, 600 units (100 + 500) of finished goods costing $5,016 ($836 + $4,180) were available for sale. If 400 units are sold, 200 units remain in the Finished Goods Inventory account. Accordingly, the cost of the 600 boxes ($5,016) must be allocated between the Finished Goods Inventory account and the Cost of Goods Sold account. The amount of the allocation is computed by first determining the cost per unit of jewellery boxes. Given 600 boxes at a cost of $5,016, the cost per unit is $8.36 ($5,016 ÷ 600). On the basis of this cost per unit, $3,344 ($8.36 × 400 boxes) is transferred from Finished Goods Inventory to Cost of Goods Sold. This leaves an ending balance of $1,672 in the Finished Goods Inventory account.

The transfer of cost from Finished Goods Inventory to Cost of Goods Sold is an asset use event. Total assets and owners' equity shown on the balance sheet decrease. The asset account Finished Goods Inventory decreases, and the expense account Cost of Goods Sold acts to decrease owners' equity (retained earnings). Net income decreases. However, cash flow is not affected by the expense recognition. Be aware that the sales transaction is composed of two events. The following shows the effects of the expense recognition. The effects of the corresponding revenue recognition are discussed in the following section as a separate event.

Assets	=	Liabilities	+	Equity	Revenue	− Expenses	= Net Income	Cash flow
Finished Goods Inventory				Retained Earnings				
(3,344)	=	n/a	+	(3,344)	n/a	− 3,344	= (3,344)	n/a

The cost-per-unit information just computed is useful for many purposes. For example, the amount of the allocation between ending Finished Goods Inventory and the Cost of Goods Sold accounts is necessary for the preparation of financial statements. Accordingly, Ventra must compute the cost-per-unit data if the company desires to prepare interim (monthly or quarterly) financial reports. The cost per unit for the month of January also could be compared with the cost-per-unit for the previous accounting period or to standard cost data to evaluate cost control and performance. Finally, the cost-per-unit data are useful in setting the price under a cost-plus-pricing strategy. To illustrate, assume that Ventra desires to earn a gross margin of $5.64 per jewellery box. Under these circumstances, it would charge $14 ($8.36 cost + $5.64 gross profit) per unit for each jewellery box. Indeed, when recording the effects of the revenue recognition for the 400 boxes sold, we assume that Ventra does, in fact, charge its customers $14 per unit.

Event 8
Revenue
Recognized on
Jewellery Boxes
Sold

Ventra recognizes $5,600 ($14 per unit × 400 units) of sales revenue. This is an asset source transaction. The asset account Cash increases and the owners' equity account **Retained Earnings** increases. Net income increases as does the operating activities section of the cash flow statement. The effects of the revenue recognition follow:

As with manufacturing companies, service companies, such as Management Consultants, must use estimated costs for decision-making purposes. Consultants must estimate all the overhead costs associated with serving a client. The estimated costs are then allocated to the cost objects (i.e., clients) to accomplish pricing and other managerial decisions.

Assets	=	Liabilities	+	Equity	Revenue	−	Expenses	=	Net Income	Cash flow
5,600	=	n/a	+	5,600	5,600	−	n/a	=	5,600	5,600 OA

Event 9
Actual Cash
Overhead Costs
Incurred

Ventra pays $1,200 cash for manufacturing overhead costs including indirect labour, utilities, and rent. The amount of actual overhead is an asset exchange event. The event acts to transfer cost from the asset account, Cash, to the temporary asset account, Manufacturing overhead. Total assets on the balance sheet are unaffected as is net income. However, the cash outflow reduces the operating activities section of the cash flow statement. These effects follow:

Assets			=	Liabilities	+	Equity	Revenue	−	Expenses	=	Net Income	Cash flow
Cash	+	Work in Process Inventory										
(1,200)	+	1,200	=	n/a	+	n/a	n/a	−	n/a	=	n/a	(1,200) OA

Recall that $1,680 of overhead was applied to the Work in Process Inventory account. This amount is significantly more than the $1,200 of actual overhead recognized earlier. The difference occurs because the estimated overhead includes several costs that have not yet been incurred. For example, the amount of supplies used and amortization expense are not recognized until an adjusting entry is made on December 31. Although these costs are recognized in December, an appropriate portion of the cost must be included in the measurement of the cost of products made in January. Otherwise, all of the cost of supplies and amortization would be assigned to the products made in December. Because the manufacturing equipment and supplies are actually used throughout the accounting period, assigning the entire cost of these resources to December alone overstates the cost of December production and understates the cost of production during other months. Such distortions in the measurement of product cost could mislead management in the decision-making process. By using *estimated* overhead costs during the accounting period, management is able to reduce the distortions that occur if actual costs are used. The difference between actual and estimated overhead is rectified through a *year-end adjusting entry*. No attempt is made to reconcile differences on an interim basis.

Summary of Events Occurring in January

Refer again to Exhibit 11–4, which summarizes the events that occurred during January. The top section of the exhibit provides a graphic illustration of the *physical flow* of the resources used to make the jewellery boxes. The bottom section shows the effects of product *cost flow* through Ventra's ledger accounts. As indicated, the January balances in the Finished Goods Inventory and Cost of Goods Sold accounts include the cost of materials, labour, and an *estimated* amount of overhead. Estimated overhead cost continues to be applied to the Work in Process Inventory account throughout the year. Actual overhead costs are accumulated in the Manufacturing Overhead account as they are incurred. The accounts are adjusted at year end to reconcile the difference between the estimated and actual overhead costs.

LO7
Record product costs in T-accounts.

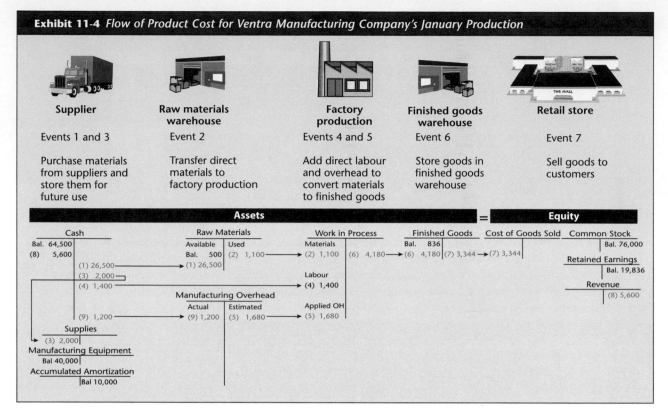

Exhibit 11-4 *Flow of Product Cost for Ventra Manufacturing Company's January Production*

Events Affecting Manufacturing Cost Flow for February through December

LO8

Understand the cyclical nature of product cost flows.

The events affecting Ventra Manufacturing Company for the months of February through December are summarized here. The sequence of events is numbered in a manner that reflects a continuation of the activity that occurred in January. Because nine events occurred in January, the first event, which represents activity from February through December, is Event 10. The list includes the following:

10. Ventra uses $24,860 of raw materials.
11. The company pays production workers $31,640 cash.
12. Because production is started on an additional 11,300 jewellery boxes, $37,968 (11,300 units × the predetermined overhead rate of $3.36 per unit) of overhead is applied to the Work in Process Inventory account.
13. The company completes work on 10,300 units of product and transfers $86,108 of cost of goods manufactured from the Work in Process Inventory account to the Finished Goods Inventory account.
14. Ventra sells 9,600 units of product and records $80,256 of cost of goods sold.
15. The company recognizes $134,400 of cash revenue for the products sold in Event 14.
16. The company pays $30,500 cash for overhead costs including indirect labour, rent, and utilities.
17. The year-end count of production supplies indicates that $300 of supplies are on hand as of December 31. Accordingly, $1,700 ($2,000 supplies available − $300 ending balance) of indirect materials cost is recognized as being used during the accounting period. Note that this is a year-end recognition of actual overhead cost.
18. Ventra recognizes $10,000 of actual overhead cost for amortization of manufacturing equipment.
19. The company pays $31,400 cash for general, selling, and administrative expenses.
20. A year-end review of the Manufacturing Overhead account reveals that overhead cost is underap-

plied by $3,752. In other words, actual overhead ($43,400) is higher than the estimated amount of overhead ($39,648). Because estimated overhead cost passes through the ledger accounts (from Work in Process Inventory, to Finished Goods Inventory, and ultimately to Cost of Goods Sold), the balance in the Cost of Goods Sold account is understated. The adjusting entry to close the Manufacturing Overhead account and to increase the balance in the Cost of Goods Sold account is made.

The flow of these costs through the ledger accounts is shown in Exhibit 11–5. The exhibit includes the effects of the January events as well as those described for February through December. The January data are shown in green to distinguish them from the data for the remainder of the year. The flow of product costs are highlighted with blue arrows to facilitate your review of the exhibit. Carefully trace the effects of each transaction to ensure that you understand product costs flow in a manufacturing entity.

LO7
Record product costs in T-accounts.

Analyses of Underapplied Overhead

What caused the overhead to be underapplied by $3,752? Recall that the predetermined overhead rate is based on two estimates including the estimated overhead cost and the estimated volume of production. At the beginning of the accounting period, Ventra estimated that total overhead cost would be $40,320, but actual overhead costs were $43,400. Accordingly, Ventra spent $3,080 more than it expected to spend for overhead cost. Having identified the *spending variance*, a $672 portion of the underapplied overhead ($3,752 − $3,080) remains unexplained. This variance is the result of the difference between the actual and estimated volume of activity and is appropriately called a volume variance. Recall that Ventra estimated production volume to be 12,000 units, but actual volume was only 11,800 units (500 units made in January + 11,300 units made from February through December). As a result, the predetermined overhead rate of $3.36 per unit was applied to 200 fewer units (12,000 units − 11,800 units) than expected. This results in a volume variance of $672 ($3.36 predetermined overhead rate × 200 units). The combination of the spending and volume variances[2] explains the total amount of the underapplied overhead ($3,080 + $672 = $3,752).

LO9
Comprehend the relationship between over- or underapplied overhead and variance analysis.

Because the actual cost is higher than the expected cost, the spending variance is unfavourable. In addition, the volume variance is unfavourable because the actual volume is less than expected, thereby implying that the manufacturing facilities were not utilized to the extent anticipated. In other words, fixed costs, such as amortization, rent, and supervisory, salaries, were spread over fewer units of product than expected, thereby increasing the cost per unit of product. If the variances are significant, estimated product costs would have been understated by an amount that could have distorted the decision-making process. For example, products could have been underpriced, thereby adversely affecting profitability. Accordingly, making estimates as accurately as possible is critically important. Even so, some minimal degree of inaccuracy is inevitable. No one knows exactly what the future will bring. Remember that managers are seeking to improve decision making. Although perfection is unattainable, responsible estimation will certainly provide timely information that is useful for decision making.

∎ Preparation of Schedule of Cost of Goods Manufactured and Sold

LO10
Prepare a schedule of cost of goods manufactured and sold.

In practice, the general ledger system depicted in Exhibit 11–5 may include millions of events. The vast amount of data makes analysis exceedingly difficult. To facilitate the analytical process, the information in the ledger accounts is summarized in a *schedule* that explains the determination of the cost of goods

---

[2]The predetermined overhead rate used in this chapter represents the standard cost and quantity of both variable and fixed inputs. As discussed in Chapter 8, separate standards can be established for variable versus fixed costs. In this chapter, we assume that the variable cost variances are insignificant. Accordingly, the discussion focuses on the effects associated with fixed cost variances.

Exhibit 11-5 *Product Cost Flow for Ventra Manufacturing Company's 2002 Accounting Period*

| Assets | = | Equity |

Cash

Bal. 64,500	
(8) 5,600	(1) 26,500
(15)134,400	(3) 2,000
	(4) 1,400
	(11) 31,640
	(9) 1,200
	(16) 30,500
	(19) 31,400
Bal. 79,860	

Supplies

| (3) 2,000 | (17) 1,700 |
| Bal. 300 | |

Manufacturing Equip.

| Bal. 40,000 | |

Accumulated Amort.

	Bal 10,000
	(18) 10,000
(20) 3,752	
	Bal. 20,000

Raw Materials Inventory

Available	Used
Bal. 500	(2) 1,100
(1) 26,500	(10) 24,860
Bal. 1,040	

Manufacturing Overhead

Estimated	
(5) 1,680	
(12) 37,968	

Actual	
(9) 1,200	
(16) 30,500	
(19) 31,400	
(17) 1,700	
(18) 10,000	
(20) 3,752	Bal. 0

Work in Process Inventory

Materials
| (2) 1,100 | (6) 4,180 |
| (10) 24,500 | (13) 86,108 |

Labour
| (4) 1,400 | |
| (11) 31,640 | |

MOH
(5) 1,680	
(12) 37,968	
Bal. 8,360	

Finished Goods Inventory

Bal. 836	(7) 3,344
(6) 4,180	(14) 80,256
(13) 86,108	
Bal. 7,524	

Cost of Goods Sold

(7) 3,344	
(14) 80,256	
Bal. 87,352	

Common Stock

| | Bal. 76,000 |

Retained Earnings

| | Bal. 19,836 |

Revenue

| | (8) 5,600 |
| | (15) 134,400 |

G, S, &A Expense

| (19) 31,400 | |

manufactured and sold. The schedule is an internal document that does not appear in a company's published financial statements. However, the result of the schedule (i.e., cost of goods sold) does appear in the income statement. Exhibit 11–6 illustrates a **schedule of cost of goods manufactured and sold** for Ventra's 2002 accounting period.

The information in the schedule in Exhibit 11–6 mirrors the transaction data included in the ledger accounts. To verify this fact, compare the information in the Raw Materials Inventory account in Exhibit 11–5 with the computation of the cost of direct raw materials used in the schedule in Exhibit 11–6. The beginning raw materials balance, amount of purchases, and ending materials balance are identical in the ledger account and the schedule. However, the information in the schedule is presented in summary form. For example, the amount of direct materials used is shown as $25,960 in the schedule. This same amount is shown as two separate events ($1,100 + $24,860) in the T-account in Exhibit 11–5. Similarly, the $33,040 amount shown as direct labour in the schedule represents the total of the two amounts ($1,400 + $31,640) of labour cost shown in the Work in Process Inventory account in Exhibit 11–5. In practice, one number in the schedule may represent thousands of individual events that are captured in the ledger accounts. Accordingly, the schedule simplifies the process of analyzing manufacturing cost flow data for decision-making purposes.

It is important to note that the *actual* amount of overhead cost is shown in the schedule of cost of goods manufactured and sold. Remember that financial statement data are gathered at the end of the accounting period when actual cost data are available. Although the estimated cost data are used for internal decision making, actual historical cost data are presented in the schedule.

Exhibit 11-6

Ventra Manufacturing Company
Schedule of Cost of Goods Manufactured and Sold

Beginning raw materials inventory	$ 500
Plus: Purchases	26,500
Raw materials available for use	27,000
Less: Ending raw materials inventory	(1,040)
Direct raw materials used	25,960
Direct labour	33,040
Manufactured overhead applied	39,648
Total manufacturing costs	98,648
Plus: Beginning work in process inventory	0
Total work in process inventory	98,648
Less: Ending work in process inventory	(8,360)
Cost of good manufactured	90,288
Plus: Beginning finished goods inventory	836
Cost of goods available for sale	91,124
Less: Ending finished good inventory	(7,524)
Cost of goods sold – unadjusted	83,600
Plus: Underapplied overhead	3,752
Cost of goods sold – Actual	$ 87,352

LO11

Prepare a set of financial statements for a manufacturing entity.

Financial Statements

The result of schedule of the cost of goods manufactured and sold is shown as the single line item *cost of goods sold* on the company's income statement. The amount of cost of goods sold is subtracted from the sales revenue to determine the gross margin. Selling and administrative expenses are subtracted from gross margin to calculate the amount of net income. Ventra Manufacturing's income statement is shown in Exhibit 11–7 and its balance sheet is shown in Exhibit 11–8. For demonstration purposes, in Exhibit 11–8, we show the three inventory accounts (i.e., Raw Materials, Work in Process, and Finished Goods) separately. In practice, these accounts are frequently combined and shown as a single amount on the balance sheet. The cash flow statement is shown in Exhibit 11–9. Review these statements carefully to ensure that you understand how the information shown in the T-accounts in Exhibit 11–5 is ultimately presented in a company's public financial reports.

Exhibit 11-7

Ventra Manufacturing Company
Income Statement
For the Period Ended December 31, 2005

Sales Revenue	$140,000
Cost of Goods Sold	(87,352)
Gross Margin	52,648
Selling and Administrative Expenses	(31,400)
Net Income	$ 21,248

Exhibit 11-8

Ventra Manufacturing Company
Balance Sheet
As of December 31, 2005

Assets	
Cash	$ 79,860
Raw Materials Inventory	1,040
Work in Process Inventory	8,360
Finished Goods Inventory	7,524
Production Supplies	300
Manufacturing Equipment	40,000
Accumulated Amortization—Manufac. Equip.	(20,000)
Book Value Manufacturing Equipment	20,000
Total Assets	$117,084
Shareholders' Equity	
Common Share	$ 76,000
Retained Earnings	41,084
Total Shareholders' Equity	$117,084

Exhibit 11-9

Ventra Manufacturing Company
Cash Flow Statement
For the Period Ended December 31, 2005

Cash Flows from Operations	
Inflow from Customers	$140,000
Outflow for Production of Inventory*	(93,240)
Outflow for Selling and Administrative Expenses	(31,400)
Net Inflow from Operating Activities	15,360
Cash Flow from Investing Activities	0
Cash Flow from Financing Activities	0
Net Change in Cash	15,360
Plus: Beginning Cash Balance	64,500
Ending Cash Balance	$ 79,860

*See Cash account in Exhibit 11–5: $26,500 + $2,000 + $1,400 + $31,640 + $1,200 + $30,500 = $93,240.

▌Motive to Overproduce

Absorption Costing versus Variable Costing

As discussed previously, the cost of manufacturing products can be divided into fixed and variable cost categories. For example, the cost of materials, labour, and supplies, frequently increase and decrease in direct proportion to the number of units produced. Other costs incurred to make products are fixed costs. The cost of rent, amortization, and supervisory salaries remain constant, regardless of the number of products made. Generally accepted accounting principles require that *all* product costs, both fixed and variable, be accumulated in the inventory accounts until the products are sold. The product costs are expensed as cost of goods sold when the goods are sold. This practice is called **absorption costing**.[3] To illustrate, assume that Hokai Manufacturing Company incurs the following costs to produce 2,000 units of inventory:

Inventory Costs	Cost per Unit	×	Units	=	Total
Variable manufacturing costs	$9.00	×	2,000	=	$18,000
Fixed overhead				=	12,000
Total (full absorption product cost)				=	$30,000

Lo12

Distinguish between absorption and variable costing.

Suppose that Hokai sells all 2,000 units of inventory for $20 per unit (sales = 2,000 × $20 = $40,000). Under these circumstances, gross margin amounts to $10,000 ($40,000 sales − $30,000 cost of goods sold). What happens to profitability if Hokai increases production while holding sales constant? Profitability increases because cost of goods sold decreases. Exhibit 11–10 illustrates this phenomenon; it shows the cost per unit at production levels of 2,000, 3,000, and 4,000 units.

[3]Since absorption costing includes all product costs including manufacturing costs, it is sometimes called full costing.

Exhibit 11–11 is Hokai's income statements assuming a sales volume of 2,000 units and production levels of 2,000, 3,000, and 4,000 units.

Suppose that management is under pressure to increase profitability. Management cannot control sales because the purchaser makes the decision to buy. Under these conditions, management may be tempted to increase profitability by increasing production. You may wonder what is so wrong about increasing production. The problem lies in inventory accumulation. Note that the level of inventory increases by 1,000 units when 3,000 units are produced but only 2,000 are sold. Likewise, the inventory rises to 2,000 units when 4,000 are produced but 2,000 are sold. Considerable risks and costs are associated with holding excess inventory. The inventory may become obsolete, damaged, stolen, or destroyed by fire, weather, or other disasters. Furthermore, holding inventory requires warehouse space, employee handling, financing, and insurance costs. In the long term, these risks and costs reduce the company's profitability. Accordingly, the overproduction of inventory is a poor business practice. To motivate managers to increase profitability without motivating them to overproduce, many companies use an internal reporting format known as *variable costing*.

Exhibit 11-10 *Cost per Unit*

Inventory Costs			
Fixed overhead (a)	$12,000	$12,000	$12,000
Number of units (b)	2,000	3,000	4,000
Fixed overhead per unit (a ÷ b)	$ 6.00	$ 4.00	$ 3.00
Variable manufacturing costs	9.00	9.00	9.00
Full absorption product cost per unit	$ 15.00	$ 13.00	$ 12.00

Exhibit 11-11 *Absorption Income Statements at Different Levels of Production with Sales Held Constant at 2,000 Units*

Level of Production	2,000		3,000		4,000
Sales ($20 per unit × 2,000 units)	$40,000		$40,000		$40,000
Cost of goods sold ($15 × 2,000) =	30,000	($13 × 2,000) =	26,000	($12 × 2,000) =	24,000
Gross margin	$10,000		$14,000		$16,000

Variable Costing

Under **variable costing**, only the *variable* product costs are accumulated in an inventory account. The income statement is prepared under the contribution margin approach, and variable product costs are subtracted from the revenue to determine the contribution margin. Fixed costs are then subtracted from the contribution margin to determine the amount of net income. Accordingly, fixed manufacturing costs are expensed in the period in which they are incurred (i.e., the period in which the resource is used), regardless of when the inventory is sold. Under these circumstances, the amount of reported profit is not affected by increases in productivity. This point is illustrated in the variable cost income statements presented in Exhibit 11–12.

LO12
Distinguish between absorption and variable costing.

Exhibit 11-12 *Variable Income Statements at Different Levels of Production with Sales Held Constant at 2,000 Units*

Level of Production	2,000		3,000		4,000
Sales ($20 per unit × 2,000 units)	$ 40,000		$40,000		$40,000
Variable cost of goods sold ($9 × 2,000) =	(18,000)	($9 × 2,000) =	(18,000)	($9 × 2,000) =	(18,000)
Contribution margin	22,000		22,000		22,000
Fixed manufacturing costs	(12,000)		(12,000)		(12,000)
Net income	$ 10,000		$ 10,000		$10,000

Although managers may still overproduce under variable costing, at least they are not tempted to do so by the lure of reporting higher profits. Accordingly, the variable reporting format encourages management to make business decisions that have a more favourable impact on long-term profitability.

Variable costing can be used only for internal reporting because generally accepted accounting principles prohibit its use in external financial statements.

---

a look
back

Most manufacturing companies accumulate product costs in three inventory accounts. The *Raw Materials Inventory account* is used to accumulate the cost of direct *raw materials* purchased for use in production. The *Work in Process Inventory* account includes the cost of partially completed products. Finally, the *Finished Goods Inventory account* contains the costs of fully completed products that are ready for sale. When direct materials are purchased, their costs are first placed in the Raw Materials Inventory account. The costs of the materials used in production are transferred from this account to the Work in Process Inventory account. The cost of direct labour and overhead are added to the Work in Process Inventory account. As goods are completed, their costs are transferred from Work in Process Inventory to Finished Goods Inventory. When goods are sold, their cost is transferred from Finished Goods Inventory to Cost of Goods Sold. The ending balances in the Raw Materials, Work in Process, and Finished Goods Inventory accounts appear on the balance sheet. The product cost in the Cost of Goods Sold account is subtracted from revenue on the income statement to determine the gross margin.

Many of the actual indirect overhead costs incurred to make products are unknown until the end of the accounting period. Examples of such costs may include the cost of rent, supplies, utilities, indirect materials, and labour. Because many managerial decisions require product cost information before year end, companies frequently estimate the amount of overhead cost. The estimated overhead costs are assigned to products through the use of a *predetermined overhead rate*.

Actual and applied overhead costs are accumulated in the temporary account *Manufacturing Overhead*. Differences between actual and applied overheads result in a balance in the Manufacturing Overhead account at the end of the accounting period. If actual overhead is higher than applied overhead, the balance represents *underapplied overhead*. If actual overhead is lower than applied overhead, the balance represents *overapplied overhead*. If the amount of over- or underapplied overhead is insignificant, it is charged directly to cost of goods sold through a year-end adjusting entry.

Manufacturing cost information is summarized in a report known as a *schedule of cost of goods manufactured and sold*. This schedule explains the determination of the amount of cost of goods sold that appears on the income statement. The actual amount of overhead cost is used in the schedule.

Generally accepted accounting principles require all product costs (fixed and variable) to be accumulated in inventory accounts until the products are sold. This practice is called *absorption costing*. Under absorption costing, management may be tempted to increase profitability by producing more units than can be sold (overproducing). Overproducing spreads the fixed cost over more units, thereby reducing the cost per unit and the amount charged to cost of goods sold. The unfortunate effect is, however, that the extra units must be held in inventory. In the long term, the risks and costs associated with inventory accumulation will reduce profitability. To eliminate the costs of inventory accumulation associated with overproduction, many companies use *variable costing* for determining product cost for internal reporting purposes. Under variable costing, only the variable product costs are accumulated in inventory accounts. Fixed product costs are expensed in the period they are incurred, not when products are sold. As a result, overproduction does not decrease the product cost per unit and managers are not tempted to overproduce to increase profitability.

a look
forward

Would you use the same product cost system to determine the cost of a bottle of Pepsi as you use to determine the cost of a house? You will find the answer to this question in the next chapter, which expands on the basic cost flow concepts introduced in this chapter. You will be introduced to job-order, process, and hybrid cost systems. You will learn to identify the types of services and products that are most appropriate for each type of cost system.

KEY TERMS

Absorption (full) costing The practice of capitalizing all product costs, including fixed manufacturing costs in Inventory. *(p. 398)*

Cost of goods sold The product costs associated with the products that were sold during an accounting period is shown as an expense subtracted from revenues to determine gross margin on the income statement. *(p. 391)*

Estimated overhead The amount of overhead costs assigned during the period to work in process using the predetermined overhead rate. *(p. 390)*

Finished Goods Inventory The asset account used to accumulate the product costs (direct materials, direct labour, and overhead) associated with completed products that have not been sold. *(p. 386)*

Manufacturing Overhead account The temporary account used during an accounting period to accumulate the actual overhead costs incurred and the total amount of overhead applied to work in process. At the end of the period, a debit balance in the account implies that overhead has been underapplied, and a credit balance implies that overhead has been overapplied. The account is closed at year end in an adjusting entry to the Inventory and Cost of Goods Sold accounts. If the balance is insignificant, it is closed only to Cost of Goods Sold. *(p. 390)*

Overapplied or underapplied overhead The result of allocating more or less overhead costs to the work in process account than the amount of the actual overhead costs incurred. *(p. 390)*

Predetermined overhead rate A rate determined by dividing the estimated overhead costs for the period by some measure of estimated total production activity for the period, such as the number of labour hours or machine hours. The base chosen should provide some logical measure of overhead use. The rate is determined before actual costs or activity are known. Throughout the accounting period, the rate is used to allocate overhead costs to the Work in Process Inventory account on the basis of actual production activity. *(p. 390)*

Raw Materials Inventory The asset account used to accumulate the costs of materials, such as lumber, metals, paints, and chemicals, that will be used to make the company's products. *(p. 386)*

Retained Earnings An equity account that is the culmination of all earnings retained in the business since inception (all revenues minus all expenses—including cost of goods sold—and distributions for the period added to all past retained earnings). *(p. 392)*

Schedule of cost of goods manufactured and sold The schedule that summarizes the flow of manufacturing product costs; the result of this schedule, cost of goods sold, is shown as a single line item on the company's income statement. *(p. 397)*

Variable costing The product costing system that capitalizes only variable costs in inventory. The income statement under variable costing subtracts variable costs from revenue to determine contribution margin. Fixed costs, including product costs, are subtracted from the contribution margin to determine net income. Under this format, the amount of net income is not affected by the volume of production. *(p. 399)*

Work in Process Inventory The asset account used to accumulate all product costs (direct materials, direct labour, and overhead) associated with the incomplete products in production. *(p. 386)*

QUESTIONS

1. What is the difference between direct and indirect raw materials costs?

2. Direct raw materials were purchased on account, and the costs were subsequently transferred to work in process inventory. How would the transfer affect assets, liabilities, equity, and cash flows? What is the effect on the income statement? Would your answers change if the materials had originally been purchased for cash?

3. How do manufacturing costs flow through inventory accounts?

4. Goods that cost $2,000 to make were sold for $3,000 on account. How does their sale affect assets, liabilities, and equity? What is the effect on the income statement? What is the effect on the cash flow statement?

5. At the end of the accounting period, an adjusting entry is made for the accrued wages of production workers. How would this entry affect assets, liabilities, and equity? What is the effect on the income statement? What is the effect on the cash flow statement?

6. Maple Leaf Company recorded the payment for utilities used by the manufacturing facility by crediting Cash and debiting Manufacturing Overhead. Why was the debit made to Manufacturing Overhead instead of Work in Process Inventory?

7. Why is the salary of a production worker capitalized while the salary of a marketing manager is expensed?

8. Al Carmon says that his company has a difficult time establishing a predetermined overhead rate because the number of units of product produced during a period is hard to measure. What are two measures of production other than the number of units of product that Mr. Carmon could use to establish a predetermined overhead rate?

9. What do the terms *overapplied overhead* and *underapplied overhead* mean?

10. What do *product costs* and *selling, general,* and *administrative costs* mean? Give examples of costs that would be product costs and examples of costs that would be selling, general, and administrative costs.

11. How does the entry to close an insignificant amount of overapplied overhead to the Cost of Goods Sold account affect net income?

12. Why are actual overhead costs not used in determining periodic product cost?

13. Because of seasonal fluctuations, Buresch Corporation has a problem determining the unit cost of its products. For example, high heating costs during the winter months cause the cost per unit to be higher than the per unit cost in the summer months even when the same number of units of product is produced. Suggest how Buresch can improve the computation of per unit cost.

14. What is the purpose of the Manufacturing Overhead account?

15. For what purpose is the schedule of cost of goods manufactured and sold prepared? Is the statement used by all companies?

16. How does the variable costing approach differ from the absorption costing approach? Explain the differences in income statement formats under each approach.

17. How is profitability affected by increases in productivity under the variable and absorption costing approaches?

18. Under what circumstance is a variable costing statement format used? What potential problem could it eliminate?

EXERCISES

L.O. 2, 7, 10, 11   **EXERCISE 11-1**   *Product Cost Flow and Financial Statements*

Kolarik Manufacturing Company was started on January 1, 2005. The company was affected by the following events during its first year of operation:

1. Acquired capital of $800 cash from the owners.
2. Paid $250 cash for direct raw materials.
3. Transferred $200 of direct raw materials to the work in process inventory.
4. Paid production employees $300 cash.
5. Paid $150 cash for manufacturing overhead costs.
6. Completed work on products that cost $500.
7. Sold products that cost $400 for $700 cash.
8. Paid $200 cash for selling and administrative expenses.
9. Made a $25 cash distribution to the owners.

Required

a. Open T-accounts and record the events affecting Kolarik Manufacturing.

b. Prepare a schedule of cost of goods manufactured and sold, an income statement, a balance sheet, and a cash flow statement.

c. Explain the difference between net income and cash flow from operations.

L.O. 2, 7, 10, 11   **EXERCISE 11-2**   *Product Cost Flow and Financial Statements*

Morris Manufacturing Company was started on January 1, 2002, when it acquired capital amounting to $500 cash from the owners. During the first year of operation, $200 of direct raw materials was purchased on account, and $150 of the materials was used to make products. Direct labour costs of $250 were paid in cash. Cash payments of $175 were made for overhead costs. The company completed products that cost $400 and sold goods that had cost $300 for $500 cash. Selling and administrative expenses of $120 were paid in cash.

Required

a. Open T-accounts and record the events affecting Morris Manufacturing.

b. Prepare a schedule of cost of goods manufactured and sold, an income statement, a balance sheet, and a cash flow statement.

c. Explain the difference between net income and cash flow from operations.

EXERCISE 11-3   *Predetermined Overhead Rate*   **L.O. 5, 9**

Baker Company estimates that its overhead costs for 2009 will be $750,000. Output is estimated in units of product to be 300,000 units.

Required

a. Calculate Baker's predetermined overhead rate on the basis of expected production.
b. If 24,000 units of product are made in March 2009, how much overhead cost should be allocated to the Work in Process Inventory account during the month?
c. If actual overhead costs in March were $63,000, would overhead be overapplied or underapplied and by how much?

EXERCISE 11-4   *Manufacturing Inventory Accounts*   **L.O. 2, 10, 11**

Nico Corporation began fiscal year 2001 with the following balances in its inventory accounts:

Raw materials	$42,000
Work in process	63,000
Finished goods	21,000

During the accounting period, Nico purchased $180,000 of raw materials and issued $186,000 of materials to the production department. Direct labour costs for the period amounted to $243,000, and factory overhead of $36,000 was allocated to Work in Process Inventory. Assume that there was no over- or underapplied overhead. Goods costing $459,000 to produce were completed and transferred to the Finished Goods Inventory account. Goods costing $452,000 were sold for $600,000 during the period. Selling and administrative expenses amounted to $54,000.

Required

a. Determine the ending balance of each of the three inventory accounts that would appear on the year-end balance sheet.
b. Prepare a schedule of cost of goods manufactured and sold and an income statement.

EXERCISE 11-5   *Missing Information in Schedule of Cost of Goods Manufactured*   **L.O. 10**

Required

Fill in the missing information on the following schedule of cost of goods manufactured:

Veser Corporation
Schedule of Cost of Goods Manufactured
For the Year Ended December 31, 2005

Raw materials		
Beginning inventory	$?	
Plus: Purchases	90,000	
Raw materials available for use	111,000	
Minus: Ending raw materials inventory	?	
Cost of direct raw materials used		$ 93,000
Direct labour		?
Manufacturing overhead		18,000
Total manufacturing costs		$232,500
Plus: Beginning work in process inventory		?
Total work in process during the period		$?
Minus: Ending work in process inventory		34,500
Cost of goods manufactured		$229,500

L.O. 10 EXERCISE 11-6   *Schedule of Cost of Goods Manufactured and Sold*

The following information pertains to Carter Manufacturing Company for March 2005;

March 1	
Inventory balances	
Raw materials	$40,000
Work in process	65,000
Finished goods	43,000

March 31	
Inventory balances	
Raw materials	$37,000
Work in process	60,000
Finished goods	35,000

During March	
Costs of raw materials purchased	$12,000
Costs of direct labour	10,000
Costs of manufacturing overhead	16,000
Sales revenues	75,000

Required

a. Prepare a schedule of cost of goods manufactured and sold.

b. Calculate the amount of gross margin on the income statement.

L.O. 6, 9 EXERCISE 11-7   *Predetermined Overhead Rate*

Three competing manufacturing companies estimated the following costs and operating data for 2008:

	Ming	Soho	Folo
Direct labour hours	90,000	60,000	70,000
Direct materials costs	$200,000	$340,000	$280,000
Direct labour costs	$540,000	$350,000	$320,000

Estimated manufacturing overhead costs and the activity base used for computing the predetermined overhead rate for the three companies were as follows:

	Manufacturing Overhead Costs	Overhead Activity Base
Ming	$630,000	Direct labour hours
Soho	680,000	Direct materials costs
Folo	800,000	Direct labour costs

Required

a. Compute the predetermined overhead rate each company would use to allocate overhead costs.

b. If Ming actually used 85,000 direct labour hours in 2008, determine the amount of overhead that it would have applied to the work in process inventory. Determine the amount of overapplied or underapplied overhead for Ming for the 2008 period if its actual overhead costs were $605,000. If the balance in manufacturing overhead is insignificant, how would the end-of-period adjusting entry affect equity?

L.O. 6, 9 EXERCISE 11-8   *Predetermined Overhead Rate*

Heildman Inc. estimates manufacturing overhead costs for the 2002 accounting period as follows:

Equipment amortization	$174,000
Supplies	15,000
Material handling	17,000
Property taxes	12,000
Production setup	16,000
Rent	30,000
Maintenance	20,000
Supervisory salaries	152,500

The company uses a predetermined overhead rate on the basis of machine hours. Estimated 2002 hours for labour were 127,500 and for machine were 90,000.

Required
a. Calculate the predetermined overhead rate.
b. Determine the amount of manufacturing overhead applied to the work in process inventory during the 2002 period if actual machine hours were 115,000.

EXERCISE 11-9   *Predetermined Overhead Rate*   **L.O. 6, 9**

Company X and Company Y both apply overhead to the Work in Process Inventory account using direct labour hours. The following information is available for both companies for the year:

	Company X	Company Y
Actual manufacturing overhead	$20,000	$40,000
Actual direct labour hours	5,000	6,000
Underapplied overhead		$ 2,000
Overapplied overhead	$ 4,000	

Required
a. Compute the budgeted overhead rate for each company.
b. Using T-accounts, record the entry to close the overapplied or underapplied overhead at the end of the accounting period for each company, assuming the amounts are immaterial.

EXERCISE 11-10   *Predetermined Overhead Rate*   **L.O. 6, 9**

Company A and Company B assign manufacturing overhead to the work-in-process inventory using direct labour cost. The following information is available for the companies for the year:

	Company A	Company B
Actual direct labour cost	$145,000	$120,000
Estimated direct labour cost	150,000	100,000
Actual manufacturing overhead cost	56,000	92,000
Estimated manufacturing overhead cost	60,000	80,000

Required
a. Compute the predetermined overhead rate for each company.
b. Determine the amount of overhead cost that would be applied to the work in process inventory for each company.
c. Compute the amount of overapplied or underapplied manufacturing overhead cost for each company.

EXERCISE 11-11   *Recording Manufacturing Overhead Costs*   **L.O. 6**

C. A. Church manufactures model airplanes. The company purchased for $850,000 automated production equipment that can make the model parts. The equipment has a $50,000 salvage value and a 10-year useful life.

Required
a. Assuming that the equipment was purchased on March 1, record in T-accounts the adjusting entry that the company would make on December 31 to record amortization on equipment.
b. In which month would the amortization costs be assigned to units produced?

L.O. 2, 6, 9 EXERCISE 11-12   *Recording Inventory Costs*

Micro Manufacturing recorded the following amounts in its inventory accounts in 2004:

Raw Materials Inventory		Work in Process Inventory	
150,000	(a)		40,000
		80,000	
40,000		60,000	
		(c)	

Finished Goods Inventory		Cost of Goods Sold	
40,000	(d)		
5,000		(e)	

Manufacturing Inventory	
(b)	60,000
5,000	

Required

Determine the dollar amounts for (a), (b), (c), (d) and (e). Assume that underapplied and overapplied overhead is closed to Cost of Goods Sold.

L.O. 12 EXERCISE 11-13   *Variable Costing versus Absorption Costing*

Carbon Company incurred manufacturing overhead cost for the year as follows:

Direct materials	$10/unit
Direct labour	$7/unit
Manufacturing overhead	
Variable	$3/unit
Fixed	$7,500 ($5/unit for 1,500 units)
Variable selling & admin. expenses	$2,000
Fixed selling & admin. expenses	$4,000

The company produced 1,500 units and sold 1,000 of them at $45 per unit. Assume that the production manager is paid a 2 percent bonus on the basis of the company's net income.

Required

a. Prepare an income statement under absorption costing.
b. Prepare an income statement under variable costing.
c. Determine the manager's bonus under each approach. Which approach would you recommend for internal reporting, and why?

L.O. 5 EXERCISE 11-14   *Smoothed Unit Cost*

Cracas Manufacturing estimated its product costs and volume of production for 2008 by quarter as follows:

	First Quarter	Second Quarter	Third Quarter	Fourth Quarter
Direct raw materials	$200,000	$100,000	$300,000	$150,000
Direct labour	120,000	60,000	180,000	90,000
Manufacturing overhead	200,000	310,000	400,000	230,000
Total production costs	$520,000	$470,000	$880,000	$470,000
Expected units produced	40,000	20,000	60,000	30,000

Cracas Company sells souvenir items at various resorts across the country. Its management uses the product's estimated quarterly cost to determine the selling price of its product. The company expects a large variance in demand for the product between quarters due to its seasonal nature. The company does not expect overhead costs, which are predominately fixed, to vary significantly as to production volume or with amounts for previous years. Prices are established by using a cost-plus-pricing strategy. The company finds variations in short-term unit cost difficult to use. Unit cost variations complicate pricing decisions and many other decisions for which cost is a consideration.

Required
a. On the basis of estimated total production cost, determine the expected quarterly cost per unit for Cracas's product.
b. Suggest how overhead costs would be estimated each quarter to solve the company's unit cost problem. Calculate the unit cost per quarter on the basis of your recommendation.

PROBLEMS—SERIES A

PROBLEM 11-1A   *Manufacturing Cost Flow across Three Accounting Cycles*

L.O. 2, 6, 7, 8, 10, 11

The following information describes the accounting events that affected Mason Manufacturing Company during its first three years of operation. Assume that all transactions are cash transactions.

Transactions for 2001
1. Started manufacturing company by issuing $1,000 common shares.
2. Purchased $500 of direct raw materials.
3. Used $400 of direct raw materials to produce inventory.
4. Paid $200 of direct labour cost to employees to make inventory.
5. Paid $100 to rent manufacturing facilities.
6. Finished work on inventory that cost $450.
7. Sold goods that cost $300 for $550.
8. Paid $185 for selling and administrative expenses.

Transactions for 2002
1. Acquired additional $200 of cash capital.
2. Purchased $600 of direct raw materials.
3. Used $650 of direct raw materials to produce inventory.
4. Paid $300 of direct labour cost to employees to make inventory.
5. Paid $120 to rent manufacturing facilities.
6. Finished work on inventory that cost $900.
7. Sold goods that cost $800 for $1,400.
8. Paid $250 for selling and administrative expenses.

Transactions for 2003
1. Paid a cash dividend of $250.
2. Purchased $700 of direct raw materials.
3. Used $600 of direct raw materials to produce inventory.
4. Paid $220 of direct labour cost to employees to make inventory.
5. Paid $140 to rent manufacturing facilities.
6. Finished work on inventory that cost $1,000.
7. Sold goods that cost $1,100 for $1,750.
8. Paid $355 for selling and administrative expenses.

Required
a. Open T-accounts and post transactions for 2001 to them.
b. Prepare a schedule of cost of goods manufactured and sold, an income statement, a balance sheet, and a cash flow statement as of the close of business on December 31, 2001.
c. Close appropriate accounts to the Retained Earnings account.
d. Repeat Requirements *a* through *c* for years 2002 and 2003.

L.O. 2, 6, 7, **PROBLEM 11-2A** *Manufacturing Cost Flow for Monthly and Annual Accounting Periods*
8, 9, 10, 11

Paula Wilson started Advanced Manufacturing Company to make universal television remote control devices that she had invented. The company's labour force consisted of part-time employees. The following information describes the accounting events that affected Advanced Manufacturing Company during its first year of operation. (Assume that all transactions are cash transactions unless otherwise stated.)

Transactions for January, 2001 First Month of Operation
1. Issued $5,000 of common shares.
2. Purchased $700 of direct raw materials and $100 of production supplies.
3. Used $400 direct raw materials.
4. Used 80 direct labour hours; production workers were paid $10 per hour.
5. Expected total overhead costs for the year to be $5,500, and direct labour hours used during the year to be 1,000. Calculate an overhead rate and apply the appropriate amount of overhead costs to work in process.
6. Paid $240 for salaries to administrative and sales staff.
7. Paid $25 for indirect manufacturing labour.
8. Paid $350 for rent and utilities on the manufacturing facilities.
9. Started and completed 100 remote controls; all costs were transferred from the Work in Process Inventory account to the Finished Goods Inventory account.
10. Sold 90 remote controls at a price of $30 each.

Transactions for Remainder of 2001
11. Acquired an additional $20,000 by issuing common shares.
12. Purchased $6,500 of direct raw materials and $1,500 of production supplies.
13. Used $5,000 of direct raw materials.
14. Paid production workers $10 per hour for 900 hours of work.
15. Applied the appropriate overhead cost to work in process inventory.
16. Paid $2,600 for salaries of administrative and sales staff.
17. Paid $400 of indirect manufacturing labour cost.
18. Paid $4,000 for rental and utility costs on the manufacturing facilities.
19. Transferred 950 additional remote controls that cost $16.40 each from Work in Process Inventory account to Finished Goods Inventory account.
20. Determined that $275 of production supplies was on hand at the end of the accounting period.
21. Sold 850 remote controls for $30 each.
22. Determine whether the overhead is over- or underapplied. Close the Manufacturing Overhead account to the Cost of Goods Sold account.
23. Close the revenue and expense accounts.

Required
a. Open T-accounts and post transactions to the accounts.
b. Prepare a schedule of cost of goods manufactured and sold, an income statement, a balance sheet, and a cash flow statement for 2001.

L.O. 2, 7, 9, **PROBLEM 11-3A** *Manufacturing Cost Flow for One-Year Period*
10, 11

Saint Francis Manufacturing started the 2004 accounting period with the following account balances:

Cash	$5,000
Common shares	10,000
Retained earnings	15,000
Raw materials inventory	6,000
Work in process inventory	4,000
Finished goods inventory (3,200 units @ $3.125)	10,000

Transactions during 2004
1. Purchased $14,000 of raw materials with cash.
2. Transferred $18,750 of raw materials to the production department.
3. Incurred and paid cash for 1,800 hours of direct labour @$8 per hour.
4. Applied overhead costs to the work in process inventory. The predetermined overhead rate is $8.25 per direct labour hour.

5. Incurred actual overhead costs of $15,000 cash.
6. Completed work on 12,000 units for $3.20 per unit.
7. Paid $7,000 in selling and administrative expenses in cash.
8. Sold 14,000 units for $55,000 cash revenue (assume FIFO cost flow).

Saint Francis charges overapplied or underapplied overhead directly to cost of goods sold.

Required
a. Open T-accounts and post the information for the 2004 transactions, including adjusting and closing entries, to the T-accounts.
b. Prepare a schedule of cost of goods manufactured and sold, an income statement, a balance sheet, and a cash flow statement for the 2004 accounting period.

PROBLEM 11-4A *Manufacturing Cost for One Accounting Cycle*   **L.O. 2, 6, 7,**
                                                                                    10, 11
The following trial balance was taken from the records of Kramer Manufacturing Company at the beginning of 2001:

Cash	$2,000	
Raw materials inventory	500	
Work in process inventory	800	
Finished goods inventory	1,400	
Property, plant, and equipment	5,000	
Accumulated amortization		$2,000
Common shares		3,600
Retained earnings		4,100
Total	$9,700	$9,700

Transactions for the Accounting Period
1. Kramer purchased $3,800 of direct raw materials and $200 of indirect raw materials on account. The indirect materials are capitalized in the Production Supplies account. Materials requisitions showed that $3,600 of direct raw materials had been used for production during the period. The use of indirect materials is determined at the end of the period by physically counting the supplies on hand.
2. By the end of the year, $3,500 of the accounts payable had been paid in cash.
3. During the year, direct labour amounted to 950 hours recorded in the Wages Payable account at $7 per hour.
4. By the end of the year, $6,000 of wages payable had been paid in cash.
5. At the beginning of the year, the company expected overhead cost for the period to be $4,200 and 1,000 direct labour hours to be worked. Overhead is allocated on the basis of direct labour hours, which, as indicated in Event 3, amounted to 950 for the year.
6. Administrative and sales expenses for the year amounted to $600 paid in cash.
7. Utilities and rent for production facilities amounted to $3,100 paid in cash.
8. Amortization on the plant and equipment used in production amounted to $1,000.
9. Assume that $8,000 of goods were completed during the year.
10. Assume that $8,500 of finished goods inventory was sold for $12,000 cash.
11. A count of the production supplies revealed a balance of $59 on hand at the end of the year.
12. Any over- or underapplied overhead is considered to be insignificant.

Required
a. Open T-accounts with the beginning balances shown in the preceding list and record all transactions for the year including closing entries to the T-accounts. (*Note:* Open new T-accounts as needed.)
b. Prepare a schedule of cost of goods manufactured and sold, an income statement, a balance sheet, and a cash flow statement.

PROBLEM 11-5A *Manufacturing Cost Flow for Multiple Accounting Cycles*   **L.O. 2, 6, 7,**
                                                                                    8, 9, 10, 11
The following events apply to Dominion Manufacturing Company. Assume that all transactions are cash transactions unless otherwise indicated.

Transactions for the 2004 Accounting Period
1. The company was started on January 1, 2004, when it acquired $180,000 cash from the owners.
2. The company purchased $40,000 of direct raw materials with cash and used $2,700 of these materials to make its products in January.

3. Employees provided 900 hours of labour at $4 per hour during January. Wages are paid in cash.

4. The estimated manufacturing overhead costs for 2004 were $72,000. Overhead is applied on the basis of direct labour hours. The company expected to use 12,000 direct labour hours during 2004. Calculate an overhead rate and apply the overhead for January to work in process inventory.

5. The employees completed work on all inventory items started in January. The cost of this production was transferred to the Finished Goods Inventory account. Determine the cost per unit of product produced in January, assuming that a total of 1,800 units of product were started and completed during the month.

6. The company used an additional $34,500 of direct raw materials and 11,500 hours of direct labour at $4 per hour during the remainder of 2004. Overhead was allocated on the basis of direct labour hours.

7. The company completed work on inventory items started between February 1 and December 31, and the cost of the completed inventory was transferred to the Finished Goods Inventory account. Determine the cost per unit for goods produced between February 1 and December 31, assuming that 23,000 units of inventory were produced. If the company desires to earn a gross profit of $3 per unit, what price per unit must it charge for the merchandise sold?

8. The company sold 22,000 units of inventory for cash at $9.50 per unit. Determine the number of units in ending inventory and the cost per unit incurred for this inventory.

9. Actual manufacturing overhead costs paid in cash were $73,000.

10. The company paid $42,000 cash for selling and administrative expenses.

11. Close the Manufacturing Overhead account.

12. Close the revenue and expense accounts.

Transactions for the 2005 Accounting Period

1. The company purchased $45,000 of direct raw materials with cash and used $2,850 of these materials to make products in January.

2. Employees provided 950 hours of labour at $4 per hour during January.

3. On January 1, 2005, Dominion hired a production supervisor at an expected cost of $1,200 cash per month. The company paid cash to purchase $5,000 of manufacturing supplies; it anticipated that $4,600 of these supplies would be used by year end. Other manufacturing overhead costs were expected to total $72,000. Overhead is applied on the basis of direct labour hours. Dominion expected to use 14,000 hours of direct labour during 2005. On the basis of this information, determine the total expected overhead cost for 2005. Calculate the predetermined overhead rate and apply the overhead cost for the January production.

4. The company recorded a $1,200 cash payment to the production supervisor.

5. The employees completed work on all inventory items started in January. The cost of this production was transferred to the Finished Goods Inventory account. Determine the cost per unit of product produced in January, assuming that 1,900 units of product were started and completed during the month.

6. During February 2005, the company used $3,000 of raw materials and 1,000 hours of labour at $4 per hour. Overhead was allocated on the basis of direct labour hours.

7. The company recorded a $1,200 cash payment to the production supervisor for February.

8. The employees completed work on all inventory items started in February; the cost of this production was transferred to the Finished Goods Inventory account. Determine the cost per unit of product produced in February, assuming that 2,000 units of product were started and completed during the month.

9. The company used an additional $36,000 of direct raw materials and 12,000 hours of direct labour at $4 per hour during the remainder of 2005. Overhead was allocated on the basis of direct labour hours.

10. The company recorded $12,000 of cash payments to the production supervisor for work performed between March 1 and December 31.

11. The company completed work on inventory items started between March 1 and December 31. The cost of the completed goods was transferred to the Finished Goods Inventory account. Compute the cost per unit of this inventory, assuming that there were 24,000 units of inventory produced.

12. The company sold 26,000 units of product for $9.75 cash per unit. Assume that the company uses the FIFO inventory cost flow method to determine the cost of goods sold.

13. The company paid $43,000 cash for selling and administrative expenses.

14. As of December 31, 2005, $500 of production supplies was on hand.

15. Actual cost of other manufacturing overhead was $71,000 cash.

16. Close the Manufacturing Overhead account.

17. Close the revenue and expense accounts.

Required

a. Open T-accounts and record the effects of the preceding events.

b. Prepare a schedule of cost of goods manufactured and sold, an income statement, a balance sheet, and a cash flow statement for both years.

PROBLEM 11-6A *Comprehensive Review Problem* **L.O. 10**

During their final year at Seneca College, two business students, Larry Ingram and Judy Brown, began a part-time business making personal computers. They bought the various components from a local supplier and assembled the machines in the basement of a friend's house. Their only cost was $400 for parts; they sold each computer for $700. They were able to make three machines per week and to sell them to fellow students. The activity was appropriately called Ingram Brown Computers (IBC). The product quality was good, and as graduation approached, orders were coming in much faster than IBC could fill them.

A national CA firm made Ms. Brown an attractive offer of employment, and a large electronic company was ready to hire Mr. Ingram. Students and faculty at Seneca College, however, encouraged the two to make IBC a full-time venture. The college administration had decided to require all students in the schools of business and engineering to buy their own computers beginning in the coming fall term. It was believed that the quality and price of the IBC machines would attract the college bookstore to sign a contract to buy a minimum of 1,000 units the first year for $600 each. The bookstore sales were likely to reach 2,000 units per year, but the manager would not make an initial commitment beyond 1,000.

The prospect of $600,000 in annual sales for IBC caused the two young entrepreneurs to wonder about the wisdom of accepting their job offers. Before making a decision, they decided to investigate the implications of making IBC a full-time operation. Their study provided the following information relating to the production of their computers:

Components from wholesaler	$400.00 per machine
Assembly labour	12.50 per hour
Manufacturing space rent	2,500.00 per month
Utilities	500.00 per month
Janitorial services	400.00 per month
Amortization of equipment	3,200.00 per year
Labour	2 hours per computer

The two owners expected to devote their time to the sales and administrative aspects of the business.

Required

a. Classify each cost item into the categories of direct materials, direct labour, and manufacturing overhead.

b. Classify each cost item as either variable or fixed.

c. What is the cost per computer if IBC produces 1,000 units per year? What is the cost per unit if IBC produces 2,000 units per year?

d. If the job offers for Mr. Ingram and Ms. Brown totaled $80,000, would you recommend that they accept the offers or proceed with plans to make IBC a full-time venture?

PROBLEM 11-7A *Absorption versus Variable Costing* **L.O. 12**

Saskatoon Manufacturing Company makes a product that sells for $18 per unit. Manufacturing costs for the product amount to $7 per unit variable, and $20,000 fixed. During the current accounting period, Saskatoon made 4,000 units of the product and sold 3,500 units.

Required

a. Prepare an absorption costing income statement.

b. Prepare a variable costing income statement.

c. Explain why the amount of net income on the absorption costing income statement differs from the amount of net income on the variable costing income statement. Your answer should include the amount of the inventory balance that would exist under the two costing approaches.

L.O. 12 PROBLEM 11-8A   *Absorption versus Variable Costing*

Classy Glass Company makes stained glass lamps. Each lamp that it sells for $350 per lamp requires $20 of direct materials and $80 of direct labour. Fixed overhead costs are expected to be $225,000 per year. Classy Glass expects to sell 1,000 lamps during the coming year.

Required

a. Prepare an income statement under absorption costing, assuming that Classy Glass makes 1,000, 1,250, and 1,500 lamps during the year.

b. Prepare an income statement under variable costing, assuming that Classy Glass makes 1,000, 1,250, and 1,500 lamps during the year.

c. Explain why Classy Glass may produce income statements under both absorption and variable costing formats. Your answer should include an explanation of the advantages and disadvantages associated with the use of the two reporting formats.

L.O. 12 PROBLEM 11-9A   *Absorption and Variable Costing*

Sanchez Manufacturing pays its production managers a bonus based on the company's profitability. During the two most recent accounting periods, the company maintained the same cost structure to manufacture its products.

Year	Units Produced	Units Sold
Production and Sales		
2001	4,000	4,000
2002	6,000	4,000
Cost Data		
Direct materials		$5 per unit
Direct labour		$8 per unit
Manufacturing overhead—variable		$4 per unit
Manufacturing overhead—fixed		$36,000
Variable selling & administrative expenses		$3 per unit sold
Fixed selling & administrative expenses		$20,000
(Assume that selling & administrative expenses are associated with goods sold.)		

Sanchez sells its products for $36 a unit.

Required

a. Prepare income statements based on absorption costing for the 2001 and 2002 accounting periods.

b. If Sanchez sold the same amount in 2001 and 2002, why did net income go up in 2002?

c. Discuss management's possible motivation for increasing production in 2002.

d. Determine the costs of ending inventory for 2002. Comment on the risks and costs associated with the accumulation of inventory.

e. On the basis of your answers to Requirements *b* and *c*, suggest a different income statement format. Prepare income statements for 2001 and 2002 under your suggested format.

PROBLEMS—SERIES B

L.O. 2, 6, 7, 8, 10, 11 PROBLEM 11-1B   *Manufacturing Cost Flow across Three Accounting Cycles*

The following information describes the accounting events that affected Jaenicke Manufacturing Company during its first three years of operation. Assume that all transactions are cash transactions.

Transactions for 2001

1. Started manufacturing company by issuing $2,000 common shares.
2. Purchased production equipment for $1,000.
3. Purchased $800 of direct raw materials.
4. Used $600 of direct raw materials to produce inventory.
5. Paid $500 of direct labour cost to employees to make inventory.

6. Paid $100 for indirect labour.
7. Recorded $200 amortization on the production equipment.
8. Finished work on inventory that cost $900.
9. Sold goods that cost $600 for $800.
10. Paid $50 for selling and administrative expenses.

Transactions for 2002
1. Acquired additional $500 of cash capital.
2. Purchased $800 of direct raw materials.
3. Used $700 of direct raw materials to produce inventory.
4. Paid $600 of direct labour cost to employees to make inventory.
5. Paid $120 for indirect labour.
6. Recorded $200 amortization on the production equipment.
7. Finished work on inventory that cost $1,500.
8. Sold goods that cost $1,400 for $1,600.
9. Paid $100 for selling and administrative expenses.

Transactions for 2003
1. Paid a cash dividend of $400.
2. Purchased $500 of direct raw materials.
3. Used $800 of direct raw materials to produce inventory.
4. Paid $300 of direct labour cost to employees to make inventory.
5. Paid $50 for indirect labour.
6. Recorded $200 amortization on the production equipment.
7. Finished work on inventory that cost $1,650.
8. Sold goods that cost $1,800 for $2,200.
9. Paid $200 for selling and administrative expenses.

Required
a. Open T-accounts and post transactions for 2001 to them.
b. Prepare a schedule of cost of goods manufactured and sold, an income statement, a balance sheet, and a cash flow statement as of the close of business 2001.
c. Close appropriate accounts to the Retained Earnings account.
d. Repeat Requirements *a* through *c* for years 2002 and 2003.

PROBLEM 11-2B   *Manufacturing Cost for One Accounting Cycle*   **L.O. 2, 6, 7, 10, 11**

The following trial balance was taken from the records of Maslow Manufacturing Company at the beginning of 2001:

Cash	$ 2,800	
Raw materials inventory	200	
Work in process inventory	600	
Finished goods inventory	400	
Property, plant, & equipment	7,000	
Accumulated amortization		$ 2,000
Common shares		4,200
Retained earnings		4,800
Total	$11,000	$11,000

Transactions for the Accounting Period
1. Maslow purchased $4,600 of direct raw materials and $500 of indirect raw materials on account. The indirect materials are capitalized in the Production Supplies account. Materials requisitions showed that $4,000 of direct raw materials had been used for production during the period. The use of indirect materials is determined at the end of the period by physically counting the supplies on hand at the end of the period.
2. By the end of the accounting period, $3,500 of the accounts payable had been paid in cash.
3. During the year, direct labour amounted to 1,200 hours recorded in the Wages Payable account at $6 per hour.

4. By the end of the accounting period, $6,500 of the Wages Payable account had been paid in cash.
5. At the beginning of the accounting period, the company expected overhead cost for the period to be $5,500 and 1,250 direct labour hours to be worked. Overhead is applied on the basis of direct labour hours, which, as indicated in Event 3, amounted to 1,200 for the year.
6. Administrative and sales expenses for the period amounted to $1,400 paid in cash.
7. Utilities and rent for production facilities amounted to $3,000 paid in cash.
8. Amortization on the plant and equipment used in production amounted to $2,000.
9. Assume that $15,000 of goods were completed during the period.
10. Assume that $10,000 of finished goods inventory was sold for $14,000 cash.
11. A count of the production supplies revealed a balance of $150 on hand at the end of the accounting period.
12. Any over- or underapplied overhead is considered to be insignificant.

Required

a. Open T-accounts with the beginning balances shown in the preceding list and record all transactions for the period including closing entries to the T-accounts. (*Note:* Open new T-accounts as needed.)
b. Prepare a schedule of cost of goods manufactured and sold, an income statement, a balance sheet, and a cash flow statement.

L.O. 2, 6, 7, 10, 11   **PROBLEM 11-3B**   *Manufacturing Cost Flow for One-Year Period*

Dexter Manufacturing started the 2005 accounting period with the following account balances:

Cash	$25,000
Common shares	20,000
Retained earnings	15,000
Raw Materials inventory	2,000
Work in process inventory	5,000
Finished goods inventory (500 units @ $6/unit)	3,000

Transactions during 2005
1. Purchased $15,000 of raw materials with cash.
2. Transferred $10,000 of raw materials to the production department.
3. Incurred and paid cash for 800 hours of direct labour at $10 per hour.
4. Applied overhead costs to the work in process inventory. The company uses a predetermined overhead rate of $15 per direct labour hour.
5. Incurred actual overhead costs of $13,000 cash.
6. Completed 3,000 units of product for a $6 cost per unit.
7. Paid $4,000 in selling and administrative expenses in cash.
8. Sold 2,000 units of product for $25,000 cash.

Dexter charges any overapplied or underapplied overhead directly to cost of goods sold.

Required

a. Open T-accounts and post the information for the 2005 transactions, including adjusting and closing entries to the T-accounts.
b. Prepare a schedule of cost of goods manufactured and sold, an income statement, a balance sheet, and a cash flow statement for the 2005 accounting period.

L.O. 2, 6, 7, 10, 11   **PROBLEM 11-4B**   *Manufacturing Cost Flow for Monthly and Annual Accounting Periods*

Old World Masters Manufacturing Company (OWMC) manufactures puzzles that depict the works of famous artists. The company rents a small factory and uses local labour on a part-time basis. The following information describes the accounting events that affected OWMC during its first year of operation. (Assume that all transactions are cash transactions unless otherwise stated.)

Transactions for First Month of Operation 2001
1. Issued $15,000 of common shares.
2. Purchased $4,000 of direct raw materials and $300 of indirect raw materials. Indirect materials are recorded in a Production Supplies account.

3. Used $3,896 of direct raw materials.

4. Used 700 direct labour hours; production workers were paid $6 per hour.

5. Expected total overhead costs for the year to be $16,800 and direct labour hours used during the year to be 9,600. Calculate an overhead rate and apply the appropriate amount of overhead costs to work in process.

6. Paid $800 for salaries to administrative and sales staff.

7. Paid $700 for indirect manufacturing labour.

8. Paid $600 for rent and utilities on the manufacturing facilities.

9. Started and completed 956 puzzles; all costs were transferred from the Work in Process Inventory account to the Finished Goods Inventory account.

10. Sold 800 puzzles at a price of $12 each.

Transactions for Remainder of 2001

11. Acquired an additional $150,000 by issuing common shares.

12. Purchased $46,000 of direct raw materials and $4,000 of indirect raw materials.

13. Used $41,050 of direct raw materials.

14. Paid production workers $6 per hour for 9,800 hours of work.

15. Applied the appropriate overhead cost to the work in process inventory.

16. Paid $8,800 for salaries of administrative and sales staff.

17. Paid $7,700 for the salary of the production supervisor.

18. Paid $6,600 for rental and utility costs on the manufacturing facilities.

19. Transferred 9,000 additional puzzles that cost $9.75 each from Work in Process Inventory to Finished Goods Inventory accounts.

20. Determined that $2,900 of production supplies was on hand at the end of the accounting period.

21. Sold 8,000 puzzles for $12 each.

22. Determine whether overhead is over- or underapplied. Close the manufacturing overhead account to cost of goods sold.

23. Close the revenue and expense accounts.

Required

a. Open T-accounts and post transactions to the accounts.

b. Prepare a schedule of cost of goods manufactured and sold, an income statement, a balance sheet, and a cash flow statement for 2001.

PROBLEM 11-5B   *Manufacturing Cost Flow for Multiple Accounting Cycles*

L.O. 2, 6, 7, 8, 9, 10, 11

The following events apply to Illini Manufacturing Company. Assume that all transactions are cash transactions unless otherwise indicated.

Transactions for the 2006 Accounting Period

1. The company was started on January 1, 2006, when it acquired $500,000 cash from the owners.

2. The company purchased $300,000 of direct raw materials with cash and used $26,000 of these materials to make its products in January.

3. Employees provided 1,500 hours of labour at $8 per hour during January. Wages are paid in cash.

4. The estimated manufacturing overhead costs for 2006 are $650,000. Overhead is applied on the basis of direct labour costs. The company expected $130,000 of direct labour costs during 2006. Record applied overhead for January.

5. By the end of January, the employees completed work on all inventory items started in January. The cost of this production was transferred to the Finished Goods Inventory account. Determine the cost per unit of product produced in January, assuming that a total of 10,000 units of product were started and completed during the month.

6. The company used an additional $234,000 of direct raw materials and 13,500 hours of direct labour at $8 per hour during the remainder of 2006. Overhead was allocated on the basis of direct labour cost.

7. The company completed work on inventory items started between February 1 and December 31, and the cost of the completed inventory was transferred to the Finished Goods Inventory account. Determine the cost per unit for goods produced between February 1 and December 31, assuming that 90,000 units of inventory were produced. If the company desires to earn a gross profit of $3 per unit, what price per unit must it charge for the merchandise sold?

8. The company sold 60,000 units of inventory for cash at $12.80 per unit. Determine the number of units in ending inventory and the cost per unit of this inventory.

9. Actual manufacturing overhead costs paid in cash were $610,000.
10. The company paid $150,000 cash for selling and administrative expenses.
11. Close the Manufacturing Overhead account.
12. Close the revenue and expense accounts.

Transactions for the 2007 Accounting Period

1. The company acquired $300,000 cash from the owners.
2. The company purchased $200,000 of direct raw materials with cash and used $20,800 of these materials to make products in January.
3. Employees provided 1,200 hours of labour at $8 per hour during January.
4. On January 1, 2006, Illini expected the production facilities to cost $1,500 cash per month. The company paid cash to purchase $7,000 of manufacturing supplies, and it anticipated that $7,000 of these supplies would be used by year end. Other manufacturing overhead costs were expected to total $455,000. Overhead is applied on the basis of direct labour costs. Illini expects direct labour costs of $80,000 during 2007. On the basis of this information, determine the total expected overhead cost for 2007. Calculate the predetermined overhead rate and apply the overhead cost for the January production. Also, record the purchase of manufacturing supplies.
5. The company recorded a $1,500 cash payment for production facilities in January.
6. In January, the employees completed work on all inventory items started in January. The cost of this production was transferred to the Finished Goods Inventory account. Determine the cost per unit of product produced in January assuming that a total of 8,000 units of product was started and completed during the month.
7. During February 2007, the company used $15,600 of raw materials and 900 hours of labour at $8 per hour. Overhead was allocated on the basis of direct labour cost.
8. The company recorded a $1,500 cash payment for production facilities in February.
9. In February, the employees completed work on all inventory items started in February; the cost of this production was transferred to the Finished Goods Inventory account. Determine the cost per unit of product produced in February, assuming that 6,000 units of product were started and completed during the month.
10. The company used an additional $143,000 of direct raw materials and 8,250 hours of direct labour at $8 per hour during the remainder of 2007. Overhead was allocated on the basis of direct labour cost.
11. The company recorded $15,000 of cash payments for production facilities for work performed between March 1 and December 31.
12. The company completed work on inventory items started between March 1 and December 31. The cost of the completed goods was transferred to the Finished Goods Inventory account. Compute the cost per unit of this inventory, assuming that 55,000 units of inventory were produced.
13. The company sold 90,000 units of product for $14 per unit cash. Assume that the company uses the FIFO inventory cost flow method to determine the cost of goods sold.
14. The company paid $130,000 cash for selling and administrative expenses.
15. As of December 31, 2007, $1,200 of production supplies were on hand.
16. Actual cost of other manufacturing overhead was $461,000 cash.
17. Close the Manufacturing Overhead account.
18. Close the revenue and expense accounts.

Required

a. Open T-accounts and record the effects of the preceding events.
b. Prepare a schedule of cost of goods manufactured and sold, an income statement, a balance sheet, and a cash flow statement for both years.

L.O. 10 PROBLEM 11-6B *Comprehensive Review Problem*

Deanna Mueller has worked as the plant manager of Stereo Plus, a large manufacturing company, for 10 years. The company produces CD players for automotive vehicles and sells them to some of the largest car manufacturers in the country. Ms. Mueller has always toyed with the idea of starting her own stereo manufacturing business. With her experience and knowledge, she is certain that she can produce superior stereos at a low cost. Ms. Mueller's business strategy would be to market the product to smaller and more specialized car manufacturers. Her potential market would consist of the car manufacturers who sell at a lower volume to discriminating customers. She is confident that she could compete in this market that values low cost and quality production. She would not compete with Stereo Plus or the other large stereo producers that dominate the market made up of the largest automotive producers.

Ms. Mueller already has firm orders for 800 stereos from several automotive producers. On the basis of the contacts that she has made working for Stereo Plus, Ms. Mueller is confident that she can make and sell 2,000 stereos during the first year of operation. However, before making a final decision, she decides to investigate the profitability of starting her own business. Relevant information follows:

Components from wholesaler	$45.00 per stereo
Assembly labour	$10.50 per hour
Rent of manufacturing buildings	$12,000.00 per year
Utilities	$300.00 per month
Sales salaries	$600.00 per month
Amortization of equipment	$2,000.00 per year
Labour	3 hours per stereo

During the first year, Ms. Mueller expects to be able to produce the stereos with only two production workers and a part-time salesperson to market the product. Ms. Mueller expects to devote her time to the administrative aspects of the business and to provide back-up support in the production work. She has decided not to pay herself a salary but to live off the profits of the business.

Required

a. Classify each cost item into the categories of direct materials, direct labour, and manufacturing overhead.
b. Classify each cost item as either variable or fixed.
c. What is the cost per stereo if Ms. Mueller's company produces 800 units per year? What is the unit cost if the company produces 2,000 units per year?
d. If Ms. Mueller's job presently pays her $15,000 a year, would you recommend that she proceed with the plans to start the new company if she could sell stereos for $120 each?

PROBLEM 11-7B *Absorption versus Variable Costing*   **L.O. 12**

Vincent Manufacturing Company makes a product that sells for $25 per unit. Manufacturing costs for the product amount to $12 per unit variable, and $80,000 fixed. During the current accounting period, Vincent made 8,000 units of the product and sold 7,600 units.

Required

a. Prepare an absorption costing income statement.
b. Prepare a variable costing income statement.
c. Explain why the amount of net income on the absorption costing income statement differs from the amount of net income on the variable costing income statement. Your answer should include the amount of the inventory balance that would exist under the two costing approaches.

PROBLEM 11-8B *Absorption versus Variable Costing*   **L.O. 12**

Hickory Ridge Company makes ladderback chairs that it sells for $250 per chair. Each chair requires $35 of direct materials and $90 of direct labour. Fixed overhead costs are expected to be $150,000 per year. Hickory Ridge expects to sell 1,500 chairs during the coming year.

Required

a. Prepare an income statement under absorption costing, assuming that Hickory Ridge makes 1,500, 2,000, and 2,500 chairs during the year.
b. Prepare an income statement under variable costing, assuming that Hickory Ridge makes 1,500, 2,000, and 2,500 chairs during the year.
c. Explain why Hickory Ridge may produce income statements under both absorption and variable costing formats. Your answer should include an explanation of the advantages or disadvantages associated with the use of the two reporting formats.

PROBLEM 11-9B *Absorption and Variable Costing*   **L.O. 12**

Gerdsen Manufacturing pays its production managers a bonus based on the company's profitability. During the two most recent years, the company maintained the same cost structure to manufacture its products.

Year	Units Produced	Units Sold
Production and Sales		
2001	5,000	5,000
2002	7,000	5,000
Cost Data		
Direct materials		$4 per unit
Direct labour		$6 per unit
Manufacturing overhead—variable		$2 per unit
Manufacturing overhead—fixed		$45,500
Variable selling & administrative expenses		$2 per unit sold
Fixed selling & administrative expenses		$15,000
(Assume that selling & administrative expenses are associated with goods sold.)		

Gerdsen's sales revenue for both years was $140,000.

Required

a. Prepare income statements on the basis of absorption costing for the years 2001 and 2002.
b. If Gerdsen sold the same amount in 2001 and 2002, why did net income go up in 2002?
c. Discuss management's possible motivation for increasing production in 2002.
d. Determine the costs of ending inventory for 2002. Comment on the risks and costs associated with the accumulation of inventory.
e. On the basis of your answers to Requirements *b* and *c*, suggest a different income statement format and prepare income statements for 2001 and 2002 under your suggested format.

ANALYZE, THINK, COMMUNICATE

ACT 11-1 BUSINESS APPLICATIONS CASE *Predetermined Overhead Rate*

Sabain Company makes frozen dinners that it sells to short-haul passenger railroad companies. The average materials cost per meal is $1.30, and the average labour cost is $0.80. Sabain incurs approximately $240,000 of fixed manufacturing overhead costs annually. The marketing department estimated that Sabain would sell approximately 240,000 meals during the coming year. Unfortunately, Sabain has experienced a steady decline in sales even though the rail industry has had a steady increase in the number of passengers. The chief accountant, Dillard Smith, was overheard saying that when he calculated the predetermined overhead rate, he deliberately lowered the estimated number of meals expected to be sold because he had lost faith in the marketing department's ability to deliver on its estimated sales numbers. Mr. Smith explained, "This way, our actual cost is always below the estimated cost. It is about the only way we continue to make a profit." Indeed, the company had a significant amount of overapplied overhead at the end of each year.

Required

a. Explain how the overapplied overhead affects the determination of the amount of year-end net income.
b. Assume that Mr. Smith used 200,000 meals as the estimated sales to calculate the predetermined overhead rate. Determine the difference in expected cost per meal he calculated and the cost per meal that would result if the marketing department's estimate (240,000 units) had been used.
c. Assuming that Sabain uses a cost-plus-pricing policy, speculate how Mr. Smith's behaviour could be contributing to the decline in sales.

ACT 11-2 GROUP ASSIGNMENT *Schedule of Cost of Goods Manufactured and Sold*

The information described in the following was taken from the accounts of Reynard Manufacturing Company for 2002.

Required

a. Divide the class into groups of four or five students per group and organize the groups into three sections. Assign Task 1 to the first section of groups, Task 2 to the second section, and Task 3 to the third section.

Group Tasks

1. The ending balance in the Raw Materials Inventory account was $208,000. During the accounting period, Reynard used $2,348,900 of raw materials inventory and purchased $2,200,000 of raw materials. Determine the beginning raw materials inventory balance.

2. During the accounting period, Reynard used $2,348,900 of raw materials inventory and $2,780,200 of direct labour. Actual overhead costs were $3,300,000. Ending work in process inventory amounted to $450,000, and cost of goods manufactured amounted to $8,389,100. Determine the amount of the balance in the beginning Work in Process Inventory account.

3. The cost of goods manufactured was $8,389,100, and the cost of goods sold was $8,419,100. Ending finished goods inventory amounted to $360,000. Determine the amount of the balance in the beginning Finished Goods Inventory account.

b. Select a spokesperson from each section. Use input from the three spokespersons to prepare a schedule of cost of goods manufactured and sold. The spokesperson from the first section should provide information for the computation of the cost of raw materials used. The spokesperson from the second section should provide information for the determination of the cost of goods manufactured. The spokesperson from the third section should provide information for the determination of the cost of goods sold.

WRITING ASSIGNMENT *Inventory Cost Flow in Manufacturing Environment*

ACT 11-3

Barret Cameron, a student in Professor Wagner's managerial accounting course, asked the following question. "In the first accounting course, the teacher said inventory costs flow on a FIFO, LIFO, or weighted average pattern. Now you are telling us inventory costs flow through raw materials, to work in process, and then to finished goods. Is this manufacturing stuff another new cost flow method or what?"

Required
Assume that you are Professor Wagner. Write a brief memo responding to Mr. Cameron's question.

ETHICAL DILEMMA *Absorption Costing*

ACT 11-4

Martin Mendez may become a rich man. He is the creative force behind Dynamic Drives, a new company. Dynamic makes external drives that permit computer users to store large amounts of information on small floppy diskettes. Dynamic has experienced tremendous growth since its inception three years ago. Investors have recognized the company's potential, and its stock is currently selling at 60 times projected earnings. More specifically, the company's 2001 earnings forecast shows estimated income to be $0.20 cents per share. Accordingly, the current market price is $12 per share ($0.20 × 60). Mr. Mendez has stock options permitting him to buy 2,000,000 shares for $8 per share on January 1, 2002. This means that he could earn $4 per share on the options. In other words, he would buy at $8 per share and sell it at $12 per share. As a result, Mr. Mendez would earn $8,000,000 ($4 × 2,000,000 shares).

Unfortunately, weak economies in foreign countries have resulted in low demand for Dynamic's products in international markets. Company insiders are painfully aware that Dynamic Drives is going to be unable to meet its projected income numbers. If actual earnings fall short of the projected earnings, the market will manifest its disappointment by discounting the share price. Mr. Mendez is concerned that the value of his share options could plummet.

At its inception three years ago, Dynamic invested heavily in manufacturing equipment. Indeed, expecting dramatic growth, the company purchased a significant amount of excess capacity. As a result, the company incurs approximately $19,200,000 in fixed manufacturing costs annually. If Dynamic continues to produce at its current level, it will make and sell approximately 800,000 drives during 2001. In the face of declining sales, Mr. Mendez has issued a puzzling order to his production manager. Specifically, he has told the production manager to increase production so that 1,200,000 drives will be completed during 2001. Mr. Mendez has explained that he believes the economies in foreign countries will surge ahead in 2002 and that he wants Dynamic to have the inventory necessary to satisfy the demand.

Required

a. Suppose that actual earnings for 2001 are $0.12 per share. The market becomes disappointed, and the price earnings ratio falls to 40 times earnings. What is the value of Mr. Mendez's share options under these circumstances?

b. Determine the impact on income reported in 2001 if production is 800,000 units versus 1,200,000 units.

c. Why would Mr. Mendez order the increase in production?

d. Identify the features described in this case that could motivate criminal and ethical misconduct. (It may be helpful to reread the ethics material in Chapter 1 before attempting to satisfy this requirement.)

ACT 11-5 SPREADSHEET ASSIGNMENT   *Using Excel*

Refer to Problem 11–6. Assume that IBC plans to produce and sell 1,600 computers.

Required

a. Construct a spreadsheet to calculate the cost of goods manufactured and the cost per unit for IBC. Use formulas in the schedule so that the cost of goods manufactured will automatically be calculated as you change the number of units sold.

b. Add an abbreviated income statement to your spreadsheet that incorporates the cost from Requirement *a*.

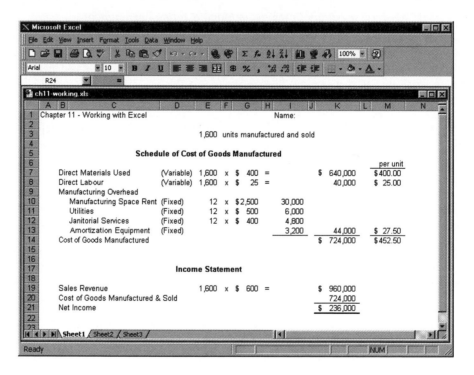

Spreadsheet Tip

Build the spreadsheet so that the number of units in Cell E3 can be changed and cost of goods manufactured and net income will be recalculated automatically.

ACT 11-6 SPREADSHEET ASSIGNMENT   *Mastering Excel*

Streezak Manufacturing Company, which sold 16,000 units of product at $20 per unit, collected the following information regarding three different levels of production:

Inventory Costs

Fixed overhead	$100,000	$100,000	$100,000
Number of units produced	16,000	20,000	25,000
Fixed overhead per unit	$6.25	$5.00	$4.00
Variable manufacturing costs	$12.00	$12.00	$12.00
Full absorption cost per unit	$18.25	$17.00	$16.00

Required

a. Construct a spreadsheet that includes the preceding data in the top of the spreadsheet. The third row (overhead per unit) and fifth row (cost per unit) should be based on formulas.

b. Include absorption costing income statements at these three levels of production as in Exhibit 11–11. Use formulas so that the number of units produced in the preceding table can be changed and net income will be recalculated automatically.

c. Include variable costing income statements at these three levels of production as in Exhibit 11–12. Use formulas so that the number of units produced in the preceding table can be changed and net income will be recalculated automatically.

Job-Order, Process, and Hybrid Cost Systems

Learning Objectives

After completing this chapter, you should be able to:

1 Distinguish between job-order and process cost systems.

2 Identify product cost flows through a job-order cost system.

3 Identify product cost flows through a process cost system.

4 Distinguish between raw materials cost and transferred-in cost.

5 Understand how hybrid accounting systems can be created by combining different components of job-order and process cost systems.

6 Identify the various forms of documentation used in a job-order cost system.

7 Understand how accounting events in a job-order system affect financial statements.

8 Understand how accounting events in a process cost system affect financial statements.

9 Convert partially completed units into equivalent whole units.

the *curious* manager

J. Caputo/Liaison

Suppose that a division of Ford Motor Company incurred approximately $76,500,000 of production cost in the process of making vehicles during the month of August. Assume that the division completed construction on 5,000 vehicles during the month and that 200 vehicles were in different stages of production at the end of the month. How would Ford managers decide the amount of the total production cost that should be charged to the partially completed vehicles? On what financial statement should the cost of these partially completed vehicles be shown?

Benchmore Boat Company made five boats during the current year, and Janis Juice Company made 500,000 cans of apple juice during the same year. Determining the cost of a boat made by Benchmore requires a different cost system from the one Janis used to determine the cost of a can of juice. Each boat has unique characteristics that affect its cost. For example, making an 80-foot yacht requires more labour and materials than making a 30-foot sailboat. Benchmore needs a system that traces product costs to individual inventory items (i.e., specific boats). *Different boats should have different costs. In contrast, one can of juice is virtually identical to another. Accordingly, each can of juice should have the same cost. Unfortunately, costs are frequently distributed unevenly over the units of production. Suppose that Janis pays $2,000 per month to rent its manufacturing facility. In a month when Janis makes 40,000 cans of juice, the rent cost is $0.05 per can ($2,000 ÷ 40,000 cans). However, if Janis makes 20,000 cans, the cost per can increases to $0.10 ($2,000 ÷ 20,000 cans).* Unlike Benchmore, Janis needs a cost system that distributes costs evenly across its total production (i.e., number of cans of juice made during an accounting period).

▌ Cost Systems

As the preceding paragraph suggests, the type of product affects the accounting system used to determine its cost. The two most common types of costing systems are a job-order cost system and a process cost system. Some companies use a hybrid costing system that incorporates some combination of the procedures used in job-order and process systems. The following section of the text will discuss the types of products most suited to each costing system. In addition, the accounting procedures used in each type of costing system will be explained.

Cost Systems and Type of Product

LO1

Distinguish between job-order and process cost systems.

A cost accounting system designed to accumulate costs by individual products is a **job-order cost system**. The boats made by Benchmore represent only one example of the products that are suited to job-order costing. Other examples include movies made by Walt Disney Productions, office buildings constructed by Rust Engineering, and airplanes made by Bombardier. Job-order cost systems apply not only to individual inventory items but also to groups or batches of inventory items. For example, the Brittwell Shirt Company may account for the production of a special order of 20,000 shirts sold to the Canadian military as a single job. Accordingly, job-order cost systems are employed when costs are accumulated by individual products or batches of products.

A cost system designed to distribute costs evenly over a homogeneous product line is a **process cost system**. In addition to beverage companies, such as Janis, process costing is frequently used by oil companies, such as Imperial Oil, chemical companies, such as Dow Chemical, food processors, such as General Mills, and paint manufacturers, such as Sherwin-Williams. The products made by these companies are normally produced in mass quantities through a continuous process that provides similar inputs to each unit produced. Under these circumstances, the *per-unit product cost* is normally determined by dividing the total product cost by the number of units of product made during some designated span of time. Accordingly, process cost systems *average* product costs across the total number of items made.

To a lesser extent, cost averaging is also used in a job-order costing system. In all situations, some costs cannot be directly traced to particular jobs. Such items as indirect materials, indirect labour, utilities, rent, amortization, and so on are not cost effectively traceable, and so these costs are normally added together and averaged across some common measure of production, such as labour hours, machine hours, area, and so forth, to determine an overhead rate that is used to allocate the total cost to individual products. Furthermore, when jobs are organized in batches of a number of similar products, the cost per unit is determined by dividing the total cost of the job by the number of units of product in the batch. Although more effort is made to trace cost to specific products under a job-order system, *both* job-order and process costing require *some form of cost averaging*.

Job-Order Cost Flow

LO2

Identify product cost flows through a job-order cost system.

The accounting systems used for job-order and process costing have been patterned after the physical flow of products as they move through the production process. For example, Benchmore Boat Company builds its boats on a custom basis. It starts each boat as a separate project when raw materials are requisitioned from the materials supply centre. Designated workers are assigned to work on specific boats. Finally, indirect (i.e., overhead) costs are assigned to each boat on the basis of the size of the project as measured by the hours of labour required to build the boat.

Benchmore uses a *job-order cost system* to accumulate cost in a manner that is consistent with the way the boats are made; for example, each boat is given a specific job identification number. The inventory accounts are maintained on a perpetual basis. Product costs are accumulated separately by designated job identification number. The costs of each boat move through the Work-in-Process Inventory to

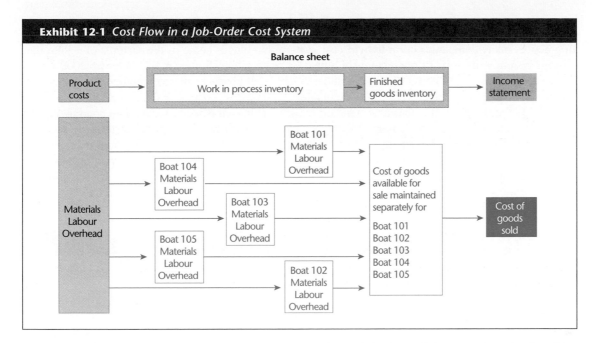

Exhibit 12-1 *Cost Flow in a Job-Order Cost System*

the Finished Goods Inventory accounts and out to Cost of Goods Sold parallel to actual production flow. Exhibit 12–1 depicts the flow of product costs for five boats that Benchmore plans to construct and sell. Note carefully that the Work in Process Inventory is composed of distinct jobs, each of which contains the costs of materials, labour, and overhead uniquely associated with a specific inventory item. In other words, one Work in Process Inventory control account has numerous subsidiary accounts. Likewise, Finished Goods Inventory contains subsidiary accounts that show the separate cost of each boat.

Process Cost Flow

Process cost systems utilize the same general ledger accounts as those used by job-order cost systems. Product costs flow from Raw Materials Inventory to Work in Process Inventory on to Finished Goods Inventory and then out to Cost of Goods Sold. The primary difference between the two systems centres on accounting for the work in process inventory. Instead of accumulating product costs by jobs in a single Work in Process Inventory control account, a process cost system accumulates these costs by departments, each of which has its own separate Work in Process Inventory account. Products normally move through a series of work centres on a continuous basis. For example, Janis Juice Company uses three distinct processes to produce its cans of apple juice. Direct raw materials enter the extraction department where juice concentrate is collected from whole fruit. The juice extract then passes to the mixing department where water, sugar, food colouring, and preservatives are added. The juice mixture then moves to the packaging department where it is poured into cans and boxed for shipment. The cost of all goods that move through a processing centre (i.e., department) is charged to that centre's Work in Process Inventory account.

Parallel to the pattern of the physical flow, cost accumulations are passed from one department to the next. In essence, the finished products of one department become the raw materials of the next department. The costs transferred from one department to the next are **transferred-in costs**. Transferred-in costs are combined with the additional materials, labour, and overhead costs incurred by each succeeding department. Accordingly, when goods are complete, the total product cost of all departments is transferred to Finished Goods Inventory. Exhibit 12–2 illustrates the cost flow for the process costing system used by Janis Juice Company. To understand the distinction between job-order and process costing systems, you should carefully compare the cost flow patterns depicted in Exhibits 12–1 and 12–2.

LO3
Identify product cost flows through a process cost system.

LO4
Distinguish between raw materials cost and transferred-in cost.

Hybrid Accounting Systems

LO5

Understand how hybrid accounting systems can be created by combining different components of job-order and process cost systems.

In practice, many companies use a **hybrid cost system** that blends some of the features of a job-order costing system with some of the features of a process cost system. For example, Gateway 2000 makes hundreds of thousands of computers with standard features. It produces these computers through a continuous-flow assembly line process that is compatible with process costing. Each unit requires the same amount of labour to assemble the same standard set of parts into finished products (i.e., computers) that are ready made for immediate delivery. However, Gateway also accepts orders for customized products that have unique features. For example, some customers may want a larger monitor, more memory, or a faster processor than the standard model has. Gateway accommodates these requests by customizing the products as they move through the production process. The customized features require cost-tracing features commonly associated with job-order costing. Accordingly, Gateway uses a hybrid costing system that combines some of the features of both process and job-order cost systems.

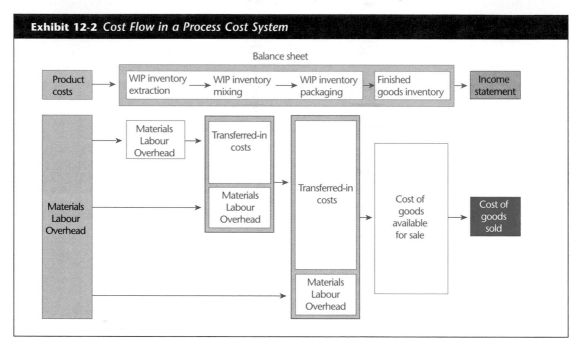

Exhibit 12-2 *Cost Flow in a Process Cost System*

Documentation in a Job-Order Cost System

LO6

Identify the various forms of documentation used in a job-order cost system.

In a job-order cost system, product costs are accumulated on a **job cost sheet**, also called a *job-order cost sheet* or a *job record*. A separate job cost sheet is prepared for each individual job. As each job moves through the various stages of production, detailed information regarding the cost of materials, labour, and overhead is added to the job cost sheet. Accordingly, when a particular job is finished, the accompanying job cost sheet contains a summary of all costs incurred to complete that job.

The information recorded on the job cost sheet has two primary source documents. The first is a **materials requisition** form. Before a designated job can be started, the job supervisor prepares a list of materials that are needed to begin work. The mechanism used to requisition the necessary materials from the materials supply centre depends on the level of technology present in the manufacturing environment. Some companies create a paper trail by delivering hard-copy documents to and from the different departments, but most modern businesses deliver requests electronically through a network of computers. Regardless of whether the information is maintained on paper documents or stored electronically, the information regarding material requisitions for each job is communicated to the accounting department where it is summarized on the job cost sheet.

©Spencer Grant/ PhotoEdit

The second source document for the job cost sheet is a **work ticket**, sometimes called a *time card*. The work ticket includes space for the job number, employee identification, and work description. The amount of time spent on each job is recorded on the work ticket, which is forwarded to the accounting department, where the wage rates are recorded and the amount of labour cost is computed on the job cost sheet. Again, information gathering can be accomplished manually or electronically. Regardless of the form used, information regarding direct labour costs is collected for each individual job and added to that job's cost sheet.

Finally, each job cost sheet provides space for the inclusion of the amount of applied overhead. The job cost sheets are maintained perpetually with new cost data being added as work on the job progresses. Accordingly, a prorated share of the estimated overhead cost is systematically added to the cost sheet through the use of a predetermined overhead rate. Exhibit 12–3 shows a job cost sheet with accompanying materials requisition forms and work tickets for Benchmore Boat Company's job-order identification number for Boat 101.

Exhibit 12-3 *Job-Order Cost Sheet and Source Documents*

Job Cost Sheet

Job Order No. Boat 101   Customer Name: Bill Clinton

Due Date: 03/15/2003   Date Started: 01/01/2002   Date Finished: 12/31/2002

Direct Materials		Direct Labour			Applied Overhead		
Req. No.	Cost	Ticket	Hours	Cost	Rate	Hours	Cost
24585	7,100	367	1,400	9,100	3.90	1,400	5,460
24600	5,600	360	1,600	10,400	3.90	1,600	6,240
24609	6,100						
Total	18,800	Total		19,500	Total		11,700

Cost summary

Direct materials	$18,800
Direct Labour	19,500
Overhead	11,700
Total	**$50,000**

Material requisitions		
	Date	Quantity
Package K	1/1	Mixed
Package R	2/1	Mixed
Package T	3/1	Mixed
Information transferred electronically		

Work tickets		
	Date	Hours
Process 1	1/30	1,400
Process 2	2/28	1,600
Information transferred electronically		

Job-Order Cost System Illustrated

LO7

Understand how accounting events in a job-order system affect financial statements.

To illustrate the use of a job-order cost system by a business, we analyze the operations of Benchmore Boat Company during its 2003 accounting period. The company's beginning account balances for 2003 are shown in Exhibit 12–4.

Benchmore's 2003 accounting events are described next. The events have been recorded in ledger T-accounts shown in Exhibit 12–5 on page 433. You may find it helpful to trace each event to the T-accounts. The events have been numbered sequentially and cross-referenced in Exhibit 12–5. The effect of each event on the financial statements is shown individually and discussed in the following sections of this chapter.

Event 1
Raw Materials Purchased

Benchmore paid cash to purchase $14,000 of raw materials. The effects of this event on the company's financial statements follow:

Assets			=	Liabilities	+	Equity		Revenue	−	Expenses	=	Net Income		Cash flow
Cash	+	Raw Materials Inventory												
(14, 000)	+	14, 000	=	n/a	+	n/a		n/a	−	n/a	=	n/a		(14,000) OA*

*Operating Activities

Exhibit 12-4 *Information Flows in the Master Budget*

BENCHMORE BOAT COMPANY
Trial Balance
As of January 1, 2003

	Debit	Credit
Cash	$ 73,000	
Production supplies	300	
Raw materials inventory	7,000	
Work in process inventory	34,000	
Finished goods inventory	85,000	
Manufacturing equipment	90,000	
Accumulated amortization		$ 32,000
common shares		200,000
Retained earnings		57,300
Total	$289,300	$289,300

Subsidiary Account Balances			
Work in Process		**Finished Goods**	
Boat 103	14,000	Boat 101	50,000
Boat 104	8,000	Boat 102	35,000
Boat 105	12,000		
Total	34,000	Total	85,000

This event is an asset exchange event; it does not affect total assets shown on the balance sheet. One asset account, Cash, decreases, and another asset account, Raw Materials Inventory, increases. The income statement is not affected. The cash outflow is shown in the operating activities section of the cash flow statement.

Benchmore used $17,000 of direct raw materials in the process of making boats. The amount used for each job was $8,000, $3,400, and $5,600 for Boat 103, Boat 104, and Boat 105, respectively. The effects of this event on the company's financial statements follow:

Event 2
Raw Materials Purchased

Assets			=	Liabilities	+	Equity		Revenue	−	Expenses	=	Net Income		Cash flow
Raw Materials Inventory	+	Work in Process Inventory												
(17,000)	+	17,000	=	n/a	+	n/a		n/a	−	n/a	=	n/a		n/a

This event is an asset exchange event that does not affect total assets shown on the balance sheet. One asset account, Raw Materials Inventory, decreases, and another asset account, Work in Process Inventory, increases. The income statement and the cash flow statement are not affected. In addition to the effects on the Work in Process Inventory control account, the individual job cost sheets are adjusted to reflect the material used on each job. Exhibit 12–5 illustrates these effects.

Event 3
Production Supplies Purchased

Benchmore paid $1,200 cash to purchase production supplies. The effects of this event on the company's financial statements follow:

Assets			=	Liabilities	+	Equity	Revenue	−	Expenses	=	Net Income	Cash flow
Cash	+	Production Supplies										
(1,200)	+	1,200	=	n/a	+	n/a	n/a	−	n/a	=	n/a	(1,200) OA

This event is an asset exchange event that does not affect total assets shown on the balance sheet. One asset account, Cash, decreases, and another asset account, Production Supplies, increases. The purchase of production supplies does not affect the income statement. The cost of supplies is allocated to the Work in Process Inventory account via the predetermined overhead rate and is expensed as part of cost of goods sold. However, the cash flow associated with the purchase of supplies is shown in the operating section of the cash flow statement.

Benchmore paid $8,000 cash to production workers who worked on Boat 103. The effects of this event on the company's financial statements follow:

Event 4
Production
Workers Paid

Assets			=	Liabilities	+	Equity	Revenue	−	Expenses	=	Net Income	Cash flow
Cash	+	Work in Process Inventory										
(8,000)	+	8,000	=	n/a	+	n/a	n/a	−	n/a	=	n/a	(8,000) OA*

Event 5
Overhead Costs
Applied

Note that these wages are *not* treated as salary expense. Because the labour was used to make inventory, the cost is included in the Work in Process Inventory account. In other words, this is an asset exchange event. One asset, Cash, decreases, and another asset, Work in Process Inventory, increases. Neither the total assets shown on the balance sheet nor the income statement is affected. The cash outflow is shown in the operating activities section of the cash flow statement. In addition to the effects on the Work in Process Inventory control account, the individual job cost sheet would be adjusted to reflect the labour used on each job. Exhibit 12–5 illustrates this effect. Note that the $8,000 labour cost is shown both in the Work in Process Inventory control account and on the job cost sheet for Boat 103.

Benchmore applied estimated manufacturing overhead costs to the job identified as Boat 103. Work on Boat 103 is complete. Even so, many of the costs associated with making it may not be known. Indeed, the boat may even be sold before all the costs associated with making it are known. Although a proportionate share of the total production supplies, amortization, supervisory salaries, rental cost, utilities, and so on were used during the early part of the year, the actual cost of these resources will not be known until the end of the year. To obtain the information needed to make decisions (e.g., the price to charge for the boat), Benchmore must estimate the overhead costs associated with making Boat 103.

To obtain as accurate an estimate as possible, Benchmore began by reviewing the overhead costs incurred during the previous year. Adjustments were made for expected changes. Assume that Benchmore's estimate of total overhead costs included the following items: production supplies, $900; amortization, $8,000; and utilities and other indirect costs, $7,090. Accordingly, the total estimated overhead is $15,990 ($900 + $8,000 + $7,090). Because boats that require more labour also require more overhead inputs, a logical relationship exists between the number of labour hours used to make a boat and the consumption of indirect overhead costs. For example, the longer people work, the more supplies they use. Similarly, more work translates into more use of the equipment, thereby causing an increase in the consumption of utilities and amortization. On the basis of the link between the amount of labour used and the consumption of indirect costs, Benchmore decided to use *direct labour hours* as the base for the allocation of overhead costs. Benchmore estimated that a total of 4,100 labour hours would be used during 2003 and established a *predetermined overhead rate* as shown below:

$$\text{Predetermined overhead rate} = \text{Total estimated overhead costs} \div \text{Total estimated direct labour hours}$$

$$\text{Predetermined overhead rate} = \$15{,}990 \div 4{,}100 \text{ per direct labour hour}$$
$$= \$3.90 \text{ per direct labour}$$

Assuming that 1,600 actual direct hours of labour were used on Boat 103, Benchmore applies $6,240 (1,600 hours 3 $3.90) of overhead to that job. The effects of this application on the company's financial statements follow:

Assets		=	Liabilities	+	Equity	Revenue	−	Expenses	=	Net Income	Cash flow
Manufacturing Overhead	+	Work in Process Inventory									
(6,240)	+	6,240	=	n/a	+	n/a	n/a	−	n/a	=	n/a	n/a

The event is an asset exchange transaction. One asset account, Work in Process Inventory, increases and another temporary asset account, Manufacturing Overhead, decreases. Overhead costs do not affect the income statement at the time they are applied to the Work in Process Inventory account. However, they do affect the income statement through the recognition of cost of goods sold at the time goods are sold. Likewise, the overhead application does not affect cash flow. Cash flow is affected when the indirect costs are paid, not when they are applied to Work in Process Inventory. The job cost sheet for Boat 103 reflects the increase in the cost associated with the application of the estimated overhead cost. The account balances in Exhibit 12–5 illustrate this.

Event 6
Product Costs
for Boat 103
Transferred to
Finished Goods
Inventory

Benchmore transferred $36,240 of product costs from Work in Process Inventory to Finished Goods Inventory. The effects of this transfer on the company's financial statements follow:

Assets		=	Liabilities	+	Equity	Revenue	−	Expenses	=	Net Income	Cash flow
Work in Process Inventory	+	Finished Goods Inventory									
(36,240)	+	36,240	=	n/a	+	n/a	n/a	−	n/a	=	n/a	n/a

This event is an asset exchange event. Costs are transferred from the Work in Process Inventory control account to the Finished Goods Inventory control account. Total assets shown on the balance sheet are unaffected as are the income statement and the cash flow statement. The job cost sheet is transferred to the Finished Goods Inventory file folder. These effects are illustrated in Exhibit 12–5.

Event 7
Selling and
Administrative
Expense Paid

Benchmore paid $24,500 cash for selling and administrative expenses. The effects of this transaction on the company's financial statements follow:

Assets	=	Liabilities	+	Equity	Revenue	−	Expenses	=	Net Income	Cash flow
(24,500)	=	n/a	+	24,500	n/a	−	24,500	=	(24,500)	(24,500) OA

This is an asset use transaction. Cash and retained earnings decrease as a result of the expense recognition. Net income decreases as a result of the expense recognition. Likewise, the cash outflow reduces the net cash flow from operating activities.

Event 8
Production
Workers Paid

Benchmore paid production workers $12,000 cash for work performed on Jobs 104 and 105. The amount of direct labour used on each job was $5,000 and $7,000 for Boat 104 and Boat 105, respectively. These jobs were still under construction at the end of 2003. The effects of this event on the company's financial statements follow:

Assets		=	Liabilities	+	Equity	Revenue	−	Expenses	=	Net Income	Cash flow
Cash	+	Work in Process Inventory									
(12,000)	+	12,000	=	n/a	+	n/a	n/a	−	n/a	=	n/a	(12,000) OA

This is an asset exchange event. It does not affect total assets as shown on the balance sheet or the income statement The cash outflow is shown in the operating activities section of the cash flow statement. In addition to the effects on the Work in Process Inventory control account, the individual job cost sheets are adjusted to reflect the labour used on each job. Exhibit 12–5 illustrates these effects.

Benchmore applied estimated manufacturing overhead costs to the jobs for Boats 104 and 105. The predetermined overhead rate was previously computed to be $3.90 per direct labour hour (see Event 5). Assume that the work described in Event 8 required 1,000 direct labour hours for Boat 104 and 1,400 direct labour hours for Boat 105. On the basis of this information, the amount of estimated overhead cost that should be applied to the two jobs is calculated.

Event 9
Overhead Costs
Applied

Job Number	Predetermined Overhead Rate	×	Actual Labour Hours Used	=	Amount of Applied Overhead
Boat 104	$3.90	×	1,000	=	$3,900
Boat 105	$3.90	×	1,400	=	5,460
Total					$9,360

The effects of applying the overhead on the company's financial statements follow:

Assets			=	Liabilities	+	Equity	Revenue	−	Expenses	=	Net Income	Cash flow
Manufacturing Overhead	+	Work in Process Inventory										
(9,360)	+	9,360	=	n/a	+	n/a	n/a	−	n/a	=	n/a	n/a

The overhead application is an asset exchange event. Total assets, net income, and cash flow are not affected. The job cost sheets for Boats 104 and 105 reflect an increase in overhead cost of $3,900 and $5,460, respectively. You should trace these allocations to the accounts shown in Exhibit 12–5.

Benchmore paid $6,100 cash for utilities and other indirect product costs. The effects of this event on the company's financial statements follow:

Event 10
Cash for
Overhead Costs
Paid

Assets			=	Liabilities	+	Equity	Revenue	−	Expenses	=	Net Income	Cash flow
Cash	+	Manufacturing Overhead										
(6,100)	+	6,100	=	n/a	+	n/a	n/a	−	n/a	=	n/a	(6,100) OA

The incurrence of the *actual overhead* costs is an asset exchange transaction. Total assets, net income, and job cost sheets are not affected. The cash outflow is shown in the operating activities section of the cash flow statement. Remember that estimated overhead costs have already been recorded in the job cost sheets.

Benchmore recognized $8,000 of amortization on manufacturing equipment. The original cost of the equipment was $90,000. It had a 10-year useful life and an estimated salvage value of $10,000. The annual amortization charge is $8,000 ([$90,000 − $10,000] ÷ 10 = $8,000). The effects of this event on the company's financial statements follow:

Event 11
Amortization on
Manufacturing
Equipment
Recognized

Assets			=	Liabilities	+	Equity	Revenue	−	Expenses	=	Net Income	Cash flow
Book Value of Equiptment	+	Manufacturing Overhead										
(8,000)	+	8,000	=	n/a	+	n/a	n/a	−	n/a	=	n/a	n/a

This amortization represents an *actual* indirect product cost (i.e., overhead), *not* an expense. Accordingly, this transaction is an asset exchange. The book value of the manufacturing equipment decreases and the Manufacturing Overhead account increases. The total amount of assets shown on the balance sheet is not affected, nor are the income statement and the cash flow statement. Finally, note that the job cost sheets are not affected by the *actual* overhead cost (i.e., amortization). Remember that *estimated* overhead flows through the inventory accounts and the associated job cost sheets.

Event 12
Actual cost of Production Supplies Recognized as Overhead

Benchmore made the year-end count of supplies and recognized actual overhead cost for the amount of supplies used. During the accounting period, $1,500 of production supplies were available for use ($300 beginning balance + $1,200 supplies purchased). Assuming that a physical count reveals that $400 of supplies is on hand at the end of the accounting period, $1,100 of supplies must have been used ($1,500 − $400). The effects of recognizing supplies used on the company's financial statements follow:

Assets		=	Liabilities	+	Equity	Revenue	−	Expenses	=	Net Income	Cash flow
Supplies +	Manufacturing Overhead										
(1,100) +	1,100	=	n/a	+	n/a	n/a	−	n/a	=	n/a	n/a

The event is an asset exchange transaction. Total assets, net income, and cash flow are not affected, nor are the job cost sheets. Remember that estimated overhead costs have already been recorded in the job cost sheets.

Event 13
Sales Revenue Recognized

Benchmore sold Boat 101 for $91,000 cash. The effects of this event on the company's financial statements follow:

Assets	=	Liabilities	+	Equity	Revenue	−	Expenses	=	Net Income	Cash flow
(91,000) =	n/a		+	91,000	n/a	−	91,000	=	(91,000)	91,000 OA

The revenue recognition from the sale of inventory is an asset source event. The asset account, Cash, and the equity account, Retained Earnings, increase. The recognition of revenue also increases the amount of net income shown on the income statement. In addition, the operating activities section of the cash flow statement increases.

Event 14
Cost of Goods Sold Recognized

Benchmore recognized cost of goods sold for Boat 101. The effects of this event on the company's financial statements follow:

Assets	=	Liabilities	+	Equity	Revenue	−	Expenses	=	Net Income	Cash flow
(50,000) =	n/a		+	50,000	n/a	−	50,000	=	(50,000)	n/a

The recognition of cost of goods sold is an asset use transaction. It acts to decrease an asset account, Finished Goods Inventory, and an equity account, Retained Earnings. The recognition of the expense decreases net income, but cash flow is not affected by the recognition of cost of goods sold. Recall that the impact on cash flow was recognized when cash was spent in the process of making the inventory. The job cost sheet for Boat 101 is transferred to the permanent files. The cost sheet is not discarded at the time of sale because it contains information that could be valuable in estimating the cost of similar special order jobs in the future.

Event 15
Cost of Goods Sold Adjusted for Overapplied Overhead

Benchmore closed the Manufacturing Overhead account and reduced the cost of goods sold by $400. Actual overhead costs amounted to $15,200 although $15,600 of overhead cost had been applied. Accordingly, the overhead has been overapplied by $400 ($15,600 − $15,200). This means that too much overhead has been transferred to the Work in Process, Finished Goods Inventory, and Cost of Goods Sold Inventory accounts. If the amount were significant, it would have to be allocated proportionately among the inventory accounts and the Cost of Goods Sold accounts. In this case, the amount is assumed to be insignificant and is assigned exclusively to cost of goods sold. The effects of this event on the company's financial statements follow:

Assets	=	Liabilities	+	Equity	Revenue	−	Expenses	=	Net Income	Cash flow
400	=	n/a	+	400	n/a	−	(400)	=	400	n/a

Exhibit 12-5 *Ledger T-Accounts for Benchmore Boat Company*

Cash

Bal. 73,000	(1) 14,000
(15) 91,000	(3) 1,200
	(4) 8,000
	(7) 24,500
	(8) 12,000
	(10) 6,100
Bal. 98,200	

Supplies

Bal. 300	(12) 1,100
(3) 1,200	
Bal. 400	

Equipment

Bal. 90,000	

Accumulated Amortization

	Bal. 32,000
	(11) 8,000
	Bal. 40,000

Raw Materials Inventory

Bal. 7,000	(2) 17,000
(1) 14,000	
Bal. 4,000	

Manufacturing Overhead

(10) 6,100	(5) 6,240
(11) 8,000	(6) 9,360
(12) 1,100	
(15) 400	
Bal. 0	

Work in Process Inventory

Bal. 34,000	(6) 36,240
(2) 17,000	
(4) 8,000	
(5) 6,240	
(8) 12,000	
(9) 9,360	
Bal. 50,360	

Boat 103

Beg. Bal.	14,000
Mat.	8,000
Lab.	8,000
O.H.	6,240
Product Cost	36,240
To Finish Goods	(36,240)
End Bal.	0

Boat 104

Beg. Bal.	8,000
Mat.	3,400
Lab.	5,000
O.H.	3,900
End Bal.	20,300

Boat 105

Beg. Bal.	12,000
Mat.	5,600
Lab.	7,000
O.H.	5,460
End Bal.	30,060

Finished Goods Inventory

Bal. 85,000	(14) 50,000
(6) 36,240	
Bal. 71,240	

Boat 101

Beg. Bal.	50,000
Sold	(50,000)
End Bal.	0

Boat 102

Beg. Bal.	35,000
Cost Added	0
End Bal.	35,000

Boat 103

Beg. Bal.	0
Cost Added	36,240
End Bal.	36,240

Common Shares

	Bal. 200,000

Retained Earnings

	Bal. 57,300

Revenue

	(13) 91,000

Cost of Goods Sold

(14) 50,000	(15) 400

Selling and Admin. Exp.

(7) 24,500	

Boat 101

Cost Sheet Data
Transferred to
Permanent Storage

Exhibit 12-6

BENCHMORE BOAT COMPANY
Trial Balance
As of December 31, 2003

	Debit	Credit
Cash	$ 98,200	
Raw materials	4,000	
Work in process	50,360	
Finished goods	71,240	
Supplies	400	
Equipment	90,000	
Accumulated amortization		$ 40,000
common shares		200,000
Retained earnings		57,300
Revenue		91,000
Cost of goods sold	49,600	
Selling and administrative expense	24,500	
Total	$388,300	$388,300

Overapplied overhead means that too much estimated cost was transferred from the asset accounts to Cost of Goods Sold. The preceding entry corrects this misstatement. When $400 is placed in the overhead account, total assets increases. The increase in assets is offset by a corresponding decrease in the Cost of Goods Sold account. This reduces expenses and increases net income, thereby resulting in an increase in the Retained Earnings equity account. Cash flow is unaffected. After this adjustment, the total increases in the overhead account (i.e., actual costs) equal the total decreases (i.e., estimated costs). Accordingly, the Manufacturing Overhead account has an ending balance of zero and does not appear on any financial statement.

The ending trial balance for Benchmore Boat Company is shown in Exhibit 12–6.

Process Cost System Illustrated

A process cost system utilizes the same general ledger accounts as those described for the job-order cost system.

LO8

Understand how accounting events in a process cost system affect financial statements.

Product costs flow through Raw Materials Inventory, Work in Process Inventory, Finished Goods Inventory, and out to Cost of Goods Sold. The primary difference between the two systems centres on accounting for Work in Process Inventory. Instead of accumulating work in process costs by job, a process cost system accumulates these costs by department for a specific period of time. The cost of all goods that move through a processing centre is charged to that centre. Because production is not divided into jobs or job lots, the need for the work in process subsidiary documents (i.e., job cost sheets) is eliminated. Accordingly, a process cost system is simpler and easier to maintain; although it offers simplicity, it does not distinguish the cost of one product from that of another. Accordingly, a process system is not appropriate for companies that manufacture products that are distinctly different from one another; it is suited to manufacturing operations characterized by the continuous production of a uniform product. In a process cost system, all products are considered to have the same cost per unit.

To illustrate the use of a process cost system by a business, we analyze the operations of Janis Juice Company during its 2003 accounting year. Recall that Janis uses three distinct processes to produce its cans of apple juice. Direct raw materials enter the *extraction department,* where juice concentrate is collected from whole fruit. The juice extract then passes to the *mixing department*, where water, sugar, food colouring, and preservatives are added. The juice mixture then moves to the *packaging department*, where it is poured into cans and boxed for shipment. The company's beginning account balances for 2003 are shown in Exhibit 12–7.

The 2003 accounting events for Janis are discussed individually in the following sections. The events, which are recorded in ledger T-accounts in Exhibit 12–9 on page 442, have been numbered sequentially and cross-referenced for your convenience. Trace each event to the T-accounts.

Exhibit 12-7

Janis Juice Company
Trial Balance
As of January 1, 2003

	Debit	Credit
Cash	$320,000	
Raw materials—fruit	7,800	
Raw materials—additives	3,100	
Raw materials—containers	9,500	
Work in process—extraction	22,360	
Work in process—mixing	7,960	
Work in process—packaging	21,130	
Finished goods	20,700	
common shares		$180,000
Retained earnings		232,550
Total	$412,550	$412,550

Janis paid cash to purchase $84,000 of raw materials. The effects of this event on the company's financial statements follow:

Assets			=	Liabilities	+	Equity	Revenue	−	Expenses	=	Net Income	Cash flow
Cash	+	Raw Materials Inventory										
(84,000)	+	84,000	=	n/a	+	n/a	n/a	−	n/a	=	n/a	(84,000) OA

This event is an asset exchange event. Total assets and net income are not affected. The cash outflow is shown in the operating activities section of the cash flow statement. The total materials cost was divided into three categories: $25,000 for whole fruit, $30,000 for additives, and $29,000 for containers. A separate inventory account is maintained for each category. Trace this event to the ledger accounts in Exhibit 12–9.

Janis used $26,720 of whole fruit to obtain extract used to make juice. The effects of this event on the company's financial statements follow:

Assets			=	Liabilities	+	Equity	Revenue	−	Expenses	=	Net Income	Cash flow
Raw Materials— Fruit	+	WIP— Extraction										
(26,720)	+	26,720	=	n/a	+	n/a	n/a	−	n/a	=	n/a	n/a

This event is an asset exchange event. It does not affect total assets, net income, or cash flow. Note carefully that the cost of the materials used is not assigned to any particular product or batch of products, but to the extraction department, which provides virtually the same value-added service to each can of juice.

Janis paid $38,000 cash to production workers who worked in the extraction department. The effects of this event on the company's financial statements follow:

Assets			=	Liabilities	+	Equity	Revenue	−	Expenses	=	Net Income	Cash flow
Cash	+	WIP— Extraction										
(38,000)	+	38,000	=	n/a	+	n/a	n/a	−	n/a	=	n/a	(38,000) OA

This is an asset exchange event. Total assets and net income are not affected. The cash outflow is shown in the operating activities section of the cash flow statement. Again, this cost is assigned to the department, rather than to individual products.

Janis applied estimated manufacturing overhead costs to work in process in the extraction department. Janis has identified a logical relationship between the number of labour dollars and the consumption of indirect overhead costs. The more dollars paid for labour, the higher is the consumption of indirect resources. Janis estimated that in 2003, $96,000 of indirect cost would be incurred and that $120,000 would be paid to production workers. On the basis of these estimates, Janis established a *predetermined overhead* rate as follows:

$$\text{Predetermined overhead rate} = \text{Total estimated overhead costs} \div \text{Total estimated direct labour hours}$$

$$\text{Predetermined overhead rate} = \$96,000 \div \$120,000$$

$$= \$0.80 \text{ per direct labour dollar}$$

On the basis of the fact that $38,000 of labour was used in the extraction department (see Event 3), Janis applied $30,400 ($38,000 $\times$ $0.80) of overhead to that department. The effects of this application on the company's financial statements follow:

Assets			=	Liabilities	+	Equity	Revenue	−	Expenses	=	Net Income	Cash flow
Manufacturing Overhead	+	WIP— Extraction										
(30,400)	+	30,400	=	n/a	+	n/a	n/a	−	n/a	=	n/a	n/a

The event is an asset exchange transaction. Total assets, net income, and cash flow are not affected.

Event 5
Overhead Costs
Applied

Convert
partially
complete
units into
equivalent
whole units

Janis finished the extraction process for some of the juice and transferred related cost from the Work in Process Inventory account of the extraction department to the Work in Process Inventory account of the mixing department. On the basis of these events, total product costs in the Work in Process Inventory account for the extraction department amounted to $117,480 ($22,360 beginning balance + $26,720 materials + $38,000 labour + $30,400 overhead). Suppose that beginning inventory had enough fruit to represent 100,000 units of product (cans) and that enough fruit was added to start an additional 485,000 units. Accordingly, the proper amount of fruit has been placed into production to make 585,000 (100,000 + 485,000 units). Furthermore, assume that enough extract has been transferred to the mixing department to make 500,000 cans of juice. Accordingly, 85,000 (585,000 − 500,000) units in ending inventory *have been started but are not complete.* The total $117,480 product cost must be allocated between the 85,000 partially completed units in ending inventory and the 500,000 completed units that have been transferred to the mixing department. To make a rational allocation, we must first convert the 85,000 partially complete units into *equivalent whole units.*

The logic employed to convert partial units into **equivalent whole units** uses simple mathematics. For example, 2 units that are 50 percent complete equal + equivalent whole unit (2 $\times$ 0.5 = 1). Similarly, 4 units that are 25 percent complete equal 1 equivalent whole unit (4 $\times$ 0.25 = 1). Likewise, 100 units that are 30 percent complete equal 30 equivalent whole units (100 units $\times$ 0.30).

Assume that an engineer estimated the 85,000 partial cans of juice in the extraction department's ending inventory to be 40 percent complete. The amount of equivalent whole units in ending inventory is therefore 34,000 (85,000 $\times$ 0.4). The total number of *equivalent units* produced during the period is 534,000 (the 500,000 units that were finished and transferred to the mixing department and the 34,000 equivalent whole units in ending inventory). On the basis of this information, the **cost per equivalent unit** can now be determined.

Cost per equivalent unit = Total cost ÷ Number of equivalent whole units
Cost per equivalent unit = $117,480 ÷ 534,000
= $0.22 per equivalent unit

The *cost per equivalent unit* can be used to allocate the total cost incurrred in the extraction department between the amount to be transferred to the mixing department and the amount to remain in the extraction department's ending Work in Process Inventory account. The allocation is as follows:

	Equivalent Units	×	Cost per Unit	Cost to Be Allocated
Transferred-out costs	500,000	×	$0.22	$110,000
Ending inventory	34,000	×	$0.22	7,480
Total				$117,480

The effects of transferring $110,000 from the extraction department's Work in Process Inventory to the mixing department's Work in Process Inventory follow:

Assets			=	Liabilities	+	Equity	Revenue	−	Expenses	=	Net Income	Cash flow
WIP— Extraction	+	WIP— Mixing										
(110,000)	+	110,000	=	n/a	+	n/a	n/a	−	n/a	=	n/a	n/a

This event is an asset exchange event. Total assets, net income, and the statement of cash flow are unaffected.

The supporting documentation for the allocation of costs between transferred out and ending inventory is frequently shown in a *cost of production report*, which is usually subdivided into three categories. The first category shows the computation of equivalent units, the second shows the determination of cost per equivalent unit, and the third shows the allocation of total cost between the amount transferred out and the amount remaining in ending inventory. A cost of production report, which is usually subdivided into three categories. The first category shows the computation of equivalent units, the second shows the determination of cost per equivalent unit, and the third shows the allocation of total cost between the amount transferred out and the amount remaining in ending inventory. A cost of production report for Janis's allocation of cost for the extraction department is shown in Exhibit 12–8.

Exhibit 12-8

JANIS JUICE COMPANY
Cost of Production Report
Extraction Department
For the Year Ended December 31, 2003

	Actual	Equivalent	
Determination of equivalent units			
Beginning inventory	100,000		
Units added to production	485,000		
Total	585,000		
Transferred to finished goods	500,000	500,000	100% Complete
Ending inventory	85,000	34,000	40% Complete
Total	585,000	534,000	
Determination of cost per unit			
Cost Accumulation			
Beginning inventory	$ 22,360		
Materials	26,720		
Labour	38,000		
Overhead	30,400		
Total	$117,480		
Divide by	4		
Equivalent units	534,000		
Cost per equivalent unit (i.e., per can)	$0.22		
Cost Allocation			
To Work in Process Overhead, Mixing Dept.			
(500,000 × $0.22)	$110,000		
To ending inventory (34,000 × $0.22)	7,480		
Total	$117,480		

The method used here to determine equivalent units is called the **weighted average method**. Note that this method ignores the state of completion of items in beginning inventory. The equivalent unit adjustment is applied *only* to the units in ending inventory. The failure to account for equivalent units in beginning as well as ending inventories can distort the accuracy of the allocation between the cost of goods transferred out and the cost of goods remaining in particular inventory accounts. Managers frequently tolerate some degree of inaccuracy because the weighted average method is relatively easy to implement. However, when accuracy is deemed to be of paramount importance, some companies use a **first-in, first-out (FIFO) method**. This method accounts for the degree of completion of both beginning and ending inventories, but its application is more complicated. Indeed, we believe that a discussion of this method is more appropriate for upper-level accounting courses. Accordingly, the FIFO method will not be covered in this text.

Event 6
Additional Raw Materials Used in Mixing Department

Janis mixed (i.e., used) $24,400 of additives with the extract obtained from the extraction department. Conceptually, the *transferred-in cost* (juice extract) from the extraction department is a raw material to the mixing department. In addition, the mixing department may obtain and add new materials to the production process. In this case, additives, such as sweetener, food colouring, and preservatives, are mixed with the juice extract. Although both *transferred-in costs* and *additives* are raw materials, it is traditional practice to classify them separately in the accounts. Review the mixing department's Work in Process Inventory account in Exhibit 12–9 to see how these costs are arranged in the ledger accounts. The effects of using additional materials in the mixing department follow:

Assets			=	Liabilities	+	Equity	Revenue	−	Expenses	=	Net Income	Cash flow
Raw Materials Additives	+	WIP— Mixing										
(24,400)	+	24,400	=	n/a	+	n/a	n/a	−	n/a	=	n/a	n/a

This event is an asset exchange event. Total assets, net income, and cash flow are not affected.

Event 7
Production Workers in Mixing Department Paid

Janis paid $48,000 cash to production workers who worked in the mixing department. The effects of this event on the company's financial statements follow:

Assets			=	Liabilities	+	Equity	Revenue	−	Expenses	=	Net Income	Cash flow
Cash	+	WIP— Extraction										
(48,000)	+	48,000	=	n/a	+	n/a	n/a	−	n/a	=	n/a	(48,000) OA

This is an asset exchange event. Total assets and net income are not affected. The cash outflow is shown in the operating activities section of the cash flow statement.

Event 8
Overhead Costs Applied to Mixing Department

Janis applied estimated manufacturing overhead costs to the Work in Process Inventory account in the mixing department. Using the *predetermined overhead* rate established in Event 4, Janis determined that $38,400 ($48,000 labour × 0.80 overhead rate) of overhead costs should be applied to the mixing department's Work in Process Inventory account. The effects of the overhead application on the company's financial statements follow:

Assets			=	Liabilities	+	Equity	Revenue	−	Expenses	=	Net Income	Cash flow
Manufacturing Overhead	+	WIP— Mixing										
(38,400)	+	38,400	=	n/a	+	n/a	n/a	−	n/a	=	n/a	n/a

The event is an asset exchange transaction. Total assets, net income, and cash flow are not affected.

Event 9
Cost of Mixed Juice Transferred to Packaging Department

Janis finished the mixing process for some of the juice and transferred the related cost from the mixing department's Work in Process Inventory account to the packaging department's Work in Process Inventory account. On the basis of these events, *total product cost* in the mixing department's

ccountants at Ford Motor Company would have to convert the partially completed units into equivalent whole units to determine the cost per equivalent unit. If we assume that the vehicles move evenly through the production process, it is reasonable to estimate that the ending inventory was 50 percent complete. Under these circumstances, the division would have 5,100 equivalent whole units of product (5,000 completed units plus 100 equivalent whole units in ending inventory [200 partial units × 0.50 percentage of completion]). Cost per equivalent whole unit could then be computed to be $15,000 ($76,500,000 ÷ 5,100 equivalent units). The portion of the total production cost allocated to the partially completed vehicles is $1,500,000 ($15,000 per unit × 100 equivalent units). This cost would be identified as ending Work in Process Inventory and would be shown on the balance sheet. The amount of work in process inventory could be shown separately or combined with other inventory costs shown on the balance sheet.

Work in Process Inventory account is $228,760 ($7,960 beginning balance + $110,000 transferred-in cost + $24,400 materials + $48,000 labour + $38,400 overhead). An engineer estimated that 510,000 units of mixed juice had been transferred from the mixing department to the packaging department and that 88,000 units of juice remaining in the mixing department were 25 percent complete. Accordingly, the equivalent whole units in ending inventory was 22,000 (88,000 × 0.25). The total *equivalent whole units* produced by the mixing department was 532,000 (510,000 + 22,000). The *cost per equivalent unit* was determined to be $0.43 ($228,760 ÷ 532,000). The allocation between the amount to be transferred out to the packaging department's Work in Process Inventory account and the amount remaining in the mixing department's *ending* Work in Process Inventory account follows:

	Equivalent Units	×	Cost per Unit	Cost to Be Allocated
Transferred-out costs	510,000	×	$0.43	$219,300
Ending inventory	22,000	×	$0.43	9,460
Total				$228,760

The effects of transferring $219,300 from the mixing department's Work in Process Inventory to the packaging department's Work in Process Inventory is as follows:

Assets			=	Liabilities	+	Equity	Revenue	−	Expenses	=	Net Income	Cash flow
WIP— Extraction	+	WIP— Mixing										
(219,300)	+	219,300	=	n/a	+	n/a	n/a	−	n/a	=	n/a	n/a

This event is an asset exchange event. Total assets, net income, and the cash flow statement are unaffected. To ensure that you understand the allocation process, find the ending balance in the mixing department's Work in Process Inventory account in Exhibit 12–9. Also find the entry that verifies $219,300 of product cost being transferred from the mixing department's Work in Process Inventory account to the packaging department's Work in Process Inventory account.

Janis added $32,000 of containers and other packaging materials to the work-in-process in the packaging department. The effects of this event on the financial statements follow:

Event 10
Additional Raw Materials Used in Packaging Department

Assets			=	Liabilities	+	Equity	Revenue	−	Expenses	=	Net Income	Cash flow
Raw Material Container	+	WIP— Packaging										
(32,000)	+	32,000	=	n/a	+	n/a	n/a	−	n/a	=	n/a	n/a

This event is an asset exchange event. Total assets, net income, and cash flow are not affected.

Event 11
Production
Workers in
Packaging
Department
Paid

Janis paid $43,000 cash to production workers who worked in the Packaging Department. The effects of this event on the company's financial statements follow:

Assets		=	Liabilities	+	Equity	Revenue	−	Expenses	=	Net Income	Cash flow
Cash	+	WIP— Packaging									
(43,000) +	43,000	=	n/a	+	n/a	n/a	−	n/a	=	n/a	(43,000) OA

This is an asset exchange event. Total assets and net income are not affected. The cash outflow is shown in the operating activities section of the cash flow statement.

Event 12
Overhead Costs
Applied to
Packaging
Department

Janis applied estimated manufacturing overhead costs to the packaging department's Work in Process Inventory account. Using the predetermined overhead rate established in Event 4, Janis determined that $34,400 ($43,000 labour × 0.80 overhead rate) of overhead costs should be applied to the mixing department's Work in Process Inventory account. The effects of the overhead application on the company's financial statements follow:

Assets		=	Liabilities	+	Equity	Revenue	−	Expenses	=	Net Income	Cash flow
Manufacturing Overhead	+	WIP— Mixing									
(34,400)	+	34,400	=	n/a	+	n/a	n/a	−	n/a	=	n/a	n/a

The event is an asset exchange transaction. Total assets, net income, and cash flow are not affected.

Event 13
Cost of Goods
Manufactured
Transferred to
Finished Goods
Inventory

Janis finished the packaging process for some of the juice and transferred the related cost from the packaging department's Work in Process Inventory account to the Finished Goods Inventory account. Total product cost in the Work in Process Inventory account for the packaging department is $349,830 ($21,130 beginning balance + $219,300 transfer-in cost + $32,000 materials + $43,000 labour + $34,400 overhead). An engineer estimated that 480,000 units of packaged juice were transferred from the packaging department to the Finished Goods Inventory account. Furthermore, the engineer estimated that 90,000 units of juice remaining in the packaging department were 30 percent complete. Accordingly, the *equivalent whole units* in ending inventory was 27,000 (90,000 × 0.30). The total equivalent whole units produced by the mixing department was 507,000 (480,000 + 27,000). The *cost per equivalent unit* was determined to be $0.69 ($349,830 ÷ 507,000). The allocation between the amount to be transferred out to the Finished Goods Inventory account and the amount remaining in the packaging department's ending Work in Process Inventory account follows:

	Equivalent Units	×	Cost per Unit	Cost to Be Allocated
Transferred-out costs	480,000	×	$0.69	$331,200
Ending inventory	27,000	×	$0.69	18,630
Total				$349,830

The effects of transferring $331,200 from the packaging department's Work in Process Inventory to the Finished Goods Inventory account follow:

Assets		=	Liabilities	+	Equity	Revenue	−	Expenses	=	Net Income	Cash flow
WIP— Packaging	+	Fiinished Goods									
(331,200)	+	331,200	=	n/a	+	n/a	n/a	−	n/a	=	n/a	n/a

This event is an asset exchange event. Total assets, net income, and the statement of cash flow are unaffected. To ensure that you understand the allocation process, you should find the ending balance in the packaging department's Work in Process Inventory account. Also find the entry that verifies

$331,200 of product cost being transferred from the packaging department's Work in Process Inventory account to the Finished Goods Inventory account.

Janis paid $106,330 cash for actual overhead costs. The effects of this event on the company's financial statements follow:

Assets		=	Liabilities	+	Equity	Revenue	−	Expenses	=	Net Income	Cash flow
Cash	+	Manufacturing Overhead									
(106,330) +	106,330	=	n/a	+	n/a	n/a	−	n/a	=	n/a	(106,330) OA

Event 14
Cash for Actual Overhead Costs Paid

The incurrence of the *actual overhead costs* is an asset exchange transaction. Total assets and net income are not affected. The cash outflow is shown in the operating activities section of the cash flow statement.

Janis sold 490,000 cans of juice at $1 per can. The effects of this event on the company's financial statements follow:

Assets	=	Liabilities	+	Equity	Revenue	−	Expenses	=	Net Income	Cash flow
490,000	=	n/a	+	490,000	490,000	−	n/a	=	490,000	490,000 OA

Event 15
Sales Revenue Recognized

The revenue recognition from the sale of inventory is an asset source event. The asset account, Cash, and the equity account, Retained Earnings, increase, and the recognition of revenue increases the amount of net income shown on the income statement. In addition, the operating activities section of the cash flow statement reflects an increase.

Janis recognized cost of goods sold for the 490,000 cans of juice sold in Event 15. Each finished can of juice cost $0.69 (see Event 13). Accordingly, cost of goods sold was $338,100. The effects of this event on the company's financial statements follow:

Assets	=	Liabilities	+	Equity	Revenue	−	Expenses	=	Net Income	Cash flow
(338,100)	=	n/a	+	(338,100)	n/a	−	338,100	=	(338,100)	n/a

Event 16
Cost of Goods Sold Recognized

The recognition of cost of goods sold is an asset use transaction. It decreases an asset account, Finished Goods Inventory, and an equity account, Retained Earnings. The recognition of the expense decreases net income. Cash flow is not affected by the recognition of cost of goods sold.

Janis paid $78,200 cash for selling and administrative expenses. The effects of this event on the company's financial statements follow:

Assets	=	Liabilities	+	Equity	Revenue	−	Expenses	=	Net Income	Cash flow
(78,200)	=	n/a	+	(78,200)	n/a	−	78,200	=	(78,200)	(78,200) OA

Event 17
Selling and Administrative Expenses Paid

The recognition of selling and administrative expense is an asset use transaction. It decreases an asset account, Cash, and an equity account, Retained Earnings. The recognition of the expense decreases net income. The cash outflow is shown as a decrease in the operating activities section of the cash flow statement.

Janis closed the Manufacturing Overhead account and increased the Cost of Goods Sold account by $3,130. Actual overhead costs amounted to $106,330 and $103,200 of overhead cost was applied. Accordingly, the overhead has been underapplied by $3,130 ($106,330 − $103,200). This means that too little overhead has been transferred to Work in Process Inventory, Finished Goods Inventory, and Cost of Goods Sold. The amount was assumed to be insignificant and was assigned directly to cost of goods sold. The effects of this event on the company's financial statements follow:

Event 18
Cost of Goods Sold Adjusted for Underapplied Overhead

Assets	=	Liabilities	+	Equity	Revenue	−	Expenses	=	Net Income	Cash flow
(3,310)	=	n/a	+	(3,310)	n/a	−	3,310	=	(3,310)	n/a

Exhibit 12-9 *Ledger T-Accounts for Janis Juice Company*

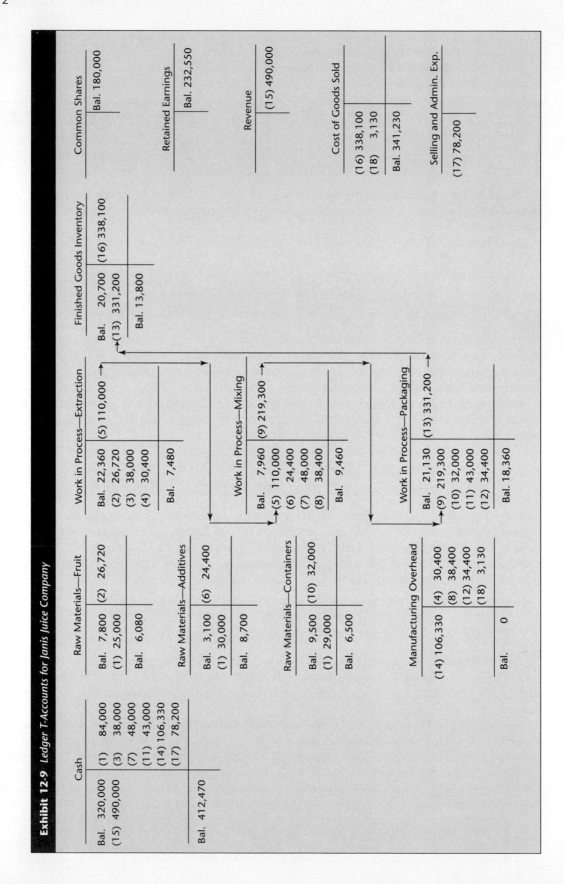

Underapplied overhead means that too little estimated cost was transferred from the asset accounts to the Cost of Goods Sold account. The preceding entry corrects this misstatement. The additional $3,130 of overhead costs is assigned to Cost of Goods Sold, thereby decreasing net income. Cash flow is unaffected. After this adjustment, the total increases in the overhead account (i.e., actual costs) equal the total decreases (i.e., estimated costs). Accordingly, the Manufacturing Overhead account has an ending balance of zero and does not appear on any financial statement.

The ending trial balance for Janis Juice Company is shown in Exhibit 12–10.

Exhibit 12-10

JANIS JUICE COMPANY
Adjusted Trial Balance
As of December 31,2003

	Debit	Credit
Cash	$412,470	
Raw materials—fruit	6,080	
Raw materials—additives	8,700	
Raw materials—containers	6,500	
Work in process—extraction	7,480	
Work in process—mixing	9,460	
Work in process—packaging	18,630	
Finished goods	13,800	
common shares		$180,000
Revenue		490,000
Cost of goods sold	341,230	
Selling and administrative expenses	78,200	
Retained earnings		232,550
Total	$902,550	$902,550

Job-order and *process cost systems* constitute the two primary methods of accounting for product cost flows in manufacturing companies. Both systems are patterned after the physical flow of products as they move through the production process. Job-order cost systems are best suited to manufacturers that make distinct products or products that are produced in distinct batches. Examples of products suited to job-order systems include buildings, ships, airplanes, and special-order batch items. A job-order cost system accumulates costs for individual products or batches of products. Each product or batch has a job identification number and its costs are accumulated separately according to the job number. A job-order cost system requires detailed accounting information. While the total cost of all jobs is accumulated in one Work in Process Inventory control account, detailed records regarding the cost of materials, labour, and overhead for each job are kept in subsidiary accounts called *job-order cost sheets*.

Process cost systems are best suited to manufacturers that make homogeneous products in a continuous production process. Examples of products suited to a process cost system include paint, gasoline, and soft drinks. A process cost system accumulates product costs for each processing department (e.g., cutting, processing, assembling, packaging). Because the units are homogeneous, the cost per unit can be determined by dividing the total processing cost by the number of units (i.e., cost averaging). Because some units are partially complete at the end of an accounting period, converting these units into equivalent whole units prior to determining the average cost per unit is necessary. The cost per equivalent whole unit is used to allocate the total processing cost among departments.

a look
back

The remaining two chapters are transitional chapters. Chapter 13 discusses financial statement analysis. Chapter 14 discusses advanced topics regarding the preparation of the cash flow statement. Some instructors choose to cover these subjects in the financial accounting course, and other instructors cover them in the managerial accounting course. When the subjects are presented in managerial accounting, there is little agreement as to whether they should be introduced at the beginning or the end of the course. Accordingly, it is likely that you have already studied the material in the next two chapters by this point. Under the assumption that this constitutes your last chapter, the author team bids you a fond farewell. We sincerely hope this text has provided you a meaningful learning experience that will serve you well as you progress through your academic training and your ultimate career. Good luck and best wishes!

a look
forward

focus on International Issues

Job-Order, Process, and Hybrid Cost Systems Cross International Borders

Companies throughout the world use job-order, process, and hybrid cost systems. Fuji film, which is made in Japan, is a small, inexpensive, homogeneous product that is suitable to a process cost system. In contrast, the French Concorde is a large, expensive, heterogeneous product that is suited to a job-order cost system.

KEY TERMS

Cost per equivalent unit The unit cost of product determined by dividing total production costs by the number of equivalent whole units. It is used to allocate product costs among processing departments (compute ending inventory and the amount of costs transferred to the subsequent department). *(p. 436)*

Equivalent whole units The result of expressing partially completed goods in an equivalent number of fully completed goods. *(p. 436)*

First-in, first-out (FIFO) method The method used to determine equivalent units when accuracy is deemed important. The method accounts for the degree of completion of both beginning and ending inventories. *(p. 438)*

Hybrid cost system A cost system that blends some of the features of a job-order cost system with some of

the features of a process cost system. *(p. 426)*

Job cost sheet A document used in a job-order cost system that accumulates the material, labour, and overhead costs of a job through the various stages of production; at job completion, contains a summary of all costs incurred to complete that job; also known as *job-order cost sheet* or *job record*. *(p. 426)*

Job-order cost system A system used to determine the cost of a distinct, one-of-a-kind product (e.g., custom-designed building) or a batch of products in batches (e.g., a special order for 100 wedding invitations). *(p. 424)*

Materials requisition The mechanism used to request or order the materials needed to begin a designated job; may be a paper document or an electronic impulse delivered through a computer. Material req-

uisitions for a job are summarized by the accounting department on a job cost sheet. *(p. 426)*

Process cost system A system used to determine the costs of homogeneous products, such as chemicals, foods, or paints, that distributes costs evenly across total production. This system determines an average unit cost by dividing the total product costs of each production department by the number of units made in that department during some designated period of time. The total costs in the last production department include all costs incurred in preceding departments so that the unit cost determined for the last department reflects the final unit cost of the product. *(p. 424)*

Transferred-in costs Costs transferred from one department to the next; combined with the materials, labour, and overhead

costs incurred in the department so that when goods are complete, the total product cost of all departments is transferred to the Finished Goods Inventory account. *(p. 425)*

Weighted average method The method often used in a process cost system for determining equivalent units; ignores the state of completion of items in beginning inventory and assumes that all items in beginning inventory are complete. *(p. 438)*

Work ticket The mechanism (paper or electronic) used to accumulate the time spent on a job by each employee; sent to the accounting department, where the wage rates are recorded and labour costs are determined. The amount of labour costs recorded on each ticket is summarized on the appropriate job-order cost sheet; sometimes called a *time card*. *(p. 427)*

QUESTIONS

1. To what types of products is a job-order cost system best suited? Provide examples.
2. To what types of products is a process cost system best suited? Provide examples.
3. What does the statement "Both job-order and process costing require some form of cost averaging" mean?
4. How is the unit cost of a product determined in a process cost system?
5. Ludwig Company, which normally operates a process cost system to account for the cost of the computers that it pro-

duces, has received a special order from a corporate client to produce and sell 5,000 computers. Can Ludwig use a job-order cost system to account for the costs associated with the special order, even though it uses a process cost system for its normal operations?

6. Which system, a job-order or a process cost system, requires more documentation?
7. How can the materials requisition form facilitate internal control?

8. In a job-order cost system, what are the Work in Process Inventory subsidiary records called? What information is included in these subsidiary records?

9. How is indirect labour recorded in the accounts? How is this labour eventually assigned to the items produced in a job-order cost system?

10. How is amortization on manufacturing equipment recorded in the accounts? How is this amortization assigned to the items produced in a job-order cost system and in a process cost system?

11. Why is a process cost system not applicable to companies that produce items that are distinctly different from one another?

12. The president of Videl Corporation tells you that her company has a difficult time determining the cost per unit of product that it makes. It seems that some units are always partially complete. Counting these units as complete understates the cost per unit because all of the units but only part of the cost is included in the unit cost computation. Conversely, ignoring the number of partially completed products overstates the cost per unit because all of the costs is included but some of the number of units are omitted from the per unit computation. How can Videl provide a more accurate cost per unit figure?

13. Bindon Furniture Manufacturing has completed its monthly inventory count for dining room chairs and recorded the following information for ending inventory: 600 units 100 percent complete, 300 units 60 percent complete, and 100 units 20 percent complete. The company uses a process cost system to determine unit cost. Why would unit cost be inaccurate if 1,000 units were used to determine unit cost?

14. What is the weighted average method? Why is it used? What are its weaknesses?

15. What is the purpose of each of the three primary steps in a process cost system? Describe each.

16. Under a process cost system, what does the term *transferred-in costs* mean? How is the amount of transferred-in costs determined?

17. The finishing department is the last of four sequential production departments for Kowalski Graphics, Inc. The company's other production departments are design, layout, and printing. The finishing department incurred the following costs for March 2006: direct material, $40,000; direct labour, $80,000; applied overhead, $90,000; and transferred-in costs, $120,000. Which department incurred the transferred-in costs? In what month were the transferred-in costs incurred?

EXERCISE 12-1   *Products Matched with a Cost System*   **L.O. 1**

Required

In the right-hand column of the following table, indicate which cost system (job-order, process, or hybrid) would be most appropriate for the type of product listed in the left-hand column. The first item is completed as an example.

Type of Product	Type of Cost System
a. Apartment building	Job-order
b. Automobile	
c. Hollywood movie	
d. Concorde aircraft	
e. Personal computer with special features	
f. Coffee table	
g. Plastic storage containers	
h. TV set	
i. Ship	
j. Boom box	
k. House	
l. Custom-made suit	
m. Van with custom features	
n. CGA review course	
o. Shirts	
p. Pots and pans	

EXERCISE 12-2   *Identification of Appropriate Cost System*   **L.O. 1**

U-Store-It, Inc. makes small aluminum storage bins that it sells through a direct marketing mail-order business. The typical bin measures 2 by 3 metres. The bins are normally used to store garden tools or other small household items. U-Store-It customizes bins for special-order customers by adding shelving, and occasionally, it makes large bins following the unique specifications of commercial customers.

Required

Recommend the type of cost system (job order, process, hybrid) that U-Store-It should use. Supply the appropriate commentary to support your recommendation.

L.O. 1 EXERCISE 12-3   *Job-Order or Process Cost System and a Pricing Decision*

Wen Lee, a tailor in his home country, recently immigrated to Canada. He is interested in starting a business making custom suits for men. Mr. Lee is trying to determine the cost of making a suit so that he can set the price at which to sell them. He estimates that his materials cost will range from $50 to $80 per suit. Because he will make the suits himself, he assumes that there will be no labour cost. Some suits will require more time than others, but Mr. Lee considers this fact to be irrelevant because he is personally supplying the labour, which costs him nothing. Finally, Mr. Lee knows that he will incur some overhead costs such as rent, utilities, advertising, packaging, delivery, and so on; however, he is uncertain as to the exact cost of these items.

Required

a. Should Mr. Lee use a job-order or a process cost system?

b. How can Mr. Lee determine the cost of suits he makes during the year when he does not even know what the total overhead cost will be until the end of the year?

c. Is it appropriate for Mr. Lee to consider labour cost to be zero?

d. With respect to the overhead costs mentioned in the problem, distinguish the *manufacturing overhead* costs from the *selling and administrative* expenses. Comment on whether the selling and administrative expenses should be included in the determination of the product cost if this information will be used for a cost-plus pricing decision. Comment on whether the selling and administrative expenses should be included in the determination of the product cost if this information will be used for financial reporting purposes.

L.O. 2 EXERCISE 12-4   *Job-Order Costing for Manufacturing Company*

Freedom, Inc. builds sailboats. Boat 356 was started on July 10 and was finished on October 31. To build the boat, Freedom incurred $34,000 of labour cost and $29,000 of materials cost. The company expects to incur $1,170,000 of overhead cost during the year. The overhead is allocated to jobs on the basis of direct labour cost. Total expected labour cost for the year is $900,000.

Required

a. If Freedom desires to earn a profit equal to 20 percent of cost, for what price should it sell the boat?

b. If the boat is not sold by year end, what amount of Work in Process Inventory and Finished Goods Inventory would appear on the balance sheet for Boat 356?

c. Is the amount of inventory you calculated in Requirement *b* the actual or the estimated cost of the boat?

d. When is it appropriate to use estimated inventory cost on a year-end balance sheet?

L.O. 2, 7 EXERCISE 12-5   *Job-Order Cost System for Manufacturing Company*

Della Robbia started a small company as a part-time business venture. The company, Robbia Special Effects, makes robotic action figures used in movies. It worked on three action figures during 2002. Beginning inventory on January 1 was zero. The following costs were incurred during the year:

Special Orders	Materials	Labour
Job 101	$6,900	$ 8,700
Job 102	9,300	12,000
Job 103	5,700	6,800

Predetermined overhead rate 60 percent of direct labour dollars

Actual overhead cost $16,900

Jobs 101 and 102 were completed and delivered to customers during the year. Job 103 was incomplete at the end of the year. Selling prices were as follows: Job 101, $28,000, and Job 102, $36,000.

Required

a. Compute the ending balance in Work in Process Inventory.

b. Determine the amount of under- or overapplied overhead for the year.

c. Determine the gross margin for the year.

EXERCISE 12-6   *Job-Order Cost System for Service Company*   L.O. 2, 7

Canmore Condos, is a small company owned by Tass Smith. It leases three condos of differing sizes to customers as vacation facilities. Labour costs for each condo consist of maid service and maintenance cost. Other direct operating costs consist of interest and amortization. The labour and direct operating costs for each condo follow:

	Direct Labour	Direct Operating Costs
Condo 1	$ 4,800	$12,000
Condo 2	6,200	14,000
Condo 3	7,500	19,000
Total	$18,500	$45,000

Indirect operating expenses, which amounted to $13,500, are allocated to the condos in proportion to the amount of direct operating costs incurred for each.

Required

a. Assuming that the amount of rent revenue from Condo 2 is $32,000, what is the amount of income it earned?

b. On the basis of the preceding information, will the company show finished goods inventory on its balance sheet? If so, what is the amount of this inventory? If not, explain why.

EXERCISE 12-7   *Job-Order Cost System*   L.O. 2

The following information applies to Project 345 completed by Jochnowitz Manufacturing Company during October, 2003. The amount of labour cost for the job was $44,900. Applied overhead amounted to $64,000. The project was completed and delivered to CSR Company at a contract price of $190,000. Jochnowitz recognized a gross profit of $34,000 on the project.

Required

Determine the amount of raw materials used to complete Project 345.

EXERCISE 12-8   *Process Cost System—Determine Equivalent Units*   L.O. 3

Fiorello Furniture Company's cutting department had 800 units of inventory in its beginning inventory. During the accounting period it began work on 3,600 units of product and had 1,100 partially complete units in its ending inventory.

Required

(Consider each requirement to be independent of the others.)

a. Assuming that the units in ending inventory were 70 percent complete, determine the total number of equivalent whole units (amount transferred out plus amount in ending inventory) accounted for by the cutting department.

b. Assuming that the total number of equivalent whole units (amount transferred out plus amount in ending inventory) accounted for by the cutting department was 3,850, what was the percentage of completion of the units in ending inventory?

EXERCISE 12-9   *Cost Allocation in a Process System*   L.O. 3

Precise Time Co. makes watches. Its assembly department started the accounting period with a beginning inventory balance of $43,000. During the accounting period, the department incurred $82,000 of transferred-in cost, $39,000 of materials cost, $120,000 of labour cost, and $130,800 of applied overhead cost. The department processed 3,050 total equivalent units of product during the accounting period.

Required

(Consider each requirement to be independent of the others.)

a. Assuming that 600 equivalent units of product were in ending Work in Process Inventory, determine the amount of cost transferred out of the Work in Process Inventory account of the assembly department to Finished Goods Inventory. What was the assembly department's cost of ending Work in Process Inventory?

b. Assuming that 2,800 units of product were transferred out of the assembly department's work in process inventory to finished goods inventory, determine the amount of the assembly department's cost of ending Work in Process Inventory. What was the cost of the finished goods inventory transferred out of the assembly department?

L.O. 3 EXERCISE 12-10   *Process Cost System—Determine Equivalent Units and Allocate Costs*

Green Mountain Ski Company manufactures snow skis. During the most recent accounting period, the company's finishing department transferred 2,400 sets of skis to finished goods. At the end of the accounting period, 300 units of product were estimated to be 60 percent complete. Total product costs for the finishing department amounted to $361,200.

Required

a. Determine the cost per equivalent.

b. Determine the cost of the goods transferred out of the finishing department.

c. Determine the cost of the finishing department's ending Work in Process Inventory.

L.O. 3 EXERCISE 12-11   *Process Cost System*

Glamour, Inc. is a cosmetics manufacturer. Its assembly department receives raw cosmetics from the moulding department. The assembly department places the raw cosmetics into decorative containers and transfers them to the packaging department. The assembly department's Work in Process Inventory account had a $59,000 balance as of August 1. During August, the department incurred raw materials, labour, and overhead costs amounting to $72,000, $85,000, and $80,000, respectively. The department transferred product that cost $342,000 to the packaging department. The balance in the assembly department's Work in Process Inventory account as of August 31 was $41,000.

Required

Determine the cost of raw cosmetics transferred from the moulding department to the assembly department during August.

L.O. 5 EXERCISE 12-12   *Selection of the Appropriate Cost System*

Angelo's Car Wash (ACW) offers customers three cleaning options. Under Option 1, only the exterior is cleaned. With Option 2, the exterior and interior are cleaned. Option 3 provides exterior waxing as well as exterior and interior cleaning. ACW completed 3,400 Option 1 cleanings, 4,800 Option 2 cleanings, and 2,100 Option 3 cleanings during 2001. The average cost of completing each cleaning option and the price charged for it are shown here:

	Option 1	Option 2	Option 3
Price charged	$14	$22	$35
Costs of completing task	7	9	28

Required

a. Is ACW a manufacturing or a service company? Justify your answer with appropriate commentary.

b. Which cost system, job-order or process, is most appropriate for ACW? Explain why.

c. What is the balance in ACW's Work in Process and Finished Goods Inventory accounts on the December 31 balance sheet?

d. Speculate as to the major costs that ACW incurs to complete a cleaning task.

PROBLEMS—SERIES A

PROBLEM 12-1A *Job-Order Cost System*   **L.O. 2, 7**

Patinkin Manufacturing Corporation was started with the issuance of $10,000 of common shares. It purchased $7,000 of raw materials and worked on three job orders during 2001 for which data follow. (Assume that all transactions are for cash, unless otherwise indicated.)

	Direct Raw Materials Used	Direct Labour
Job 1	$1,000	$2,000
Job 2	2,000	4,000
Job 3	3,000	2,000
Total	$6,000	$8,000

Factory overhead is applied using a predetermined overhead rate of $0.50 per direct labour dollar. Jobs 2 and 3 were completed during the period and Job 3 was sold for $9,000. Patinkin paid $400 for selling and administrative expenses. Actual factory overhead amounted to $3,500.

Required
a. Record the data in T-accounts.
b. Reconcile all subsidiary accounts with their respective control accounts.
c. Record the closing entry for over- or underapplied manufacturing overhead, assuming that the amount is insignificant. Close revenue and expense accounts.
d. Prepare a schedule of cost of goods manufactured and sold, an income statement, a balance sheet, and a cash flow statement for 2001.

PROBLEM 12-2A *Job-Order Cost System*   **L.O. 2, 7**

Wald Construction Company began operations on January 1, 2001, when it acquired a $200,000 cash contribution from its owners. During the year, Wald purchased $520,000 of direct raw materials and $25,000 of indirect raw materials (i.e., production supplies) on account and used $480,000 of the direct materials. There were 10,800 hours of direct labour worked at an average rate of $8 per hour paid in cash. The predetermined overhead rate was determined to be $5 per direct labour hour. The company started construction on three prefabricated buildings. The job cost sheets reflected the following allocations of costs to each building:

	Direct Materials	Direct Labour Hours
Job 1	$120,000	3,000
Job 2	200,000	5,000
Job 3	160,000	2,800

The company paid $16,000 cash for indirect labour costs. At the end of the accounting period, $1,000 of production supplies was on hand. Actual overhead cost paid in cash other than indirect materials and indirect labour amounted to $18,000. Wald completed Jobs 1 and 2 and sold Job 1 for $210,000 cash. The company incurred $20,000 of selling and administrative expenses that were paid in cash. During the year, $190,000 of accounts payable was paid. Over- or underapplied overhead is closed to Cost of Goods Sold.

Required
a. Record the data in T-accounts.
b. Reconcile all subsidiary accounts with their respective control accounts.
c. Record the closing entry for over- or underapplied manufacturing overhead, assuming that the amount is insignificant. Close revenue and expense accounts.
d. Prepare a schedule of cost of goods manufactured and sold, an income statement, a balance sheet, and a cash flow statement for 2001.

L.O. 3, 8 PROBLEM 12-3A *Process Cost System*

You-Finish-It, Inc. makes rocking chairs. The chairs move through two departments during the production process. Lumber is cut into chair parts in the cutting department, which transfers the parts to the assembly department, where they are assembled. The company sells the chairs to hobby shops as unfinished furniture. The following transactions apply to You-Finish-It's operations of the first year (2001). (Assume that all transactions are for cash, unless otherwise stated.)

1. The company was started when it acquired a $50,000 cash contribution from the owners.
2. The company purchased $15,000 of direct raw materials and $400 of indirect materials. Indirect materials are capitalized in the Production Supplies account.
3. Direct materials totalling $6,000 were issued to the cutting department.
4. Labour cost amounted to $28,200. Direct labour use for the cutting and assembly departments was $10,000 and $13,000, respectively. Indirect labour costs amounted to $5,200.
5. The predetermined overhead rate was $0.50 per direct labour dollar.
6. Actual overhead costs other than indirect materials and indirect labour amounted to $6,400 for the year.
7. The cutting department transferred $12,000 of inventory to the assembly department.
8. The assembly department transferred $20,000 of inventory to finished goods.
9. The company sold inventory costing $18,000 for $30,000.
10. Selling and administrative expenses amounted to $3,000.
11. A physical count revealed $100 of production supplies on hand at the end of the accounting period.
12. Assume that over- or underapplied overhead is insignificant.

Required
a. Record the data in T-accounts.
b. Record the closing entry for over- or underapplied manufacturing overhead, assuming that the amount is insignificant.
c. Close the revenue and expense accounts.
d. Prepare a schedule of cost of goods manufactured and sold, an income statement, a balance sheet, and a cash flow statement for 2001.

L.O. 3, 4, 8 PROBLEM 12-4A *Process Cost System*

The ending balances computed in Problem 12-3A should be used as the beginning balances for this problem. The transactions for the second year of operation (i.e., 2002) are described here. (Assume that all transactions are cash transactions, unless otherwise indicated.)

1. The company purchased $20,000 of direct raw materials and $650 of indirect materials.
2. Materials totalling $6,700 were issued to the cutting department.
3. Labour cost amounted to $23,500. Direct labour usage for the cutting and assembly departments was $11,000 and $10,000, respectively. Indirect labour costs amounted to $2,500. (*Note:* It may appear that the cash balance to pay these labour costs is insufficient, but these amounts represent summary data for the entire year. Cash revenue, which is recorded later, would also have been spread over the entire accounting period. Accordingly, these data are not presented in exact order of collection and payment. You can assume that sufficient cash is available when periodic payments are made.)
4. The predetermined overhead rate was $0.50 per direct labour dollar.
5. Actual overhead costs other than indirect materials and indirect labour for the month amounted to $7,300.
6. The cutting department transferred $15,000 of inventory to the assembly department.
7. The assembly department transferred $30,000 of inventory to finished goods.
8. The company sold inventory costing $17,000 for $32,000.
9. Selling and administrative expenses amounted to $4,200.
10. At the end of the accounting period, $150 of production supplies was on hand.
11. Assume that over- or underapplied overhead is insignificant.

Required
a. Record the data in T-accounts.
b. Record the closing entry for over- or underapplied manufacturing overhead, assuming that the amount is insignificant.
c. Close the revenue and expense accounts.

d. Prepare a schedule of cost of goods manufactured and sold, an income statement, a balance sheet, and a cash flow statement for 2002.

PROBLEM 12-5A *Inventory Cost Determined under Process Cost System*   **L.O. 3**

Bliss Company had 500 units of product in its work in process inventory at the beginning of the period and started 4,000 additional units during the period. At the end of the period, 1,500 units were in work in process inventory. The ending work in process inventory was estimated to be 60 percent complete. The cost of work in process inventory at the beginning of the period was $4,560, and $36,000 of product costs was added during the period.

Required
Prepare a cost of production report including the following:
a. The number of equivalent units of production.
b. The product cost per equivalent unit.
c. The total cost allocated between the ending Work in Process Inventory and Finished Goods Inventory accounts.

PROBLEM 12-6A *Inventory Cost Determined under Process Cost System*   **L.O. 3**

Roan Company had 100 units of product in work in process inventory at the beginning of the period, and it started 700 units during the period and transferred 600 units to finished goods inventory. The ending work in process inventory was estimated to be 80 percent complete. Cost data for the period follows:

	Product Costs
Beginning balance	$ 3,950.00
Added during period	7,260.00
	$11,210.00

Required
Prepare a cost of production report including the following:
a. The number of equivalent units of production.
b. The product cost per equivalent unit.
c. The total cost allocated between the ending Work in Process Inventory and Finished Goods Inventory accounts.

PROBLEM 12-7A *Process Cost System*   **L.O. 3**

Jordan Plastic Products, Inc. makes a plastic toy in its two departments, parts and assembly. The following are the data related to the parts department's transactions in 2003:
1. The beginning balance of the Work in Process Inventory account was $2,850. This inventory consisted of parts for 1,000 toys. The beginning balances in the Raw Materials Inventory, Production Supplies, and Cash accounts were $32,000, $500, and $100,000, respectively.
2. Direct materials costing $26,000 were issued to the parts department. The materials were sufficient to start work on 5,000 toys.
3. Direct labour cost amounted to $23,500, and indirect labour costs amounted to $2,300. All labour costs were paid in cash.
4. The predetermined overhead rate was $0.30 per direct labour dollar.
5. Actual overhead costs other than indirect materials and indirect labour for the year amounted to $4,750, which was paid in cash.
6. The department completed work on parts for 4,500 toys. The remaining toys were 60 percent complete. The completed parts were transferred to the assembly department.
7. All of the production supplies had been used by the end of the accounting period.
8. Over- or underapplied overhead was closed to the Cost of Goods Sold account.

Required
a. Determine the number of equivalent units of production.
b. Determine the product cost per equivalent unit.
c. Allocate the total cost between the ending Work in Process Inventory and parts transferred to the assembly department.
d. Record the transactions in a partial set of T-accounts.

L.O. 3 PROBLEM 12-8A *Process Cost System*

Pepper Cola Corporation, that produces a new soft drink brand, Spicy Icy, has a beginning balance of common shares at $216,000. The process includes two production departments, mixing and bottling. Some related data regarding the mixing department's activities for 2006 follow:

Accounts	Beginning Balances
Cash	$ 78,000
Raw Materials	37,000
Production Supplies	1,000
Work in Process Inventory (800,000 units)	100,000

1. Pepper Cola issued additional common shares for $100,000 cash.
2. The company purchased raw materials and production supplies for $74,000 and $2,000, respectively, in cash.
3. The company issued $100,000 of raw materials to the mixing department for the production of 1,000,000 units of Spicy Icy that were started in 2006. A unit of soft drink is the amount needed to fill a bottle.
4. The mixing department used 5,400 hours of labour during 2006, including 5,000 hours for direct labour and 400 hours for indirect labour. The average wage was $12 per hour. All the wages were paid in 2006.
5. The predetermined overhead rate was $2 per direct labour hour.
6. Actual overhead costs other than indirect materials and indirect labour for the year amounted to $3,600, which was paid in cash.
7. The mixing department completed 1,200,000 units of Spicy Icy. The remaining inventory was 50 percent complete.
8. The completed soft drink was transferred to the bottling department.
9. The ending balance in the Production Supplies account was $1,400.

Required
a. Determine the number of equivalent units of production.
b. Determine the product cost per equivalent unit.
c. Allocate the total cost between the ending Work in Process Inventory and units transferred to the bottling department.
d. Record the transactions in T-accounts.

PROBLEMS—SERIES B

L.O. 2, 7 PROBLEM 12-1B *Job-Order Cost System*

Navajo Corporation received a shareholder's contribution of $400,000 on January 1, 2004, when it was created. It purchased $79,000 of raw materials and worked on three job orders during the year. Data regarding these jobs are as follows. (Assume that all transactions are for cash, unless otherwise indicated.)

	Direct Raw Materials Used	Direct Labour
Job 1	$21,000	$ 32,000
Job 2	17,000	48,000
Job 3	35,000	56,000
Total	$73,000	$136,000

The average wage rate is $16 per hour. Factory overhead is applied using a predetermined overhead rate of $7.50 per direct labour hour. Jobs 1 and 3 were completed during the year, and Job 1 was sold for $98,000. Navajo paid $14,000 for selling and administrative expenses. Actual factory overhead amounted to $63,500.

Required
a. Record the data in T-accounts.
b. Reconcile all subsidiary accounts with their respective control accounts.

c. Record the closing entry for over- or underapplied manufacturing overhead, assuming that the amount is insignificant. Close revenue and expense accounts.

d. Prepare a schedule of cost of goods manufactured and sold, an income statement, a balance sheet, and a cash flow statement for 2004.

PROBLEM 12-2B *Job-Order Cost System*   L.O. 2, 7

Gerald Corporation was founded on January 1, 2002, when shareholders contributed $350,000 for common shares. During the year, Gerald purchased $300,000 of direct raw materials and $37,000 of production supplies, all on account. The company used $270,000 of direct materials. There were 8,000 hours of direct labour worked at an average rate of $10 per hour paid in cash. The predetermined overhead rate was determined to be $8 per direct labour hour. The company started making three custom-ordered sailboats. The job cost sheets reflected the following allocations of costs to each boat:

	Direct Materials	Direct Labour Hours
Boat 1	$100,000	2,000
Boat 2	50,000	1,200
Boat 3	120,000	4,800

The company paid $22,000 cash for indirect labour costs. At the end of year, $7,000 of production supplies was on hand. Actual overhead cost paid in cash other than indirect materials and indirect labour amounted to $18,000. Gerald completed Boats 1 and 2 and sold Boat 1 for $270,000 cash. The company incurred $62,000 of selling and administrative expenses that were paid with cash. During the year, $240,000 of accounts payable was paid. Over- or underapplied overhead is closed to Cost of Goods Sold.

Required
a. Record the data in T-accounts.
b. Reconcile all subsidiary accounts with their respective control accounts.
c. Record the closing entry for over- or underapplied manufacturing overhead, assuming that the amount is insignificant. Close revenue and expense accounts.
d. Prepare a schedule of cost of goods manufactured and sold, an income statement, a balance sheet, and a cash flow statement for 2002.

PROBLEM 12-3B *Process Cost System*   L.O. 3, 8

Mandy Food Company makes frozen vegetables. The production involves two departments, processing and packaging. Raw materials are cleaned and cut into proper sizes in the processing department and then transferred to the packaging department, where they are packaged and frozen. The following transactions apply to Mandy's first year (2001) of operations. (Assume that all transactions are for cash, unless otherwise stated.)

1. The company was started when it acquired a $160,000 cash contribution from the shareholders.
2. Mandy purchased $84,000 of direct raw materials and $15,000 of indirect materials. Indirect materials are capitalized in the Production Supplies account.
3. Direct materials totalling $76,000 were issued to the processing department.
4. Labour cost amounted to $154,000. Direct labour usage for the processing and packaging departments was $65,000 and $51,000, respectively. Indirect labour costs amounted to $38,000.
5. The predetermined overhead rate was $0.80 per direct labour dollar.
6. Actual overhead costs other than indirect materials and indirect labour amounted to $45,000 for the year.
7. The processing department transferred $121,000 of inventory to the packaging department.
8. The packaging department transferred $140,000 of inventory to finished goods.
9. The company sold inventory costing $126,000 for $235,000.
10. Selling and administrative expenses amounted to $47,000.
11. A physical count revealed $6,000 of production supplies on hand at the end of the year.
12. Assume that over- or underapplied overhead is insignificant.

Required
a. Record the data in T-accounts.
b. Record the closing entry for over- or underapplied manufacturing overhead, assuming that the amount is insignificant.
c. Close the revenue and expense accounts.
d. Prepare a schedule of cost of goods manufactured and sold, an income statement, a balance sheet, and a cash flow statement for 2001.

L.O. 3, 4, 8 PROBLEM 12-4B *Process Cost System*

The ending balances computed in Problem 12-3B should be used as the beginning balances for this problem. The transactions for the second year of operation (i.e., 2008) are described here. (Assume that all transactions are cash transactions, unless otherwise indicated.)

1. The company purchased $102,000 of direct raw materials and $18,000 of indirect materials.
2. Materials costing $82,000 were issued to the processing department.
3. Labour cost amounted to $179,000. Direct labour usage for the processing and packaging departments was $72,000 and $59,000, respectively. Indirect labour costs amounted to $48,000. (*Note:* It may appear that the cash balance to pay these labour costs is insufficient, but these amounts represent summary data for the entire year. Cash revenue, which is recorded later, would also have been spread over the entire year. Accordingly, these data are not presented in exact order of collection and payment. You can assume that sufficient cash is available when periodic payments are made.)
4. The predetermined overhead rate was $0.80 per direct labour dollar.
5. Actual overhead costs other than indirect materials and indirect labour for the year amounted to $50,000.
6. The processing department transferred $250,000 of inventory to the packaging department.
7. The packaging department transferred $350,000 of inventory to finished goods.
8. The company sold inventory costing $342,000 for $650,000.
9. Selling and administrative expenses amounted to $64,000.
10. At the end of the year, $4,000 of production supplies was on hand.
11. Assume that over- or underapplied overhead is insignificant.

Required
a. Record the data in T-accounts.
b. Record the closing entry for over- or underapplied manufacturing overhead, assuming that the amount is insignificant.
c. Close the revenue and expense accounts.
d. Prepare a schedule of cost of goods manufactured and sold, an income statement, a balance sheet, and a cash flow statement for 2002.

L.O. 3 PROBLEM 12-5B *Inventory Cost Determined under Process Cost System*

At the beginning of 2005, Templeton Company had 3,000 units of product in its work in process inventory, and it started 32,000 additional units of product during the year. At the end of the year, 10,000 units of product were in the work in process inventory. The ending work in process inventory was estimated to be 50 percent complete. The cost of work in process inventory at the beginning of the period was $7,500, and $90,000 of product costs was added during the period.

Required
Prepare a cost of production report including the following:
a. The number of equivalent units of production.
b. The product cost per equivalent unit.
c. The total cost allocated between the ending Work in Process Inventory and Finished Goods Inventory accounts.

L.O. 3 PROBLEM 12-6B *Inventory Cost Determined under Process Costing*

El Norte Company's beginning balance of work in process inventory was 9,000 units of product in 2003, and during the period, the company started 48,000 units of product and transferred 47,000 units to finished goods inventory. The ending work in process inventory was estimated to be 30 percent complete. Cost data for the period follow:

	Product Costs
Beginning balance	$ 19,000
Added during period	151,000
	$170,000

Required

Prepare a cost of production report including the following:

a. The number of equivalent units of production.

b. The product cost per equivalent unit.

c. The total cost allocated between the ending Work in Process Inventory and Finished Goods Inventory accounts.

PROBLEM 12-7B *Process Cost System*   **L.O. 3, 8**

Wilford Corporation makes blue jeans. Its process involves two departments, cutting and sewing. The following are the data related to the cutting department's transactions in 2006:

1. The beginning balance of the Work in Process Inventory account was $14,620. This inventory consisted of fabric for 6,000 pairs of jeans. The beginning balances in the Raw Materials Inventory, Production Supplies, and Cash accounts were $75,000, $3,500 and $226,000, respectively.

2. Direct materials costing $46,780 were issued to the cutting department; this amount of materials was sufficient to start work on 15,000 pairs of jeans.

3. Direct labour cost amounted to $56,000, and indirect labour costs amounted to $4,500. All labour costs were paid in cash.

4. The predetermined overhead rate was $0.25 per direct labour dollar.

5. Actual overhead costs other than indirect materials and indirect labour for the year amounted to $6,400, which was paid in cash.

6. The cutting department completed 16,000 pairs of jeans. The remaining jeans were 40 percent complete.

7. The completed units of cut fabric were transferred to the sewing department.

8. All of the production supplies had been used by the end of the year.

9. Over- or underapplied overhead was closed to the Cost of Goods Sold account.

Required

a. Determine the number of equivalent units of production.

b. Determine the product cost per equivalent unit.

c. Allocate the total cost between the ending Work in Process Inventory and units transferred to the sewing department.

d. Record the transactions in a partial set T-accounts.

PROBLEM 12-8B *Process Cost System*   **L.O. 3, 8**

Stain Paper Products Corporation, that produces paper cups, has a beginning balance of common shares at $171,000. The process includes two production departments, printing and forming. Some related data regarding the printing department's activities for 2003 follow:

Accounts	Beginning Balances
Cash	$91,000
Raw Materials	41,000
Production Supplies	3,000
Work in Process Inventory (300,000 units)	36,000

1. Stain Paper Products issued additional common shares for $220,000 cash.

2. The company purchased raw materials and production supplies for $80,000 and $7,000, respectively, in cash.

3. The company issued $114,000 of raw materials and $7,200 of production supplies to the printing department for the production of 800,000 paper cups.

4. The printing department used 6,200 hours of labour during 2003, including 5,600 hours for direct labour and 600 hours for indirect labour. The average wage was $10 per hour. All the wages were paid in 2003.

5. The predetermined overhead rate was $0.50 per direct labour hour.

6. Actual overhead costs other than indirect materials and indirect labour for the year amounted to $14,800, which was paid in cash.
7. The printing department completed 700,000 paper cups. The remaining cups were 50 percent complete.
8. The completed paper cups were transferred to the forming department.
9. The ending balance in the Production Supplies account was $2,800.

Required
a. Determine the number of equivalent units of production.
b. Determine the product cost per equivalent unit.
c. Allocate the total cost between the ending Work in Process Inventory and units transferred to the forming department.
d. Record the transactions in T-accounts.

ANALYZE, THINK, COMMUNICATE

ACT 12-1 BUSINESS APPLICATIONS CASE *Missing Information*

Dana Sudzina, who was recently employed by CamCo has discovered that the accounting records for the past month are incomplete. His search of the records and supporting documents revealed the following fragments of information:

	September 1	September 30
Raw materials inventory	$21,300	$ 19,500
Work in process	26,100	28,350
Finished goods	50,150	46,925
Raw materials purchased		(h) = ?
Raw materials available		(g) = ?
Raw materials used		(f) = ?
Labour (overhead is 150% of labour cost)		(e) = ?
Manufacturing overhead		112,500
Total manufacturing costs		(d) = ?
Total work in process		(c) = ?
Cost of goods manufactured		(b) = ?
Cost of goods available for sale		(a) = ?
Cost of goods sold		221,500

Required
a. Compute the missing amounts.
b. If a physical count of the ending raw materials inventory revealed that the balance shown above was understated by $500, how would this error have affected the income statement?

ACT 12-2 GROUP ASSIGNMENT *Job-Order Cost System*

Wexler Bridge Company constructs bridges for the province of New Brunswick. During 2002, Wexler started work on three bridges. The cost of materials and labour for each bridge follows:

Special Orders	Materials	Labour
Bridge 101	$407,200	$352,700
Bridge 102	362,300	375,000
Bridge 103	801,700	922,800

The predetermined overhead rate has been established at $1.20 per direct labour dollar. Actual overhead costs were determined to be $2,170,800. Bridge 102 was constructed for a contract price of $1,357,000 and was turned over to the province. Construction on Bridge 101 was also completed, but the province had not yet finished its inspection process. General selling and administrative expenses amounted to $210,000. Over- or underapplied overhead is closed directly to the Cost of Goods Sold account. The company recognizes revenue when it turns over a completed bridge to a customer.

Required

a. Divide the class into groups of four or five students each and organize the groups into three sections. Assign Task 1 to the first sections of groups, Task 2 to the second sections, and Task 3 to the third sections.

   Group Tasks
   1. Determine the cost of construction for Bridge 101.
   2. Determine the cost of construction for Bridge 102.
   3. Determine the cost of construction for Bridge 103.

b. Select a spokesperson from each section. Use input from the three spokespersons to prepare an income statement and the asset section of the balance sheet.

c. Does the net income accurately reflect the profitability associated with Bridge 102? Provide an appropriate explanation.

d. Would converting to a process cost system improve the accuracy of the amount of reported net income? Provide an appropriate explanation.

WRITING ASSIGNMENT *Determination of a Proper Cost System*   **ACT 12-3**

Professor Julia Silverman received the following e-mail message:

"I don't know if you remember me. I am Tim Wallace. I was in your introductory accounting class a couple of years ago. I recently graduated and have just started my first real job. I remember your talking about job-order and process cost systems. Indeed, I looked the subject up in the textbook you wrote. In that book, you say that a process cost system is used when a company produces a single, homogeneous, high-volume, low-cost product. Well, the company I am working for makes T-shirts. All the shirts are the same. They don't cost much, and we make nearly a million of them every year. The only difference in any of the shirts is the label we sew on them. We make the shirts for about 20 different companies. It seems to me that we should be using a process costing system. Even so, our accounting people are using a job-order cost system. Unfortunately, you didn't tell us what to do when the company we work for is screwed up. I need some advice. Should I tell them they are using the wrong accounting system? I know I am new around here, and I don't want to offend anybody, but if your book is right, the company would be better off if it started using a process cost system. Some of these people around here didn't go to college, and I'm afraid they don't know what they are doing. I guess that's why they hired someone with a degree. Am I right about this or what?"

Required

Assume that you are Professor Silverman. Write a return e-mail responding to Mr. Wallace's inquiry.

ETHICAL DILEMMA   *Amount of Equivalent Units*   **ACT 12-4**

René Alverez knew that she was in over her head soon after she took the job. Even so, the opportunity for promotion comes along rarely and she believed that she would grow into the job. Ms. Alverez is the cost accounting specialist assigned to the finishing department of Standard Tool Company. Bill Sawyer, the manager of the finishing department, knows exactly what he is doing. In each of the three years he has managed the department, the cost per unit of product transferred out of his Work in Process Inventory account has declined. His ability to control cost is highly valued, and it is widely believed that he will be the successor to the plant manager, who is being promoted to manufacturing vice-president. One more good year would surely seal the deal for Mr. Sawyer. It was little wonder that Ms. Alverez was uncomfortable in challenging Mr. Sawyer's estimate of the percentage of completion of the department's ending inventory. He contended that the inventory was 60 percent complete, but she believed that it was only about 40 percent complete.

   After a brief altercation, Ms. Alverez agreed to sign off on Mr. Sawyer's estimate. The truth was that although she believed that she was right, she did not know how to support her position. Besides, Mr. Sawyer was about to be named plant manager, and she felt it unwise to challenge such an important person.

The department had beginning inventory of 5,500 units of product, and it started 94,500 units during the period. It transferred out 90,000 units during the period. Total transferred-in and production cost for the period amounted to $902,400. This amount included the amount of cost in beginning inventory plus additional costs incurred during the period. The target (i.e., standard) cost per unit is $9.45.

Required

a. Determine the equivalent cost per unit, assuming that the ending inventory is considered to be 40 percent complete.

b. Determine the equivalent cost per unit, assuming that the ending inventory is considered to be 60 percent, complete.

c. Comment on Mr. Sawyer's motives for establishing the percentage of completion at 60 percent, rather than 40 percent.

ACT 12-5 SPREADSHEET ASSIGNMENT   *Using Excel*

Bucyrus Company had 4,000 units of product in work in process inventory at the beginning of the period, and started 8,000 units during the period. At the end of the period, 2,000 units remained in work in process. The ending work in process inventory was estimated to be 40 percent complete. The cost of the units in beginning work in process inventory was $11,040. During the period, $19,200 of product costs were added.

Required

a. Construct a spreadsheet that incorporates the preceding data into a table. The following screen capture is an example.

b. Insert a section into the spreadsheet to calculate total manufacturing costs.

c. Insert a section into the spreadsheet to calculate equivalent units and cost per equivalent unit.

d. Insert a section into the spreadsheet to allocate the manufacturing costs between finished goods and ending work in process.

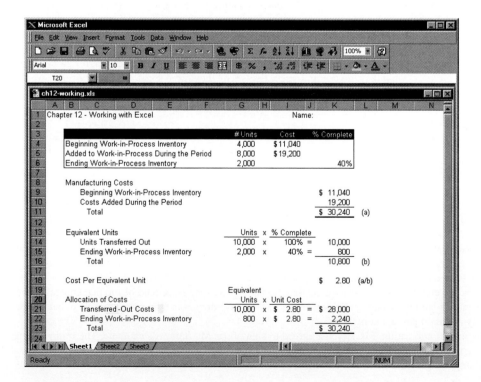

Spreadsheet Tip

The cells that contain numbers below Row 7 should all be formulas to allow changes to the data in Rows 3 to 6. Any changes in the data will automatically be reflected in the rest of the spreadsheet.

SPREADSHEET ASSIGNMENT   *Mastering Excel*   **ACT 12-6**

Refer to the job cost sheet in Exhibit 12–3.

Required

Construct a spreadsheet that recreates the job cost sheet in Exhibit 12–3. Use formulas wherever possible, such as in the total row.

Spreadsheet Tips

1. The headings for direct materials, direct labour, and applied overhead can be centred across two or three columns by choosing Format and Cells and checking the Merge box under the alignment tab. A shortcut to centre these is to click on the Merge and Centre icon in the formatting tool bar.
2. All lines in the job cost sheet can be drawn using Format and Cells and then choosing the border tab.

Financial Statement Analysis

Learning Objectives

After completing this chapter, you should be able to:

1 Describe the factors associated with the communication of useful information.

2 Differentiate between horizontal and vertical analyses.

3 Understand what the term *ratio analysis* means.

4 Calculate the ratios that facilitate the assessment of a company's debt-paying ability.

5 Calculate the ratios that facilitate the assessment of a company's solvency.

6 Calculate the ratios that facilitate the assessment of a company's managerial effectiveness.

7 Calculate the ratios that facilitate the assessment of a company's position in the stock market.

8 Identify different forms for presenting analytical data.

9 Understand the limitations of financial statement analysis.

the *curious* manager

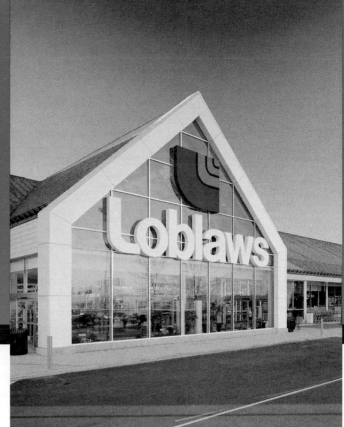

© Loblaw Companies Limited

Loblaw Companies Limited's annual financial statements for the year ending December 31, 2000, stated that the company had a net income of $473 million. In comparison, Sobeys Inc. reported net income of $42 million for its year ending May 5, 2001. Does this suggest that Loblaw's performance is better than that of Sobeys? The answer is, no. What the comparison says more than anything else is that Loblaw Company is a much larger company than Sobeys. How do you compare the performance of companies of such vastly different sizes?

The utility of financial statement information can be enhanced when it is expressed in the form of ratios that permit comparisons across time and among companies. Accordingly, both internal and external users can benefit from a knowledge of common techniques to analyze these statements. Before we begin a detailed explanation of numerous ratios and percentages, however, we look at the factors involved in communicating useful information.

❚ Factors in Communicating Useful Information

The primary objective of accounting is to provide information that is useful for decision making. To prepare information that will meet this objective, accountants must give consideration to the intended users, the purpose for which the information is being prepared, and the process by which the information is analyzed.

The Users

The users of financial information include managers, creditors, shareholders, potential investors, and regulatory agencies. Each of these groups represents many strata of individuals and organizations, all with different purposes and varying levels of sophistication concerning the activities of the business world. For example, an investor may be the individual who knows little about financial statements, a large investment house whose expertise in analysis includes the use of complex statistical procedures, or someone whose expertise falls between that of these two. One financial reporting issue concerns the level of knowledge to which the information should be aimed. Condensing the complexities of business to a level easily understood by the uninformed investor has become increasingly difficult. It is generally recognized that the user should be considered to be a person with a reasonable knowledge of business or one who has the capacity and willingness to achieve a reasonable knowledge. Such terms as "reasonable, average, prudent, informed, and sophisticated" are often used in trying to describe the users of information, yet such ambiguous qualities are difficult to define.

The Purpose of the Desired Information

Just as each potential user possesses a different level of knowledge, each also requires different information, depending on the decision at hand. Financial statements are general-purpose statements, meaning that they are prepared to be used by a wide variety of parties, rather than being aimed at one specific group. For this reason, some disclosed information may be irrelevant to some users but vital to others. Different forms of analysis are necessary to identify the information that is most relevant to a particular decision.

Financial statements can be only synopses of economic information. The costs of providing all information about a firm would be prohibitive to the business. **Information overload** is also a consideration. When too much information is presented, the important pieces of information can often be obscured by trivialities. The user confronted with reams of data may become so frustrated in attempting to isolate desired information that the value of what *is* provided may be lost.

Information Analysis

Because of the many categories of users, the different levels of knowledge, the varying needs of decision makers, and the general nature of financial statements, a number of techniques are used in analysis. In the following sections, we consider a number of methods of analysis commonly employed. No method of analysis is right or wrong; the choice depends on which tool appears to provide information that is most relevant to an individual situation.

Methods of Analysis

Analysis of financial statements should focus primarily on isolating those pieces of information that will provide the desired input to a decision. The information required can take many forms but usually involves some form of comparison. This may entail comparing changes in the same item over a number of years, key relationships within the same year, or the operations of several firms in the same industry. Although many of these comparisons overlap, this chapter discusses methods of analysis in three categories: horizontal, vertical, and ratio. Exhibits 13–1 and 13–2 represent comparative financial statements for Milavec Company and will be referred to in the examples of analysis techniques.

Horizontal Analysis

Horizontal analysis refers to the study of an individual item over a period of time. This period of time may be only the current operating period or may be many years. Several approaches may be taken in reviewing one account: study of absolute amounts, percentages, and trends.

Absolute Amounts

Financial statement users are interested in the **absolute amounts** of various accounts for many reasons. Economic statistics are built on totals of absolute amounts as reported by businesses. These include gross national product figures and the amount spent to replace productive capacity. Financial statement users with expertise in particular industries can look at costs, such as research and development, and know whether a company is spending excessively or conservatively.

Exhibit 13-1

MILAVEC COMPANY
Income Statement and Statement of Retained Earnings
For the Years Ending Decemer 31

	2004	2003
Sales	$900,000	$800,000
Cost of Goods Sold		
Beginning Inventory	43,000	40,000
Purchases	637,000	483,000
Goods Available for Sale	680,000	523,000
Ending Inventory	70,000	43,000
Cost of Goods Sold	610,000	480,000
Gross Margin from Sales	290,000	320,000
Operating Expenses	248,000	280,000
Income before Taxes	42,000	40,000
Income Taxes	17,000	18,000
Net Income	25,000	22,000
Plus: Retained Earnings, Beginning Balance	137,000	130,000
Less: Dividends	0	15,000
Retained Earnings, Ending Balance	$162,000	$137,000

Exhibit 13-2

MILAVEC COMPANY
Balance Sheet
As of December 31

	2004	2003
Assets		
Cash	$ 20,000	$ 17,000
Marketable Securities	20,000	2,000
Notes Receivable	4,000	3,000
Accounts Receivable	50,000	56,000
Merchandise Inventory	70,000	43,000
Prepaid Expenses	4,000	4,000
Property, Plant, and Equipment (net)	340,000	310,000
Total Assets	$508,000	$455,000
Equities		
Accounts Payable	$ 40,000	$ 38,000
Salaries Payable	2,000	3,000
Taxes Payable	4,000	2,000
Bonds Payable, 8%	100,000	100,000
Preferred Stock, 6%, $100 par, cumulative	50,000	50,000
Common Stock, $10 Par	150,000	125,000
Retained Earnings	162,000	137,000
Total Equities	$508,000	$455,000

Simply using absolute amounts has many drawbacks, however. The major problem is that the **materiality** level differs from firm to firm. *Materiality* is a term that is difficult to define but nevertheless is used constantly in accounting. Firms are not required to account strictly for *immaterial* items, yet it is very difficult to look at an absolute amount and fully appreciate its significance without considering the size of other accounts of the business. Exxon Corporation's financial statements are presented in millions of dollars, indicating that amounts are rounded to the nearest million for reporting purposes. In that case, a $400,000 account may be considered immaterial and may be omitted altogether. This $400,000 amount, however, could represent total sales to a much smaller firm and therefore is material to it. No comparisons would

Exhibit 13-3

MILAVEC COMPANY
Comparative Income Statement
For the Years Ending December 31

	2004	2003	Percentage Difference
Sales	$900,000	$800,000	+12.5%*
Cost of Goods Sold	610,000	480,000	+27.1
Gross Margin from Sales	290,000	320,000	−9.4
Operating Expenses	248,000	280,000	−11.4
Income before Taxes	42,000	40,000	+5.0
Income Taxes	17,000	18,000	−5.6
Net Income	$ 25,000	$ 22,000	+13.6

*100,000 ÷ 800,000; all changes expressed as percentages of previous totals.

be possible between the two companies' operating performance using only absolute amounts.

Percentage Analysis

Percentage analysis involves establishing the relationship of one amount to another. In horizontal analysis, an account is expressed as a percentage of the previous balance of the same account. This type of analysis attempts to eliminate the materiality problems of comparing firms of different sizes by putting each on the same basis: 100 percent. Exhibit 13–3 presents a condensed version of Milavec's income statement showing horizontal percentages of each item.

The percentage changes reveal some interesting features. Even though Milavec's net income has increased slightly more than total sales, it may be pricing its products too low. The cost of goods sold increased much more than sales, resulting in a lower gross margin. A more detailed analysis would also investigate the substantial decrease in operating expenses despite the increase in volume.

In any analysis, whether of percentages, absolute amounts, or ratios, you must be careful to avoid making simplistic conclusions about the resulting information. Numerical relationships should be used to identify areas requiring further study. Recall from Chapter 8 that a change in what may appear to be a favourable direction may not necessarily be a good sign. The underlying reasons must be considered.

Trend Analysis

Trend analysis is simply an extension of percentage analysis to cover several periods of time. When more than two figures are studied, two basic approaches could be used: choosing one base year on which to base increases or decreases or calculating the percentage of change from each preceding figure. For example, assume that Milavec's sales for 2001 and 2002 had been $600,000 and $750,000, respectively.

	2004	2003	2002	2001
Sales	$900,000	$800,000	$750,000	$600,000
Increase over 2001 sales	50.0%	33.3%	25.0%	—
Increase over preceding year	12.5%	6.7%	25.0%	—

From this analysis, Milavec's 2004 sales represent a 50 percent increase over 2001 sales, and a very large increase (25 percent) occurred in 2002. From 2002 and 2003, sales increased only 6.7 percent but increased much more (12.5 percent) in the following year.

Vertical Analysis

Vertical analysis is a procedure that uses percentages to compare each of the parts of an individual statement to the whole. Horizontal analysis considers one item over many time periods, and vertical analysis considers many items in the same interval of time.

Percentages and ratios provide a common base that facilitates comparisons among companies of divergent sizes. For example, horizontal analysis reveals that Loblaw Company's 2000 earnings were approximately 26% higher than its 1999 earnings. In contrast, Sobeys experienced a decrease in earnings of approximately 47%. Although Loblaw Company is a much larger company that Sobeys, the increase in income for Loblaw could be due to the fact that Loblaw is a national company and Sobeys is more of a regional company. It could be that the economy of the region in which Sobeys operates was not as dynamic as the national economy. It could be that there was a company restructure that is not apparent in a numbers comparison. Being a good financial analyst is more that just calculating ratios. It is interpreting the ratios as well as considering qualitative factors.

Vertical Analysis of the Income Statement

In this type of analysis, each item is generally shown as a percentage of sales. Even though vertical analysis pertains to one statement, its usefulness is enhanced when vertical analysis of several years is performed. Exhibit 13–4 presents Milavec's income statements for 2004 and 2003. From this analysis, interesting relationships or changes in relationships can be identified. For example, the cost of goods sold has increased significantly as a percentage of sales. However, operating expenses and income taxes have decreased in relation to sales. Each of these points bears more analysis as to the trends they may be exhibiting for future profits.

Exhibit 13-4

MILAVEC COMPANY
Vertical Analysis of
Comparative Income Statements

	2004		2003	
	Amount	Percentage of Sales	Amount	Percentage of Sales
Sales	$900,000	100.0%	$800,000	100.0%
Cost of Goods Sold	610,000	67.7	480,000	60.0
Gross Margin from Sales	290,000	32.3%	320,000	40.0%
Operating Expenses	248,000	27.6	280,000	35.0
Income before Taxes	42,000	4.7	40,000	5.0%
Income Taxes	17,000	1.9	18,000	2.3
Net Income	$ 25,000	2.8%	$ 22,000	2.7%

Vertical Analysis of the Balance Sheet

When vertical analysis of the balance sheet is performed, each asset is presented as a percentage of total assets and each equity account is presented as a percentage of total equity. The vertical analysis of Milavec's balance sheets in Exhibit 13–5 reveals few large changes in percentages from the preceding year; however, when percentages are analyzed, small changes may represent a substantial increase in current assets, and because inventory is one of the less liquid current assets, this change may have significant consequences. Another pitfall to avoid in this analysis is the temptation to perceive that the decrease in the percentages of the nonchanging accounts indicates decreasing absolute amounts. Bonds payable and preferred shares have not changed, although their percentages to the total have decreased.

Exhibit 13-5

MILAVEC COMPANY
Vertical Analysis of Corporation Balance Sheets

	2004	Percentage of Total	2003	Percentage of Total
Assets				
Cash	$ 20,000	3.9%	$ 17,000	3.7%
Marketable Securities	20,000	3.9	22,000	4.8
Notes Receivable	4,000 0.	8	3,000	0.7
Accounts Receivable	50,000	9.8	56,000	12.3
Merchandise Inventory	70,000	13.8	43,000	9.5
Prepaid Expenses	4,000	0.8	4,000	0.9
Total Current Assets	168,000	33.0	145,000	31.9
Property, Plant, and Equipment	340,000	67.0	310,000	68.1
Total Assets	$508,000	100.0%	$455,000	100.0%
Equities				
Accounts Payable	$ 40,000	7.9%	$ 38,000	8.3%
Salaries Payable	2,000	0.4	3,000	0.7
Taxes Payable	4,000	0.8	2,000	0.4
Total Current Liabilities	46,000	9.1	43,000	9.4
Bonds Payable, 8%	100,000	19.7	100,000	22.0
Total Liabilities	146,000	28.8	143,000	31.4
Preferred Shares 6%, $100 par	50,000	9.8	50,000	11.0
Common Shares, $10 par	150,000	29.5	125,000	27.5
Retained Earnings	162,000	31.9	137,000	30.1
Total Shareholders' Equity	362,000	71.2	312,000	68.6
Total Equities	$508,000	100.0%	$455,000	100.0%

Ratio Analysis

LO3

Understand what the term *ratio analysis* means.

Ratio analysis is a form of vertical analysis in that it involves comparisons among different accounts in the same set of statements. It differs in that individual ratios indicate relationships between specific accounts, rather than between an account and the designated total on the statement. Numerous ratios are used for a wide variety of purposes, and the remainder of this chapter will be devoted to a discussion of some of the more commonly used ones.

Objectives of Ratio Analysis

As stated earlier, the various users of financial statements approach analysis with many different objectives. Although managers often use internally generated data to analyze operations, much information prepared for external purposes can be quite useful in examining past operation and determining future policies. Creditors are interested in assurances that the firm will be able to repay its debts on a timely basis. Both creditors and shareholders are concerned with the various means used to finance the company, whether through debt, equity transactions, or earnings. Shareholders and potential investors desire indicators of the future value of their investments and look to past performance of earnings and dividend policy to provide information that they hope will provide clues to the future. Although it is difficult to draw strictly defined lines among all of these objectives, we study debt-paying ratios grouped into three specific categories: liquidity ratios, solvency ratios, and profitability ratios.

▌ Measures of Debt-Paying Ability

Liquidity Ratios

Liquidity ratios as defined in this context are those that indicate a firm's short-term debt-paying ability. As such, they deal primarily with current assets and liabilities. The examples in the following section are taken from information presented in the financial statements of Milavec Company.

LO4

Calculate the ratios that facilitate the assessment of a company's debt-paying ability.

Working Capital

Working capital is defined as current assets minus current liabilities. Because current liabilities represent debts that must be satisfied in the current operating period and current assets are those assets that can be most easily converted into funds in the current period, working capital theoretically represents the funds that the company will have remaining to operate. Another way to look at working capital is to think of it as the cushion against short-term debt-paying problems. The amount of working capital at the end of 2004 and 2003 for Milavec Company is the following:

	2004	2003
Current assets	$168,000	$145,000
− Current liabilities	46,000	43,000
Working capital	$122,000	$102,000

Milavec's working capital experienced a dramatic increase from 2003 to 2004, but the numbers themselves tell us little. Whether $122,000 is a sufficient amount or not depends on many factors, among them the industry in which Milavec operates, its size, and the maturity dates of its current obligations. We can see, however, that the increase in working capital is primarily due to the increase in inventories.

Current Ratio

Working capital is an absolute amount and suffers from the difficulties of comparison that were mentioned earlier. It would be very difficult to compare Milavec's $122,000 with working capital from another firm of $122,000 and come to meaningful conclusions. However, by expressing the same information as a ratio, we have a better measure of the strength of the company's debt-paying ability in relation to other firms. The **current ratio**, also frequently called the **working capital ratio**, is calculated as follows:

$$\text{Current ratio} = \frac{\text{Current assets}}{\text{Current Liabilities}}$$

To illustrate the usefulness of the current ratio, consider Milavec's position in relation to a larger firm with current assets of $500,000 and current liabilities of $378,000.

	Milavec	Other Firm
Current assets (a)	$168,000	$500,000
− Current liabilities (b)	46,000	378,000
Working capital	$122,000	$122,000
Current ratio (a ÷ b)	3.65:1	1.32:1

The current ratio is expressed as the number of dollars of current assets to one dollar of current liabilities. In our example, despite the identical amount of working capital, Milavec appears to be in a much stronger working capital position. Any conclusions to be drawn from this analysis must consider the particular circumstances of the firm; there is no "good" current ratio for which to strive. Many financial statement users consider 2:1 to be an acceptable level; however, some industries may require more or less. A current ratio could also be too high, indicating poor management of investment opportunities in relation to current operational requirements.

Quick Ratio

The **quick ratio**, also known as the **acid-test ratio**, is a more conservative form of the current ratio. The quick ratio considers the fact that some accounts classified as current assets are less liquid than others. For example, inventories may take several months to sell; also, prepaid expenses serve only to offset otherwise necessary expenditures as time elapses. The quick ratio attempts to measure the firm's *immediate* debt-paying ability by considering only cash, receivables, and current marketable securities (known as *quick assets*) in relation to current liabilities.

$$\text{Quick ratio} = \frac{\text{Quick assets}}{\text{Current liabilities}}$$

The current ratios and quick ratios for 2004 and 2003 for Milavec Company follow:

	2004	2003
Current ratio	168,000 ÷ 46,000	145,000 ÷ 43,000
	3.65:1	3.37
Quick ratio	94,000 ÷ 46,000	98,000 ÷ 43,000
	2.04:1	2.13:1

The decreasing quick ratio from 2003 to 2004 reflects the larger investment in inventory in 2004.

Accounts Receivable Ratios

In an era when credit plays an enormous role in defining purchasing power, it is imperative for a company to manage its receivables in an effective manner. Two relationships are often examined to indicate a firm's collection record: **accounts receivable turnover** and **number of days' sales in receivables**.

1. *Turnover.* Accounts receivable turnover is calculated as follows:

$$\text{Accounts receivable turnover} = \frac{\text{Net credit sales}}{\text{Average accounts receivable}}$$

Net credit sales refers to sales on account after discounts and returns. When credit sales make up the bulk of sales or when the sales figure is not divided into cash and credit sales, the total sales figure must be used. *Net accounts receivable* refers to receivables after subtracting the allowance for bad debts, and it is preferable to use an average figure, when available. With comparative statements, a beginning and ending balance can be used, but it is even better if monthly data are available. Milavec Company's accounts receivable turnover is computed as follows:

	2004	2003
Net sales (assume all on account) (a)	$900,000	$800,000
Beginning receivables	$ 56,000	$ 55,000*
Ending receivables	50,000	56,000
Average receivables (b)	$ 53,000	$ 55,500
Turnover (a ÷ b)	16.98	14.41

*Additional data are not in illustration.

The 16.98 turnover figure for 2004 indicates that the company collects its average receivables almost 17 times a year. The higher the number, the faster the collections. A company can have a cash flow problem and lose substantial purchasing power if sales are tied up in receivables for long periods of time.

2. *Average collection period.* This ratio is sometimes called number of days' sales in receivables. Another way to look at the turnover figure is to determine the number of days, on average, it takes to

collect a receivable. If receivables are collected 16.98 times in 2004, the average is 365 ÷ 16.98 (the number of days in the year divided by turnover), in this case 21 days. For 2003, it took 25 days to collect the average receivable (365 ÷ 14.41). In summary, the *average collection period* can be calculated as follows:

$$\text{Average collection period} = \frac{\text{Number of days in the year}}{\text{Accounts receivable turnover}}$$

Although the time required for collection improved, no other conclusions can be reached without an analysis of the industry, Milavec's past performance, and the general economic environment.

Inventory Ratios

A fine line exists between having too much and too little inventory in stock. Insufficient inventory can lead to lost sales and time-consuming delays. Too much inventory can use needed space, cost extra insurance coverage, and become obsolete. In analyzing the funds tied up in inventory, the same two ratios are used as in accounts receivable analysis.

1. *Turnover.* **Inventory turnover** indicates the number of times, on the average, that total inventory is replaced during the year. The relationship is computed as follows:

$$\text{Inventory turnover} = \frac{\text{Cost of Goods sold}}{\text{Average inventory}}$$

Again, it is preferable to use as many figures as are available for the average calculation. Inventory turnover for Milavec is as follows:

	2004	2003
Cost of goods sold (a)	$610,000	$480,000
Beginning inventory	43,000	40,000
Ending inventory	70,000	43,000
Average inventory (b)	$ 56,500	$ 41,500
Inventory turnover (a ÷ b)	10.80	11.57

Generally, a higher turnover indicates that merchandise is being handled more efficiently. However, trying to compare firms in different industries can be dangerous. Grocery stores and many retail outlets have high turnover, while appliance and jewellery stores have much lower turnover due to the nature of the goods being sold. We will look at this issue in more detail when we discuss return on investment.

2. *Number of days' sales in inventory.* By dividing the number of days in the year by inventory turnover, we calculate the **number of days' sales in inventory**, a figure that approximates the number of days the firm could sell inventory without purchasing more. For Milavec, this figure was 34 days in 2004 (365 ÷ 10.80) and 32 days in 2003 (365 ÷ 11.57). In summary, the number of days required to sell inventory can be computed as follows:

$$\text{Number of days' sales in inventory} = \frac{\text{Number of days in the year}}{\text{Inventory turnover}}$$

Solvency Ratios

Solvency ratios are used to analyze a firm's long-term debt-paying ability and the composition of its financing structure. These ratios measure the relationships between different portions of the equity section of the balance sheet. Creditors are concerned about the firm's ability to satisfy outstanding obliga-

LO5

Calculate the ratios that facilitate the assessment of a company's solvency.

tions. The larger the percentage of liabilities, the greater is the risk that the company could fall behind or default on payments. Shareholders, too, are concerned about the firm's ability to pay debts; their interest is in the company's ability to maintain high earnings per share and dividend payments. Each group desires that financing be undertaken in such a way as to minimize the risk of its investment, whether that investment is in debt or shareholders' equity.

Debt/Equity Ratios

The following ratios are simply three ways to express the same relationship; however, each is frequently used. You should be familiar with all three.

1. *Ratio of liabilities to total equity.* This ratio is presented as a percentage. It simply notes the percentage of the company that is financed by debt. Often you will see this ratio presented as a percentage of liabilities to total assets.
2. *Shareholders' equity ratio.* This ratio, also a percentage, is the difference between the debt/equity ratio and 100 percent. It is the percentage of total equity (or total assets) represented by shareholders' equity.
3. *Debt/equity ratio.* In this ratio, *equity* is a shortened form of shareholders' equity. The previous two ratios considered parts of equity in relation to total equity; this ratio examines the parts in relation to each other, resulting in a dollar amount of liabilities for every dollar of shareholder's equity. The calculations for these three common ratios can be summarized as follows:

$$\text{Liabilities to total equity} = \frac{\text{Total liabilities}}{\text{Total equity}}$$

$$\text{Shareholders' equity ratio} = \frac{\text{Total shareholders' equity}}{\text{Total equity}}$$

$$\text{Debt/equity ratio} = \frac{\text{Total liabilities}}{\text{Total shareholders' equity}}$$

Using these formulas for Milavec Company produces the following.

	2004	2003
Total liabilities (a)	$146,000	$143,000
Total shareholders' equity (b)	362,000	312,000
Total equity (c)	$508,000	$455,000
Liabilities to total equity (a ÷ c)	29%	31%
Total shareholders' equity ratio (b ÷ c)	71%	69%
Debt to equity ratio (a ÷ b)	0.40:1	0.46:1

Each year the company's liabilities accounted for slightly less than one-third of total equity. The amount of liabilities per dollar of shareholders' equity declined by 0.06. It is impossible to say whether this slight reduction in the percentage of liabilities is a favourable trend. Perhaps the company is in a strong enough position to incur more liabilities. However, a lower level of liabilities generally suggests greater security because the likelihood of foreclosure is lessened.

Number of Times Bond Interest Is Earned

This ratio provides a quick look at the burden that long-term debt interest payments pose for the company. This is often calculated with the debt/equity ratios.

$$\text{Number of times bond interest is earned} = \frac{\text{Income before taxes and bond interest expense}}{\text{Bond interest expense}}$$

The numerator is the income of the company before taxes and before bond interest expense. The result of dividing this figure by bond interest expense indicates how often the interest obligation could be satisfied. Obviously, interest will be paid only once, but the more often it *could* be paid, the stronger is the company's ability to meet its obligations. For Milavec, this calculation is as follows:

	2004	2003
Income before taxes	$42,000	$40,000
Bond Interest (100,000 × 0.08) (b)	8,000	8,000
Income before taxes and interest (a)	$50,000	$48,000
Times interest earned (a ÷ b)	6.25 times	6 times

This type of analysis can be done with any expense or dividend payment. The other calculation most frequently seen is the number of times the preferred dividend is earned. The ratio takes much the same form except that the numerator is net income (after taxes), and the denominator, naturally, is the preferred dividend.

Plant Assets to Long-Term Liabilities

Often, a company secures its long-term liabilities by indenture. Financial statement users are interested in analyzing a firm's long-term ability to borrow funds on the strength of its asset base. This ratio provides such a measure and is calculated as follows:

$$\text{Plant assets to long-term liabilities} = \frac{\text{Net plant assets}}{\text{Long-term liabilities}}$$

For Milavec Company, these ratios follow:

	2004	2003
Net plant assets (a)	$340,000	$310,000
Bonds payable (b)	100,000	100,000
Plant assets to long-term liabilities (a ÷ b)	3.4:1	3.1:1

▌ Measures of Profitability

Profitability refers to the company's ability to generate earnings. Numerous ratios can be used to measure different aspects of profitability. Both management and external users desire information about how a firm is succeeding in generating profits and how these profits are being used to reward investors. The following two sections discuss ratios designed to measure managerial effectiveness and ratios frequently used by investors to measure return. This is simply a convenient way to categorize **profitability ratios** because investors often use measures of managerial effectiveness to predict future returns.

LO6

Calculate the ratios that facilitate the assessment of a company's managerial effectiveness.

Measures of Managerial Effectiveness

The most common ratios used to evaluate managerial effectiveness involve measurement of how the assets are generating sales and what percentage of these sales result in earnings. It is important to remember that an *absolute amount* of sales or earnings has little meaning unless the size of the company is considered.

Net Margin

You are probably familiar with the terms *gross margin* and *gross profit*, which refer to the amount of sales dollars remaining after a major expense, cost of goods sold, is subtracted. Net margin refers to the amount of the sales dollar remaining after all expenses are subtracted. **Net margin** can be calculated in several ways; some of the most common methods limit the expenses to normal operating expenses or expenses other than tax expense. For our purposes, however, we will use all expenses for simplicity. By dividing net income by net sales, we arrive at net margin expressed as a percentage of sales.

$$\text{Net margin} = \frac{\text{Net income}}{\text{Net sales}}$$

For Milavec Company, the net margins for the two years presented are as follows:

	2004	2003
Net income (a)	$ 25,000	$ 22,000
Net sales (b)	900,000	800,000
Net margin (a ÷ b)	2.78%	2.75%

Milavec is maintaining approximately the same net margin. Obviously, the larger the percentage, the better it is; however, it is difficult to analyze whether the net margin is adequate without considering factors such as the particular industry and the history of the company.

Turnover of Assets

Turnover of assets is a ratio that measures how many sales dollars are being generated for each dollar of assets. Like the margin calculation, the parts of this ratio can be defined in several different ways. Assets may be limited to operating assets, or a total assets figure may be desired. Also, when the amount of assets changes significantly during the year, it is desirable to use the average asset base, rather than the year-end balance. We use the latter to promote simplicity.

$$\text{Turnover of assets} = \frac{\text{Net sales}}{\text{Total assets}}$$

For Milavec, the turnover of assets calculations are as follows:

	2004	2003
Net sales (a)	$900,000	$800,000
Total assets (b)	508,000	455,000
Asset turnover (a ÷ b)	1.77	1.76

Analysis of asset turnover is also subject to other considerations. The particular industry may have high turnover if only minimal investment is required to operate the business. On the other hand, industries that require large amounts of machinery may be characterized by lower asset turnover.

Return on Investment

Return on investment combines the two preceding ratios (net margin and turnover of assets) to produce a measure that is easier to use in comparing different industries. Return on investment (ROI), often called **return on assets** or *earning power*, is calculated as follows:

$$\text{ROI} = \text{Net margin} \times \text{Asset turnover}$$

Remember that these two ratios consist of the following parts:

$$\frac{\text{Net income}}{\text{Net sales}} \times \frac{\text{Net sales}}{\text{Total assets}}$$

By cancelling net sales from both fractions, ROI can also be expressed as follows:

$$\text{ROI} = \frac{\text{Net income}}{\text{Total assets}}$$

When the amount of assets changes significantly during the year, it is desirable to use the average asset base, rather than the year-end balance. Although it may seem easier to think of ROI simply as the last fraction, it is very important to understand that it is a result of two considerations: how earnings are generated from sales and how sales are generated from assets. For Milavec, the calculation of ROI is as follows:

2004
2.78% × 1.77 = 4.92%
2003
2.75% × 1.76 = 4.84%

Using the fraction approach produces the same result. To understand how ROI can be used to compare different industries, consider the following figures for a retail clothing store and an appliance store:

	Margin		Turnover		ROI
Clothing store	2%	×	3.0	=	6%
Appliance store	4%	×	1.5	=	6%

Each has the same ROI, but it is arrived at in a different manner. The appliance store must earn a higher percentage of sales because its turnover is lower. Grocery stores often have net margins far less than 1 percent, yet the extremely high turnover results in significant profitability.

Return on Equity

Return on equity (ROE) is often used to measure the profitability of the firm in relation to the amount invested by shareholders. ROE is higher than ROI simply because the ratio does not consider that part of the business that is financed by debt. This ratio is really another way to look at leverage, much like the debt/equity ratios discussed earlier. ROE is computed as follows:

$$\text{ROE} = \frac{\text{Net income}}{\text{Total shareholders' equity}}$$

When the amount of shareholders' equity changes significantly during the year, it is desirable to use the average equity base, rather than the year-end balance. The formula above produces the following ROE figures for Milavec Company:

	2004	2003
Net income (a)	$ 25,000	$ 22,000
Preferred shares, 6%, $100 par, cumulative	50,000	50,000
Common shares, $10 par	150,000	125,000
Retained earnings	162,000	137,000
Total shareholders' equity (b)	$362,000	$312,000
ROE (a ÷ b)	6.9%	7.1%

The slight decrease in ROE is primarily due to the increase in common shares from 2003. Although earnings were higher, the increase in total shareholders' equity offsets this. From the information provided, we do not know whether Milavec had the use of these additional funds all or part of the year. If these data are available, it is best to calculate a weighted average amount of shareholders' equity.

LO7

Calculate the ratios that facilitate the assessment of a company's position in the stock market.

Stock Market Ratios

Present and potential investors in a company's share employ many common ratios. The ratios are primarily used in analyzing companies of different sizes and different industries in relation to their earnings and dividends. Remember that a purchaser of shares can profit in two ways: the dividends paid and the increase in the value of the shares. Thus, although investors consider dividends to be important, they are also interested in the overall earnings performance of the company as an indication of the value of the shares they own.

Earnings per Share

Perhaps the most frequently quoted ratio of earnings performance is **earnings per share** (EPS), which attempts to measure the value of a share by attributing to it a portion of the company's earnings. Do not confuse EPS with *dividends per share*. Rarely would a company distribute all the year's earnings to the shareholders. EPS calculations are among the most complex in accounting, and more advanced textbooks devote entire chapters to their calculation. At this level, we deal with the following basic formula:

$$\text{Earnings per share} = \frac{\text{Net earnings available for common shares}}{\text{Average number of outstanding common shares}}$$

By limiting the net earnings figure to earnings available for common shares, we eliminate the amount of the preferred dividend (i.e., $0.06 \times \$50,000 = \$3,000$) from consideration. Note that Exhibit 13–1 indicates that preferred dividends were not paid in 2004. However, since the preferred shares are cumulative, the preferred dividend is in arrears and not available to the common shareholders. The number of common shares outstanding is determined by dividing the book value of the shares by the par value per share (i.e., $\$150,000 \div \$10 = 15,000$ for 2004 and $\$125,000 \div \$10 = 12,500$ for 2003). With these considerations in mind, the 2004 EPS figure for Milavec is as follows:

$$\frac{\$25,000 \text{ (net income)} - \$3,000 \text{ (preferred dividend)}}{(15,000 + 12,500)/2 \text{ (average common shares outstanding)}} = \$1.60 \text{ per share}$$

A great deal of importance is attached to EPS figures, so it is important to understand the many limitations involved. Numerous variables are involved in calculating income, including different methods for amortization, inventory cost flow and revenue recognition, to name only a few. The denominator is also very much in question because various factors affect the number of shares to include. Numerous opportunities exist for manipulation of the EPS figure, and the prudent investor must consider all these in deciding how much weight to attach to earnings per share.

Book Value

Book value per share is another frequently quoted measure of a share. It is calculated as follows:

$$\text{Book value per share} = \frac{\text{Shareholders' equity} - \text{Preferred rights}}{\text{Average outstanding common shares}}$$

Instead of using shareholders' equity as the numerator, we could have easily used assets minus liabilities, which is the formula for determining a company's "net worth." Net worth is a misnomer because a company's worth is not reflected in the accounts. Because assets are recorded at historical costs and different methods are used to transfer their costs to expense, the book value of assets remaining after liabilities have been deducted really means little if anything. Nevertheless, because the term *book value per share* is used frequently, you should be aware of its definition.

Preferred rights refers to the amount of money that would be required to satisfy the claims of preferred shareholders. If a call premium exists, that must also be considered. In our example, we assume that the preferred shares can be retired at par; thus, book value per share for 2004 is as follows:

$$\frac{\$362{,}000 - \$50{,}000}{(15{,}000 + 12{,}400)/2} = \$22.69 \text{ per share}$$

Price-Earnings Ratio

The **price-earnings ratio**, often called the *PE ratio*, is a measure that weighs the earnings per share of each firm by the price of a share. Assume that Firms A and B have an EPS of $3.60 and Firm C has an EPS of $4.10. On the basis of these data alone, you may prefer the higher EPS of Firm C. However, your decision may change when you consider that the price of one share in each firm is $43.20, $36, and $51.25, respectively. Now, which share should you buy? The price of Firm C's shares is higher, but then, its EPS is higher, too. Using the PE ratio can reduce all three firms to the same comparison basis:

$$\text{Price-earnings ratio} = \frac{\text{Market price per share}}{\text{Earnings per share}}$$

Thus, the PE ratios for the three firms are:

A	B	C
12.0	10.0	12.5

An immediate reaction to this might be to consider Firm B to be the best buy for your money. On the other hand, there must be some reason that Firm C's stock is selling at 12½ times earnings. Perhaps technology or expert management is keeping the price high. It is difficult, therefore, to use these ratios in a simple manner to make shares decisions as the reasons behind the ratios must be examined as well.

Dividend Yield

The **dividend yield** is a measure of the profitability of particular interest to those investors who are primarily investing to receive short-term returns in the form of dividends. Dividend yield gives a measure of the dividends received as a percentage of the market price of the shares.

$$\text{Dividend yield} = \frac{\text{Dividends per share}}{\text{Market price per share}}$$

As an example, consider Firms D and E. The information required to calculate dividend yield is as follows:

	Firm D	Firm E
Dividends per share (a)	$ 1.80	$ 3.00
Market price per share (b)	40.00	75.00
Dividend yield (a ÷ b)	4.5%	4.0%

Even though the actual dividend per share is higher for Firm E ($3 versus $1.80), the yield is lower (4.5% versus 4%) because the price of the shares is so high.

Other Ratios

In actuality, a wide array of other ratios may be used to analyze profitability. Most of these ratios follow the logic of many of the ratios presented. For example, you should be able to calculate the *yield* of a number of factors. Yield can be simply expressed as what is received as a percentage of what is given up. We calculated the dividend yield, which could be either for common or preferred shares. The earnings yield would be earnings per share as a percentage of market price. Yield on a bond can be calculated in much the same way (interest received divided by the price of the bond).

Another category of ratios includes those used to calculate the number of times a particular item is earned as a measure of the safety of that item. Although the most commonly calculated measures involve bond interest and the preferred dividend, the same format can be used for any expense or other payout. The specific ratios presented in this chapter are summarized in Exhibit 13–6.

The last category we discuss consists simply of other percentages. A ratio is, by definition, a percentage. It is a measure of one item (the numerator) in terms of another (the denominator). In this chapter, we have discussed the major percentages, but different circumstances could call for the calculation of less common ratios. You should be able to calculate a ratio of *any* two items that are of interest in your analysis. In the Milavec example, you may be interested in the percentage of its operating expenses that are prepaid at the end of the year. The answer is 1.6 percent (2004 prepaid expenses ÷ 2004 total operating expenses).

Exhibit 13-6 *Summary of Key Relationships*

Liquidity Ratios	1. Working capital	**Current assets − Current liabilities**
	2. Current ratio	**Current assets ÷ Current liabilities**
	3. Quick (acid-test) ratio	**(Current assets − Inventory − Prepaids) ÷ Current liabilities**
	4. Accounts receivable turnover	**Net credit sales ÷ Average net receivables**
	5. Average collection period	**Days in year ÷ Accounts receivable turnover**
	6. Inventory turnover	**Cost of goods sold ÷ Average inventory**
	7. Number of days required to sell inventory	**Days in year ÷ Inventory turnover**
Solvency Ratios	8. Liabilities to total equity	**Total liabilities ÷ Total equity**
	9. Shareholders' equity ratio	**Total shareholders' equity ÷ Total equity**
	10. Debt/equity ratio	**Total liabilities ÷ Total shareholders' equity**
	11. Number of times bond interest earned	**Income before taxes and bond interest expense ÷ Bond interest expense**
	12. Plant assets to long-term liabilities	**Net plant assets ÷ Long-term liabilities**
Profitability Ratios	13. Net margin	**Net income ÷ Net sales**
	14. Turnover of assets	**Net sales ÷ Total assets**
	15. Return on investment (also: return on assets)	**Net income ÷ Total assets**
	16. Return on equity	**Net income ÷ Total shareholders' equity**
Stock Market Ratios	17. Earnings per share	**Net earnings available for common shares ÷ Average number of outstanding common shares**
	18. Book value per share	**(Shareholders' equity − Preferred rights) ÷ Average outstanding common shares**
	19. Price-earnings ratio	**Market price per share ÷ Earnings per share**
	20. Dividend yield	**Dividends per share ÷ Market price per share**

▌ Presentation of Analytical Relationships

LO8

Identify different forms for presenting analytical data.

Analytical information can be presented in endless ways in annual reports; the only limits are the creativity of the individual firm and the costs involved. Although most of the information included in annual reports is not required, companies often aid the user of the statements by preparing and presenting the information in a manner that can be more easily understood than simple numbers. Some of the more common forms of presentation are bar charts, pie charts, and graphs. Examples of these three forms are presented in Exhibits 13–7, 13–8, and 13–9.

The most widely recognized source of financial information is a company's annual report. Most companies provide copies of their annual report free of charge. Normally, a person can obtain a copy of the annual report simply by calling the corporate office and asking the receptionist to direct the call to the appropriate department. Another source for public companies registered with the Securities and Exchange Commission is the SEDAR, which can be accessed through the Internet address www.SEDAR.com. Also, many brokerage houses offer free financial information through their web pages. As an example, we suggest that you try the Internet address www.schwab.com.

Myrleen Ferguson Cate/ PhotoEdit

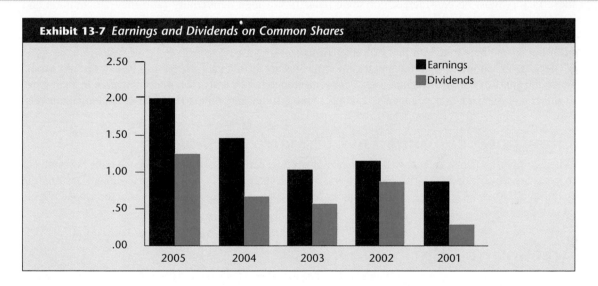

Exhibit 13-7 *Earnings and Dividends on Common Shares*

▮ Limitations of Financial Statement Analysis

Analyzing financial statements is much like buying a new car. Each car is different, and each one has applicable statistics to be considered: gas mileage, size of engine, reputation of maker, colour, accessories, and price, to name a few. Just as it is difficult to compare a Toyota station wagon with a Ferrari sports car, so it is difficult to compare a small textile firm with a giant oil company. This is the classic situation of comparing apples and oranges. The only way the potential buyer can compare the two cars is to focus on key pieces of data expressed on the same basis for each car. Gas mileage is a comparable factor. The superior gas mileage of the station wagon may pale in comparison with the thrill of driving the sports car, yet the price of the latter may prove to be the statistic that determines the ultimate choice.

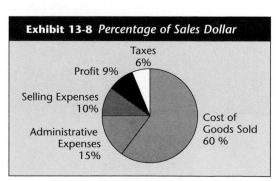

Exhibit 13-8 *Percentage of Sales Dollar*

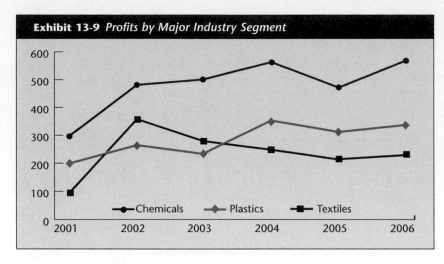

Exhibit 13-9 *Profits by Major Industry Segment*

An investor, or any other external user, can use ratios only as a general guide or set of clues to the potential of the business. It is very easy to place too much weight on any one figure. From the preceding discussion, you should realize that many factors must be considered before deciding how much faith to place in a ratio and what the ratio really means.

Different Industries

LO9

Understand the limitations of financial statement analysis.

Different industries may be affected by unique social policies, special accounting procedures, or other individual industry attributes. Before the ratios of the companies in different industries can be compared, these factors must be considered. For some industries, a high debt/equity ratio may be common and much more acceptable than in other industries. A particular line of business may require more or less working capital than some average. In this case, the working capital and quick ratios would have little meaning when compared with those of other firms.

Because of industry-specific factors, most professional analysts specialize in certain industries. Financial analysts for brokerage houses, banks, insurance funds, and so on may specialize in such areas as mineral or oil extraction, chemicals, banking, retail, insurance, bond markets, and international markets.

Changing Economic Environment

When comparing firms, an analyst must realize that the general state of the economy changes from year to year. Significant decreases in fuel costs and drops in interest rates in recent years make old rule-of-thumb guidelines for analysis of these factors obsolete. In addition, inflation is a factor whose effects cannot be ignored.

Accounting Principles

An analysis technique is only as reliable as the data on which it is based. Although the great majority of firms follow generally accepted accounting principles, a wide variety of methods is available from which to choose in certain categories, including different inventory and amortization methods, different schedules for recognizing revenue on construction projects, and different ways to account for oil and gas exploration costs. Companies that may otherwise be identical may use different accounting methods and therefore produce noncomparable ratios. For this reason, many analysts try to recast statements by estimating what the results would have been under the same methods.

Accrual accounting requires the use of many estimates; bad debts expense, warranty expense, asset lives, and salvage are just a few. The reliability of the resulting income figures depends on the expertise and the integrity of the persons responsible for the estimates.

Specific characteristics of the accounting model affect the numbers that are produced. Two underlying concepts in particular, *conservatism* and *historical cost*, have a tremendous impact on financial reporting. By accruing estimated losses and deferring gains until realization, conservatism biases financial statements in a downward direction. There are persuasive reasons for the conservatism principle, but it does distort the use of accounting figures as indicators of the potential for future gains.

The historical cost concept is probably the greatest single culprit in distorting the results of financial statement analysis. The historical cost of an asset does not represent its value in the present. To make matters worse, the $10,000 asset purchased in 1960 cannot even be compared with the $10,000 asset purchased in 1975 because of the difference in the value of the dollar. Because of historical cost, financial statements are full of dollars of different sizes. By adding and subtracting these dollars, the result is much like adding miles to kilometers.

Financial statement analysis involves many factors, among them the characteristics of the users, what information is desired, and how the information is to be used. Three general methods of analysis are *horizontal*, *vertical*, and *ratio analyses*. The ratios that are commonly calculated can be analyzed in terms of their ability to measure a firm's liquidity, solvency, and profitability. The specific ratios presented in this chapter are summarized in Exhibit 13–6. Despite the ease of calculation and the apparent insights provided by ratios, they have limitations involving differing industry characteristics, differing economic conditions, and the fundamental principles of the accounting system used to produce the numbers.

a look **back**

The next chapter covers the cash flow statement. In this chapter, you will learn how to identify cash transactions into one of three categories, including financing activities, investing activities, and operating activities. In addition, the chapter explains how to prepare a cash flow statement using the T-account method and how to distinguish the direct method of presentation from the indirect method. The level and timing of coverage of the cash flow statement differs among schools. Accordingly, your instructor may or may not cover this chapter.

a look **forward**

KEY TERMS

Absolute amounts Dollar totals reported in accounts on financial reports that can be misleading because they make no reference to the relative size of the company being analyzed. *(p. 463)*

Accounts receivable turnover A ratio measuring the quality of accounts receivable; calculated by dividing net sales by average net accounts receivable. *(p. 468)*

Acid-test ratio A measure of immediate debt-paying ability; calculated by dividing very liquid assets (cash, receivables, and marketable securities) by current liabilities. *(p. 468)*

Book value per share A measure of the value of a common share; calculated by dividing shareholders' equity less preferred rights by the average number of

common shares outstanding. *(p. 474)*

Current ratio A measure of liquidity; calculated by dividing current assets by current liabilities. *(p. 467)*

Dividend yield A ratio for comparing shares dividends paid in relation to the market price; calculated as dividends per share divided by market price per share. *(p. 475)*

Earnings per share A measure of the value of a share of common shares in terms of company earnings; calculated as net income available to common shareholders' divided by the average number of outstanding common shares. *(p. 474)*

Horizontal analysis An analysis technique that compares amounts of the same item over several time periods. *(p. 463)*

Information overload A situation in which presentation of too much information confuses the user of the information. *(p. 462)*

Inventory turnover A measurement of the volume of sales in relation to inventory levels; calculated as the cost of goods sold divided by average inventory. *(p. 469)*

Liquidity ratios Measures of short-term debt-paying ability. *(p. 467)*

Materiality The characteristic that designates the point at which the knowledge of or lack of information would make a difference in a decision; may be measured in absolute, percentage, quantitative, or qualitative terms. *(p. 463)*

Net margin A profitability measurement that indicates the percentage of each sales dollar resulting

in profit; calculated as net income divided by net sales. *(p. 472)*

Number of days' sales in inventory Another way to look at the inventory turnover by converting the inventory turnover ratio into a number of days; calculated by dividing average inventory by the average cost of goods sold. *(p. 469)*

Number of days' sales in receivables (average collection period) Another way to look at the accounts receivable turnover by converting the turnover ratio into a number of days; calculated by dividing 365 days by the turnover ratio. *(p. 468)*

Percentage analysis Analysis of relationships between two different items to draw conclusions or make decisions. *(p. 464)*

Price-earnings ratio A measurement used to compare the values of different shares in terms of earnings; calculated as market price per share divided by earnings per share. *(p. 475)*

Profitability ratios Measurements of a firm's ability to generate earnings. *(p. 471)*

Quick ratio Same as acid-test ratio. *(p. 468)*

Ratio analysis Same as percentage analysis. *(p. 466)*

Return on assets Same as return on investment. *(p. 472)*

Return on equity A measure of a firm's profitability based on earnings generated in relation to shareholders' equity; calculated as net income divided by shareholders' equity. *(p. 473)*

Return on investment A measure of profitability based on a firm's asset base; calculated as net income divided by total assets. ROI is a product of net margin and asset turnover. *(p. 472)*

Solvency ratios Measures of a firm's long-term debt-paying ability. *(p. 469)*

Trend analysis The study of the performance of ratios over a period of time. *(p. 464)*

Turnover of assets A measure of sales in relation to assets; calculated as net sales divided by total assets. *(p. 472)*

Vertical analysis An analysis technique that compares items on financial statements to significant totals. *(p. 464)*

Working capital An absolute dollar amount calculated by subtracting current liabilities from current assets. *(p. 467)*

Working capital ratio Another term for the current ratio; calculated by dividing current assets by current liabilities. *(p. 467)*

QUESTIONS

1. Why are ratios and trends used as an approach to financial analysis?
2. What do the terms *liquidity* and *solvency* mean?
3. What can be analyzed from a horizontal presentation of financial statement information? a vertical presentation?
4. What is the significance of inventory turnover, and how is it calculated?
5. What is the difference between the current ratio and the quick ratio? What does each measure?
6. Why are absolute amounts insufficient for comparing firms?
7. What is the difference between return on investment and return on equity?
8. Which ratios are used to measure long-term debt-paying ability? How is each calculated?
9. What are some of the limitations of the earnings per share figure?
10. What are the components of return on investment? What does each measure?
11. What is information overload?
12. What is the price-earnings ratio? Explain the difference between this and the dividend yield.
13. What are some environmental factors that must be considered in analyzing firms?
14. How do accounting principles affect financial statement analysis?

EXERCISES

L.O. 4 EXERCISE 13-1   *Inventory Turnover*

The Adams Company's merchandise inventories and other related accounts for 2004 follow:

Sales	$3,000,000
Cost of goods sold	2,200,000
Merchandise inventory:	
Beginning of year	500,000
End of year	600,000

Required

Assuming that the merchandise inventory buildup was relatively constant, how many times did the merchandise inventory turn over during 2004?

EXERCISE 13-2   *Number of Times Bond Interest Earned*   **L.O. 5**

The following data were abstracted from the financial records of Baker Corporation for 2004:

Sales	$3,600,000
Bond interest expense	120,000
Income tax expense	600,000
Net income	800,000

Required
How many times was bond interest earned in 2004?

EXERCISE 13-3   *Current Ratio*   **L.O. 4**

Camden Corporation collected a $100 account receivable from the $1,200 balance in its receivables account.

Required
Compare the current ratio before the collection with the current ratio after the collection.

EXERCISE 13-4   *Working Capital and Current Ratio*   **L.O. 4**

On June 30, 2003, Gamma Company's total current assets amounted to $400,000 and the total current liabilities equalled $200,000. On July 1, 2003, Gamma issued a *short-term* note to a bank for $50,000 cash.

Required
a. Compare the working capital before and after this transaction.
b. Compute the current ratios before and after this transaction.

EXERCISE 13-5   *Working Capital and Current Ratio*   **L.O. 4**

On June 30, 2003, Gamma Company's total current assets amounted to $400,000 and the total current liabilities equalled $200,000. On July 1, 2003, Gamma issued a *long-term* note to a bank for $50,000 cash.

Required
a. Compare the working capital before and after this transaction.
b. Compute the current ratios before and after this transaction.

EXERCISE 13-6   *Horizontal Analysis*   **L.O. 2**

Hiyakawa Corporation over the last two years showed the following operating results from its income statement:

	2004	2003	Percentage Change
Sales	$1,000,000	$900,000	
Cost of Goods Sold	750,000	600,000	
Gross Margin on Sales	$ 250,000	$ 300,000	
Operating Expenses	205,000	225,000	
Income before Taxes	$ 45,000	$ 75,000	
Income Taxes	17,100	30,000	
Net Income	$ 27,900	$ 45,000	

Required
a. Compute the percentage changes of items in Hiyakawa Corporation's income statements from 2003 to 2004.
b. Comment on the features revealed by the percentage changes computed in Requirement *a*.

EXERCISE 13-7   *Vertical Analysis*   **L.O. 2**

Charlotte Company shows the following operating results for the last two years of its operations:

2004	Amount	Percentage of Sales
Sales	$300,000	
Cost of Goods Sold	200,000	
Gross Margin on Sales	$100,000	
Operating Expenses	65,000	
Income before Taxes	$ 35,000	
Income Taxes	15,000	
Net Income	$ 20,000	

2005	Amount	Percentage of Sales
Sales	$290,000	
Cost of Goods Sold	188,500	
Gross Margin on Sales	$101,500	
Operating Expenses	75,000	
Income before Taxes	$ 26,500	
Income Taxes	11,500	
Net Income	$ 15,000	

Required

Prepare vertical analysis income statements by computing each item as a percentage of sales for each of the two years shown.

L.O. 2 EXERCISE 13-8   *Ratio Analysis*

The balance sheet for Mecklenburg Corporation follows:

Current Assets	$ 250,000
Long-Term Assets (net)	1,590,000
Total Assets	$1,840,000
Current Liabilities	$ 175,000
Long-Term Liabilities	980,000
Total Liabilities	$1,155,000
Capital Shares and Retained Earnings	685,000
Total Liabilities and Capital	$1,840,000

Required

Compute the following:
Working capital _____
Current ratio _____
Liabilities to total assets _____
Shareholders' equity ratio _____
Debt/equity ratio _____

L.O. 7 EXERCISE 13-9   *Ratio Analysis*

During 2003, TIS Corporation reported total after-tax net income of $2,368,500. During the year, the number of shares remained constant at 10,000 of $100 par, 9 percent preferred shares and 400,000 common shares. The company's total equity is $11,500,000 including the income for the year. TIS Corporation's common shares were selling at $26 per share at the end of its fiscal year. All dividends for the year have been paid, including $2.40 per share to common shareholders.

Required

Compute the following:
a. Earnings per share
b. Book value per share of common shares

c. Price-earnings ratio
d. Dividend yield

EXERCISE 13-10   *Ratio Analysis*   **L.O. 2, 3, 4,
                                                                              5, 6, 7**

Required

Match the following desired computation with the correct formula that should be used to make the calculation:

_____ 1. Working capital	A. Net income ÷ Total shareholders' equity
_____ 2. Current ratio	B. Cost of goods sold ÷ Average inventory
_____ 3. Quick ratio	C. Current assets − Current liabilities
_____ 4. Accounts receivable turnover	D. Days in year ÷ Inventory turnover
_____ 5. Average collection period	E. Net income ÷ Total assets
_____ 6. Inventory turnover	F. (Net income − Preferred dividends) ÷ Average outstanding common shares
_____ 7. Number of days' sales in inventory	G. (Current assets − Inventory − Prepaid expenses) ÷ Current liabilities
_____ 8. Liabilities to total equity	H. Total liabilities ÷ Total equity
_____ 9. Shareholders' equity ratio	I. Days in year ÷ Accounts receivable turnover
_____ 10. Return on investment	J. Total shareholders' equity ÷ Total equity
_____ 11. Return on equity	K. Net credit sales ÷ Average net receivables
_____ 12. Earnings per share	L. Current assets ÷ Current liabilities

EXERCISE 13-11   *Horizontal and Vertical Analyses*   **L.O. 2**

Income statements for Wimbleton Company for 2002 and 2003 follow:

	2003	2002
Sales	$121,000	$92,000
Cost of Goods Sold	$ 75,000	$51,000
Selling Expenses	20,000	11,000
Administrative Expenses	12,000	14,000
Interest Expenses	3,000	5,000
Total Expenses	$110,000	$81,000
Income before Taxes	$ 11,000	$11,000
Income Taxes Expense	3,000	2,000
Net Income	$ 8,000	$ 9,000

Required

a. Perform a horizontal analysis of 2003 compared with 2002.
b. Perform a vertical analysis for both years.

EXERCISE 13-12   *Ratio Analysis*   **L.O. 2, 3, 4,
                                                                              5, 6, 7**

Compute the following ratios using Beta Company's balance sheet for 2001:

Assets	
Cash	$ 6,000
Marketable Securities	3,200
Accounts Receivable	5,200
Inventory	4,400
Property and Equipment	68,000
Accumulated Amortization	(5,000)
Total Assets	$81,800

(Continued on the following page.)

Equities	
Accounts Payable	$ 3,400
Current Notes Payable	1,400
Mortgage Payable	1,800
Bonds Payable	8,600
Common Shares, $50 Par	44,000
Paid-in Capital in Excess of Par	1,600
Retained Earnings	21,000
Total Equities	$81,800

The average number of common shares outstanding during 2001 was 880 shares. Net income for the year was $6,000.

Required
Compute each of the following:
a. Current ratio
b. Earnings per share
c. Quick (acid-test) ratio
d. Return on investment
e. Return on equity
f. Debt/equity ratio

L.O. 4, 5, 6, 7   **EXERCISE 13-13**   *Comprehensive Analysis*

Required
For each of the following transactions, indicate the effect on (1) the current ratio, (2) working capital, (3) shareholders' equity, (4) book value per share of common shares, (5) retained earnings:
a. Sold merchandise on account for a profit.
b. Issued share dividend.
c. Paid account payable.
d. Sold building for a loss.
e. Collected account receivable.
f. Wrote off account receivable.
g. Purchased inventory on account.
h. Declared cash dividend.

L.O. 4, 7   **EXERCISE 13-14**   *Accounts Receivable Turnover, Inventory Turnover, and Net Margin*

Selected data of Campbell Company are as follows:

Balance Sheet As of December 31		
	2006	2005
Accounts Receivable	$500,000	$470,000
Allowance for Doubtful Accounts	(25,000)	(20,000)
Net Accounts Receivable	$475,000	$450,000
Inventories, Lower of Cost or Market	$600,000	$550,000

Income Statement
For the Year Ended December 31

	2006	2005
Net Credit Sales	$2,500,000	$2,200,000
Net Cash Sales	500,000	400,000
Net Sales	$3,000,000	$2,600,000
Cost of Goods Sold	$2,000,000	$1,800,000
Selling, General, & Administrative Expenses	300,000	270,000
Other Expenses	50,000	30,000
Total Operating Expenses	$2,350,000	$2,100,000

Required

Find the following:

a. The accounts receivable turnover for 2006.
b. The inventory turnover for 2006.
c. The net margin for 2005.

EXERCISE 13-15 *Comprehensive Analysis*   **L.O. 4, 5**

The December 31, 2005, balance sheet of Glenn, Inc. is presented here. These are the only accounts in Glenn's balance sheet. Amounts indicated by a question mark (?) can be calculated from the additional information given.

Assets	
Cash	$ 25,000
Accounts Receivable (net)	?
Inventory	?
Property, Plant, and Equipment (net)	294,000
	$432,000
Liabilities and Shareholders' Equity	
Accounts Payable (trade)	$?
Income Taxes Payable (current)	25,000
Long-Term Debt	?
Common Shares	300,000
Retained Earnings	?
	$?

Additional Information:

Current Ratio (at year end)	1.5 to 1.0
Total Liabilities ÷ Total Shareholders' Equity	0.8
Gross Margin	30%
Inventory Turnover (Cost of Goods Sold ÷ Ending Inventory)	10.5 times
Gross Margin for 2005	$315,000

Required

Find the following:

a. The balance in trade accounts payable as of December 31, 2005.
b. The balance in retained earnings as of December 31, 2005.
c. The balance in the inventory account as of December 31, 2005.

L.O. 2 **PROBLEM 13-1A** *Vertical Analysis*

The following percentages apply to Lingleton Company for 2006 and 2007:

	2007	2006
Sales	100.0%	100.0%
Cost of goods sold	61.0	64.0
Gross margin	39.0%	36.0%
Selling and administrative expense	26.5%	20.5%
Interest expense	2.5	2.0
Total expenses	29.0%	22.5%
Income before taxes	10.0%	13.5%
Income tax expense	5.5	7.0
Net Income	4.5%	6.5%

Required

Assuming that sales were $700,000 in 2006 and $900,000 in 2007, prepare income statements for the two years.

L.O. 5, 6, 7 **PROBLEM 13-2A** *Ratio Analysis*

The following is River Road's income statement information:

	2005	2004
Net sales	$1,260,000	$780,000
Net income before interest and taxes	330,000	255,000
Net income after taxes	166,500	189,000
Bond interest expense	27,000	24,000
Shareholders' equity, December 31 (2003: $600,000)	915,000	705,000
Common shares, par $50, December 31	780,000	690,000

The average number of shares outstanding was 15,600 for 2005 and 13,800 for 2004.

Required

Compute the following ratios for River Road for 2005 and 2004:

a. Number of times bond interest was earned.

b. Earnings per share based on the average number of shares outstanding.

c. Price-earnings ratio (market prices: 2005, $96 per share; 2004, $116 per share).

d. Return on average equity.

e. Net margin.

L.O. 4 **PROBLEM 13-3A** *Ratio Analysis*

Limon Manufacturing has a current ratio of 3:1 on December 31, 2008. The following are transactions in which the company engaged. Indicate whether each transaction would (+) increase, (−) decrease, or (NE) not affect Limon's current ratio. Do the same for the effect on its working capital.

Required

a. Collected accounts receivable.

b. Invested in current marketable securities.

c. Paid cash for a trademark.

d. Wrote off an uncollectible account receivable.

e. Sold equipment for cash.

f. Sold merchandise for a profit (cash).
g. Declared a cash dividend.
h. Purchased inventory on account.
i. Scrapped a fully amortized machine (no gain or loss).
j. Issued a shares dividend.
k. Purchased a machine for a long-term note.
l. Paid a previously declared cash dividend.

PROBLEM 13-4A *Ratio Analysis*   L.O. 7

The following are selected data for Faneburg Company for 2004 and additional information on industry averages:

Earnings (i.e., net income)		$ 217,500
Preferred shares (16,500 shares at $50 par, 4%)		$ 825,000
Common shares (37,500 shares at $1 par, market value $56)		37,500
Paid-in capital in excess of par—common		600,000
Retained earnings		703,125
		$2,165,625
Less: Treasury shares		
Preferred (1,500 shares)	$ 67,500	
Common (1,500 shares)	30,000	97,500
Total shareholders' equity		$2,068,125

Note: Dividends in arrears on preferred shares: $30,000. The preferred shares can be called for $51 per share.

Industry averages:	
Earnings per share	$ 5.20
Price-earnings ratio	9.5
Return on equity	11.2%

Required
a. Calculate and compare Faneburg Company's ratios with the industry averages.
b. Discuss whether you would invest in the company and any other factors that should be considered.

PROBLEM 13-5A *Missing Numbers on Balance Sheet*   L.O. 2

The bookkeeper of Bendigo's Country Music Bar fell ill and left this incomplete balance sheet. Bendigo's working capital is $60,000 and the shareholders' equity ratio is 60 percent.

Assets	
Current Assets	
Cash	$ 14,000
Accounts Receivable	28,000
Inventory	(A)
Prepaid Expenses	6,000
Total Current Assets	$ (B)
Long-Term Assets	
Building	$ (C)
Less: Accumulated Amortization	(26,000)
Total Long-Term Assets	140,000
Total Assets	$ (D)

(Continued on the following page.)

Equities		
Liabilities		
Current Liabilities		
Accounts Payable	$	(E)
Notes Payable		8,000
Income Tax Payable		7,000
Total Current Liabilities		$25,000
Long-Term Liabilities		
Mortgage Payable		(F)
Total Liabilities	$	(G)
Shareholders' Equity		
Common Shares		70,000
Retained Earnings		(H)
Total Shareholders' Equity		(I)
Total Equities	$	(J)

Required

Complete the balance sheet by filling in the blanks.

L.O. 2, 3, 4, 5, 6, 7   **PROBLEM 13-6A** *Ratio Analysis*

The following are the financial statements of McKeown Company:

	2002	2001
Revenues		
Net Sales	$315,000	$262,500
Other Revenues	6,000	7,000
Total Revenues	$321,000	$269,500
Expenses		
Cost of Goods Sold	$189,000	$154,875
Selling Expenses	32,000	29,000
General and Administrative Expenses	16,000	15,000
Interest Expense	4,000	4,500
Income Tax Expense (40%)	32,000	26,450
Total Expenses	$273,000	$229,825
Earnings from Continuing Operations before Extraordinary Items	48,000	39,675
Extraordinary Gain (net of $8,000 tax)	6,000	0
Net Earnings	$ 54,000	$ 39,675

Assets		
Current Assets		
Cash	$ 6,500	$ 11,500
Marketable Securities	1,000	1,500
Accounts Receivable	50,000	47,500
Inventories	150,000	145,000
Prepaid Expenses	5,000	2,500
Total Current Assets	$212,500	$208,000
Plant and Equipment (net)	157,000	157,000
Intangibles	30,500	0
Total Assets	$400,000	$365,000
Equities		
Liabilities		
Current Liabilities		
Accounts Payable	$ 60,000	$ 81,500
Other	25,000	22,500
Total Current Liabilities	$ 85,000	$104,000
Bonds Payable	100,000	100,000
Total Liabilities	$185,000	$204,000
Shareholders' Equity		
Common Shares ($3 par)	150,000	150,000
Paid-in Capital in Excess of Par	20,000	20,000
Retained Earnings	45,000	(9,000)
Total Shareholders' Equity	$215,000	$161,000
Total Equities	$400,000	$365,000

Required

Calculate the following ratios for 2001 and 2002. When insufficient data prohibit the computation of averages, year-end balances should be used in the calculations.

a. Net margin
b. Return on investment
c. Return on equity
d. Earnings per share
e. Price-earnings ratio (market price at end of 2002 and 2001 was $5.94 and $4.77, respectively)
f. Book value per share of common shares
g. Times bond interest earned
h. Working capital
i. Current ratio
j. Quick (acid-test) ratio
k. Accounts receivable turnover
l. Inventory turnover
m. Shareholders' equity ratio
n. Total liabilities to total shareholders' equity

PROBLEM 13-7A *Horizontal Analysis*   **L.O. 2**

Financial statements of Strasbourg Company follow:

Strasbourg Company
Balance Sheets
As of December 31

Assets	2007	2006
Current Assets		
Cash	$ 94,000	$ 72,000
Marketable Securities	124,000	36,000
Accounts Receivable (net)	320,000	280,000
Inventories	800,000	860,000
Prepaid Items	160,000	60,000
Total Current Assets	$1,498,000	$1,308,000
Investments	$ 160,000	$ 120,000
Plant (net)	1,600,000	1,530,000
Land	172,000	146,000
Total Assets	$3,430,000	$3,104,000
Equities		
Liabilities		
Current Liabilities		
Notes Payable	$ 100,000	$ 40,000
Accounts Payable	640,000	600,000
Salaries Payable	124,000	98,000
Total Current Liabilities	$ 864,000	$ 738,000
Noncurrent Liabilities		
Bonds Payable	600,000	600,000
Other	200,000	160,000
Total Noncurrent Liabilities	$ 800,000	$ 760,000
Total Liabilities	$1,664,000	$1,498,000
Shareholders ' Equity		
Preferred Shares (par value $100, 5% cumulative, non-participating; 4,000 shares authorized and issued no dividends in arrears)	$ 400,000	$ 400,000
Common Shares ($5 par; 100,000 shares authorized; 60,000 shares issued)	300,000	300,000
Paid-In Capital in Excess of Par—Preferred	60,000	60,000
Paid-In Capital in Excess of Par—Common	200,000	200,000
Retained Earnings	806,000	646,000
Total Shareholders' Equity	$1,766,000	$1,606,000
Total Equities	$3,430,000	$3,104,000

Strasbourg Company		
Statement of Income and Retained Earnings		
For the Years Ended December 31		
	2007	**2006**
Revenues		
Sales (net)	$1,400,000	$1,260,000
Other Revenues	26,000	30,000
Total Revenues	$1,426,000	$1,290,000
Expenses		
Cost of Goods Sold	$ 700,000	$ 617,400
Selling, General, and Administrative	330,000	300,000
Interest Expense	46,000	43,000
Income Tax Expense (40%)	140,000	131,840
Total Expenses	$1,216,000	$1,092,240
Net Earnings (Net Income)	$ 210,000	$ 197,760
Retained Earnings, January 1	646,000	498,240
Less: Preferred Stock Dividends	20,000	20,000
Common Stock Dividends	30,000	30,000
Retained Earnings, December 31	$ 806,000	$ 646,000

Required

Prepare a report for horizontal analysis of both the balance sheet and the income statement.

PROBLEM 13-8A *Ratio Analysis*

L.O. 2, 3, 4, 5, 6, 7

Required

Use the financial statements of Strasbourg Company in Problem 13-7A to calculate the following ratios for 2007 and 2006:

a. Working capital
b. Current ratio
c. Quick ratio
d. Receivables turnover (Beginning receivables at January 1, 2006, was $280,000.)
e. Number of days' sales in receivables (average collection period)
f. Inventory turnover (Beginning inventory at January 1, 2006, was $840,000.)
g. Number of days' sales in inventory
h. Shareholders' equity ratio
i. Debt/equity ratio
j. Number of times bond interest earned
k. Plant assets to long-term debt
l. Net margin
m. Turnover of assets
n. Return on investment
o. Return on equity
p. Earnings per share
q. Book value per share of common shares
r. Price-earnings ratio (market price per share: 2006, $35.25; 2007, $37.50)
s. Dividend yield on common shares

PROBLEM 13-9A *Vertical Analysis*

L.O. 2

Required

Use the financial statements of Strasbourg Company in Problem 13-7A to perform a vertical analysis of both the balance sheets and the income statements for 2007 and 2006.

PROBLEMS—SERIES B

L.O. 2 PROBLEM 13-1B *Vertical Analysis*

Lowder Corporation's controller has prepared the following vertical analysis for the president:

	2007	2006
Sales	100.0%	100.0%
Cost of goods sold	57.0	54.0
Gross margin	43.0%	46.0%
Selling and administrative expense	18.0%	20.0%
Interest expense	2.8	4.0
Total expenses	20.8%	24.0%
Income before taxes	22.2%	22.0%
Income tax expense	10.0	8.0
Net income	12.2%	14.0%

Required

The sales were $500,000 in 2002 and $800,000 in 2003. Convert the report to regular income statements for the two years.

L.O. 5, 6, 7 PROBLEM 13-2B *Ratio Analysis*

Information from Land's financial statements follows:

	2007	2006
Net Sales	$3,600,000	$2,500,000
Net Income before Interest and Taxes	800,000	650,000
Net Income after Taxes	350,000	240,000
Bond Interest Expense	90,000	60,000
Shareholders' Equity, December 31 (2005: $1,200,000)	1,800,000	1,500,000
Common Shares, Par $30, December 31	1,050,000	900,000

Average number of shares outstanding was 32,000 for 2007 and 30,000 for 2006.

Required

Compute the following ratios for Lando Company for 2007 and 2006.
a. Number of times bond interest was earned.
b. Earnings per share based on the average number of shares outstanding.
c. Price-earnings ratio (market prices: 2007, $75 per share; 2006, $60 per share).
d. Return on average equity.
e. Net margin.

L.O. 4 PROBLEM 13-3B *Ratio Analysis*

Jentry Company has a current ratio of 2:1 on June 30, 2005. The following are examples of transactions in which the company engaged. Indicate whether each transaction would (+) increase, (−) decrease, or (NE) not affect Jentry's current ratio. Do the same for the effect on its working capital.

Required

a. Issued a 10-year bond for $100,000 cash.
b. Paid cash to settle an account payable.
c. Sold merchandise for more than cost.
d. Recognized amortization on plant equipment.
e. Purchased a machine by issuing a long-term note payable.
f. Purchased merchandise inventory on credit.
g. Received customer payment on accounts receivable.
h. Paid cash for federal income tax expense (assume that the expense has not been previously accrued).

i. Declared cash dividend to be paid three months later.
j. Received cash for interest of a long-term note receivable (assume that interest has not been previously accrued).
k. Received cash from the issue of a short-term note payable.
l. Traded a truck for a sedan.

PROBLEM 13-4B   *Ratio Analysis*

L.O. 7

Selected data for Sawyer Company for 2006 and additional information on industry averages follow:

Earnings (i.e., net income)	$ 420,000
Preferred shares (40,000 shares at $35 par, 6%)	$1,400,000
Common shares (81,000 shares at $10 par, market value $38)	810,000
Paid-in capital in excess of par—common	900,000
Retained earnings	1,200,000
Total Shareholders' Equity	$4,310,000

Note: Dividends in arrears on preferred shares: $79,800. The preferred shares can be called for $46 per share. There are 1,000 common shares in Treasury.

Industry averages:

Earnings per share	$2.50
Price-earnings ratio	8
Return on equity	7.3%

Required
a. Calculate and compare Sawyer Company's ratios with the industry averages.
b. Discuss whether you would invest in the company and any other factors that should be considered.

PROBLEM 13-5B   *Missing Numbers on Balance Sheet*

L.O. 2

Ivana Halvorsen discovered a piece of wet and partially burned balance sheet after her office was destroyed by fire. She could recall a current ratio of 1.75 and a shareholders' equity ratio of 55 percent.

Assets	
Current Assets	
Cash	$25,000
Accounts Receivable	(A)
Inventory	42,000
Prepaid Expenses	9,000
Total Current Assets	$ (B)
Long-Term Assets	
Building	$ (C)
Less: Accumulated Amortization	(30,000)
Total Long-Term Assets	180,000
Total Assets	$ (D)
Equities	
Liabilities	
Current Liabilities	
Accounts Payable	$42,000
Notes Payable	(E)
Income Tax Payable	18,000
Total Current Liabilities	$80,000
Long-Term Liabilities	
Bonds Payable	45,000
Mortgage Payable	(F)
Total Liabilities	$ (G)

Table is continued on the following page.

Shareholders' Equity		
Common Shares		90,000
Retained Earnings		(H)
Total Shareholders' Equity		(I)
Total Equities	$	(J)

Required

Complete the balance sheet by filling in the blanks.

L.O. 2, 3, 4, 5, 6, 7   **PROBLEM 13-6B**   *Ratio Analysis*

The following are the financial statements for Theta, Inc.:

Theta, Inc. Balance Sheets As of December 31		
Assets	**2007**	**2006**
Current Assets		
Cash	$ 392,000	$ 304,000
Marketable Securities	80,000	60,000
Accounts Receivable (net)	372,000	360,000
Inventories	600,000	640,000
Prepaid Items	90,000	46,000
Total Current Assets	$1,534,200	$1,410,000
Investments	$ 400,000	$ 400,000
Plant (net)	800,000	780,000
Other	200,000	180,000
Total Assets	$2,934,200	$2,770,000
Equities		
Liabilities		
Current Liabilities		
Notes Payable	$ 20,000	$ 30,000
Accounts Payable	330,000	300,000
Other	120,000	60,000
Total Current Liabilities	$ 470,000	$ 390,000
Noncurrent Liabilities		
Bonds Payable	500,000	500,000
Other	120,000	60,000
Total Noncurrent Liabilities	$ 620,000	$ 560,000
Total Liabilities	$1,090,000	$ 950,000
Shareholders ' Equity		
Preferred Shares, ($100 par, cumulative, non-participating; $100 liquidating value; 2,000 shares authorized and issued; no dividends in arrears)	$ 200,000	$ 200,000
Common Shares ($10 par; 100,000 shares authorized; 40,000 shares issued)	400,000	400,000
Paid-in Capital in Excess of Par —Preferred	120,000	12,000
Paid-in Capital in Excess of Par —Common	400,000	400,000
Retained Earnings	724,200	808,000
Total Shareholders' Equity	$1,844,200	$1,820,000
Total Equities	$2,934,200	$2,770,000

Theta, Inc. Statement of Income and Retained Earnings For the Years Ended December 31		
	2007	**2006**
Revenues		
Sales (net)	$800,000	$760,000
Other Revenues	24,000	14,000
Total Revenues	$824,000	$774,000
Expenses		
Cost of Goods Sold	$464,000	$433,200
Selling, General, and Administrative	230,000	192,000
Interest Expense	33,000	32,000
Income Tax Expense (40%)	38,800	46,720
Total Expenses	$765,800	$703,920
Net Earnings (Net Income)	$58,200	$70,080
Retained Earnings, January 1	700,000	663,920
Less: Preferred Shares Dividends	14,000	14,000
Common Shares Dividends	20,000	20,000
Retained Earnings, December 31	$724,200	$700,000

Required

Calculate the following ratios for 2007:

a. Working capital
b. Current ratio
c. Quick ratio
d. Accounts receivable turnover
e. Average collection period
f. Inventory turnover
g. Number of days' sales in inventory
h. Shareholders' equity ratio
i. Debt/equity ratio
j. Times bond interest earned

k. Plant assets to long-term debt
l. Net margin
m. Turnover of assets
n. Return on investment
o. Return on equity
p. Earnings per share
q. Book value
r. Price-earnings ratio (market price: $13.26)
s. Dividend yield on common shares

PROBLEM 13-7B *Ratio Analysis*

L.O. 2, 3, 4, 5, 6, 7

Rothenburg Company's shares is quoted at $16 per share at December 31, 2005 and 2004. Rothenburg's statements follow:

Rothenburg Company Statement of Income and Retained Earnings For the Years Ended December 31		
	2005	**2004**
Net Sales	$600,000,000	$500,000,000
Costs and Expenses		
Cost of Goods Sold	490,000,000	400,000,000
Selling, General, and Administrative Expenses	66,000,000	60,000,000
Other	7,000,000	6,000,000
Total Costs and Expenses	$563,000,000	$466,000,000
Income before Income Taxes	$ 37,000,000	$ 34,000,000
Income Taxes	16,800,000	15,800,000
Net Income	$ 20,200,000	$ 18,200,000
Retained Earnings at Beginning of Period	134,000,000	126,000,000
Less: Dividends on Common Shares	12,000,000	10,000,000
Dividends on Preferred Shares	200,000	200,000
Retained Earnings at End of Period	$142,000,000	$134,000,000

Rothenburg Company
Balance Sheets
As of December 31

Assets	2005	2004
Assets		
Current Assets		
Cash	$ 3,500,000	$ 3,600,000
Marketable Securities at cost which approximates market	13,000,000	11,000,000
Accounts Receivable, net of allowance for doubtful accounts	105,000,000	95,000,000
Inventories, lower of cost or market	126,000,000	154,000,000
Prepaid Expenses	2,500,000	2,400,000
Total Current Assets	$250,000,000	$266,000,000
Property, Plant, and Equipment, net of accumulated amortization	311,000,000	308,000,000
Investments	2,000,000	3,000,000
Long-Term Receivables	14,000,000	16,000,000
Goodwill and Patents, net of accumulated amortization	6,000,000	6,500,000
Other Assets	7,000,000	8,500,000
Total Assets	590,000,000	608,000,000
Liabilities and Shareholders' Equity		
Current Liabilities		
Notes Payable	$ 5,000,000	$ 15,000,000
Accounts Payable	38,000,000	48,000,000
Accrued Expenses	24,500,000	27,000,000
Income Taxes Payable	1,000,000	1,000,000
Payments Due within one year	6,500,000	7,000,000
Total Current Liabilities	$ 75,000,000	$ 98,000,000
Long-Term Debt	169,000,000	180,000,000
Deferred Income Taxes	74,000,000	67,000,000
Other Liabilities	9,000,000	8,000,000
Total Liabilities	$327,000,000	$353,000,000
Shareholders ' Equity		
Common Shares, $1 par value; 20,000,000 shares authorized and 10,000,000 shares issued and outstanding	$ 10,000,000	$ 10,000,000
5%Cumulative Preferred Shares, par value $100 per share; $100 liquidating value; authorized 50,000 shares; issued and outstanding 40,000 shares	4,000,000	4,000,000
Additional Paid-in Capital, common	107,000,000	107,000,000
Retained Earnings	142,000,000	134,000,000
Total Shareholders' Equity	$263,000,000	$255,000,000
Total Liabilities and Shareholders' Equity	$590,000,000	$608,000,000

Required

On the basis of the preceding information, compute the following for 2005 only:

a. Current ratio
b. Quick (acid-test) ratio
c. Number of days' sales in average receivables (average collection period), assuming a business year consisting of 300 days and all sales on account
d. Inventory turnover
e. Book value per share of common shares
f. Earnings per share on common shares
g. Price-earnings ratio on common shares
h. Shareholders' equity ratio
i. Return on investment
j. Return on equity

PROBLEM 13-8B   *Horizontal Analysis*   **L.O. 2**

Required

Use the financial statements of Rothenburg Company in Problem 13-7B to perform a horizontal analysis of both the balance sheets and income statements for 2005 and 2004.

PROBLEM 13-9B   *Vertical Analysis*   **L.O. 2**

Required

Use the financial statements of Rothenburg Company in Problem 13-7B to perform a vertical analysis (based on total assets, total equities, and sales) of both the balance sheets and income statements for 2005 and 2004.

ANALYZE, THINK, COMMUNICATE

BUSINESS APPLICATIONS CASE   *Horizontal Analysis*   **ACT 13-1**

During 1997, the Philip Morris Company reached agreements with the states of Mississippi, Florida, and Texas to make current and future payments related to health-care costs that these states had incurred to treat certain illnesses of smokers.[*] As a result, on its 1997 income statement, Philip Morris recognized the expense settlement charges for $1.457 billion. This type of expense had not been recognized in 1995 or 1996. The settlement charges were included in operating income; they were *not* classified as extraordinary. Philip Morris's operating incomes, before subtracting income taxes, for 1995, 1996, and 1997 were as follows:

1995	1996	1997
$9.347 billion	$10.683 billion	$10.611 billion

Required

a. Compute the percentage growth in Philip Morris's operating income before taxes from 1995 to 1996 and from 1996 to 1997.

b. Determine what Philip Morris's operating income before taxes would have been in 1997 if there had been no settlement charges expense. Using this revised number, compute the percentage growth in operating income before taxes from 1996 to 1997.

c. Assuming Philip Morris experiences the same average growth rate in earnings from 1997 to 1998 that it did from 1995 to 1996 to 1997, develop a rough estimate of its 1998 operating income before taxes under two separate assumptions:

   (1) No settlement charges were shown in 1998.

   (2) The settlement charges in 1998 are the same amount as they were in 1997.

GROUP ASSIGNMENT   *Ratio Analysis and Logic*   **ACT 13-2**

Presented here are selected data from the annual reports of four companies for the most recent reporting period. (2000/2001). The four companies in alphabetical order are:

Bell Canada – a utility company – telephone, wireless, satellite television

Big Rock Brewery Ltd. – consumer products – beverages

Hudson's Bay Company – consumer goods – department stores

Visionwall Incorporated – industrial products – building materials

The data, presented in the order of the amount of sales, are as follows. Dollar amounts are in millions.

	A	B	C	D
Sales	13,230	7,075	32.2	13
Net Earnings	1,314	39.6	1.4	.05
Inventory		1,655.6	2.7	1.0
Accounts Receivable	2,108	888	1.6	2.5
Total Assets	22,826	4,604	31.3	7.9

[*]This precedent has significant impact here in Canada, where provincial governments have gone to the courts to establish similar agreements.

Required

a. Divide the class into groups of four or five students per group and then organize the groups into four sections. Assign Task 1 to the first section of groups, Task 2 to the second section, Task 3 to the third section, and Task 4 to the fourth section.

   Group tasks

   1. Assume that you represent Bell Canada. Identify the set of financial data (i.e., Column A, B, C, or D) that relates to your company.
   2. Assume that you represent Big Rock Brewery Ltd. Identify the set of financial data (i.e., Column A, B, C, or D) that relates to your company.
   3. Assume that you represent Hudson's Bay Company. Identify the set of financial data (i.e., Column A, B, C, or D) that relates to your company.
   4. Assume that you represent Visionwall Incorporated. Identify the set of financial data (i.e., Column A, B, C, or D) that relates to your company.

   (*Hint:* Use ratios to facilitate the identification of the financial data related to your particular company.)

b. Select a representative from each section. Have the representatives explain the rationale for the group's selection. The explanation should include a set of ratios that support the group's conclusion.

ACT 13-3 WRITING ASSIGNMENT *Interpretation of the Ratios*

The following are the debt to assets, return on assets, and return on equity ratios for four companies from two different industries. The range of interest rates each company was paying on its long-term debt is provided. Each of these public companies is a leader in its particular industry, and the data are for the fiscal years ending in 2003. All numbers are percentages.

	Debt to Assets*	Return on Assets	Return on Equity	Interest Rates
Banking Industry				
Brook Banking Corporation	92	1.0	11.5	5.7–7.0
Wells Fargo & Co.	87	1.2	9.0	6.1–11.0
Home Construction Industry				
Henderson Homes, Ltd.	62	2.5	6.5	7.0–10.1
Longo Brothers, Ltd.	66	5.8	16.9	7.8–10.5

*Debt-to-Assets Ratio is defined as total liabilities divided by total assets.

Required

a. On the basis of only the debt-to-assets ratios, the banking companies appear to have the most financial risk. Generally, companies that have lower financial risk are charged lower interest rates. Write a brief explanation of why the banking companies can borrow money at lower interest rates than can the construction companies.

b. Explain why the return on equity ratio for Brook Banking is more than 10 times higher than its return on assets ratio, and Henderson Homes' return on equity ratio is less than three times higher than its return on assets ratio.

ACT 13-4 ETHICAL DILEMMA   *Making the Ratios Look Good*

J. Talbot is the accounting manager for Kolla Waste Disposal Corporation. Kolla is having the worst financial year since the its inception. Indeed, the company is expected to report a net loss. In the midst of such bad news, Ms. Talbot surprised the company president, Mr. Winston, by suggesting that the company write off approximately 25 percent of its garbage trucks. Mr. Winston responded by noting that the trucks could still be operated for another two or three years. Ms. Talbot replied, "We may use them for two or three more years, but you couldn't sell them on the street if you had to. Who wants to buy a bunch of old garbage trucks, and besides, it will make next year's financials so sweet. No one will care about the additional write-off this year. We are already showing a loss. Who will care if we lose a little bit more?"

Required

a. How will the write-off affect the following year's return on assets ratio?
b. How will the write-off affect the asset and income growth percentages?
c. Assuming that Ms. Talbot writes off the garbage trucks, is this action ethical?

SPREADSHEET ASSIGNMENT   *Using Excel*

ACT 13-5

Hiyakawa Corporation's 2005 income statement is as shown in the spreadsheet.

Required

Construct a spreadsheet to conduct horizontal analysis on the income statements for 2005 and 2004.

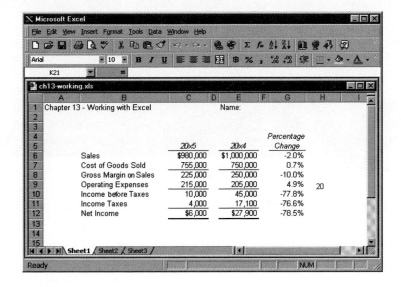

SPREADSHEET ASSIGNMENT   *Mastering Excel*

ACT 13-6

Refer to the data in ACT 13-5.

Required

Construct a spreadsheet to conduct vertical analysis for both years, 2005 and 2004.

Learning Objectives

After completing this chapter, you should be able to:

1 Identify the types of business events that are reported in the three sections of the cash flow statement.

2 Convert an accrual account balance to its cash equivalent.

3 Prepare a cash flow statement using the T-account method.

4 Explain how cash flow from operating activity reported under the indirect method differs from that reported under the direct method.

5 Explain how the classifications used on the cash flow statement could provide misleading information to decision makers.

the *curious* manager

Photodisc/Janis Christie

The following information is available for Northampton Group Inc., a mid-range hotel operator and Georgian Court Hotel Limited Partnership, owner of the Georgian Court in Vancouver B.C:

	Northampton Group Inc.	Georgian Court Hotel Limited Partnership
Revenues	$24,447,845	$6,144,980
Amortization	1,836,782	669,218
Net Cash Spent on Capital Assets	4,822,791	59,822

Both these businesses are in the hotel industry. Why did Northampton spend two and a half times more cash on capital assets than it had in amortization, whereas Georgian Court spent only one-ninth as much cash on capital assets than it had in amortization?

*The cash flow statement explains how a company obtained and used cash during some period. The sources of cash are known as **cash inflows**, and the uses are called **cash outflows**. The statement classifies cash receipts (i.e., inflows) and payments (i.e., outflows) into three categories: operating activities, investing activities, and financing activities. The following sections define these activities and outline the types of cash flows that are normally classified under each category.*

LO1

Identify the types of business events that are reported in the three sections of the cash flow statement.

Operating Activities

Operating activities include cash inflows and outflows generated by running (i.e., operating) the business. Some of the specific items that are shown under this section are as follows:

1. Cash receipts from sales, commissions, fees, and receipts from interest and dividends.
2. Cash payments for inventories, salaries, operating expenses, interest, and taxes.

Note that *gains* and *losses* are not included in this section. The total cash collected from the sale of assets is included in the investing activities section.

Investing Activities

Investing activities include cash flows that are generated through a company's purchase or sale of long-term operational assets, investments in other companies, and its lending activities. Some items included in this section follow:

1. Cash receipts from the sale of property, plant, equipment or of marketable securities as well as the collection of loans.
2. Cash payments used to purchase property, plant, equipment or marketable securities as well as loans made to others.

Financing Activities

Financing activities include cash inflows and outflows associated with the company's own equity transactions or its borrowing activities. The following are some items appearing under the financing activities section:

1. Cash receipts from the issue of shares and borrowed funds.
2. Cash payments for the repayment of debt and payment of dividends.

When you are trying to classify transactions into one of the three categories, it is helpful to note that the identification of the proper category depends on the company's perspective, rather than on the type of account being considered. For example, a transaction involving common shares is considered an investing activity if the company is purchasing or selling its investment in another company's common shares. In contrast, common share transactions are classified as financing activities if the company is issuing its own shares or is buying back its own shares. Similarly, the receipt of dividends is classified as an operating activity, but the payment of dividends is classified as a financing activity. Furthermore, lending cash is considered to be an investing activity, and borrowing cash is a financing activity. Accordingly, proper classification centres on the behaviour of the company involved, rather than the type of instrument being used.

Noncash Investing and Financing Transactions

Occasionally, companies will engage in significant **noncash investing and financing transactions**. For example, a company may issue some of its common shares in exchange for the title to a plot of land. Similarly, a company could accept a mortgage obligation in exchange for the title of ownership to a building (i.e., a 100% owner-financed exchange). Since these types of transactions do not involve the exchange of cash, they cannot be included as cash receipts or payments on the cash flow statement. However, the Canadian Institute of Chartered Accountants (CICA) has concluded that full and fair reporting requires the disclosure of all material investing and financing activities, regardless of whether they involve the exchange of cash. Accordingly, the CICA requires that the cash flow statement include a separate schedule for the disclosure of noncash investing and financing activities.

Reporting Format for Cash Flow Statement

The cash flow statement is arranged with operating activities shown first, investing activities second, and financing activities last. Under each category, individual cash inflows are shown first, with cash outflows being subtracted and the net difference being carried forward. The schedule of noncash investing and financing activities is typically shown at the bottom of the statement. Exhibit 14–1 demonstrates this format of statement presentation.

With respect to the placement of the four primary financial statements, the cash flow statement is usually presented last. However, a sizable number of companies show the cash flow statement immediately after the income statement and balance sheet. These companies place the cash flow statement before the other three statements.

Converting from Accrual to Cash-Basis Accounting

The operating activities section of the cash flow statement is essentially a cash-basis income statement. Since accounting records are normally maintained on an accrual basis, it is necessary to convert data based on accruals and deferrals to cash equivalents to determine the amount of cash flow from operating activities. The following section discusses the conversion process.

LO2
Convert an accrual account balance to its cash equivalent.

Operating Activities
Converting Accruals to Cash

Accrual accounting is the process through which revenues and expenses are recognized before cash is exchanged. When accrual accounting is applied, revenue and expense items recognized in the current period may have cash consequences in a later period. Furthermore, revenue and expense items recognized in a past period may result in cash receipts or payments that materialize in the current period. Accordingly, the amount of cash receipts and payments realized during any particular accounting period may be larger or smaller than the amount of revenue and expense recognized during that period. The following section discusses the adjustments needed to convert accrual accounting to cash-basis accounting.

Revenue Transactions With regard to **revenue transactions**, the application of accrual accounting means that some revenue is likely to be reported on the income statement before the cash is received. Accordingly, the amount of revenue recognized is normally different from the

---

Exhibit 14-1

WESTERN COMPANY
Cash Flow Statement
For the Year Ended 2001

Cash Flows from Operating Activities		
Plus: List of Individual Inflows	$XXX	
Less: List of Individual Outflows	(XXX)	
Net Increase (Decrease) from Operating Activities		$XXX
Cash Flows from Investing Activities		
Plus: List of Individual Inflows	XXX	
Less: List of Individual Outflows	(XXX)	
Net Increase (Decrease) from Investing Activities		XXX
Cash Flows from Financing Activities		
Plus: List of Individual Inflows	XXX	
Less: List of Individual Outflows	(XXX)	
Net Increase (Decrease) from Financing Activities		XXX
Net Increase (Decrease) in Cash		XXX
Plus: Beginning Cash Balance		XXX
Ending Cash Balance		$XXX
Schedule of Noncash Investing and Financing Activities		
List of Noncash Transactions		$XXX

Northampton operates mid-range hotels, such as Holiday Inn Express, Best Western, Sheraton Hotels and Suites, in various locations in Ontario and Quebec. The company is growing and expanding. As a result, it is continually adding properties to its portfolio of hotels. Georgian Court, on the other hand, operates one hotel in Vancouver and, other than minor additions, has no expansion plans on the horizon.

amount of cash that the company realizes during any particular accounting period. Some customers purchase goods or services in the current accounting period but pay for them in a later period. Other customers may pay cash in the current period for goods or services purchased in a prior period. As a result, the cash received may be more or less than the amount of revenue recognized.

To convert revenue recognized to the corresponding amount of cash collected, it is necessary to analyze both the amount of revenue appearing on the income statement and the change in the balance of the accounts receivable account. For example, assume that a company reported $500 of revenue on its income statement. Furthermore, assume that during the accounting period under consideration, the beginning and ending balances in the company's Accounts Receivable account were $100 and $160, respectively. Accordingly, the balance in the receivables account increased by $60 ($160 − $100). Taking this fact into consideration, we can conclude that $60 of the $500 in sales was not collected in cash. Therefore, the amount of cash collected must have been $440 ($500 − $60).

LO3

Prepare a cash flow statement using the T-account method.

The conclusion that $440 of cash was collected from the revenue transactions was derived through logic. This conclusion can be confirmed through a process commonly called the T-account method. The **T-account method** begins with the opening of the Accounts Receivable T-account with the appropriate beginning and ending balances displayed. In this case, the beginning balance is $100, and the ending balance is $160. Next, a $500 debit is added to the account to record the recognition of the revenue. The resultant T-account appears as follows:

	Accounts Receivable	
Beginning Balance	100	
Debit to Record Sales	500	?
Ending Balance	160	

Mathematically, adding $500 to a beginning balance of $100 does not result in an ending balance of $160. A $440 credit to the receivables account would be required to arrive at the $160 ending balance. Since cash collections result in credits to the Accounts Receivable account, it can be assumed that the Cash account was debited when the receivables account was credited. Accordingly, the analysis of the T-account also leads to the conclusion that $440 of cash was collected as a result of activities associated with the generation of revenue.

Expense Transactions Accrual accounting results in the recognition of **expense transactions** before the payment of cash occurs, which means that a liability is normally recorded at the time the expense is recognized. The liability is later reduced as cash payments are made. Accordingly, the amount of accrued expense displayed on the income statement must be analyzed in conjunction with any change in the balance of the related liability account in order to determine the amount of cash outflow associated with the expense recognition. For example, assume that a company reports $200 of utilities expense on its income statement. Furthermore, assume that the beginning and ending balances in the Utilities Payable account are $70 and $40, respectively. This situation implies that the company not only made payments to cover the use of the utilities in the current period but also paid an additional $30 ($70 − $40) to reduce the obligations of prior periods. Accordingly, the amount of cash outflow associated with utility use is $230 ($200 + $30).

The T-account method can also be used to verify the $230 cash payment. A T-account for Utilities Payable is opened with beginning and ending balances placed into the account. Furthermore, a credit amounting to $200 is made to the account to reflect the recognition of the current period's utility expense. The resultant T-account appears as follows:

Utilities Payable

	70	Beginning Balance
?	200	Credit to Record Expense
	40	Ending Balance

Mathematical logic dictates that a $230 debit is required to arrive at the $40 ending balance ($70 + $200 − $230 = $40). Since debits to payable accounts are normally offset by credits to the Cash account, the T-account analysis indicates that cash outflows associated with utility expenses amounted to $230.

Converting Deferrals to Cash

Deferral transactions are events in which cash receipts or payments occur before the associated revenue or expense is recognized. Since revenue and expense recognition occurs in one accounting period and the associated cash receipts and payments occur in a different accounting period, differences arise between income reported in the financial statements and the cash-basis income. The following section discusses the procedures necessary to convert deferrals to their cash-basis equivalents.

Revenue Transactions When cash is collected before the completion of the earnings process, a company incurs an obligation (i.e., liability) to provide goods or services at some future date. The revenue associated with the cash receipt is recognized in a later period when the work is accomplished. As a result, *the amount of revenue reported on the income statement and the amount of cash receipts normally differ*. The conversion of deferrals to cash requires an analysis of the amount of revenue reported and the change in the balance of the liability account, *Unearned Revenue*. For example, assume that the amount of revenue recognized was $400 and that the Unearned Revenue account increased from a beginning balance of $80 to an ending balance of $110. The increase in the liability account implies that the company received cash in excess of the amount of the revenue recognized. Not only did the company earn the $400 of revenue reported on the income statement, but it also received $30 ($110 − $80) for which it became obligated to provide goods and services in a future period. Accordingly, cash receipts associated with earnings activities amounted to $430 ($400 + $30).

An analysis of the T-account for unearned revenue confirms the receipt of $430 cash. The Unearned Revenue account is opened with the appropriate beginning and ending balances. A debit is made to the account to record the recognition of $400 of revenue. The resultant account appears as follows:

Unearned Revenue

		80	Beginning Balance
Credit to Recognize Revenue	400	?	
		110	Ending Balance

Clearly, $430 must have been added to the beginning balance of $80 so that when the $400 debit entry was subtracted, the resulting ending balance was $110. Since credit entries to the Unearned Revenue account are normally offset by corresponding debits to the Cash account, the analysis suggests that $430 of cash receipts was associated with revenue activities.

Expense Transactions On many occasions, companies pay cash for goods or services that are not used immediately. The cost of the goods or services is normally capitalized in an asset account at the time the cash payment is made. The assets are then expensed in later periods when the goods or services are used in the process of earning revenue. Consequently, some items paid for in prior periods are expensed in the current period, while other items that are paid for in the current period are not expensed until later periods. *Accordingly, the amount of cash outflows normally differs from the amount of expense recognized for any given accounting period.*

To convert recognized expenses to cash flows, it is necessary to analyze the amount of change in the balance of certain asset accounts as well as the amount of corresponding expense that is recognized on the income statement. For example, assume that the beginning and ending balances in the Prepaid Rent account are $60 and $80, respectively, and that the amount of reported rent expense is $800. This situation suggests that the company not only paid enough cash to cover the $800 of recognized expense but also paid an additional $20 ($80 − $60). Therefore, the cash outflow associated with the rent payments amounted to $820 ($800 + $20).

The cash outflow of $820 for rent payments can be confirmed through T-account analysis. The beginning and ending balances are placed in a T-account for prepaid rent. The account is then credited to reflect the rent expense recognition of $800. The resultant T-account appears as follows:

	Prepaid Rent		
Beginning Balance	60		
	?	800	Credit to Recognize Expense
Ending Balance	80		

To have an ending balance of $80, there must have been an $820 debit to the account ($60 + $820 − $800 = $80). Since a debit to the Prepaid Rent account is normally offset by a credit to Cash, the analysis confirms that the cash outflow associated with rent payments is $820.

Investing Activities

Determining cash flow from investing activities may also require an analysis of changes in the beginning and ending account balances along with certain income statement data. For example, assume that the Land account had a beginning and ending balance of $900 and $300, respectively. Furthermore, assume that the income statement contained the recognition of a $200 gain on the sale of land. The $600 ($900 − $300) decline in the book value of the land suggests that the land was sold. The gain from the income statement implies that the land was sold for $200 more than its book value. Accordingly, the analysis suggests that the land was sold for $800 ($600 + $200) cash. Note that the amount of cash flow is different from the amount of gain appearing on the income statement. Indeed, the full $800 cash inflow appears in the investing activities section of the cash flow statement. The operating activities section of the statement is not affected by the gain from the land sale.

The amount of cash inflow ($800) from investing activities can also be verified through the T-account method. An analysis of the beginning and ending balances in the Land account suggests that land costing $600 ($900 beginning balance − $300 ending balance) was sold. This amount, coupled with the $200 gain shown in the Retained Earnings account, suggests that $800 cash was collected from the sale. The appropriate T-accounts are as follows:

Cash		Land		Retained Earnings	
?		900	600		200
		300			

It is possible that the company could have received some resource other than cash when the land was sold. However, other alternative explanations would be discovered when the other balance sheet accounts were analyzed.

Financing Activities

Cash flow from financing activities can frequently be determined by simply analyzing the change in the balances of liability and shareholders' equity accounts. For example, an increase in bond liabilities from

$500 to $800 implies that the company issued new bonds that resulted in the receipt of $300 cash. This conclusion can be supported by an analysis using the T-account method. A T-account is opened with the beginning and ending balances shown here:

Bonds Payable

	500 Beginning Balance
	?
	800 Ending Balance

A $300 credit must be added to the $500 opening balance in order to arrive at the $800 ending balance. Since cash is normally increased when bond liabilities increase, the analysis supports the conclusion that $300 of cash inflow was derived from the incurrence of debt.

Other explanations are also possible. Perhaps some of the company's shareholders decided to exchange their equity securities for debt securities. Or the company may have been willing to incur the obligation in exchange for some asset (i.e., property, plant, or equipment) other than cash. Such transactions would be reported in the schedule of noncash investing and financing transactions.

▌ Comprehensive Example Using the T-Account Approach

The preceding discussion emphasized the need to analyze financial statements and supporting data in the process of preparing a cash flow statement. The beginning and ending balances in the accounts being analyzed can be drawn from two successive balance sheets. The revenues, expenses, gains, and losses can be found on the income statement. Also, notes to the financial statements may contain information needed to identify noncash transactions. Exhibits 14–2 and 14–3 are the balance sheets, income statement, and additional information needed to prepare a cash flow statement.

LO3

Prepare a cash flow statement using the T-account method.

Exhibit 14-2

THE NEW SOUTH CORPORATION
Comparative Balance Sheets
As of December 31

	2004	2005
Current Assets		
Cash	$ 400	$ 900
Accounts Receivable	1,200	1,000
Interest Receivable	300	400
Inventory	8,200	8,900
Prepaid Insurance	1,400	1,100
Total Current Assets	11,500	12,300
Long-Term Assets		
Marketable Securities	3,500	5,100
Equipment	4,600	5,400
Less: Accumulated Amortization	(1,200)	(900)
Land	6,000	8,500
Total Long-Term Assets	12,900	18,100
Total Assets	$24,400	$30,400

Continued on following page.

Current Liabilities		
Accounts Payable—Inventory Purchases	$ 1,100	$ 800
Salaries Payable	900	1,000
Other Operating Expenses Payable	1,300	1,500
Interest Payable	500	300
Unearned Rent Revenue	1,600	600
Total Current Liabilities	5,400	4,200
Long-Term Liabilities		
Mortgage Payable	0	2,500
Bonds Payable	4,000	1,000
Total Long-Term Liabilities	4,000	3,500
Shareholders' Equity		
Common Shares	8,000	10,000
Retained Earnings	7,000	12,700
Total Shareholders' Equity	15,000	22,700
Total Liabilities and Shareholders' Equity	$24,400	$30,400

Exhibit 14-3

THE NEW SOUTH CORPORATION
Income Statement
For the Period Ended December 31, 2005

Sales		$20,600
Cost of Goods Sold		(10,500)
Gross Margin		10,100
Operating Expenses		
Amortization Expense	$ 800	
Salaries Expense	2,700	
Insurance Expense	600	
Other Operating Expenses	1,400	
Total Operating Expenses		(5,500)
Operating Income		4,600
Other Operating Income—Rent Revenue		2,400
Total Operating Income		7,000
Nonoperating Revenue and Expenses		
Interest Revenue	700	
Interest Expense	(400)	
Loss on Sale of Equipment	(100)	
Total Nonoperating Items		200
Net Income		$ 7,200

Additional information:
1. The corporation sold equipment for $300 cash. This equipment had an original cost of $1,500 and accumulated amortization of $1,100 at the time of the sale.
2. The corporation issued a $2,500 mortgage note in exchange for land.
3. There was a $1,500 cash dividend paid during the accounting period.

Preparation of Cash Flow Statement

Begin the process of analyzing the financial statements by opening a T-account for each item on the balance sheets. Enter the beginning and ending balances for each item into the T-accounts. Use the 2004 balance sheet (see Exhibit 14–2) to determine the beginning balance of each account and the 2005 balance sheet to get the ending balances. The Cash account should be large enough to be divided into three

Exhibit 14-4 Balance Sheet T-Accounts

Assets	=	Liabilities	+	Shareholders' Equity

Cash

Bal.	400		

Operating Activities

(a2)	20,800	11,500	(b3)
(g2)	1,400	2,600	(d2)
(h2)	600	300	(e2)
		1,200	(f2)
		600	(i2)

Investing Activities

(k1)	300	1,600	(j1)
		2,300	(l1)

Financing Activities

(o1)	2,000	3,000	(n1)
		1,500	(p1)
Bal.	900		

Accounts Receivable

Bal.	1,200	20,800	(a2)
(a1)	20,600		
Bal.	1,000		

Interest Receivable

Bal.	300	600	(h2)
(h1)	700		
Bal.	400		

Inventory

Bal.	8,200	10,500	(b1)
(b2)	11,200		
Bal.	8,900		

Prepaid Insurance

Bal.	1,400	600	(e1)
(e2)	300		
Bal.	1,100		

Marketable Securities

Bal.	3,500		
(j1)	1,600		
Bal.	5,100		

Equipment

Bal.	4,600	1,500	(k1)
(l1)	2,300		
Bal.	5,400		

Accumulated Amortization

(k1)	1,100	1,200	Bal.
		800	(c1)
		900	Bal.

Land

Bal.	6,000		
(m1)	2,500		
Bal.	8,500		

Accounts Payable—Inventory

(b3)	11,500	1,100	Bal.
		11,200	(b2)
		800	Bal.

Salaries Payable

(d2)	2,600	900	Bal.
		2,700	(d1)
		1,000	Bal.

Operating Exp. Payable

(f2)	1,200	1,300	Bal.
		1,400	(f1)
		1,500	Bal.

Interest Payable

(i1)	600	500	Bal.
		400	(i1)
		300	Bal.

Unearned Rent Revenue

(g1)	2,400	1,600	Bal.
		1,400	(g2)
		600	Bal.

Mortgage Payable

		0	Bal.
		2,500	(m1)
		2,500	Bal.

Bonds Payable

(n1)	3,000	4,000	Bal.
		1,000	Bal.

Common Shares

		8,000	Bal.
		2,000	(o1)
		10,000	Bal.

Retained Earnings

(b1)	10,500	7,000	Bal.
(c1)	800	20,600	(a1)
(d1)	2,700	2,400	(g1)
(e1)	600	700	(h1)
(f1)	1,400		
(i1)	400		
(k1)	100		
(p1)	1,500		
		12,700	Bal.

components representing cash flows from operating, investing, and financing activities. Exhibit 14–4 contains a full set of T-accounts with all analytical transactions included. Each transaction is labelled with a lowercase letter. Since some analysis requires more than one entry, each letter is also followed by a number, which permits detailed labelling for each transaction. The following section explains each transaction in full detail.

Cash Flows from Operating Activities

Cash flow from operating activities is essentially a cash-basis income statement. Since accrual accounting is normally used in the preparation of formal financial statements, it is necessary to convert the income statement data to cash equivalents. Accordingly, each item on the income statement should be analyzed separately to assess its cash flow consequences.

Cash Receipts from Sales

The first item appearing on the income statement is $20,600 of sales revenue. Assuming that all sales transactions were on account, the entry to record sales would have required a debit to Accounts Receivable and a credit to Sales Revenue. Because the T-account analysis includes only balance sheet accounts and sales revenue acts to increase Retained Earnings, the entry to record sales in the T-accounts is shown as a debit to Accounts Receivable and a credit to Retained Earnings. This entry is labelled (a1) in Exhibit 14–4. After the sales revenue transaction is recorded, the cash inflow from sales can be determined by analyzing the Accounts Receivable T-account. Note that the beginning balance of $1,200 plus the debit to receivables of $20,600 resulting from sales transactions suggests that $21,800 of receivables was available for collection. Since the ending balance in the receivables account amounts to $1,000, there must have been $20,800 (i.e., $21,800 − $1,000) of receivables collected. This cash inflow is recognized with a debit to the Cash account under the operating activities section and a credit to the Accounts Receivable account. This entry is labelled (a2) in Exhibit 14–4.

The preceding discussion introduces several practices that apply to the analysis of all cash flows from operating activities. First, note that all revenue, expense, gain, and loss transactions ultimately affect the Retained Earnings account. Accordingly, to reconcile the beginning and ending balances in Retained Earnings, all income statement items are posted directly to the Retained Earnings account. Second, the determination of when to stop the analysis depends on the reconciliation between the beginning and ending account balances. In this case, the analysis of Accounts Receivable stopped with the $20,800 credit because the beginning balance plus the debit and minus the credit equalled the ending balance. Accordingly, the analysis of the account is completed because the beginning and ending balances have been reconciled (i.e., the change in the account has been fully explained). The analysis for the entire statement is completed when the beginning and ending balances in all the balance sheet accounts are reconciled. Since many of the balance sheet accounts remain to be reconciled, the cash flow analysis in this case will continue.

Cash Payments for Inventory Purchases

It is helpful to make two simplifying assumptions in analyzing cash payments for inventory purchases. First, assume that the company employs the perpetual inventory method; second, assume that all purchases are made on account. On the basis of these assumptions, the entry to record the cost of goods sold ($10,500, as shown on the income statement in Exhibit 14–3) would have required a credit to the Inventory account and a debit to Retained Earnings (i.e., cost of goods sold). This entry is labelled (b1) in the exhibit. This entry only partly explains the change in the beginning and ending balances of the Inventory account. A closer analysis of this account suggests that some inventory must have been purchased. Given that the beginning balance in the Inventory account was $8,200 and that $10,500 of inventory cost was transferred to cost of goods sold, it is logical to assume that $11,200 of inventory was purchased to arrive at the ending Inventory balance of $8,900. The entry to record the inventory purchase, labelled (b2), includes a debt to Inventory and a credit to Accounts Payable. This entry completes the explanation of the change in the beginning and ending balances but only partly explains the change in the beginning and ending balances in the Accounts Payable account. Given a beginning balance in Accounts Payable of $1,100 and additional purchases on account amounting to $11,200, there must have been $12,300 of accounts payable available for payment. Since the ending balance in the Accounts Payable account amounted to $800, there must have been cash payments of $11,500 ($12,300 − $800). The entry to record this cash outflow, labelled (b3), includes a credit to the operating activities section of the Cash account and a debit to the Accounts Payable account.

Noncash Effects of Amortization

The next item on the income statement is amortization expense. Amortization expense is a noncash charge against revenues. In other words, no cash changes hands at the time the amortization expense is recorded. Indeed, the entry to record amortization expense (c1) includes a debit to Retained Earnings (i.e., amortization expense) and a credit to Accumulated Amortization. This entry only partly explains the change in accumulated amortization, indicating that further analysis is required. However, cash flow consequences associated with long-term assets and their respective contra-accounts affect the investing activities section of the cash flow statement. Accordingly, further analysis is delayed until investing activities are considered. At this stage, the analysis of cash flows from operating activities continues.

Cash Payments for Salaries

The entry to record $2,700 of salary expense includes a debit to Retained Earnings (i.e., salary expense) and a credit to Salaries Payable. This entry, labelled (d1), partly explains the change in beginning and ending balances in the Salaries Payable account. The beginning balance of $900 plus the $2,700 increase for the current period's expense suggests that there were $3,600 of salaries available for payment during the period. Since the ending balance amounted to $1,000, there must have been a cash payment for salaries amounting to $2,600 ($3,600 − $1,000). The entry to record the cash payment for salaries includes a debit to the Salaries Payable account and a credit to the operating activities section of the Cash account. This entry is labelled (d2) in the exhibit.

Cash Payments for Insurance

The entry to record $600 of insurance expense requires a debit to Retained Earnings (i.e., insurance expense) and a credit to Prepaid Insurance. This entry, labelled (e1), partly explains the change in the beginning and ending balances in the Prepaid Insurance account. The beginning balance of $1,400 less the reduction of $600 associated with the recognition of insurance expense suggests an ending balance of $800. However, the balance sheet shows an actual ending balance of $1,100. Accordingly, a purchase of $300 ($1,100 − $800) of prepaid insurance must have been made during the accounting period. The cash outflow for the purchase of insurance is labelled (e2) and includes a debit to the Prepaid Insurance account and a credit to the operating activities section of the cash flow statement.

Cash Payments for Other Operating Expenses

The $1,400 of other operating expenses appearing on the income statement is recorded in the T-accounts with a debit to Retained Earnings and a credit to the Operating Expenses Payable account. This entry, labelled (f1), partly explains the change in the beginning and ending balances in the Operating Expenses Payable account. Given a beginning balance of $1,300 and the $1,400 addition for current expenses, the total amount available for payment was $2,700 ($1,300 + $1,400). Since the ending balance amounted to $1,500, the cash payments must have amounted to $1,200 ($2,700 − $1,500). The entry to record the cash payment is labelled (f2) and includes a debit to the Operating Expenses Payable account and a credit to the operating activities section of the Cash account.

Cash Receipts for Rent

The entry to record $2,400 of rent revenue includes a debit to the Unearned Rent Revenue account and a credit to the Retained Earnings account. This entry, labelled (g1), partly explains the change in the beginning and ending balances in the Unearned Rent Revenue account. The beginning balance of $1,600 less the $2,400 reduction caused by the recognition of the rent revenue suggests that there must have been a credit (i.e., increase) in the account in order to arrive at an ending balance of $600. Since increases in the unearned account are offset by increases in cash, collections must have been equal to $1,400 ($1,600 + $1,400 − $2,400 = $600). The required entry for the cash receipt includes a credit to the Unearned Rent Revenue account and a debit to the operating activities section of the Cash account. This entry is labelled (g2) in Exhibit 14–4.

Cash Receipts from Interest

The entry to record $700 of interest revenue includes a debit to the Interest Receivable account and a credit to Retained Earnings (i.e., interest revenue). This entry, labelled (h1), partially explains the change in the beginning and ending balances in the Interest Receivable account. Given the beginning balance of $300 plus the $700 debit created through the recognition of interest revenue, the receivables account indicates that there was $1,000 ($300 + $700) of interest receivables available for collection. The ending balance of $400 implies that $600 ($1,000 − $400) of cash was collected. The entry to record this cash inflow is labelled (h2) and includes a credit to Interest Receivable and a debit to the operating activities section of the Cash account.

Cash Payments for Interest

The entry to record $400 of interest expense is labelled (i1) and includes a debit to Retained Earnings (i.e., interest expense) and a credit to Interest Payable. The entry partly explains the change in the beginning and ending balances in the Interest Payable account. The beginning balance of $500 plus the $400 that resulted from the recognition of interest expense suggests that there was $900 of interest obligations available for payment. The ending balance of $300 implies that $600 ($900 − $300) was paid in cash. The entry to recognize the cash outflow for this interest payment is labelled (i2) and includes a debit to the Interest Payable account and a credit to the operating activities section of the Cash account.

Noncash Effects of Loss

The loss on the sale of equipment does not affect cash flows from operating activities. The full proceeds from the sale constitute the amount of cash flow. The amount of any loss or gain is irrelevant. Indeed, the sale involves the disposal of an investment and therefore is shown under the investing activities section. Cash flow from operating activities is not affected by gains or losses on the disposal of long-term assets.

Completion of Analysis of Operating Activities

Since no other items appear on the income statement, the conversion process from accrual to cash is completed. The operating activities section of the Cash account contains all the cash receipts and payments necessary to determine the net cash flow from operations. This information is placed into the formal cash flow statement (presented later in the chapter). With the completion of the assessment of cash flow from operating activities, the analysis proceeds to the cash flow effects associated with investing activities.

Cash Flows from Investing Activities

Investing activities generally involve the acquisition (i.e., purchase) or disposal (i.e., sale) of long-term assets. Accordingly, the analysis of cash flows from investing activities centres on changes in the beginning and ending balances in long-term assets.

Cash Payments to Purchase Marketable Securities

The first long-term asset shown on the balance sheets is Marketable Securities. An analysis of this asset account indicates that the balance in the account increased from $3,500 at the beginning of the period to $5,100 at the end of the period. The most reasonable explanation for this increase is that the corporation purchased additional securities in the amount of $1,600 ($5,100 − $3,500). In the absence of information to the contrary, it is assumed that the purchase was made with cash. The entry to record the purchase includes a debit to the Marketable Securities account and a credit to the investing activities section of the Cash account. This entry is coded (j1) in Exhibit 14–4.

Cash Receipts from Sale of Equipment

The next asset on the balance sheets is Equipment. Our earlier review of the income statement disclosed a loss on the sale of equipment, which suggests that some equipment was sold during the period. This sale is expected to result in a cash inflow in the amount of the sales price. The additional information at the bottom of the income statement discloses that equipment costing $1,500 with accumulated amortization of $1,100 was sold for $300. The difference between the $400 ($1,500 − $1,100) book value and the $300 sales price explains the $100 loss on the income statement. The cash receipt from the sale is $300. The original cost, accumulated amortization, and loss do not affect cash flow. The entry to recognize the cash receipt includes a debit to the investing section of the Cash account, a debit to Retained Earnings (i.e., loss), a debit to the Accumulated Amortization account, and a credit to the Equipment account. The entry is labelled (k1) in the exhibit.

Cash Payments to Purchase Equipment

The sale of equipment partially explains the change in the beginning and ending balances in the Equipment account. However, further analysis suggests that some equipment must have been purchased. A beginning balance of $4,600 less $1,500 for the equipment that was sold suggests that $2,300 of equipment must have been purchased in order to arrive at the ending balance of $5,400 ($4,600 − $1,500 + $2,300 = $5,400). The cash payment necessary to purchase the equipment is labelled (l1) and includes a debit to the Equipment account and a credit to the investing activities section of the Cash account.

Noncash Transaction for Land Acquisition

The Land account increased from a beginning balance of $6,000 to an ending balance of $8,500, thereby suggesting that $2,500 ($8,500 − $6,000) of land was acquired during the accounting period. The additional information at the bottom of the income statement discloses the fact that the corporation acquired this land through the issuance of a mortgage. Accordingly, no cash consequences are associated with the transaction. The transaction recording this event is labelled (m1) in Exhibit 14–4. Since the transaction does not affect cash, it is shown in the separate schedule for noncash investing and financing transactions on the cash flow statement.

Since all long-term asset accounts have been reconciled, the analysis of cash flows from investing activities is completed. The process continues with an assessment of cash flows associated with financing activities.

How did Florida Power and Lighting (FPL) acquire $501 million of property and equipment without spending any cash? Oddly enough, the answer can be found in the company's cash flow statement. The supplemental schedule of noncash investing and financing activities section of FPL's cash statement shows that it acquired $81 million of equipment by accepting lease obligations and that it acquired $420 million of property by assuming debt. In other words, FPL acquired $501 million (i.e., $81 million + $420 million) in property and equipment by agreeing to pay for it later.

©Telegraph Colour Library/FPG

Cash Flows from Financing Activities

The long-term liability and shareholders' equity sections of the balance sheets are analyzed to assess the cash flows from financing activities. Note that the first long-term liability account on the balance sheet is Mortgage Payable. The change in this account was explained in the analysis of the land acquisition, discussed earlier in this chapter. As explained, this financing activity is shown along with the investing activity in the separate schedule for noncash transactions. Accordingly, the analysis of cash flows proceeds with the change in the Bond Liability account.

Cash Payment for Bonds

The balance in the Bonds Payable account decreased from $4,000 to $1,000. In the absence of information to the contrary, it is logical to assume that $3,000 ($4,000 − $1,000) was paid to reduce bond liabilities. The entry to record the cash outflow includes a debit to the Bonds Payable account and a credit to the financing activities section of the Cash account. This entry is coded (n1) in the exhibit.

Cash Receipt from Shares Issue

The balance in the Common Shares account increased from $8,000 to $10,000. In the absence of information to the contrary, it is logical to assume that $2,000 ($10,000 − $8,000) of cash was collected as proceeds from the issuance of common shares. The entry to record this cash inflow is labelled (o1) and includes a credit to Common Shares and a debit to the financing activities section of the Cash account.

Cash Payments for Dividends

Finally, additional information at the bottom of the income statement discloses a cash dividend of $1,500. The transaction to record this cash outflow includes a debit to the Retained Earnings account and a credit to the financing activities section of the Cash account. It is labelled (p1) in Exhibit 14–4.

Presenting Information in the Cash Flow Statement

Since all income statement items have been analyzed, changes in balance sheet accounts have been explained, and all additional information has been considered, the analytical process is completed. The data in the T-account for cash must now be organized in appropriate financial statement format. Recall that cash flow from operations is presented first, cash flow from investing activities second, and cash flow from financing activities third. Noncash investing and financing activities are shown in a separate schedule or in the footnotes. Exhibit 14–5 is a cash flow statement and a separate schedule for non-cash activities.

LO4

Explain how cash flow from operating activity reported under the indirect method differs from that reported under the direct method.

Cash Flow Statement Presented under the Indirect Method

Up to now, the cash flow statement has been presented in accordance with the **direct method**. The direct method is intuitively logical and is the method recommended by the Canadian Institute of Chartered Accountants. Even so, most companies use an alternative known as the **indirect method**. The difference between the two methods is in the presentation of the operating activities section. The indirect method uses net income as reported on the income statement as the starting point. The method proceeds by showing the adjustments necessary to convert the accrual-based net income figure to a cash-basis equivalent. The conversion process can be accomplished by the application of three basic rules, which are discussed next.

An increase in the balance of the Accounts Receivable account would suggest that not all sales were collected in cash. Accordingly, the amount of revenue shown on the income statement would overstate the amount of cash collections. Therefore, it is necessary to subtract the amount of the increase in the receivables account from the amount of net income to convert the income figure to a cash-equivalent basis. Similarly, a decrease in the receivables balance has to be added to the net income figure. Extending this logic to all current asset accounts results in the first general rule of the conversion process. **Rule 1: Increases in current assets are deducted from net income**, and decreases in current assets are added to net income.

The opposite logic applies to current liabilities. For example, an increase in accounts payable suggests that not all expenses were paid in cash. Accordingly, it is necessary to add the increase in the payables account to the amount of net income to convert the income figure to a cash-equivalent basis. Conversely, decreases in payable accounts are deducted from net income. Extending the logic to all the current liability accounts produces the second general rule of the conversion process. **Rule 2: Increases in current liabilities are added to net income, and decreases in current liabilities are deducted from net income.**

Finally, note that some expense and revenue transactions do not have cash consequences. For example, although amortization is reported as an expense, it does not require the payment of cash. Similarly, losses and gains reported on the income statement do not have consequences that are reported in the operating activities section of the cash flow statement. **Rule 3: All noncash expenses and losses are added to net income, and all noncash revenue and gains are subtracted from net income.**

These three general rules apply only to items affecting operating activities. For example, Rule 2 does not apply to an increase or decrease in the current liability account for dividends because dividend payments are considered to be financing activities, rather than operating activities. Accordingly, some degree of judgment must be exercised in applying the three general rules of conversion.

Exhibit 14–6 shows the presentation of a cash flow statement under the indirect method. The statement was constructed by applying the three general rules of conversion to the data for The New

Exhibit 14-5

THE NEW SOUTH CORPORATION
Cash Flow Statement
For the Period Ended December 31, 2005

Cash Flows from Operating Activities
Cash Receipts from

Sales	$20,800		
Rent	1,400		
Interest	600		
Total Cash Inflows		$22,800	
Cash Payments for			
Inventory Purchases	11,500		
Salaries	2,600		
Insurance	300		
Other Operating Expenses	1,200		
Interest	600		
Total Cash Outflows		(16,200)	
Net Cash Flow from Operating Activities			$6,600
Cash Flows from Investing Activities			
Inflow from Sale of Equipment		300	
Outflow to Purchase Marketable Securities		(1,600)	
Outflow to Purchase Equipment		(2,300)	
Net Cash Flow from Investing Activities			(3,600)
Cash Flows from Financing Activities			
Inflow from Shares Issue		2,000	
Outflow to Repay Debt		(3,000)	
Outflow for Dividends		(1,500)	
Net Cash Flow from Financing Activities			(2,500)
Net Increase in Cash			500
Plus: Beginning Cash Balance			400
Ending Cash Balance			$ 900
Schedule of Noncash Investing and Financing Activities			
Issue of Mortgage for Land			$2,500

South Corporation shown in Exhibits 14–2 and 14–3. Note that the only difference between the statement presented under the indirect method (Exhibit 14–6) and the statement shown under the direct method (Exhibit 14–5) is the Cash Flow from Operating Activities section. Cash flows from investing and financing activities and the schedule of noncash items are not affected by the alternative reporting format.

▌ Consequences of Growth on Cash Flow

LO5

Explain how the classifications used on the cash flow statement could provide misleading information to decision makers.

Why do decision makers in business need a cash flow statement? Why is the information provided on the income statement not sufficient? Although it is true that the income statement shows how well a business is doing on an accrual basis, it does not show what is happening with cash. Understanding the cash flows of a business is extremely important because cash is used to pay the bills. A company, especially one that is growing rapidly, can have substantial earnings but be short of cash because it must buy goods before they are sold, and it may not receive cash payment until months after revenue is recognized on an accrual basis. To illustrate, assume that you want to go into the business of selling computers. You borrow $2,000 and use the money to purchase two computers that cost $1,000 each. Furthermore,

Exhibit 14-6

THE NEW SOUTH CORPORATION
Cash Flow Statement (Indirect Method)
For the Period Ended December 31, 2005

Cash Flows from Operating Activities		
Net Income	$7,200	
Plus: Decreases in Current Assets		
and Increases in Current Liabilities		
Decrease in Accounts Receivable	200	
Decrease in Prepaid Insurance	300	
Increase in Salaries Payable	100	
Increase in Other Operating Expenses Payable	200	
Less: Increases in Current Assets		
and Decreases in Current Liabilities		
Increase in Interest Receivable	(100)	
Increase in Inventory	(700)	
Decrease in Accounts Payable for Inventory Purchases	(300)	
Decrease in Interest Payable	(200)	
Decrease in Unearned Revenue	(1,000)	
Plus: Noncash Charges		
Amortization Expense	800	
Loss on Sale of Equipment	100	
Net Cash Flow from Operating Activities		$6,600
Cash Flows from Investing Activities		
Inflow from Sale of Equipment	300	
Outflow to Purchase Marketable Securities	(1,600)	
Outflow to Purchase Equipment	(2,300)	
Net Cash Flow from Investing Activities		(3,600)
Cash Flows from Financing Activities		
Inflow from Shares Issue	2,000	
Outflow to Repay Debt	(3,000)	
Outflow for Dividends	(1,500)	
Net Cash Flow from Financing Activities		(2,500)
Net Increase in Cash		500
Plus: Beginning Cash Balance		400
Ending Cash Balance		$900
Schedule of Noncash Investing and Financing Activities		
Issue of Mortgage for Land		$2,500

assume that you sell one of the computers on account for $1,500. At this point, if you had a payment due on your loan, you would be unable to pay the amount due. Even though you had a net income of $500 (i.e., revenue of $1,500 − cost of goods sold of $1,000), you would have no cash until you collected the $1,500 cash due from the account receivable.

Real-World Data

The cash flow statement frequently provides a picture of business activity that would otherwise be lost in the complexities of the application of accrual accounting. For example, consider the effects of restructuring charges on operating income versus cash flow experienced by IBM Corporation. For 1991, 1992, and 1993 combined, IBM reported operating *losses* (before taxes) of more than $17.9 *billion*. During this same period, it reported "restructuring charges" of more than $24 billion. Therefore, without the restructuring charges, IBM would have reported operating profits of about $6 billion (before taxes). Are restructuring charges an indication of something bad or something good? Who knows? Different financial analysts have different opinions about this issue. There is something about IBM's performance dur-

Exhibit 14-7 *Operating Income versus Cash Flow from Operations (amounts in $000)*

Company		Current	Past
Air Canada	Income from Operations	$86,000	$377,000
	Cash Flow from Operating Activities	115,000	680,000
Bombardier Inc.	Income from Operations	975,400	718,800
	Cash Flow from Operating Activities	899,900	913,000
Westjet Airlines Ltd.	Income from Operations	53,462	30,469
	Cash Flow from Operating Activities	51,930	29,831
McGraw-Hill Ryerson Ltd.	Income from Operations	4,639	5,849
	Cash Flow from Operating Activities	(294)	12,312
Rainmaker Entertainment Ltd.	Income from Operations	2,777	2,060
	Cash Flow from Operating Activities	6,554	4,837
Corel Corporation	Income from Operations	(61,050)	13,438
	Cash Flow from Operating Activities	(28,030)	9,855

ing these years that can be more easily understood. The company produced over $21 billion in positive cash flow from operating activities. It had no trouble paying its bills.

Exhibit 14–7 is a comparison of the income from operations and the cash flow from operating activities for six real-world companies for the 2001/2000 and 2000/1999 fiscal years.

The conclusion one must reach about using the cash flow statement is the same as that for using the balance sheet or the earnings statement. Users cannot simply look at the numbers. They must analyze the numbers based on a knowledge of the particular business being examined.

Accounting alone cannot tell a businessperson how to make a decision. Making good business decisions requires an understanding of the business in question, the environmental and economic factors affecting the operation of that business, and the accounting concepts on which the financial statements of that business are based.

---

a look **back**

Throughout this course, you have been asked to consider many different accounting events that occur in the business world. In many cases, you were asked to consider the effects that these events have on a company's balance sheet, income statement, and cash flow statement. By now, you should be aware that each of the financial statements shows a different, but equally important, view of the financial situation of the company in question.

This chapter provided a more detailed examination of only one financial statement, the cash flow statement. The chapter presented a more comprehensive review of how an accrual accounting system relates to a cash-based accounting system. It is important that you understand not only both systems but also how the two systems relate to each other. This is the reason that a formal cash flow statement begins with a reconciliation of net income, an accrual measurement, to net cash flow from operating activities, a cash measurement. Finally, this chapter explained how the idiosyncrasies of classifying cash events as operating, investing, or financing activities may cause an inadequately educated user of financial information to reach incorrect conclusions.

a look **forward**

This chapter probably completes your first course in accounting. We sincerely hope that this text has provided you a meaningful learning experience that will serve you well as you progress through your academic training and your ultimate career. Good luck and best wishes!

Accrual accounting An accounting system that recognizes expenses or revenues before the associated cash payments or receipts occur. *(p. 503)*

Cash inflows Sources of cash. *(p. 501)*

Cash outflows Uses of cash. *(p. 501)*

Deferral transactions Accounting transactions in which cash payments or receipts occur before the associated expense or revenue is recognized. *(p. 505)*

Direct method The method of preparing the cash flow statement that reports the total cash receipts and cash payments from each of the major categories of activities (i.e., collections from customers, payment to suppliers). *(p. 515)*

Expense transactions Transactions completed in the process of operating a business that decrease assets or increase liabilities. *(p. 504)*

Financing activities Business activities that generate cash inflows and cash outflows from transactions with a company's owners (i.e., shares or dividend transactions) or its creditors (i.e., borrowing or repayment transactions). *(p. 502)*

Indirect method A method of preparing the cash flow statement that uses the net income from the income statement as a starting point for the reporting of cash flow from operating activities. The adjustments necessary to convert accrual-based net income to a cash-equivalent basis are shown in the operating activities section of the cash flow statement. *(p. 515)*

Investing activities Business activities that generate cash inflows and cash outflows through a company's purchase or sale of long-term operational assets, investments, and lending activities. *(p. 502)*

Noncash investing and financing transactions Business transactions that do not directly affect cash, such as exchanging shares for land or purchasing property by using a mortgage. These transactions are reported as both an inflow and an outflow in a separate section of the cash flow statement. *(p. 502)*

Operating activities Business activities that generate cash inflows and cash outflows through the process of operating the business. *(p. 502)*

Revenue transactions Transactions completed in the process of operating a business that increase assets or decrease liabilities. *(p. 503)*

T-account method A method of determining net cash flows by analyzing beginning and ending balances on the balance sheet and inferring the periods transactions from the income statement. *(p. 504)*

1. What is the purpose of the cash flow statement?
2. What are the three categories of cash inflows and cash outflows shown on the cash flow statement? Discuss each and give an example of an inflow and an outflow for each category.
3. What are noncash investing and financing activities? Give an example. How are these transactions shown on the cash flow statement?
4. Best Company had a beginning balance in its Accounts Receivable account of $12,000 and ending Accounts Receivable of $14,000. If total sales were $110,000, what amount of cash was collected?
5. Best Company's Utilities Payable account had a beginning balance of $3,300 and an ending balance of $5,200. Utilities expense reported on the income statement amounted to $87,000. What was the amount of cash payment for utilities for the period?
6. Best Company had a balance in the Unearned Revenue account of $4,300 at the beginning of the period and an ending balance of $5,700. If the portion of unearned revenue that was recognized as being earned during the period amounted to $15,600, what amount of cash was collected?
7. Which of the following activities are financing activities?
   a. Payment of accounts payable

   b. Payment of interest on bonds payable
   c. Sale of common shares
   d. Sale of preferred shares at a premium
   e. Payment of a dividend on the shares
8. Does amortization expense affect net cash flow? Explain.
9. If Best Company sold land that cost $4,200 for a $500 gain, how much cash was collected from the sale of land?
10. If Best Company sold office equipment that originally cost $7,500 and had $7,200 of accumulated amortization for a $100 loss, what was the selling price for the office equipment?
11. In which section of the cash flow statement would the following transactions be reported?
    a. Cash receipt of interest income
    b. Cash purchase of marketable securities
    c. Cash purchase of equipment
    d. Cash sale of merchandise
    e. Cash sale of common shares
    f. Payment of interest expense
    g. Cash proceeds from loan
    h. Cash payment on bonds payable
    i. Cash receipt from sale of old equipment
    j. Cash payment for operating expenses

12. What is the difference between preparing the cash flow statement using the direct approach and using the indirect approach?

13. Which method (i.e., direct or indirect) of preparing the cash flow statement is more intuitively logical? Why?

14. What is the major advantage of using the indirect method in preparing the cash flow statement?

15. What is the advantage of using the direct method of preparing the cash flow statement?

16. How would the following transactions of Best Company be shown on the cash flow statement?
   a. Purchased new equipment for $46,000 cash.
   b. Sold old equipment for $8,700 cash. The equipment had a book value of $4,900.

17. Can a company have a negative cash flow from operations for the year on the cash flow statement but still have a net income on the income statement? Explain.

EXERCISES

L.O. 1 EXERCISE 14-1   *Classifying Transactions into Categories of Cash Flows—Direct Method*

Required

Identify each of the following activities as operating activities, investing activities, or financing activities for the cash flow statement (assume that the direct method is used):
a. Sale of merchandise for cash
b. Purchase of equipment for cash
c. Payment of employee salary
d. Interest income received on a certificate of deposit
e. Sale of shares for cash
f. Cash proceeds from bank loan
g. Payment of interest on loan
h. Payment of dividends
i. Repayment of bank loan
j. Sale of used equipment

L.O. 1 EXERCISE 14-2   *Identifying Operating Activities Cash Inflows—Direct Method*

Required

Which of the following transactions produce cash inflow from operating activities? (Assume the direct method is used.)
a. Cash payment for salaries
b. Cash payment for equipment
c. Provision of services for cash
d. Cash receipt from interest
e. Cash payment for dividends
f. Collection of cash from accounts receivable

L.O. 2 EXERCISE 14-3   *Using Account Balances to Determine Cash Flow from Operating Activities—Direct Method*

The following account balances are available for Joy Gift Shop for 2009:

Account Title	Beginning of Year	End of Year
Accounts Receivable	$19,000	$22,000
Interest Receivable	6,000	3,000
Accounts Payable	25,000	26,500
Salaries Payable	13,500	12,000

Other Information for 2009:

Sales on Account	$250,000
Interest Income	20,000
Operating Expenses	154,000
Salaries Expense for the Year	106,000

Required

a. Compute the amount of cash *inflow* from operating activities. (*Hint:* It may be helpful to assume that all revenues and expenses are on account.)

b. Compute the amount of cash *outflow* from operating activities.

EXERCISE 14-4   *Using Account Balances to Determine Cash Flow from Operating Activities—Direct*   **L.O. 2**
Method

The following account balances were available for Dream Furniture Company for 2009:

Account Title	Beginning of Year	End of Year
Unearned Revenue	$9,000	$4,000
Prepaid Rent	1,900	800

The portion of the unearned revenue that was recognized as having been earned during the period was $32,000. Rent expense for the period was $6,000. Dream Furniture Company maintained its books on the accrual basis.

Required

Using the T-account approach, determine the amount of cash inflow from revenue and cash outflow for rent based on the preceding information.

EXERCISE 14-5   *Using Account Balances to Determine Cash Flow from Investing Activities*   **L.O. 2**

The following account information is available for Action Construction Company for 2009:

	Land				Marketable Securities	
Bal.	10,000	25,000		Bal.	150,000	31,000
	50,000				60,000	
Bal.	35,000			Bal.	179,000	

The income statement contained a $9,000 gain on the sale of land and a $1,200 loss on the sale of marketable securities.

Required

Prepare the investing activities section of the cash flow statement for 2009.

EXERCISE 14-6   *Using Account Balances to Determine Cash Flow from Financing Activities*   **L.O. 2, 3**

The following account balances were available for Goldfish, Inc. for 2007:

	Mortgage Payable				Capital Shares				Paid-in Capital in Excess of Par	
		131,000	Bal.			100,000	Bal.			
55,000						30,000			33,000	Bal.
		76,000	Bal.			130,000	Bal.		56,000	
									89,000	Bal.

Required

Prepare the financing activities section of the cash flow statement for 2007.

EXERCISE 14-7   *Using Account Balances to Determine Cash Outflow for Inventory Purchases*   **L.O. 2, 3**

The following account information is available for Filex Cruise Company. The company uses the perpetual inventory method.

	Inventory				Accounts Payable	
Bal.	82,000				27,200	Bal.
	?	149,000		?	152,000	
Bal.	85,000				40,500	Bal.

Required

Compute the amount of cash paid for the purchase of inventory.

L.O. 2, 4 EXERCISE 14-8   *Using Account Balances to Determine Cash Flow from Operating Activities—*
Indirect Method

Lemon Company uses the indirect method for preparing the cash flow statement. The following accounts and corresponding balances were drawn from Lemon's accounting records:

Account Titles	Beginning Balances	Ending Balances
Accounts Receivable	$15,000	$17,200
Prepaid Rent	1,500	800
Interest Receivable	600	200
Accounts Payable	9,050	9,450
Salaries Payable	2,100	1,750
Unearned Revenue	1,000	1,850
Net income for the period was $35,000.		

Required

Using the preceding information, compute the net cash flow from operating activities using the indirect method.

L.O. 2-4 EXERCISE 14-9   *Using Account Balances to Determine Cash Flow from Operating Activities—Direct*
and Indirect Methods

The following information was drawn from the accounting records of Ming Company:

	2008	2009
Cash	$ 35,000	$ 84,700
Accounts Receivable	165,000	159,800
Prepaid Rent	4,200	5,600
Accounts Payable	124,000	125,000
Utilities Payable	13,200	8,400
Revenue		$240,000
Operating Expenses		(155,000)
Utilities Expense		(15,300)
Rent Expense		(20,000)
Net Income		$ 49,700

Required

a. Prepare the operating activities section of the cash flow statement under the direct method for 2009.
b. Prepare the operating activities section of the cash flow statement under the indirect method for 2009.

L.O. 3, 5 EXERCISE 14-10   *Explaining Information Contained in the Cash Flow Statement*

The following selected transactions are for Jackson Corp. for the 2009 period:
1. Purchased new office equipment for $4,500.
2. Sold old office equipment for $800 that originally cost $6,000 and had accumulated amortization of $5,700.
3. Borrowed $10,000 cash from the bank for six months.
4. Purchased land for a cost of $115,000 by paying $30,000 in cash and issuing a note for the balance.
5. Exchanged no-par common shares for an automobile valued at $14,500.

Required

a. Prepare the appropriate sections of the cash flow statement for the 2009 period.
b. What information does the noncash investing and financing activities section of the statement provide? If this information were omitted, could it affect a decision to invest in a company?

PROBLEM 14-1A *Classifying Transactions on the Cash Flow Statement*   **L.O. 1**

Required

Identify each of the following transactions as an operating activity (OA), an investing activity (IA), a financing activity (FA), or a noncash transaction (NT):

a. Declared a shares split.

b. Provided services for cash.

c. Bought land with cash.

d. Issued common shares for cash.

e. Issued a note payable in exchange for equipment.

f. Recorded amortization of goodwill.

g. Provided services on account.

h. Paid cash for rent.

i. Purchased office supplies on account.

j. Paid cash for salaries.

k. Collected cash from accounts receivable.

l. Received interest on note receivable.

m. Paid a cash dividend.

n. Recorded amortization expense.

o. Received advance payment for services.

p. Purchased marketable securities with cash.

q. Paid insurance with cash.

r. Purchased inventory with cash.

s. Repaid principal and interest on a note payable.

PROBLEM 14-2A *Using Transaction Data to Prepare a Cash Flow Statement*

May & Company engaged in the following transactions during the 2009 accounting period. The beginning cash balance was $24,400.

L.O. 2, 3

1. Credit sales were $110,000. The beginning receivables balance was $86,000 and the ending balance was $92,000.

2. Salaries expense for the period was $34,000. The beginning salaries payable balance was $2,500 and the ending balance was $1,300.

3. Other operating expenses for the period were $32,000. The beginning Operating Expense Payable account was $3,100 and the ending balance was $7,200.

4. Recorded $14,300 of amortization expense. The beginning and ending balances in the Accumulated Amortization account amounted to $12,000 and $26,300, respectively.

5. The Equipment account had beginning and ending balances of $103,000 and $136,000, respectively. The increase was caused by the cash purchase of equipment.

6. The beginning and ending balances in the Notes Payable account were $30,000 and $45,000, respectively. The increase was caused by additional borrowing for cash.

7. There was $5,600 of interest expense reported on the income statement. The beginning and ending balances in the Interest Payable account were $2,500 and $2,000, respectively.

8. The beginning and ending Merchandise Inventory account balances were $25,000 and $22,000, respectively. The company sold merchandise with a cost of $51,000 (cost of goods sold for the period was $51,000). The beginning and ending balances of Accounts Payable were $7,200 and $5,000, respectively.

9. The beginning and ending balances of Notes Receivable were $7,500 and $12,500, respectively. The increase resulted from a cash loan to one of the company's employees.

10. The beginning and ending balances of the Common Shares account were $50,000 and $75,000, respectively. The increase was caused by the issue of common shares for cash.

11. Land had beginning and ending balances of $22,500 and $16,500, respectively. Land that cost $6,000 was sold for $14,700, resulting in a gain of $8,700.

12. The tax expense for the period was $3,500. The Tax Payable account had a $320 beginning balance and a $220 ending balance.

13. The investments account had beginning and ending balances of $10,000 and $19,000, respectively. The company purchased investments for $17,000 cash during the period, and investments that cost $8,000 were sold for $6,000, resulting in a $2,000 loss.

Required

Convert the preceding information to cash-equivalent data and prepare a cash flow statement.

L.O. 2, 3

PROBLEM 14-3A *Using Financial Statement Data to Determine Cash Flow from Operating Activities*

The following account information is available for Star Dust Company for 2009:

Account Title	Beginning of Year	End of Year
Accounts Receivable	$ 50,000	$ 42,500
Merchandise Inventory	190,000	174,600
Prepaid Insurance	4,500	4,000
Accounts Payable (Inventory)	72,500	87,500
Salaries Payable	8,800	7,250

Other Information
1. Sales for the period were $325,000.
2. Purchases of merchandise for the period were $243,000.
3. Insurance expense for the period was $6,000.
4. Other operating expenses (all cash) were $42,600.
5. Salary expense was $60,000.

Required
a. Compute the net cash flow from operating activities.
b. Prepare the cash flow from the operating activities section of the cash flow statement.

L.O. 2, 3 **PROBLEM 14-4A** *Using Financial Statement Data to Determine Cash Flow from Investing Activities*

The following information pertaining to investing activities is available for Turner Company for 2009:

Account Title	Beginning of Year	End of Year
Machinery and Equipment	$310,000	$334,000
Marketable Securities	51,000	19,500
Land	67,000	94,000

Other Information for 2009
1. Marketable securities were sold at book value. No gain or loss was recognized.
2. Machinery was purchased for $60,000. Old machinery with a book value of $8,000 (cost of $36,000, accumulated amortization of $28,000) was sold for $8,500.

Required
a. Compute the net cash flow from investing activities.
b. Prepare the cash flow from the investing activities section of the cash flow statement.

L.O. 2, 3 **PROBLEM 14-5A** *Using Financial Statement Data to Determine Cash Flow from Financing Activities*

The following information pertaining to financing activities is available for V-Tech Company for 2009:

Account Title	Beginning of Year	End of Year
Bonds Payable	$250,000	$180,000
Capital Shares	100,000	156,000
Paid-in Capital in Excess of Par	72,000	107,000

Other Information
1. Dividends paid during the period amounted to $31,000.
2. No new funds were borrowed during the period.

Required
a. Compute the net cash flow from financing activities for 2009.
b. Prepare the cash flow from the financing activities section of the cash flow statement.

PROBLEM 14-6A *Using Financial Statements to Prepare a Cash Flow Statement—Direct Method*   **L.O. 2, 3**

The following financial statements were drawn from the records of Blue Mountain, Incorporated:

Balance Sheet As of December 31	2008	2009
Assets		
Cash	$ 1,400	$24,200
Accounts Receivable	600	1,100
Inventory	3,000	2,800
Equipment	11,000	9,000
Accumulated Amortization—Equipment	(8,700)	(9,000)
Land	5,200	8,600
Total Assets	$12,500	$36,700
Liabilities and Equity		
Accounts Payable	$ 2,100	$ 2,600
Long-Term Debt	3,200	2,800
Common Shares	5,000	9,700
Retained Earnings	2,200	21,600
Total Liabilities and Equity	$12,500	$36,700

Income Statement for the Year Ended December 31, 2009	
Revenue	$33,650
Cost of Goods Sold	(12,050)
Gross Margin	21,600
Amortization Expense	(2,800)
Operating Income	18,800
Gain on Sale of Equipment	1,450
Loss on Disposal of Land	(50)
Net Income	$20,200

Additional Data
1. During 2009, the company sold equipment for $4,450. The equipment originally cost $5,500. Accumulated amortization on this equipment was $2,500 at the time of the sale. Also, the company purchased equipment for $3,500 cash.
2. The company sold land that cost $1,300. This land was sold for $1,250, resulting in the recognition of a $50 loss. Also, common shares were issued in exchange for title to land that was valued at $4,700 at the time of exchange.
3. Paid dividends of $800.

Required
Use the T-account method to analyze the data and prepare a cash flow statement.

PROBLEM 14-7A *Using Financial Statements to Prepare a Cash Flow Statement—Direct Method*   **L.O. 2, 3**

The following financial statements were drawn from the records of Grace Corporation:

Balance Sheet As of December 31

	2005	2006
Assets		
Cash	$ 14,100	$ 61,800
Accounts Receivable	33,000	28,500
Inventory	57,000	63,000
Notes Receivable	15,000	0
Equipment	127,500	73,500
Accumulated Amortization—Equipment	(70,500)	(37,370)
Land	26,250	41,250
Total Assets	$202,350	$230,680
Liabilities and Equity		
Accounts Payable	$ 24,300	$ 21,000
Salaries Payable	12,000	15,000
Utilities Payable	600	300
Interest Payable	900	0
Note Payable	30,000	0
Common Shares	120,000	150,000
Ratained Earnings	14,550	44,380
Total Liabilities and Equity	$202,350	$230,680

Income Statement for the Year Ended December 31, 2006

Revenue	$290,000
Cost of Goods Sold	(144,000)
Gross Margin	146,000
Operating Expenses	
Salary Expense	(92,000)
Amortization Expense	(8,870)
Utilities Expense	(6,100)
Operating Income	39,030
Nonoperating Items	
Interest Expense	(1,500)
Gain or (Loss)	(900)
Net Income	$ 36,630

Additional Information
1. Sold equipment costing $54,000 with accumulated amortization of $42,000 for $11,100 cash.
2. Paid a $6,800 cash distribution to owners.

Required
Use the T-account method to analyze the data and prepare a cash flow statement.

L.O. 2, 4 PROBLEM 14-8A *Using Financial Statements to Prepare a Cash Flow Statement—Indirect Method*

The comparative balance sheet for Triumph Company for 2008 and 2009 is as follows:

Balance Sheet As of December 31		
	2008	**2009**
Assets		
Cash	$ 20,300	$ 34,400
Accounts Receivable	11,000	15,000
Merchandise Inventory	88,000	80,000
Prepaid Rent	2,400	1,200
Equipment	144,000	128,000
Accumulated Amortization	(118,000)	(73,400)
Land	40,000	96,000
Total Assets	$187,700	$281,200
Liabilities		
Accounts Payable (Inventory)	$ 38,000	$ 33,500
Salaries Payable	12,000	14,000
Shareholders' Equity:		
Common Shares, $25 Par Value	100,000	125,000
Retained Earnings	37,700	108,700
Total Liabilities and Equity	$187,700	$281,200

Income Statement for the Year Ended December 31, 2009	
Sales	$ 750,000
Cost of Goods Sold	(398,600)
Gross Profit	351,400
Operating Expenses	
Amortization Expense	(11,400)
Rent Expense	(12,000)
Salaries Expense	(128,000)
Other Operating Expenses	(129,000)
Net Income	$ 71,000

Other Information

1. Purchased land for $56,000.
2. Purchased new equipment for $50,000.
3. Sold old equipment that cost $66,000 with accumulated amortization of $56,000 for $10,000 cash.
4. Issued common shares for $25,000.

Required

Prepare the cash flow statement for 2009, using the indirect method.

PROBLEMS—SERIES B

PROBLEM 14-1B *Classifying Transactions on the Cash Flow Statement*   **L.O. 1**

Required

Identify each of the following transactions as an operating activity (OA), an investing activity (IA), a financing activity (FA), or a noncash transaction (NT):

a. Purchased supplies on account.
b. Collected cash from accounts receivable.
c. Accrued warranty expense.
d. Borrowed cash by issuing a bond.
e. Loaned cash to a business associate.
f. Paid cash for interest expense.
g. Incurred a loss on the sale of equipment.
h. Wrote down inventory because the year-end physical count was lower than the balance in the Inventory account.

i. Paid cash to purchase inventory.
j. Paid cash for operating expenses.
k. Wrote off an uncollectible account receivable under the allowance method.
l. Wrote off an uncollectible account receivable under the direct write-off method.
m. Issued common shares for cash.
n. Declared a shares split.
o. Issued a mortgage to purchase a building
p. Purchased equipment with cash.
q. Repaid the principal balance on a note payable.
r   Made a cash payment for the balance due in the Dividends Payable account.
s. Received cash dividend from investment in marketable securities.

L.O. 2, 3 PROBLEM 14-2B *Using Transaction Data to Prepare a Cash Flow Statement*

Clair Cosmetics Co. engaged in the following transactions during the accounting period. The beginning cash balance was $43,000.

1. Credit sales were $24,000. The beginning receivables balance was $64,000 and the ending balance was $45,000.
2. Salaries expense for the period was $16,000. The beginning salaries payable balance was $8,000 and the ending balance was $4,000.
3. Other operating expenses for the period were $18,000. The beginning operating Expense Payable account was $8,000 and the ending balance was $5,000.
4. Recorded $15,000 of amortization expense. The beginning and ending balances in the Accumulated Amortization account amounted to $6,000 and $21,000, respectively.
5. The Equipment account had beginning and ending balances of $22,000 and $28,000, respectively. The increase was caused by the cash purchase of equipment.
6. The beginning and ending balances in the Notes Payable account were $22,000 and $18,000, respectively. The decrease was caused by the cash repayment of the debt.
7. There was $2,300 of interest expense reported on the income statement. The beginning and ending balances in the Interest Payable account were $4,200 and $3,750, respectively.
8. The beginning and ending Merchandise Inventory account balances were $11,000 and $14,700, respectively. The company sold merchandise with a cost of $41,800. The beginning and ending balances of Accounts Payable were $4,000 and $3,200, respectively.
9. The beginning and ending balances of Notes Receivable were $50,000 and $30,000, respectively. The decline resulted from the cash collection of a portion of the receivable.
10. The beginning and ending balances of the Common Shares account were $60,000 and $80,000, respectively. The increase was caused by the issue of common shares for cash.
11. Land had beginning and ending balances of $12,000 and $7,000, respectively. Land that cost $5,000 was sold for $3,000, resulting in a loss of $2,000.
12. The tax expense for the period was $3,300. The Tax Payable account had a $1,200 beginning balance and a $1,100 ending balance.
13. The Investments account had beginning and ending balances of $10,000 and $30,000, respectively. The company purchased investments for $25,000 cash during the period, and investments that cost $5,000 were sold for $11,000, resulting in a $6,000 gain.

Required
Convert the preceding information to cash-equivalent data and prepare a cash flow statement.

L.O. 2, 3 PROBLEM 14-3B *Using Financial Statement Data to Determine Cash Flow from Operating Activities*

The following account information is available for Zoom-In Photo Shop for 2009:

Account Title	Beginning of Year	End of Year
Accounts Receivable	$ 8,900	$10,500
Merchandise Inventory	68,000	71,400
Prepaid Insurance	800	600
Accounts Payable (Inventory)	9,400	9,800
Salaries Payable	3,200	2,900

Other Information
1. Sales for the period were $124,000.
2. Purchases of merchandise for the period were $93,000.
3. Insurance expense for the period was $4,000.
4. Other operating expenses (all cash) were $13,700.
5. Salary expense was $21,300.

Required
a. Compute the net cash flow from operating activities.
b. Prepare the cash flow from the operating activities section of the cash flow statement.

PROBLEM 14-4B *Using Financial Statement Data to Determine Cash Flow from Investing Activities*   **L.O. 2, 3**

The following information is available for Fresh Fish Mart Co. for 2009 pertaining to investing activities:

Account Title	Beginning of Year	End of Year
Machinery and Equipment	$81,000	$85,000
Marketable Securities	33,000	25,600
Land	21,000	17,000

Other Information for 2009
1. Marketable securities were sold at book value. No gain or loss was recognized.
2. Machinery was purchased for $20,000. Old machinery with a cost of $16,000 and accumulated amortization of $12,000 was sold for $5,500.
3. Land that cost $4,000 was sold for $5,000.

Required
a. Compute the net cash flow from investing activities.
b. Prepare the cash flow from the investing activities section of the cash flow statement.

PROBLEM 14-5B *Using Financial Statement Data to Determine Cash Flow from Financing Activities*   **L.O. 2, 3**

The following information is available for Sturdy Marble Company for 2009 pertaining to financing activities:

Account Title	Beginning of Year	End of Year
Bonds Payable	$ 85,000	$ 90,000
Capital Shares	105,000	140,000
Paid-in Capital in Excess of Par	42,000	58,000

Other Information
1. Dividends paid during the period amounted to $14,000.
2. Additional funds of $20,000 were borrowed during the period by issuing bonds.

Required
a. Compute the net cash flow from financing activities for 2009.
b. Prepare the cash flow from the financing activities section of the cash flow statement.

PROBLEM 14-6B *Using Financial Statements to Prepare a Cash Flow Statement—Direct Method*   **L.O. 2, 3**

The following financial statements were drawn from the records of Slim Line Products Co.:

Balance Sheet As of December 31		
	2008	2009
Assets		
Cash	$ 970	$ 8,060
Accounts Receivable	1,000	1,200
Inventory	1,300	1,000
Equipment	8,550	6,850
Accumulated Amortization—Equipment	(6,475)	(5,650)
Land	4,000	6,500
Total Assets	$9,345	$17,960
Liabilities and Equity		
Accounts Payable	$1,200	$ 1,800
Long-Term Debt	2,000	1,600
Common Shares	5,000	8,500
Retained Earnings	1,145	6,060
Total Liabilities and Shareholders' Equity	$9,345	$17,960

Income Statement for the Year Ended December 31, 2009	
Revenue	$8,740
Cost of Goods Sold	(3,100)
Gross Margin	5,640
Amortization Expense	(875)
Operating Income	4,765
Gain on Sale of Equipment	900
Loss on Disposal of Land	(300)
Net Income	$5,365

Additional Data

1. During 2009, the company sold equipment for $3,400. The equipment originally cost $4,200. Accumulated amortization on this equipment was $1,700 at the time of the sale. Also, the company purchased equipment for $2,500 cash.
2. The company sold land that cost $1,000. This land was sold for $700, resulting in the recognition of a $300 loss. Also, common shares were issued in exchange for title to land that was valued at $3,500 at the time of exchange.
3. Paid dividends of $450.

Required

Use the T-account method to analyze the data and prepare a cash flow statement.

L.O. 2, 3 PROBLEM 14-7B *Using Financial Statements to Prepare a Cash Flow Statement—Direct Method*

The following financial statements were drawn from the records of Prestige Novelty Design Co.:

Balance Sheet As of December 31		
	2008	2009
Assets		
Cash	$ 7,050	$ 47,150
Accounts Receivable	20,000	18,000
Inventory	32,000	36,000
Notes Receivable	8,000	0
Equipment	85,000	49,000
Accumulated Amortization—Equipment	(47,000)	(23,900)
Land	15,000	23,000
Total Assets	$120,050	$149,250
Liabilities and Equity		
Accounts Payable	$ 13,200	$ 12,000
Salaries Payable	5,000	7,500
Utilities Payable	700	400
Interest Payable	500	0
Note Payable	12,000	0
Common Shares	55,000	75,000
Ratained Earnings	33,650	54,350
Total Liabilities and Equity	$120,050	$149,250

Income Statement for the Year Ended December 31, 2009	
Revenue	$150,000
Cost of Goods Sold	(72,000)
Gross Margin	78,000
Operating Expenses	
Salary Expense	(44,000)
Amortization Expense	(4,900)
Utilities Expense	(3,200)
Operating Income	25,900
Nonoperating Items	
Interest Expense	(1,200)
Loss	(400)
Net Income	$ 24,300

Additional Information
1. Sold equipment costing $36,000 with accumulated amortization of $28,000 for $7,600 cash.
2. Paid a $3,600 cash distribution to owners.

Required
Use the T-account method to analyze the data and prepare a cash flow statement.

PROBLEM 14-8B *Using Financial Statements to Prepare a Cash Flow Statement—Indirect Method*   **L.O. 2, 4**

The comparative balance sheet for Ajax Food Research Centre for 2008 and 2009 is as follows:

Balance Sheet As of December 31		
	2008	**2009**
Assets		
Cash	$24,200	$ 3,150
Accounts Receivable	3,630	5,100
Merchandise Inventory	28,000	22,600
Prepaid Rent	1,070	350
Equipment	72,000	70,000
Accumulated Amortization	(59,000)	(36,700)
Land	25,000	58,000
Total Assets	$94,900	$122,500
Liabilities and Equity		
Accounts Payable (Inventory)	$20,000	$ 18,600
Salaries Payable	5,300	6,100
Shareholders' Equity		
Common Shares, $50 Par Value	60,000	75,000
Retained Earnings	9,600	22,800
Total Liabilities and Equity	$94,900	$122,500

Income Statement for the Year Ended December 31, 2009	
Sales	$240,000
Cost of Goods Sold	(132,000)
Gross Profit	108,000
Operating Expenses	
Amortization Expense	(5,700)
Rent Expense	(3,500)
Salaries Expense	(47,600)
Other Operating Expenses	(38,000)
Net Income	$ 13,200

Other Information
1. Purchased land for $33,000.
2. Purchased new equipment for $31,000.
3. Sold old equipment that cost $33,000 with accumulated amortization of $28,000 for $5,000 cash.
4. Issued common shares for $15,000.

Required
Prepare the cash flow statement for 2009 using the indirect method.

ANALYZE, THINK, COMMUNICATE

ACT 14-1 REAL-WORLD CASE *Following the Cash*

During 1997, as part of a major restructuring plan, Reynolds Metals Company sold at least nine plants that produced aluminum or aluminum products. It also sold coal properties and several distribution facilities. The cash flow statement for Reynolds Metals for 1997, 1996, and 1995 are shown on the next page.

Required
a. During 1997, how much cash did Reynolds Metals receive from the sales of assets that resulted from its restructuring efforts?
b. What did Reynolds apparently do with the cash it received from the sales of the plants and other assets? The answer to this question requires the use of judgment. It might be helpful to rephrase the question as: What was Reynolds able to spend money on that would not have been possible had it not sold the assets? Write a brief explanation and justification of your conclusions.

Reynolds Metals Company Consolidated Cash Flow Statement (dollars in millions)			
	Years Ended December 31		
	1997	1996	1995
Operating Activities			
Net Income	$136	$ 89	$389
Adjustments to Reconcile Net Income to Net Cash Provided by Operating Activities			
Amortization	368	365	344
Operational Restructuring Effects	58	37	—
Cumulative Effect of Accounting Change	—	15	—
Other	28	26	18
Changes in Operating Assets and Liabilities Net of Effects from Acquisitions and Dispositions			
Accounts Payable, Accrued and Other Liabilities	74	(110)	(173)
Receivables	(194)	67	(59)
Inventories	(108)	93	17
Other	1	(62)	(47)
Net Cash Provided by Operating Activities	363	520	489
Investing Activities			
Capital Investments			
Operational	(152)	(195)	(219)
Strategic	(120)	(237)	(626)
Maturities of Investments in Debt Securities	—	—	125
Sales of Assets—Operational Restructuring	367	—	—
Other	(3)	(5)	(20)
Net Cash Provided by (used in) Investing Activities	92	(437)	(740)
Financing Activities			
Proceeds from Long-Term Debt	—	40	106
Reduction of Long-Term Debt and Other Financing Liabilities	(245)	(105)	(22)
Increase (decrease) in Short-Term Borrowings	(138)	111	(18)
Cash Dividends Paid	(99)	(135)	(106)
Stock Options Exercised	59	5	22
Net Cash Used in Financing Activities	(423)	(84)	(18)
Cash and Cash Equivalents			
Net Increase (decrease)	32	(1)	(269)
At Beginning of Year	38	39	308
At End of Year	$ 70	$ 38	$ 39
Supplemental Disclosure of Cash Flow Information			
Cash Paid during the Year for			
Interest	$164	$176	$179
Income Taxes	21	2	56
See Notes beginning on page 44. [Refers to the 10K report.]			

GROUP ASSIGNMENT   *Preparing a Cash Flow Statement*   **ACT 14-2**

The following financial statements and information are available for Bravo Ent.:

Balance Sheet As of December 31

	2008	2009
Assets		
Cash	$ 60,300	$ 80,100
Accounts Receivable	42,500	51,600
Inventory	85,900	93,200
Marketable Securities (Held-to-Maturity)	110,000	142,000
Equipment	245,000	325,000
Accumulated Amortization	(120,000)	(155,000)
Land	60,000	40,000
Total Assets	$483,700	$576,900
Liabilities and Equity		
Liabilities		
Accounts Payable (Inventory)	$ 33,100	$ 18,200
Notes Payable—Long-Term	125,000	115,000
Bonds Payable	50,000	100,000
Total Liabilities	208,100	233,200
Shareholders' Equity		
Common Shares, No Par	80,000	100,000
Preferred Shares, $50 Par	50,000	55,000
Paid-in Capital in Excess of Par—Preferred		
Shares	13,400	17,200
Total Paid-in Capital	143,400	172,200
Retained Earnings	132,200	171,500
Total Shareholders' Equity	275,600	343,700
Total Liabilities and Shareholders' Equity	$483,700	$576,900

Income Statement for 2009

Sales Revenue		$ 525,000
Cost of Goods Sold		(383,250)
Gross Profit		141,750
Operating Expenses		
Supplies Expense	$10,200	
Salaries Expense	46,000	
Amortization Expense	45,000	
Total Operating Expense		101,200
Operating Income		40,550
Nonoperating Items		
Interest Expense		(8,000)
Gain from the Sale of Marketable Securities		15,000
Gain from the Sale of Land and Equipment		6,000
Net Income		$ 53,550

Additional Information

1. Sold land that cost $20,000 for $22,000.
2. Sold equipment that cost $15,000 and had accumulated amortization of $10,000 for $9,000.
3. Purchased new equipment for $95,000.
4. Sold marketable securities that cost $20,000 for $35,000.
5. Purchased new marketable securities for $52,000.
6. Paid $10,000 on the principal of the long-term note.

7. Paid off a $50,000 bond issue and issued new bonds for $100,000.
8. Issued some new common shares.
9. Issued some new $50-par preferred shares.
10. Paid dividends. (*Note:* The only transactions to affect retained earnings were net income and dividends.)

Required

a. Organize the class into three sections, and divide each section into groups of three to five students. Assign each section of groups an activity section of the cash flow statement (i.e., operating activities, investing activities, and financing activities).

Group Task

Complete your assigned portion of the cash flow statement. Have a representative of your section put your activity section of the cash flow statement on the board. As each adds its information on the board, the full cash flow statement will be presented.

Class Discussion

Have the class finish the cash flow statement by computing the net change in cash. Also have the class answer the following questions:

b. What was the issue price of the preferred shares?
c. What was the book value of the equipment sold?

WRITING ASSIGNMENT *Explaining Discrepancies between Cash Flow and Operating Income*   **ACT 14-3**

The following selected information was drawn from the records of Neon Company:

Assets	2008	2009
Accounts Receivable	$200,000	$420,100
Merchandise Inventory	360,000	740,000
Equipment	742,000	930,600
Amortization	(156,000)	(201,200)

Neon is experiencing cash flow problems. Despite the fact that the company reported significant increases in operating income, operating activities produced a net cash outflow. Indeed, recent financial forecasts indicate that Neon will have insufficient cash to pay its current liabilities within three months.

Required

Write a memo that provides a logical explanation for Neon's cash shortage. Include a recommendation for remedying the problem.

ETHICAL DILEMMA   *Would I Lie to You, Baby?*   **ACT 14-4**

Bill and Sue Fullerton are involved in divorce proceedings. When discussing a property settlement, he told her that he should take over their investment in an apartment complex because she would be unable to absorb the loss that the apartments are generating. Mrs. Fullerton was somewhat distrustful and asked Mr. Fullerton to support his contention. He produced the following income statement, which was supported by a CA's unqualified opinion that the statement was prepared in accordance with generally accepted accounting principles.

Fullerton apartments Income Statements For the Year Ended December 31, 2003		
Rent Revenue		$290,000
Less: Expenses		
Amortization Expense	$140,000	
Interest Expense	92,000	
Operating Expense	44,000	
Management Fees	28,000	
Total Expenses		(304,000)
Net Loss		($14,000)

All revenue is earned on account. Interest and operating expenses are incurred on account. Management fees are paid in cash. The following accounts and balances were drawn from the 2002 and 2003 balance sheets:

Account Title	2002	2003
Rent Receivable	$20,000	$22,000
Interest Payable	6,000	9,000
Accounts Payable (Oper. Exp.)	3,000	2,000

Mrs. Fullerton is reluctant to give up the apartments but feels that she must because her present salary is only $25,000 per year. She says that if she takes the apartments, the $14,000 loss would absorb a significant portion of her salary, leaving her only $11,000 with which to support herself. She tells you that while the figures seem to support her husband's arguments, she feels that she is failing to see something. She knows that she and her husband collected a $10,000 distribution from the business on December 1, 2003. Also, $75,000 cash was paid in 2003 to reduce the principal balance on a mortgage that was taken out to finance the purchase of the apartments two years ago. Finally, $12,000 cash was paid during 2003 to purchase a computer system used in the business. She wonders, "If the apartments are losing money, where is my husband getting all the cash to make these payments?"

Required

a. Prepare a cash flow statement for the 2003 accounting period.

b. Compare the cash flow statement prepared in Part *a* with the income statement and provide Sue Fullerton with recommendations.

c. Comment on the value of an unqualified audit opinion when using financial statements for decision-making purposes.

ACT 14-5 SPREADSHEET ANALYSIS   *Preparing a Cash Flow Statement Using the Direct Method*

Refer to the information in Problem 14-8A. Solve for the cash flow statement using the direct method. Instead of using the T-account method, set up the following spreadsheet to work through the analysis. The Debit/Credit entries are very similar to the T-account method, except that they are entered onto a spreadsheet. Two distinct differences are as follows:

1. Instead of making entries on Row 2 for Cash, cash entries are made beginning on Row 24 under the heading Cash Transactions.

2. Entries for Retained Earnings are made on Rows 15 through 20 since there are numerous revenue and expense entries to that account.

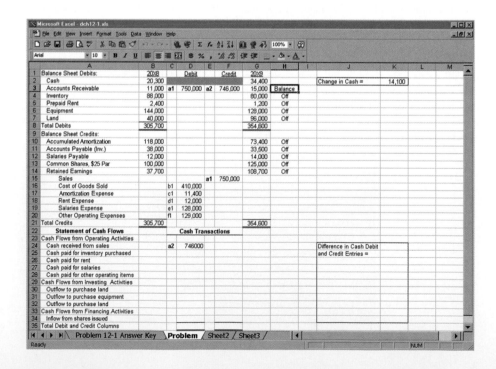

Required

a. Enter information in Column A.

b. Enter the beginning balance sheet amounts in Column B and ending balances in Column G. Total the debits and credits for each column.

c. To prevent erroneous entries to Cash in Row 2, darken the area in Columns C through F.

d. In Columns C through F, record entries for the revenue and expenses and then the related conversions to cash flow. The first entry (a1) and (a2) converting Sales to Cash Received from Sales has been provided for you. So has the labelling for the expense entries (b1 through f1).

e. Record the four entries from the Other Information provided in Problem 14-8A. These are investing and financing activities.

f. In Column H, set up the IF function to determine whether the balance sheet accounts are in balance or not ("off"). Cell H3 for Accounts Receivable is provided for you. Cell H3 can be copied to all the balance sheet debit accounts. The balance sheet credit account formulas will differ given the different debit/credit rules for those accounts. The formula for Retained Earnings will need to include Rows 14 through 20. *When the word "Balance" is reflected in every balance sheet cell in column H, the spreadsheet analysis is complete.*

g. Total the Debit and Credit columns to ensure that the two columns are equal.

h. As a final check, beginning in Cell J2, compute the change in the Cash account by subtracting the beginning balance from the ending balance. The difference will equal $14,100. Also beginning in Cell J24, compute the difference in the debit and credit cash entries in Rows 24 through 34. The difference should also equal $14,100.

Spreadsheet Tip
Darken cells by highlighting the cells to be darkened. Select Format and then Cells. Click on the tab titled Patterns and choose a colour.

SPREADSHEET ANALYSIS   *Preparing a Cash Flow Statement Using the Indirect Method*   **ACT 14-6**

(*Note:* If you completed ACT 14-5, that spreadsheet can be modified to complete this problem.)

Refer to the information in Problem 14-8A. Solve for the cash flow statement using the indirect method. Instead of using the T-account method, set up the following spreadsheet to work through the analysis. The Debit/Credit entries are very similar to the T-account method, except that they are entered onto a spreadsheet. Instead of making entries on Row 3 for Cash, Cash Flow entries are made beginning on Row 18.

	A	B	C	D	E	F	G	H	I	J	K
1	Balance Sheet Debits:	20X6		Debit		Credit	20X7				
2	Cash	20,300					34,400			Change in Cash =	14,100
3	Accounts Receivable	11,000	◎	4,000			15,000	Balance			
4	Inventory	88,000					80,000	Off			
5	Prepaid Rent	2,400					1,200	Off			
6	Equipment	144,000					128,000	Off			
7	Land	40,000					96,000	Off			
8	Total Debits	305,700					354,600				
9	Balance Sheet Credits:										
10	Accumulated Amortization	118,000			(b)	11,400	73,400	Off			
11	Accounts Payable (Inv.)	38,000					33,500	Off			
12	Salaries Payable	12,000					14,000	Off			
13	Common Shares, $25 Par	100,000					125,000	Off			
14	Retained Earnings	37,700			(a)	71,000	108,700	Balance			
15	Total Credits	305,700					354,600				
16	Statement of Cash Flows										
17	Cash Flows from Operating Activities										
18	Net Income		(a)	71,000						Difference in Cash Debit	
19	Plus Noncash Charges									and Credit Entries =	
20	Amortization Expense		(b)	11,400							
21	Changes in Current Assets & Liab.										
22	Increase in Accounts Receivable				◎	4,000					
23	Decrease in Inventory										
24	Decrease in Prepaid Rent										
25	Decrease in Accounts Payable										
26	Increase in Salaries Payable										
27	Cash Flows from Investing Activities										
28	Outflow to purchase land										
29	Outflow to purchase equipment										
30	Inflow from sale of equipment										
31	Cash Flows from Financing Activities										
32	Inflow from shares issue										
33	Total Debit and Credit Columns			86,400		86,400					
34											
35											

Problem 12-2 Answer Key   **Problem**   Sheet2   Sheet3

Required

a. Enter information in Column A.

b. Enter the beginning balance sheet amounts in Column B and ending balances in Column G. Total the debits and credits for each column.

c. To prevent erroneous entries to Cash in Row 2, darken the area in Columns C through F.

d. Record the entry for Net Income. This is entry (a) provided.

e. Record the entry for Amortization expense. This is entry (b) provided.

f. Record the entries for the changes in current assets and liabilities. The entry for the change in Accounts Receivable has been provided and is referenced as entry (c).

g. Record the four entries from the Other Information provided in Problem 14-8A. These are the investing and financing activities.

h. In Column H set up the IF function to determine whether the balance sheet accounts are in balance or not ("off"). Cell H3 for Accounts Receivable is provided for you. Cell H3 can be copied to all the balance sheet debit accounts. The balance sheet credit account formulas will differ given the different debit/credit rules for those accounts. *When the word "Balance" is reflected in every balance sheet cell in column H, the spreadsheet analysis is complete.*

i. Total the Debit and Credit columns to ensure that the two columns are equal.

j. As a final check, beginning in Cell J2, compute the change in the Cash account by subtracting the beginning balance from the ending balance. The difference will equal $14,100. Also beginning in Cell J18, compute the difference in the debit and credit cash entries in Rows 18 through 32. The difference should also equal $14,100.